Vouchers
and the
Provision of
Public Services

Vouchers and the Provision of Public Services

C. Eugene Steuerle
Van Doorn Ooms
George E. Peterson
Robert D. Reischauer
Editors

BROOKINGS INSTITUTION PRESS
COMMITTEE FOR ECONOMIC DEVELOPMENT
URBAN INSTITUTE PRESS
Washington, D.C.

Copyright © 2000
THE BROOKINGS INSTITUTION
COMMITTEE FOR ECONOMIC DEVELOPMENT
URBAN INSTITUTE

Vouchers and the Provision of Public Services
may be ordered from:

BROOKINGS INSTITUTION PRESS
1775 Massachusetts Avenue, N.W.
Washington, D.C. 20036
Tel.: 1-800-275-1447 or (202) 797-6258
Fax: (202) 797-6004
www.brookings.edu

Library of Congress Cataloging-in-Publication data
Vouchers and the provision of public services / C. Eugene Steuerle ...
[et al.], editors.
    p. cm.
ISBN 0815781547 (alk. paper)
ISBN 0815781539 (pbk. : alk. paper)
1. Subsidies. 2. Social services. 3. Subsidies—United States.
4. Social services—United States. I. Steuerle, C. Eugene, 1946–
II. Title.
    HC79.S9 V68 2000   00-009439
    361'.05—dc21   CIP

9 8 7 6 5 4 3 2 1

The paper used in this publication meets minimum requirements of the
American National Standard for Information Sciences—Permanence of Paper
for Printed Library Materials: ANSI Z39.48-1984.

Typeset in Adobe Garamond

Composition by
R. Lynn Rivenbark
Macon, Georgia

Printed by
R. R. Donnelley and Sons
Harrisonburg, Virginia

Foreword

OVER THE PAST few decades, the use of vouchers for the delivery of public services has proliferated. They are now used in many programs—including food stamps, housing assistance, and grants for higher education—that, while well known, are seldom identified as voucher programs. Other programs, such as Medicare and primary and secondary education, are experimenting with vouchers. Some of these experiments have been controversial. In fact, the word *voucher* has often taken on positive or negative connotations in political debates without there being any dispassionate examination of the merits of using vouchers versus alternative approaches to delivering particular public goods or services.

This volume provides the most comprehensive examination available of the use of vouchers. While many past studies have focused on the use of vouchers in a single service area, this book examines a wide variety of applications in such areas as education, child care, employment training, housing, food, and health care. The studies in this volume discuss the dimensions along which vouchers should be compared to alternative delivery mechanisms and analyze the social, political, and economic conditions that might make vouchers an effective mechanism for delivering services. Our hope is that certain lessons can be drawn from the use of vouchers in one service area and applied to others.

The idea for this set of studies was born when William Beeman, then a vice president of the Committee for Economic Development, observed that economics and public finance textbooks paid scant attention to vouchers; if they did, it was only in reference to school vouchers. The Brookings Institution, the Urban Institute, and the Committee for Economic Development decided to launch a collaborative effort to fill this void.

Initial drafts of the chapters in this volume were presented at a conference on October 2 and 3, 1998. At that conference, the authors benefited from the comments of Ophelia Basgal, Gordon Berlin, David Breneman, Steve Carlson, E. J. Dionne Jr., Christine Ferguson, Carol Graham, Jane Hannaway, Ron Haskins, Elliot Mincberg, and Lester Salamon. Mike Petro and Chris Dreibelbis of the Committee for Economic Development and Kathleen Elliott Yinug of Brookings were instrumental in organizing the conference.

Producing a volume with so many authors from so many institutions proved a Herculean task on the part of many individuals. Gary Kessler was patient and methodical in editing the manuscript, Inge Lockwood proofread and Shirley Kessel indexed the pages, and Janet Walker shepherded the volume through the production process at the Brookings Institution Press. Andrea Barnett, Joe Pickard, and Chris Spiro of the Urban Institute provided invaluable administrative and research assistance throughout the project.

The views expressed in this book are those of the authors and should not be ascribed to any of the persons acknowledged above or to the trustees, officers, or other staff members of the Brookings Institution, the Urban Institute, or the Committee for Economic Development.

> MICHAEL H. ARMACOST
> *President, Brookings Institution*
>
> CHARLES E. M. KOLB
> *President, Committee for Economic Development*
>
> ROBERT D. REISCHAUER
> *President, Urban Institute*

Washington, D.C.
May 2000

Contents

PART ONE

Framework

C. EUGENE STEUERLE

1 | *Common Issues for Voucher Programs*

IN RECENT years vouchers have come to be used pervasively in most modern economies. Yet debates over different types of vouchers often proceed in isolation, as if no learning can be applied from one area to another. These debates can even take on an ideological fervor. Considered as a tool of public policy, however, a voucher is ideologically neutral and can be compared to other components of a tool chest—helpful for some purposes, less appropriate for others. Even where potentially useful, there may be alternative tools that may be applied to the task, while the voucher itself comes in all sizes and shapes. Put another way, a voucher is simply a means of subsidy or payment, it can be designed in an almost infinite (although bounded) number of ways, and it is always a means to an end, not an end in itself.

Consider the range of services and goods to which vouchers are applied: food, higher education, primary and secondary school education, housing, employment and training, child care, and medical insurance for the nonelderly and for the elderly are among the best-known. But vouchers are also made available for such items as low-flush toilets, taxi rides for the intoxicated, food for panhandlers, neutering of pets, and much else. (For a more comprehensive list, see the chapter by Paul Posner and others). This wide range implies that vouchers are here to stay but does not speak to their

3

merit relative to alternative means of the dispersing of funds. Moreover, it does not help explain why in one area there will be furious controversy over their use, while in another there will be little disagreement at all.

This chapter provides an overview of issues that tend to arise in voucher programs and proposals—more in some than in others. Some of these issues will be addressed in more depth in other studies in this book. Because of its overview nature, this chapter does not attempt to ascertain the relevance or applicability of vouchers to any one area nor to catalogue their availability.

Definition and Boundaries

To begin with, a definition of a voucher is necessary: *a voucher is a subsidy that grants limited purchasing power to an individual to choose among a restricted set of goods and services.*[1] Some elaborations are in order:

—A voucher can give purchasing power to an individual directly or indirectly. While food stamps may be given directly to an individual to spend at a grocery store, for instance, a housing voucher might be paid indirectly through the rental housing owners as long as the subsidized individual is given some choice of where to live. In effect, the payment itself may be made to either the consumer or the provider. The flow of payment tells us little about where the incidence of the benefit lies.[2]

—A voucher can be in the form either of an expenditure or a tax subsidy. A housing voucher, for example, can be designed as either a direct grant or a tax credit. Issues of administration, such as the ability of tax authorities to administer a subsidy for those with no tax liability, may affect whether a program should be *designed* as an expenditure or tax subsidy but not necessarily whether it should be *defined* as a voucher.

—A voucher is normally limited or capped as to how much an individual can spend. It is often set at a particular value, for example, $50 a month for food stamps. Thus an open-ended subsidy, such as a traditional Medicare policy that could cover any and all qualifying medical expenses without limit, does not quite fit the definition. Because it provides a choice of providers to subsidized individuals, however, traditional Medicare is very close to a voucher, and capped vouchers are now offered within Medicare as an alternative to the traditional package of benefits. (See the chapter by Robert Reischauer as well as that by David Bradford and Daniel Shaviro.) Up to the capped amount, however, a voucher can be designed to have co-payment rates or deductibles or otherwise cover only a share of costs.[3]

—A voucher both *prescribes* and *proscribes*. On the one hand, the subsidized consumer must have some choice of providers of goods or services (for example, of apartments, schools, or medical plans). Depending on the voucher, providers can be public or private, profit seeking or nonprofit. On the other hand, a voucher restricts the types of goods and services that can be purchased: housing vouchers cannot be spent on clothing; a combined housing and clothing voucher cannot be spent on education. (For a discussion on combined, or "bundled," vouchers, see the chapter by Robert Lerman and C. Eugene Steuerle.)

The range is wide within these boundaries. Vouchers are well suited to provide an intermediate level of choice. Thus choices are proscribed to remain within a particular set, but within this set the consumer has a fair amount of freedom. At one extreme, choices might be extraordinarily restricted. For instance, a voucher might be (and one actually is) provided for food items available in only one cafeteria. At another extreme, a voucher could be provided for almost everything consumable except, say, vacations and alcoholic beverages; for all intents and purposes (other than administration), this latter style of voucher would be almost equivalent to cash.[4] Policymakers, of course, should set boundaries for a program according to goals and principles, not according to whether it will, by definition, be called a voucher.

—All voucher programs are accompanied by regulation, although not necessarily by more or less regulation than would accompany alternative programs. The government always regulates what it subsidizes. While vouchers are often designed to involve less regulation than direct provision of the same goods and services, they tend to regulate more than cash subsidies do.

Government regulations apply to both consumers and producers. Eligibility rules, for instance, determine which consumers can be subsidized and how changes in their behavior (for example, movement to another jurisdiction, attainment of income through work or marriage) might affect their qualification. Suppliers are regulated in the goods and services they can provide (for example, only certain types of food) and in their quality (for example, child care provided in certified settings, education at accredited institutions).

Goals

Most of the discussion of vouchers, whether academic research, policy analysis, or political assertion, tends to address one or two goals only. The selection of goals and the ability of a voucher to meet them tend to vary significantly from one voucher program to another. By scanning the types of goals typically articulated—revealed preferences of a sort—a good deal can be learned about the relative concerns that prevail in the policy process and whether alternative mechanisms are likely to be considered. Almost all of these goals relate to issues of efficiency or equity, broadly defined. Among the goals commonly associated with vouchers are the following:

—*Choice and efficiency.* "Choice" is often the first buzzword that comes up when the potential advantages of vouchers are being discussed. Among policy analysts the emphasis is on improving efficiency by avoiding or reducing the regulation of individual purchases. In choosing, individuals will get greater satisfaction or value if they can decide how to spend a given amount of money in accord with their own preferences. This is the base on which much of the economic theory of the household proceeds.

Sometimes efficiency gains are measured not by the value added by additional options for consumers, but by the cost of production, such as lower cost per unit of output or lower cost for the same "amount" of output. For example, greater efficiency in education might lead to greater levels of "learning" for the same cost or the same level of learning at a lower cost.

Greater freedom of choice may also encourage more competition among suppliers. For example, suppliers of housing may have to compete more if they must regularly face the demands of consumers than if they obtain once-for-all contracts (for example, to construct some permanent housing in particular locations).

Quality improvements are one way that efficiency might be obtained. In his chapter, Robert Reischauer suggests that voucherlike managed-care options under Medicare were favored by some who believed these options would improve the quality of medical care provided.

—*Choice and equity.* While the efficiency aspects of choice are quite appealing, the public—perhaps even more than researchers and analysts—is often attracted by what it considers to be "fair" or equitable. However, efficiency and equity concerns often run in parallel. For example, the rich can easily choose what school their children attend, either by moving across jurisdictions or by simply paying for private school. "Why can't others also have this choice?" the fairness argument goes. A counterargument is that the benefits of choice will not, in practice, inure to those who need help the most, but this again is posed as much as an equity as an efficiency argument. (See the discussion below on adverse selection and on consumers' ability to choose.)

The equity issue comes up in different ways in voucher programs. For example, vouchers for primary and secondary school students are still largely experimental. (For a discussion of these experiments, see the chapter by Isabel Sawhill and Shannon Smith.) Voucher proposals have often succeeded or failed in state legislatures according to the degree to which these equity arguments were persuasive. Indeed, in his chapter in this volume, Burdett Loomis emphasizes that vouchers sometimes bring about coalitions of conservatives who argue for efficiency and liberals who argue for equity, especially for low-income students. The chapter by Arthur Hauptman similarly indicates that access as a matter of equity has displaced quality and efficient choice as a primary goal of higher education vouchers. In the case of child care, some argue that it is unfair to pay neighborhood providers but not grandparents, so grandparents are also made eligible on this equity (as well as efficiency) criterion. In housing programs, it is sometimes deemed unfair (and inefficient) not to permit public housing occupants to take their subsidy to move closer to work or to a better school. Indeed, the chapter by George Peterson notes that vouchers have been used, as a matter of justice or equity, to comply with court-ordered desegregation.

While equity and efficiency arguments are often mutually reinforcing, they may be at odds when efficiency of choice is allowed to create greater disparities in outcomes among recipients. Choice, for instance, can reallocate a greater share of benefits to the more knowledgeable of recipients. Sometimes choice may be sold as a matter of equity but may not efficiently reach that goal if the symbolism has no substance. For example, some individuals may have little choice with a voucher if they lack mobility and knowledge. (See the chapter by Loomis.)

—*Increased competition.* Sometimes vouchers are favored as a way to improve efficiency through more competition among suppliers than is thought to prevail under public provision, especially where there are public monopolies.[5] Where entry of new providers is feasible, vouchers may allow alternative types and quantities of services to be provided. For example, public schools might behave in a monopolistic fashion if the majority of parents are deterred from using alternative providers by prohibitive costs. (One needs to be careful here to distinguish just what characteristic of the good or service is considered worrisome. For example, some parents may not be concerned about teachers but about disruptive settings or uninviting physical structures.) Using an alternative private provider is expensive to the individual if he or she must give up the full value of any public subsidy when turning to a private provider, as in the case of many national health care systems outside the United States and in public education in the United States. As yet another example, housing vouchers may have reduced the power of small groups of construction companies that might have dominated the bidding market for building public housing. At least in theory, housing vouchers could make it more difficult for powerful groups to use anticompetitive zoning restrictions to force subsidized persons to live in selected areas.

The goal of increased competition as a mechanism for enhancing efficiency and equity does not necessarily mean the absence of public providers. Vouchers can exist side by side with publicly provided goods and services, as in the cases of Early Start education and child-care vouchers, or of public housing and housing vouchers. Competition may be enhanced, especially if public and private provisions are subsidized roughly to the same degree and under the same rules.

—*Replacement of other programs.* With significant government presence in a wide variety of social areas, it should not be surprising that new vouchers are often favored—or opposed—not so much on what the voucher may do per se but whether it will be more efficient or equitable than some already established program. It is doubtful, for instance, that opposition to vouchers for primary and secondary education or for capitated payments (limited payments per person or illness) to managed-care institutions under Medicare would be so strong if there were no existing public school or Medicare system. By the same token, vouchers especially come into the limelight as a possible public policy tool when an existing institutional structure for transferring benefits is viewed as inadequate. Here the voucher is often viewed as potentially improving quality, rather than the quantity, of the good or service involved. Thus housing vouchers have been favored as a substitute for public housing for some time now by many liberals and conservatives and by Republican and Democrat presidents alike.[6] Primary and secondary school education vouchers are more controversial, but they, too, are suggested primarily in contrast to public education as it is currently provided.[7] Often only limited comparisons are made in the public debate. For example, a debate over replacing public housing construction with housing vouchers will often dodge the question of whether a subsidy only for housing might be more efficient if it could be spent on education as well.

—*Restriction of choice, or proscription along with prescription.* By the very act of designating a voucher for a specific set of goods and services, policymakers formally restrict what can be bought. Thus vouchers are often intended to restrict the ability of recipients—especially of those on public assistance—to spend their money on items thought less needed or desirable by the majority of voters, legislators, or taxpayers. For example, assistance to low-income individuals might be provided for food but not for recreation. This makes a voucher a two-edged sword.

Why does proscription typically accompany prescription? Efficiency in the broadest sense requires considering both those subsidized and those who are subsidizing—considering preferences of donors as well as those of recipients and considering whether the actions of recipients produce external costs or benefits for others, whether donors or not. Those who are paying may prefer to provide basic or "merit" goods and services such as clothing, food, or other necessities of life more than other goods and services. A balancing act between preferences of recipients and concerns of taxpayers, therefore, is required.

Often the concern for transferors' interests goes under the general heading of "paternalism": those providing assistance, like parents, restrain the choices of the recipient for his or her own good. But in another sense the efforts may be nothing more than attempts to target specific needs and adopt the most efficient method of achieving an equity goal. For example, if the goal is to alleviate poverty—defined as some minimal standard of consumption—then items of consumption not in that standard are not meant to be subsidized.

Similarly, the target of many programs is to get the necessary goods and services to different members of a household even though the payment may be made through one member only. Concentrating assistance on food, housing, and medical care tends to restrict the ability of adults to garner welfare benefits for themselves rather than for their children. Thus proscriptions on use can also be considered administrative devices to ensure that the subsidies go to intended beneficiaries.

Once again, the coin has an equity, as well as an efficiency, side. It might be deemed unfair for the child in one poor family to get less food than a child in another poor family if parents differentially spend assistance on items that are not necessities. Or transferors who pay taxes and live under a tight budget may deem it unfair to be taxed to provide higher levels of subsidized recreation to transferees. Or it may be considered only fair that the young children of a single parent who is required to work receive necessary adult supervision (through child-care vouchers) during the day. Or more equal access to higher education (through educational vouchers) may be considered a matter of equality of opportunity for those with fewer resources, whereas cash or even food assistance to young adults without children does not meet this same equity standard.

—*Budget control.* Vouchers can be and often are designed to provide budget control. A voucher grants a "limited" subsidy to each individual, and typically the maximum is an exact dollar value (for example, food stamps) or a maximum subsidy (for example, rental assistance) placed on the voucher itself. These limits usually give legislatures control over growth in costs over time, at least on a per-recipient basis. Contrast this with programs that are open ended in the sense of allowing new goods and services to be provided continually, or higher prices to be charged, without requiring further decisions by sitting legislators or current voters.[8] For example, many of the Medicare benefits now scheduled for the year 2065 were put in place by legislators 100 years before then.[9]

Vouchers usually try to provide cost control by limiting the subsidy to some maximum amount (which can vary over time) and then encouraging choice within that subsidy amount. Increases in payments generally derive from legislative action, not simply as a response to producers supplying or individuals demanding more goods and services. (In the language of "entitlements," the voucher may or may not be an entitlement—that is, avoid the annual appropriations process—but it is less likely to grow automatically over time.) As opposed to direct public provision, which tries to regulate prices and quantities more directly, vouchers are also argued in many cases to reduce overhead and administrative expense. Some, for instance, believe that public school systems tend to have higher costs because the political decisionmaking process results in a ratio of nonteaching to teaching staff that is too high.[10]

Not all vouchers save on costs. Vouchers may make subsidies more explicit because of expanded choice. They could then become *more valuable*, demand might rise, and more eligible individuals might apply, thereby adding to costs. Similarly, a voucher (or other reform) could increase the accessibility of services, again leading to higher demand and greater costs.

Vouchers may also represent one way that legislators simply dodge the cost of what they have mandated, in effect proscribing what they themselves have prescribed. For example, legislators may mandate that schools perform a variety of functions, that public housing contain certain features and amenities, and that health plans accede to wants such as choice of doctors or limited waiting periods. Then, lacking funds to pay for these mandates, these same legislators may try to put some overall cap on total or per capita expenditures. In effect, the voucher can become a convenient tool to try to put a ceiling on the cost of the very things legislators have mandated. Loomis suggests that cost containment often makes vouchers politically appealing to legislators. Sometimes this approach may work, as when prices paid to providers are above market price and can be reduced; other times, the system may simply be overconstrained, and the balloon simply cannot be shoved into the box. A managed-care plan, for instance, might have trouble accommodating government mandates to provide more services at a reduced voucher payment.

—*Both open-ended and capped incentives.* Vouchers are sometimes chosen as a policy tool because they offer the opportunity to address incentive structures in a very direct way. A typical (but not necessary) design is for a voucher to provide a zero price to the individual (or 100 percent subsidy) for initial purchases but no subsidy beyond some cap. (This structure is more applicable to necessities and less applicable to other items, such as higher education.) This may have the disadvantage of leading individuals to buy more than would be efficient from their own or society's perspective. Moreover, some of the subsidy almost inevitably covers expenditures that individuals would have made anyway. Nonetheless, it helps ensure that at least the voucher amount is spent on the particular good or service if it is considered to be a necessity. Per dollar of expenditure, it also leads to the greatest level of subsidy for the first dollars spent. If there are diminishing returns—less and less benefit from additional amounts for the person assisted—needs are more likely to be concentrated on the first, not last, dollars of expenditure.

While open-ended incentives tend to lead to excessive marginal purchases of the subsidized good or service, a limit or cap on a voucher means that it eventually will provide zero subsidy beyond some limit.[11] At some point this leaves the full cost of the *marginal* purchase (for example, of food beyond the cost of a healthy diet) to the individual.

As demonstrated by Bradford and Shaviro, the "optimal" subsidy rate for the marginal purchase is not necessarily zero, depending on what goals are being pursued and on the response rates of consumers and providers to different price subsidies. Nonetheless, for many practical applications— when the "merit" good sought is some minimum level of well-being, when the response rates of consumers and providers cannot be estimated well, and when there are declining returns to the consumer from additional consumption of the item—a zero rate at some level of consumption has very strong appeal.

One reason is that in the general marketplace a zero rate of subsidy is the rate applied to most goods and services purchased by most individuals. (That is, most goods and services are neither taxed nor subsidized selectively for the population as a whole.) In most applications of public finance, the burden of proof for nonzero tax or subsidy rates is normally placed on the advocate, or else any market interference could be justified. Put another way, assume that the burden of proof is deemed to have been met with respect to subsidizing *some* minimal level of consumption of a merit good or service. Such evidence does not carry over to *all* levels of consumption of that good or service for those who are subsidized. Hence subsidies that are designed mainly to provide assistance will usually be capped at some level or another.

If the goal is not assistance to individuals but subsidization of the general activity—for example, a subsidy for pollution abatement or investment in education that inures to the larger benefit of society—then the logic of a limit or cap does not necessarily apply, or it does not apply in the same way.

Alternative and Related Mechanisms

None of the preceding goals—choice and efficiency, choice and equity, replacement of other programs, restriction of choice, increased competition, budget control, and both open-ended and capped subsidies—are necessarily met better by a voucher than by any and all alternatives. Again, the voucher must simply be considered one of several tools that are available. For some purposes, more than one tool is required. Nor does the inferiority, if any, of current law to vouchers establish the a priori superiority of any particular style of voucher to all alternatives. Among the many alternative tools are the following:

—*Direct noncompetitive public provision.* By longstanding tradition, goods and services can be provided directly by government. Health care can be provided through veterans' hospitals, education through public schools, child care through a public child-care center, housing through the building of public housing projects. Before the existence of food stamps, the government distributed surplus commodities directly to consumers. Even direct public provision, however, entails many private, rent-seeking activities, the most obvious being wage-seeking on the part of those who are paid by government for their labor. The relative cost of direct public provision is affected by whether workers receive more or less when working for the government and by the relative effectiveness of private nonprofit and profit-making suppliers. The efficiency of direct public provision is also affected by the extent to which innovation is allowed to displace less-efficient activity. For example, monopoly or monopsony practices in a government enterprise or in a government union can vary widely.

—*Competitive public suppliers and contracting out to private suppliers.* Competition and choice sometimes can be enhanced through competition among public providers. Public charter schools or even magnet schools, for example, may be an alternative way of providing some choice and competition in education. In a variety of areas, government might give greater choice by setting up alternative programs and letting them compete among themselves. In his chapter, John Bishop implies that the ability of parents and students to choose among public schools and the independence of these schools may be more important than whether the schools are publicly or privately owned. A select list of public training programs, with complete choice for individuals, is very close to a voucher that can be spent only on training programs from a restricted list that includes private providers. In other words, there are a variety of ways to enhance competition.

When government contracts out its work, it uses public funds but private suppliers. Although contracting out is considered relatively new in fields like primary and secondary education, it has always been the common practice in programs like Medicare, which contracts out for almost all its services. Some types of contracts are fairly far from vouchers: they may give little or no choice to recipients, they may maintain a public monopoly of sorts, or they may be open ended in terms of benefits. Other types of contracts can be made to look like vouchers or are vouchers. For instance, a variety of housing vouchers involve contracts with private suppliers of rental housing. Government health payments of a fixed amount to government-selected health maintenance organizations (HMOs) or preferred provider organizations (PPOs) should be considered vouchers if the individual can choose among these provider organizations but the size of the subsidy is limited per individual.

Even if there is only one supplier under a contract, some of the inefficiencies associated with public monopoly provision of public goods and services can be reduced. At least at the time of bidding there is some competition among suppliers for the government contract.

—*Other supplier subsidies and controls.* At times government may try to influence the consumption of particular items simply by increasing their supply. It may, for instance, try to reduce the price of food by providing crop subsidies to farmers. Producer subsidies for items that everyone may purchase, like food, may not always result in the desired targeting of the subsidy. In many less-developed countries, nonetheless, a subsidy to suppliers of some basic staples has been tried, with mixed effect, simply because poverty was spread among a large target population and because of administrative inability to distinguish well among individuals (for example, being unable to "means test" individuals for eligibility). In his chapter, Hugo Priemus notes that property subsidies were used in Europe after World War II to respond to a shortage in housing supply before being gradually replaced with voucherlike allowances.

At other times government tries to control or regulate what producers can do. In the case of rent controls, for instance, government attempts to keep down the price of housing. Limits on what can be charged for basic food items, such as bread, have also been attempted, especially in socialized or less-developed countries. In these cases, however, the government often keeps down the supply as well, usually with bad and sometimes disastrous results for the very groups it is trying to help. Rent controls have been tried in some American cities and in many European countries. (See the Priemus chapter.)

—*Cash payments.* The case for vouchers in some ways takes off from a negative income tax literature arguing that the greatest freedom of choice is established by the provision of cash assistance.[12] Milton Friedman and James Tobin, two economists often on very different sides of many fiscal and government policy issues, are often cited together because of their collaboration at one point in time in favoring the negative income tax.[13] Barring any extenuating circumstances—paternalism, desire of funders that only certain types of goods be purchased—consumers would prefer (or at a minimum, find equally valuable) more options to fewer.[14] Following this logic to its limit, cash should be favored over any in-kind benefit because of the additional options the former provides. It might also reduce administrative costs (more money for recipients, less for government workers) and avoid a stigma (for example, spending cash rather than food stamps at the grocery store).[15] As emphasized above, therefore, vouchers can be considered a hybrid or compromise between cash and complete government determination of how money will be spent (for example, on this particular apartment in this particular block of public housing).[16]

When might cash be preferred? On this question, the United States has experienced an almost complete reversal of attitudes in recent years. Cash used to go mainly to those who did not work, and little or no cash went to those who did. Now more cash is going to those who work and less to individuals who do not work and who rely only on welfare. This change has been reflected partly in the adoption and expansion of a cousin to the negative income tax, the earned income tax credit (EITC), which is now a significant component of income-conditioned assistance in the United

States. The EITC effectively provides a "work test" before it is granted, and it provides higher levels of benefits as earnings increase over certain ranges (for example, for a household with one child in 1997, the credit equals 34 percent of earnings on a base of up to $6,500 of earnings, although it phases out at slightly higher income levels).[17]

Why, one might ask, is society willing to provide cash assistance to those who earn some amount of money from work but not to others? Apparently, where the work requirement is met, many voters who would otherwise reject a pure negative income tax are willing to accept the underlying argument that cash can be an efficient form of transfer. Cash programs may simply be cheaper as well, both because administrative costs are lower and because the recipient may be glad to trade $12 of in-kind benefits, say, for $10 in cash. Such differential valuation of cash and in-kind benefits not only reflects the inefficiency of in-kind benefits but also sometimes leads to fraud and black markets. (See the chapter by Robert Moffitt.)

In balancing the gains from greater choice with the demands of taxpayers and providers, recent experience may imply that U.S. policymakers prefer choice mainly for those individuals who convey through their willingness to work that they are likely to spend the assistance in a form desired by those paying for the transfers. Work becomes an indicator that the transferee has a greater probability of somehow being more competent, trustworthy, or knowledgeable than otherwise. Therefore, some of the extra management and efficiency costs that derive from in-kind provision can be avoided. Or, more simply, the new consensus may be that willingness to work implies an attitude ("personal responsibility") that ought to be funded (with cash).

For those who do not work, in contrast, the federal government has now moved to a situation in which no permanent cash assistance will be available except for those who qualify on the basis of age or disability.[18] The long-term poor will no longer be able to receive Aid to Families with Dependent Children (AFDC) or its replacement, Temporary Assistance for Needy Families (TANF). Thus the EITC has replaced AFDC as the one cash assistance item that will be available to (working) lower-income individuals on a consistent basis.

In practice, of course, a voucher may be very close to cash assistance if it is easily transferable in the market. (See the discussion on food stamps by Moffitt.) From the beneficiaries' perspective, a voucher is as good as cash if they likely would have spent at least that much on the subsidized commodity anyway. (See the Bradford and Shaviro chapter.) In this last respect, the smaller the size of the voucher—especially when it comes to necessities—the more likely it merely covers what would have been purchased with cash. Note, however, that even in this last case, what may be true in general for beneficiaries may not be true for all beneficiaries (for example, 10 percent of beneficiaries would have purchased not food but some less necessary item if given cash instead).

—*Loans and guarantees*. Vouchers, grants, or credits may be inappropriate forms of subsidies for dealing with certain types of market failures. In the case of higher education, for instance, the market failure might result from the lack of efficient lending markets for borrowing against future earnings. Similarly, the market failure in question may relate to inadequate access to loans (for example, in a low-income area with higher rates of default). Here a government guarantee might help someone obtain a loan at a rate closer to what could be obtained elsewhere. Even loan and guarantee programs raise issues of choice, for instance, among potential lenders. A voucher can also be made in the form of loans or guarantees as long as the beneficiary is given some choice over how to allocate the implied subsidy.

—*Block grants*. Although block grants are an intermediate and not a final mechanism for delivery, they deserve at least brief mention, because they are promoted as encouraging competition within the public sector. The competition derives from greater experimentation at lower levels of government. Unlike competition among suppliers for each customer's business, here competition is achieved mainly through comparisons across jurisdictions: approaches that are successful for one state or locality may be adopted by others. Like vouchers, block grants (for example, from states to localities) are also used as a device to restrict budgetary cost by pushing requirements to control costs onto lower levels of government. Block grants sometimes combine and consolidate programs in ways that may provide more choice to the individual as well (for example, when the consolidated program includes more individual options).

Categorical block grants could even be thought of as vouchers for lower levels of government. Many block grants give other levels of government the flexibility to make payments to individuals in the form of vouchers.

—*Combinations of mechanisms*. Alternative mechanisms are not mutually exclusive. They can be combined and spliced together in multiple ways. Indeed, today's income-conditioned assistance programs are an amalgamation of all sorts of program approaches—public schools, vouchers for housing and food, contracted-out medical services, and so on. In addition, subsidies for the same service or commodity are often provided through multiple mechanisms: vouchers and loans for higher education, vouchers and public housing for housing assistance, for example. This does not imply that these combinations are ideal or even effective, only that they are not exclusive.

Market Conditions

A variety of issues come to the fore in determining the effectiveness of a voucher. Many of these relate to the market conditions in which the voucher operates.

Competition among Suppliers

When it comes to a voucher's purported efficiency gains, one of the first issues raised is whether or not it provides greater competition among suppliers. Housing vouchers, for instance, may yield a more competitive supply of housing than public housing contracts will yield, not only initially but also years after the housing has been built. Whether education vouchers provide greater competition depends on many factors, such as the extent of the market. (See the Sawhill and Smith chapter.) For example, there may be a national market for higher education, a regional market for some primary and secondary schools, and a small local market for schooling in rural communities. Vouchers might not do much to improve competition in a rural market with only one school, although even here there may be some enhancement if the voucher is somehow portable or could be used to bargain for other inputs (for example, books and computer learning). In the case of higher education, Hauptman argues that vouchers worked well in the case of the G.I. Bill after World War II because there was adequate supply of places in colleges and universities but that expansion of public institutions may have been the appropriate policy to meet the exploding demand created by the baby boom population. Linda Bilheimer's chapter suggests that the supply of commercial HMO plans for Medicaid recipients might be inadequate because they would face low payment rates from the government and because there may be few health care providers in the inner city. Of course, in a heavily regulated market like health care, potential suppliers react not just to the availability of a voucher but also to the other costs and benefits implied by regulations—such as requirements to accept all applicants, even those that may be costly to the supplier. In some cases, there is a concern that what is sought—for example, training customized for the real needs of employers—cannot really be supplied through a voucher, or through any other public program, for that matter. (See the chapter by Burt Barnow.)

One needs to be careful to distinguish between short-term and long-term supply. If a voucher is newly introduced, especially in a market where government control and regulation has previously dominated, it will take time for alternative suppliers to make their services available. Moreover, if it is a partially regulated market, such as for education or health care, it will often take time for the regulations surrounding the new voucher—for example, legal specification of the service to be provided and to whom the supplier must sell—to sort themselves out.

To make matters yet more complicated, markets can be made more competitive simply by making entry easier, even when there are still limited suppliers. The existing suppliers must meet demands of customers to avoid loss of some of their market. Occasionally, advocates for educational vouchers for primary and secondary education will argue that the threat or presence of a voucher creates significant improvement in public schools as well.

Competition among suppliers depends partly on access by demanders. Housing vouchers can be very restrictive in their use—although there are exceptions, they often cannot be carried across jurisdictions, and in practice their use might be confined to a few areas zoned adequately for low-income housing to be built. Thus suppliers from alternative jurisdictions might be excluded from the market. Even with a voucher for higher education, many individuals with family ties (such as care-taking responsibilities) may be able to use only the nearest college, regardless of the potential for supply competition.[19]

Effect of Vouchers on Prices

Because vouchers may effectively increase the demand for certain goods and services, they may also increase prices. The more prices increase, of course, the more the subsidy goes to suppliers rather than to those who are intended to receive it. Hauptman notes that federal student loans, which effectively operate like vouchers, have been a factor in the rapid growth of college tuitions over the past two decades. Peterson indicates that prices also tend to rise in areas where there is a high concentration of housing (Section 8) vouchers. In both these cases, supply is somewhat constrained or expanded only at higher marginal cost. Douglas Besharov and Nazanin Samari voice concern that if the supply of providers does not expand to meet increased demand arising from vouchers for child care, the price of child care will rise and the subsidy will accrue to providers.

Providers may also gain larger shares of the subsidy if they can discriminate among consumers in pricing (somewhat like airlines do when charging different fares to different types of customers). Bradford and Shaviro raise this as a theoretical consideration, while Besharov thinks that some child-care providers charge lower prices to nonvoucher customers. Since child-care vouchers can also go to grandparents and other family providers, it would not be surprising if those relatives would provide child care even at a zero price in absence of the voucher.

Through regulation, the government itself may influence how much of the voucher is taken up in higher prices. For example, if it sets minimum standards for child care, housing, education, and so forth—and if those minimum standards are beyond what is provided in other parts of the market (regulated or not)—a higher price for the good or service may be required. Whether these regulations result in a net gain must be determined on a case-by-case basis. Few of these issues are unique to vouchers; most arise in the case of almost all types of subsidies.

The broader the market in which the voucher can be spent, the less likely it is to run into conditions of limited supply. Lerman and Steuerle suggest that combining various goods and services into a bundled voucher is one way to give greater choice to individuals. They might then have the ability to change what they buy and therefore deflect increases in price in one good simply by switching some of their purchases to another good.

Ability to Choose by Demanders

In addition to access (raised above also as a supply issue), vouchers constantly raise issues as to the capability of recipients to choose. They could lack either competence or resources. Can they pick an appropriate diet with food vouchers or the right type of college with vouchers for higher education? Is information reasonably accessible and cheap, or are consumers either incapable of shopping around or unmotivated to do so? Is a public service something that has to be experienced (an "experience" good or service), in which case knowledge about it is acquired mainly by trying it out? If so, it may be impractical for consumers to experience all alternatives. A related problem is whether or not there is "asymmetrical information," in which producers know more about their own products than consumers do and, as a result, can mislead consumers.

Problems regarding the ability of consumers to decide vary widely. Moffitt argues that there are few informational problems with food vouchers, because food quality is easily determined and mistakes in choosing can easily be corrected the next time. Search costs are also low. Conversely, Peterson suggests that search costs can be quite high in the case of a housing voucher emphasizing "mobility" in which recipients are given choices among different jurisdictions. This problem in making informed choices is usually not uniform among all recipients but varies according to their perceived capabilities. For example, mentally impaired individuals may not be able to make the same informed decisions as others regarding vocational rehabilitation providers. (See the Barnow chapter.) However, even in this case, their parents or friends may have information not available to a government worker who decides how to allocate the subsidy.

The information issue almost always comes up when a voucher is controversial, especially a new one, as in primary and secondary education and in health care.[20] Note that in both of these cases government already presumes limited information among demanders, whether they have vouchers or not. This is reflected in licensing or certification of a professional class (teachers, doctors) that is given certain powers to make decisions for consumers (prescribing homework or drug treatment).[21] Bilheimer indicates that some Medicaid recipients may be unwilling or unable to make informed choices. Many beneficiaries who are required to enroll in managed care plans do not exercise their right to chose among the available plans. Consequently, they end up being assigned to plans by the state.

COMPETITION AND INEQUALITY. One fear with respect to individual decisionmaking is that not all will get the same benefit for each dollar of voucher spent. Let me be quite direct here: competition by its very nature does imply some amount of inequality. If not all are getting the same product, then those with the least information or competence in choosing are more likely, all other things being equal, to get a lower-quality good or service. This does not mean, however, that they are worse off under a voucher or other device that involves greater choice or competition. An analogy can be made with markets for nonsubsidized goods and services. When savvy consumers compete in the market for cars, they create a demand that leads suppliers to furnish better automobiles to everyone, not just to those who are initially the most savvy. Also, while decisions may not be optimal, they may still be better than in the absence of vouchers.

Whether a market with some choice results in relatively greater inequality is also uncertain. To do a fair comparison, all sources of inequality, of which competition is merely one, must be taken into account. The value of Medicare, for example, varies widely across states and among doctors. Well-informed patients have always done better at picking more capable doctors. The quality of child-care providers differs. Access varies. Ability to vote with one's feet—to move within or across jurisdictions—is far from equal.

With competition, information markets expand in ways that help promote greater equality (for example, toward informing consumers if they are getting a worse deal for their dollars and toward allowing the same good to be purchased for the same price by all customers). In some noncompetitive public goods markets, by the same token, there are only pretenses of equality. Sources of disparity are often kept hidden to try to maintain support for the programs. For example, some children in some inner-city public schools, as in the District of Columbia, may have as much spent on them as children in suburban schools, but the expenditure may not provide an equal-value education or a value to consumers anywhere near to its cost. Large disparities in age-specific Medicare expenditures by different states seem to be related more to different health care practices by providers than to the differential health of the recipients.

Regulation can be and often is invoked to try to reduce or minimize potential disparities in outcomes because of differences in abilities of consumers to choose. Of course, with enough regulation, a voucher could be made to look almost exactly like direct public provision of a good or service. At least some regulation, however, is always required. For example, racially segregated schooling and noncertified education classes generally would not qualify for an education voucher.

INFORMATION SYSTEMS. Information systems for consumers serve vital roles but vary in quality.[22] Small-scale systems might not be able to provide sufficient information for choice, while large-scale systems could inundate consumers with too much or inappropriate information. Information systems themselves may be regulated, leading to more administrative costs. Government may produce or require production of consumer reports, specify formats for information provided to consumers, or serve as an adviser. One "Moving to Independence" program, for example, provides counseling and apartment search assistance for housing certificate holders. Reischauer notes that under 1997 legislation dealing with voucher options under Medicare, the Health Care and Financing Administration (HCFA) must send participants materials describing all the options available to them, including data comparing plans in a given market area. Bilheimer notes that some states are also using enrollment brokers to provide information and assistance to Medicaid beneficiaries to help them choose among managed care plans.

Government may also attempt to restrict what it believes to be misleading or inappropriate advertising. Under the legislation just noted, HCFA regulates marketing materials sent to participants by HMOs. Bishop argues that educational vouchers work best in countries with government-required standardized assessment, which focuses parents' attention on learning rather than on less important criteria. One interpretation of this result is that the publication of standardized test results provides a simplified guide for citizens. It leaves open the question of whether other guides would do as well or better.

The case of training vouchers provides a striking example of the interplay between government-provided information and vouchers. Barnow emphasizes the importance of "individual referrals" to ensure that recipients go to vendors with good performance and reasonable costs that supply training both for occupations in demand and for the recipients' level of skill and aptitude. Lessons learned there may well be applicable elsewhere. Lerman and Steuerle suggest that systems of structured choice, in which a voucher may cover more than one good or service, may require some interplay between the recipient and government workers. For example, a voucher helping a welfare recipient with a wide variety of work-related costs may require both a caseworker and the recipient to choose together among a set of options.

Adverse Selection

Allowing choices, especially among individuals with different capabilities and different needs, sometimes raises issues of adverse selection. Adverse selection generally arises when individuals can sort or "select" themselves into groups in ways that exclude other groups. It typically reduces the amount of redistribution intended. Note that this occurs in the case of a voucher (or other form of subsidy) when it has some inherent characteristic that makes what at first may appear to be the same entitlement to be of different value to different persons, yet in a way that is not explicitly stated or priced on the voucher itself. There is no argument about adverse selection in the case of food stamps, where $10 worth of food stamps provides essentially the same buying potential to almost everyone. Some people may get more food stamps because they have lower income, but the difference is explicit. In this case, individuals cannot further sort themselves into groups that would increase the basic value of their voucher.

With some other types of vouchers, recipients may cluster together in a group to avoid paying for some implicit cross-subsidization. If the healthy buy their insurance together, then the value of their vouchers of fixed monetary value can buy more insurance than if they insure with a group of unhealthy individuals whose vouchers do not cover their expected costs.[23] If a school can avoid taking in more expensive students—those impaired or in need of greater supervision—the remaining students can buy more education with their own vouchers than otherwise. The adverse selection issue is raised mainly in health and education, but it can also occur in housing and other areas. The specific issue at hand is usually whether the neediest (of students, medically insured, tenants, and so forth) will receive some inappropriately low level of benefits.

When there are some externally determined and objectively measurable characteristics that can be used to differentiate among recipients, a subsidy can be designed better to prevent adverse selection. While implicit redistribution formulas often create an incentive for the observant to reorganize to maximize their own benefits, explicit formulas are less likely to offer such options. In health care, therefore, a common explicit alternative suggested is to create subsidies according to different levels of risk. A proposal for voucherlike tax credits for universal health care under President Bush in 1992, for instance, attempted to provide higher levels of subsidy both for those with lower incomes and those with higher risks.[24] Educational vouchers adjusted by income could deal with some of the potential adverse selection against disadvantaged students, at least to the extent that income and disadvantage are correlated. Sawhill and Smith suggest that the subsidy level could vary with student characteristics, such as poverty, disability, or the need to take English as a second language (ESL) to make all types of students attractive to schools.

As long as risk pools contain differences in expected need, however, even subsidized risk pools can only reduce, not eliminate, adverse selection. Reischauer describes how federal legislation (the Tax Equity and Fiscal Responsibility Act of 1982) provided risk adjustment for Medicare vouchers according to age, gender, Medicaid enrollment, and institutional status, but these adjustments covered only a small percentage of the variation in health care costs. Accordingly, sicker individuals still opted for traditional Medicare, while on the supply side HMOs became reluctant to sign up costlier individuals. The government ended up paying more because those who chose vouchers on average already had costs below the voucher amount. Bilheimer raises similar issues with respect to proposed vouchers for the nonelderly. Although no vouchers are generally available for this population yet, low-cost options are sometimes hard to find for individuals operating outside of employer pools because of adverse selection and high administrative costs. Indeed, part of the debate over vouchers or credits for the nonelderly centers on how large adverse selection would be in this market.

Implicit, as opposed to explicit, redistribution, of course, suffers from its own set of problems. Often the implicit redistribution is arbitrary and even regressive. For example, in health insurance it is at least questionable whether nonsmokers should cover all the costs incurred by smokers, or lower-income younger workers cross-subsidize higher-income older workers, or citizens in low-cost states subsidize health care and health providers in high-cost states—implicit redistributions that occur under the current system.[25]

A significant difficulty with denying choice simply for the sake of maintaining implicit redistribution patterns is that it may also deter other equity and efficiency gains that choice would help bring about. For example, would one want to hold back upwardly mobile, disadvantaged students from choosing a school with higher educational standards for the purpose of maintaining educational equality among those in poor schools? The dilemma is that more choice can mean both more efficiency and greater adverse selection at the same time. The two often go hand in hand. The relative importance of each will depend on the nature of the markets and on the extent to which explicit forms of redistribution can be used to deter the adverse selection.

One way to limit increases in inequality through adverse selection is to turn to regulation and ensure that all choices are available to as many people as possible. For instance, a health insurance pool might be required to accept all comers, thus reducing the extent to which the healthy can band together and exclude the unhealthy. An educational institution might be required to accept all applications, or at least to give each an equal probability of acceptance. Even if some inequality still remains, it is more tolerable on equity and efficiency grounds if each person has the same choices and greater equality of opportunity, if not equality of result. By the same token, equal opportunity can be nominal rather than real. It still might be quite easy for groups to sort by employment status or geography even if technically each group is open to all comers. For example, it may not be practical for those in the inner city to travel to a richer suburb for education or to join a health insurance plan whose main constituents are workers cared for by preferred providers near an outlying plant.

Substitutability

Although vouchers can be spent directly only on the authorized category of spending, they free up other household resources for spending on other goods and services. The incremental effect on spending for the targeted category may be quite small—that is, there can be a high degree of substitution in household budgets. Empirical questions have been raised about the substitution effect (or budget fungibility) in all fields where vouchers have been used. Among the many factors affecting substitutability are the level of subsidy and degree of individual differences in tastes. Food stamps have often been considered highly substitutable for cash, especially in a world where the size of the voucher is modest and hence unlikely to purchase more than a basic level of food consumption. Moffitt, however, notes that even food stamps are less than cash equivalent. Regulatory attempts, moreover, have been made to limit substitution through such activities as sales of vouchers to others. These regulations, however, necessarily detract from the value of vouchers to users. (See the chapter by Bradford and Shaviro and that of Moffitt.)

In his chapter, Michael McConnell raises the issue of substitutability to contend with judicial arguments that government should subsidize only secular inputs into primary and secondary education. That is, if the government subsidizes bus transportation to religious schools, the schools can raise tuition because they know parents will now have some money freed up that they would have otherwise spent on transportation. McConnell, who favors vouchers for primary and secondary education, believes that this type of distinction has no economic substance.

The issue of substitution comes up also in a fiscal context—the extent to which the voucher simply substitutes for private spending that otherwise would have taken place. Sawhill and Smith raise this concern for school vouchers that may replace private spending among higher-income individuals who would have purchased education in absence of the voucher. When vouchers are offered in lieu of public education, they may also end up supporting those who already had left public education for private alternatives. This may be considered "fair" by those who don't benefit from current public education expenditures, but it still may raise the net public cost of offering an alternative.

Of course, if vouchers are cash equivalent, they are hardly worth the effort, especially given the extra administrative cost they may entail. Here, once again, we may want to distinguish between a voucher that is cash equivalent for all recipients and one for whom cash equivalence only applies to some. A voucher may still be preferred if it encourages purchase of the subsidized good or service among a subset of individuals who might otherwise spend the money on something society considers less valuable. (See the discussion on restriction of choice or proscription, above.)

Some Issues of Structural Design

A variety of design features determine the effectiveness of the voucher and the way it affects the market for the good or service that is subsidized. The following sections discuss some of the most prominent of these issues.

Universality and Permanence of the Voucher

In a number of cases, policymakers feel that they cannot afford to expand a voucher (or other subsidy) to cover all those who meet the eligibility criteria. In the United States, child care, training, housing, and school vouchers, among others, reach only a small proportion of those who are eligible.[26] Less than full universality, however, raises a number of issues:

—*Queues.* Even when conditioned on the basis of income, many programs still generate queues of "eligible" clients who cannot get vouchers.[27] This excess demand creates its own set of market distortions. For example, it greatly increases the extent to which existing recipients become reluctant to move to find better jobs, educational facilities, or support from related family members, as movement to another jurisdiction may require reentering a queue. Queues are also open invitations for corruption, ranging from the petty brokering of inside information about how to enter the queue to explicit bribes paid to move up in the queue, as was found rampant in the District of Columbia system for housing vouchers and public housing.[28]

With queues, allocation is usually made according to a first come, first served or lottery basis, neither of which is wholly satisfactory for equity or efficiency purposes. Bradford and Shaviro indicate that these secondary criteria sometimes affect other choices, such as the length of time individuals are willing to stay in an area to meet residency requirements. Peterson points out, however, that whether federal or local preference rules are used is crucial, as the wider the jurisdiction in which the queue occurs, the less mobility is affected. Although the issue of queues comes up quite often in the United States in the case of housing, Priemus notes that the issue seems to arise more in the United States than in Europe, because housing is more of an entitlement in Europe.

Although queues usually derive from budget constraints, the same amount of money often could be spread among more or all eligible recipients. Peterson raises the issue of whether housing benefits should be reduced so that housing vouchers can be made more universal.

—*New tax structures.* The income-conditioning of vouchers creates phaseouts that raise marginal tax rates and add, often capriciously, to work, saving, and marriage disincentives for recipients. Typically, these multiple tax and phaseout systems are uncoordinated. This issue is addressed in more detail elsewhere. (See the chapter by Bradford and Shaviro as well as that by Lerman and Steuerle.) Here, note simply that the combined tax rate structures in place in all or almost all countries around the globe show little rationality, system, or development by principles.

Even though they often operate capriciously, hidden tax rate structures achieve political acceptance because they are hidden. Take a voucher system of universal health care. It could be phased out as income increases. Or a voucher or subsidy of the same value could be provided to all individuals, and the cost then covered through direct taxes. In universal systems, it is possible to duplicate almost the same economic structure with direct taxes as with phaseouts, but for budget accounting purposes, the phaseout is not counted as a tax but rather as a reduction in expenditures.[29] That latter makes it "appear" less expensive or intrusive even when it is not.

—*Lack of complete market testing.* When vouchers are limited by income or targeted to one area or group, they may fail to provide a full market test of their effectiveness. For instance, when housing vouchers are available only in limited quantity, the change in demand is restricted and the capability of attracting competitive suppliers is decreased. Similarly, a voucher may have weak effects on competition in markets when it is only temporary. Alternative suppliers of services often will not enter a market if it is not believed to be permanent or long term. Education vouchers in the United States to date have never been supplied on a permanent enough basis (or universal enough basis) to provide a comprehensive test of how well they work. One can, however, draw some inferences from other countries or jurisdictions if vouchers in the area of examination have become a more permanent feature of the policy landscape.

Migration and Mobility

Federal vouchers that may be spent anywhere within the nation make migration across jurisdictions easier than would grants to states for the same purposes; similarly, state vouchers may be superior on this criterion to grants to localities. The amount of mobility or migration in voucherlike programs varies widely. For example, vouchers in higher education can be applied almost anywhere and food stamps are universally available (although one needs to reapply after moving and may receive a different amount), while housing, child care, and training subsidies often require waiting in a queue in a jurisdiction or region. Peterson notes that consolidation of public housing authorities (PHAs) has often increased portability across jurisdictions, while residency preferences have been removed from many PHAs as well. Expanding the boundary within which a voucher may be spent clearly enhances both migration and mobility and generally improves efficiency.

Decentralization

"Devolution" and "decentralization" could be considered ways of putting decisionmaking closer to the level of the individual. In one sense, vouchers might be considered an ultimate form of devolution when choice of suppliers is left to the individual. A corollary is that increasing the regulatory power of states and localities may actually centralize power up from the individual unless it displaces, rather than adds to, the regulatory power the federal government would have exercised anyway.

This issue has come to the fore for the income-conditioned transfer programs financed by the federal government. It turns out that efforts at devolution in the 1990s have actually centralized larger portions of the financing portion of these programs at the federal level, even if there has been some decentralization of some decisionmaking about how to spend a portion of funds.[30] One reason for the centralization of financing is that states have fewer incentives to add to the federal payments when each additional dollar of expense is covered entirely out of state funds. As states have contributed less, the federal government's share of total financing has risen. Even on the expenditure (rather than financing) side, moreover, the more universal voucherlike programs like food stamps and cash programs like the earned income tax credit leave little leeway for state involvement in how to spend funds. Because these latter programs have become an even larger share of the income assistance pie, the devolution of TANF expenditure decisions to the states has actually left a larger share of all expenditure decisions to the federal government.

Ironically, if more controls are given to state and local governments relative to the individual, these programs could become more, not less, centralized. Whether greater regulation improves or hurts the programs is another question. Many who claim they are for decentralization actually mean that they want federal subsidization and state and local control rather than federal subsidization and individual control. Since variations abound, it is difficult to come up with any hard-and-fast conclusion about the influence of vouchers on devolution. For example, a new federal voucher for health care for the nonelderly might be spendable only on a health insurance policy that meets state regulations. Here, there would be devolution of regulatory control but possible further centralization of the financing of medical payments to the national level.

Decentralization, therefore, often means that the federal government (or state government) will provide a national benefit but leave a variety of choices over administration and regulation to the states (or localities). Such decentralization may invite experimentation and push controls closer to a level where they can be administered, which is a primary advantage. By the same token, it can cause headaches. Geographic variation is a major concern in such areas as housing, primary and secondary education, and health care for the elderly. (See the chapters by Peterson, Sawhill and Smith, and Reischauer.) Each case is unique, but all share the attribute that the benefit level can vary not according to the needs or characteristics of individual beneficiaries, but rather by their geographic location. Thus, when benefits vary in value by geographical location, they tend to be less equitably distributed and less portable.

With decentralization, one also needs to worry about what may work well in one area but not in another—for example, vouchers for primary education in urban versus rural areas where selection may be more difficult. Where wide variation already exists in a nonvoucher program, it becomes impossible to substitute some vouchers and still hold harmless all states or localities as well as all producers and consumers. A different type of program inevitably will involve a different distribution of benefits—a major obstacle to voucher reform in Medicare, among other programs.

Loomis notes that decentralization versus centralization debates are often not what they at first appear to be—debates over the proper location for decisionmaking. Instead, they may reflect venue-shopping among interest groups to change the balance of power in their favor.

Methods of Delivery and Control

Vouchers can be provided to suppliers or to the beneficiaries themselves. They may take the form of tax subsidies or direct expenditures. They may be refundable or not, and the degree of regulation and quality control will vary. These and many other choices mean that there are a wide variety of types of vouchers. (See the chapter by Posner and others.)

— *Tax subsidies versus direct expenditures.* The choice of delivery mechanism may be led by political considerations. For example, tax subsidies are recorded in the budget as a negative tax rather than as a positive expenditure. As a matter of budget policy, such accounting tends to hide the additional interference in the economy that the tax subsidy entails. Still, in some cases tax subsidies may be easier to deliver administratively, especially if eligibility for the subsidy can and should be easily determined from the data already reported on tax returns. Although almost never done, there is no reason tax administration authorities could not deliver exactly the same subsidy if the budget authorities more accurately reported it as an expenditure rather than a tax cut.

— *Payment to beneficiaries or suppliers.* Vouchers tend to be delivered to suppliers mainly when administrative considerations dominate. When done this way, there usually will be some type of contractual relationship between the beneficiary and the supplier, as in the case of higher education and some forms of rental housing, but it is simply easier or more enforcable for the government to send its check to the supplier chosen by the beneficiary. Note, however, that the beneficiary still needs a means of certifying eligibility to potential suppliers of the goods or services. Food stamps have recently moved toward a hybrid system where one probably cannot even define whether beneficiaries or suppliers are getting the initial payment. Essentially, it will operate somewhat like a credit card that delivers lines of credit but not actual script to the beneficiary; payments of money rather than credit lines will be made to grocery stores and other suppliers when the card is used. (See the Moffitt chapter.) This new system may both reduce paperwork and at the same time make more difficult the spending of food stamps by anyone other than beneficiary.

— *Refundable or nonrefundable credits.* Refundable vouchers allow recipients to keep the difference between expected purchases to be subsidized and actual purchases. Suppose, for instance, that the expected level of food or education or housing purchase is $300 a month but that the voucher is worth $200. This type of differential arises in programs with a phaseout of benefits, because the beneficiary earns income and is expected to contribute some amount toward the expected purchase amount. If the credit is refundable, the recipient essentially gets the $200 even if less than $300 is spent. For every potential expenditure above $200, in fact, the recipient either pays or saves the full cost. Refundable vouchers are generally viewed as encouraging more cost consciousness by beneficiaries and allowing them to gain by efficiently choosing how to spend their vouchers. Among the vouchers that provide for refundability are the G.I. Bill, Section 8 housing, and, in recent years, food stamps. By the same token, refundability tends to make the voucher more like cash, especially when the voucher amount falls below some minimum that might be expected to be spent by almost any beneficiary.

—*Regulation and quality control.* At times advocates for vouchers will argue that they wish to move away from the regulations that apply to direct expenditures. Such an argument, for instance, is made with respect to health care vouchers in lieu of traditional Medicare. However, some standards and regulation are inevitable. At a minimum, the government will try to ensure that the voucher is spent on the goods and services prescribed and not on those proscribed, and that only "eligible" individuals receive the vouchers.

Quality control arises when there is a potential that the good or service being purchased is not really what is intended. In the case of higher education, for instance, concerns are often raised about schools that promise some form of technical training that is unlikely to lead to jobs or for which advertising costs and profits eat up a large chunk of the voucher. Health care and health insurance already tend to be regulated to a significant extent. But a new program creates its own set of regulatory needs. For instance, should individuals be allowed to spend a medical voucher on an insurance policy that doesn't cover catastrophic care? The government would then be on the hook again if the individual could not cover these costs when they arose.

In some cases, like child care, there are no easy choices. If child-care vouchers must be spent on highly regulated quality care, costs could be raised considerably. Moreover, this would tend to exclude parents and neighbors from providing the care. To complicate matters further, caregiving relatives sometimes give some kickback to beneficiaries.

Quality control within the voucher program itself is required less if the good or service already has to meet various local, state, or national standards. For example, the food offered in grocery stores may already be considered adequately safe to eat.

As always, balance is required. Some regulation is needed to provide quality control, but too much regulation will hamper efficiency. Bishop notes that vouchers to private schools are more effective in countries with exit exams but are less effective when schools do not compete for students or are not allowed to remove disruptive students or incompetent teachers. While private schools need true independence to be effective, complete laissez-faire would result in "diploma mills."

Combined Effects

As vouchers grow in number and value, overlapping issues of efficiency, design, and administration arise. For example, it may be inefficient and restrictive of choice for housing and food stamp vouchers to be separated. There is also a learning curve: individuals who have learned how to use one type of voucher may be much more adept at using another, so that consumer knowledge could grow more than proportionately with expenditures on vouchers. Small vouchers that were at first ineffective might be more effective in a more voucher-oriented world. Administrative efficiency and practicality are also affected by whether or not vouchers are provided on a more general basis: for example, by how many places a poor individual must apply to for different types of assistance. (For a discussion of bundled vouchers or "structured choice," see the chapter by Lerman and Steuerle.)

Constituencies

Vouchers are no different from other programs in the sense that constituencies will develop for the preservation of the program. (See the Loomis chapter.) These constituencies form among both consumers and providers of the good or service. The agricultural lobby, for instance, has become a mainstay of support for food stamps. (See the Moffitt chapter.) When new vouchers are proposed, they are more likely to be supported if they do not threaten any established constituency, that is, if they are complements of, rather than substitutes for, what already exists. Vouchers for higher education were generally viewed as expansive and good for existing educators, who came quickly to support these efforts. Conversely, vouchers for primary and secondary education may threaten those already providing services in public schools. Similarly, vouchers for Medicare may threaten either the level of benefits already received by Medicare beneficiaries or the ability of medical suppliers to charge amounts that may be in excess of what a voucherized system would support. As always, much depends on the actual design of the voucher itself.

The power of constituencies can have an influence on market conditions. Traditional government programs create two types of interest groups that may tend to work against future reform or amendment: the beneficiaries of the program and the public employees who serve them. Vouchers may limit the role of the second category of interest groups if the size of the bureaucracy can be kept smaller. This difference could also make vouchers more adaptable and easier to reform over time.

In some voucher programs, more administrative involvement may be highly desirable (see the Lerman and Steuerle chapter), while competition among public suppliers can be achieved through methods other than vouchers. Therefore, there is no *necessary* reason why vouchers must have a reduced constituency of public employees. Rather, the structure of interest groups and constituencies must be taken into account to determine the long-term advantages and disadvantages of using vouchers versus other alternatives.

Constitutional Issues

Constitutional issues may also arise when vouchers are offered. In this case, the issue becomes the interpretation of constitutional meaning rather than the principles of efficiency and equity invoked from a public finance or administration perspective. Perhaps the most difficult constitutional issue of all within the United States has been over vouchers and similar payments to students who might use them in sectarian schools. (See the chapters by McConnell and by Elliot Mincberg and Judith Schaeffer.)

Opponents of vouchers for primary and secondary schools sometimes emphasize that the *effect* of a voucher would be primarily sectarian today because of the dominance of sectarian schools among those that are now private and would receive the voucher (Mincberg and Schaeffer). Proponents believe that the restrictions placed by the courts on vouchers for primary and secondary education are simply not consistent today with the allowance of many other payments to flow through sectarian organizations, such as institutions of higher learning (McConnell). Opponents would stress the extent to which sectarian education could subsidize sectarian beliefs over other forms of knowledge; proponents point to the success of existing church-related schools in educating students well—often better than public schools—in reading, arithmetic, and other subjects. Opponents believe that little choice is provided by vouchers, because, considered by themselves, vouchers would favor the sectarian schools that exist. Proponents think that vouchers are "neutral" among all forms of education and help establish neutrality when education subsidies are considered as whole.

These issues do not go away when voucher payments are allowed. Once payments flow, government inevitably places some regulation on what is being subsidized, as it wants to ensure that minimal learning and educational standards are met. In turn, church-related schools must cope with the government regulation that results, thus, according to some, opening the door for excessive entanglement between church and state. Many of these issues already play out to some extent with vouchers for higher education.

Measuring Success

Whatever the initial assessment of the merit of vouchers as a mechanism, they also need to be reevaluated over time. Like many government programs, it is often difficult to get good measures of outputs, much less outcomes, as opposed to inputs or dollars spent. Sometimes it is hard even to agree on what the outputs and outcomes should be in the first place! When a program such as vouchers is promoted as a means of fostering competition, however, another measurement problem arises. Take, for example, the common approach of evaluating the success of a voucher program by comparing outcomes for voucher recipients with outcomes for a control group that does not have access to vouchers. If a voucher is ultimately successful in promoting competition, it might improve conditions for both those who receive the voucher and those in the control group, who only have access to some alternative. (For a discussion of experiments designed to measure the effect on public schools without vouchers, see the chapter by Sawhill and Smith.)

A voucher that is truly successful in introducing competition into a given market should improve conditions everywhere. In theory, individuals may not even have to use the voucher, because its potential use may induce other public sector providers to be efficient in their provision of goods and services. Thus even the threat of potential competition may help keep a single supplier more productive. Competition forces all providers to move toward equal value of output per dollar spent; otherwise they will have difficulty surviving. Thus vouchers, like Pell grants for private or public higher education, may improve the quality of output within both types of institutions and for the system as a whole. (See the Hauptman chapter.) This equalization effect of vouchers makes it harder to verify empirically the advantages of alternative delivery systems simply by comparing the quality or price of their output. Even in the absence of empirically measurable differentials, other evidence (although not conclusive) includes theory, the introduction of new levels of competition, or a time series indicating a higher level of average output per dollar spent.

Finally, even when it appears that success is possible with a voucher, other factors must be examined. A voucher may be successful relative to having no program, but less successful than an alternative program that has never been tried. It may also appear to be more successful under some circumstances or at different levels of intervention than others. For example, Bishop's finding that school vouchers seem to work better in countries with standardized testing than in those without does not tell us whether any particular form of standardized testing is the best form of information system to supplement a voucher. Perhaps even more improvement would come from measuring growth in knowledge rather than level of attainment at the end of the year. In effect, attempting to measure success—and to test that success against alternatives—is a never-ending requirement for almost any public program.

Conclusion

The goal of vouchers is to improve efficiency and equity in the provision of public services. Vouchers must compete with direct government delivery, contracting of government services, competitive public suppliers, cash payments, and loans, among alternative delivery mechanisms.

While vouchers work well under the right circumstances, much attention must be given to their market conditions and structural design. Among the market conditions that must be examined are the access of beneficiaries to alternative suppliers, the effect of a subsidy on prices, the ability of those with a voucher to choose and obtain information about the value of services, the amounts of adverse selection that might take place (along with any explicit means of adjusting for risk differentials among recipients), and the extent to which the voucher simply substitutes for purchases that otherwise would have taken place. Structural issues arise over the universality and permanence of the voucher, the tax rate structure to which it implicitly contributes, the allowed migration and mobility of recipients, and the amount of decentralization involved. Structural choices must be made to design a voucher as an expenditure or tax credit, pay beneficiaries or suppliers, make the subsidy refundable or nonrefundable, and decide how far to go with regulations or quality controls. The role of constituencies must be taken into account, including their ability to restrict competition. And, of course, vouchers cannot be implemented unless they are constitutional in the first place.

While it is not always easy to measure the success of vouchers vis-à-vis other government programs, they are a powerful tool in the government's tool chest. Their expansion in recent years attests to their usefulness. Most of all, it increases our responsibility to learn better how to structure and channel this growing body of public expenditures.

Notes

1. *Random House Dictionary of the English Language*, 2d edition unabridged (New York: Random House, 1987).

2. In almost all cases, a stated *intent* of policymakers is that the subsidy inure to the benefit of the consumer, although providers are also sometimes favored in the next breath (for example, farm state politicians favoring the provision of food stamps). Market forces, such as the availability and responsiveness of supply to price changes, obviously may shift the incidence of benefits and mitigate against any initial intent. Of course, just as intended benefits may not inure to consumers, so also suppliers may not gain under a variety of circumstances. For example, food stamp purchases may not help farmers if there is no increase in demand for food.

3. Using the language of David Bradford and Daniel Shaviro's chapter in this volume, a cap implies a declining marginal rate of reimbursement (ending at zero percent). Traditional Medicare is not a voucher, because it does not have a final marginal rate of reimbursement of zero percent.

4. Although no voucher program is this broad, there are at least some that attempt to cover reimbursement for all "employment-related" expenses.

5. Milton Friedman argues that government may *fund* certain services (public goods) to ensure an optimal level of investment, but it does not necessarily have to be the provider. See Milton Friedman, *Capitalism and Freedom* (University of Chicago Press, 1962), pp. 85–107. At times public monopolies can be even more deleterious or harder to change through eventual competition than private monopolies.

6. For example, Jimmy Carter proposed placing an emphasis on existing housing as opposed to the construction of new public housing, Ronald Reagan called vouchers the "cornerstone" of his housing policy and proposed the establishment and expansion of rural housing vouchers, George Bush requested a 27 percent increase in voucher funding in 1992, and Bill Clinton proposed replacing fifty-four thousand public housing units with rental certificates.

7. In their influential book *Politics, Markets, and America's Schools* (Brookings, 1990), John Chubb and Terry Moe begin their argument with a criticism of the bureaucratic constraints of the current system.

8. A very good example is the design of health care programs. In the United States, much of government health insurance for the elderly remains on a fee-for-service basis, with government continually paying larger shares of the nation's income to meet a demand that can only be expected to expand. This approach has made it quite difficult for government to regulate either the quantity of care provided or the payments made to suppliers, although selective restrictions on both have been tried continually. As only one example, diagnosis-related groups (reimbursement for specific treatments) attempted to provide some restriction on cost, but providers responded partly by upgrading their diagnoses (pneumonia became pneumonia with complications), as well as expanding their use of new, better, and more expensive equipment.

9. For a discussion of how automatic growth distorts decisions on national priorities, see C. Eugene Steuerle, Edward M. Gramlich, Hugh Heclo, and Demetra Smith Nightingale, *The Government We Deserve: Responsive Democracy and Changing Expectations* (Urban Institute, 1998).

10. Vouchers, of course, are not the only means of trying to solve any of these problems.

11. If a dollar's worth of consumption costs individuals eighty cents, for example, they will tend to purchase the subsidized item up to the point that its value to them, regardless of cost to society, has been reduced to eighty cents. At that point, the other twenty cents, paid by society, is likely to represent a dead weight loss, barring any "externality" gains to other individuals in society.

12. See C. Eugene Steuerle, "Uses of the Negative Income Tax Framework," *Focus*, vol. 12, no. 3 (1990), pp. 30–32.

13. See, for example, Friedman, *Capitalism and Freedom*, and James Tobin, Joseph A. Pechman, and Peter M. Mieszkowski, "Is a Negative Income Tax Practical?" *Yale Law Journal* (November 1967).

14. See Francis J. Cronin, "A Household's Decision to Accept or Reject a Conditional Transfer Offer," *Southern Economic Journal*, vol. 49, no. 1 (1982), pp. 218–34.

15. For example, Christine Ranney and John Cushman conclude that the welfare stigma associated with food stamps make them considerably less valuable to recipients than cash payments. See Christine K. Ranney and John E. Cushman, "Cash Equivalence, Welfare Stigma, and Food Stamps," *Southern Economic Journal*, vol. 53, no. 4 (1987), pp. 1011–27.

16. Lester Thurow argues that in-kind transfers such as vouchers may be more effective than cash payments in achieving a minimum consumption level of certain goods and services because recipients would spend a lot of the cash on other goods and services. See Lester C. Thurow, "Cash Versus In-Kind Transfers," *American*

Economic Review, vol. 64, no. 2 (1974), pp. 190–95. Edwin West argues that vouchers are superior to cash because they lack fungibility. See Edwin G. West, "Education Vouchers in Principle and Practice: A Survey," *World Bank Research Observer*, vol. 12, no. 1 (1997), pp. 83–103.

17. For 1997, if there is one child, the credit equals 34 percent of earnings up to $6,500 of earnings for a maximum credit of $2,210; this maximum credit phases out between $11,930 and $25,750 of income at a 15.98 percent rate. Other rates and credit amounts apply for different types of families. See *Green Book*, Committee Print, House Committee on Ways and Means, 105 Cong. 2 sess. (Government Printing Office, 1998).

18. Cash transfers through Social Security and Supplemental Security Income remain available for the aged and disabled.

19. To ensure adequate access to health care, a clinic in rural Wisconsin issued vouchers to individuals living too far away to use the clinic or requiring services the clinic could not provide. See Doris P. Slesinger and Cynthia Ofstead, "Using a Voucher System to Extend Health Services to Migrant Farm Workers," *Public Health Reports*, vol. 111, no. 1 (1996), pp. 57–62.

20. Even in housing programs, differences in information among demanders may lead to inequities. Francis Cronin argues that, compared with white families at equal income levels, black families tend to search in fewer neighborhoods and are less likely to search in neighborhoods of different socioeconomic status than their own. See Francis J. Cronin, "How Low-Income Households Search for Housing: Preliminary Findings on Racial Differences," *Urban Institute Working Paper Series*, no. 249 (1975).

21. An important distinction can still be made. In the case of primary and secondary schooling, voucher proponents argue that demand is too constrained because parents and children can contribute more to determining conditions under which education is received. In the case of medical care, voucher proponents assert that demand is too unconstrained, as individuals have little or no understanding of the marginal cost of insurance because existing tax subsidies and expenditure programs encourage purchases to come from government or employers. In one case, demanders know too little about benefits; in the other, about costs.

22. One set of advocates for educational vouchers want to set up a "Parent Information Center" to help parents pick the best school for their children. See Chubb and Moe, *Politics, Markets, and America's Schools*.

23. For a discussion of the problem of adverse selection in health care, see Linda J. Blumberg and Len M. Nichols, *Health Insurance Market Reforms: What They Can and Cannot Do* (Urban Institute, 1998).

24. This effort to subsidize different risk pools was led by David Bradford when he was on the Council of Economic Advisers and is reflected in an important government report sometimes ignored because it was issued at the end of the Bush administration. See White House Task Force on Health Risk Pooling, "Health Risk Pooling for Small-Group Health Insurance" (GPO, January 1993).

25. With automobile insurance, worse drivers pay higher rates even though they also tend to be cross-subsidized by state rules requiring insurance coverage and effectively capping rates that can be charged.

26. For example, until 1998 only 1.5 percent of children were eligible for the Milwaukee school choice program. (See the chapter by Isabel Sawhill and Shannon Smith.)

27. For a discussion on the market distortions caused by queues for housing vouchers, see George E. Peterson and Kale Williams, "Housing Mobility: What Has It Accomplished and What Is Its Promise?" in Alexander Polikoff, ed., *Housing Mobility: Promise or Illusion?* (Urban Institute, 1995).

28. See Cindy Loose, "5 D.C. Housing Employees Charged; Only 10 of 400 New Rent Vouchers Issued since 1990 Didn't Involve Bribery, Probe Finds," *Washington Post*, April 13, 1994, p. A1.

29. The real-world applicability of this point can again be seen in the proposal by President Bush for a universal health care tax credit or voucher. It provided for combined tax rates of 100 percent or so for many individuals between 100 percent and 150 percent of poverty. See C. Eugene Steuerle, "Beyond Paralysis in Health Policy: A Proposal to Focus on Children," *National Tax Journal*, vol. 45, no. 3 (1992), pp. 357–68.

30. See C. Eugene Steuerle and Gordon Mermin, "Devolution as Seen from the Budget," *New Federalism: Issues and Options for States*, no. A-2 (Urban Institute, 1997).

DAVID F. BRADFORD
DANIEL N. SHAVIRO

2 The Economics of Vouchers

THIS CHAPTER provides a swift tour of the economic issues presented by vouchers, which have been defined as "grants earmarked for particular commodities, such as medical care or education, given to individuals."[1] Among its main conclusions are the following:

—A voucher is cash equivalent if the allocation between commodities that the recipient chooses at her budget line is identical to that which she would have chosen if she instead had been given cash in the amount of the voucher. In practice, vouchers may be cash equivalent more often than is commonly believed. The greater the recipient's preference for the commodities the voucher can be used to purchase, and the smaller the amount of the voucher relative to her other resources, the greater likelihood of cash equivalence.

—Since non-cash-equivalent vouchers are inferior to cash from the standpoint of a recipient with stable and well-defined preferences, replacing them with cash would be a Pareto improvement in the absence of other

The authors are grateful to Barbara Fried, Helen Hershkoff, Van Doorn Ooms, Michael Schill, and Eugene Steuerle, along with participants at the Brookings Institution conference and the New York University Law School Colloquium on Tax Policy and Public Finance, for helpful comments.

considerations. That is, it would leave recipients better off and no one else worse off. Among the other considerations that may support using vouchers are paternalism, externalities (including preferences by those who pay for the vouchers to induce a particular commodity choice), and the distributional aim of measuring need when it cannot be observed directly. An example related to the latter is a wage tax—in some respects a negative voucher program that conditions negative grants on the commodity choice of market goods rather than leisure.

—Any voucher program can be said to have a marginal reimbursement rate (MRR) structure, describing the size of the grant per dollar of earmarked expenditure as the amount of such expenditure by the consumer increases. The programs most likely to be characterized as involving "vouchers" are those that have an MRR structure of 100 percent-0 percent. For example, someone who has $10 worth of food stamps can use them to pay 100 percent of qualifying food purchases up to $10, and 0 percent thereafter. By contrast, a food subsidy program with a flat MRR structure would pay a fixed percentage of the cost of all the consumer's qualifying food expenditures.

—Determining appropriate MRRs presents an optimal tax problem that can be compared to that of setting marginal tax rates, or MTRs. Where a voucher responds to paternalism or externalities, Pigovian taxes (such as a pollution tax that requires polluters to bear the costs they impose on others) provide a useful analytical tool for solving this optimal tax problem, since they similarly attempt to alter marginal incentives. Where a voucher program serves the distributional aim of measuring need that cannot be observed directly, the optimal income tax perspective with respect to wage taxes may provide a better analogy.[2] In some circumstances, either of these perspectives can suggest that the classic 100 percent-0 percent MRR structure of vouchers is inappropriate. That structure is perhaps most likely to be optimal in the Pigovian setting if at some point the extra utility from increasing recipients' choice of earmarked commodities steeply declines.

—One rationale for vouchers' typical MRR structure of 100 percent-0 percent that is not generally persuasive, however, is that of using the top rate of zero as a cap for "budget control" purposes. This rationale ignores the likely option of holding expenditure constant by increasing the top MRR while reducing lower-tier MRRs, and it treats a nominal accounting measure of dollars spent in a given program as normatively significant. If a terminal MRR of zero is desirable, this presumably is because an underlying rationale based on paternalism or externalities has ceased to apply.

—The incentive effects of voucher eligibility criteria, such as income or asset tests, can be important. Poor households often face effective MTRs on their earning or saving that approach or even exceed 100 percent, because of the combination of explicit income and other tax liability with multiple phaseouts of transfers under both voucher and nonvoucher programs. Such MTRs, which can produce "poverty traps," may become likely (even if they look unappealing when considered directly) if policymakers fail to integrate their consideration of "poverty" with that of distribution generally or of specific income-conditioned transfer programs with the overall tax-transfer system.

—Vouchers do not have uniform allocation and price effects, given variations in how they affect demand and supply. To the extent that particular vouchers are cash equivalent, only income effects could lead them to increase demand for earmarked commodities. The direction and magnitude of the income effects of vouchers on demand are a function of the relative income and price elasticities of beneficiaries and others. In cases where a voucher increases demand, its price effects depend on supply elasticity, which tends to be greater in the long run than the short run.

—In markets such as housing that are thought to have fixed short-term supply, concern about a price increase if direct grants to consumers (such as vouchers) increase demand, resulting in transition gain to suppliers if demand is not fully anticipated, may motivate the use of public supply instead of direct grants. Yet any such transition gain can be reduced without regard to the choice between public and private supply. Moreover, short-term supply may be less fixed than is commonly thought (for example, because housing is a multidimensioned commodity), and the prospect of transition gain may have desirable incentive effects, inducing short-term supply to increase in anticipation of the adoption of direct grants. Thus the choice between public and private supply should depend in large part on how well each responds in a given setting to the underlying incentive and information problems posed by supply of the particular commodities at issue.

—Both the transitional and the long-term effects of increasing demand for a commodity are easier to analyze where the suppliers are for-profit firms than otherwise. Thus in primary education, where nonprofit firms dominate private supply, transition gain from an underanticipated demand increase (such as from newly provided school vouchers) would be locked into the industry by the lack of owners with a claim on residual profits. The use of the transition gain in the industry would likely depend on the consumption preferences of the managers or of those with whom they had dealings, with the prestige effects of alternative uses possibly playing an important role.

—In choosing a supply mode for a given commodity, the level of supplier competition can be important and is distinguishable from, although potentially affected by, the choice between public and private supply. Government supply through vouchers or other mechanisms is most likely to be successful (whether or not preferable on balance to private supply) in industries where nonprofit firms have proven to be competitive among private suppliers.

Defining Vouchers and the Reasons for Using Them

What are vouchers? Definition suggests a particular economic substance, but it also implicates mere form.[3] How relevant is it whether a given program involves issuing scrip to consumers that they hand over to suppliers for reimbursement? Can a special tax benefit for medical or educational expenses constitute a voucher, and does this depend on whether one considers the benefit a "tax expenditure"? Would a program cease to involve vouchers if recipients could (lawfully) sell their scrip for cash rather than use it to acquire for themselves the earmarked commodities?

Plainly, there are no platonic vouchers, nor any absolute distinction between voucher and other programs. Even as the term is commonly used in public policy debate, the mechanism would be expected both to have unclear boundaries and to be sufficiently sensitive to form that programs of identical economic content might be called "vouchers" or not, at the designers' discretion. For example, consider a program providing free public education with some degree of student choice among schools and providing the schools with state funds that are conditioned on the number of qualified students who enrolled. Whether or not people called this a voucher program might depend on whether the schools nominally charged "tuition" that the students paid with state-issued scrip the schools then submitted to receive state funds, or instead charged zero tuition and separately received identical enrollment-based compensation from the state. Yet this design choice might make no difference so far as the program's real character and effects were concerned.

Ultimately, the precise definitional boundary that one draws between "vouchers" and "nonvouchers" is of little import. What matters are the actual effects of programs, given their characteristics, which can vary continuously along multiple dimensions. The term "voucher" is useful, however, insofar as people actually use it in a particular fashion. Information therefore can be conveyed by describing various programs as more or less voucher-like, even if it is not particularly useful to say which of them cross some arbitrary threshold of voucherdom. The best way to capture what a "voucher" is in public policy debate is therefore both to describe such economic substance as the term has and to explore some prominent examples that show how it is used. As to economic substance, the following four characteristics appear to be critical, if not in all cases indispensable:

—*Grant to consumers based on personal or household characteristics.* The grant provided by a voucher goes directly to consumers rather than to suppliers (or, if directly to the supplier, on behalf of a particular consumer). Moreover, this typically is not solely a matter of nominal incidence, as under the rule—generally viewed by economists as "irrelevant"—that splits nominal payroll tax liability between workers and employers.[4] Rather, personal or household characteristics must have some bearing on who receives the grants and uses them to consume the earmarked commodities. Vouchers therefore help pay for earmarked commodities, but just for beneficiaries, not for other consumers. This voucher characteristic accordingly is not present to the extent that all of the prospective consumers of a given commodity are offered the same grant.

—*Intermediate choice.* The fact that a voucher is earmarked for specific commodities suggests that consumers have what might be called an intermediate range of choice. For example, a voucher for medical care or education allows some choice within the favored category, such as between schools, doctors, and alternative expenditures, that fit the definition of medical care. Given this feature, in the public education example described above, even the use of tuition and scrip probably would not suffice to create what people considered a "voucher" program, if each student were mandatorily assigned to a particular school. The provision of intermediate consumer choice raises two questions: why not more choice (at the limit by providing cash), and why not less choice? Of course, for these questions to be significant, the upper and lower boundaries must both be meaningful.

—*Supplier competition.* Typically associated with consumer choice is the allowance of competition between suppliers. (The extent to which competition actually arises may depend on the particular market.) Suppliers often are mainly or wholly private firms, with or without limitation to nonprofits. They may, however, face significant government regulation of the earmarked commodities they provide or of their operations more generally.

—*Declining marginal rate of reimbursement.* Considered as a government co-payment for particular commodities, vouchers tend toward a declining marginal rate structure per dollar of earmarked expenditure by the consumer—at the limit, 100 percent reimbursement up to a dollar ceiling, followed by zero reimbursement. To the extent this is so, each consumer's potential reimbursement is capped. While there are no bright lines, an uncapped program, especially if it used a rising or relatively flat reimbursement rate, typically would not be described as providing vouchers. On this ground alone, an unlimited income tax deduction for, say, education expenditure probably would not be called a voucher program even though its value gradually declines as it pushes the taxpayer into lower-rate brackets and becomes zero on the elimination of net taxable income. Conversely, the Helping Outstanding Pupils Educationally (HOPE) education credit (Internal Revenue Code, section 25A), which provides certain federal income taxpayers with a tax credit that is capped at $1,500 per student per year, might be considered a voucher despite not using scrip that the supplier must redeem.

Some Typical Voucher and Related Programs

We next consider four leading areas where "voucher" programs are or might be used. Three involve current federal programs, while the fourth is a hypothetical state government program of a sort that has been widely discussed. We start by describing the programs and then ask what problems they are trying to address, how what were clearly nonvoucher programs might address the same problems, and how the voucher versus nonvoucher approaches should be evaluated. We do not limit our discussion to programs that fully meet the "voucher" definition, since such a limitation would impede evaluating the significance of the various strict voucher characteristics.

FOOD STAMPS. Households that satisfy a considerable list of criteria may receive food stamps from the federal government. These may actually be stamps, denominated in dollars, or they may take the form of a plastic electronic benefit transfer (EBT) card, like a phone card, loaded with a certain dollar total. Food stamps are an entitlement, guaranteed to any applicant household that satisfies the requirements. These would include an income test, a liquid assets test, and a requirement that unemployed adults, if not exempted, register for work and stand ready to participate in certain training programs.

The number of food stamps a qualified household receives is determined by formula. Roughly speaking, a household receives the difference between 30 percent of "counted monthly cash income" and an amount deemed sufficient to buy an adequate low-cost diet (given household composition). Thus suppose a given household was deemed to need $4,500 a year to eat adequately. It would receive $4,500 in food stamps if it had no income for the year, phasing down to no food stamps as its income increased to $15,000.

Food stamps may be used at approved grocery stores to buy approved products, basically food items for home preparation. (A household living in certain remote areas of Alaska may also use food stamps to pay for equipment for procuring food by hunting and fishing.) The retailer obtains cash reimbursement or, in the case of the EBT card, a bank account credit from the federal government.[5]

MEDICARE. Medicare is a nationwide federal health insurance program for the aged and certain disabled persons. Hospital insurance ("Part A coverage") is provided automatically and covers most costs above a deductible amount, up to a temporary ceiling that has little effect in practice. Coverage for items such as physicians' and laboratory services ("Part B coverage") may be purchased at a fixed monthly premium and pays 80 percent of amounts above a deductible. Patients can purchase supplemental "Medigap" coverage that eliminates their liability to pay deductibles and coinsurance, thus reducing marginal cost to zero (the Part A coverage ceiling aside).

The monthly premium is zero for Part A coverage, and even for Part B coverage it is far less than what an arm's-length insurance provider would charge. Qualifying individuals identify themselves to service providers, who are reimbursed by Medicare. Reimbursements are for fixed amounts that depend on the diagnosis for Part A coverage and on prescribed fee schedules for Part B coverage. Any deductibles and co-payments are billed by the providers to the covered individuals.

Although the individual has considerable latitude to choose the supplier of services paid for by Medicare, some forms of purchase may not be allowed because of the difficulty of adapting them to the program's basic structure. It has, for example, been difficult to develop an option for beneficiaries to enroll in qualifying health maintenance organizations (HMOs). Moreover, holders of Medigap coverage have virtually no incentive to engage in cost-conscious shopping.

Medicare is not a "voucher" program, as the term is generally defined in this book, because of the lack of a final MRR of zero. By contrast, a replacement program that made fixed payments to a managed-care provider chosen by the consumer would qualify as a voucher program. We will discuss the current Medicare system, however, because it is otherwise voucherlike, helps illuminate design questions pertaining to the optimal MRR structure, and could conceivably be made a full-fledged voucher program through the enactment of reimbursement ceilings.

HOUSING. Federal subsidies to housing (other than through the income tax) come in two main forms: project-based assistance and tenant-based assistance.[6] Only the latter provides enough consumer choice to meet our "voucher" definition, but both are worth describing briefly to illuminate comparisons between voucher and alternative programs.

Under project-based assistance, which includes but is not limited to public housing, a qualifying tenant who makes it to the top of a local jurisdiction's waiting list is offered a specific unit (or a choice of up to three). She must then either accept what is offered or return to the bottom of the waiting list. Similarly, a still-qualifying incumbent tenant who wants to leave her unit without exiting the program can only do so at the cost of returning to the bottom of the waiting list. Qualification depends on income, asset tests, and family size. It is determined by the public housing authority (PHA) in the case of public housing and by the landlord (subject to verification) in the case of privately owned projects. The qualifying tenant pays in rent 30 percent of an income measure specified for this purpose. The federal government makes up the difference between this amount and an allowable rent that is based on the estimated cost of providing the unit, with some reference to comparable rents in the area. (No higher rent can be charged, even if the tenant would be willing to pay it, without making the unit nonqualifying.) The grant is phased out as income increases in much the same manner as under the food stamps program.

Tenant-based assistance meets the voucher definition, although it involves the use of items called both vouchers and certificates. In each case, tenants who have been approved for the grant search for qualifying housing units, which must meet program quality standards. In the case of the certificates, rent for the unit must be less than or equal to the "fair market rent" (FMR) in the area, "based on the cost of modest, decent private housing on the local market."[7] The voucher program makes use of an FMR computation, but it permits rent to exceed the FMR.

In the case of a voucher, the landlord receives the amount by which the FMR exceeds 30 percent of the tenant's income. The tenant pays the balance of the rent and thus bears the consequences of any difference, up or down, between it and the FMR. By contrast, under the certificate program, where the rent cannot exceed the FMR, the landlord receives the difference between 30 percent of the tenant's income and the rent charged. Thus the fiscal benefit if the rent is below the FMR accrues to the government rather than to the tenant by reducing its outlay in that case.

In contrast to food stamps and Medicare, the various housing programs are not entitlements. Housing that qualifies for project-based assistance is in fixed supply at any time, and it generally cannot meet the demand for it by qualified applicants. The tenant-based subsidies are subject to budget limits that likewise fall short of demand by families that meet the qualifications. The programs therefore have queues, and "only one eligible applicant in three ever receives federal housing assistance."[8] Queuing has encouraged the use of subsidiary criteria for qualification, and it has made willingness to stay in a given area while one moves up the waiting list and thereafter (perhaps in an inferior housing unit) an informal prerequisite for receiving assistance. It is worth noting, however, that some subsidiary criteria, such as requirements that one accept available work or undergo job training, may have some tendency to offset other distortive features of the voucher program, such as the effect of an income phaseout of the voucher amount on incentives to work.

EDUCATION. Public education through high school is generally free to all resident children in the United States.[9] It typically is financed through local property taxes, along with state and federal aid. Below the college level, government generally has provided no direct aid to assist particular private school students in paying their tuition. Recent years, however, have seen increased discussion of proposed school vouchers that could be used on private school tuition, and Milwaukee, Wisconsin, recently adopted such a program on a limited test basis.[10]

Under a hypothetical school voucher program resembling the Milwaukee experiment, a qualifying family would receive from its state government a voucher for a fixed amount of money. Qualification and the amount of the voucher would depend on family attributes such as income relative to the number of school-age children. The vouchers would be usable towards paying tuition at all qualifying schools (possibly limited to those that were nonsectarian), although they would be set too low to pay it in full. The schools would be able to submit vouchers from their students to the state government for reimbursement.

Problems Addressed by Voucher and Related Programs

Through each of these voucher and related programs, the government intervenes in the economy with respect to a particular consumer transaction. For food stamps, the transaction is provision of food to people who do not have enough to eat. For Medicare, it is the provision of medical care to elderly people who are sick. For housing vouchers, it is the provision of adequate accommodations to people who either are homeless or live in substandard accommodations such as the stereotypical tenement or slum. For education vouchers, it is the provision of adequate education to children.

Each program therefore seems to rest on the view that nonoccurrence of the identified transaction in circumstances where the voucher is used to ensure its occurrence would be undesirable.[11] Since consumer transactions ordinarily are the province of the particular consumers and suppliers who decide whether or not to engage in them, it is worth asking what really is thought to be the problem in each of these cases. The main possibilities—apart from simply a convenient political alliance between supporters of progressive redistribution and of business subsidies—are the following:[12]

—*Distribution.* Each of the above commodities might be thought important enough to suggest that almost anyone who was not facing a severe budget constraint would purchase it. Thus, at a minimum, nonoccurrence of the consumer transactions helps to dramatize broader distributional problems. Starvation, for example, is more vivid than generalized poverty. If vividness were the only issue, this might suggest broadening the programs' focus to address poverty in general, without limitation to an arbitrary subset of the commodities that poor people may be unable to afford. In some cases, however, the voucher programs' focus on satisfying consumer demand for a particular commodity may advance the core requirement of distributional policy that one correctly identify the needy. Thus if sick elderly people are needier than healthy ones who otherwise have the same resources, Medicare arguably directs its aid to the "right" group by subsidizing the medical expenditure that results from being sick. (One could argue that other programs, such as the income tax, adjust for nonhealth differences in elderly people's resources.) Or, if a household's overall level of need is significantly conditioned on the educational needs of its children, then school vouchers may tend to direct aid to where the need is greater.

—*Externalities.* A second rationale for focusing on the above consumer transactions is that they have positive externalities that are not fully reflected in the incentives of consumers and suppliers who decide whether to engage in them. An example would be the possibility that schooling shapes children's tastes and abilities in a way that will benefit others when they grow up, such as by encouraging productive work relative to crime or relying on transfers. Living in adequate housing in a decent neighborhood might have similar effects. Or the externality might involve reaching inside the household to overcome parental disregard of the children's interests, such as by requiring the household to allocate a given portion of its total budget to commodities, such as education and housing, of which the children can claim a large or even exclusive share.

A distinctive kind of externality relates to the donative preferences of those who vote and pay for government transfers. Suppose that one derives utility from enabling a poor person to eat but not from enabling her to do something that she prefers (even rationally) at the margin to eating—say, purchasing alcohol or entertainment. The resulting positive externality to her food consumption can be addressed by subsidizing it, such as through a voucher.[13] Or suppose one's preference is simply that the particular funds one gives the donee be used in a specified way, such as to purchase food, without regard to the overall effect on her budget allocation between commodities. (This could reflect "voucher illusion," or a failure to understand how the recipient's other commodity choices may adjust.) Here, earmarking the transfer addresses an externality, even if its marginal effect on the donee is equivalent to that from receiving cash.

—*Paternalism.* A third rationale for focusing on the above consumer transactions is that voucher recipients who would fail to engage in them if given unrestricted cash instead of vouchers would be making a mistake from the standpoint of their own interests. Here, the alcoholic is required to eat rather than drink for her own good, and not because donors would prefer that she eat, or schooling is forced on households that underestimate its real value to them.

Paternalism is least ambiguous in cases where the recipient has stable, well-defined preferences (of the sort normally assumed in neoclassical models) that would lead inexorably to a change in budget allocation if vouchers were replaced by cash. Some voucher recipients, however, may not exhibit such preferences. Instead, framing effects or the exhortatory influence of receiving a voucher that one is told should be spent in a particular way may end up influencing consumer choices. Thus suppose that an individual with income of $50 a week, $30 of which he spends on food, would in fact increase his weekly food expenditure to $40 if he received $10 of food stamps, but only to $35 if he received an extra $10 of cash. The decision to give him food stamps instead of cash would not be paternalistic in the sense of requiring him to depart from stable consumer preferences of the sort one could depict with an indifference map. It might still, however, be paternalistic in the sense of reflecting a judgment from the outside that a $40 food expenditure was better for him than one of $35, and thus that the government should try (through framing or exhortation) to influence his allocative choice.

—*Other market failure.* Other market failures, such as monopoly, supplier bias, regulatory distortions, thin markets, or lag in adjusting to new consumer demand, may also be blamed for the nonoccurrence of desirable consumer transactions. Low-income housing, for example, might be undersupplied as the result of zoning restrictions or union rules in the construction industry. Or public education might be protected from private competition despite any deficiencies because it is provided free, thus potentially making extension of the subsidy to private schools efficient even if a first-best approach would eliminate all education subsidies.

Nonvoucher Alternatives to Problems Addressed by Vouchers

A voucher program provides only one possible response to the aim of intervening with respect to the consumer transaction it identifies. At least in principle, alternatives always include at least the following:

—Providing voucher recipients with cash, or amounts not conditioned on their spending decisions. Thus food stamps, housing vouchers, and hypothetical school vouchers could be replaced with cash. Medicare could in principle be replaced by a program of paying cash to elderly individuals that was conditioned on an assessment of their medical needs without regard to their actual expenditures. In practice, households that receive vouchers frequently also receive cash grants, as in the case of food stamp households that also receive Temporary Aid to Needy Families (TANF), or Medicare recipients who also receive Social Security payments. However, the exclusive use of cash may fail to address some of the rationales for voucher programs, such as those based on externalities or paternalism.

—Providing suppliers of earmarked commodities with direct subsidies, with or without reliance on the identity of their consumers. This, too, is currently done to some extent. Consider low-income housing tax credits as well as charitable income tax deductions along with exemptions from various taxes for nonprofit suppliers in the medical and education industries.

However, the incidence of such supplier subsidies may be hard or impossible to direct to transactions involving the particular consumers that voucher programs typically are intended to benefit.

—The government can itself supply earmarked commodities rather than using vouchers to reimburse private suppliers. Public housing and education are the obvious current examples, but in principle the government could also replace Medicare with public hospitals for the elderly and food stamps with public food commissaries that handed out food conditioned on people's household circumstances. Because of its similar focus on a particular consumer transaction, this option often provides the closest substitute and leading political alternative to a voucher program.

How should the choice be made between voucher programs and their nonvoucher alternatives? Obviously, the underlying rationales for relating government grants to specific consumer transactions need to be evaluated carefully. However, even within the framework of accepting these rationales, incentive and underlying information issues arise on both the consumer and the supplier sides of the transactions. The rest of this chapter, therefore, looks first at the consumer-side issues and then at supplier-side issues.

Consumer-Side Issues

In general, when a tax or transfer is generated by a transaction, its economic incidence is unrelated to its nominal incidence but depends instead on supply and demand elasticities. The standard example is the payroll tax, the economic incidence of which is thought to be unaffected by its nominal fifty-fifty split between workers and employers.[14] Special considerations, such as effects on transaction costs or the existence of separate government programs that are conditioned on nominal (pretax or transfer) prices or wages, may cause nominal incidence to matter in some cases.[15]

The significance of vouchers providing a grant to consumers rather than suppliers does not rest on nominal incidence. Thus in the case of a school voucher program, it might not matter whether the vouchers were given to consumers to reimburse their tuition payments or to the schools to supplement any such payments. Likewise, in the case of Medicare, the fact that the government directly pays suppliers of medical services does not prevent the program from being viewed as consumer directed.

Rather than nominal incidence, the key feature separating a voucher from a business subsidy is differential provision of the grant for transactions involving different consumers, based on the consumers' personal or household characteristics. This feature may cause consumers to face different prices for the same commodity, depending on whether they can use vouchers or not, unless suppliers can price discriminate (net of the proceeds from any vouchers) between consumers in voucher and nonvoucher transactions.

As an example of such price discrimination, suppose that a school voucher program provided $1,000 tuition vouchers to a specific group of students but that the schools could respond by charging these students $1,000 more in tuition (net of the vouchers) than other students. If this were a stable outcome, it would convert the grant into a supplier subsidy, without permitting vouchered students to pay less out of pocket than unvouchered students. Under fully competitive markets, however, this result is impossible. After all, so long as vouchered students are worth more in revenue to the schools than unvouchered but otherwise identical students, the schools would be expected to compete for them by cutting the price, until at equilibrium the vouchered students paid $1,000 less out of pocket.

Yet noncompetitive situations where suppliers capture the benefit are not uncommon. Consider universities, which may charge less than a market-clearing tuition, using legislative subsidies or their endowments (which are locked in by nonprofit status) to pay their bills and selective admissions to choose within the queue of applicants. If the federal government enacts a voucher program (such as the HOPE credit) for selected students, the universities may respond by increasing tuition for people who meet the voucher criteria.[16]

Or consider cases where suppliers have some degree of local monopoly power that they use to price discriminate based on their assessment of different customers' reservation prices. (A standard example would be car dealers if some or all of their customers have significant search costs.) In such cases, the fact that a consumer either must communicate bearing a voucher or has observable characteristics from which this can be inferred may lead to price discrimination that effectively converts the voucher into a business subsidy. Medicare might provide an example in markets where competition is limited or where searching for health care would be costly if it were not for the system's use of prescribed fee schedules.

Extent to Which Vouchers Are Cash Equivalents

It is natural to think of vouchers as inherently noncash equivalent from the recipient's standpoint, because they can only be used to purchase

Figure 2-1. *Effect of Cash versus a Food Voucher on Alice's Budget Line*
Nonfood (dollars)

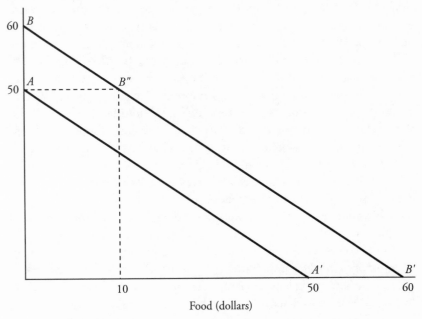

Food (dollars)

earmarked commodities. In fact, however, a voucher is equivalent to a cash grant unless the earmarking alters the recipient's overall budget allocation between commodities. Cash equivalence may be common and depends on both the consumer's preference for earmarked relative to other commodities and the voucher's size relative to the consumer's other spendable resources. (For discussion on the actual cash equivalence of food stamps, see the chapter by Robert Moffitt in this volume.)

The point can be illustrated through a hypothetical example in which there are only two commodities, food and nonfood. Suppose that before the adoption of the voucher program, Alice has a weekly income of $50. She thus can spend $50 on food and nothing on nonfood, $50 on nonfood and nothing on food, or any intermediate combination that does not cost more than $50, as shown by line *AA'* in figure 2-1.

Now suppose a new voucher program is enacted under which Alice receives $10 a week in food stamps in addition to her other income. Had she instead been given an extra $10 of cash a week, her budget line would

Figure 2-2. *When Alice's Food Vouchers Are Equivalent to Cash*

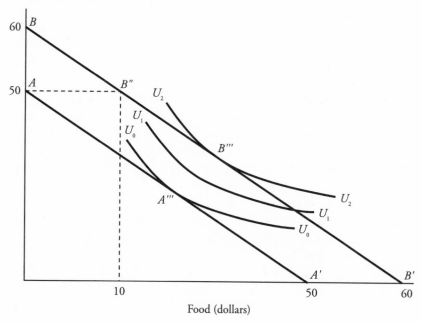

Nonfood (dolllars)

Food (dollars)

have shifted outwards to embrace combinations from $60 on food and no nonfood, to no food and $60 on nonfood, as shown by line BB'. However, given the requirement that the food stamps be spent on food—assuming this cannot be circumvented, such as by selling them for cash—the attainable combinations must include at least $10 of food. Thus she still cannot afford more than $50 of nonfood. Her actual new budget line therefore differs from BB' by the subtraction from it of the triangle ABB''. Yet it remains at all points above AA', since any affordable quantity of nonfood can now be combined with $10 more food than previously.

To what extent is Alice made better off by the food stamp program? This depends on how her preferences for food and nonfood lead her to value alternative combinations of the two. This can be shown by superimposing indifference curves on her new budget line. In figure 2-2 we see an outcome where the voucher program happens to permit her to select the same new combination—involving increases in both food and nonfood consumption—that she would have chosen if offered cash. In either case, she moves to B''' whether she receives cash or the voucher. Thus in this case, giving her $10 of food stamps leads to the same budget allocation as giving her $10 of cash and increases her utility by the same amount (from A''').

More generally, the voucher program gives Alice the same benefit as cash whenever B'''—the point of tangency of line BB' with the highest indifference curve that touches it (U_2)—lies to the right of B'', which is the point where the amount of the earmarked commodity that she purchases equals the amount of her vouchers. In figure 2-2 the constraint requiring Alice to spend at least $10 out of her $60 budget on food is no constraint at all, since she meets it of her own volition. Replacing the voucher with a $10 cash grant would therefore make no difference. Indeed, replacing it with a $10 nonfood voucher would likewise make no difference, since B''' is shown as being above $10 on the vertical (nonfood) axis. Under any of these alternatives, Alice uses the extra $10 to move from A''' to B''', increasing both her food and her nonfood consumption in proportions that depend purely on the preferences that underlie her indifference curves as distinct from how (if at all) the $10 grant is earmarked.

Now suppose instead that B''' lay to the left of B''. Holding everything else on figure 2-2 the same, this would require some combination of (a) shifting curve U_2 to the left to reflect Alice's having a greater taste for nonfood relative to food consumption at that utility level, and (b) shifting B'' to the right by increasing the portion of Alice's budget line that was earmarked for food expenditure. Now, if Alice were allowed to spend $60 however she liked, she would buy less food than the amount of her food vouchers. Under this condition, the vouchers are worth less to her than cash in the same amount, because they leave her on an indifference curve that lies below U_2. This is shown in figure 2-3, in which her relevant indifference curves lie further to the left (towards nonfood) and the composition of her $60 budget has changed to consist of $20 of food vouchers and only $40 of other goods. Here, the result of earmarking the food vouchers is that her utility increases only from U_0 to U_1, rather than to U_2.

At the limit, if Alice placed no value on any food, food vouchers would be worthless to her. Although they would permit her to add food in the vouchered amount to her otherwise exclusive nonfood consumption, they would keep her on the same indifference curve (a horizontal line in which only the quantity of nonfood mattered). Even short of that extreme, however, whenever B''' lies to the left of B'', replacing the voucher with a cash grant would make her subjectively better off at no added budgetary cost to the government. Accordingly, absent externalities or grounds for paternal-

Figure 2-3. *When Alice's Food Vouchers Are not Equivalent to Cash*

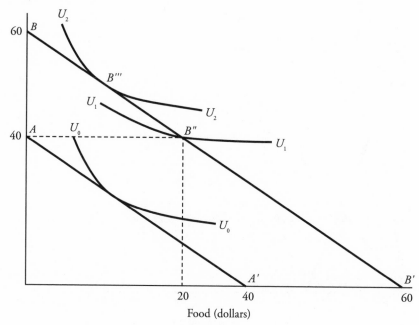

Nonfood (dollars)

Food (dollars)

ism, this would be a Pareto improvement, making her better off and no one worse off.

What determines whether one has the cash-equivalence case depicted in figure 2-2 or, instead, the non-cash-equivalence case depicted in figure 2-3? This depends on two things. The first is the consumer's relative preference for the earmarked commodity at the relevant budget level. Consumers with different preferences will have different income-expansion paths. In the standard textbook picture, an income-expansion path is a smooth, northeast-inclined curve that shows the combination of, in this case, food and nonfood (in dollars spent) chosen by the household at various budget levels, given prices. The typical shape is that of the segments $OG''X$ and $OI''X'$ in figure 2-4. $OI''X'$ belongs to a consumer with a strong taste for nonfood (an alcoholic, for example), relative to the consumer with expansion path $OG''X$. The voucher program gives rise to a kinked shape for the income-expansion paths, so that $MI''X'$ describes the income expansion path of the alcoholic and $MG''X$ that of the ordinary consumer. The portions of the

Figure 2-4. *Expansion Paths under a Typical Food Voucher Regime*

Nonfood (dollars)

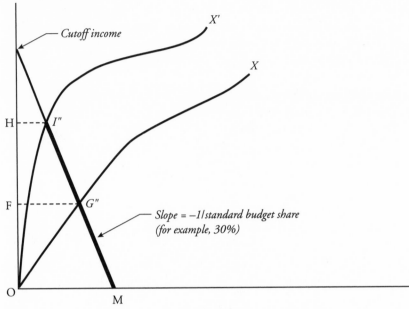

Food (dollars)

paths sloping up to the northwest (*MI″* and *MG″*) constitute the choices made when the requirement that the vouchers be used on food is binding on the consumer in question. That constraint cuts in at a higher preprogram income (*H* instead of *F*) for the alcoholic, the consumer with the lesser relative preference for food.

As the examples in figure 2-4 suggest, the second determinant of the degree of cash equivalence is the amount of the voucher relative to the consumer's other resources. Thus consider the cash equivalence of food stamps for two households that are identical except that their other (cash) incomes are zero and $12,000, respectively, where the allowable benefit is $4,500 minus 30 percent of income. ("Identical" thus means they have the same income-expansion paths in figure 2-4, *MG″X*, for example.) The first household receives $4,500 in food stamps (the only resources it has) and the second $900. Here, food stamps very likely are a cash equivalent for the second household (which surely would spend at least $900 of its total $12,500 on food items for home consumption in any event), but very likely is not a cash equivalent for the first. Moreover, the less the first household's taste for spending its first few thousand dollars of resources on food, the less cashlike the benefit is. Note that the second household will spend less on food than the first household, despite being better off overall. The situation is illustrated in figure 2-4. The household with the greater income is at a point like A, whereas the household with zero cash income is at a point like M.

These results can perhaps be rationalized if an important motivation for using food vouchers is paternalism and if cash income is a proxy for the ability to make good decisions. Thus suppose that alcoholism induces behavior contrary to self-interest but cannot be observed directly. At all income levels up to a certain point, the food voucher interferes more with the exercise of consumer choice by alcoholics than by nonalcoholics. And the intervention extends to a higher level of cash income for alcoholics than for nonalcoholics.

Externality arguments also might in some circumstances support allowing the voucher to become more cashlike as other income increases. Suppose that voters and taxpayers want the specific resources they transfer to be used for food and nothing else. Here, increasing cash equivalence as nonvoucher income increases is a by-product of satisfying this preference, and the welfare loss to the lowest-income households from having to buy extra food ought in principle to be compared to the welfare gain to third parties from making them do this. One also might consider the reduced disincentive effect of an income-conditioned voucher on work if it is not cash equivalent.

Now consider Medicare, where the marginal reimbursement rate remains indefinitely at 80 percent or 100 percent, rather than going to 0 percent once a fixed expenditure limit has been reached. The size of the grant is therefore conditioned on the amount that the consumer decides to spend. (Medicare also, unlike Medicaid, provides sufficiently generous reimbursement to avoid giving suppliers any strong financial incentive to act as gatekeepers.) Thus in figure 2-5, AA' is Bob's budget line absent a Medicare program, which he can allocate between health-care and non-health-care expenditure. AB' is the new budget line resulting from Medicare's 80 percent reimbursement rate for his medical expenditures. (AB' would be horizontal at a 100 percent reimbursement rate.) For any point B' that Bob picks on this budget line, we can specify a budget line CC' that Bob would have had if given an unconditional cash grant in the same amount.

Medicare's extremely pronounced effect on the budget lines of beneficiaries makes its historical growth pattern unsurprising. The increase in

Figure 2-5. *Effect of 80 Percent Medicare Reimbursement on Bob's Budget Line*

Non-health care (dollars)

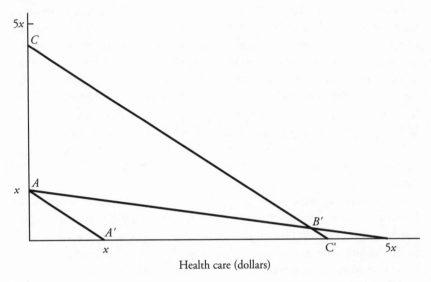

Health care (dollars)

medical expenditure would probably have been even greater if not for (a) the noncash costs of receiving health care, such as in personal time or discomfort, and (b) the role doctors may play, even when generous payment is available, in deciding what health care to supply. Indeed, without these factors, beneficiaries whose Medigap coverage placed them on a horizontal budget line might be expected to demand all medical expenditure that conveyed even a penny of benefit, without regard to its cost.

Although we do not show indifference curves in figure 2-5, the skew towards medical expenditure that even 80 percent reimbursement induces suggests a possibility that Bob could increase his utility at no extra budgetary cost to the government, if he were permitted to move to the left from *B'* along *CC'* by shifting toward nonhealth-care expenditure without a reduction in his grant. This would not be the case, however, for medical expenditure that was sufficiently urgent for Bob to want to allocate to it all available resources above those required for minimum subsistence.

Where Bob would prefer to move to the left along *CC'*, this is a figure 2-3–type case in which the Medicare grant is not cash equivalent. In such a case, the argument against permitting Bob to achieve the commodity allocation he wants given his budget line probably cannot rest on paternalism. Even to the extent that increasing medical expenditure correlates with increased sickness, how plausible is it that the sicker one is the greater the likelihood that one will misunderstand one's own interest in allocating one's consumption to health care? Thus the argument for non-cash-equivalent Medicare grants probably must rest either on distributional grounds (if we cannot tell whom we want to benefit without observing medical expenditure) or on an externality claim, perhaps concerning voters' and taxpayers' donative preference for having Medicare beneficiaries consume health care rather than other commodities.

Relative Choice under Voucher Programs versus Government Supply

The prior section's comparison of vouchers to cash grants still holds if one substitutes government-supplied commodities for cash grants. Thus suppose that, in lieu of giving someone a $10,000 voucher to purchase housing or education, the government spent $10,000 to provide her with free public housing or education. One could identically analyze whether her budget allocation and utility would change if she were instead handed $10,000 in cash and permitted (but not required) to purchase the same commodity for that amount. After all, free supply is a kind of implicit voucher transaction; the government spends a sum of money on the beneficiary but specifies its use.

As we will see in a later section of this chapter, some crucial differences between vouchers and free (or below-cost) government supply lie on the supplier side. Vouchers may use private rather than public suppliers, often accompanied by greater competition between suppliers, and thus affect the incentive structure of commodity supply. On the consumer side, however, there often are important differences as well between vouchers and free government supply. Voucher programs often permit greater consumer choice than government supply programs, both of specific commodities within the earmarked category and of suppliers.

In illustration, consider programs relating to housing and schools. In housing, the tenant-based voucher and certificate programs allow beneficiaries to select the qualified housing unit of their choice, whereas project-based assistance, much of which involves public housing, offers no more than three units on a take-it-or-leave-it basis. Similarly, while school choice can to some extent be accommodated in the public school structure, advocates of school voucher programs argue that choice should be greater still, going both to the particular school and to what sort of education is being purchased (for example, religious content).

We should note, however, that this distinction in consumer choice is not inherently related to whether one uses actual vouchers or merely (through free government supply) implicit ones. After all, public housing or education can be structured to offer extensive consumer choice of specific commodity or supplier, while the use of a voucher does not prevent choice from being limited. The frequent difference in practice may reflect supplier-side incentive issues of the sort that we discuss in a later section.

Why might greater consumer choice of specific commodity and supplier be desirable? Apart from its effect on supplier incentives, the main argument rests on consumer sovereignty. Even if consumer sovereignty is rejected at some margins of choice—say, between food and alcohol—based on externalities and paternalism, there may be other choices, including those within a broad category—say, a food choice between pasta and hamburgers—as to which the reasons for limiting it do not apply.[17]

The downside of providing greater consumer sovereignty is that, depending on how the (voucher or nonvoucher) program is structured, it may ease consumer choice that is inconsistent with any externality or paternalism-based rationales. It also, depending on program structure, raises issues of consumer cost consciousness—the degree of incentive to secure earmarked commodities at a low rather than high price, which we consider next.

Consumer Incentives to Be Cost Conscious

Consumers have every reason to be cost conscious when they are spending their own money. Moral hazard arises if they are spending someone else's money and their behavior cannot be perfectly observed. In the voucher setting, cost consciousness plays a complicated role, because one may want consumers to take the cost of earmarked commodities into account in some respects but not in others. For example, the whole point of providing food stamps rather than cash in cases where the two are not equivalent is to induce a kind of departure by recipients from full cost consciousness when they buy food. Yet this aim of the program would presumably be subverted if people bought food wastefully and thus remained ill-nourished—a danger that the program design helps to minimize through its incentive structure. Suppose, however, that the food stamps program was revised to be more like Medicare, in the sense that beneficiaries were reimbursed for whatever costs they incurred to acquire food of a given caloric content. Now the diminished incentive to be cost conscious in buying food might begin to pose major problems for the system (for example, people could buy beluga caviar and be reimbursed), notwithstanding the aim of eliminating cost consciousness in certain trade-offs between food and nonfood.

MARGINAL REIMBURSEMENT RATES AS POSING AN OPTIMAL TAX PROBLEM. In general, the cost consciousness of consumers who receive vouchers or other earmarked grants depends on the marginal rate of reimbursement (MRR)—the percentage of a dollar of extra expenditure for an earmarked commodity that the government, rather than the consumer, would bear. Under the definition stated earlier (and generally applied throughout this volume), the classic voucher has an MRR structure of 100 percent-0 percent, and nothing too far from that even qualifies as a voucher. Nonetheless, we examine the question of setting optimal MRRs more broadly, since policymakers can choose the MRRs they prefer without being constrained by artificial definitional boundaries.

Setting MRRs in a voucher or similar program is very similar to setting marginal tax rates (MTRs) in a tax system. At a broad level of generality, only the direction of the cash flow—from government to consumer in the voucher and from taxpayer to government in a tax system—distinguishes the two cases. Consider a Pigovian pollution tax, which attempts to discourage the taxed activity to the extent of that activity's negative externalities. Or consider an optimal income tax (OIT) in the literature inspired by James Mirrlees in his 1971 study entitled "An Exploration in the Theory of Optimum Income Taxation," carried in the *Review of Economic Studies*. An OIT is in some respects a negative voucher program that taxes the commodity choice of market goods that are paid for through market work, although here the aim is distributional rather than based on considering market participation akin to pollution.

It should be clear, therefore, that setting MRRs presents an optimal tax problem, the analysis of which depends on the underlying reason for altering the relative prices of different commodities for program beneficiaries. We first discuss the case where the program responds to paternalism or externalities and thus resembles a Pigovian tax. Second, we discuss the case where the program serves distributional purposes and thus resembles the OIT. Third, we discuss the case where the program's effects on consumer choice are undesirable in terms of the policy objectives usually adduced in welfare economics and where it ought (apart perhaps from political considerations) to be replaced by a cash grant. Finally, we discuss issues of "program cost" that are sometimes described as justifying the classic voucher's 100 percent-0 percent MRR structure.

First, suppose that choice is limited by externalities or paternalism. Thus alteration of consumer choice is affirmatively desirable up to a given point but not beyond—just as Pigovian taxes should be set at the right level, given externalities, rather than too high or too low. The goal therefore is to induce some choice of earmarked commodities that the voucher recipient would not have selected if given cash. However, the extent to which the alteration of choices is desirable depends on the relationship between the allocation that the consumer would actually choose at the budget line she would face if the vouchers were converted to cash and the socially preferred allocation at this budget line. In effect, the problem is to select the correct Pigovian subsidy at each point.

To show how optimal MTRs depend on this relationship, suppose we start with a zero-income household that, absent paternalism or externalities relating to its food consumption, would simply receive a cash grant. To be optimal, any food voucher component of this grant would have to be a cash-grant equivalent with a zero MTR at the household's actual decision point regarding food expenditure.

Then suppose we adopt the paternalistic view that zero-income households underestimate by 20 percent the benefit of eating food, while otherwise making rational choices. Or, equivalently, suppose that the benefit to other people (perhaps from donative preferences) of food consumption by such households equals 20 percent of the cost of the food, without regard to the amount of food consumed. Under this view, optimal MRR analysis would suggest providing unlimited 20 percent reimbursement for the household's food purchases and presumably reducing the cash grant.

Suppose instead, however, that the paternalistic view holds that zero-income households are being irrational if they do not spend enough on food to buy an adequate low-cost diet (assuming a cash grant of at least that amount) but that decisions whether to spend more than this minimum threshold are presumptively within consumer sovereignty. Or, equivalently, suppose that voters and taxpayers derive substantial utility from increasing the food consumption of zero-income households up to the amount needed to buy an adequate low-cost diet but zero utility from supporting further food consumption (apart from any utility that they assign to progressive redistribution through cash grants). Now, reducing cash grants and enacting a food voucher program with a 100 percent-0 percent MRR (like that of the actual food stamps program) begins to look plausible. Further specification of the paternalism or externalities would be needed to explain the gradually increasing cash-grant equivalence of food stamps as income increases and the amount of the grant decreases.

Even under this assumption that the extra utility from the grantees' increasing their food consumption suddenly declines from significant to zero, a 100 percent-0 percent MRR is not necessarily optimal under limited information. If the exact point where this happens for given households is unknown, the aim of minimizing error costs might suggest a range of intermediate MRRs. However, the assumption of a sudden decline in extra utility would still tend to justify MRRs that swiftly went from very high to very low if the drop generally occurred in a fairly narrow and predictable expenditure range.

Why should the extra utility from grantees' increasing their consumption of a specific commodity be expected to decline so steeply in a narrow range? The question is well taken, and we do not assert that in any of the cases covered by voucher programs it actually does. The assumption does, however, appear to underlie various voucher programs. Thus in the food stamps setting, paternalistic claims may emphasize the case of the zero-income household headed by an alcoholic who prefers to drink his dinner rather than uniform underappreciation by zero-income households of the value of food. In addition, voters' and taxpayers' donative preferences may induce them to value on altruistic grounds providing the poor with enough food to forestall starvation or malnutrition, along with housing and education that meet some minimum standard, without extending these altruistic preferences either to further increases in poor people's utility from these forms of consumption or to other consumption (such as entertainment) that the poor value. Consider the charitable impulse that, in contrast to a welfare economics view, treats alms for the poor as somehow different in kind from progressive redistribution generally. Or consider normative views that emphasize providing specified commodities (whether material or not) that are selected by the observer rather than the consumer on the ground that these items are "merit goods" or "primary goods."[18]

We next consider the case where the grant program is not intended to alter consumer choices, even though it may have this effect, but rather bears on commodity choice as an indirect signal of need. Suppose, for example, that Medicare subsidizes medical expenditure by the elderly as a proxy for redistributing wealth from the healthy to the sick on the ground that the latter are worse off but that health (as distinct from medical expenditure) is hard to observe directly. If given this interpretation, Medicare naturally brings to mind the OIT, which taxes earnings (and thus the commodity choice of market consumption over leisure) as a proxy for taxing earning ability that cannot be directly observed.

Figure 2-6. *Effect of 30 Percent Earnings Tax on Carol's Budget Line*

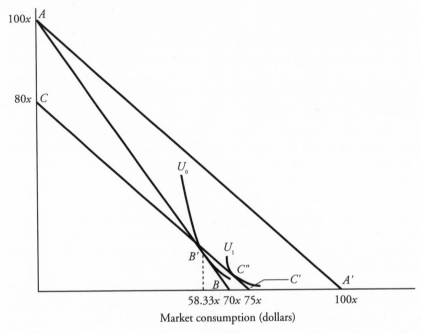

Figure 2-6 drives home the similarity between the OIT and Medicare (as depicted in figure 2-5) by showing how the imposition of a 30 percent earnings tax affects Carol's budget line and her commodity allocation between leisure and market consumption. Her budget line shifts from AA' (with $100x$ of earnings at A', where she exclusively chooses market consumption) to AB (where the same choice yields her only $70x$ of earnings). Her budget line continues to reach A on the vertical (leisure) axis because the tax is zero if she does not earn.

Suppose that Carol chooses point B' on her new budget line, where she earns $83.33x$ before tax and pays taxes of $25x$, leaving after-tax income of $58.33x$. If policymakers had known that she would choose this point, in principle they could have created a Pareto improvement by simply charging her a $25x$ lump-sum tax. This would have made her budget line CC', which is parallel to AA' but $25x$ lower. B' is on this budget line, but she now would be able to move from it to some point C'', where she substitutes additional work for leisure and earns more than $83.33x$. (The fact that $B'C'$ lies above the budget line segment $B'B$ that she actually faces, given the earnings tax, makes it likely that she would move in this direction.) She thereby would be able to increase her utility by moving from indifference level U_0 to U_1.

OIT analysis involves determining the optimal rate structure under various assumptions by quantifying the trade-off between utility gain from transferring resources from high- to low-wage rate individuals (possibly explained on the ground that people have similar utility functions characterized by declining marginal utility) and utility loss from inducing workers to substitute away from market consumption (as from moving Carol to U_0 rather than U_1). The Medicare version would simply substitute health levels for wage rates (perhaps on the assumption that health expenditure has declining marginal utility as one grows healthier) and nonmedical consumption for market consumption.

Two main findings in the OIT literature are of potential interest to the analysis of Medicare. First, no plausible estimates of labor supply elasticity produce MTRs anywhere near 100 percent. For optimal MRRs under Medicare to be anywhere near 100 percent, the relevant elasticity would have to be considerably lower or the relevant marginal utility curves would have to be a lot steeper.

Second, Mirrlees, while expecting to find that optimal tax rates were highly graduated, found instead that they were relatively linear or at some point even modestly declining under a variety of alternative specifications. This is now a common result in the OIT literature, which indeed finds that the marginal tax rate should in principle be zero at the very highest income level in the society, if this point can be determined.[19]

The intuitive explanation for this result is that marginal tax rates at inframarginal income levels are in effect lump sum and thus nondistortive. A tax rate at the very highest income level in the society is at the margin for one individual and inframarginal for no one. As the income level drops, the tax rate becomes inframarginal for increasing numbers of individuals, although the number for whom it is at the margin may fluctuate, depending on wage rates and preferences in the population. This constant increase in inframarginality as the amount of income declines provides the reason, even far below the hypothetical zero point, for lesser rate graduation than one might have thought followed from declining marginal utility.

The same general trade-offs should apply to Medicare as to the optimal income tax, although the relevant elasticity and rate of declining marginal utility might be very different. This suggests the possibility that an approximately linear MRR structure—more like the current Medicare MRR structure (apart from its being set at 100 percent) than like the classic voucher MRR structure of 100-0—might conceivably be optimal below the very highest medical expenditure level in society.

Suppose that we eliminate paternalism, externalities, and distributional measurement as reasons for conditioning voucher amounts on earmarked expenditures but put nothing in their place. Thus there is no good reason for limiting the consumer's use of the grant (apart, perhaps, from increasing the program's political feasibility), and the voucher is in all cases either functionally identical to a cash grant or else inferior. Here, the optimal marginal reimbursement rate for everyone is 0 percent. Positive inframarginal rates, which have the figure 2-2 result of leaving the recipient's budget allocation unchanged, do no harm, however.

This case is analogous to OIT in the absence of declining marginal utility, where, assuming that lump-sum taxation (the analog to cash grants) was unavailable, one would want a sharply declining analogous MTR structure in order to keep people's actual marginal rates as low as possible. In the MRR, just like the MTR, setting, the rate structure would not necessarily be 100-0, given limited information about people's marginal decision points, but it presumably would tend in that direction rather than toward linearity.

The prior discussions showed that in different settings a variety of arguments may support decreasing the MRR to zero as consumption of the earmarked commodities increases. This is typically described as "capping" the voucher, thus giving it a determinate or at least maximum value. We should note, however, that perhaps the most common argument for this MRR feature—that it provides "budget control" or helps to limit "program cost"—is in two respects mistaken. First, the relationship between a final MRR of zero and advancing these goals is unclear. Second, "budget control" and "program cost" are questionable normative goals that in some cases merely reflect fiscal language, rather than economic substance.

As a simple matter of arithmetic, the budget cost of a voucher program (ignoring administrative costs) equals the dollars spent by program beneficiaries on earmarked commodities, multiplied by the average MRR per dollar spent. Hence increasing the MRR on some of these dollars need not increase the program cost so long as it drops for other dollars. To be sure, changing the MRRs may change the dollars spent, as in the case where MRRs at consumers' marginal decision points increase and inframarginal MRRs decline. Yet the dollars spent by a given set of consumers on any particular commodities are inevitably finite. Thus it should always be possible to pay for increasing the final MRR above zero by reducing prior

MRRs. Perhaps the most that can be said from a program cost perspective about a final MRR of zero, other than that lower MRRs in general are cheaper than higher MRRs, is that it may tend to reduce budgetary variance. However, pure variance in the overall budget matters little if the government is risk neutral and can arise as well from uncertainty about, say, the number of covered dollars that will end up being spent under voucher programs that use a 100 percent-0 percent MRR structure.[20] Consider food stamps, where the performance of the economy may have a major effect on program cost, given the income qualification tests.

Even insofar as a final MRR of zero reduces the absolute level or variance of program costs, however, the normative significance of its doing so is unclear. Variance is a problem for consumers with uncertain needs as well as for taxpayers with uncertain budget costs, and it is plausible that the former will often face less diversifiable risk exposure than the latter (whence the common description of various voucher and other programs that address the problems of poverty or age as "social insurance"). As to absolute "program cost," the term often involves a myopic focus on a particular set of rules best viewed as part of the total tax-transfer system.

Thus suppose initially that food stamps are always cash equivalent to the recipients. Increasing the size of the food stamps program merely means that some people receive larger net transfers than previously or pay smaller net taxes. Surely the overall tax-distributional picture is what matters, not the details of how formally distinct programs contribute to this picture.[21] Even where food stamps are not cash equivalent and thus induce substitution by the consumer relative to the allocation she would have chosen at a cash-equivalent budget line, one who is concerned about these effects should focus directly on them rather than on the distinct accounting question of how many dollars were nominally "spent" (that is, transferred to consumers) under the program—a number that has no necessary relationship to the real allocative effect.

This overall budgetary perspective is worth keeping in mind even though real-world policymakers typically face more limited or marginal decisions. Suppose, for example, that there is concern about the "size of government" or the amount of "new government spending" that is being authorized. From any plausible underlying motivation for such a view, transfers (that is, negative taxes) should not be viewed as akin to, say, building new bridges or naval bases or comprehensively regulating a given industry.

The income tax equivalent of the "program cost" argument for a final MRR of zero would hold that potential income tax liability should be capped, through a final MTR of zero, not for OIT-type reasons but to provide "revenue control," ensuring that the income tax will not raise too much overall revenue. This argument (as distinct from one for lowering tax rates generally) is little heard despite its similarity to the "program cost" argument described above.[22]

Cash Rebates When Less than the Voucher Value Is Spent on the Earmarked Commodity

So far we have assumed that, whatever the MRR, no portion of a voucher can be traded in for increasing spending other than on earmarked commodities. However, a voucher can be designed to provide cash reimbursement if what is deemed enough of the earmarked item is bought without spending the entire voucher. Thus the tenant-based housing voucher program permits beneficiaries to keep the cost saving from paying less than the applicable FMR for a qualified housing unit.

The significance of this cash rebate feature can easily be misunderstood. Its absence in, say, the tenant-based housing certificate program may seem to induce overpaying the landlord (up to the certificate amount) for a given housing unit, since no cost saving can be captured anyway. (This includes the possibility of collusion between the landlord and tenant in setting the rent.) However, assuming perfectly competitive low-income housing markets with zero search costs, where (ignoring differences in taste) the more one paid the more one got, one would never want to overpay in this sense, since it would mean accepting less valuable housing than one could have demanded for the same cost. Under this assumption, providing cash reimbursement in the housing voucher program merely increases the grant's cash equivalence by permitting the beneficiary to purchase commodities that she values more at the margin than extra housing. This is desirable under consumer sovereignty, but it could conceivably conflict with externality or paternalism rationales for providing grants that are tied to housing.

The overpayment view may hold, however, to the extent of any departure from perfect competition and zero search costs. Suppose that the nonfungibility of housing units and one's own distinctive taste (for example, to live near family or work) caused one to prefer a given unit to any other available unit charging up to the FMR. Only a cash refund feature would provide any incentive to bargain for a rent below the FMR. Or suppose that housing search costs discourage looking for the best value that the FMR can buy. Once again, the voucher program's cash refund feature increases incentives to bargain, since the value of a cash refund is unlikely to be similarly limited by search costs.

Incentive and Distributional Effects of Rules Determining Voucher Eligibility

Eligibility to receive vouchers typically depends on personal or household characteristics apart from simply purchasing earmarked commodities. Thus the food stamps program uses income and liquid asset tests. Various housing programs use income tests, and school voucher programs might do so as well (as does the current pilot program in Milwaukee). In addition, various housing programs require that one stay within the same jurisdiction to move up on the waiting list for rationed benefits and may also use subsidiary criteria to allocate benefits (although, as noted previously, these may tend to offset other distortions). Since all of these various attributes are typically measured at the household level, eligibility generally depends on household composition. Finally, Medicare relies on an attribute—age—that consumers cannot directly affect, although they can affect the age at which they seek medical treatment. We next briefly examine the basic incentive and distributional effects of these various criteria for voucher eligibility.

INCOME TESTS. Reliance on some measure of income to determine voucher eligibility presents the classic OIT trade-off. While income is presumably a signal of some distributionally important underlying attribute, such as low wage rate or bad luck, an income test creates moral hazard because of the incentive effect of conditioning the grant on income when earning effort cannot be well observed.

While income-conditioned vouchers are in no way unique in this regard, they may exacerbate the resulting incentive problems when they are layered on top of each other *and* on other income-conditioned aspects of the overall tax-transfer system. Consider, for example, that as a low-income household's earnings increase, it may not only be phased out of food stamps, housing benefits, and other income-conditioned voucher programs such as Medicaid, but it may also lose welfare benefits under TANF, face phaseout of the earned income tax credit, and bear federal income and payroll taxes along with state and local income, sales, and property taxes. The combined effective marginal tax rate in some cases approaches or may even exceed 100 percent.[23] The incentive effects are likely to be particularly acute, given the general rule of thumb that distortion increases with the square of the tax rate.

The MTR effects of multiple income-conditioned tax and transfer programs could be mitigated by shifting to the use of "bundled vouchers," as discussed in the chapter in this volume by Robert Lerman and C. Eugene Steuerle. Or the different income measures of programs could take account of changing benefits and burdens under other such programs. Although the issue extends well beyond the voucher setting, addressing it solely with vouchers might already have a significant effect. Thus suppose a given household faced a marginal income tax rate of 15 percent and phaseout rates of 30 percent with regard to both food stamps and housing vouchers. An extra dollar of earnings would therefore face a combined 75 percent MTR from these three programs if they took no account of each other's benefits and burdens. However, just including the value of food stamps in income for housing voucher purposes and vice versa—without adjusting or taking any account of income tax liability—would reduce the MTR to about 61 percent.

Including program benefits and burdens in each other's income measures can be made quite complicated by the interactions, and therefore might seem to call for a uniform, integrated measure. However, the income tests for various voucher and other income-conditioned tax and transfer programs differ in various respects. These differences may reflect distinct distributional aims in different settings, or else they simply may be artifacts of historically separate design. Whether the differences have good rationales or not, they increase the complexity of determining one's status under the various programs even without regard to the problem of reciprocal inclusion.

In general, while the use of separate income tests by multiple income-conditioned programs does not make overly steep MTRs a logical necessity, it may tend in practice to encourage them. One reason is what one might call the pathology of bounded rationality. If policymakers only focus on one problem at a time, they may be prone to overlook the consequences of so pervasively using income tests in an uncoordinated fashion. A second reason for overly steep MTRs arises from the inclination to think of voucher and other transfer programs as providing distinct benefits that ought to be limited to the poor, rather than as components in an integrated tax-transfer system that is progressive across the entire income range. As soon as one concludes that, say, a four-person household with $5,000 of income is poor and thus should receive various benefits (TANF, food stamps, housing vouchers, Medicaid, and so forth), whereas a four-person household with income of $25,000 is not poor and hence should receive no such benefits, one is committed to MTRs that might be far in excess of what one would consider reasonable if one were asked directly about appropriate MTRs as income increases from $5,000 to $25,000. Substance may therefore be driven by framing and fiscal language.

ASSET TESTS. Liquid asset tests such as those used in the food stamps program distort both savings decisions (that is, when to consume) and asset choices by savers. For example, since homes are not included in liquid assets, food stamps provide an incentive to own a home rather than hold liquid assets and pay rent, even though this choice has a weak relationship if any to the distributional purpose of measuring need. (Home ownership may reduce one's short-term ease of substitution between housing and food expenditure, but to condition the grant on reduced ease of substitution may have undesirable incentive effects.)

The desirability of conditioning distribution policy on savings decisions, rather than just on work decisions as under a wage tax, is a familiar topic in the public finance literature—underlying, for example, the income versus consumption tax debate and consideration of wealth taxes and estate taxes. One distinctive feature here, however, is the steepness of the incentive effects at some margins. Food stamps are denied to a household with counted liquid assets above $2,000, or $3,000 if the household has an elderly member. For a household that has liquid assets below the ceiling and is considering crossing the threshold, the consequences can be quite severe. For example, suppose that, but for the asset test, one would expect to receive food stamp benefits of about $1,000 a year for the next five years. At a 5 percent discount rate, the present value of the lost benefits from exceeding the asset limit would be about $4,333. This might well swamp the expected benefit from increasing one's saving by a couple of thousand dollars, or it might have an income effect that made continued saving impossible. Features of this sort have helped to prompt the discussion in the welfare literature of "poverty traps" that deprive work and saving of their reward to low-income households.[24]

HOUSEHOLD COMPOSITION. The treatment of household status presents another classic dilemma in distribution policy. One person's income or assets may significantly increase the well-being of others in the same household, but determining tax or transfer consequences at the household level may distort decisions whether to form a household (or at least one that is observable). Often, the incentive effect is to discourage household formation, despite policy aims that may lie in the opposite direction.[25]

Transfer programs, including income-conditioned vouchers, tend to inquire into (and penalize) household status more aggressively and consistently than does, say, the federal income tax. This presumably reflects the practice of abstracting programs that benefit the poor from any integrated view of progressive tax-transfer policy, thus inducing rigorous testing at the household level of whether one is truly poor. For example, a change in the income tax liability of Mr. and Mrs. Bill Gates by reason of their forming a one-earner household would be unlikely to excite the same controversy as giving food stamps to Mrs. Gates if the program ignored household status.

Food stamps provide a good example of the incentive issues that may arise in income-conditioned voucher and other transfer programs. Having two adults rather than one in a household with children may increase the countable income and assets or, if the second adult is unemployed, risk disqualifying the household if he or she fails to meet the work requirement. The resulting deterrence of two-adult households could be reduced without ceasing to measure income and assets at the household level, but this would require raising the income and asset thresholds for such households relative to one-adult households. The deterrence could also be eased by making the MTRs from phasing out transfers less steep.

STAYING WITHIN THE JURISDICTION AND OTHER SUBSIDIARY CRITERIA. Other preconditions for voucher eligibility may have incentive effects that are not even discernibly related to distribution policy. Consider the effective requirement under housing programs that one remain in the same jurisdiction in order to move up on the waiting list for units, vouchers, or certificates. Other subsidiary criteria that local housing authorities apply may have incentive effects as well, although in some cases they may counteract the income and asset phaseouts by encouraging work.

The subsidiary incentive effects result from the queuing that arises once housing benefits do not go to all households that meet the formal eligibility requirements. For vouchers and certificates that are not tied to the level of public housing stock, this reflects deliberate budget limits. The decision to impose these limits and thus create queuing has distributional as well as incentive consequences. For example, it ensures that households defined as equally deserving or needy end up being treated differently, notwithstanding the standard public finance norm of horizontal equity along with the related utilitarian principle that treating equals unequally may reduce welfare, all else equal, as a consequence of declining marginal utility.[26]

AGE. Age, the chief prerequisite for Medicare eligibility, stands alone among the requirements in the programs we have been examining in being outside the recipient's direct control. Its effects on medical expenditure aside, Medicare therefore chiefly raises distributional rather than incentive issues. These go to optimal life cycle distribution to the extent that age cohorts pay for their own benefits—as generally has not been the case since the program was introduced, given the "pay-as-you-go" structure whereby current workers finance current retirees' benefits and the significant long-term financing and sustainability problems. Insofar as younger age cohorts pay for the benefits of older cohorts and cannot realistically expect similar support when they retire, the distribution of Medicare benefits is conditioned on one's year of birth and raises issues of generational distribution.[27]

Supplier Incentives and Market Structure

Perhaps the most important issue at stake in the choice between vouchers and other methods of delivering earmarked commodities to specified beneficiaries is the incentives bearing on suppliers. Differences in the incentives faced by the personnel (such as landlords, teachers, and the like) in public agencies as compared to private firms are often considered the most important factors at stake in voucher debates. And the relevant incentives are not limited to satisfying static consumer demand today. Innovation and responsiveness to changing conditions, while critical as well, are not well modeled by the textbook description of a firm deploying a known technology in the face of clearly revealed prices of inputs and outputs. Yet these factors are of the essence in the choice between competitive market and political "command and control" mechanisms of service delivery.

The classic argument for competitive private supply, going back to Adam Smith's "invisible hand," is that the profit motive, when combined with the need to satisfy customers who have other options for awarding their business, is the best available goad to inducing both economizing behavior in production and socially valuable innovation. Government provision, under this view, suffers both from a tendency to encourage the creation of monopoly power (although competing government institutions are possible, especially at the local scale famously discussed in a 1956 article by Charles Tiebout) and from underpowered or misdirected bureaucratic incentives.[28] There is obviously significant ideological disagreement in our society concerning how severe these problems are and how to assess the relative desirability of competitive private supply.

Adding to the complexity of the supplier incentive issue is the factor that responsiveness to consumers may not be the only objective of a program providing consumer grants that are earmarked to specific commodities. If complete cash equivalence is not intended because of paternalism or externalities, consumers have an incentive, which suppliers may share, to seek to evade the earmarking. Examples include using food stamps to buy nonfood items or school vouchers to pay for educational content that is inconsistent with the state's education policy. Consumers and suppliers may also have an incentive, depending on program structure, to pass on various costs to taxpayers.

Thus, even assuming private supply, a government agency may be required to monitor constraints on the commodities provided under the program, the reimbursable costs, and the identity and qualification of beneficiaries. In the absence of information costs, these functions could arguably be most simply served by direct provision by the same agency. However, the ubiquity of information asymmetries (how does one monitor the monitors?) suggests that there is no easy or uniform solution to the problem of designing institutions to induce economizing (and otherwise appropriate) behavior.

Ronald Coase is generally credited with the seminal work leading to the modern theory of the firm as a web of contractual relations, driven in equilibrium by competitive forces and designed to overcome agency costs.[29] The related contract, finance, and organizational theories have exploded in recent years. "Privatization" is the buzzword for the problem addressed by an important subset of this work, in which outsourcing a variety of functions to private firms is often a suggested solution.[30]

While we cannot go far beyond noting the importance of these supplier incentive issues, two brief observations are worth making. The first is that, under a variety of incentive structures, competition may have important effects on quality. These effects are likely to be positive for consumer satisfaction, although the effects on policy goals underlying earmarking may be more ambiguous. There can be significant competition in the public as well as the private setting, as exemplified by the Tiebout model and by arguments for increasing public school choice within a school district or larger jurisdiction.

Competition between public suppliers often requires decentralization. Thus in the Tiebout model, small jurisdictions help keep exit costs low and the number of competing local governments high. Similarly, some school reformers argue for decentralizing authority over public schools from school boards appointed at the city or county level either to school principals or, depending on the public choice problems, to local boards elected by parents or voters generally. Competition can also be increased in various other supply dimensions by, say, localizing decisions about teaching qualifications, administrative structure, and supported extracurricular activities. At least to some extent, then, design choices concerning the use of competition to improve supplier incentives can be separated from design choices regarding public versus private supply.

Our second observation concerns evidence from the private sector that may shed light on when public supply can be effective. A government agency is a kind of nonprofit firm that may resemble private nonprofit firms if it is similarly subject to competitive pressures, insulated from direct control by elected officials, and entrusted only with operational authority in running well-defined programs, as distinct from the power to make broad public policy decisions. Thus evidence concerning the suitability of the nonprofit firm for operations in different industries may shed light on how well government suppliers can perform in the same industries.

Among private firms, there is suggestive evidence that the nonprofit form is distinctly more suitable for providing some commodities than others. Nonprofit firms (other than joint-venture organizations such as cooperatives) are common only in the provision of commodities that have "a loosely charitable, virtuous, or public-spirited halo or aura"—for example, alms, education, religion, health care, and the high arts but not housing, retail food supply, or automobile repair.[31] This pattern predates the prominence of tax benefits that are tied to charitable status.

The most prominent economic theory explaining nonprofit firms has come from Henry Hansmann, who argued that they address "contract failure" where supplier performance is so hard to monitor that the profit motive reduces, rather than increases, consumer (including donor and employee) trust.[32] As an example, if a major research university became privately owned, with shareholders who had a right to residual profits, not only donors but students and faculty might become suspicious of its commitment to maximizing teaching and research quality that were hard to observe.

The main problem with Hansmann's theory is that it fails to explain the observed association between the nonprofit firm and the provision of broadly "charitable" commodities. Why should monitoring problems that give rise to contract failure be so concentrated in this realm? For example, is it really more difficult, as Hansmann suggested, to monitor the handful of prominent nonprofit firms, such as the United Way, that provide foreign famine relief (in effect posting reputational bonds), than the many small-scale automobile repair firms that tell suspicious but ill-informed customers what repair services are needed?[33]

The answer may lie in the black box nature of the nonprofit constraint, which gives critical importance to the preferences and incentives that guide behavior in a nonprofit firm (and are relied on by others as a substitute for direct monitoring). Thus in the case of higher education, both the worker preferences that make a university career attractive and the structure of the particular "market" for prestige may have a sufficient correlation, even if imperfect, with the aims of various consumers (such as students and donors) to present a better solution to the basic information problems than a for-profit firm can offer. In the case of health care, where the industry is mixed, the for-profit and nonprofit solutions may be comparably good. In the case of automobile repair, one would be hard pressed to find either workers with consumption motives akin to those in the classic nonprofit setting or customers who would expect any such motives to improve service quality rather than simply leaving the nonprofit supplier with the underpowered incentives that may be familiar from one's dealings with, say, the Department of Motor Vehicles.[34]

The implication we would draw for public supply is that it is most likely to be successful where evidence from private firms suggests that the nonprofit form is feasible—say, schooling and health care, as distinct from housing or retail food supply. In areas where the functioning of private nonprofit firms suggests that public supply may be feasible, the question whether to select it may turn on such considerations as those of public choice, or how best to maximize beneficial competition, or how regulatory goals external to the basic consumer transaction are best determined and served.

The decision whether to use vouchers is affected by these considerations because they are typically associated with the decision to use private supply. They can, however, conceivably be adapted to circumstances of mixed public and private supply (as with schools) or even solely public supply so long as prices are being charged at least to some consumers.

Allocative and Price Effects in Competitive Markets

The allocative and distributional consequences of voucher programs depend on how they affect equilibrium quantities and prices for the earmarked and other commodities. In figure 2-7 the market demand curve in the absence of a voucher program for a good, x, is shown as curve D^0D^0; market supply is SS, with equilibrium price p^0 and equilibrium quantity OB. The curve $D_B^0D_B^0$ represents the amount demanded by the beneficiaries

Figure 2-7. *Voucher with No Effect on Equilibrium Price or Quantity*

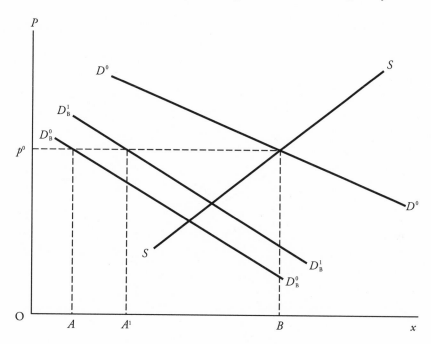

of the voucher program; the demand by everyone else constitutes the remainder of the horizontal difference to D^0D^0. Under the impact of the voucher program (even if it is cash equivalent), beneficiary demand shifts out to $D_B^1D_B^1$. Yet the net impact of the program in the market for x depends as well on how it affects nonbeneficiary demand. For example, if the program simply transfers income in a lump-sum fashion from the one group to the other, its influence on the market demand curve will depend purely on the income elasticities of the two groups. If the marginal effect of a dollar of income is the same for both groups, the program will have no effect on the market demand. Assuming that the program has no impact on suppliers, there will accordingly be no change in equilibrium price or the total quantity demanded, but instead simply a shift in the composition of the consumption between the two groups of demanders. In figure 2-7 the net effect is a shift in the consumption of x, with the consumption by the beneficiary group increasing by AA^1 to OA^1, and the consumption by the remainder of the demanders decreasing by AA^1, from AB to A^1B.

If the inward shift of the demand curve by the group financing the program is less than the outward shift in demand by the beneficiaries (because

Figure 2-8. *Voucher That Increases Equilibrium Price and Quantity*

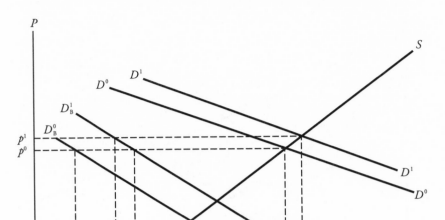

of differences in the marginal effect of income on demand, for example, or because the voucher program incorporates some price incentives for beneficiaries), some of the program's impact will be translated into an increase in the equilibrium price.[35] Figure 2-8 illustrates such a case; the net effect of the program is an outward shift of the market demand curve from D^0D^0 to D^1D^1 and no shift in the supply curve. In this case, the equilibrium price increases from p^0 to p^1. The increase in consumption by the beneficiary group is therefore diminished, from AA^1 to AA^2. At the higher price, nonbeneficiaries consume less than they otherwise would, although there remains an overall increase, from OB to OB^1, in x consumed in equilibrium. Part of the program's effect is to increase the surplus of suppliers. However, this need not translate into a net gain by suppliers, since, like everybody else, they experience the full range of effects in all markets and in the tax-transfer system.

Focusing just on the market for x, the effect of the program depends on the income and price elasticities of demand by beneficiaries and nonbeneficiaries as well as on the price (and perhaps income) elasticity of supply. In the special case of a horizontal supply curve, there will be no change in the equilibrium price. Price and income elasticities of demand will figure in the determination of the overall effect of the program on the total amount consumed and the distribution of that consumption between beneficiaries and others.

Effects of a Competitive Market and Choice between Voucher Programs and Public Supply

Analysis of supply and demand curves also has an important time element. As a general rule, short-run price elasticities are lower (in absolute value) than long-run price elasticities. In some settings, policy may be influenced by the belief that short-run supply price elasticities, in particular, are low. In housing, for example, the adjustments in stock may be very slow, so that the immediate impact of an outward shift in demand may be no change in the equilibrium quantity. Figure 2-9 illustrates this view for the two competing assumptions about overall demand shift that might accompany an outward shift in the demand by beneficiaries from $D_B^0 D_B^0$ to $D_B^1 D_B^1$. Supply is here assumed fixed at OB. With no outward shift in the market demand, the outcome is the same as in figure 2-7. Increased consumption by beneficiaries is matched by decreased consumption by nonbeneficiaries, with no change in the equilibrium price. With an outward shift in demand, by assumption there still is no change in the total amount consumed in equilibrium. The suppliers enjoy a price increase to p^2, which is greater than p^1, at the expense of consumers (beneficiaries and nonbeneficiaries alike) and of the taxpayers. Beneficiaries' consumption increases by AA^3, which is less than in the previous case (because the price increase is greater); nonbeneficiary consumption is still reduced.

Beliefs of this sort about short-term supply conditions may influence the choice of methods of delivering services to beneficiaries. Food stamps, like housing, may induce a net increase in demand for the earmarked commodities, or at least food of certain types. However, supply conditions may be roughly approximated by an infinitely elastic supply curve (taking into account the possibility of substitution among qualities of food), so that the spillover of effects through prices onto nonbeneficiary consumers and onto suppliers is likely to be small. This supply elasticity may be particularly clear to voters at the retail level (even if it holds equally throughout the production chain). Thus the lack of consumer political demand that the government enter the food supply business upon enacting or expanding food stamps, in order to avoid handing retailers a transition gain at their expense, is unsurprising. (Farmers who provide important

Figure 2-9. *Transition Effect of a Voucher when Supply Is Fixed*

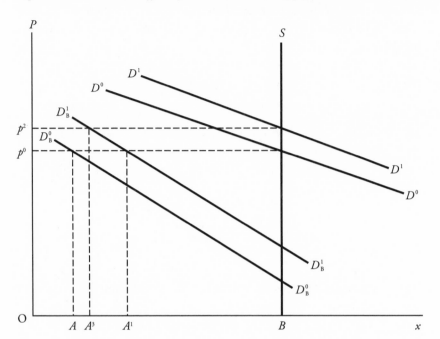

political support to the food stamp program might not object to such a demand so long as the government purchased its retail supply from them.)

By contrast, it is generally taken for granted that the supply of housing is relatively fixed in the short run. This may be a reason why policymakers in the past tended to favor direct provision of housing to beneficiaries, via public housing or publicly subsidized private projects. Government entry into the housing business may have been rationalized as a way to prevent transition gain to landlords at the expense of consumers on the expansion of demand for housing (with builders being indifferent since they would construct the extra housing either way).

Figure 2-10 sketches the analysis of why public provision might be thought for this reason a preferable alternative to the voucher solution described in figure 2-9. The effect of providing some amount of public housing directly to the beneficiary population is to induce a leftward shift of their demand curve on the private market, indicated as the shift from $D_B^0 D_B^0$ to $D_B^2 D_B^2$. The decline in their demand equals the amount of publicly

Figure 2-10. *Transition Effect of New Public Housing when Private Supply Is Fixed*

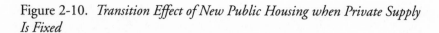

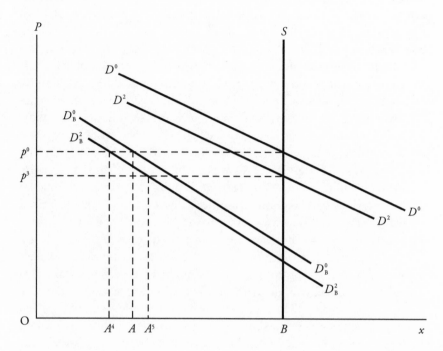

provided housing, represented by AA^4. If financing the program induces some reduction in demand for housing by nonbeneficiaries, then the leftward shift in overall demand on the private market will be greater than AA^4 to D^2D^2. The consequence is a reduction in the price on the private market, from p^0 to p^3, inducing an increase in demand on the private market by the residual beneficiary population from OA^4 to OA^5. In the example, net impact on the amount of housing consumed by the nonbeneficiary population is a reduction from AB to A^5B.

We should reemphasize that, if the view that figures 2-9 and 2-10 illustrate is accurate at all, it pertains purely to the short run, since this is the only period over which it is plausible to treat the housing supply as fixed (regulatory restrictions such as through zoning codes and rent control aside). However, the view can be challenged even on its own terms as a description of the short run and even if the government program, in fact, increases demand for housing. For one thing, the construction of public, like private, housing is not instantaneous. If it is acceptable to await the completion of public housing construction before program beneficiaries actually begin to receive aid, then it is unclear why the delay involved in deferring the effective date of the voucher program until supply has been able to adjust should be unacceptable.

In addition, in evaluating the extent to which short-term supply is fixed, the complexity of a "commodity" such as housing should be kept in mind. While it is helpful in clarifying ideas to think of housing as a single-dimensioned good, managing its many physical, service, and neighborhood dimensions has been central to the policy problem. One consequence of these multiple dimensions is that the inelasticity of supply suggested by the longevity and rigidity of structures may be misleading. Quality changes, upgrading a kitchen or bath, landscaping, security provision, and so on, as well as deterioration, can potentially respond quickly to prices, probably on a roughly constant-cost basis. The horizontal supply curve may therefore be a decent approximation to reality even in the short run.

Finally, even if short-term supply is fixed, it presumably reflects beliefs about prices in the long run. Landlords might be expected to take into account the possibility of government interventions that would affect the spot price of housing. Thus only if a given intervention was unexpected would it offer them anything but a normal return, and each surprise might have reputation effects on what they expected the next time. Given these effects, a decision to build public housing that reduced demand for private housing, rather than supplying vouchers that increased such demand, might lead landlords to reduce rather than increase supply if they expected new housing programs for the poor to be adopted shortly.[36]

Suppose that the long-run supply of housing, as depicted in figure 2-10, is horizontal at the price p^0, and that the long run arrives fairly quickly (whether because of advance anticipation or otherwise). Then the long-run effect of providing public housing is to reduce the equilibrium quantity on the private market by the sum of the amount of the public supply and reduced demand by the nonbeneficiary population, with no change in price either to the nonbeneficiary population or to the portion of the beneficiary population that remains in private market housing. Under these conditions, the main significance of the spot response of building public housing is that now an increased portion of housing supply is in public rather than private hands. The consequences depend on public versus private supplier incentives of the sort that we discuss in the next section. In some cases, however, public housing may have been built without focusing primarily on this question of relative incentives.

Noncompetitive and Nonprofit Markets

The analysis in the chapter's first section assumed competitive markets and conventional for-profit firms. Relaxing either of these assumptions may change the analysis. For example, if suppliers possess significant monopoly power (say, in small local markets), the case for direct government supply is strengthened, along with that for standard antimonopoly policies such as regulation or antitrust enforcement. (For a market-power example that may be comparable, consider the labor market for nurses, in which various studies have concluded that small-town hospitals act as monopsonists.)[37]

The implications of a substantial nonprofit presence in an industry are more complicated, as a discussion of primary and secondary schooling may show. Schooling, like housing, is a complex service with multiple dimensions, but one with a considerably different supply structure. In the United States, such schooling is provided by public agencies at the local level and by private, typically nonprofit charitable entities, which are subject to licensing or other forms of government supervision. Public schools do not ordinarily charge tuition (although there may be exceptions for nonresident students); instead, residence in the sponsoring jurisdiction constitutes the price of admission. They are typically financed by local property taxes, along with state and federal government aid. Private schools generally charge tuition, although they may rely as well on charitable contributions (mainly from alumni and parents), subsidiary fund-raising activities, and whatever state and federal tax benefits are afforded to charitable institutions generally.

Both sorts of organizations compete in some degree for "customers," based on price and quality. For public schools, the competition is effected largely through the mechanism of "voting with your feet," the analogy of which to ordinary competitive processes was first emphasized by Charles Tiebout.[38] Sometimes parents may choose among schools in a public school district, and sometimes particular schools limit enrollment on the basis of selective admission. (This is an aspect of product quality, essentially a network externality that takes into account the importance for education of interaction with other customers.) Private schools may emphasize particular philosophical or religious perspectives in addition to being selective. They may also, where better financed than the public schools with which they compete, permit parents with sufficient resources to select a more capital-intensive education for their children.

Given these market features, school voucher programs raise two complications that were absent in our discussion of housing. First, they extend direct aid to consumers who use private suppliers, in a setting where these consumers may be more distinct (for example, in income or taste) from consumers who use public suppliers than from consumers of low-income housing. Second, the fact that most or all of the private suppliers are non-profits may complicate the analysis. Even in highly competitive markets, nonprofit firms are harder to model than for-profit firms. Nonprofit status is something of a black box, since it is not clear what is being maximized once conventional owners with a demand for residual profits are eliminated. Plainly, tastes in consumption play an important role. Consider not only a donor whose preferences help shape what the nonprofit firm does, but the employee of a nonprofit firm who foregoes the higher salary she could have earned elsewhere to "spend" some of her implicit wage on doing this work rather than, say, purchasing restaurant meals or ski vacations.[39] Eliminating residual owners may also give important scope to managerial compensation in the form of prestige—inherently a hard thing to model from parsimonious assumptions. University officials in 1998, for example, may attach greater prestige to attracting qualified minority students than their predecessors did in 1948.

Against this background, consider a hypothetical school voucher program, adopted by a state government, with the following characteristics. Each voucher is good for a fixed amount (conditioned on the beneficiary's household income and jurisdiction) that can be used at either a public school or a qualifying private school. Public schools continue not to charge tuition but can turn in their students' vouchers to the state government and receive the face amount. The program is financed by increasing the state's income or sales tax.

An alternative program that increased the state's education spending exclusively through public supply would have involved giving grants solely to the public schools. Adopting the voucher program instead changes the characteristics of the average beneficiary if public and private school students differ systematically in any way. It also increases the size of the benefited population by extending aid to private as well as public school students, thus requiring either a costlier program or a smaller grant per student (assuming no cost savings from resulting student transfers).

An initial question that the adoption of either program would present concerns the effect on public schools of receiving additional state financing. To a first approximation, it is plausible that all of the new public school funds would end up being restored to local taxpayers. On average, taking into account the need to pay for the new state spending, local taxpayers face the same trade-offs as previously in the local school political process. That is, they pay more in state sales and income taxes than previously but benefit from additional state spending on their public schools. Thus the new state program places them in roughly the same position on average that they could have reached on their own by taxing themselves at a higher rate to increase local school spending. Reducing their own public school spending and property taxes by the amount of the new funds their schools received from the state would roughly restore them to the average position they had previously selected. It therefore is plausible that the local public schools would end up on average exactly where they started, although interjurisdictional effects, along with those between taxpayers in a given jurisdiction, might affect political outcomes.

Extending the analysis to consider the consequences of the voucher program's extension of direct aid to private school students, a full incidence analysis, working primarily through the value of local real estate, would be quite complex. (See the 1992 study by William Bogart, David Bradford, and Michael Williams for an incidence analysis of a similar program.)[40] Such an analysis would be necessary to specify the program's income effects on the school sector, even assuming that the income elasticities of different groups for education spending were known. It is plausible, however, that demand for private schooling would increase, given the income and substitution effects on voucher recipients and notwithstanding the income effect on other taxpayers.[41]

To the extent that this increase in demand for private schooling was underanticipated, and assuming adjustment costs, private schools would have a one-time surplus that, as nonprofit firms, they could not distribute to owners. With the transition gain locked into the industry (or at least the nonprofit sector), the schools would have to choose among such disparate uses for it as increasing salaries, providing greater financial aid, reducing tuition across the board, expanding special educational programs, or increasing physical plant. The choice among these alternatives would depend on the preferences of school administrators and those with whom they had dealings (such as students' households, employees, and donors). In addition, assuming the importance of a taste for prestige in the education industry, the choice might depend on the prestige provided by different alternatives at the time the surplus arose.

Whether or not the increased demand for private schooling from providing school vouchers was anticipated, in equilibrium it would result in a larger private school sector than otherwise. One likely effect would be a net shift of students from public to private schools. However, other likely effects on the mix and character of the services provided by private (and public) schools are hard to determine without further specification of the various actors' preferences.

Conclusion

This chapter's tour of the basic economic issues presented by voucherlike government programs has found a number of consumer-side and supplier-side issues. On the consumer side, perhaps the central issue is the extent to which a voucher or similar grant is and, given the program objectives, should be cash equivalent. The perspective on this issue may have implications for determining the optimal marginal reimbursement rate (MRR) as earmarked expenditures by the consumer increase. A further issue goes to the effect of income-conditioned programs on people's incentives relating to work, saving, and household formation. Poorly integrated multiple income-conditioned voucher and other programs can result in the (perhaps accidental) imposition of punitive-effective marginal tax rates on members of low-income households who are considering increasing their labor market participation.

On the supplier side, the core questions go to the choice between private and public supply and the level of supplier competition. Vouchers are often associated with the decision to make greater use of competitive private supply, whether through for-profit or nonprofit firms. Issues of how to optimize supplier incentives and establish the desired degree of competition may therefore be crucial to voucher debates, although they may be hard to capture in standard economic models and not strictly related to the issues of voucher design that this chapter has emphasized.

Voucher and related programs can also have at times surprising allocative and price effects. An example that may be quite unusual but that should help dramatize the complexity of the underlying causation is that vouchering a given commodity may actually reduce its equilibrium quantity if the income elasticity of demand by the recipients for the commodity generally is less than that of the individuals who pay for the program.

By focusing only on the economics of vouchers, as distinct from their politics, this chapter ignores an important element of why they are used and why one might reasonably decide to advocate them in lieu of programs that are superior except for their dim political prospects. We leave political issues to the chapter in this volume by Burdett Loomis. However, even though the economics and politics ultimately need to be integrated, focusing on the economics alone is useful as a stage in one's thinking. Good political choices cannot be made without understanding what different alternatives would accomplish.

Notes

1. Harvey S. Rosen, *Public Finance*, 4th ed. (Chicago: Richard D. Irwin, 1995), p. 584.

2. James Mirrlees, "An Exploration in the Theory of Optimum Income Taxation," *Review of Economic Studies*, vol. 38 (1971), pp. 175–208.

3. Rosen, *Public Finance*, p. 584.

4. Ibid., p. 285.

5. *Green Book: Background Material and Data on Programs within the Jurisdiction of the Committee on Ways and Means*, Committee Print, House Committee on Ways and Means, 104 Cong. 2 sess. (Government Printing Office, 1996).

6. John C. Weicher, *Privatizing Subsidized Housing* (Washington, D.C.: AEI Press, 1997).

7. Ibid., p. 3.

8. Helen Hershkoff and Stephen Loffredo, *The Rights of the Poor* (Southern Illinois University Press, 1997), p. 229.

9. Ibid., p. 269.

10. *Milwaukee Parental Choice Program*, Wisconsin Stat. Sec. 119-23, 1998.

11. Housing and education vouchers often are described as responding to the failures of public housing and education rather than to underprovision of the earmarked commodities in private consumer transactions. However, an important motivation for providing the public housing and education whose quality has attracted criticism was presumably to address underprovision of these commodities in private transactions.

12. The statutory preambles to both the food stamps and certain housing programs set forth legislative aims of providing aid both to particular industries and to the poor.

13. Rosen, *Public Finance*, p. 163.

14. Ibid., p. 285.

15. See Stephen A. Woodbury and Robert G. Spiegelman, "Bonuses to Workers and Employers to Reduce Unemployment: Randomized Trials in Illinois," *American Economic Review*, vol. 77 (1987), pp. 513–30, in which offering a cash bonus to unemployed workers upon securing a new job had markedly different effects than letting the workers assign such a bonus to the employer. This appears to have reflected transaction costs. Only workers selected under new pilot programs initially

knew that the bonuses were available, thus making the transaction where the employer paid a high nominal wage cost and was reimbursed "more complicated" than the one where the employer paid a low nominal wage that was supplemented.

16. Along these lines, upon enactment of the HOPE credit, the Massachusetts Board of Higher Education scaled back a proposal to eliminate certain community college tuition, proposing instead to charge students whose income made them likely candidates for the credit a tuition roughly in the amount that was HOPE-creditable (Richard Chacon, "Board Trims Its Plan for Free Tuition," *Boston Globe*, September 23, 1997). The net effect, compared to giving such students free tuition, would be to transfer revenue from the Federal Treasury to Massachusetts in the amount of the HOPE credits claimed.

17. Non-cash-equivalence in the case of prescribed consumption also becomes more likely as one moves to finer categories, such as types of food rather than all food. The taste for a type of food is likely to vary more between consumers than the taste for all food, since one can live without, say, meat or ice cream but not without calories.

18. Richard A. Musgrave, *The Theory of Public Finance* (McGraw-Hill, 1959); John Rawls, *A Theory of Justice* (Harvard University Press, 1971).

19. Joel Slemrod, "Optimal Taxation and Optimal Tax Systems," *Journal of Economic Perspectives*, vol. 4 (1990), p. 164.

20. K. J. Arrow and R. C. Lind, "Uncertainty and the Evaluation of Public Investment Decisions," *American Economic Review*, vol. 60 (1970), pp. 364–78.

21. Daniel N. Shaviro, "The Minimum Wage, the Earned Income Tax Credit, and Optimal Subsidy Policy," *University of Chicago Law Review*, vol. 64 (1997), pp. 463–64.

22. While the income tax differs from a voucher program that responds to paternalism or externalities in not being deliberately aimed at altering people's marginal decisions, the "program cost" argument seems to rest on the idea that such alteration is desirable only up to a point and not beyond.

23. Andrew B. Lyon, "Individual Marginal Tax Rates under the U.S. Tax and Transfer System," in David F. Bradford, *Distributional Analysis of Tax Policy* (Washington, D.C.: AEI Press, 1995); Linda Giannarelli and C. Eugene Steuerle, *The Twice-Poverty Trap: Tax Rates Faced by AFDC Recipients* (Urban Institute, 1995); Shaviro, "The Minimum Wage"; Daniel N. Shaviro, *Effective Marginal Tax Rates on Low-Income Households* (Washington, D.C.: Employment Policies Institute, 1999).

24. Giannarelli and Steuerle, *The Twice-Poverty Trap*, p. 1.

25. C. Eugene Steuerle, *Removing Marriage Penalties* (Washington, D.C.: The Communitarian Network, forthcoming).

26. Musgrave, *Theory of Public Finance*; Rosen, *Public Finance*; Alan J. Auerbach and Kevin A. Hassett, *A New Measure of Horizontal Equity* (Washington, D.C.: AEI Press, 1999); Louis Kaplow, "A Fundamental Objection to Tax Equity Norms: A Call for Utilitarianism," *National Tax Journal*, vol. 48 (1994), pp. 497–514.

27. Laurence J. Kotlikoff, *Generational Accounting: Knowing Who Pays, and When, for What We Spend* (New York: Free Press, 1992); Daniel N. Shaviro, *Do Deficits Matter?* (University of Chicago Press, 1997).

28. Charles M. Tiebout, "A Pure Theory of Local Expenditures," *Journal of Political Economy*, vol. 44 (1956), pp. 416–24.

29. Ronald Coase, *The Firm, the Market, and the Law* (University of Chicago Press, 1988).

30. Oliver Hart Andrei Shleifer, and Robert W. Vishny, "The Proper Scope of Government: Theory and an Application to Prisons," Working Paper 5744 (Cambridge, Mass.: National Bureau of Economic Research, 1996).

31. Daniel N. Shaviro, "Assessing the 'Contract Failure' Explanation for Nonprofit Organizations and Their Tax-Exempt Status," *New York Law School Law Review*, vol. 41 (1997), p. 1001.

32. Henry B. Hansmann, "The Role of Nonprofit Enterprise," *Yale Law Journal*, vol. 89 (1980), p. 835.

33. Ibid., pp. 868–72.

34. Shaviro, "Contract Failure," p. 1003.

35. At least in principle, the opposite result is also possible: a decline in demand for the earmarked commodity as a result of the income effect of the transfer.

36. Daniel N. Shaviro, *When Rules Change: An Economic and Political Analysis of Transition Relief and Retroactivity* (University of Chicago Press, forthcoming).

37. Daniel Sullivan, "Monopsony Power in the Market for Nurses," *Journal of Law and Economics*, vol. 32, no. 2 (1989), p. S135.

38. Tiebout, "A Pure Theory of Local Expenditures," pp. 416–24.

39. Shaviro, "Contract Failure."

40. William T. Bogart, David F. Bradford, and Michael G. Williams, "Incidence Effects of a State Fiscal Policy Shift: The Florio Initiatives in New Jersey," *National Tax Journal*, vol. 45 (1992), pp. 371–87.

41. David F. Bradford and Wallace E. Oates, "The Analysis of Revenue—Sharing in a New Approach to Collective Fiscal Decisions," *Quarterly Journal of Economics*, vol. 85 (1971), pp. 416–39. See this source for an attempt to model a somewhat similar situation.

BURDETT LOOMIS

3 | *The Politics of Vouchers*

I N EARLY August 1998, as debate in the House of Representatives on school vouchers within the District of Columbia drew to a close, Majority Leader Dick Armey (R-Tex.) called on
Speaker of the House Newt Gingrich (R-Ga.) to offer his side's concluding
comments. The hour was late, and the bill—to approve the District's
appropriations for the 1999 fiscal year—was scarcely earth shattering. Yet
the GOP's biggest guns were making emotional pleas to provide about
2,000 students with vouchers that would allow them to attend the public
or private school of their choice. At the culmination of ten hours of debate,
Speaker Gingrich spoke in an accusing tone toward the Democrats, "*You're*
denying the children of this District money. They are desperate to leave the
schools you have trapped them in."[1] Gingrich laid the blame at the hands
of the teachers' unions, with their vigorous opposition to vouchers, and
made the attack personal—directing his words toward Eleanor Holmes
Norton (D-D.C.). Norton rushed to the microphone, defending both her-

Special thanks go to Heather Hoy, my research assistant and program assistant
at the Robert J. Dole Institute for Public Service and Public Policy, and to Eric
Sexton.

self and her position, noting that she had won more than 90 percent of the District vote and was scarcely beholden either to teachers' unions or any other given interest. Rather, she observed that the District appropriation legislation has "become an excuse for indulging the controversial, social and financial, whims of some members of this body. It's unfair to you, it's unfair to me, and it's unfair to District residents."[2]

The vouchers amendment—the same as a stand-alone bill vetoed three months earlier by President Clinton—passed on a 214-206 party-line vote. In turn, the entire $6.8 billion budget was placed in jeopardy, as most observers expected another presidential veto, even though the vouchers program would have cost only $6.4 million annually (2,000 students receiving $3,200 each).

Why such bitterness and emotion over an item that would directly affect so few students? Both politics and policy considerations come into play. First, Congress can directly impose policies on the District, and thus the instrument of the appropriations bill offers an attractive opportunity to make a political statement through a pilot program. Second, given the overwhelming number of African Americans in the District's schools, the Republicans can make a pitch to members of a population that has embraced vouchers in increasing numbers. Various surveys have demonstrated support for vouchers by substantial majorities of blacks.[3] Finally, a federal program—or even legislation that is vetoed—offers a model for those states that wish to develop their own vouchers initiatives. After all, education remains essentially a state function. As a Heritage Foundation scholar put it, "If this goes through at the federal level . . . some state legislatures will jump on the bandwagon right away." Conversely, defeat in the District "will slow the statewide movement."[4] In the end, the stakes were much higher than just providing 2,000 vouchers to a relative handful of the District's 70,000 schoolchildren. Speaker Gingrich's unusual appearance on the House floor and his emotional appeals dramatized the political importance of the vouchers issue, even as it was headed for a presidential veto. This was merely one battle in a long-term war over school vouchers; more hard-fought, emotional skirmishes were sure to come, on the House floor, in state capitols, in courtrooms, and in any number of other venues, across the country.

As the D.C. school vouchers issue played out between April and August 1998, another voucher bill was wending its way through the legislative process on Capitol Hill. Although it received some attention, the consolidation of more than sixty job training programs into a single simplified package (S.1186) received broad bipartisan support as it sailed through both the House and Senate. In many ways, the acknowledged ineffectiveness of the confusing array of job training programs differed only modestly from the situation created by the weak public schools in the District of Columbia. But in this instance a bipartisan coalition endorsed vouchers as a way to improve both choice and accountability in job training policy. At least one conservative group—Phyllis Schlafly's Eagle Forum—actively opposed the training legislation, and the American Policy Center warned that "the Secretary of Education [would gain] control over secondary and post-secondary education over and above the governors of each state, and would also designate appropriate career choices for individuals involved in the 'program'."[5] This attempt to reframe the issue in alarmist, government-control terms failed, as mainstream business groups such as the Business Roundtable and the U.S. Chamber of Commerce lobbied for and then hailed the passage of the legislation. The bill and its reliance on vouchers were endorsed by President Clinton and embraced by all Democratic senators. The only Senate opposition came from seven conservative Republicans; the House vote was similarly overwhelming.

Despite some earlier far-right successes in blocking similar legislation, senators from Mike DeWine (R-Ohio) to Paul Wellstone (D-Minn.) enthusiastically backed the legislation, both to increase job training efficiency and to address (in DeWine's words) "the unfinished business of welfare reform."[6] As a major part of the legislative package, training vouchers won support as a reasonable policy solution within a fragmented issue domain. In addition, there were classic elements of distributional politics at work—the $10 billion bill offered enough resources to attract Democratic backing, and the local control and choice elements of the legislation allowed state and local chambers of commerce to seek funding as "One-Stop Customer Service Delivery Systems."[7]

Thus, within a few days in August 1998, two voucher bills won passage in Congress. One—D.C. school vouchers worth $6.4 million—attracted the energetic support of the Republican party leadership and the lobbying efforts of dozens of groups, ranging from the Heritage Foundation to the National Education Association; a vigorous struggle ensued, with the final budget bill excluding the program. The other bill—with a $10 billion price tag and a heavy emphasis on vouchers for job training—breezed through both houses and obtained almost immediate presidential approval. Such a juxtaposition emphasizes that there is no single "politics of vouchers." Rather, like many other policy tools, vouchers are most usefully viewed within the many contexts of politics and interest group activities.

Vouchers, Interests, and Politics: Some Promising Perspectives

This chapter describes the political contexts that frame policymaking where vouchers are considered as a possible tool for addressing a host of problems that range from feeding the poor to providing medical care. There has been, to date, no attempt to describe (to say nothing of analyze) vouchers from a political perspective. Indeed, when most people think of vouchers and politics together, they immediately associate these notions with issues of K–12 school choice. To be sure, that is the most visible, most combustible issue in which vouchers have emerged as a possible policy tool. But it is not the whole story. Vouchers have often existed, often with little or no controversy, in various policy arenas since the 1960s and 1970s (as early as the 1940s for the GI Bill). This is important because some clear stakeholders in these programs can be identified, as can the coalitions of interests that have supported particular initiatives over the years.

For example, food stamps, Section 8 housing vouchers, and Pell higher education grants have long histories, and although voucher-related controversies remain within the nutrition, housing, and higher education policy communities, the use of vouchers is well established. It seems likely that job training will soon enjoy a similar status, and Medicare capitation payments—a voucher-like tool—are growing in importance without engendering much controversy. Conversely, the subject of K–12 vouchers remains highly controversial and unsupported at present by any federal funds. The mix of public and (mostly) private voucher pilot programs derive from state and (mostly) local efforts whose results continue to be subject to often-politicized evaluations, often sponsored by foundations and institutes that have some stake in the outcome.

Vouchers and Interest Group Politics

To make sense of how organized interests relate to voucher policies, proposals, and politics requires a little backtracking to examine the nature of contemporary interest group politics. In particular, this approach will employ the broad notion of "organized interest" that will include entities ranging from groups inside Congress (the Rural Caucus) to state universities to political action committees to think tanks—to say nothing of conventional membership groups like the American Association of Retired People (AARP) or the National Education Association (NEA). In other words, many different kinds of interests have a stake in the outcomes of the politics and policymaking that surround vouchers.

Organized interests seek to affect policies in various venues, and they use two basic tools: money and information. The Common Cause/Center for Responsive Politics version of interest group influence—legalized bribery in the form of an exchange of campaign contributions and favors for legislators' votes—is not so much wrong as incomplete. Most contemporary interest group politics revolve around the politics of ideas and information. This does not mean that money is unimportant. But campaign contributions pale before the incredible costs of integrated lobbying campaigns (by tobacco firms, Microsoft, telecommunications interests, health care associations, and other interests) that include insider access, public relations, grass-roots cultivation of key constituents, advertising, and other techniques. Money and information overlap a lot because modern lobbying has grown increasingly expensive, for a host of reasons. Especially important are the rising stakes of many policy decisions, whether in changing bankruptcy laws, rewriting telecommunications regulations, or—on point for this project—establishing the rules of the game for school (or Medicare) vouchers. Billions of dollars are at stake in these policies; investing tens of millions in lobbying would seem to make good economic sense. At the same time, many other policies exist within a safe-haven, low-profile "niche," where interests combine quietly to protect their advantages.

Once a context for the contemporary politics of interests has been established, the chapter will focus on a set of broad themes that structure how groups address voucher issues. These include the following:

—Who are the stakeholders, real and potential? Perhaps the key question here is to what extent we can clearly establish who has concrete stakes in a voucher policy—for example, when the interest receives a current benefit (for example, food stamp recipients). Who are these interests, and are they actual players in the controversies that most affect them? Are there potential players who seek major changes in the nature of continuing program? And what stakes are involved?

—What is the scope of conflict or the number of interests affected? Drawing on E. E. Schattschneider, among others, it is important to understand the "scope of conflict" (how public it is) and the actual number of individuals or interests affected by a policy decision.[8] The politics of a "niche" issue, such as a technical aspect of food stamps eligibility, is structured very differently from a highly public issue that affects a lot of individuals, such as the Clinton health care reform proposals.

—What are the venues? The venues for politics often shape outcomes. Thus, venue shopping (for example, courts versus legislatures) is an important element of contemporary interest group politics. Because the politics of influence often plays out differently in state capitals than in Washington, moving particular controversies to the states (or to local units of government) can change the balance of power among interests. Organized interests may thus develop strategic visions that encourage them to embrace devolution, not based on any principle but for political advantage (for example, conservative dominance of a state legislature).

—What is the relationship between choice and accountability? As governments adopt voucher programs, the relationship between choice and accountability stands at the heart of the politics. Although there may not be a direct trade-off (more choice, less accountability), interests will work hard to structure the conditions of choice and accountability. Moreover, these considerations are crucial to the core public-private relationships inherent in vouchers. And many significant issues will be complex, which increases the importance of lobbying over the details.

—How is "choice" used as a symbol? Choice is a powerful argument across most policy areas (telecommunications, health, education, abortion, and on and on). But we should be highly skeptical of how choice is used. Often it conveys more symbolic than substantive meaning (for example, in health care policy), or it may be used to mask a basic lack of real choice (in much of telecommunications policy). Interests may well publicly endorse choice while privately seeking to structure actual choices in their own favor.

—What politics of ideas or think tank politics are involved? Although some voucher issues are well grounded in practice (for example, food stamps), a lot of voucher politicking takes place within the nexus of think tanks, op-ed pages, and sponsored research. Organized interests are involved here, but often at one remove. Interests use the narratives constructed by scholars and think tank fellows as they further their own policy preferences.

—What is the relationship between vouchers and budgets? To what extent do interests embrace vouchers as an element of fiscal restraint and control? This gets at broader questions of coalition politics, in which advocates for vouchers on the perceived merits of the policy join with those who see vouchers as a means to cut governmental expenditures, either overall or at a given level of government. At the same time, vouchers can serve as an effective tool in capping governmental expenditures that threaten to explode (Medicare) or simply to keep on growing steadily.

These themes surely do not exhaust the ways in which the politics of vouchers can be usefully examined, but, given the dearth of any comprehensive political analysis of vouchers, they do provide some starting points. In particular, the first perspective noted above offers a way to place the politics of vouchers across policies.

Interests and Venues: The Scope and Breadth of Conflict

Although organized interests continue to lobby in time-honored ways within the corridors of Washington institutions, such as Congress and bureaucratic agencies, they have begun to spend more time shaping perceptions of problems and political agendas. In addition, they are devoting more and more attention to earlier stages of policy formulation—especially the fundamental defining and redefining of issues. In doing this, they are following the insights of academic writers Roger Cobb and David Rochefort, who have noted that narrowing or broadening participation are key goals of activists and organized interests.[9] Indeed, successfully defining conditions as problems (such as smog, learning disabilities, or global warming) often represents the single most important step in changing policies.[10]

Influencing final governmental decisions is ordinarily very difficult for all but a few political players and the best-connected interest group representatives. When major changes occur, especially in an era of divided government, a small "gang" of executive and legislative personnel hammer out the eventual solution.[11] In this situation, access must be limited, or decisionmaking will grind to a halt.

But in the politics of problem definition, everyone can play by calling a press conference, releasing a study, going on a talk show, commissioning a poll, or buying an advertisement. There is no shortage in Washington of either well-defined problems or potential solutions. Indeed, the capital is awash in arguments and evidence that seek to define problems and set agendas. What is more difficult to understand is how certain definitions come to prevail within the context of political institutions that often, though not always, resist the consideration of new—or newly packaged—ideas.

We do have some clues, however. Frank Baumgartner and Bryan Jones have sought to study agenda setting within the context of political institutions, both in terms of how items get considered and what implications may flow from agenda change. Issue definitions remain crucial, but they are placed within the framework of "policy image" and "policy venue," both of which have roots in Schattschneider's concept of expanding conflict to increasingly broad audiences.[12] The construction of policy images, such as those debating whether slowing the growth of Medicare spending reflects an actual cut in the program, lies at the heart of policy formulation. But the search for a hospitable decisionmaking venue is scarcely less important.

Policy venues can range from the state and federal courts to U.S. Senate committees to state legislatures. They are crucial in understanding how the politics of problem definition and agenda setting relate to political institutions. As has been demonstrated on environmental and agricultural issues, venue change is central to understanding the evolution and impact of issue networks on policy outcomes.[13] The growth of government has expanded the number of venues, as well as their diversity. Multiple venues offer widely varied opportunities for shaping issues in broader arenas like elections or narrower ones such as congressional subcommittees.

As problem definition, agenda status, and venue shopping become increasingly important elements of policymaking, organized interests have stepped up their attempts to expand, restrict, or redirect conflict. The public interest and environmental movements of the 1960s often led the way in understanding these elements of political life, leaving business to catch up in the 1970s and 1980s.[14] Based on this development, a longtime student of public interest groups, Jeffrey Berry, has concluded that citizen groups have driven the policy agenda since the 1960s, thus forcing business interests to respond to sets of issues developed by groups such as Common Cause and the Sierra Club.[15]

Following on the heels of these agenda successes has been the institutionalization of interests within the government, especially when broad public concerns are at stake.[16] For instance, many of the 1995 battles over the Contract with America placed legislators in sharp conflict with programs supported by governmental administrators and professionals who ran programs, like those within the Department of Education, that were slated for elimination.

And there's the rub. As more interests seek to define problems and push agenda items, more messages emanate from more sources.[17] For threatened interests, whether corporate, environmental, or professional, the decision to "socialize" a conflict has no meaning unless it can be accomplished. Even Ralph Nader, the past master of using the press to expand the scope of conflict, has recently found it difficult to attract media attention.[18] In 1996 this longtime crusader for safety and environmental issues had to run for president as a Green Party candidate to generate coverage of his message. Some interests can cut through the cacophony of voices; in particular, those in Schattschneider's affluent "heavenly chorus" can—at a price—get their message across by spending lavishly on public relations campaigns or by buying advertising time and space. Moreover, if such messages are directed toward legislators who have received substantial campaign contributions from these same interests, they typically reach an already receptive audience.

The emphasis on problem definition looms large when public policy is on the table. In policy controversies, tremendous uncertainty is unleashed within the political process. Lots of substantive interests are in play, many competing scenarios are put forward, legislative decisions are always contingent, and public policy outcomes are often filled with unanticipated consequences.[19] As cozy policymaking triangles have been replaced by loose, ill-defined policy communities, decisionmaking under conditions of great uncertainty has become more common.[20]

In policy battles, the capacity to obtain information and control its dissemination is the most important political power of all. Political scientist James Thurber argues that if participants cannot resolve conflict on their own turf, "'outsiders' from other committees, agencies, bureaus, groups, the media, or the general public will take the issue away from them."[21] This "scope of conflict" perspective is extremely important to the dynamics of policy formulation and a source of the greatest type of uncertainty of all—conflict redefinition.

As shown in table 3-1, there are different types of group conflict structured by two dimensions: (1) the scope of conflict; and (2) the breadth of impact, that is, the number of people and interests affected. In previous decades, interest groups active on small, technical issues could count on the policy conflict being restricted to niche politics, a narrow scope of conflict affecting just a few interests. From the standpoint of interest groups, the beauty of these types of controversies—especially the low-visibility ones—was that they were stable and therefore predictable. Conflicts that started out as one type generally stayed in that domain. There were few explicit efforts at conflict redefinition and even fewer cases of successful redefinition. Even for an issue like abortion, which illustrates the politics of public confrontation, the highly visible, often symbolic, nature of the battle has meant a certain kind of stability.

Today, the situation is radically different. Changes in the contemporary political process give groups more strategic options. Depending on their self-interest, groups can seek to reduce or expand the scope of conflict. At some points in time, it may be advantageous to restrict conflict to restricted policy niches where particular interests can dominate. At other times, a group might embrace the competition among many interests in a more open policy community to make its political points. Whatever the policy

Table 3-1. *Scope and Breadth of Group-Related Conflict*

Breadth: number of people and interests affected	Scope	
	Narrow	Broad
Few	Niche politics (for example, small farm loan program)	Symbolic politics (for example, flag-burning amendment)
Many	Policy community politics (for example, banking)	Public confrontation politics (for example, NAFTA)

issue, considerable effort must go into strategic calculations regarding the costs and benefits of changing the scope of conflict.

It is here that policymaking uncertainty is greatest. Groups interested in particular issues never know exactly what the venue is going to be, which factors will shape the institutional arena, or how the conflict will develop. Particular controversies can metamorphose over night into the realm of symbolism, policy niches, or public confrontation, each necessitating very different kinds of political approaches. Thus, to return to the politics of vouchers, it makes a great deal of difference if jobs or voucher reforms are defined by the job training policy community as a set of moderate, sensible changes (as it was in July 1998), rather than as a radical attempt to impose federal control over career choices and local programs (as the Eagle Forum sought to do).

The Politics of Vouchers across Issues

What follows will be brief considerations of the politics of several issues in which vouchers play (or might play) a major role as a policy tool. Beyond the most obvious, K–12 school vouchers, these will include housing, food stamps, higher education, and health care. In all these areas, the very notion of vouchers is most tempting, not just for policy wonks but for politicians as well. In the words of one analysis, "The White House has proposed converting most of the money spent on federal-housing and job-training programs into vouchers. Conservatives—longtime champions of vouchers for education and low-income housing—have recently proposed vouchers for Medicaid, Medicare, and veterans' health care."[22] Given such interest across political parties, and from minority populations for school vouchers, a reasonable conclusion is that vouchers are on the policy agenda across many issue areas. And no agenda has received more attention than that of elementary and secondary education.

K–12 School Vouchers: Substance and Symbol

The K–12 voucher debate is by far the most public and the most acrimonious of all the voucher policy controversies. In terms of table 3-1, most of the politics take place on the right side of the figure, either as public confrontations or as symbolic politics. For the foreseeable future, K–12 voucher politics will be played out in highly public ways, in that the conflict has already been "socialized," whether at the local, state, or national level. The question is more often the extent to which the debate is essentially symbolic.[23] To the extent that symbolism (of quality education, choice, opportunity, whatever) dominates, few meaningful changes are likely to occur. If, however, various interests can manage to hold a coherent public debate (in Congress or the Supreme Court, as well as in the states), the use of vouchers as a policy tool could well become routine (if contentious) within the K–12 policy community.

The very richness of school voucher politics makes the issue simultaneously useful and atypical in thinking through the more general politics of vouchers. The issue generates much more controversy and energetic position taking than most others; it thus sheds light on how vouchers can be politicized and with what results. A quick tour through the key elements of voucher politics is thus enlightening.

—*Constituencies and stakeholders.* As school voucher controversies extend into the late 1990s, the attitudes of urban minority populations have become especially important elements of the debate. In the 1997 Delta Kappa/Gallup Poll, for example, between 62 percent and 72 percent of African Americans expressed their support for vouchers.[24] Other surveys have reported similar results, which means serious trouble for Democratic legislators and school choice opponents, given blacks' status as the most loyal of all Democratic constituencies. As John Jennings, director of a think tank that opposes vouchers, put it: "Blacks are finally saying, "We've had enough with inner-city schools . . . [which] could be a problem for Democrats."[25] In particular, members of the Congressional Black Caucus might well listen to their constituents and open the door to national experimentation with vouchers, although such an alliance did not materialize in the 1998 D.C. voucher initiatives.

Still, the positions of racial and ethnic minorities could change the traditional balance of power among stakeholders in this issue area. The public school defenders—unionized teachers (the NEA and the American
Federation of Teachers) and the school board associations—have historically succeeded in blocking the use of public funds for vouchers.[26] But
supporters of vouchers have grown consistently in number and visibility
since the mid-1980s, with a loose coalition of "pro-family" groups, conservative think tanks, and various elected officials and candidates. In particular, the backing of the Reagan administration and a number of governors, such as Wisconsin's Tommy Thompson, helped move vouchers on
to both the public and governmental policy agendas.[27] As the voucher
issue has matured in the 1990s, the opponents have had an increasingly
difficult time holding their coalition together, not necessarily because
pilot programs have proven vouchers successful but largely because proponents have combined the "choice" argument with the continued perception that—especially in low-income areas—public schools are failing.
This combination produces a climate in which the voucher story line
sounds more and more appealing, most notably to minorities in urban
settings.[28] As African American columnist William Raspberry notes,
approvingly quoted by Peterson and Greene, "It's time for some serious
experimentation."[29]

—*Scope and breadth of politics.* Among all voucher-related issues, only
K–12 education has been played out consistently with great publicity (an
"expanded scope of conflict"). Most school voucher politics takes place
within the "symbolic politics," or the "public confrontation" quadrants, of
table 3-1. Thus, Speaker Gingrich castigates the Democrats over a minor
provision in a D.C. funding bill, and voucher opponents place great public pressure on the president to veto the legislation.

Even when the immediate impact of legislation (as with public funding
for vouchers in Wisconsin) is modest, the stakes are regarded as high by
most groups. And since opponents and proponents have taken turns winning and losing battles over school vouchers, all interests, as sometime
losers, have had an incentive in the past fifteen years to expand the scope
of conflict to bring in a wider audience. This is especially true for school
choice supporters, in that surveys have demonstrated a steady growth of
backing for vouchers among the public at large, as well as in pockets of
minority populations. The 1998 Phi Delta Kappa-Gallup survey demonstrated, for example, that for the first time a majority of respondents
(51 percent) voiced support for allowing children to "attend *any* public,
private or church-related school."[30]

The public nature of these politics is important because high visibility renders meaningful debate more difficult and serious deliberation and informed compromise more unlikely, when contrasted to the low-visibility politics within a particular policy community (such as higher education). Moreover, given the number of venues and the role of the states in voucher policymaking, national debates in Congress may simply bear little fruit in determining some definitive national policy on this issue.

—*Venues.* In the United States, K–12 education policymaking lies mostly in the province of state and local politics. As such, the national politicking on vouchers runs through Milwaukee and Cleveland as much as on Capitol Hill, given these cities' status as running publicly funded voucher programs. Thus, a governor like Wisconsin's Republican Tommy Thompson sees school choice, along with welfare reform, as a potential signature accomplishment of his four-term administration. Such experimentation takes advantage of both the traditional federal division of responsibilities and the current trends on devolution. When thirty-plus privately funded voucher programs are added to the mix, the local nature of the policy venues is reinforced.[31]

As political support for vouchers increases, the most important venues for national policy change will probably be found within the court systems at both the federal and state levels. In June 1998, the Wisconsin Supreme Court ruled that public funding for vouchers for religious school education violated neither the state constitution nor the U.S. Constitution, and four months later the U.S. Supreme Court refused to review the case. This ruling opens the door for other states to experiment with legislation of their own.[32] As Jersey City mayor Bert Schundler, a fervent advocate of vouchers, notes, "The question has always been when do we get our grass-roots supporters cranking to put pressure on the Legislature? I think it's time to start cranking."[33] More generally, the constitutional issues of church-state cooperation offer voucher opponents structural opportunities to move controversies into judicial venues, even when the core arguments may be as much about the distribution of resources as about more profound constitutional issues. In sum, the numerous venues contribute to the complexity and fragmentation of school voucher politics, yet the combination of symbol and substance, along with the drumbeat of think tank pronouncements, illustrates how much of the debate on local and state programs is filtered through inside-the-beltway sources.

—*Think tanks and the politics of symbols.* For all the fierce local battles over vouchers in Milwaukee and Cleveland, the most sustained political rhetoric has emanated from (mostly conservative) think tanks in Washington, D.C. Only a visit to a Heritage Foundation web site or selection of publications is needed to gain a flavor of the pro-vouchers narrative. Ironically, the seminal event of the intellectual debates over school choice was publication of John Chubb and Terry Moe's *Politics, Markets, and America's Schools* by the Brookings Institution Press. Jeffery Henig noted that four elements combine to give this book its substantial legitimacy: an emphasis on democracy; an empirical focus; a relatively detailed model for school choice; and its publication by Brookings, "perhaps the nation's premier think tank . . . [with] a moderately liberal reputation [that] made its endorsement all the more potent."[34]

More generally, the very notion of choice resonates broadly in American society. The idea of freedom is often corralled by interests that seek to push (or oppose) a specific set of proposals. For example, public debate over both Clinton's health care reforms and the 1996 telecommunications legislation hinged largely on the idea that individual choices should be maximized. The symbolism of greater choice bore little relationship to the legislative outcomes on either of these issues, but the symbolism of choice emerged as a powerful (and winning) narrative for many interests.[35] Indeed, many contemporary think tanks have used expertise "more as ammunition for partisan and ideological causes than as balanced or objective information."[36] Nor are advocacy think tanks the only ones that weave narratives around choice, as Brookings demonstrated with Chubb and Moe's work. Still, it is the conservative advocacy think tanks that push choice narratives most fervently. As the Hudson Institute's Gregg Vanourek hotly proclaimed, "With all of its moral underpinnings, charismatic leadership, political battles, and courtroom dramas, the *school choice movement is a natural and worthy heir to the original civil rights movement. . . . Someday we will come to view school choice as a fundamental civil right in this country.*"[37]

—*Choice and accountability.* In virtually all voucher programs, the virtues of choice must be balanced by the overall requirements of accountability. For school vouchers, accountability comes in various possible forms—from meeting accepted education standards to using certified teachers to measuring parental satisfaction to following the letter of federal law concerning the special populations that public schools are required to serve. The public at large, which by a slim majority favors governmental funding of school choice, overwhelmingly (76 percent) endorses the idea that private schools should be held to the same standards of accountability as public schools.[38] Various groups that oppose school vouchers on constitutional grounds are reflecting this view and moving accountability arguments to the fore. This makes sense to the extent that the lack of any obligation to serve special populations provides both financial and operational advantages for private schools.

Most supporters of vouchers see accountability as relatively unimportant; after all, getting choice on the agenda has been their emphasis for fifteen years. Moreover, competition in itself is seen as adequate to ensure quality. As Senator Larry Craig (R-Idaho) concluded, "We are not going to worry about the private system. It competes. It has to be good or it will not get the kids."[39]

Accountability also comes into play in the evaluation of extant voucher programs. Many of the battles fought during the agenda-setting phase of policymaking are refought over evaluation and interpretation of results. Stanford professor of economics and higher education Henry M. Levin notes, "Most of the stuff written on the subject is very tendentious. It supports a particular viewpoint that starts with ideology, not with evidence, and looks for evidence that buttresses its views."[40] Stronger, theory-based analyses have begun to appear, but the results remain mixed, and there are some indications that accountability criteria have begun to shift—from putatively objective standards to parental satisfaction—essentially a market response.

—*Vouchers, spending, and budgets.* Providing public education is the most costly element of state and local government in the United States, and increasing per student expenditures has not proved effective in improving educational quality. Given these circumstances, K–12 vouchers present a set of opportunities for conservatives and a set of threats to a host of established interests. Most states have benefited from good times in recent years, yet there is only modest support for increased spending on public education.[41] Although both Republicans and Democrats have proposed some funding increases and program changes at the federal level, the minimal federal contribution to K–12 education spending means that the major struggles occur in the states' respective school finance politics.[42]

The NEA argues that vouchers—even modest ones—will increase costs by paying for "students already in private schools."[43] Conversely, voucher advocates see the potential for holding state costs down, as with the Wisconsin program that provides $5,000 vouchers to a maximum of 15,000 Milwaukee students whose families are near the poverty level. The state will trim approximately $5,000 from the Milwaukee public schools' budget for each student that opts to use a voucher for private education.[44] Thus politics swirls around both the total level of spending and the (re)distribution of that spending. The teachers' unions remain the most self-interested, but—

at $5,000 a head—private schools have real incentives to step up to the table. The financial health of the states allows for the possibility of increased funding for education that combines vouchers and continued support for public education, but economic weakness would place the states under great stress—turning distributive politics into a redistributive struggle.

Established Programs: Food Stamps, Housing, and Higher Education

In considering vouchers beyond the K–12 issue area, the most important initial line of demarcation appears to be whether the policy tool is firmly in place or not. This puts well-established food stamps, housing vouchers, and Pell grants and loans for higher education in one category, evolving voucher programs for Medicare and Medicaid recipients in another, and the new job-training vouchers—in the initial stages of implementation—in still another.

Established voucher programs often face challenges, but they have created strong sets of advocates, both inside Congress and out. For the most part, the politics of food stamps, housing vouchers, and Pell grants and student loans fall into the "policy community" category (table 3-1). That is, they affect large numbers of individuals, but the scope of conflict remains relatively narrow. This means that members of the policy community (for example, from universities to loan processor Sallie Mae to trade associations for higher education, plus parts of the Department of Education and appropriate congressional committees and subcommittees) will typically decide the fate of the programs, usually outside the glare of publicity.[45] This does not mean that the politics will not be intense—just ask a lobbyist about the ins and outs of reauthorizing higher education legislation—but the conflict will not be socialized to bring new participants into a highly public fray.

Important to understanding the politics of vouchers within these issue areas is the relative *weakness* (at least in terms of lobbying) of their core constituencies—the poor for food stamps and housing vouchers and students from poor to lower-middle-class families for Pell grants and student loans. The program constituents themselves are both represented by others (for example, members of Congress) and supported by more powerful coalition partners, such as various higher education organizations. This plays out somewhat differently across the three issues, but in each instance the politics of vouchers is thoroughly enmeshed with other unconnected items the core constituents often have little capacity to affect.

For example, food stamp politics has become tied to the often ideological politics of welfare reform and anti-immigrant sentiments, in addition to its traditional linkages to farmers and grocers.[46] In the end, the long-standing (if sometimes shaky) coalition has hung together from the late 1960s through the 1990s.[47] Still, welfare reforms and provisions restricting aid to legal immigrants have demonstrated the weakness of the core constituency. As Representative Ileana Ros-Lehtinen (R-Fla.) rhetorically asked, "Who is going to give a seventy-five-year-old legal resident a job? . . . The welfare bill is loaded with such injustices, affecting only the neediest families. As a group, they are a constituency for no one."[48]

To an extent, the congressional Republicans did succeed in expanding the scope of the conflict on food stamps by relating the program to a broader conservative agenda and their version of welfare reform, signed into law by President Clinton. But in 1998 the food stamp policy community, represented by substantial congressional majorities, overwhelmed the Republican leadership and the hard-core welfare reformers by first defeating a restrictive rule that would have allowed food stamps to be decoupled from a farm bill authorizing research funding and then by passing the research/food stamp/crop insurance bill.[49] More important, food stamp supporters beat back an attempt to reconfigure food stamps into block grants for the states. Despite its weakness, the food stamp constituency once again got by with a little help from its friends—especially Republicans from farm belt states and agricultural interests such as the American Farm Bureau Federation (AFBF).

The politics of housing vouchers resembles those of food stamps, but if anything, the constituents are weaker and the allies less reliable.[50] Not only do they have no linkage to groups like the powerful AFBF, but their major allies in the bureaucracy (the Department of Housing and Urban Development) and Congress (the banking committees) do not wield the same kind of clout that the Agriculture Department and the agriculture committees (and the respective appropriations subcommittees) do. Vouchers have constituted about 30 percent of HUD housing assistance (which altogether serves less than a third of those eligible), and this form of assistance has become an increasingly important option as both the Clinton administration and the Republican Congress seek to overhaul federal housing policy.

Vouchers are attractive because they do not require that any new housing be built. Rather, legislators can argue that vouchers will allow clients to enter the private housing market, even though vouchers may not be adequate to allow the poor to rent in a tight housing market. Vouchers thus can offer symbolic cover, while not necessarily addressing substantive problems. At the same time, vouchers do offer much more potential immediate impact than does the building of new public housing units. Still, budget cutters will find it easier to eliminate "paper apartments" (vouchers) than to reduce funding for the maintenance of existing structures.[51] Moreover, many of those individuals who are eligible for housing vouchers simply do not choose to use them, either remaining in public housing or not facing the bureaucratic requirements.

In short, housing vouchers have never received quite the acceptance of food stamps, in part because they represent only a single element within a much larger set of housing subsidies, including the 800-pound gorilla of the home-mortgage tax deduction. Over time, legislators have proven wary of the housing marketplace, and no strong political force has pushed them hard to overcome their qualms.

The final voucherlike programs considered, Pell grants and student loans, have generated a fairly strong constituency within the higher education community. Organizations representing state colleges and universities, community colleges, land-grant universities, private colleges, and other higher education interests have consistently defended Pell grants and loans for a quarter century. Yet this policy community has experienced serious divisions over the distribution of Pell funds, even as they have lobbied for more funds in total. With grants covering only $2,500 or so in expenses, the more pricey, private schools have historically desired higher limits for awards, which recently have been raised to $4,500. Their major opponents have been low-tuition community colleges, whose desire has been to offer awards to as many students as possible. In recent years, state universities, with their own tuition escalating, have moved their position closer to that of the private institutions.[52] In other words—despite some rhetoric about low grant levels as denying students opportunities (private schools) or helping more students move beyond high school (community colleges)—this has been traditionally an old-fashioned fight over who gets what in the distribution of funds, although the 1998 higher education reauthorization markedly increased levels of Pell grants and some other voucherlike assistance.[53] Members of the higher education policy community were long regarded as ineffective, or at least nonaggressive, lobbyists.[54] In the wake of the Republican takeover of Congress, they became more energetic, more sophisticated, and more successful.

In food stamps, housing vouchers, and higher education vouchers, the traditional policy community politics of (re)distribution dominates, although the twin desires of most Republicans and more than a few Democrats to shrink the federal government and hold down federal spending have played out in different ways across these issue areas. And account-ability has sometimes come to the fore as a political consideration (for example, food stamp fraud, local control of public housing). Still, in the end, the politics of these programs reflects the more or less conventional struggles over who gets what and under what conditions.

Health Care: Vouchers in a Complex Policy Community

In his chapter for this volume, Robert Reischauer writes of extensive (if lit-tle used) vouchers within the Medicare system, dating from 1982 tax leg-islation.[55] In an early draft of their paper that catalogs all voucher pro-grams, Paul Posner and his coauthors did not even list Medicare as an issue area in which vouchers existed.[56] Nor did an Internet search come up with any meaningful hits when "Medicare" and "vouchers" were joined in a series of searches.

What gives? Some hidden agenda? Hardly. Rather, the fact is that many programs that contain the attributes of vouchers, as defined academically, are not labeled "voucher" policies. All in all, that works to their benefit, given the public's linkage of the term to K–12 education. Moreover, as Reischauer demonstrates, voucherlike policy can insinuate itself over time, with little controversy (or even recognition). Sooner or later, however, groups of stakeholders, such as health maintenance organization (HMO) participants, will recognize their common interests and may become a powerful political force in changing policies.

The 1982 adoption of Medicare vouchers as an option for participants flowed directly out of the health care policy community—"a small group of influential analysts and policy makers" who saw HMOs as superior delivery systems in terms of both quality and efficiency.[57] This top-down decision had the potential to affect large numbers of individuals, but relatively few took advantage of the choice. In the 1990s, with HMOs gaining popular-ity, about 15 percent of all Medicare recipients chose the voucher option, although most would not have thought about it in those terms. Given the myriad problems with and complexities of the health care system, it is no wonder that a voucherlike program received little attention. Still, as Reischauer notes, "The Medicare option has . . . created a constituency" that has the potential to become an important political force, especially as Medicare becomes increasingly involved with questions of cost and afford-ability, as opposed to quality of care and administrative efficiency.[58]

This nascent interest is especially significant in the wake of the Balanced Budget Act of 1997, which expanded and restructured the Medicare option in light of the goal of reducing the program's rate of growth. As questions of equity, adequate information, and quality inevitably emerge, the HMO-voucher stakeholders of the 2010 period—given their age, education, and income—have the potential to speak loudly and expand the scope of the controversy. In that instance, members of the health care policy community could well lose control of the Medicare issue, much as Bill Clinton threatened them with his 1993–94 reform proposals.

Medicare (and health care more generally) arguably constitutes the most complex policy arena and the most difficult political context for the introduction of vouchers. The policy obstacles are formidable (see the chapter in this volume by Robert Reischauer), but no more so than the political difficulties. Ironically, the very complexity of health care policies may simultaneously increase and decrease the potential for meaningful change that includes the extensive use of vouchers. At some point, the participant-stakeholders will constitute a powerful interest, which may work against a considered consensus by most policy community members; expanding the scope of the conflict would not likely produce better policy outcomes, given the symbolic politics that would emerge. Conversely, the complexity of Medicare policies in the next decades may push public consideration of vouchers into the background, where they have remained since 1982. With so many other important issues in the mix, voucherlike options have the chance to appear as the policy tools that they are. And unlike K–12 vouchers, they do not intersect with a cultural divide over the role of a public institution. Indeed, Medicare vouchers may allow at least a modicum of choice for most participants.

A Politics of Vouchers?

In many environments, vouchers are viewed as a tried-and-true policy tool that requires little more than some occasional tinkering. On occasion, values-driven politics (food stamps for legal immigrants or mixing poor and middle-income populations in housing) intervenes, but for the most part, major decisions are made within the low-profile politics of established policy communities. These voucher programs offer cost containment, some real choice, and low administrative expenses—a combination that draws the support of lots of interests and legislators. In these contexts, vouchers reflect the ordinary distributional (and sometimes redistributional) politics that we have come to expect and understand in post-1960 U.S. policymaking.

In other policy arenas, ranging from K–12 education to veterans' health care, vouchers come across as promising initiatives in addressing difficult and intractable policy problems—and the adoption of voucher innovations may well become more likely to the extent that public education and veterans' health care can be labeled as crises. In contrast to the stable policy community politics of established voucher programs, K–12 proposals (and health care packages, too, if they came close to fruition) generate a very different kind of politics. With a broad scope of conflict and high stakes for many interests, such voucher politics is less predictable, more heavily lobbied, and more susceptible to venue shopping both in terms of state and federal venues and of decision points across the branches of government (and especially the courts). At the same time, as Douglas Besharov and Nazanin Samari note, one new set of programs—child-care vouchers—has received "apparently smooth implementation . . . in all states."[59]

To the extent that issues remain unsettled or tentative, the politics of ideas, expertise, and advocacy comes into play, with many arguments being filtered through (mostly) Washington-based think tanks. School vouchers represent a mature form of this politicking, while health care advocacy (very public and involved in the 1993–94 era of proposed reforms) has now retreated to address choice issues as one element of incremental change within a complex policy environment.

In the end, the theoretical attraction and practical virtues of vouchers as a policy tool will keep the idea well positioned to serve as the basis for proposals in any number of issue areas. Established voucher policies also show few signs of losing their core supporters. But does this mean there is some distinctive "politics of vouchers?" Probably not, beyond their continuing attractiveness in bringing together sometimes unlikely coalitions and offering the possibility for new thinking around difficult societal problems. Still, questions of accountability and ideology remain important obstacles to further adoption, especially in areas where major interests (teachers' unions and school board associations, the American Association of Retired Persons and veterans organizations, for example) retain their political clout.

Notes

1. Matthew Tully, "School Vouchers, Other Issues Push Parties into Confrontation over District of Columbia Bill," *CQ Weekly*, August 8, 1998, p. 2183.

2. David A. Vise and Michael H. Cottman, "House Adds Vouchers in Approving D.C. Budget," *Washington Post*, August 7, 1998, p. B1.

3. See Rochelle L. Stanfield, "Preaching against Vouchers," *National Journal*, April 4, 1997, p. 769; Rochelle L. Stanfield, "A Turning Tide on Vouchers," *National Journal*, September 27, 1997, p. 1911.

4. Quoted in *Education Week on the Web* (www.edweek.org [January 10, 1996]).

5. "Stop the New 'Careers' Act"(www.americanpolicy.org [September 12, 1998]).

6. Frederic J. Froomer, "DeWine's Job-Training Bill Passes Senate," *Associated Press Dispatch*, July 31, 1998.

7. U.S. Chamber of Commerce press release (www.uschamber.org.NEWS [August 5,1998]).

8. See E. E. Schattschneider, *The Semi-Sovereign People* (Holt, Rinehart, Winston, 1960); William E. Browne, "Organized Interests and Their Issue Niches," *Journal of Politics*, vol. 52 (May 1990), pp. 477–509.

9. David Rochefort and Roger Cobb, eds., *The Politics of Problem Definition* (University Press of Kansas, 1994), p. 5.

10. Christopher Bosso, "The Contextual Bases of Problem Definition," in Rochefort and Cobb, eds., *The Politics of Problem Definition*, pp. 182–203.

11. Paul Light, *Artful Work: The Politics of Social Security Reform* (Random House, 1983).

12. Frank Baumgartner and Bryan Jones, *Agendas and Instability in American Politics* (University of Chicago Press, 1993), p. 25ff.

13. Christopher Bosso, *Pesticides and Politics* (University of Pittsburgh Press, 1987).

14. David Vogel, *Fluctuating Fortunes* (Basic Books, 1989), pp. 295–97.

15. Jeffrey Berry, *The New Liberalism: The Rising Power of Citizen Groups* (Brookings, 1999).

16. Gary Mucciaroni, *Reversals of Fortune* (Brookings, 1995), p. 180ff.

17. Hugh Heclo, "Our Changing Political Process," in C. Eugene Steuerle, ed., *The Government We Deserve* (Urban Institute, 1998).

18. Ralph Nader, "Minimal Media Coverage of Auto Safety Initiative," *Liberal Opinion*, March 27, 1995, p. 25.

19. James Thurber, *Divided Democracy* (Washington, D.C.: CQ Press, 1991); Browne, "Organized Interests and Their Issue Niches."

20. William E. Browne, *Cultivating Congress* (University Press of Kansas, 1995); John Wright, *Interest Groups and Congress* (Allyn and Bacon, 1996); David Whiteman, *Communication in Congress* (University Press of Kansas, 1996).

21. Thurber, *Divided Democracy*, p. 336.

22. John Hall and William D. Eggers, "Health and Social Services in the Post-Welfare State: Are Vouchers the Answer?" Policy Study 192, Reason

Foundation, Los Angeles, California (www.reason.org [August 8, 1998]). To their credit, the authors discuss various possible unintended consequences of adopting vouchers to address problems not currently considered entitlements.

23. Murray Edelman, in *The Symbolic Uses of Politics* (University of Illinois Press, 1964) and *Political Language* (Academic Press, 1977), emphasized the intertwining of the symbolic and the substantive, but symbolism may well keep both policymakers and audiences from fully addressing the issues at hand.

24. Stanfield, "A Turning Tide on Vouchers," p. 1911.

25. Ibid, p. 1912.

26. Jeffery Henig, *Rethinking School Choice* (Princeton University Press, 1994), p. 68ff.

27. Henig provides a clearheaded recounting of this agenda-building stage for school vouchers in *Rethinking School Choice*, pp. 71–4.

28. See, for example, the clearheaded article by Michael Winerip, "School for Sale," *New York Times Magazine*, June 14, 1998, p. 42ff.

29. Paul E. Peterson and Jay P. Greene, "Race Relations and Central City Schools," *Brookings Review* (Spring 1998), p. 37.

30. "Poll: More Americans Favor Public Funding in Public Schools," CNN interactive (cnn.com [August 25, 1998]).

31. See the chapter in this volume by Paul Posner and others.

32. Joan Biskupic, "Wisconsin Wins School Vouchers Case; State Ruling, Allowing Tax Money for Religious Education, Could Become Test Case," *Washington Post*, June 11, 1998, p. A1; Jacques Steinberg, "Advocates of School Vouchers Heartened by Ruling," *New York Times*, June 13, 1998, p. B1.

33. Quoted in Steinberg, "Advocates of School Vouchers Heartened by Ruling," p. B1.

34. Henig, *Rethinking School Choice*, p. 87.

35. See Darrell West and Burdett Loomis, *The Sound of Money* (W. W. Norton, 1999), chaps. 4, 6; on telecommunications, in particular, see Tom W. Bell and Solveig Singleton, eds., *Regulators' Revenge* (Cato Institute, 1998).

36. Andrew Rich and R. Kent Weaver, "Advocates and Analysts: Think Tanks and the Politicization of Expertise," in Allan J. Cigler and Burdett A. Loomis, eds., *Interest Group Politics*, 5th ed. (Washington, D.C.: CQ Press, 1998), p. 237.

37. Gregg Vanourek, "The Choice Crusade," *Educational Excellence Network*, December 1996, (edexcellence.net [September 7, 1998]). Emphasis added.

38. "Poll: More Americans Favor Public Funding in Private Schools," p. 3.

39. Statement of Senator Larry E. Craig, concerning the District of Columbia Appropriations Act, 1998 (www.senate.gov/~craig [September 25, 1997]).

40. Quoted in Rochelle Stanfield, "Education Wars," *National Journal*, March 7, 1998, p. 509.

41. Ironically, it is Republican governors who have increased spending the most. See Peter Beinart, "Republican Heartthrobs," *New Republic,* December 8, 1998, p. 27.

42. Stanfield, "Education Wars," pp. 508–09.

43. "Vouchers," National Education Association, "In brief" (www.nea.org [September 12, 1998]).

44. Biskupic, "Wisconsin Wins School Vouchers Case," p. A1.

45. For a discussion of the idea of policy community as it applies to higher education, see Constance E. Cook, "The Washington Higher Education Community: Moving beyond Lobbying 101," in Cigler and Loomis, *Interest Group Politics*, 5th ed., pp. 97–117; Constance Cook, *Lobbying for Higher Education* (University of Tennessee Press, 1998).

46. Curt Anderson, "House Sends President Immigrant Food Stamp-Farm Bill," *Associated Press Newswire*, via Lexis-Nexis, June 5, 1998.

47. See James C. Ohls and Harold Beebout, *The Food Stamp Program* (Urban Institute, 1993).

48. Ruth Coniff, "Going Hungry: Congressional Republicans Block Food Stamps for Immigrants," *Progressive* (June 1998), p. 9.

49. Sue Kirchhoff, "House Clears Agriculture Bill, Restoring Food Stamps to Legal Immigrants," *CQ Weekly*, June 6, 1998, p. 1532.

50. See Peter Dreier and John Atlas, "Housing Policy's Moment of Truth," *American Prospect* (Summer 1995), pp. 68–77.

51. Rochelle Stanfield, "Communities Reborn," *National Journal*, June 22, 1998, p. 1373.

52. Stephen Burd, "Proposed Pell-Grant Limits Split 2-Year and 4-Year Colleges," *Chronicle of Higher Education*, April 4, 1994, p. A28.

53. See the chapter in this volume by Arthur M. Hauptman.

54. Cook, "The Washington Higher Education Community," p. 112.

55. See the chapter in this volume by Robert Reischauer. This section draws considerably on several of the arguments and some of the data presented there.

56. See the chapter in this volume by Paul Posner and others.

57. See the chapter in this volume by Robert Reischauer.

58. Ibid.

59. See the chapter in this volume by Douglas Besharov and Nazanin Samari.

PART TWO

Practice

ROBERT A. MOFFITT

4 | *Lessons from the Food Stamp Program*

O F ALL THE programs discussed in this volume, food stamp benefits come the closest to a universal, portable, uniform-benefit voucher. Benefits are issued in the form of dollar-denominated coupons to eligible households, which can use them, within certain restrictions, to purchase food at a wide variety of outlets.

An important question is whether the food stamp program can offer lessons to other areas of public service provision regarding the advantages and disadvantages—and general issues—that arise from using vouchers as a mechanism to deliver public services. The conclusion of this chapter is that there are few such lessons. The subsidization of food through the voucher mechanism works well for a number of reasons, few of which are present in other areas in which the government provides or subsidizes goods or services. However, there are a few issues that arise in the food stamp program and that have received attention in the policy and research discussions surrounding it that would be quite relevant should subsidies in other service areas be converted to vouchers.

In addition to thanking the editors, the author would like to thank Steven Carlson and James Ohls for comments.

119

The first section of this chapter outlines the history of the program, its current operation, and its rules. The following section discusses the features of the food market that make the use of vouchers for food subsidization so much more natural than vouchers for many of the other goods and services discussed in this volume. Political considerations and federalism issues are discussed in the third section, while the fourth section examines some of the issues that would be relevant to other programs should they be converted to vouchers, issues related to participation, access, and fraud (or trafficking). The final section discusses the in-kind nature of the food stamp program and the related issue of its effect on food expenditures.

Background: History and Rules of the Program

The provision of food to individuals and families in need by those who are better off has taken many forms in the United States. In the first half of the twentieth century, the best-known forms of food assistance in this country were soup kitchens and related food distributions to the unemployed and the destitute of the Great Depression. Beginning in the late 1930s, however, a more systematized form of food provision was initiated, one that channeled surplus agricultural commodities to the poor through the use of color-coded coupons.[1] The coupons were provided to those who were eligible for local assistance programs; commodities that were in different degrees of excess supply could be purchased using the different colored coupons. The system lapsed in 1943, when World War II absorbed surplus commodities. After the war the federal farm price support systems generated surplus commodities, and direct commodity distribution administered by local food agencies was used to provide food assistance. As might be expected, the attempt to distribute food in that way to large numbers of families led to difficulties in moving and storing food as well as to fluctuating and limited choice of types of food.

In the early 1960s, the Kennedy administration initiated a pilot food coupon system in several counties: between 1961 and 1964 the existing commodity distribution system in these counties was replaced. The Food Stamp Act of 1964, which created the modern Food Stamp Program (FSP), gave to all counties in the country the option of participating in the coupon system. However, counties were not required to participate. Even though benefits were financed completely by the federal government, federal eligibility criteria were not used; eligibility was determined by state-level welfare rules.

Initially, only twenty-two states took up the coupon option, and even then not all counties in those states joined the program. Over the first decade increasing numbers of counties dropped their commodity distribution programs and adopted the new FSP. Growing public and media attention to the issue of hunger led to the adoption of federal eligibility criteria and benefit schedules as well as to the indexation of benefits to inflation. In 1973 the program was mandated for all counties.

Historically, then, the only major alternative to vouchered provision of food assistance to the poor in the United States has been the direct distribution of commodities to the poor. The obvious inefficiency of such a delivery mechanism for large-scale distribution is the reason this mechanism no longer plays a significant role. It has not completely disappeared, however. The Emergency Food Program, which provides surplus commodities to emergency food facilities around the country; the Nutrition Program for the elderly, which reimburses facilities for the elderly for preparation of meals; the Commodity Supplemental Food Program, which provides food commodities to low-income mothers and children and to the low-income elderly; the Special Milk Program, which serves milk to low-income children in schools and summer camps; meals-on-wheels programs for the elderly; commodity distribution programs to soup kitchens, food banks, and other charitable institutions; and several other programs provide food commodities directly to the poor.[2] However, the total value of commodities distributed through all of these programs is only a small fraction of that purchased with food stamps.

Operation and Rules

The FSP is a federal program; 100 percent of benefits are paid by the federal government from general tax revenues. The program is run by the states, however, which pay approximately 50 percent of the program's administrative costs. On a day-to-day basis, two types of organizations are involved in the FSP. First, there are welfare agencies, which certify the eligibility of households. Although these certifications take place in welfare agencies, many who are not eligible for cash assistance are eligible for food stamps. The welfare agencies issue stamps to those who are certified as eligible.[3] States are required to maintain a quality control program that audits eligibility records and that is reviewed by the federal government. The federal government assesses error rates in the eligibility and benefit determination process, and states can be penalized for excessive errors.

The second type of organization involved in the FSP on a daily basis is the retail outlet. Such stores are authorized to sell food to those who wish to pay for it with the food coupons they have received from the welfare department. There are almost 200,000 participating retail outlets in the United States. These outlets collect the stamps and take them to banks, which credit the retailer's account for the value. The banks then send the coupons to the Federal Reserve Board, which destroys them. The welfare agencies and the retail outlets are under the oversight of the Food and Nutrition Service of the Department of Agriculture (USDA/FNS).

Only certain types of outlets are authorized by USDA to accept stamps. Many convenience stores and almost all supermarkets are authorized. However, restaurants and stores that sell a high portion of their stock as ready-to-eat cooked food are not eligible. This restriction reflects the program's objective, which is to subsidize food intended for home preparation.

At the household level, eligibility has always been more or less universal with respect to family structure—that is, eligibility is not conditioned on family structure per se, as was the case with the Aid to Families with Dependent Children (AFDC) welfare program. Instead, eligibility is determined on the basis of income, assets, and household size. A food stamp unit, or "household," is a group of individuals living together and commonly purchasing food, preparing meals, and eating together. Certain individuals (spouses, children) who are related by blood ties are considered part of the food stamp household even if they purchase food and prepare meals separately.

To be eligible for stamps, a household must have gross and net monthly income that falls below certain maximum levels, which vary with the household's size. (Net income is gross income minus housing expense deductions, work-related expenses and earned income deductions, dependent care deductions, and a variety of other miscellaneous deductions.) In addition,there are specified maximum levels for various types of assets (cars, houses, financial assets, and so forth). Once a household has been certified, it must be recertified every three to twelve months.

The benefit amount (the "allotment") of an eligible household is determined by a formula that, roughly speaking, is equal to a guarantee amount that varies with household size minus 30 percent of net monthly income. The benefit equals the dollar value of the food coupons the eligible unit receives. The nominal, or statutory, marginal tax rate in the program is thus 30 percent. However, the effective marginal tax rate is quite different, because the deductions themselves vary with income and because the maximum income limits create notches at which the tax rate exceeds 100 percent. Temporary Assistance to Needy Families (TANF, which replaced AFDC) and other benefits are included in countable income, which has implications for cumulative marginal tax rates of those who participate in multiple programs.[4] Coupons are indexed for inflation in food prices.

Before 1977, households with benefits that were less than the guarantee amount were required to pay this difference in cash (the "purchase requirement") in return for coupons equal in value to the guarantee. This purchase requirement, which was thought to discourage participation, was eliminated in 1977, and since that time eligible households have been given coupons equal in value to their benefit amount.

Stamps can be used for most food purchases but not all. Excluded are hot foods intended for immediate consumption, vitamins, medicines, pet foods, alcoholic beverages, and any nonfood items (except seeds and plants).

In fiscal year 1997 the federal government spent approximately $21 billion on the benefits, and an additional 15 percent of this amount was spent on administrative expenses. There were 23 million individuals living in households receiving stamps. Table 4-1 shows the caseload and participation rates in the program from 1975 to 1996 (participation rates of eligibles are discussed later in this chapter).

Other Cash Programs

The other major cash-oriented food programs are the Supplemental Nutrition Program for Women, Infants, and Children (WIC), the School Lunch Program, and the School Breakfast Program. The benefits for these programs are also 100 percent federally funded. The WIC program provides nutritional education, health services, special nutritious foods, and food vouchers for special foods to low-income pregnant women, mothers, infants, and children who are judged to be at "nutritional risk." The vouchers can be used only for a restricted set of foods, and the number of authorized retail outlets is much smaller than is the case with the FSP. The School Breakfast and School Lunch programs offer reduced-price or free meals to low-income children enrolled in school.

Why Vouchers Are Used for Food Redistribution

Of all the programs discussed in this volume, the FSP comes closest to being a pure voucher program. Is this a historical accident or are there compelling reasons why vouchers are the most efficient or sensible way to

Table 4-1. *Food Stamp Participation Rates, 1975–96*

Year	Number of participants (millions)	Participation as a percentage of	
		Total population	Poor population
1975	16.3	7.6	63.0
1976	17.0	7.9	68.1
1977	15.6	7.2	63.1
1978	14.4	6.5	58.8
1979	15.9	7.1	61.0
1980	19.2	8.4	65.6
1981	20.6	9.0	64.7
1982	20.4	8.8	59.3
1983	21.6	9.2	61.2
1984	20.9	8.8	62.0
1985	19.9	8.3	60.2
1986	19.4	8.0	59.9
1987	19.1	7.8	59.1
1988	18.7	7.6	58.9
1989	18.8	7.6	59.6
1990	20.0	8.0	59.6
1991	22.6	9.0	63.3
1992	25.4	10.0	68.9
1993	27.0	10.4	68.7
1994	27.5	10.5	72.1
1995	26.6	10.1	73.0
1996	25.5	9.6	69.8

Source: *Background Material and Data on Programs within the Jurisdiction of the Committee on Ways and Means*, Committee Print 105-7, House Ways and Means Committee, 105 Cong. 2 sess. (GPO, 1998), p. 874.

provide food subsidies to low-income households? There are several reasons to conclude the latter.

Existence of a Well-Established Market for the Good

Clearly the market for food is well established and well organized. It is a massive market with a large number of buyers and sellers and where the transaction costs of trades are quite small. Competition is strong and prices are kept in line by that competition. Contrast this with education, for which there has been no established market at the primary and secondary level, or with the day-care industry, which has only in recent years established a significant market.

A Well-Defined Good with Easily Identifiable Quality Characteristics

This is perhaps the most important characteristic that differentiates food from medical care, day care, and education. Food products, while highly heterogeneous and differentiated in the market both in "real" ways and in brand-identification ways, are nevertheless easily characterized as to quality, and information on that quality is widely available. (Preferences over quality, of course, vary tremendously.) There is relatively little scope for private information on the quality of the good and for asymmetric information leading to suboptimal provision.[5] Contrast this with education, the quality of which has been debated since mass education began and the economic payoff of which, even if that is taken to be the quality standard, is highly uncertain at the individual level. For example, the economic value in terms of future earnings of differing educational philosophies is essentially unknown. Likewise, medical care is a service where the asymmetric information of the seller and buyer has played a major role in the organization of the market and has resulted in many abridgements of pure consumer sovereignty (for example, through the existence of insurers).

This is not to say that the issue of allowing complete consumer sovereignty has not been discussed in the FSP as it has in other areas of subsidy, where it has sometimes been suggested that consumers will not make "good" choices. In the FSP this takes the form of arguments that recipients do not purchase nutritionally beneficial foods. Because the restrictions on the types of food that can be purchased with stamps are so minimal, recipients have great scope to choose foods with wide ranges of nutritional content. Research on the nutritional content of food purchased with food stamps indicates that nutrient availability is considerably enhanced by the FSP—even more than cash.[6] Whether the food purchased by recipients is exactly what the voter-taxpayers would prefer the recipients to buy is, however, not known.

Nevertheless, the vastly weaker magnitude and force of the argument in the case of food has led to the current situation, in which nutrition education and the nutritional content of the food purchased by food stamp recipients are major issues among those who participate in policy discussions of the program but have never gained enough force to seriously challenge the existence of the program or to cause policymakers to significantly

restrict the types of food that can be purchased with stamps. While everyone prefers that parents purchase the most nutritious food possible, especially for the sake of their children, there is insufficient evidence that the
foods that they do buy are harmful enough to outweigh the benefits of the
additional food purchasing power that the FSP coupons provide.

Low Transaction Cost of Purchase of the Good

Here the most useful contrasts are with housing and education. In rental
housing, the cost of search and relocation are nontrivial and this allows
some collusion between landlords and tenants or some exploitation of
recipients by landlords. While competition in the market is strong, the relatively high costs of searching for a new housing unit reduce mobility in
the short run. This also holds true for education, which represents an
investment in time and effort. In the market for food, however, where a
consumer can cross the street to purchase food from a different store, the
possibilities for these types of suboptimal arrangements are far less likely.

Consumption in Groups No Larger than the Family

Here the contrast is with education and housing, where externalities bring
other considerations into play. Peer group educational effects, for example,
as well as the neighborhood effects of low-income housing, which both
result from sorting of consumers by type, are issues often brought up in
voucher discussions. These factors do not play a role in the FSP.

Political Considerations

The FSP is one of the nation's most popular welfare programs and, as a
result, has been subject to few changes in its basic structure over the past
thirty years. This can be contrasted with the experience of cash welfare,
housing, medical care, child care, and other programs that have undergone
major reforms. Of the three largest income-conditioned transfer programs
for the nonelderly poor—the other two are TANF and Medicaid—the FSP
is the only one with benefits that are entirely federally financed and with
benefits and eligibility conditions that are uniform nationwide.[7] As other
programs have been devolved to the state level, converted to block grant or
matching form, or otherwise moved to local levels, the FSP has remained
in its original Great Society form at the federal level.

This longevity and support has been traced to a number of factors.[8] One is the emotive power of hunger, which was demonstrated early in the history of the program, when television brought the issue to the attention of American voters in the 1960s. As an image, hunger has proven more powerful than homelessness, lack of health insurance, inadequate child care, or poor schools. The risk of being accused of reducing poor children or the low-income elderly to starvation has given the program a political invulnerability that other programs do not have.

In addition to this issue is the long-noted support of mainstream political interests, most notably a powerful agricultural lobby.[9] While all in-kind transfers have lobbies backed by the suppliers of the commodity in question, the agricultural lobby is particularly strong. Members of Congress and senators from farm states and states with strong rural constituencies have been consistent supporters of the program. In addition to the agricultural lobby, the FSP has enjoyed strong support among a number of public-interest and low-income advocacy groups. They have played a major role in recent food stamp debates.[10]

The strength of the hunger issue and the political support of the agricultural lobby and advocacy groups probably explains the puzzle of the FSP's federal nature. There is little economic rationale or reason of governmental organization why food stamps should be provided at the federal level while housing, cash assistance, medical-care assistance, and other benefits for the low-income population should be provided at the state and local levels or shared between different levels of government. As recently as 1995, when congressional debates over the AFDC program led to legislation devolving it to the states, similar legislative proposals to block grant the FSP were soundly rejected.[11] Predictions that such legislation would reduce food expenditures of the poor no doubt played a role in the efforts of both the agricultural lobby and advocacy groups to defeat the proposals.[12] Thus the program has continued to demonstrate strong survival in a political environment in which retrenchment has occurred in many other programs for the poor.

Participation, Access, Trafficking, and Fraud

Even though the characteristics of the market and the political environment make the situation facing food stamps somewhat unique, the experience of food stamps, to a greater or lesser degree, provides some lessons that are relevant for vouchers in other service areas. Among these are issues related to participation rates—sometimes also called take-up rates—and fraud and illegal trading of stamps, known as trafficking.

Participation Rates

One long-standing concern of those involved with the FSP has been the relatively low participation rates of eligible households. Although the participation rate among eligibles has been rising since the mid-1970s, it hovers around only 60 percent.[13] Researchers have studied and debated extensively the reasons for nonparticipation. One popular explanation for the lack of participation is the notion of "stigma," the embarrassment that eligible households would experience from receiving welfare. Stigma could arise in the grocery line, where the recipient must publicly reveal his or her recipient status to the clerk and to other shoppers. There is also more general welfare stigma, which arises from feelings of negative self-worth and loss of pride at being dependent on welfare. These phenomena have been documented by sociologists and psychologists. Stigma also arises when the individual applies for benefits. The procedures required to establish eligibility expose the applicant's status to others when the caseworker verifies the applicant's income, family size, assets, and characteristics.

A distinction should be made between the types of stigma that are unique to food stamps, those that are associated with any voucher, and those that accompany any income-tested government program. Generalized stigma that is entirely internal to the recipient would occur for any welfare program, whether cash or in-kind and whether the service is delivered through a voucher or through some other mechanism, such as direct provision. Likewise, the stigma associated with the verification of eligibility would occur for any welfare program that has similar eligibility determination procedures. The FSP is unique in that stigma could arise in the grocery line. Clearly, this would be missing in a cash transfer program. However, the question is not over the merits of cash transfers versus vouchers, but rather between vouchers and other delivery mechanisms, such as direct provision. Direct service provision may generate greater stigma than vouchers. For example, living in a public housing project may stigmatize residents more than receiving a Section 8 voucher, and placing one's children in a day care center restricted to low-income children may involve more embarrassment than receiving a day care voucher, if public revelation is the primary principle at work. In other words, one cannot conclude that vouchers per se necessarily have a stronger stigma-inducing effect than other forms of transfer.

While researchers tend to regard participation rates below 100 percent as acceptable, particularly if they result from welfare stigma, policymakers often view less than full participation as a sign of program failure. Most researchers regard welfare stigma as a legitimate individual preference (or a negative preference against being a welfare recipient). They consider it rational for an individual or family to accept lower income in return for the ability to say it is self-sufficient. Policymakers, however, are more likely to judge a feeling of stigma as an unfortunate side effect, one that needs to be overcome.

While stigma is thought to be an important deterrent to participation, food stamp policy analysts believe that access, convenience, and knowledge also play major roles in determining participation. Access to the welfare offices is a problem, particularly in rural areas. The burden of paperwork in establishing eligibility often requires multiple trips to the welfare office. Recertification, which takes place every three to twelve months, requires that repeated trips be made. Access to authorized outlets can also be a problem in less densely populated areas and in areas in which there are few participating households. Transportation can be a barrier for low-income families, particularly those without access to cars. Some families also appear to be unaware of their own eligibility and, when informed, apply for and are accepted in the program, suggesting that lack of information is sometimes a barrier.[14]

For whatever reason, the effect on participation rates of eligibles is an important issue when considering conversion of a program from cash or direct provision to vouchers. While it is difficult to make generalizations, it is reasonable to guess that with vouchers participation rates would rise relative to direct provision of benefits but fall relative to cash provision. The greater feeling of stigma in public housing has already been noted and, although it is a special feature of that program, public housing is rationed. (See the chapter by George Peterson in this volume.) But the greater desirability of housing vouchers as compared to public housing would probably raise participation rates even if both were available in equal supply. The greater flexibility of vouchers and the greater rein it provides to consumer sovereignty are likely to apply to other areas such as child care, medical care, and education.

Fraud and Trafficking

Another issue that has generated considerable discussion in the FSP and that should be relevant to vouchers in other areas concerns the opportunities for illegal trading of stamps, known as trafficking. There is a black market for food stamps that functions with the cooperation of authorized retail outlets. The classic case is that in which individual recipients sell their stamps at less than face value to merchants operating outlets authorized to accept stamps. Prices range from 50 cents to 70 cents per dollar of face value. The merchants then redeem the stamps for full face value, without actually having sold the food to justify them.

There are other methods of trafficking besides this classic method.[15] For example, recipients who have been allotted more stamps than they desire might sell some of their stamps at a discount to other recipients who have been allotted fewer stamps than they need. Studies reveal that recipient households can be both buyers and sellers of stamps, sometimes even within the same month. Such behaviors can be understood as representing trades between those with different preferences for food and as a means of intertemporal smoothing in response to uneven cash income flows, an issue that is discussed later in the context of the cash-equivalent value of stamps.

Another method of trafficking, "evasion trafficking," is practiced by merchants to create a paper record of having sold food equivalent in value to the stamps the merchant redeems. Under this scheme, the merchant buys stamps from a recipient at a discount and uses them to purchase food goods from a different retail outlet. The merchant then stocks that food on his own shelf, and the food is eventually sold in the normal course of business. Both merchants have sold goods in the same amount as their cash-plus-stamps receipts. One merchant did not incur the cost of purchasing the food in the first place, but this requires a different level of detection.

The relevant question is whether trafficking is extensive or not. There are no reliable figures showing what voters might regard as the most important measures of trafficking: the number of recipients who engage in trafficking or the percent of food expenditure that is trafficked.[16] In other words, we do not know whether trafficking is practiced by a substantial fraction of recipients or only by a small minority. Nevertheless, investigative and audit studies of merchants have generated reliable estimates suggesting that approximately 4 percent of the value of food stamps is trafficked and that approximately 9 percent of retail outlets engage in such deception.[17] Trafficking is less likely at supermarkets, chains, and gasoline station minimarkets and is more common at individually owned convenience stores.

Trafficking is a popular staple of local newspaper reports and has attracted the attention of Congress, which has held hearings on the matter. The Food and Nutrition Service has responded to the problem by pushing forward with electronic benefit transfer (EBT) and by preauthorizing stores. With EBT, recipients are given a debit card that can only be used to pay for purchases. The balance on the card is replenished automatically each month, without any action on the beneficiary's part. Thus the recipient has an incentive not to sell the card.[18] The recipient is supposed to show identification when using the card, but this requirement is rarely imposed at the cash register in the grocery store. So, while fraud is reduced, it is not eliminated. One study reported that EBT made trafficking more complex because it required recipients to bring their trafficking collaborators with them to the grocery store rather than simply conducting the transaction beforehand and separately.[19]

Preauthorization of stores entails visiting and examining retail outlets before authorizing them for participation in the program. Some observers feel that such measures can reduce the incidence of fraudulent merchants. Preauthorization, however, has made relatively little headway, and there is no consensus on how effective it might be.

Trafficking would naturally seem to be easier if benefits were provided through vouchers rather than through direct provision, for the cost of trading should be easier with vouchers. In public housing, for example, the closest activity to trafficking would be allowing someone else rather than the eligible family to occupy the unit in return for a payment.[20] The costs of such transactions would seem to be greater than those incurred by simply trading a voucher. In direct provision of child care, education, and similar programs, use of the services by someone other than the correct recipient would be easily detected.

Under the voucher mechanism, there is a trade-off between opportunities for illegal trading and access and participation. If participation and access are to be maximized, stamps must be easily available and as many stores as possible should be authorized to participate. But easy access and authorization of borderline stores increases the opportunities for fraud and raises the cost of enforcement. Such a trade-off would be present in any voucher program.

Effect of FSP on Food Expenditure: In-Kind Value

The value of food stamps to recipients—that is, their cash-equivalent value (CEV)—has been a major subject of research; similar questions have been raised about other in-kind transfer program benefits. With food stamps, the issue has policy relevance because analysts and policymakers periodically have proposed cashing out stamps. Some advocate this because the CEV of food stamps is thought to be close to one, which means that cashing them out would lead to a relatively trivial reduction in food expenditure while reducing administrative costs, stigma, and the like. In contrast, the CEVs of other vouchers are thought to be far less than one, and hence cashing them out would result in significant reductions in expenditures on the particular good or service the program was intended to boost. This is an important issue, because both voters and agricultural lobbies prefer food stamps to cash because they presume the former will lead to more food expenditure than the latter.

As was noted earlier, vouchers are not equivalent to in-kind transfer, but rather are a type of delivery mechanism for in-kind transfer. A variety of other mechanisms, such as direct provision and its many variants, are available.[21] In this context, CEV issues are relevant because it would be desirable to compare the CEVs of the different delivery mechanisms for each service. These differences could be used as one criterion, among others, in deciding the most appropriate mechanism to use to deliver the particular good or service. The CEV of housing vouchers, for example, is probably greater than the CEV for public housing, holding constant the dollar size of the subsidy.

If the CEV of food stamps were one (that is, if food stamps were equivalent in value to cash), there would be considerable administrative savings from cashing them out, because the complicated chain of issuance of scrip, use of scrip in retail outlets, redemption at banks, and final receipt at Federal Reserve banks could all be eliminated. The possibilities for trafficking and fraud would be greatly reduced, although all stigma and fraud practices at the eligibility determination point would remain. Participation rates possibly would increase, and hence more of the eligible population would be served.

The findings from the research literature on the CEV of food stamps go against the conventional wisdom among economists that food stamps are essentially equivalent to cash. The theory of the consumer implies that households that spend more on food than they are allotted in food stamps—that is, those that spend some of their own cash on food—necessarily will treat the coupons as inframarginal. They will, in other words, regard the stamps as increased income and will allocate that income across all categories of expenditures, not just food.[22] Because FSP allotments are set quite low, all but the very lowest income households tend to supplement their coupons with additional purchases out of their own funds and therefore are in this situation.[23]

Nevertheless, two pieces of evidence suggest that stamps are not treated simply as an addition to general income. First, a sizable body of econometrics evidence suggests that food stamps boost the food expenditures of participant households more than an equivalent increase in cash income. These studies estimate regression equations of food expenditure on the size of the food stamp allotment and on cash income, both measured over the same time interval. If food stamps were essentially equivalent to cash, the co-efficients on food stamps and cash would be expected to be roughly the same. However, the estimated coefficients on food stamps are generally double those of cash. Whereas the marginal propensity to consume (MPC) food out of food stamps ranges from 0.20 to 0.45, that out of ordinary cash income ranges from 0.05 to 0.10.[24] There are a number of explanations for this puzzling result, which suggest that it is a statistical artifact, but on the whole none has been convincing.[25]

The other source of evidence on the issue comes from the cash out experiments in which a random sample of families have had their food coupons replaced by cash. The food expenditures of these households are then compared to those of a control group that continues to receive coupons. It was initially thought that cash out would have little effect on food expenditures. This view was supported by the Puerto Rican experience. Stamps were cashed out entirely in the early 1980s in Puerto Rico, and most analyses found that there was no effect on food expenditures.[26] However, this result could have arisen because incomes are very low in Puerto Rico, while the FSP coupon allotments were the same there as on the mainland. So it should have been expected that the stamps would be more or less equivalent to cash. Several subsequent randomized trials of FSP cash out were conducted on the U.S. mainland. They showed that food expenditures were indeed reduced by cash out, by between 18 and 28 cents per dollar of stamps.[27] Thus both this evidence and the econometric evidence suggest that food stamps are not inframarginal and have genuine extra effects on food expenditure.

Squaring these results with the fact that food expenditures are generally higher than FSP allotments is not easy and there is no consensus explanation. One possibility is that the FSP alters preferences and that recipients are simply persuaded by the existence of stamps to spend more on food than they would otherwise. This is difficult to test, but it would be surprising if low-income families, which are usually desperately in need of cash to pay for electricity, rent, telephones, and shoes for their children, would be willing to forego some of those expenditures because the government told them they should spend their income on food instead. Another explanation that has been advanced is that FSP-recipient households engage in splurge buying after initially receiving stamps and then are forced to purchase food out of their own cash reserves later in the month, before the next issuance of their FSP allotment. However, while this does demonstrate that an excess of food expenditure over food stamp amounts—measured on a monthly basis—does not necessarily imply that food stamps are equivalent to cash, it does not by itself prove that the FSP is not equivalent to cash either. An increase in the FSP allotment amount would lead households to exhaust their food coupons at a later point in the month, but this does not necessarily mean that their food expenditures out of their own cash over the rest of the month would stay the same, rather than fall. It is still the increment in total food expenditure after an increase in the food allotment that measures fungibility, and the timing of food purchases out of food coupons and cash over the month has no necessary implication for that measure.

For the timing of food expenditures and food coupons to have a constraining effect on food expenditures requires either that there are liquidity constraints present that prevent smoothing of food expenditures over the month, or that discount rates are very high among recipients, or both. But liquidity constraints seem implausible, at least on average, for there would seem to be little barrier to holding onto stamps and using them later in the month. For high discount rates to be the explanation requires, conversely, that food expenditures actually fall over the month following receipt of the FSP allotment. There is apparently no evidence on this question, so it remains a possibility.

The evidence that food stamps are not equivalent to cash also implies, parenthetically, that trafficking must not be pervasive among the recipient population. Pervasive trafficking should lead to high cash-equivalent values in general and may even be a mechanism for getting around liquidity constraints, as families sell food stamps when their cash income is low and buy stamps when their cash income is high to smooth food consumption. The anecdotal evidence that some recipient families do exactly this—sell during part of the month and buy during other parts of the month—is consistent with this notion. However, the econometric and cash out evidence suggests, indirectly, that such behavior cannot be sufficiently widespread to make coupons equivalent to cash.

A simpler explanation is that the minority of households for which the stamps are constraining is nevertheless sufficiently large to generate the larger regression coefficients and the cash out experiment results that constitute the evidence against cash equivalency. The coefficients and results are only averages over the entire population of recipients and hence are not inconsistent with the existence of a majority of recipients for whom the stamps are inframarginal. Crude estimates put the percentage of recipients who spend more on food each month than the value of their stamps at 89 percent. Therefore, 11 percent spend all, or less than all, of their stamps.[28] The 11 percent who are constrained could explain some of the differences between estimated MPCs and the cash out experiment estimates, although those estimates seem a bit too high to be explained by the small fraction of constrained households.

Whatever the explanation for the less-than-complete cash equivalency, current policy discussions take the evidence as genuine and have concluded that cashing out would reduce food expenditures, on average. Consequently, cashing out the FSP is not on the current policy agenda.

Conclusions

Are there lessons from the FSP for the use of vouchers for the delivery of goods and services of the other types discussed in this volume? For the most part, the answer is no. The food stamp program has unique characteristics, at least relative to child care, housing, education, and health care, that make vouchers a more natural mechanism through which to subsidize the service—food expenditures of the poor. At the same time, there are a few voucher-related issues in the food stamp program that can inform those interested in extending vouchers in other areas. One is the problem of low participation rates that arises from voluntary application for the voucher. Participation rates in voucher programs could easily be far less than 100 percent, and usually are, although they may be higher than participation rates under direct provision and other delivery mechanisms. A second issue is the problem of fraud and trafficking, which is likely to be more prevalent when goods and services are delivered through vouchers than through other mechanisms. The administrative procedures associated with the voucher determine, in large degree, the possibilities for trafficking. A third is the surprising effect of vouchers on food expenditures, which suggests that the leakage from using vouchers into other expenditures may not be as large as some have feared. If food vouchers increase food expenditures more than cash, it is even more likely that other vouchers would do so for expenditures on other relevant goods. An issue in nonfood voucher applications, however, is whether alternative delivery mechanisms like direct provision would have a more or less constraining effect on expenditures and hence a higher or lower cash equivalent value than vouchers. This has not been examined for the case of food because there are no major alternative mechanisms.

Notes

1. This discussion of early history is largely taken from James Ohls and Harold Beebout, *The Food Stamp Program: Design Tradeoffs, Policy, and Impacts*, (Urban Institute, 1993). See also Peter Rossi, *Feeding the Poor: Assessing Federal Food Aid* (Washington, D.C.: AEI Press, 1998).

2. Vee Burke, *Cash and Noncash Benefits for Persons with Limited Income: Eligibility Rules, Recipient and Expenditure Data, FYs 1992–94* (Congressional Research Service, December 1995).

3. Stamps can also be issued by banks and check-cashing establishments.

4. *Background Material and Data on Programs within the Jurisdiction of the Committee on Ways and Means*, Committee Print, House Ways and Means Committee 104-14, 104 Cong. 2 sess. (Government Printing Office, 1996), p. 397.

5. Isolated instances of this occur when merchants sell mislabeled or other fraudulently identified goods.

6. Barbara Devaney and Robert Moffitt, "Dietary Effects of the Food Stamp Program," *American Journal of Agricultural Economics*, vol. 73 (February 1991), pp. 202–11; Thomas Fraker, *The Effects of Food Stamps on Food Consumption: A Review of the Literature* (Washington, D.C.: Food and Nutrition Service, 1990); Ohls and Beebout, *The Food Stamp Program*.

7. There are other federally funded cash transfer programs of importance, however, such as Social Security income, Pell grants, and veterans' pensions.

8. See Ohls and Beebout, *The Food Stamp Program*, for a good discussion of this issue.

9. "Agricultural lobby" here includes food retailers as well as the farm sector.

10. Ohls and Beebout, *The Food Stamp Program*, chapter 7.

11. However, benefits were reduced for immigrants and for unemployed individuals, so the program did not escape completely unscathed.

12. Betsey Kuhn and others, "The Food Stamp Program and Welfare Reform," *Journal of Economic Perspectives*, vol. 10 (Spring 1996), pp. 189–98.

13. In the early 1990s, the participation rate rose to over 60 percent, but subsequently it has declined slightly (Scott Cody and Carole Trippe, "Trends in FSP Participation Rates: Focus on August 1995," USDA Food and Consumer Service, October 1997). The nature of the data permits only the calculation of an average monthly participation rate. This is not equivalent to, say, the percentage of eligible households that ever participate over a longer period (such as a year), which is necessarily higher.

14. B. Daponte, Seth Sanders, and Lowell Taylor, "Why Do Eligible Households Not Use Food Stamps? Evidence from an Experiment," *Journal of Human Resources* (forthcoming).

15. Anne Ciemnecki and others, *Final Report for the Food Stamp Participant Trafficking Study* (USDA Food and Consumer Service, May 1998); Theodore F. Macaluso, *The Extent of Trafficking in the Food Stamp Program* (USDA Food and Consumer Service, August 1995).

16. See Ciemnecki and others, *Final Report*, however, for reports by focus groups. The authors concluded that most of the reports by the respondents on frequency of trafficking were not reliable and were still significantly underreported.

17. The 4 percent figure is, in some respects, an overestimate, because only a fraction of the value of the food stamps trafficked has actually been pocketed by the merchant. Over half ends up as cash for the recipient, some portion of which may be spent on food, as the taxpayer-voter desires. Because some of the cash received by the recipient who sells the stamps will not be used on food, the face value of the stamps is not an accurate measure of the true food expenditure of the recipient.

18. Another barrier to trafficking EBT cards is that the buyer of a card cannot verify the current balance on the card.

19. Ciemnecki and others, *Final Report*.

20. A more plausible form of illegal use of a housing unit is to allow more family members or friends to use the unit than were stated when eligibility was determined. But this can occur with either direct provision or vouchers. Likewise, fraud can occur in the falsification of income at the time of eligibility determination. But this can occur with either type as well, and with cash transfers.

21. See the introduction to this volume by C. Eugene Steuerle for a discussion of those variants and the chapter by David Bradford and Daniel Shaviro for a discussion of both consumer- and supply-side differences between vouchers and direct provision.

22. See the chapter by Bradford and Shaviro in this volume for a discussion of the relevant theory.

23. An early estimate of high CEV for food stamps can be found in Timothy Smeeding, *Alternative Methods for Valuing Selected In-kind Transfer Benefits and Measuring Their Effect on Poverty*, Technical Paper 50 (Bureau of the Census, 1982).

24. Fraker, *The Effects of Food Stamps*.

25. One possibility is that a higher degree of measurement error in cash income biases its coefficient toward zero. However, tests of this hypothesis have not shown it to explain the difference. Another econometric explanation that has been advanced is that selection bias arises in the FSP because different families have different MPCs and that participants are drawn from the upper tail of the distribution of the MPCs for food (Devaney and Moffitt, "Dietary Effects of the

Food Stamp Program," pp. 208–09). However, econometric tests for selection bias have not shown this to explain the difference either. Thus, at least to date, the difference in MPCs seems to be genuine.

26. Harold Beebout and others, "Evaluation of the Nutrition Assistance Program in Puerto Rico—Volume II: Effects on Food Expenditures and Diet Quality," (Washington, D.C.: MPR, 1985); Barbara Devaney and Thomas Fraker, "Cashing Out Food Stamps: Impacts on Food Expenditures and Diet Quality," *Journal of Policy Analysis and Management*, vol. 5 (1986), pp. 725–41; Robert Moffitt, "Estimating the Value of an In-Kind Transfer," *Econometrica*, vol. 57 (March 1989), pp. 385–409.

27. Thomas Fraker, Alberto Martini, and James Ohls, "The Effect of Food Stamp Cashout on Food Expenditures," *Journal of Human Resources*, vol. 30 (Fall 1995), pp. 633–49.

28. Ohls and Beebout, *The Food Stamp Program*, p. 106.

GEORGE E. PETERSON

5 Housing Vouchers: The U.S. Experience

VOUCHERS HAVE been a part of American housing policy since 1974, when the first "housing certificate" program was introduced. Today, more than 1.4 million low-income households receive federal voucher assistance to help pay for rental housing. The voucher approach has been used both as a general form of housing assistance and as a strategy to address specific problems in the housing market. Court-supervised consent decrees, for example, have provided central-city minority households with vouchers that can be used throughout the metropolitan region in an attempt to break up historical patterns of segregation perpetuated by the location of public housing.

Vouchers also have been at the heart of the last quarter century of housing policy debate in the United States. A ten-year experimental program in voucher design and voucher administration, carried out in twelve cities starting in the 1970s, preceded adoption of the key voucher legislation. This program remains one of the largest and most ambitious social experiments ever conducted in the United States. It sought to demonstrate that demand-side subsidies provided to low-income housing consumers could improve housing outcomes more cost effectively than would supply-side subsidies for housing construction. In terms of policy influence, the voucher demonstration project was successful. Since the mid-1980s, demand-side assistance to renters has been the dominant form of subsidization for new low-income housing programs.

Housing vouchers are again generating policy attention today, as other types of federal housing assistance are "vouchered out." U.S. housing policy now calls for demolition of the least successful public housing projects and replacement of some of the demolished units by vouchers awarded to displaced residents. The privately owned low-income housing built with federal subsidies in the late 1970s and early 1980s is now coming "off contract" as it reaches the end of its twenty-year contractual dedication to low-income occupancy. Part of this housing also is being replaced, not with other physical units, but with vouchers given to residents. The heightened reliance on vouchers has raised anew questions as to whether vouchers in practice possess the cost and market-choice advantages claimed for them, and, if so, whether these advantages hold true under different types of housing market conditions, including the tight housing markets now found in many metropolitan areas.

Experience in implementing housing vouchers offers some lessons for the use of vouchers in other fields where voucher initiatives are under consideration. Housing vouchers are not entitlements. They are subject to annual budgetary review. They also are limited by a budget ceiling that restricts voucher participation to a relatively modest share of families meeting the income eligibility test. Vouchers in fields like child care, job training, and education are likely to face similar budget constraints, rather than be open-ended entitlements like food stamps. All housing subsidies, including both demand-side and supply-side assistance, together reach only slightly more than a third of the households eligible for housing assistance on income grounds, resulting in excess demand for participation in every type of public program. This excess demand leads to tough choices as to who should receive housing vouchers and invites arbitrariness or even corruption in local program administration. Finally, though housing markets are competitive, they also are marked by a variety of local restrictions on the kind of housing that can be built and where it can be built; by relatively high household search costs; by neighborhood externalities such as the quality of schools and the neighborhood crime rate; by attempts to discourage the entry of low-income households or racial minorities into some jurisdictions; and by an unequal distribution of information between owners or landlords, on one side of the housing market, and low-income renters, on the other. Similar conditions often prevail in other areas where vouchers are being debated. The experience of using housing vouchers may therefore shed light on the kinds of problems likely to arise in other fields where the relevant market is not a straightforward competitive market in a single-dimensioned commodity.

Vouchers in the Context of Overall Housing Assistance

Vouchers presently are part of a four-pronged approach to housing subsidies for low- and moderate-income households in the United States. The other programs provide "project-based" assistance, intended to increase the supply of basic-quality housing. Together, all forms of federal, state, and local housing assistance reach about 36 percent of the households eligible for assistance on income grounds.

Public Housing

The oldest form of housing subsidy is public housing, introduced as part of the Housing Act of 1937. Construction of public housing was intended to help upgrade the quality of the U.S. housing stock by building units that met society's basic standards for satisfactory housing. According to the legislative language, provision of public housing was designed to help "remedy . . . unsafe and insanitary housing conditions and the acute shortage of decent, safe, and sanitary dwellings for families of low income."[1] Approximately 1.3 million households now live in public housing. Most of the public housing stock was built between 1950 and 1975. Only a hundred thousand new units (gross) have been built since the mid-1980s. Over the past five years, the stock of public housing in the United States has shrunk, as federal policy has called for demolishing units in bad physical condition that either cannot be upgraded cost effectively or are contributing to neighborhood concentrations of poverty and racial isolation. A former rule requiring that demolished public housing units be replaced on a one-for-one basis with new construction has been dropped in favor of a policy of thinning out concentrations of public housing and replacing some of the lost units with vouchers that residents can use to rent housing on the private market.

Subsidized Private Housing

A second supply-side effort has involved the federal government in subsidizing new construction or substantial rehabilitation of privately owned rental housing intended for low- and moderate-income occupancy. The shift to private-sector subsidies was motivated in part by disillusionment with the results of public housing, which in the public mind became identified with high-density, central-city projects of concentrated poverty. A variety of mechanisms have been used to subsidize the owners and developers of private rental housing for the low-income market, including below-market construction financing, accelerated depreciation, and other tax breaks. In the largest such program, the project-based portions of Section 8, the government guaranteed developers a rental stream scaled to construction cost in return for their contractual commitment to rent the units for a period of at least twenty years to low-income tenants eligible for rental assistance. Federal subsidies for private rental construction began in 1961 and reached their height between 1974 and 1983, when the Section 8 new construction program largely replaced public housing construction. By the late 1980s, Section 8 new construction subsidies were phased out in favor of demand-side vouchers.

In all, there are now about 2.1 million federally subsidized private rental units on the low-income urban market. Although no new housing has been built under Section 8 for many years, most of the units remain "on contract" to federally assisted low-income renters. Two types of policy issues presently face the federally subsidized private housing stock. Vouchers have been advanced as part of the solution for both. At one end of the low-income housing market, there are projects built with federal subsidies that have a long history of operating and occupancy problems. Many of these projects have received special below-market federal loans to keep them operating. By the mid-1990s, however, conditions had become so deplorable in some of these projects that the Department of Housing and Urban Development (HUD) concluded that the only cost-effective option was to shut them down and provide displaced tenants with vouchers so that they could find adequate housing on their own. At the other end of the low-income market are well-maintained and well-located housing units with Section 8 subsidies. The projects are now coming off their contract period of twenty years' dedication to low-income occupancy. Good-quality basic housing in strong local markets can command rental rates that substantially exceed the rates paid under existing HUD rental contracts. Owners of such housing are removing the units from the (government-supported) low-income stock and offering them on the regular market. The government responded by offering to raise rents to market rates, up to a ceiling, and by providing vouchers to households that are displaced from Section 8 project housing.

Tax Credits

In addition to the subsidy programs administered at the federal level by HUD, the Low Income Housing Tax Credit (LIHTC), administered by the Treasury Department, provides tax benefits to developers of low-income housing. Under this program, enacted in 1986, principally non-profit developers build moderately subsidized rental housing, most of which is affordable to households with incomes at or below 60 percent of the area median income. The developers package the tax credits generated by their investment and sell them to corporate or other investors, then use the proceeds to subsidize rent levels. Because the Treasury Department does not maintain records on the volume of housing built with LIHTC assistance, estimates of production vary. Nonprofit development associations assert that some nine hundred thousand affordable units had been built or authorized for construction with LIHTC subsidies by the end of 1998. HUD found three hundred and thirty thousand completed units to be in operation as of 1996.[2] Still another estimate was that four hundred and ninety-five thousand units were in operation by 1997. Unlike the other main supply-side programs, the LIHTC is currently producing new housing in significant volume. Production is capped by a legislative ceiling on the volume of tax credits.[3]

Table 5-1 summarizes the distribution by program type of the stock of publicly subsidized low-income housing in the United States, as of 1997.

Although table 5-1 shows that units built under subsidized construction programs account for the largest component of the assisted low-income housing stock, this is a legacy of past subsidy programs. The 1997 allocation of new federal rental assistance, for example, was split 72 percent for vouchers and 28 percent for all types of project-based programs.

How the Housing Voucher Program Works

As the fourth leg in the national housing assistance strategy, vouchers and certificates work from the demand side of the housing market.[4] The voucher program operates as follows:

—HUD contracts with a local public housing authority (PHA), or sometimes with another local or regional administrative agency, to operate the voucher program locally. Households are precertified based on income and family composition as eligible for voucher participation.

Table 5-1. U.S. *Distribution of Low-Income Assisted Housing by Program Type, 1997*

Program	Percentage of total[a]
Public housing	21
Certificates and vouchers	24
HUD-assisted private projects	35
Low-income housing tax credit	9
Rural loan program[b]	9
State-level programs	3

Source: Sandra J. Newman and Ann B. Schnare, *Beyond Bricks and Mortar: Re-examining the Purpose and Effects of Housing Assistance* (Urban Institute, 1997).

a. Total number of assisted housing units = 6,002,000. This total excludes housing for Native Americans on reservations. Some units participate in more than one subsidy program.

b. The Rural Rental Housing Direct Loan Program was administered by the Farmers Home Administration (FmHA) until 1994, when the FmHA was abolished and the program was transferred to the Department of Agriculture.

—The voucher program is designed to fill the gap between the cost of decent, sanitary, and physically safe housing and 30 percent of a household's adjusted income. In practice, the cost of basic housing is estimated through the local area fair market rent (FMR). The fair market rent is determined by HUD from census statistics and special local surveys. It is defined as the 40th percentile of the local area rent distribution for recently rented housing suitable for the household's composition.

—Upon application to a PHA, an eligible family usually is placed on a waiting list. When the family rises to the top of the list, it receives a voucher, which promises rent assistance if the family can locate a suitable dwelling unit. At one time, certain forms of housing vouchers could be used only within the market area of the PHA issuing the voucher. Today, all vouchers can be used anywhere in the country. The value of the voucher depends on the family's income and family size, as well as on the local FMR.

—The family then conducts a market search either on its own or, in some program variants, with assistance from housing counselors. The family has sixty days for the basic search period, which typically can be renewed once. When it finds a suitable unit, the family negotiates the rent and other conditions of the lease. The PHA generally does not participate in the market search or rent negotiation, but it must certify that the unit meets HUD's standards for decent, safe housing that is not overcrowded and that the rental agreement protects the rights of the tenant. The initial lease is for one year.

—The landlord enters into two separate contracts and receives two monthly rental checks. One contract is with the tenant; the other is with the PHA. The family is assumed to be able to pay up to 30 percent of its adjusted income for rent. The PHA pays the difference between this amount and the standardized fair market rent. The family pays the remainder of the rent bill. Because the PHA's payment is based on the FMR, the family has a direct financial incentive to seek out attractively priced units and to negotiate a favorable lease. If it is able to find adequate housing at less than the FMR, it pockets all of the savings. If it selects a dwelling unit that costs more than the FMR, the family pays 100 percent of the additional rent.

—A Section 8 voucher tenant enjoys the same market rights as other tenants. At the end of the lease period, such a family may elect to move, with its voucher, to another unit. If a tenant fails to make rent payments during the lease period, the landlord can pursue the usual remedies, including eviction. The landlord is responsible for maintaining the unit in a safe and sanitary condition. Units are supposed to be inspected at least once a year by the PHA to confirm that they continue to meet program standards. Tenants are supposed to report changes in income, but in practice, monitoring usually is done on an annual basis at the time of voucher renewal.

—Landlords are not required by federal law to accept Section 8 tenants, and some landlords refuse to participate in the program.[5] However, a few states have held that state law prohibits landlords from denying rental units to Section 8 voucher holders who otherwise are qualified to rent.[6]

—The average Section 8 voucher costs the government about $6,000 a year in rent subsidy.

Housing vouchers thus share fundamental characteristics with vouchers in other program areas. They provide market choice to the consumer and are designed to stimulate competition in the basic rental housing market. In project-based housing programs, tenants are matched with housing units by the local public housing authority through administrative assignment. Because there is excess demand for subsidized housing of all kinds, landlords of subsidized projects (whether a public housing authority or a private owner) do not have to compete for tenants. They are essentially assured of occupancy as long as their housing units meet HUD standards. In effect, their primary "client" is HUD.[7] In the freestanding voucher program, private-sector owners must compete for subsidized tenants just as they compete for other tenants.

Housing vouchers do have some distinctive features that set them apart. One critical element is the concept of fair market rent. The fact that a household's voucher amount is calculated with respect to FMR, rather than actual rent, allows market incentives for efficient shopping to be transmitted to the voucher holder. If actual rent, or actual rent up to a ceiling, is the basis for reimbursement (as it formerly was in the "housing certificate" program), tenants have no financial incentive to find and negotiate the best deal possible. Empirical studies confirm that "voucher" holders, subject to the shopping incentive, did in fact spend less on rent than did comparable "certificate" holders, who did not have the shopping incentive. However, the difference was modest—averaging only about 3 percent of monthly rent.

The backup role of the PHA is another important feature of housing voucher operation. The PHA must certify that the unit selected by the voucher holder is in safe and sanitary condition at the time of leasing, must certify that the lease contract is fair to the tenant, and is supposed to inspect the unit's physical condition annually. The PHA also often maintains a listing of available rental units that fit within voucher guidelines, which the voucher holder can use in her search for housing.

The appropriate degree of PHA or other institutional intervention in the voucher holder's market search has been the subject of considerable debate over the years. In some of the early experimental versions of the voucher program, voucher holders searched for housing entirely on their own, without institutional involvement and without mandatory minimum housing standards. Tenants in these unrestricted programs tended to occupy somewhat lower-quality housing—measured for an array of internal and external housing characteristics—for which they paid lower average rent. Household (or at least, parental) utility presumably was maximized by converting the housing voucher, at the margin, into cash by accepting lower-quality housing.

An unrestricted housing voucher was never seriously considered by Congress for the national housing program. The legislative conviction that "housing programs" should be used to address housing needs meant that housing vouchers were tied to minimum housing standards. In part, the insistence on minimum housing standards was justified by the belief that unsanitary or unattractive housing exerted strong negative externalities, making it appropriate for society to demand minimum standards of housing consumption by those receiving voucher assistance. In practice, HUD regulations also restrict aspects of what might be regarded as a household's private choice—for example, they constrain the trade-off between location and housing size by limiting the number of persons per bedroom.

Recently, debate has centered around whether voucher holders should receive counseling assistance as part of the housing search. Counseling often is intended to introduce tenants to housing possibilities outside the neighborhoods they already know, as well as to build self-esteem and interviewing skills for the voucher holder, thereby making them better prepared as shoppers. Counseling of this kind may be accompanied by programs that provide transportation so that voucher holders can inspect suburban rental units or by programs that provide child care during a parent's housing search. In recent voucher programs, the trend has been to build in a larger role for support institutions in the housing search. Programs designed to encourage households to move out of concentrated poverty areas in the central city, for example, usually contain a counseling element.[8]

Brief History of Housing Vouchers

In some other sectors, the voucher approach to social welfare assistance evolved over time, without a conscious decision to change policy course, in such a way that the dividing line between "vouchers" and other kinds of assistance programs can be difficult to define. That is not true of federal housing policy. The shift toward vouchers reflected a sharp change in perception of the nature of the nation's housing problems. It represented a deliberate if partial replacement of project-based assistance (supply-side housing programs) in favor of demand-side supplements of low-income households' rental purchasing power. The change in policy direction was thoroughly debated and analyzed.

Before vouchers, U.S. social housing policy had been based on two premises. First, there was assumed to be a shortage of physically adequate housing, which had to be met through new, subsidized supply. The social housing subsidies introduced after World War II are perhaps best seen as part of a national effort to increase housing supply and housing quality across the entire income spectrum. Far more costly subsidies were provided to middle-class homeowners in terms of subsidized mortgages, along with the nontaxation of imputed rent and tax deductibility of mortgage interest.

At the lower end of the income distribution, housing need was measured in terms of tangible deficiencies in the housing stock. Typical of the definition of housing need in this era was the 1970s census definition that classified as "inadequate" housing that (a) lacked indoor plumbing; (b) lacked kitchen facilities; or (c) suffered from two or more major physical defects, such as dilapidated exterior conditions, "three or more breakdowns of six or more hours each time in the heating system during the previous winter," or "three or more times completely without water for six or more hours each time during the preceding 90 days, with the problem inside the unit."

The second premise concerned the externalities generated by low-quality housing. Poor-quality housing was believed to undermine the health and morals of inhabitants and to place the rest of the community at risk as well. Further, physically dilapidated housing was held to exercise a blighting influence on an entire neighborhood. These same perceptions about the importance of externalities led to the slum eradication and urban renewal efforts of the 1950s and 1960s. In the housing literature, public spending for low-income families was justified as vigorously by the external benefits that the improvements would generate for others as by the benefits that the occupants would reap from living in better-quality housing. Even the "supply" orientation of construction subsidies is somewhat ambiguous in this context. It was as important to the policy approach that hazardous or blighted units be torn down and removed as it was that new, adequate units be built.[9]

The importance attributed to adverse externalities helped reinforce the supply-side emphasis of housing policy. The specific characteristics of the housing bundle that gave rise to community health risks and other negative externalities—like the lack of indoor plumbing or exterior decay—could be identified and corrected in supply-side programs without running the risk that residents might have other priorities of their own.

To their credit, the construction programs of the 1950s, 1960s, and early 1970s helped transform the physical quality of the American housing stock. Household income growth and rural-to-city migration were more important, but together these factors largely eliminated the physical deficiencies that until then had provided the rationale for federal housing assistance. Table 5-2 shows the vast improvement that occurred in terms of traditionally defined housing need. In 1940, 44.6 percent of all occupied dwelling units in the United States lacked complete indoor plumbing. By 1977 that proportion had fallen to 2.4 percent. The proportion of physically dilapidated housing declined so steeply that the census stopped reporting it as a separate category of deficiency.

By the 1970s it was evident to many housing experts that the war on physically substandard housing had been largely won, at least to the extent that was feasible for supply-side programs. Not only had the quality of housing been greatly improved, but the American housing system had demonstrated that it could build good-quality housing for every household that could afford to pay for it. The remaining problem was affordability. A significant portion of the American population consisted of households whose incomes did not permit them to purchase decent hous-

Table 5-2. *Changes in Housing Conditions, 1940–77*
Percent

Condition	1940	1950	1960	1970	1977
Lacking some or all plumbing	44.6	34.0	15.2	5.1	2.4
Dilapidated	18.1	9.1	5.8	3.7	...
Either lacking plumbing or dilapidated	48.6	35.4	17.0	7.4	...
In need of rehabilitation[a]	...	...	...	...	7.4

Source: Congressional Budget Office, *Federal Housing Assistance: Alternative Approaches* (GPO, 1982).

a. Two or more serious deficiencies of the kind described in the text.

ing at market prices while at the same time providing for the other necessities of life, such as food, clothing, and medical care.

It was in this context that housing vouchers were initially recommended. A National Housing Policy Review conducted in the early 1970s under Richard Nixon urged replacing the hodgepodge of construction and rehabilitation subsidy programs that then existed with "housing allowances" or "vouchers" provided to low-income households. Vouchers were recommended largely because of their transfer efficiency and their use of the competitive market. Vouchers could be targeted on households of specified income levels meeting specific needs criteria. The size of the voucher could be adjusted to individual household circumstances. Use of the voucher could be tied to consumption of minimum-quality housing as defined in federal housing regulations, so as to take into account externalities as well as consumer preferences. Vouchers, it was maintained, would call forth their own supply response once fully built into low-income households' demand for housing. Advocates of the voucher approach argued that the timing was right precisely because the housing market had demonstrated its ability to deliver an adequate supply of decent housing when demand conditions justified it. Vouchers were viewed, in principle, as a replacement for all other types of housing assistance that would eventually reach the entire low-income population.

Experimental Housing Allowance Program

Not surprisingly, the recommendation to "voucher out" other housing assistance encountered opposition. Believers in the supply-side approach to housing assistance objected that, without construction programs to add to housing supply, vouchers for the poor would merely result in an escalation of housing rents, adding to program costs while at the same time inflicting hardships on families in the same housing submarket that did not receive vouchers. In effect, this argument held either that there was a low elasticity of supply for basic housing, so that injections of new demand financed by vouchers would drive up housing prices, or that the administratively determined fair market rents and minimum quality standards established by HUD would set a new floor for the local market, eliminating all competition below the HUD-authorized threshold rent and quality levels.

To test supply and demand propositions and to evaluate the market impacts of alternative program designs, HUD decided to launch what at the time was the largest social experiment in U.S. history.[10] The Experimental Housing Allowance Program (EHAP) operated in twelve cities over a period of ten years. More than 30,000 households participated in the experiment by receiving housing allowances. Variations in housing allowance design were tested at different sites and times. The reactions of households, landlords, and local housing markets were monitored through detailed interviewing, administrative records, and analytical studies. The EHAP experiment ran from 1972 to 1981. More than $53 million (in 1970s dollars) were paid out as housing allowances to participating families, research costs totaled $82 million more, and program administration cost another $23 million.

Without waiting for full results from EHAP, Congress and the administration began to modify Section 8, the basic piece of housing legislation, to accommodate the voucher principle. Changes made in 1974 allowed some households to use housing certificates to search the market for suitable units in "existing housing," rather than be matched with new housing built specifically for the program. After EHAP was concluded, Section 8 was again modified to include the freestanding voucher program based on reimbursement of fair market rent as described above.

Current Voucher Policy and Housing Needs

In recent years, housing vouchers have expanded at the expense of other HUD subsidy programs, but overall expansion has been limited by budget restrictions. Between 1990 and 1994, approximately 4.75 vouchers were issued by HUD for every incremental unit of project-based assistance.[11] Under its "vacancy consolidation" program, HUD has begun demolishing

100,000 severely distressed public housing units and (since 1995) has been replacing some of them not with other "hard" units but with vouchers for the displaced tenants. Vouchers also have been the instrument of choice for many of HUD's experimental programs. The fiscal year 1999 budget proposal, for example, contained funding for 50,000 Welfare to Work vouchers designed to allow welfare recipients to move to housing closer to job opportunities. The measure eventually was passed by Congress. A number of special voucher allocations have been made to support the movement of low-income households into suburban communities where school and other opportunities are thought to be better.

Total voucher growth has often lagged behind intent. For example, despite congressional authorization for 100,000 new housing vouchers in fiscal year 2000 and 200,000 new vouchers in fiscal year 2001, only 60,000 new vouchers actually were funded under the fiscal year 2000 budget agreement. The principal obstacle to faster growth has been the high cost of housing assistance. Although less costly than other forms of aid, the average cost to the federal government of a housing voucher is now $6,000 a year. That annual cost will persist indefinitely, tending to grow with rent levels, unless Congress expressly rescinds some of the voucher authorizations.

In one important respect the designers of the original voucher recommendations have been vindicated. At least by the standards that have become conventional in housing analysis and housing policy, today's housing problem is overwhelmingly a problem of housing affordability not housing condition, as shown in table 5-3.

Policy Issues Surrounding Housing Vouchers

Vouchers in the housing sector have raised a mix of policy issues. These range from fundamental questions about the role of vouchers as one of several federal housing strategies for low-income households, all of which together assist only a fraction of those theoretically eligible for assistance, to practical questions about how a national housing program gets implemented efficiently at the local level when some jurisdictions do not want more poor people as residents.

Rationing Excess Demand

Housing subsidies are limited by budgetary ceilings. Therefore, there is excess demand for all types of federal housing assistance, including vouchers. What

Table 5-3. *Renter Households with Different Types of Housing Needs*[a]
Thousands

Problem	Worst-case needs[b]	Total poverty needs[c]
Affordability burden	4,931	6,055
Inadequate housing condition	381	...
Both problems	141	...
Total	5,453	...

Sources: Joint Center for Housing Studies, Harvard University, *The State of the Nation's Housing—1998* (Cambridge, Mass., 1998); Jennifer Daskal, *In Search of Shelter: The Growing Shortage of Affordable Rental Housing* (Washington, D.C.: Center on Budget and Policy Priorities, 1998).

a. Need is measured after housing subsidies. Households receiving federal subsidies are assumed not to be needy.

b. As defined by the Department of Housing and Urban Devlopment (HUD): households with incomes of less than 50 percent of local median that spend more than 50 percent of income on housing (affordability burden) or have severe problems with plumbing, heating, electrical systems, or maintenance/repairs (housing condition).

c. Households below poverty line that spend more than 30 percent of income on housing.

rationing rules are used to allocate housing vouchers and what market distortions have resulted?

ELIGIBILITY AND TENURE. In principle, vouchers could be provided to low-income homeowners as well as low-income renters. In two of its sites, the EHAP experiment offered vouchers to all households meeting the program's income test, including homeowners. No special difficulties of administration were observed; in fact, the supply response was greater in owner-occupied units than in rental units.

The restriction of voucher eligibility to renters is first and foremost a budgetary measure. As of 1995, about 3.8 million owner-occupant households with very low incomes met the federal standard for severe housing problems. This compares with 5.5 million rental households. (See table 5-3.) Eliminating homeowners from the eligibility pool thus reduces the high-priority need group by more than 40 percent. Many of the owner-occupant households in severe need are elderly poor. Their exclusion from housing assistance, besides restraining total subsidy costs, has been rationalized by their presumably higher permanent incomes, as evidenced by their ownership of housing assets.

Until recently, the prohibition on owner-occupied housing applied as well to renter households that, once enrolled in the voucher program, wanted to use their voucher assistance to buy a home. In 1992 Congress for the first time authorized the use of Section 8 certificates to pay for home purchases. HUD subsequently took the position that all agencies administering Section 8 certificates or vouchers should permit their use for home mortgage payments, as long as households met lending standards. In principle, this step corrects a bias toward renting that was paradoxical in view of the avowed goals of recent national administrations to increase homeownership rates among low-income and minority households. In practice, however, only a handful of households (far below 1 percent) have used vouchers for home purchases. Section 8 households rarely can meet mortgage lending standards, since future voucher payments are not guaranteed by the government, and they have difficulty financing down payments.[12]

FEDERAL AND LOCAL PREFERENCE RULES. Formal preference rules are used to allocate vouchers and other housing subsidies among the pool of eligible renters. Until 1997 these rules were established primarily at the federal level and served to focus assistance on households judged to be in greatest housing need. The federal preferences gave priority to households in three categories: those paying more than 50 percent of income for housing, those living in severely deficient housing conditions, and those that had been involuntarily displaced from their housing. A total of 90 percent of Section 8 certificates and vouchers had to be awarded to households in one of these federal preference categories. Local preferences could be used to allocate the remaining 10 percent of vouchers as well as to establish priorities within the group of households that met federal preference standards. In 1997, as part of the effort to decentralize the administration of federal housing programs, federal preference rules were scrapped. Devolution to the local level of the responsibility for setting priority rules has potentially strong implications for the way housing vouchers and other forms of housing assistance will be allocated in the future.

The decision to abandon federal preferences was part of a broader rethinking of housing subsidy policy. By giving priority to the poorest of the poor and those in greatest housing need, federal preference rules had converted many public housing and Section 8 projects into congregations of extremely poor, socially dependent households.[13] The negative impact of concentrated poverty environments like these has been the subject of a great deal of analysis in the social sciences.[14]

At the same time it devolved responsibility for establishing preference rules, the federal government encouraged local PHAs to experiment with new criteria for program entry that would generate a broader mix of income levels in housing projects, create a stronger core of employed heads of household living in subsidized units, and, in the process, generate more favorable neighborhood effects.

The rationale for encouraging a greater income mix is less clear for the voucher program than it is for project-based assistance. Voucher households select their preferred neighborhoods individually. Although there is some clustering of voucher families in practice, voucher tenants are considerably more dispersed geographically than are households living in subsidized housing projects and are considerably less likely to live in neighborhoods with high poverty rates or homogeneous racial profiles.[15] If local PHAs adjust their preference criteria for voucher programs along the same lines as for project-based housing, so as to increase the coverage of working households, the population of very poor households not covered by any housing subsidy is almost certain to grow.

In the past many PHAs have made residence in the community a local preference criterion. Local residency preferences, in fact, have been one of the primary obstacles to greater mobility under all housing subsidy programs. Some suburbs have been willing to accept low-income housing projects for their own poor but have used residency preferences to prevent central-city households from moving into subsidized housing in their jurisdictions and have adopted parallel restrictions to limit eligibility of "outsiders" for locally issued vouchers. Devolution to the local level of responsibility for establishing preference criteria may help revive this exclusionary posture.[16]

QUEUING. Queuing is the final step in rationing excess demand. In the standard case, a household applies to its PHA for rental assistance, is screened for eligibility on income and other grounds, is classified under the local preference system, and then joins a waiting list. When the family rises to the top of the waiting list, it has the option of accepting the next unit that becomes available or of turning down that unit and staying at the head of the waiting list. Typically, a household is allowed to turn down up to three housing offers, though some PHAs are more stringent and allow only one rejection. If the household does not accept any of the choices offered to it, it goes back to the bottom of the waiting list. Some PHAs maintain separate waiting lists for public housing, Section 8 project-based housing, and vouchers. Others operate a unified waiting list.

How long are the queues? Nationwide, in 1998–99 the average voucher or certificate holder had had to wait twenty-eight months before receiving a voucher. In large PHAs, those with 10,000 to 30,000 Section 8 recipients, the average waiting time was forty-two months. Even this figure understates the full extent of queuing. Those who receive vouchers must meet the local priority tests. Other eligible households of lower priority can remain on the waiting list without ever obtaining a voucher but are not counted in computing the average waiting period. In August 1994, for example, the Section 8 voucher waiting list for the Chicago Housing Authority contained 46,812 names and had been closed for several years to new applicants.[16] Other big cities also had long waiting lists that were closed. In Miami, successful applicants for housing vouchers or certificates had to wait an average of eighty-two months before obtaining one. In 1998–99 the average wait in Los Angeles and Newark had been ten years.

Among successful applicants, the national average wait for a voucher (twenty-eight months) is more than twice the average waiting time for entry into public housing (eleven months) and also longer than the wait for entry into Section 8 project-based assistance. This suggests that, at the margin and relative to supply levels in the different programs, recipients prefer the market choice that the voucher system provides. However, the existence of parallel queues distorts consumer choice. The prospect of waiting several years for entry into the voucher program, with the ultimate outcome uncertain, will prompt some households in need of housing also to apply for and accept a project-based unit, even though this is not their first choice. Under the present combination of subsidy programs, PHAs have no discretion to react to demand signals by increasing their voucher pool, say, while reducing public housing units. Over the intermediate term, local PHAs and HUD are moving gradually in this direction by demolishing public housing units in the worst condition or in the worst locations and replacing them not with new public housing but with vouchers for the displaced tenants.

Housing Benefit Formula

Housing vouchers illustrate formula design issues that are common to many voucher programs. Because housing vouchers have been used in so many countries, many of the basic formula variations, which are only theoretical possibilities in other sectors, have actually been adopted by national housing programs somewhere in the world.

Essentially all of the housing voucher or housing allowance programs that have been proposed follow the same basic formula design, which also is used in many other income-related voucher programs. This can be expressed as

$$B = R - t\,(Y - N),$$

where B is the value of the voucher benefit; R is rent or annual housing cost; Y is household income; N is the household "basic needs" income level, or poverty line; and t is the "tax" rate—that is, rate at which voucher benefit is reduced as household income rises.[18]

An economic margin and set of economic incentives is associated with each of the variables in this equation. A good deal of the policy choice in housing voucher design has involved deciding which of the economic margins is most important and how preservation of the market incentives associated with different margins should be traded off against one another.

"TAX" RATE. Consider first the relationship between t, the "tax" rate, or rate at which the voucher benefit is reduced as household income rises, and N, the household basic needs income level. To stay within budgetary constraints, a voucher formula can either cover all of a household's housing expense at the basic needs income level, then withdraw benefits rapidly as income grows beyond the basic needs level, or it can maintain a tax rate that is less steep but that is applied starting at very low income levels, below the basic needs or poverty-line threshold.

The choice of formula design can be illustrated by comparing the current voucher benefit formula in the United States with the housing allowance formula in use in Great Britain during the mid-1990s. In the United States, t is now set equal to 0.3 and N equals 0. That is, households contribute 30 percent of income to their housing costs, starting with the first dollar of income. In Great Britain, t was set equal to 0.65 for income above the basic needs level, but was 0 up to the basic needs level. This implies that all of a household's rent was covered by the housing allowance, as long as household income was below the basic needs level, but that housing allowance benefit was withdrawn at a steep rate (65 percent) for income earned above this threshold.

Economists tend to think of t, the tax rate on benefits, in terms of the incentive to work and earn income. As pointed out by C. Eugene Steuerle and by David Bradford and Daniel Shaviro in this volume, it is the cumulative t across all social benefit and tax programs that determines the work incentive. This cumulative t is much higher than t in any single benefit program and in certain circumstances may exceed 1.0. The benefit tax rate t has other behavioral impacts. Just over two-thirds of the nonelderly households receiving federal housing subsidies in the United States are headed by single women. For these households, the withdrawal of housing benefit at the rate t in relation to household income acts as a marriage tax, or a tax on formally acknowledged two-adult living arrangements, since the partner's income figures into the household income calculation.

In the housing literature, t has been more often viewed, at least in the United States, as a needs standard. Low-income households, it is maintained, should not have to spend more than 30 percent of their incomes on housing. If they do, they are deemed to have housing "need"—specifically, to face a "housing affordability" problem. The basis of this needs standard is murky at best, as is its presumed constancy.[19] Nonetheless, the ratio of 0.3 has been accepted in the United States since the Reagan years as both a measure of housing affordability and as the appropriate cost-sharing ratio to include in the housing voucher benefit formula. Essentially the same formula, with the same value of t, is used to determine tenant benefits in public housing and in Section 8 project housing.

HOUSEHOLD INCOME. In the housing benefit formula, the term Y refers to adjusted household income. It includes earned income plus cash transfer payments such as welfare—now Temporary Aid to Needy Families (TANF)—payments. It excludes the value of in-kind transfers.

HOUSING RENT. The most powerful housing market incentives surround the term R in the voucher benefit formula. If R is set equal to actual rent (or actual rent up to some ceiling, as formerly in the housing certificate program), participating households have no incentive to shop for and negotiate the best housing price. They are prohibited from spending more than the ceiling R and have no incentive to spend less, since they cannot keep for themselves any of the program savings. In the voucher program, R is defined as the fair market rent for a suitably sized basic housing unit in the local housing market. Fair market rent is measured as rent at the 40th percentile of the local rent distribution among suitably sized units leased within the previous eighteen months. Defining reimbursable rent in this manner implies that, at the margin, the household bears 100 percent of the cost of its housing choice.

The concept of reimbursing households based on a third-party, independent determination of the cost of a "basic" or "minimally adequate" service bundle can be applied to some other sectors that use vouchers. A household might be reimbursed at the 40th percentile of the local cost distribution of standard and acceptable child care, for example, leaving it to the family to seek out the best child-care opportunity and best price. The feasibility of such a system depends on two factors: the ability to determine the price of a standardized bundle of services in the local market and (where this is thought to be important) the inspection capacity to confirm that the service solution purchased by the household actually offers the characteristics that society wants included. The federal Food Stamp Program provides vouchers of a standardized amount, but it prescribes little about the necessary characteristics of the food bundle that is purchased, except to exclude alcohol, tobacco, and certain other items. Vouchers for child care or job training presumably would require more thorough inspection and verification, if voucher amounts were tied to the standardized cost of a "minimally adequate" service package.

Other margins are associated with FMR. The FMR procedure recognizes variations in rent levels across metropolitan regions and reimburses households accordingly. This policy compensates voucher holders for regional housing cost differentials, but it should not create significant incentives for intermetropolitan migration. Variations in fair market rents across submarkets within a single metropolitan area are a different matter. Present HUD policy allows use in the subsidy formula of "exception rents" for specific submarkets. Exception rents can be up to 120 percent of the metropolitan-wide FMR, if justified by adequate information about actual rent levels. Thus households moving into a particular, higher-priced geographical subarea (like a middle-class suburb) can be reimbursed for higher rents than if they moved elsewhere in the metropolitan area. The exception rent policy can significantly affect mobility incentives and it raises fundamental issues about voucher design, which are addressed in the next section.

MODIFYING THE BENEFIT FORMULA. One way to reduce the excess demand for housing subsidies is to modify the benefit formula so as to cut benefit levels. Within a fixed budget constraint, more eligible households could then actually receive vouchers or other benefits. There is precedent for changing parameters in the benefit formula. In 1981 the marginal tax rate, t, in the housing benefit formula was raised from 25 percent to 30 percent. This increased the cost-sharing burden on households by requiring them to contribute 30 percent rather than 25 percent of household income to housing expense. In 1995 measurement of FMR was changed from the 45th percentile of the local rent distribution to the 40th percentile, thereby lowering the subsidy amount for program participants. Both changes were made to hold back spending on federal housing subsidies, rather than to increase program coverage.

Household Mobility and Voucher Portability

Housing vouchers are intended to expand tenant choice by allowing poor households to shop the entire rental market, rather than be limited to public housing and the neighborhoods where federally assisted housing units have been built. Relative to other HUD programs, the voucher program has succeeded in opening up new locational possibilities and has reduced the geographical concentration of assisted households.

Table 5-4 summarizes the census tract characteristics where voucher and certificate holders are located as compared to the census tract characteristics where households participating in public and private project-based housing assistance live. The table also shows the census tract concentration of all welfare households and all renter households of any income level. Along the two dimensions that have received the most attention in studies of negative neighborhood effects—concentrations of poverty and concentrations of racial minorities—the voucher and certificate programs show a good deal of neighborhood dispersion as compared to public housing and to the neighborhood location of all welfare households.

The degree of locational choice that vouchers *should* confer, however, has become one of the more controversial aspects of the voucher program. The policy debate has entangled three issues that it is helpful to differentiate.

ADMINISTRATIVE PORTABILITY. Originally, a local PHA's housing certificate could be used only within the issuing authority's area of operation. Thus for the typical case where a central-city PHA has jurisdiction only within the central city's boundaries, the practical mobility conferred on certificate holders in conducting their housing search was much less than the principles of a housing voucher program would imply. In practice, a household had to limit its search to a single jurisdiction.

In 1987 Congress amended the terms of Section 8 certificates to make them "portable"—that is, to allow recipients to use the certificates throughout the state and in contiguous metropolitan areas of different states.[20] However, the principle of portability was slow to be translated into administrative practice. A national survey of portability, conducted in 1991 by the National Association of Housing and Redevelopment Officials (NAHRO) and covering 750 PHAs, found that just 3 percent of all outstanding Section 8 certificates and vouchers were subject to interjurisdictional portability agreements and had been used outside the issuing authority's jurisdiction.[21] Cost was one limiting factor. The "exporting" PHA

Table 5-4. *Distribution of Housing Units by Program and
Census Tract Characteristics*
Percent[a]

Census tract concentration characteristic	Program				
	Public housing	Subsidized private projects	Vouchers and all certificates	Welfare households	All rental households
Poverty rate					
30–39	17.1	11.5	9.5	12.1	6.8
>40	36.5	10.4	5.3	11.6	5.7
Percent minority population					
50–79	13.3	10.4	11.1	10.6	7.5
>80	37.6	15.1	9.9	17.8	9.4

Source: Newman and Schnare, *Beyond Bricks and Mortar.*
a. Percentage of program households living in census tracts that meet concentration standard.

must count the portable voucher against its voucher allocation, even though the household takes up residence in another jurisdiction. The issuing PHA also must surrender most of the administrative fee it receives from HUD.

A more potent factor behind the resistance to portability has been the unwillingness of many communities to accept or attract other jurisdictions' poor. Some suburbs have declined to enter into portability agreements with the region's central city out of the same fear of income, racial, and behavioral mixing that lies behind other exclusionary practices, from restrictive zoning to residency preferences.

Nonetheless, portability has made great strides since 1991. All federal housing vouchers can now legally be used anywhere in the nation. Interjurisdictional administrative agreements between PHAs have become much more common. A number of metropolitan regions have consolidated local PHAs or established larger regional authorities for the purpose of administering housing vouchers. These arrangements make it simpler for a voucher holder to rent housing anywhere within the much larger service area of the regional authority. At the same time, there has been a fairly steep decline in local residency requirements for obtaining a voucher. Together, these steps have made it much easier, administratively, to use vouchers to move from one community to another.[22]

ADDRESSING SEGREGATION. Some vouchers expressly require house-holds to move to other locations. In the *Gautreaux* cases, the U.S. Supreme Court found that the Chicago Housing Authority and HUD, through its funding and oversight of the Chicago Housing Authority, had deliberately sited public housing so as to perpetuate and intensify racial segregation.[23] The Court upheld the plaintiffs' right to interjurisdictional remedy. The central element in the remedy was a special "voucher mobility" program that enabled current and past residents of Chicago public housing to move to other locations, primarily in the suburbs. African American households using the mobility vouchers were required to move to neighborhoods with low concentrations of black population (not higher than 30 percent) to further the desegregation goals of the program. More than 6,500 house-holds, almost all of them African American, have moved from inner-city locations as part of the court-supervised consent decree.

Gautreaux spawned similar successful litigation in Buffalo, Cincinnati, Dallas, Memphis, Minneapolis, Yonkers, and other cities.[24] "Mobility vouchers" were part of the court-supervised remedy in each instance. These programs mostly involve mandatory mobility. Households must move in order to take advantage of the voucher. Moreover, they typically must move to census tracts that have low concentrations of African American or minor-ity population, and sometimes must accept constraints on subsequent moves, as well. The programs typically provide tenant counseling to prepare households for the moves and to assist them in locating rental units.

MOVING TO OPPORTUNITY. The most recent generation of mobility vouchers has been designed to support moves from high-poverty neigh-borhoods, mostly in the central city, to low-poverty neighborhoods, mostly in the suburbs. HUD launched what was intended to be a ten-year social experiment called Moving to Opportunity to stimulate such moves and to analyze the effect that residing in lower-poverty neighborhoods has on the work histories of households, children's school achievement, family crime victimization, and other outcomes. To participate in the program, house-holds had to move from census tracts that had poverty rates greater than 40 percent to census tracts that had poverty rates below 10 percent.

It is still too early to judge whether voucher-related moves to the sub-urbs are a cost-effective way to address problems of concentrated poverty or problems associated with racial isolation. We do know that households making voluntary moves under voucher programs tend to move to neigh-borhoods with moderately less poverty and less minority racial concentra-tion. In interviews, households cite the desire to reduce their exposure to crime and violence as the overwhelming rationale for their moves. The impact of moves on the earnings or work experience of adults appears to be quite modest, but there is evidence to suggest that the impact on the subsequent educational attainment and earnings history of children may be significantly greater.[25] And even if the gains are moderate, they may come with little or no financial cost when the same amount of housing assistance is at stake.

VOUCHER POLICY ISSUES RELATED TO MOBILITY. Let us assume that neighborhood effects are as substantial as the proponents of mobility programs maintain, and that households moving to "better" neighborhoods are able to capture these externalities. The importance of neighborhood characteristics to the housing market certainly is supported by evidence that favorable crime rates, favorable school performance, good job access, and higher average household income are all characteristics that influence rent levels and are capitalized into housing prices.

In the unsubsidized housing market, households have to trade off neighborhood attributes against other characteristics of the housing bundle, like housing size and condition, as well as against nonhousing consumption. Then they must make a joint choice of where to live and how much housing to consume. Subsidized tenants whose purchasing power has been augmented by vouchers face the same choice, as long as they are reimbursed according to the regionwide FMR.

The use of exception rents to substitute for FMR in the subsidy benefit formula, however, changes the locational calculus. When exception rents are used, voucher holders, unlike other participants in the housing market, do not have to trade off neighborhood attributes against other housing characteristics, at least within the up to 20 percent rent premium recognized in exception rents. Instead, tenants are fully reimbursed for the extra costs of living in a higher-priced neighborhood. Whereas use of a regionwide FMR creates for the tenant both a shopping incentive and a budget constraint, FMRs that are differentiated by submarket within the region create a situation where choosing a higher-cost neighborhood (up to the exception rent ceiling) has no cost consequences for the tenant. Instead of the tenant bearing 100 percent of the cost of her housing choice at the margin, as for physical characteristics, the tenant bears none of the cost at the margin of buying a better neighborhood, up to the FMR adjustment ceiling.

The use of vouchers to stimulate mobility also implies that some subsidized households, those that are consuming at the 40th percentile of the rent distribution in higher-priced suburbs, will be able to afford better housing—in particular, better neighborhood attributes—than some unsubsidized households. It is an open question whether this relationship is desirable in order to stimulate dispersion of poor households, but it underlies some of the hostility expressed toward voucher mobility programs in working-class neighborhoods. Critics have argued that providing better neighborhoods for free to subsidized households eliminates one of the most important aspects of the American social ladder—the principle that a household earns its way into a better neighborhood through labor effort and by making neighborhood quality a budget priority.[26] Facing political controversy of this kind, Congress terminated the Moving to Opportunity demonstration project in early 1999, halfway through its intended life.

Empirical Estimates of Important Parameters

This section summarizes empirical findings regarding some of the important parameters relevant to housing vouchers and the market's response to them. The estimates can be compared to those reported for vouchers in other fields.

VOUCHER ENROLLMENT RATES. Because the volume of housing subsidies is severely limited by budget constraints, the rate of enrollment desired by households in voucher programs cannot be estimated easily from program data. Many households are discouraged from applying for vouchers by the lengthy waiting lists; others cannot apply because local waiting lists are closed to new applicants. The EHAP experimental design, however, in some sites offered voucher participation to all income-eligible households, without the possibility of other kinds of housing subsidy.

Enrollment rates were surprisingly low. Households already living in units that met the program's standard for housing quality enrolled at approximately a 95 percent rate.[27] These households did not have to move or change their behavior in any way to receive benefits. Among households living in units that failed the housing quality test, enrollment rates approximated 50 percent. These households were obliged either to upgrade their units or to move to other locations to qualify for voucher payments. Variations in program design confirmed that the more detailed the specification of minimally adequate housing standards, the lower the overall participation rate in the voucher program.

Over time, as households have become more familiar with the voucher program, the proportion of households voluntarily changing residence after they obtain vouchers has risen. Desired enrollment rates are likely also to have increased, since reluctance to move was a primary reason offered for nonparticipation. Still, the experience in implementing housing vouchers justifies caution in projecting how rapidly households will enroll in a new voucher program that requires them to make significant changes in lifestyle. In the housing sector, most of the recent voucher programs with specific mobility goals have included counseling assistance to make households feel more comfortable with their moves.

SUCCESS IN FINDING HOUSING. Administrative "success" in the housing voucher program is measured by the proportion of voucher recipients that finds suitable housing and is able to use the voucher. Search costs in the rental housing market can be high, especially for minority households seeking to move from the inner city to new neighborhoods and for households without access to an automobile or child care. Landlords often resist renting to Section 8 voucher holders, especially in tight housing markets.

The initial success rates reported for voucher programs were disturbingly low. Success rates were lowest for minority households and for households starting with the poorest-quality housing conditions. In the EHAP experiment, only 40 to 50 percent of voucher recipients that had to move in order to use their vouchers were successful in finding housing.[28] Later, under the freestanding voucher program, success rates rose to 70 percent or more in a majority of the study locations, although they remained below 50 percent in the tightest housing markets. Studies in the early and mid-1990s reported much higher success rates. One analysis of 1993 data found that 87 percent of voucher recipients were able to find eligible housing, including those who did not have to move.[29] The gap in placement rates between white households and minority households also narrowed. This was a period of generally weak housing markets, with high vacancy rates.

The tight housing markets of the late 1990s appear to have negatively affected voucher placements, though there is little more than anecdotal evidence on this score at present. In 1998 only 60 percent of the families awarded housing vouchers in St. Louis, for example, were able to find housing. The other 40 percent had to return the vouchers because of their inability to locate qualifying units where the landlord would accept vouchers. The evidence, slim as it is, suggests a housing market in which many landlords accept voucher households as tenants only as a second choice. They prefer the private market to the bureaucratic arrangements for receiving voucher payments from HUD. In weak housing markets, this landlord preference is overridden by the reality that voucher holders are one of the few sources of active demand. In tight housing markets, landlords have more choice of tenants.

IMPACT OF VOUCHERS ON HOUSING PRICES. Analyses of the impact of vouchers on housing prices have reported no effect or negligible effect. This is consistent with most empirical estimates of a highly elastic housing supply curve in the intermediate and longer term. Informal reports, however, have suggested that in certain neighborhoods where there has been a high rate of Section 8 voucher in-migration, landlords have been able to raise rents on lower-quality units to near the FMR at which voucher households are reimbursed. Whether these price increases have been offset by quality upgrading is unclear. As long as voucher holders have a preference for living in certain neighborhoods and this preference is reinforced by informal steering by the PHA and landlords, rental increases in zones of high Section 8 voucher concentration are a realistic possibility.

HOUSING DEMAND FROM VOUCHERS VERSUS GENERAL INCOME SUPPLEMENTS. The EHAP experiment compared the effect on housing demand of housing vouchers versus general income assistance of the same magnitude.[30] Estimated elasticities in both cases were low. Approximately 10 percent of additional, unrestricted cash grants were spent on housing. Approximately 20 percent of housing allowance payments were spent on incremental housing. Analysts attributed almost all of the difference in housing consumption to the fact that some households participating in the voucher program had to improve their housing conditions in order to meet the program's minimum housing standards. The overall low response of housing consumption to increases in income is consistent with the view that low-income households assign a high priority to obtaining minimally satisfactory housing and spend a high proportion of their income to pay for it—that is, today's low-income housing problem is primarily an affordability problem. When households receive moderate increments of income, whether in the form of cash or housing vouchers, they spend most of the increase for other goods rather than for additional housing.

COST OF VOUCHERS VERSUS SUPPLY SUBSIDIES. Since Section 8 "new construction" and Section 8 "voucher" programs use essentially the same benefit formula to calculate household payments, and since both programs draw from the same pool of subsidy applicants and have the same standards for acceptable housing, it is easier to compare the costs of demand-side and supply-side housing subsidies than it is in most sectors. In project-based assistance, reimbursable rent, R, in the benefit formula is calculated as a fair market return on the cost of constructing unsubsidized rental units of comparable quality, rather than on market rents in the competitive rental market. Weicher reports that internal HUD studies have found that Section 8 project-based rents are, on average, 24 percent higher than the FMRs used in the voucher benefit formula for housing of the same size and location.[31] Other studies have estimated that the lifetime costs to the federal government of Section 8 subsidized project housing average about 40 percent to 50 percent more than the cost per unit of Section 8 vouchers.[32]

Explanations for the higher cost of supply-side subsidies are varied. The HUD inspector general has found numerous cases of collusion between developers and HUD inspectors to inflate the "comparable cost" estimates of subsidized housing. Since a handful of developers have accounted for a large share of low-income housing production under this and other HUD programs, collusion of this kind could contribute significantly to average supply cost. An important part of the cost differential reflects the means of producing housing. In the unsubsidized housing market, very little privately owned housing comparable to Section 8 housing is newly constructed. Housing for this submarket usually filters down from more expensive use, or, in certain circumstances, is upgraded from poorer-quality stock. The rarity of new construction makes cost comparisons between the subsidized market and the private market extremely difficult. It also suggests that new construction generally is not a cost-effective way of serving this submarket.

Reform Proposals

Housing vouchers originally were conceived as an income-contingent entitlement that would replace all other forms of low-income housing subsidy. The idea of universal housing vouchers has now disappeared from policy debate because of budget constraints. The practical range of reforms has been limited to those that can be implemented with approximate budget neutrality.

Vouchering Out Housing Assistance

One policy option is for HUD to "voucher out" all of its project-based housing assistance programs. That strategy was recommended by Henry

Cisneros when he was secretary of HUD and has been advocated by a range of other housing experts. The basic principles behind vouchering out are simple. The current set of subsidies to housing providers would be terminated as soon as legally possible, including both subsidies to public housing authorities to operate public housing and subsidies to private owners to supply project-based housing to the low-income market. The tenants living in these units would be given vouchers. They could use the vouchers to continue living in the same units, or they could move to other housing that better met their needs. Tenants would be better off because of their expanded choice, while formerly subsidized providers would be forced by competition to become more efficient and more customer oriented.

Vouchering out of this kind could be expected to be broadly cost neutral. The savings realized from substituting vouchers for subsidies to private owners of project-based units would be approximately offset by the higher costs of providing vouchers to residents of public housing. The construction costs of public housing are now a sunk cost. The operating, maintenance, and repair costs of public housing are below the per-unit subsidy cost of vouchers, so that vouchering out this segment of the subsidized housing stock would involve a net budget cost, at least in the short and intermediate terms.[33]

The principal obstacles to full-scale vouchering out lie elsewhere. HUD, through FHA, has guaranteed mortgages for the majority of the privately owned subsidized housing stock. Because HUD pays above-market rents for most of these properties and has recognized above-market construction costs, the mortgage values also are inflated. If HUD were to terminate its rental contracts when the current contracts expire and force the owners of Section 8 housing to compete for tenants in the market, the expected rents and therefore property values would decline. The value of many projects would decline below the amount of the outstanding mortgage, triggering mortgage defaults that HUD would have to cover. It has been estimated that HUD would have to foreclose on as much as half of the 900,000 subsidized apartment units insured by FHA, involving some $15 billion of outstanding mortgages.

This is not an additional economic cost. The true cost has already been created by subsidizing the construction of uncompetitive housing units. If that cost is not recognized today in the form of mortgage defaults resulting from exposure to competitive rents, it will have to be recognized tomorrow, in the form of deepening annual rent subsidies to keep the units operating in the black. The magnitude of the one-time mortgage liability, and the difficulty of designing a strategy that avoids it, nonetheless has been a major roadblock to across-the-board vouchering out, given the federal budget rules that limit annual expenditure increases.

Immediate vouchering out also would shrink the stock of low-income housing. Providing vouchers to tenants of public housing and project-based housing would trigger a large amount of out migration. If public and private owners had to operate this housing on a market basis, some projects would be deemed able to compete fully with private market housing and would opt out of the low-income market. Other housing projects would be allowed to move down in quality, competing in the market for cheaper housing. Some projects would not be able to compete at all without project subsidies—that is, they could not generate rents to cover their operating and maintenance costs. These units would be squeezed out of the housing supply. Weicher conjectures that 165,000 to 265,000 public housing units would be retired from the housing stock as the consequence of full vouchering out, but he points out that there is no firm basis for a projection. The subsidized housing in private hands is mostly of sufficient quality and recent vintage that it should be able to generate positive operating income on the private market, and thus stay in use. However, the operating income of these properties in many cases would not be sufficient to repay the outstanding mortgages on the properties. These projects would have to pass through mortgage default, HUD foreclosure, and resale before they could be placed on a financially sound operating basis. Foreclosure and liquidation of several hundred thousand low-income housing units would, at a minimum, temporarily disrupt the supply of low-income housing and quite possibly would make private landlords unwilling to accept participation in government voucher programs in the future.

These adjustment costs may seem to be a high cost to pay for the rapid conversion of project-based housing subsidies to vouchers. A similar policy, spread over a longer period of time, would accomplish many of the same objectives without the market disruption. Every year, under current policy, a portion of the public housing stock is judged to be in too poor condition to continue to operate as is or to justify the expense of modernization. If HUD were to adopt a policy of demolishing these poorest-quality units when they reach the end of their useful lives and replacing them with vouchers, over a period of ten to fifteen years a large part of the public housing stock would have been converted to vouchers. A similar option faces policymakers in designing policy for privately owned subsidized units. As the mortgages on these units are paid off, HUD can decline to renew subsidized rental contracts on poor-quality units and can replace them with vouchers, without the complications and expense of handling mortgage defaults. Such a policy seems to be the general approach that HUD, in fact, is now following.

Are Demand-Side Subsidies Sufficient in Tight Housing Markets?

One of the fundamental policy issues concerning housing vouchers is whether vouchers can or should be the sole subsidy instrument for delivering low-income housing subsidies in a period of tight housing markets. Low-cost housing is produced in the private market primarily through filtering—by permitting older housing to deteriorate in quality or by subdividing larger housing into smaller rental units. During periods of economic strength, such as the nation has witnessed since 1994, the filtering process slows down, or may even reverse itself. With strong demand for better-quality housing, fewer units are allowed to deteriorate and more units are upgraded to meet market demand.

As a result of this process, the inventory of low-cost housing can erode. HUD estimates that between 1996 and 1998, the supply of rental units costing less than $300 per month (in inflation-adjusted dollars) fell by 19 percent, from 6.8 million units to 5.5 million units. HUD and Congress have drawn the conclusion that demand-side subsidies must be supplemented by supply-side subsidies to produce more low-income housing or at least to keep existing project units in the low-income stock. First priority has been given to preserving Section 8 project-based units as they come off contract. For project-based housing that now commands market rents in excess of the original contract amount, HUD and Congress have authorized an emergency initiative that will increase program contract rents to the comparable private market level or to 150 percent of the FMR, whichever is lower. For project-based housing that cannot generate an economic return at market rents, HUD and Congress have authorized continued and deepening subsidies to pay above-market rents after expiration of the original project contract. It is hoped that these measures will keep the bulk of Section 8 project-based housing in the low-income housing stock, lessening the need to displace tenants and to give tenants demand-side vouchers.

Although many policy analysts have interpreted this situation as a supply-side problem that necessitates a targeted, supply-side response, in reality it reflects a strengthening housing market in which low-end demand financed through a combination of vouchers and household income growth has not kept pace with privately financed middle-income demand resulting from economic growth. Rents in the low-income housing market have risen at approximately the same rate as rents in the rest of the housing market. However, as long as only 36 percent of income-eligible households receive housing assistance, and if household incomes at the lower end of the income distribution continue to lag behind growth in the rest of the economy, housing "affordability" for unsubsidized households in the low-income market will worsen. Some owners of rental housing will find it to their advantage to exit the low-income market in favor of higher income submarkets where demand is stronger. The widening affordability gap does not imply that supply-side subsidies are more cost-effective than demand-side subsidies for those who receive housing benefits. However, it can be argued that supply-side measures are more beneficial to low-income residents who do not receive subsidies, because the increased supply tends to dampen overall rents in the low-income submarket.

Time Limits for Housing Vouchers

Federal housing assistance is out of sync with the spirit of federal welfare reform. Long queues of applicants wait for entry into all types of assisted housing. Yet, once a household obtains a housing voucher or a public housing unit, in practice it enjoys lifetime possession, as long as its income does not exceed program limits and the family does not engage in egregious behavior. In the twelve largest PHAs, the average family in public housing stays in the same unit for fourteen years and then may move to another subsidized unit or subsidy program.

It would seem to be more consistent with the current welfare reform philosophy to redefine housing programs so that they, too, provide temporary support to needy households, assuming that the head of household is able to work. The same five-year lifetime limitation applied to welfare assistance could be applied to rental assistance. Or a two-tier housing support system could be introduced in which household heads able to work can benefit from housing subsidies at the current level for five years but must accept a lower level of housing support thereafter. Rather than the social lottery that now occurs—where the "winners" get the right to lifetime housing assistance, but the "losers" get nothing—every household could receive a time-limited right to housing assistance similar to the right to welfare assistance. Housing assistance would be bundled together with other types of assistance that dependent families need to access the labor force.

HUD has experimented with comprehensive, time-limited programs of this type under the labels of Project Self-Sufficiency, Operation Bootstrap, and Family Self-Sufficiency. All involve the idea of supplementing social housing subsidies by giving households access to many of the resources they need to gain an economic foothold—such as child care, job training, social services, and transportation support.[34] In exchange for the augmented resources, households have been asked to accept limits on their eligibility to receive federal housing assistance.

Three clear findings have emerged from these experiments. First, very few households proved willing to voluntarily trade their long-term right to housing subsidies for up-front investments in job training and other support services that would help equip them for the job market. Public housing authorities reported widespread reluctance to sign up for the various self-sufficiency programs, even when they included two years of job training and free child care during the training period. Second, while households that complete the self-sufficiency programs on average increase their hours of work and their earned incomes, few households come close to achieving self-sufficiency, in the sense of no longer requiring federal assistance for food, welfare, or housing. The increases in work and pay are modest. This market reality is consistent with the unwillingness of households to surrender their entitlement to long-term federal housing assistance in order to participate in programs that generate only modest economic returns. Third, current law does not permit HUD to cut off housing assistance benefits for households that remain income eligible. Even though households participating in the self-sufficiency programs voluntarily signed contracts allowing HUD to terminate their housing benefits after the program period, the courts later ruled that HUD did not have the legal authority to terminate benefits. Paradoxically, at the same time as Congress has passed time limits for welfare participation, it has forbidden the administration, through newly passed legislative language, to impose time limits on housing benefits.

Notes

1. 50 Stat. 888 (1937), Sec. 1.

2. Department of Housing and Urban Development, *A Picture of Subsidized Households*, vol. 11, *United States: Large Projects and Agencies* (1996).

3. The LIHTC ceiling for each state is $1.25 per capita per year, or about $338 million in total in 1999. States also can issue tax-exempt housing bonds to help finance low-income housing construction. There is a separate ceiling on the annual volume of such bonds.

4. Historically, the Section 8 "housing certificate" and "housing voucher" programs operated separately but according to very similar principles and rules.

The main differences involved (a) the mechanism for rent reimbursement, as described later, and (b) portability. A locally issued voucher always could be used anywhere in the nation. A certificate could be used only in a restricted area. The two programs were consolidated under a single set of regulations in June 1998. The consolidated regulations follow the "voucher" rules in most respects. In this chapter, I frequently use the term "voucher" generically to describe both programs. Specific program characteristics refer to the formal "voucher" program except where otherwise noted.

5. Formerly, federal rules required that if a landlord accepted *any* Section 8 voucher holder, the landlord had to accept *all* qualified Section 8 applicants. This rule dissuaded some landlords from participating in the Section 8 program and helped promote a specialized submarket of housing that served primarily Section 8 voucher holders. The requirement has now been dropped.

6. The New Jersey Supreme Court, for example, has upheld a state law that prohibits landlords from refusing to rent to a person based only on the source of a person's lawful income and has held that the law prohibits landlord discrimination against Section 8 voucher holders.

7. John C. Weicher, *Privatizing Subsidized Housing* (Washington, D.C.: AEI Press, 1997).

8. Margery Austin Turner and Kale Williams, *Housing Mobility: Realizing the Promise* (Urban Institute, 1998).

9. The public housing law, for example, originally required that at least one blighted housing unit be *demolished* for each unit of public housing that was built. Later, the law was amended to reverse the requirement: at least one public housing unit had to be *built* for each housing unit demolished as part of urban renewal or other programs.

10. Ira C. Lowry, *Rent Control and Housing Assistance: The U.S. Experience* (Urban Institute, 1996).

11. John M. Hartung and Jeffrey R. Henig, "Housing Vouchers and Certificates as a Vehicle for Deconcentrating the Poor: Evidence from the Washington, D.C., Area," *Urban Affairs Review*, vol. 32, no. 3 (1997), pp. 403–19.

12. In spring 2000, Republican presidential candidate George W. Bush proposed allowing local PHAs to provide Section 8 renters one year's worth of vouchers in a lump sum to cover the down payment and closing costs of a home purchase.

13. Lawrence J. Vale, "Beyond the Problem Projects Paradigm: Defining and Revitalizing 'Severely Distressed' Public Housing," *Housing Policy Debate*, vol. 4, no. 2 (1993), p. 155.

14. William Julius Wilson, *The Truly Disadvantaged: The Inner City, the Underclass, and Public Policy* (Chicago University Press, 1987); Christopher Jencks and Susan E. Mayer, "The Social Consequences of Growing Up in a Poor Neighborhood," in Laurence E. Lynn Jr. and Michael G. H. McGeary, eds., *Inner-City Poverty in the United States* (National Academy Press, 1990).

15. HUD, *A Picture of Subsidized Households*; Sandra J. Newman and Ann B. Schnare, *Beyond Bricks and Mortar: Re-examining the Purpose and Effects of Housing Assistance* (Urban Institute, 1997).

16. See the following section, entitled "Household Mobility and Voucher Portability," however, for a discussion of the legal and administrative limitations on residency preferences.

17. George E. Peterson and Kale Williams, "Housing Mobility: What Has It Accomplished and What Is Its Promise?" in Alexander Polikoff, ed., *Housing Mobility: Promise or Illusion?* (Urban Institute, 1995).

18. P. A. Kemp, "Housing Allowances and the Fiscal Crisis of the Welfare State," *Housing Studies*, vol. 9, no. 4 (1994).

19. J. David Hulchanski, "The Concept of Housing Affordability: Six Contemporary Uses of the Housing Expenditure-to-Income Ratio," *Housing Studies*, vol. 10, no. 4 (1995). Given the relatively low price elasticity of demand for housing usually found in empirical estimates, it would be expected that, as housing prices rise relative to the prices of other goods, housing's share of household income also would rise, while the share of income spent on other basic goods would decline. In legislative practice, countries have adopted many different "housing affordability" standards. The ratio formerly used for public programs in the United States was 0.25.

20. This is one area where the housing "certificate" and "voucher" programs differed. Vouchers, introduced in 1982, always could legally be used anywhere in the country.

21. National Association of Housing and Redevelopment Officials, *Report on NAHRO's 1991 Section 8 Portability Survey* (December 1991).

22. It is useful to distinguish between *obtaining* a voucher in a community outside one's residence and *using* a voucher in another location. Federal rules allow households to obtain vouchers from jurisdictions other than their own; only locally established residency preferences have stood in the way. However, these restrictions are by no means universal. In 1994 HUD found that 54 percent of 2,541 PHAs surveyed did not have residency preferences for admission to their voucher waiting list. For example, when West Hartford, Connecticut, closed its Section 8 voucher waiting list in 1993, only 120 of the nearly 900 families on the list lived in West Hartford; almost all of the rest lived in Hartford, the central city. Similarly, approximately 60 percent of the households on the voucher waiting list for New Castle County, Delaware, gave neighboring Wilmington as their present address.

The use of vouchers outside the issuing authority's boundaries is gathering steam. All vouchers now can legally be used anywhere in the nation. Portability in practice has lagged, but is accelerating. In July 1994 the Housing Authority of Alameda County, California, was administering 1,230 vouchers from other jurisdictions, up more than 100 percent from 1992. (See Peterson and Williams, "Housing Mobility," and Philip D. Tegeler, Michael L. Hanley, and Judith Liben,

"Transforming Section 8 into a Regional Housing Mobility Program," in Alexander Polikoff, ed., *Housing Mobility: Promise or Illusion?*) The "vouchering out" experience of subsidized housing projects closed by HUD provides further evidence of the moderate use of portability. In case studies of four such housing projects in Baltimore, Newport News, Kansas City, and San Francisco, researchers found that in two of the sites about half the respondents reported that they had considered using their vouchers in another jurisdiction, and in the other two sites about one-quarter of respondents did so. In the end, the proportion of voucher households that did move to another jurisdiction ranged from 23 percent in San Francisco to 10 percent or less in Baltimore and Kansas City. The researchers attributed the differences in actual portability to (a) tenant preferences to remain in the same broad neighborhood, (b) the need to move further to find satisfactory housing in a tight housing market such as San Francisco's, and (c) differences in the degree of counseling support for portability. See Rutgers University, Center for Urban Research Policy, *Case Studies of Vouchered-out Assisted Properties* (HUD, 1998).

23. *Gautreaux* v. *Chicago Housing Authority*, 304 F. Supp. 736 (N.D. Ill. 1969); *Hills* v. *Gautreaux*, 425 U.S. 284 (1976); *Gautreaux* v. *Landrieu*, 523 F. Supp. (N.D. Ill. 1981).

24. Peterson and Williams, "Housing Mobility"; Turner and Williams, *Housing Mobility: Realizing the Promise*.

25. James E. Rosenbaum, Nancy Fishman, Alison Brett, and Patricia Meaden, "Can the Kerner Commission's Housing Strategy Improve Employment, Education, and Social Integration for Low-Income Blacks?" *North Carolina Law Review* (Special Issue: *Symposium: The Urban Crisis: The Kerner Commission Report Revisited*), vol. 71, no. 5. (1993), pp. 1519–72; Julie E. Kaufman and James E. Rosenbaum, "The Education and Employment of Low-Income Black Youth in White Suburbs," *Educational Evaluation and Policy Analysis*, vol. 14, no. 3 (1992), pp. 229–40.

26. Howard Husock, "Voucher Plan for Housing: A Trojan Horse," *Wall Street Journal*, December 12, 1994, p. A14; James Bovard, "Suburban Guerrilla," *American Spectator* (September 1994), pp. 26–32.

27. Stephen D. Kennedy, *Housing Allowance Demand Experiment: Final Report* (Boston, Mass.: Abt Associates, 1980).

28. Ira S. Lowry, *Experimenting with Housing Allowances: The Final Report of the Housing Assistance Supply Experiment* (Cambridge, Mass.: Oelgeschalger, Gunn, and Hain, 1980).

29. Stephen D. Kennedy and Meryl Finkel, *Section 8 Rental Voucher and Utilization Study, Final Report* (HUD, 1994).

30. Kennedy, *Housing Allowance Demand Experiment: Final Report*.

31. Weicher, *Privatizing Subsidized Housing*.

32. Kirk McClure, "Housing Vouchers versus Housing Productions: Assessing Long-term Costs," *Housing Policy Debate*, vol. 9, no. 2 (1998), pp. 355–71.

33. See Weicher, *Privatizing Subsidized Housing*, for a cost comparison. Weicher includes in the cost of operating public housing the level of repair and maintenance spending that would be necessary to make the public housing stock competitive with private housing.

34. Amy Bogdon, "What Can We Learn from Previous Housing-Based Self Sufficiency Programs?" paper presented at a Fannie Mae Foundation-sponsored seminar on the Implications of Welfare Reform for Housing, Washington D.C., 1997; William M. Rohe and Rachel Gorshick Kleit, "Housing, Welfare Reform, and Self-Sufficiency: An Assessment of the Family Self-Sufficiency Program," *Housing Policy Debate*, vol. 10, no. 2 (1999), pp. 333–69.

HUGO PRIEMUS

6 | *Housing Vouchers: A Contribution from Abroad*

T HIS CHAPTER discusses the issue of housing affordability and four strategies to facilitate it. Drawing heavily on the recent work of Peter Kemp in the United Kingdom, the chapter will also provide an overview of housing allowances—policies and experiences— around the world, specifically in Australia, New Zealand, Canada, Germany, the Netherlands, Sweden, and Great Britain.

A number of questions pertaining to housing allowances and housing vouchers are posed, which I attempt to answer on the basis of experiences in the Netherlands and other European countries. The conclusion considers the pros and cons of housing allowances and housing vouchers and what form of housing subsidy can be recommended.

Four Strategies to Ensure Housing Affordability

Housing vouchers and housing allowances are instruments to realize the policy goal of ensuring decent and affordable housing for low-income households.[1] The assumptions here are that, without policy measures, some low-income households would not be able to afford housing of a reasonable quality or that affordable housing for low-income households would be of insufficient quality. This, in turn, suggests the existence of implicit values about housing quality and affordability.

Let us assume that reasonable housing is defined as independent housing (according to the statistical definition of housing) that complies with current building codes. And let us also assume affordable housing to be housing that leaves the household sufficient resources to live comfortably after having paid all housing costs. This minimum budget depends on prevailing norms and standards in a specific country, era, and culture.

Four strategies exist to tackle the problem of low-income households living in housing that they cannot afford or living in substandard housing.

—*No financial instruments.* A policy of actively encouraging tenants to move on to more expensive housing when their incomes rise and they can afford to do so should increase the availability of affordable housing for low-income households. However, this filtering strategy by no means guarantees that sufficient vacancies will arise for such housing in the foreseeable future. Thus a low-income household might not find a solution to their problem in this strategy. If the bottleneck persists, the household may fall victim to a series of external negative effects: a greater chance of unemployment, health-related problems, and poor conditions for raising children, which may lead to resistance, social protest, violence, and criminal behavior.

—*Income distribution.* This strategy, using, for example, income tax measures such as a negative income tax, does not ensure that a household succeeds in obtaining affordable housing (after all, this depends on the situation in the housing market: the supply of affordable housing, rent policy, allocation systems, and so forth). Provided that this bottleneck is tackled successfully, this is the strategy of choice for theoretical economists. Households most value those resources they are free to spend as they see fit. Scarcity and other supply shortages can seriously limit a household's choice, but there is another serious objection to this strategy. If households choose to spend the extra resources on sex, drugs, and rock and roll instead of decent housing, taxpayers' support for the strategy will be short-lived. No one is prepared to pay taxes toward a system that fails to solve blatant social problems.

—*Targeted housing support.* From a theoretical economic view, this strategy, which includes housing vouchers and housing allowances, is imperfect, but it works in practice. Housing vouchers and housing allowances can only be spent on decent housing. If households refuse to use housing allowances, their problem will not be solved, but this will not cost society anything. In such a situation, it is up to social workers and community organizations to convince such households to use housing allowances to improve their living situation.

—*Property subsidies.* A major advantage of this policy instrument, which was adopted on a large scale in Europe after 1945, is that it works to solve the supply side of the problem. Theoretically, this instrument could alleviate shortages in affordable decent housing. Unfortunately, experience shows that low-income households are not the main beneficiaries of property subsidies. The instrument is usually used to stimulate new housing development and renovations, and such projects are typically aimed at average and above-average income groups. Even with property subsidies, low-income households are usually unable to afford new houses.

If property subsidies were to make new housing affordable to low-income households, and if an effort were made to establish a consistent relationship between rent and quality, then the stock of housing in general would be underpriced. In that case, property subsidies would spread out and apply to almost the entire stock.

Other disadvantages of property subsidies are that they usually go hand in hand with some form of rent control and considerably distort the housing market, since prices lose much of their indicative function. Property subsidies might be implemented temporarily in situations of acute housing shortages, but they have too many disadvantages to be recommended as a general policy measure.

There is one case in which property subsidies can be highly effective. When interest rates rise steeply, housing costs tend to rocket upward and as a result new housing developments can come to an almost complete standstill.[2] In this case, property subsidies provided as interest subsidies may considerably mitigate the effects of interest rate fluctuations on house rents. Such solutions are actually forms of treasury management.

Generally, in situations without a large housing shortage, it would appear that housing vouchers and housing allowances are the best strategy to ensure affordable housing for low-income households.

Housing Allowances: Policies and Experiences Abroad

Much of this section is distilled from Kemp's *Comparative Study of Housing Allowances.*[3] He defines housing allowances as demand subsidies that provide income-related help in paying the costs of housing. The sum provided depends on a household's income and housing costs and often on household composition as well. Housing allowances provide direct revenue support to consumers on the demand side.[4] Housing vouchers, as the term is used by Kemp and in this chapter, are similar to housing allowances, except that payment is based on a standardized rent level, rather than on a household's actual rent.

Housing allowances and vouchers are generally assumed to have a smaller regulatory effect on individuals than the direct provision of goods and services have. However, they regulate household expenditure more than cash subsidies do. Vouchers are not uncapped, open-ended subsidies; if a household exceeds the limit of the voucher, it must pay the full amount in excess of the limit or it may lose the housing voucher altogether.

In some countries, social assistance schemes also include housing assistance. In these cases, housing assistance is embedded, as it were, in the general social assistance system (in the United States, in the former Aid to Families with Dependent Children program; in Germany, Sozialhilfe; and also in Austria and Canada).

After World War II, Western Europe suffered an acute housing shortage. Combinations of rent control and property subsidies were implemented to alleviate this problem. The first measure of keeping rents low initially had more success than the second measure of increasing housing supply. However, continued rent control led private landlords to neglect property maintenance and to disinvest by selling rental properties to owner-occupiers.

Thereupon governments decided to relax rent control in stages and to reduce supply subsidies. In the 1960s and 1970s, housing allowances were introduced in most Western European countries to bring rent-to-income ratios to an acceptable level for low-income households. Sometimes fixed maximum rent-to-income ratios were introduced, as for example in the Netherlands, where a 10 percent rent-to-income ratio initially applied to households with a minimum income and a 16 percent ratio to average-income households.[5]

The first rent subsidy program in Europe in the form of housing allowances was launched in France in 1948. Germany followed suit with its Wohngeld program in 1965. In the Netherlands, rent subsidies were introduced experimentally in 1970. In 1975 the system became common policy there and was implemented on a large scale. Britain's national rent rebate and allowance scheme was launched in 1972. In Australia, rent rebates for public housing were introduced in 1981.[6] In most countries, the rise of housing allowances was linked to a reduction or even the elimination of producer subsidies. Oddly, countries such as Italy and Spain insisted on upholding property subsidies. In these countries, housing allowance schemes were not introduced.

Table 6-1. *Housing Tenure in Selected Countries*[a]
Percent

Type of tenure	Australia (1991)	New Zealand (1991)	Canada (1993)	Germany (1987)	Nether- lands (1993)	Sweden (1990)	Great Britain (1993)
Owner-occupied	67	74	65	38	47	41	67
Private rented	21	15	30	43	17	19	10
Social rented[b]	6	8	6	15	36	21	24
Other[c]	6	3	. . .	4	. . .	19	. . .

Source: Kemp, *A Comparative Study*, p. 23.
a. Totals may not sum to 100 because figures are rounded.
b. Includes publicly owned housing and housing that is privately owned by nonprofit housing associations.
c. Includes cooperative housing; in Sweden, 15 percent of housing consisted of cooperative housing.

The shift away from supply subsidies to demand subsidies was prompted on the one hand by an improved housing supply and on the other hand by a perceived need to curtail subsidies. In the 1970s and 1980s, in particular, many Western European countries struggled to cope with major budget deficits. Drastic budgets cuts were called for, and as housing was no longer a pressing problem, cuts in public housing expenditure were inevitable.

By largely replacing producer subsidies with housing allowances, total government spending was reduced and market forces were given a looser rein. The years of rent control and producer subsidies had led to a web of bureaucratic procedures—in particular for new housing development and housing allocation—that had all but stifled market forces in many countries.

A correct view of the distribution of housing supply with respect to tenure, shown in table 6-1, is vital for a correct interpretation of the application of housing allowances in the countries being discussed.

In Australia, Canada, Germany, and New Zealand, the housing market is dominated by the commercial (private) sector. In contrast, the Netherlands, Sweden, and, to a lesser extent, Britain have a more mixed housing market with a considerable social rental housing segment operating in parallel with the private market. The countries also differ strongly with respect to the rate of owner-occupied houses. Owner-occupation is the main form of tenure (65 to 74 percent) in New Zealand, Australia, Britain, and Canada. Germany, Sweden, and the Netherlands have much lower owner-occupation rates (38 to 47 percent).

Table 6-2. *Gross Rent and Gross Rent, Fuel, and Power as a Share of Household Final Consumption Expenditures, Selected Countries*[a]
Percent

Country	1980		1985		1990		1992	
	Gross rent	*Gross rent and fuel and power*	*Gross rent*	*Gross rent and fuel and power*	*Gross rent*	*Gross rent and fuel and power*	*Gross rent*	*Gross rent and fuel and power*
Australia	17	19	17	19	18	21	18	20
New Zealand	...	...	17	19	20	22	...	...
Canada	...	20	...	22	...	23	...	24
Germany	14	19	16	22	17	21	17	21
Netherlands	...	...	13	19	15	18	15	18
Sweden	19	25	20	26	21	25	26	31
Great Britain	14	19	15	20	14	18	15	19

Source: Kemp, *A Comparative Study*, p. 51.

a. Includes households of all tenures, renters and owner-occupiers. Gross rent includes estimates for the imputed rents of owner-occupiers.

Table 6-2 shows the magnitude of gross rent and of gross rent plus fuel and power, measured in a percentage of household final consumption expenditure, for households in several countries in the 1980s and early 1990s. The data refer to housholds in all forms of tenure, rental and owner occupied.

The steepest rise in rent burden during this period occurred in Canada and Sweden. In Canada, the estimated proportion of total household expenditure spent exclusively on rent rose from 15 percent to 21 percent; the expenditure spent on rent, fuel, and power increased from 20 percent to 24 percent. However, Kemp did note that these figures are not completely reliable.[7] In Sweden, expenditure on rent increased from 19 percent of total consumption in 1980 to 26 percent in 1992. The modest increase in rent burden in Britain can be explained by the inclusion of data on imputed rents for owner-occupiers.

In 1992 the Swedes spent more of their income on rent than citizens of any other country did. By comparison, Britain and the Netherlands were relatively low-rent countries. In Canada, rents in 1992 were moderately high when viewed as a proportion of household income, while Australia and Germany could be termed countries with average rents.

Table 6-3, taken from Kemp, describes the key objectives and some of the defining characteristics of housing allowances as implemented in the selected countries.[8]

In Australia, housing allowances for tenants receiving social security benefits, pensions, and allowances take the form of rent assistance provided by the Department of Social Security and the Department of Veterans' Affairs. Implicit rent rebates may also take the form of income-related rents for public housing tenants. While the Department of Social Security acknowledges that rent assistance fulfills a specific housing policy role, the scheme's objectives are related to social security rather than housing policy.

Rent assistance is provided as a component of the core social security programs for social security clients. Accordingly, rent assistance is designed to support the primary objective of these programs—to provide adequate income support for clients and their dependents—through supplements to meet the additional costs of private rental housing. This is similar to the function of other supplementary payments made within the social security system.

In contrast, rent rebates are regarded as an instrument of housing policy. The aim of public housing is generally to provide affordable housing to people in need. With the shift away from bricks and mortar subsidies toward national market rents, implicit rent rebates are becoming the principal means to ensure the affordability of public housing for tenants.

Housing allowances may be seen as an instrument of social security or as one of housing policy, depending on which ministry implements the measure. And that, in turn, depends on how the instrument is designed (especially if it is linked to a change in income and the overall cost of living or to changes in housing costs).

In New Zealand, the accommodation supplement is considered a housing policy instrument. According to an official of the Social Policy Agency, the aim of accommodation supplements is to direct accommodation assistance to those who need it most, and to encourage those who are able to take care of their own needs to do so.[9]

In Canada, the basic aim of housing allowances is to make housing more affordable for people who neither receive social assistance nor live in subsidized (rent geared to income) housing.[10] Affordability is recognized as one of the three major housing problems, the others being adequacy and suitability. An affordability problem is said to exist when a household's rent-to-income ratio is greater than 30 percent. In fact, norms such as this one are politically determined; they have no objective rationale. Housing allowances are designed to help solve affordability problems. A secondary aim of Canadian housing allowances is to reduce the demand on social housing and hence to reduce the pressure to build more public housing.[11] Housing allowances are in keeping with the Canadian policy of providing welfare through the market system. The housing assistance provided to social security recipients is seen as part of the welfare system and not as an instrument of housing policy.

The primary aim of housing allowances in Germany is to ensure that the cost of adequate housing is reasonably congruent with household income. Housing allowances have traditionally been regarded as a housing policy instrument. However, since the late 1980s, housing allowances have increasingly been seen as a component of social assistance. The housing supplement provided to social assistance recipients has always been regarded as part of the income support system.

In the Netherlands, housing allowances are very much considered a housing policy instrument.[12] The Dutch scheme has two main goals: to prevent excessive rent burdens on low-income tenants and to ensure that low-income households can obtain accommodation of a certain standard and have a sufficient range of housing possibilities to choose from.[13]

In Sweden, the aim of housing allowances for nonpensioners is to enable economically weak households to live in good-quality and sufficiently spacious housing. A long-term aim of the allowances is to enable families to take up accommodation that is large enough for every child to have his or her own room. The scheme also acts as a form of income support, since it includes a "fixed sum" for children in the calculation of housing allowances. Pensioner housing allowances in Sweden supplement the general pension system. Thus housing allowances for nonpensioners are directed at both housing and income support, while the housing supplement for pensioners primarily serves as income support.

In Britain, the aim of the Housing Benefit scheme is defined as helping people on low incomes to pay rent for accommodation that is reasonably priced and appropriate to the size of household. Implicitly, the scheme's primary role is to provide income support. It is administered by local authorities on behalf of the Department of Social Security, which is responsible for social policy. The scheme ensures that a household's net income after housing costs is at least equal to the social assistance benefit rates. Moreover, housing benefit is limited to households with incomes under or around the social assistance level (income support).[14] Even so, housing benefit is viewed as an important element of housing policy in Britain and, as such, is highly valued. Conversely, income support through mortgage interest payments to homeowners is regarded to be part of the social security system rather

Table 6-3. Role of Housing Allowances in Selected Countries

Country	Housing allowance or voucher scheme	Aims of scheme	Housing policy or social security instrument?
Australia	Rent assistance; rent rebates	Supplementary income; affordability	Income support; housing policy
New Zealand	Accommodation supplement	Affordability	Housing policy
Canada	Shelter allowances	Affordability; reduce demand for social housing	Housing policy
	Housing component of social assistance	Supplementary income	Income support
Germany	Wohngeld	Affordability of adequate housing	Housing policy, but increasingly income support
	Housing component of Sozialhilfe	Supplementary income	Income support
Netherlands	Individuele Huursubsidie	Affordability; housing adequacy; housing opportunity	Housing policy
Sweden	Housing allowances for nonpensioners	Affordability; housing adequacy; supplementary income	Housing policy
	Pensioners' housing allowance supplement	Supplementary income	Income support
Great Britain	Housing Benefit	Minimum income	Income support
	ISMI[a]	Minimum income	Income support

Source: Kemp, *A Comparative Study*, p. 57.
a. The ISMI program provides homeowners aged sixty or more with income support for the full amount of their mortgage interest payments (maximum is £100,000 of a mortgage loan).

than an instrument of housing policy, though it is recognized that both instruments have implications for the housing market.

Thus in most of the selected countries, housing allowances traditionally have been seen as an explicit housing policy instrument but are becoming more integrated with general social support. The situation in Britain stands out because housing allowances in that country are part of the social security system and effectively constitute an income support scheme; by definition, this is also true of the mortgage interest payments made to recipients of income support. Australia's rent assistance scheme is also an implicit form of income support. In other countries where social assistance includes a variable component for individual housing expenditure, this is regarded as income support.

There are considerable differences between the housing allowance systems in the countries discussed here. Kemp provides an elaborate overview, which we can summarize as follows:[15]

—Six of the seven countries operate national housing allowance schemes, with the exception of Canada, where such schemes exist in only five provinces.

—In all schemes, all renter households may apply for housing allowances; however, in Australia assistance is limited to renters on social security benefits, and in the five Canadian provinces eligibility is limited to elderly households, with the exception of Manitoba, where families are also eligible.

—Owner-occupiers are eligible for housing allowances in the Canadian province of Quebec (provided they are elderly), Germany, New Zealand, and Sweden; they are not eligible for assistance in Australia, the Netherlands, or Britain.

—In Canada, Germany, Sweden, and Britain (owner-occupiers only), social assistance payments are adjusted to include a component covering all or some of the housing costs of recipients.

—In all of the selected countries, except Britain, housing allowances take the form of "housing gap" schemes in which part of the difference between a set minimum rent and the actual rent (up to a rent ceiling or benefit maximum) is covered by the subsidy.

—The housing allowance scheme in Britain most resembles the housing component of social assistance schemes in the other selected countries.

—In Sweden and Britain especially, housing allowances cover a considerable percentage of rents or gross domestic product compared to the other countries. In Britain, this is because social assistance does not include a rent component, therefore housing allowances pertain to the full cost of rent; in

Sweden, a much greater proportion of households receive housing allowances than in other countries.

—Britain's housing allowance scheme provides much more assistance in proportion to the housing costs than other schemes. This is partly because of Britain's meager social security benefits for the unemployed compared to other countries, and again, because social assistance does not include a provision for rent.

—In Britain, entitlement to housing allowances is restricted to the lowest incomes, unlike in other countries; therefore it targets the poorest households more than elsewhere.

The countries also have different experiences regarding use, incentives, and eligible housing costs.[16] Kemp summarized the main findings on these topics as follows:

—The assessment of eligible costs varies in the selected countries; in some countries, gross rent is eligible for an allowance, while others ignore certain items; some countries include all homeowner costs in housing allowances (including capital repayments), while others cover interest payments only.

—Cost ceilings are used by all countries (though in Britain this only applies to the income support for homeowners aged sixty or more; in the Netherlands, renting a house over the ceiling amount disqualifies the tenant completely from any housing allowance, while in other countries, that part of the rent exceeding the ceiling is simply disregarded).

—Most countries set limits on the total housing allowance that may be granted.

—Regulations to investigate whether applicants' housing costs are excessive exist only in Britain and to a lesser extent in the Netherlands.

—Except in Britain, recipients are required to pay a minimum amount of the housing costs themselves; in some countries, however, social assistance schemes may cover all of a recipient's housing costs.

—The marginal subsidy rate varies; an increase in housing costs is only reimbursed in full in Britain and in some countries' social assistance schemes.

—Work incentives are regarded as a problem in some countries but not in others; the income taper on housing allowances in Britain is much steeper than in other countries (though social assistance schemes in some countries have a 100 percent withdrawal rate).

—There is little evidence of a stigma attached to housing allowances in any of the countries; the degree of awareness and concern about the use of such schemes varies.

Table 6-4. *Share of Households Receiving Housing Allowances,*
Selected Countries, 1993
Percent

Country	Share of households
Australia	16
New Zealand	13
Canada	<1
Germany	6
Netherlands	15
Sweden	27
Great Britain	19

Source: Kemp, *A Comparative Study,* p. 75.

—Landlords' attitudes toward housing allowance recipients also vary; in some countries, landlords are not likely to know whether or not tenants are on housing allowances.

Finally, table 6-4 gives an overview of the percentage of households receiving housing allowances in 1993 in each country. The differences are large, ranging from less than 1 percent in Canada to 27 percent in Sweden.

Questions about Housing Allowances and Housing Vouchers

Once a system of income-related subsidies has been chosen to alleviate housing affordability problems for households with a modest income, several other choices will have to be made to further develop a policy instrument (as shown in the previous section). In this section, we will discuss the most important policy questions.

Range of Available Housing

Should the system apply only to rented dwellings or to owner-occupied housing as well? With respect to rental housing, should the system apply only to social housing or also to private rentals?

If the regulation is to apply to various tenures, should the regulation make distinctions for the different tenures? The general aim should be tenure-neutral housing policy, and both rentals and owner-occupied housing should qualify for housing allowances. Nor is there reason to distinguish between social and private rentals. Nevertheless, home ownership is not the most obvious form of tenure in any country for those with a low income and little capital of their own. Governments therefore generally have far more experience with housing allowances for tenants than with housing allowances for owner-occupiers.

Forms of Housing

Should only those occupying housing in the strict sense (dwellings meeting the minimum standards) qualify for housing allowances or should other forms of housing (shared housing, bedsitters, houseboats, and so on) also qualify, as well as housing in poor physical condition?

In general, policymakers insist on providing housing allowances only to housing of acceptable quality and link housing allowances to (official) dwellings. Other forms of housing act as informal buffers to the housing market.

Household Range

Should each household with a high housing expenditure-to-income ratio qualify for housing allowances? What procedure should apply to households with subminimal incomes? Should a maximum income apply?

Usually a (legal) minimum income applies. Households with a subminimal income are primarily considered to have an income problem. Their housing problem comes secondary to that. Income problems could be alleviated through social security or negative income tax. Housing allowances for households at the other end of the income range miss their mark. Therefore most housing allowance systems have income ceilings. Finally, distinctions are usually made between households of different sizes (in relation to financial capacity) and sometimes of different ages (people aged sixty-five years and over are thought not to have much chance of improving their income situation).

Housing Expenses Definition

Rent may be defined as rent alone, rent and compulsory service charges (for example, elevator maintenance), or gross rent and other housing costs, such as heating. The sum may be based on current rent, the previous year's rent, or a standard, virtual rent.

Income may be defined as the breadwinner's income, breadwinner and spouse's combined income, or household income. The figure used to calculate entitlement may represent net, taxable, or gross income. Finally, entitlement may be based on the current year's income or the previous year's income.

It is easiest to take the current year's rent and the previous year's income, since an exact calculation of current income is often difficult to provide and to verify. Compulsory service charges may be included in the definition of rent. Income is usually defined as household income; after all, a household applies for a housing allowance as a unit. Financial capacity is preferably based on tax income. In the case of owner-occupied housing, housing allowances could be based on a home's rental value and any compulsory and unavoidable service charges.

Basis of Housing Allowances

Applications for housing allowances based on real rent must be made after the fact or else subtracted from the rent each month. In a supplier's market, this could have an undesirable impact on rents: landlords think they can get away with raising the rent, as tenants end up paying a reduced rent anyway. When housing allowances are based on standard rents, housing vouchers can be distributed beforehand (as in the United States). However, the downside of housing vouchers is that if real rent is (much) higher than the standard rent sum, tenants continue to have a housing affordability problem. The concluding section will go into this matter in more detail.

Application Frequency and Duration of Entitlement

Rents and household income change each year. A government's budget also varies from year to year. An annual housing subsidy application, entitlement granted for only a year at a time, thus appears the most logical choice. Property subsidies, however, provide long-term security, even in subsidized housing where the rents are adjusted each year.

System Implementation

Should the system be implemented centrally or regionally? By which organization? Does the system provide a budget or an entitlement?

The preceding section showed that most housing allowance schemes operate nationwide. Income data must be verified, and this is best done on the basis of revenue data. Thus housing allowances seem to lend themselves best to centralized implementation by a ministry for housing or by the revenue service. If implementation is delegated to, for example, the municipal authorities, an own-risk provision should be drawn up so that municipalities cannot allocate expensive housing to low-income families at the cost of the national budget. A budget ceiling could also be drawn up. However, there is a risk that households applying for housing allowances at the end of the year miss out simply because the budget has been spent. A budget ceiling may cause queues of applicants, as is the case in the United States.

If housing allowances are regarded as an entitlement, the scheme should be open-ended. But such schemes are by definition difficult to manage financially.[17] A private organization could also be charged with implementing the scheme. Whoever implements the scheme, however, the responsible authority will have to make sure of a watertight agreement.

Policy Instrument

Should housing allowances be regarded as a housing policy instrument or an income policy instrument? Different views of housing allowances exist in different countries.[18] (See table 6-3.) In the past, housing allowances were generally regarded as housing policy instruments. The housing ministry controlled expenditure through its entitlement policy and rent policy.

However, as housing policy becomes less restrictive and support for income support to owner-occupiers grows, housing allowances are shifting toward the domain of income policy, responding more and more to changes in income and costs of living. Increasingly, they are an instrument to combat poverty, moving from the housing ministry to the social security ministry.

Fraud Prevention

The simplest way of preventing abuse of the system is to verify stated income and rent and check up on household composition. This last aspect, however, is generally regarded as the Achilles heel of any housing allowance system as well as for the revenue system.

Regulation Design

A recurring question is: which part of excessive housing costs should qualify for compensation and within which margins? In some countries, standard rents apply; housing expenses over and above the standard rents are compensated for by means of subsidies. In that case, however, the government has no control whatsoever of household expenditure. In effect, households are encouraged to live it up at the government's cost. What's more, the threat of the poverty trap is greatest here: households benefit little from a rise in income.[19]

That is why most governments are moving away from rigid standard rents in favor of the direct-benefit principle. If people want to live in a house with a higher rent (and presumably a higher living quality), it is only reasonable that they should pay a greater net amount of rent. A maximum is set on rents qualifying for subsidy, and a so-called "quality reduction" is applied in the case of rents that exceed a basic rent level. Housing allowances do not cover the sum of the quality reduction; households wanting a higher quality of living must pay for this themselves.

Finally, governments have become wary of measures that negatively affect the job market, especially when it comes to young people. Generous housing subsidies are thought to weaken the incentive to work. Concern about this negative secondary effect of housing subsidies is greatest in Britain. Traditionally, this effect does not apply to pensioners, but for demographic and labor market reasons this may change in the future.

Concluding Remarks

In times of overall housing shortage, property subsidies are recommended as a temporary measure to increase supply. Housing allowances are the instrument of choice in "normal" situations, for both tenants and owner-occupiers. The direct benefit principle is recommended to limit the poverty trap effect. According to the direct benefit principle, net household expenditure for a household rises with rent and dwelling quality.

The advantages of housing allowances compared with property subsidies are that they do not distort the housing market so much, households retain considerable freedom of choice, and certain housing complexes are less likely to be stigmatized. The disadvantages are that they generally constitute open-end schemes, which are vulnerable to public budget cuts in hard times;[20] the costs of administering the scheme are relatively high, particularly in the private rental sector (compared to property subsidies); the effects on housing supply are unclear; fraud is difficult to combat; and a poverty trap cannot be avoided entirely.

This final section discusses three fundamental questions concerning housing allowances: are they primarily instruments of housing policy or income policy, should allowances be paid to the tenant or the landlord, and should support be provided beforehand or after the fact?

Housing Policy or Income Policy?

Housing allowances are shifting away from housing policy and becoming an instrument of income policy. As a housing policy instrument, the system is managed by the housing ministry; as part of income policy, it is managed by the social services or tax authority. Housing allowances, in which rent and household income are the two main variables, illustrate the overlap in housing policy and income policy.[21] High rents affect both a household's net buying power (after housing costs) and the housing supply and development of rents. Kemp pointed out that housing allowances should not be studied as an isolated instrument, but rather should be kept in the context of housing policy, tax regime, social security system, and even the welfare state.[22]

Payment to Tenant or Landlord?

Housing allowances usually entail cash payments to the landlord (lender) or tenant (homeowner). Sometimes housing allowances take the form of rent rebates in which the housing tenant is charged a rent reduced by the allowance sum.

In the Netherlands, *both* procedures apply: a tenant may choose whether he wishes to receive the housing allowances directly or whether he wants to pay a reduced rent to the landlord, who receives the subsidy. This appears to be a sensible approach.

Housing Support: Beforehand or After the Fact?

Mostly, households must have taken up a tenancy or bought a house before they can apply for a subsidy, since it is based on actual housing costs. This is referred to as a housing allowance after the fact. In the United States, applicants for the housing voucher scheme may apply for a voucher before finding accommodation, although actual payments are made to the landlord, and only for suitable accommodation. Within a given urban market (a submarket), the U.S. voucher is related to standardized rent rather than actual rent. (See the chapter by George Peterson in this volume.)

Which formula is better? If the value of a housing voucher has no relation to the actual gross rent, large variations in net rent and rent-to-income

ratios may persist. In an operational market where rent and housing quality are closely related, better quality is paid for in its entirety by households.
Housing vouchers of this kind are more market oriented than housing
allowances, which appear to be more policy oriented. Housing allowances
are usually only moderately related to quality differences. Thus, in a system
based on housing allowances after the fact, seniors with a low income just
might be able to afford an expensive nursing apartment, while the same
apartment would be unaffordable in a voucher system. It is hard to say
which system is better. In western Europe, most governments favor housing allowances after the fact. In the United States, preferences may differ.

Notes

1. See O. A. Papa, *Housing Systems in Europe: Part II. A Comparative Study
of Housing Finance,* (Delft University Press, 1992); and H. Priemus, *Housing
Allowances in the Netherlands: Product of a Conservative or Progressive Ideology?*
(Delft University Press, 1984).

2. H. Priemus, "How to Abolish Social Housing? The Dutch Case," *Inter-
national Journal of Urban and Regional Research,* vol. 19 (1995), pp. 145–55; and
H. Priemus, "Recent Changes in the Social Rented Sector in the Netherlands,"
Urban Studies, vol. 33, no. 10 (1996), pp. 1891–908.

3. P. A. Kemp, *A Comparative Study of Housing Allowances* (London:
HMSO, 1997).

4. Ibid., p. 15.

5. H. Priemus, "Housing Allowances in the Netherlands," in P. A. Kemp,
ed., *The Future of Housing Benefits* (Centre for Housing Research, University of
Glasgow, 1986), pp. 150–96.

6. Kemp, *A Comparative Study,* p. 17.

7. Ibid., p. 51.

8. Ibid., pp. 57–59.

9. J. Kuila, "Integrating Government Assistance for Accommodation,"
Social Policy Journal of New Zealand, vol. 1 (1993), pp. 44–50.

10. M. Steele, "A Model Success Story from the Provinces to a Fiscal
Calamity," mimeo (Toronto, 1995).

11. Ibid.; M. Steele, *Housing Allowances: An Econometric Analysis* (University
of Toronto Press, 1985); and M. Steele, *Housing Allowances: An Assessment of the
Proposal for a National Program for Canada* (Toronto: Canadian Home Builders'
Association, 1985).

12. See P. J. Boelhouwer, *De Individuele Huursubsidie en de Lokale
Woningtoewijzing* [Housing allowances and the local allocation of dwellings],
Volkshuisvestingsbeleid en Bouwmarkt 3 (Delft University Press, 1989); and

P. J. Boelhouwer, *De Individuele Huursubsidie en het Woningmarktgedrag van Huishoudens* [Housing allowances and the housing market behavior of households], Volkshuisvestingsbeleid en Bouwmarkt 4 (Delft University Press, 1989).

13. A. Buys and I. Mütter, *IHS in Perspectief. F. Verhuurders* [Housing allowances in perspective. F. Landlords] (Amsterdam: RIGO, 1994); R. Donninger, G. Dozeman, and M. Schellekens, *IHS in Perspectief. B. Samenhang met Terreinen van Volkshuisvestingsbeleid* [Housing allowances in perspective. B. Cohesion with areas of housing policy] (Amsterdam: RIGO, 1994); R. Donninger, G. Dozeman, J. van der Schaar, M. Schellekens, and A. Zandstra, *IHS in Perspectief. C. Constante Waarde in het Volkshuisvestingsbeleid* [Housing allowances in perspective. C. Constant value in housing policy] (Amsterdam: RIGO, 1994); M. G. Lijesen, "IHS, de Fiscale Behandeling van de Eigen Woning en de Werking van de Woningmarkt" [Housing allowances, fiscal aspects of homeownership and the functioning of the housing market] *Openbare Uitgaven*, vol. 4 (1994), pp. 154–63; J. Van der Schaar, *IHS in Perspectief. G. De Toekomst van het Instrument Individuele Huursubsidie* [Housing allowances in perspective. G. The future of housing allowances as policy instruments] (Amsterdam: RIGO, 1994); J. Van der Schaar and A. Zandstra, *IHS in Perspective. A. Besluitvorming Belicht* [Housing allowances in perspective. A. Decisionmaking processes clarified] (Amsterdam: RIGO, 1994); M. Schellekens, *IHS in Perspectief. E. In- En Uitstroom Huurders* [Housing allowances in perspective. E. Inflow and outflow tenants] (Amsterdam: RIGO, 1994); M. Schellekens and L. Leidelmeijer, *IHS in Perspectief. D. Gedrag van Huurders* [Housing allowances in perspective. D. Behavior of tenants] (Amsterdam: RIGO, 1994).

14. J. Hills, *Unraveling Housing Finance* (Oxford: Clarendon, 1991).

15. Kemp, *A Comparative Study*, pp. 61–91.

16. Ibid., pp. 92–107.

17. H. Priemus, "The Uncontrollability of the Housing Allowance," *Netherlands Journal of Housing and Environmental Research*, vol. 5, no. 2 (1990), pp. 169–80.

18. Kemp. *A Comparative Study*, p. 57.

19. P. A. Kemp, *Housing Benefit: Time for Reform* (York, U.K.: John Rowntree Foundation, 1998).

20. I. L. Ooms and O. A. Papa, *De Lange-Termijnontwikkeling van de Individuele Huursubsidie* [The long-term development of housing allowances], Volkshuisves-Tingsbeleid en Bouwmarkt 2 (Delft University Press, 1989); H. Priemus, "Improving or Endangering Housing Policies? Recent Changes in the Dutch Housing Allowance Scheme," *International Journal of Urban and Regional Research*, vol. 22, no. 2 (1998), pp. 319–30.

21. Kemp, *Housing Benefit*.

22. Kemp, *A Comparative Study*, p. 22; P. A. Kemp, "Housing Allowances and the Fiscal Crisis of the Welfare State," *Housing Studies*, vol. 9, no. 4 (1994), pp. 531–42.

DOUGLAS J. BESHAROV
NAZANIN SAMARI

7 *Child-Care Vouchers and Cash Payments*

B ETWEEN 1991 AND 1997, federally related support to
low-income families for child care more than doubled,
going from about $5.1 billion to about $10.7 billion (in 1998 dollars).
Since 1990 a portion of these funds have been subject to a requirement
that states give parents the option of receiving a child-care voucher, or "certificate." Currently, nearly half of these funds are subject to the voucher
requirement. Giving parents checks or cash is also allowed, and at least sixteen states and Puerto Rico do so, usually in the form of a check.

This chapter summarizes what is known about the use of vouchers and
cash to enable low-income parents to select the child-care providers of their
choice. It also makes some tentative judgments about the impact of vouchers and the operational issues that have arisen. Most of the other chapters
in this volume explore the differences between vouchers and government-
provided services (provided either directly or through grants and contracts). However, because all states already offer child-care vouchers, this
chapter focuses more on implementation experiences. In addition, because
some states are now making cash payments, this chapter also addresses the
relative advantages of vouchers versus cash payments.

Unfortunately, there is little systematic research on these subjects, so
major portions of this chapter are based on our own informal survey of

state officials and child-care providers, as well as on various indirect measures of program operations.[1]

Child-Care "Certificate"

Before the Family Support Act of 1988 was implemented, most federally subsidized child care was funded through the Social Services Block Grant (SSBG), Title XX of the Social Security Act. Under the SSBG, which is still law, states may fund various social service programs. About 20 percent of SSBG funds have traditionally been used for day care, which can be provided either directly by the state, through state-owned and operated centers, or indirectly, through grants and contracts for child-care "slots" with selected providers, including centers and licensed family day-care homes.[2]

Statutory Requirement

The Family Support Act of 1988 created two additional child-care funding streams: (1) AFDC/JOBS (Aid to Families with Dependent Children/Job Opportunities and Basic Skills Training Program) Child Care and (2) Transitional Child Care. Under both, states were authorized to operate their own centers and issue grants and contracts with private agencies. In a break from past rules, states were also *authorized* to give parents certificates (vouchers) or even cash (either in advance of payment or as subsequent reimbursement). Only a few states took advantage of this new authority to provide parents with vouchers or cash.

In 1990 Congress made child-care vouchers mandatory under the new Child Care and Development Block Grant (CCDBG). At the urging of Representatives Charles W. Stenholm (D-Tex.) and E. Clay Shaw Jr. (R-Fla.), the CCDBG required states to offer voucherlike "certificates." Child-care "certificates" were defined as "a certificate, check, or other disbursement that is issued . . . directly to a parent."[3] Of equal importance to the shape of state voucher systems is another provision of the same law that, in effect, guaranteed that the vouchers could be used for unlicensed child care.

In 1996 Congress applied these voucher-related provisions to the Child Care and Development Fund (CCDF), created under the Personal Responsibility and Work Opportunity Reconciliation Act (P.L. 104-193). This act repealed the legislative authority of three child-care programs related to the Aid to Families with Dependent Children program with differing program rules—At-Risk Child Care, AFDC/JOBS Child Care, and Transitional Child Care—and replaced them with the CCDF block grant.

Vouchers

Before the use of vouchers, once eligibility for child-care aid was established, parents were typically referred to an available center-based program, such as a community-based child-care program or Head Start, or to other providers, including family day-care homes, with which the state had a contract to provide services. Now that vouchers are required under federal law, all states offer them (or cash). In fact, as a U.S. Department of Health and Human Services (HHS) report concludes, "During the last few years, *certificate use has become the primary method of financing care.*"[4]

The form of vouchers varies by state, but most include the name of the provider chosen by the parent, the name of the child authorized to receive care, the hours of care authorized, the amount of reimbursement and parental co-payment, and an expiration date. Most often the authorization must be signed by the public assistance caseworker, the provider, and the parent. Providers usually submit to the government an invoice for the hours of care provided. The government then pays providers directly for their services and they are responsible for collecting any required parental co-payments.

Checks and Cash

As mentioned, since 1990 federal law has also authorized states to offer parents checks, cash, or other disbursements with which to pay for child care. Why?

According to Kristine Iverson, who worked on this provision as a senior aide to Senator Orrin Hatch (R-Utah), authorizing checks and cash was a response to state officials who were concerned about administering a voucher program. Grants and contracts seemed simpler to administer: states paid a limited number of providers a set amount to reserve space for subsidized children, and parents needing care were simply referred to the providers. In contrast, vouchers required a whole new payment apparatus capable of receiving and processing hundreds or thousands of individual payments in a confusing array of amounts to an almost unlimited number of providers. (As will be discussed below, this proved to be an initial challenge in some places.) Allowing states to use checks was thought to make the process much simpler to administer because it takes one step out of the process: the state would give a check to the parents who would then be responsible for paying providers.[5]

According to our telephone survey, at least sixteen states and Puerto Rico issue checks or cash to parents.[6] Thirteen states and Puerto Rico issue one-party checks, although two of those states, Alaska and Kansas, are issuing checks only as pilot programs to test their feasibility. At least two of these states issue two-party checks, which must be coendorsed by the parent and the child-care provider, and one state, Utah, makes a cash transfer to the parents' bank account.

States differ in the circumstances under which they will provide checks or cash. Some states provide checks or cash to any income-eligible family, regardless of welfare participation, for any type of care (center-based, family, or relative-provided care). Other states, such as Pennsylvania and Alaska, distinguish between welfare and nonwelfare families. In Pennsylvania, welfare families receive checks for all types of child care, but nonwelfare income-eligible families receive checks only to pay for informal care. Alaska offers checks only to nonwelfare, income-eligible families, which may use the subsidy to purchase any kind of care.

Some states issue checks only for relative-provided care (for example, Indiana, New Mexico, New York, and North Carolina). Others offer checks as reimbursement to parents only for emergency child-care arrangements made when a parent's primary arrangement falls through unexpectedly (for example, Missouri and Wisconsin).

Implementation

For a voucher system to work, the state must have a system for smoothly processing hundreds or thousands of vouchers. In broad outline, this means preparing individual authorizations in almost infinite variation, receiving payment requests from an uncounted number of providers, and then issuing hundreds or thousands of checks a month—all in specific amounts, depending on the amount and type of child care provided and the parents' required co-payment, if any. No wonder the states had lobbied for the right to issue checks.

It appears that some states had difficulty at least in the start-up phases of voucher systems. The initial unpreparedness of state agencies, complicated and confusing program rules, and miscommunication between agencies all resulted in late, withheld, or inaccurate payments. In almost all communities, such administrative problems seem to get worked out in relatively short order and there is no evidence that these were more than passing problems during the early stages of implementation.[7]

Otherwise, implementation seems to have gone smoothly. However, the basis of this conclusion is a little like the mouse who did not roar: neither the child-care literature nor child-care advocates complain about the implementation of voucher systems. Instead, generalized accounts are seen of successful implementation, with the partial exception of some providers not always being paid by parents, as described below.[8]

Controlling Costs

In grant and contract systems, aggregate child-care costs are controlled by the number and size of grants and contracts awarded. Per-child prices are set through the government's agency-by-agency negotiation of rates. Often these arrangements provide far fewer slots than are needed by income-eligible families, in which case rationing is accomplished by allowing agency-level waiting lists to develop. Total costs are also kept down by low participation rates by parents, who are often unhappy with the choices they are given.

In voucher systems, it is more difficult to provide less than full coverage for income-eligible families. In grant and contract systems, the central authority's rationing need not be explicit and can therefore be relatively invisible. In voucher systems, however, if funds do not exist to provide vouchers for all those formally eligible, there must be explicit rationing. The central political authority, in a relatively visible manner, must decide who gets the voucher, what service is provided, and so forth. Hence, voucher systems make it politically more difficult to provide fewer slots than there are eligible children. In addition, because vouchers give parents more choice of providers, they are more likely to use available child-care benefits, including payments for services that were once provided free by friends and relatives.

This makes controlling per-child costs even more important in voucher systems. The government, however, cannot negotiate directly with providers, because it is the parent, not the government, who selects the provider from a broad range of potential providers (with substantially different cost and price structures). Thus, under voucher systems, states seek to control per-child costs by instituting (1) calibrated reimbursement schedules that are meant to cap payment levels, depending on the type of care, and (2) co-payment requirements that are meant to create price-sensitive shoppers.

Calibrated Reimbursement Schedules

The applicable federal law originally required states to offer payment rates based on the 75th percentile of local market rates (that is, equal to or above the rate that 75 percent of local providers charge). But because of local conditions, this national standard was too high in some communities and too low in others. The 1996 CCDF lifted this requirement. About twenty-nine states and jurisdictions have used this freedom to set lower rates.[9] This seems to make sense.

Payment rates have to reflect the conditions of the local market for child care. If the rates are too low, providers will not accept publicly subsidized families or will cut back on the scope or quality of their services. If they are too high, providers will raise prices without necessarily benefiting the family or the government, and, if enough children are involved, overall market prices may rise. Or providers may give illegal rebates to subsidized families, as discussed in a later section, or they may attempt to price discriminate, setting a lower price for parents without subsidies.

The latter situation apparently occurred in Alabama and Connecticut. Officials in both states report that some providers in their states offered hefty discounts from their published rates for families not receiving government aid. (The mechanism for discriminating between the two was to offer the discount to parents who paid in advance or by a certain date.) Thus state funds for low-income families were essentially subsidizing more affluent families or increasing profits for providers.[10] In Wisconsin, state officials tried to reduce this problem by requiring providers to post their payment rates and practices and to report them to the state agency administering child-care subsidies.

Moreover, payment rates also need to take into account price differentials among different types of providers. Centers, licensed family day-care homes, and unlicensed care each have different cost and price structures. For example, according to the Survey of Income and Program Participation (SIPP), in 1993 the average weekly full-time child-care payments by families with preschoolers were $63.58 for center-based care, $51.52 for family day care, and $42.04 for relative-provided care.[11]

Co-Payments

All states impose some sort of co-payment, at least for those families toward the upper end of income eligibility, as required by the CCDBG (which allows exemptions for low income). According to the HHS Child Care Bureau, in twenty-two states and jurisdictions, co-payments can exceed 10 percent of family income.[12]

One purpose of co-payments is to make parents price sensitive by having them pay more for higher-priced care and less for lower-cost care. As with reimbursement schedules, states must be careful not to set co-payment rates too high, lest they discourage the use of child care or encourage the use of inadequate child care, nor too low, lest they have no effect on parental decisionmaking.

Thirty-two states and jurisdictions set specific co-payment amounts based on family income. They range from a minimum of $8 a month per child for families below the federal poverty level in Wyoming to a maximum of $491 a month for families at the high end of the sliding scale in Minnesota. Two states (Maine and Virginia) set the co-payment as a percentage of family income. In Maine, families pay between 2 and 10 percent of their income, according to a sliding scale. In Virginia, families pay between 10 and 12 percent of their gross income, depending on the number of children they have, although some families below the federal poverty line are exempted. Fourteen states and jurisdictions charge a percentage of the cost of care, ranging from Vermont's 1 percent to Idaho's maximum of 90 percent for families at the high end of the income scale. Three states and the District of Columbia use a combination of these approaches.[13]

There is widespread anecdotal evidence that some parents have difficulty making their co-payments. It is not clear whether their nonpayment is caused by the inability to pay, a desire to pay for other things, or simple neglect or inattention. The seriousness of the problem is also difficult to gauge. Apparently, no state systematically collects information on the subject. In any event, parental nonpayment does not seem to have been a serious enough problem for any state to have taken concerted corrective action, although some states have attempted to improve payment rates by lowering co-payment rates.

Substitution and Monetization

Most low-income parents have traditionally relied on other household members for child care, as well as on friends, neighbors, and relatives, who provide it free or at low cost. For example, as late as 1994, over half of the children in families with incomes up to 150 percent of poverty were in relative-provided care—even when the mother worked full time.

One of the reasons many income-eligible parents did not take advantage of child-care subsidies (before vouchers) was because the subsidies were only for center-based care, which the parents either did not want or found inconveniently located. Or the parents worked part time and could not find a contracted-for provider who would take their children only part time. Often, they just paid for the care themselves.

Vouchers, and especially vouchers to unlicensed providers, remove these barriers to accepting child-care assistance—because most voucher systems enable parents to use a wider array of informal providers, including friends, relatives, and neighbors. Thus to some unmeasured but undoubtedly large degree, vouchers have resulted in both the substitution of government spending for parental spending and the monetization (at the full market price) of services that were once provided for free or at low cost.[14] To quote one Alabama official, "once child-care money was available, grandma wouldn't do it for free."

Of course, from a social cost point of view, grandma never did it "for free." But that is a different issue. In addition, it appears that many of these informal providers are turning back to the parents some portion of the voucher's value. (More on this in the last section.)

How large an issue is this? No one knows for sure, but consider the following: In 1993 there were about 135,000 paid relative-provided care arrangements for poor children, for which payments totaled an estimated $423 million. In addition, there were about 295,000 unpaid relative-provided care arrangements. If the government had paid for the care of all the poor children now being cared for by relatives, the annual cost would have been $1.3 billion—more than three times actual expenditures. This rough estimate, based on 1993 data, is only meant to suggest the potential amount of monetization. It does not reflect the large increase in the number of children in child care brought on by welfare reform, nor does it include likely price increases caused by the newly or more easily available subsidies for relative-provided care.

The issue of monetization has taken on sufficient momentum that officials in some states are considering whether to prohibit the use of vouchers for family members. Wisconsin already prohibits the use of vouchers for relatives who live in the child's home. In addition, regardless of training, relatives are not eligible to receive the higher reimbursement rates that Wisconsin offers to providers who have completed training in child development, unless they are also caring for unrelated children. In New York City, officials are considering whether to eliminate reimbursement for relative-provided care entirely.

Child-Care Market

Just about all experts agree that a functioning, diverse market for child-care services has existed for some time. Not every service has been available for all families. Infant care, for example, is a long-standing problem. But by and large, supply seems to meet demand (and more so, actually), parents seem to act like price-sensitive consumers, and child-care agencies seem to compete for customers. What has happened with the introduction of vouchers?

More Choices

For their proponents, one of the great advantages of vouchers is that they have vastly broadened parental choice. In the years since vouchers were introduced, there has been an unprecedented increase in the number and variety of providers now available to low-income families receiving child-care assistance. Based on a 1993 study of child-care agencies in fifteen states, for example, Christine Ross and Stuart Kerachsky of Mathematica Policy Research describe how, by "using vouchers, parents can shape the child care market to provide more of the types and features of child care that they want. Vouchers expand parents' choice of providers to include relatives and informal providers—persons who are generally not included in contract systems."[15]

Some parents need only half-day care; some need evening or after-hours care; and others need full-day care, perhaps with extended hours. Some parents want their children cared for by other family members; some want to use neighbors; others want a nursery school; and still others want a care center, perhaps in a church. Some parents may want all their children of different ages in one place; others may not care. Some parents will want their children close to home; others will want them close to work. The variations are almost infinite.

Under a grant or contract system, it is a practical impossibility for public authorities to enter into contracts or make grants that cover all these possibilities. Vouchers, however, can accommodate such variation with relative ease.

There is also some evidence that vouchers have reduced the economic (and racial) segregation of clients inherent in programs based on grants and contracts. For reasons of administrative practicality, under a grant or contract system there is a tendency to fund only those providers that serve a large number of economically disadvantaged families or that are located in neighborhoods where such families predominate. These facilities then become de facto segregated by income—and often by race. In one of the few studies on the subject, Yale professor of law and public policy Susan Rose-Ackerman analyzed the use of grants and contracts for subsidized day care in the 1970s and early 1980s. She concluded that "the level of segregation by race and class is high under existing programs."[16]

Vouchers remove the government's inadvertent role in fostering this level of economic and racial segregation, because they decentralize the decisionmaking process. Giovanna Stark, president of Government Action and Communication (GAC), a consulting group, and former executive director of California's Child Development Policy Advisory Committee, explains, "Vouchers can result in mixing children from different economic backgrounds. The more socioeconomic integration there is in a residential community or an employment center, the more useful vouchers are in allowing that larger integration to be reflected within a child care setting."[17] Of course, the agencies or firms serving the middle class must be willing to accept the voucher.

Increased Supply

The expanded use of vouchers happens to have coincided with a major increase in the demand for child care. By almost all accounts, the supply of child care easily expanded in response to this increased demand.

If the supply of providers had not risen to meet this increase in demand, all other things being equal, the price of child care could have been expected to increase. There apparently is no evidence of widespread price increases.[18] Thus a December 1997 report by the President's Council of Economic Advisers that examined the effect of subsidies on the cost of child care concluded that "the available evidence indicates that the supply of care will rise to meet an increase in demand for care without much of a change in the current price. For example, although the number of children in paid care has approximately doubled over the past twenty years, the real price of care has not changed. In addition, direct estimates indicate that small changes in the price of child care induce large supply responses. As a result, in the absence of other changes, the benefits of a subsidy accrue to the consumer."[19]

The existence of a functioning, decentralized market for child-care services—with relatively low barriers to entry, especially for family day care—has contributed to the apparently easy expansion of child-care slots. Unlike some of the other program areas considered in this volume, before the widespread introduction of vouchers, the government did not maintain a near monopoly on services (as in the case for elementary and secondary schools, for example). Instead, there was a plethora of formal and informal, for-profit and not-for-profit providers.

Vouchers seem to have facilitated the market's response. They allowed parents to go directly to providers, especially informal providers, that had vacancies or that could expand to meet the increased demand, thus avoiding a cumbersome, slow-moving contract and grant-making process. For center providers as well, vouchers have greatly reduced the paperwork and other administrative tasks related to serving subsidized clients. The director of a center in Boston noted that contracts with the state to purchase slots required the completion of over fifty pages of forms each year. Establishing eligibility to serve clients with vouchers, conversely, only required the completion of a five-page form each year.

Competition for Customers

In theory, vouchers should also improve the quality of child-care services. "Customer-driven systems force service providers to be accountable to their customers," argue David Osborne and Ted Gaebler in their influential book *Reinventing Government*.[20] Service providers need to win the patronage of the clients they are meant to serve, in both senses of the word. Vouchers also make it easier to defund obviously unsuccessful or unsatisfactory programs—because recipients will simply stop selecting them.[21]

Moreover, in a market with a substantial proportion of voucher holders, providers would be expected to compete for customers by tailoring services to their needs and preferences. That is what seems to have happened in inner-city Milwaukee under the Wisconsin voucher system.

Wisconsin's system, revised to accommodate its welfare reform program (W-2), opened up the entire child-care market to voucher holders, who, because of the required co-payment, were also encouraged to be price sensitive. At the same time, Wisconsin's welfare reform, which paired a guaranteed child-care subsidy with a requirement for all able-bodied recipients to work or participate in a work preparation activity, expanded the child-care market with a flood of voucher-holding parents seeking child care.

The question was: Which child-care providers would the W-2 parents choose? In inner-city Milwaukee, a coalition of about sixty inner-city providers, Day Care Advocates of Milwaukee (DCAM), decided to compete against lower-cost family day-care homes and unlicensed providers by offering enhanced services geared to the needs of W-2 participants. With the help of foundation grants, the DCAM members expanded their services to meet the needs of working mothers as well as their children. These services included extended-hours care plus meals; psychological, cognitive, and social development testing; stress management and employment counseling; parenting and nutrition classes; teen-parent centers; help with W-2 requirements; and family advocacy.[22]

How unusual is it for centers to offer these enhanced services? In 1990 Mathematica Policy Research conducted a national survey of 1,581 child-care centers, 231 Head Start programs, and 583 family day-care homes.[23] According to the survey, only about one-third of the centers in the national survey offered physical exams and psychological, cognitive, and social development testing (presumably mostly the Head Start centers)—compared to about 60 percent of DCAM centers. More telling was the absence of work-related services. For example, only 3 percent of the centers in the national sample provided dinner, compared to 20 percent of DCAM centers.

It remains to be seen whether this kind of provider response will occur in other places. Milwaukee enjoyed a unique combination of carefully crafted policy, supportive foundations that funded the initial expansion of services, and DCAM's coalition of savvy and caring inner-city providers.[24] Moreover, DCAM's grass-roots providers served the neighborhoods that were the heart of welfare reform. Between 80 and 90 percent of its clients were in W-2. So their decision to focus on W-2 recipients should not have been surprising. Nevertheless, the Milwaukee example does reveal the promise of bottom-up, market-driven approaches fueled by vouchers.

The "Problem" of Unlicensed Care

Vouchers have made government aid available for unlicensed child care because of the federal mandate mentioned above. As a result, reports the HHS inspector general, "Approximately half of parents using certificates obtain care from informal providers—neighbors or relatives. Most of these informal providers are license-exempt—they operate legally outside of the states' regulatory framework."[25]

Incentives for Lower-Cost Care

Many child-care experts believe that parents are being forced into home-based and unlicensed child care—through low reimbursement rates and high co-payment requirements that encourage parents to seek low-cost care. And they worry about the quality of such child care.

In Wisconsin, for example, a family at the federal poverty level with two children in care must pay $112.58 a month in co-payments for licensed care, compared to $77.94 a month in co-payments for unlicensed care. In fourteen other states, co-payments are determined as a percentage of the cost of care. Since unlicensed, informal care is significantly less expensive than licensed care, this creates a strong incentive for parents to seek lower-cost, informal care.

Thus state voucher systems can create strong incentives for parents to use less expensive care, which generally means unlicensed, home-based care. In many states, these informal providers may not even be subject to government health and safety regulations.

The evidence is mixed, however, about whether these incentives actually change many parental decisions. Even in states where the co-payment is based on a straight percentage of family income regardless of the cost of the care, parents seem to be choosing informal care in accord with their pre-existing preferences. For regardless of family income, informal, home-based care is the most common form of child care for all children under age five. A total of 70 percent of the children of all working mothers are in home-based care, which encompasses care by all relatives (including fathers), in-home babysitters or nannies, and family day care.[26] This overall statistic, however, obscures very real differences in parental preferences based on the child's age and developmental needs.

Parents tend to prefer informal or home-based care for younger children, that is, infants and toddlers. The picture changes sharply for three- and four-year-olds. Parents tend to prefer center-based programs for older children because of their emphasis on cognitive and social development and structured educational curriculums. Ellen Kisker and Rebecca Maynard, in their study of quality, cost, and parental choice in child care, report that parents with older children in care are highly concerned about "whether the environment promotes learning."[27] One-third of the mothers they surveyed reported that they would change arrangements if cost was not a factor; "most of these mothers would prefer center-based care for their child because [they think that] the child would have better learning opportunities."[28]

If cost were no object, more low-income as well as lower-middle-class parents would probably use high-cost, center-based care, especially for their older preschoolers. For example, the 1990 National Child Care Survey asked parents two questions to gauge their child-care preferences:

(1) "How satisfied are you with your [current arrangement]?" and (2) "Assuming you could have any type or combination of care arrangements . . . would you prefer some other type or combination of types instead of what you have now?" A total of 96 percent of the respondents reported being either "very satisfied" or "satisfied." Despite this high rate of satisfaction, 26 percent of the parents said they would "prefer some other type" of care, and about half of these parents said they wanted to switch to center-based care.[29]

This apparent preference, however, should be interpreted with care. First, we do not know the age of the children involved, which could be significant, as parents tend to prefer centers for older children. Second, parents were asked what child-care arrangement they would "prefer," suggesting that cost should not be a factor. This is like asking "If I gave you a car for free, which would you prefer, a Chevrolet or a Cadillac?" When given a free choice between goods with such different prices, one would expect consumers to choose the higher-priced good, because they think price indicates product quality or because they want to maximize the value of what is being given to them for free.

Nevertheless, it is undoubtedly the case that, if given free access to the most expensive, center-based child care, many parents would accept it, at least for their older children. Thus the question is: Is licensed family day care and center-based care sufficiently better for children that taxpayer funds should be used to fund them? Surprisingly little evidence suggests that they are.

Nonenforcement of Licensing Standards

The argument in favor of licensed care presupposes that licensing standards are enforced. Enforcement, however, seems uneven at best. David Blau and Naci Mocan, for example, examined detailed data on the characteristics of quality that are regulated and the child-care environment from a random sample of 400 day-care centers in four states collected in 1993 as part of the Cost, Quality, and Child Outcomes in Child Care Centers (CQCO) study. Blau and Mocan concluded that

> if regulations affected the behavior of centers, then [they] would expect to find many centers with a group size and/or child staff ratio at or close to the regulation. However, the great bulk of firms substantially exceed the regulations (i.e. they have a group size smaller

than the regulated maximum, and a staff-child ratio higher than the regulated maximum), suggesting that the regulations are not binding. Those firms that do not exceed the regulation are often well below it (or above, in the case of group size). This suggests that not only are the regulations not binding, but they are not strictly enforced, either.[30]

Does Licensing Improve Child Outcomes?

One of the major assumptions in the child-care field is that the standards of care that professional and advocacy organizations propound (often called "quality" standards) lead to better physical, emotional, and cognitive outcomes for children. As a general principle, this makes sense. The way children are cared for during the day ought to affect their development. The existing research, however, provides no persuasive evidence that the characteristics of child care that can be effectively regulated result in better outcomes for children.

Studies that have attempted to evaluate the effects of child-care quality on child outcomes have come to inconsistent and contradictory conclusions. Findings vary by age of the child, child-care arrangement, and outcomes examined. Some studies find no correlation between characteristics subject to regulation (such as staff-to-child ratios, staff training, and group size) and child outcomes (such as social and cognitive development); others find small correlations between some characteristics and some outcomes for some groups of children.[31] As Ron Haskins writes, one "problem with studies of child care quality is that the observed correlations are modest and nearly all the studies are short-term."[32]

Not only are the correlations small, but they are plagued with unresolved questions of selection bias. That is, they cannot adequately control for family background or child characteristics, which also strongly influence child development as well as the choice of provider.[33] Ellen Kisker and Rebecca Maynard, for example, after reviewing much of the available literature on characteristics of child-care quality and child outcomes, concluded that "due to the limitations of the research showing that these characteristics of care are associated with child development outcomes, the levels of these indicators of quality that constitute acceptable, good quality care have not been well established . . . there is no strong empirical basis for suggesting particular thresholds for each of the child care quality indicators."[34]

The lack of definitive findings in this large body of research should not be overinterpreted. It is unlikely that the "quality" of child care is irrelevant to child development. It must matter what kind of environment a child is in for many hours of the day. There are at least two possible explanations for the absence of clear research results: either impacts cannot be measured using current research tools (perhaps because the qualitative differences among programs are not as great as supposed) or the characteristics of child care that lead to good child outcomes are not those subject to regulation. As Sandra Scarr concludes, "regulations affect actual quality of care only tangentially. . . . States cannot legislate warm, sensitive interactions or rich learning opportunities provided by talented teachers. Therefore, regulations that directly produce higher costs improve quality of care only indirectly."[35]

The point is that current research is simply too slender a reed for aggressive policymaking, especially given the inarguable costs of regulation. Even home-based care is substantially more expensive when it is licensed. Although estimates vary and undoubtedly depend on the types of care provided, regulated home-based child care costs from 10 to 30 percent more than unregulated care.[36] William Gormley, a professor of government and public policy at Georgetown University, surveyed local regulation in cities with populations greater than 50,000 and "found extensive local regulation of relatively small family day care homes. For example, family day care providers who care for six children are required to have a business license in 39 percent of these cities; an occupancy permit in 43 percent; and a zoning permit in 28 percent."[37] In his study of family day-care home regulation in Milwaukee County, Wisconsin, Gormley "found cost increases directly attributable to regulation. The cost of home improvements alone was $936 per provider."[38]

Besides raising costs for parents (or government), Gormley found that these regulatory burdens reduced the supply of family day-care homes. He found that regulation was responsible both for declines in the growth of new licensed providers and for declines in the actual numbers of licensed providers of family day care.[39]

Vouchers versus Cash

As mentioned above, about sixteen states and Puerto Rico give parents checks and cash instead of vouchers. Thirteen of these states and Puerto

Rico issue one-party checks, two issue two-party checks, and one makes a cash transfer to the parents' bank account. Since two-party checks are more like vouchers than cash, this discussion is largely about one-party checks and cash transfers.

Even More Parental Choice

A major reason for allowing states to use cash payments was concern over the difficulty of administering voucher systems. But cash subsidies have another benefit: they seem to increase parental options by widening their choice of providers.

First, some states are unwilling to directly support unlicensed care. They seem worried that honoring vouchers from unlicensed child-care providers might be interpreted as endorsing the particular provider, which could be an embarrassment should there be a problem later. Cash payments to the parents thus insulate the state from criticism if a provider is subsequently found to be inadequate or worse.[40]

Second, like food stamps, there is some stigma associated with child-care vouchers. Some providers do not want to serve present or even former welfare recipients. Cash assistance prevents the provider—and other families—from knowing that the family is receiving government aid. That also tends to prevent providers from overcharging subsidized clients or engaging in cross-subsidization.

Cathie Pappas, Utah's block grant administrator for child care, believes that her state's replacement of its voucher system with a cash payment system not only greatly increased parents' flexibility in choosing care, but has also reduced fraud committed by providers. (Previously, Utah paid providers directly, and providers would often accept payment and continue billing the state even if the subsidized parent had not been receiving care or received fewer hours of care than the amount subsidized.)[41]

Conversely, knowing that parents are receiving their child-care assistance in cash may make some providers unwilling to serve them—for fear that they will not pay their bills. Several states reported that some providers were refusing to serve clients with cash or check subsidies for fear they would not be paid on time. States such as Alaska, Kansas, and Utah have tried to ameliorate this problem by eliminating three-way payment agreements that required signatures from the parent, provider, and caseworker. Payment agreements are now made between the parent and the caseworker only. That way providers no longer know which parents are receiving subsidies.

Ensuring Parental Payments

These cash payments to parents through either one-party checks or bank transfers are in direct opposition to an HHS "strong" recommendation to the states.

> We strongly discourage a cash system, because providers must meet health and safety standards, and we believe that the use of cash can severely curtail the Lead Agency's ability to conform with this statutory requirement. If, nevertheless, a Lead Agency chooses to provide cash, it must be able to demonstrate that: (1) CCDF funds provided to parents are spent in conformity with the goals of the child care program as stated at section 658A of the Act, i.e., that the money is used for child care; and (2) that child care providers meet all applicable licensing and health and safety standards, as required by section 658E(c)(2) (E) and (F) of the Act. Lead Agencies, therefore, may wish to consider having parents who receive cash attest that the funds were used for child care and to identify the provider. Such a statement would help assure that the funds were expended as intended by the statute and lessen the possibilities for fraud. Finally, Lead Agencies are reminded that they must establish procedures to ensure that all providers, including those receiving cash payments from parents, meet applicable health and safety standards.[42]

Left unsaid in the HHS comment, of course, is the fear that parents may misuse the money. One danger is that they will either leave the children home, unattended, or that they will use grievously inadequate caretakers. No state, however, reported this as a serious or substantial problem.

The other danger is that parents will arrange child care but not pay for it. Although there are no estimates of the prevalence of nonpayment, this was a problem reported by some states. The providers then complained to the state. But the state, having already issued a payment to the parents, could not issue the same payment twice. The states then undertook the difficult, time-consuming, and often unsuccessful effort to recover payment from the parents. For this reason, Alabama and Connecticut are both in the process of phasing out their cash programs; Arizona and Nevada have already terminated theirs.[43]

In all states that give cash, therefore, monitoring parental payments is an important issue. All states require the parent to present a receipt indicating how the provider can be contacted, the hours of care used, the payment rate, and the amount paid. This can even be a handwritten note from an informal provider. In Kansas, for example, the parent must present a receipt for child care received and paid for each month in order to get the next month's subsidy. Some states also require that both parents and providers sign the receipt. Other states, such as Colorado, issue three-party payment agreements between the parent, provider, and agency that define the type of care and the amount of the subsidy.

States also have adopted a variety of sanctions for parents who fail to present a receipt for services, or for parents who use less care than provided by the cash subsidy and pocket the rest. Some states reduce the next month's subsidy by the amount unaccounted for; others terminate the subsidy until the parent reimburses the state for the amount unaccounted for or produces a receipt. In some states, repeated problems may result in parents losing their eligibility to participate in the program.

Forced Consumption versus True Cash Out

As we have seen, the diversity of the child-care market and of parental needs for care mean that the price of care can vary widely—even in the same community. Moreover, the evidence suggests that parents are in a better position to judge the quality of care and are much better positioned to obtain a lower price than is the government.

What happens when the actual price of child care is substantially below the value of the cash payment to the parent so that the parent might be able to bargain for a lower payment? This often is the case with informal care, but it is also possible in regard to center care. Or what happens if the caretaker is a good friend or relative who is willing to take less money so that the family has more? In both situations, the parent may be tempted to keep the difference.

Call it a rebate, a kickback, or a side payment, the dynamic is the same: the value of the voucher exceeds what the parent must spend to obtain child care—and the provider is willing to return at least some of this excess payment to the parent. As we saw, one way to deal with this problem is to have a three-tiered price structure—for center-based care, licensed family day care, and unlicensed care. That helps. But given the vast array of providers and the different needs of parents, the government cannot set the one right price for each tier of child care, because there is none. That is why states also impose co-payments.

The plain fact, however, is that many parents simply would not want to consume as much child care as the government apparently wants them to spend. Consider a close parallel: the thriving black market for food stamps.[44]

No one knows the extent of informal child-care rebates. Many state officials seem to be going along with, or at least taking no action to curtail, them. These side payments are most easily made when the parties are close and the child-care subsidy is in the form of a one-party check. But they seem to occur even when a two-party check or an actual voucher is used, and even when the parent and provider are strangers. It is only that the transaction seems more natural and hence more likely when it is the parent holding the cash.

This is an entirely understandable process, and, unless the parents are using terribly inadequate caregivers, it ought to be legal. Just give the parents money and make them responsible for finding child care for their children. Besides recognizing the inevitable, there is otherwise no incentive for parents who do not face a co-payment to select a low-cost provider.

There is a precedent for cashing out child-care expenses, and a pretty good one: the now-defunct Aid to Families with Dependent Children dependent care disregard, which was offered to parents combining work with AFDC payments. The disregard allowed for the offsetting of parents' work-related child-care expenses up to $175 a month for each child age two or older, and up to $200 a month for each child less than two years old. The disregard reduced parents' "countable earned income," which increased their AFDC grant amount.[45] Parents could claim the disregard for any kind of child care, including relative-provided care. Parents were required to present receipts for child care purchased, and, in the case of relative-provided care, the receipt could be a note designating the hours of care used and the amount paid. In 1996, the last year of the program, 73,351 families claimed an average of $183.69 a month in child-care fees. Total federal expenditures were $162 million in 1996.[46]

The public, however, may not be ready for such a radical idea as a full cash out of child-care benefits. There is a less extreme alternative.

Refundable Vouchers?

If simple cash payments are politically unattainable, or if society determines that it wants to encourage a level of child-care consumption higher than parents would otherwise want, consideration should nevertheless be given to making vouchers refundable.

Recipients who can pocket the difference between a lower-cost provider and the dollar value of the voucher have a strong incentive to be cost conscious. Indeed, refundability may be the only way to create cost consciousness among recipients whose incomes are too low to impose a co-payment of any meaningful size.

Actually, the idea of refundability is not that radical. For many years, the United States has offered a refundable education voucher to service members and veterans. Authorized by what is commonly referred to as the GI Bill and administered by the Department of Veterans Affairs, the federal government currently provides $528 a month to service members and veterans pursuing education or vocational training. Eligibility is based on months of service—to receive thirty-six months of benefits (four academic years), participants must serve at least forty months of a forty-eight-month enlistment or thirty months of a thirty-six-month enlistment.

The voucher is for tuition and living expenses, and full-time participants receive $528 a month regardless of whether they choose to attend a private or public college or university or a vocational training program. The amount is adjusted depending on hours in school. If the student attends an institution for which tuition is less than $528 a month, students can keep the difference and attribute it to living expenses.[47]

Section 8 housing vouchers also have an aspect of refundability. "If a household can find an acceptable unit renting for less than [the amount of the voucher], it can keep the difference."[48] In essence, refundability is a reality when there is (or can be) a black market for the vouchers, such as with the food stamp program. And it can also develop in those systems, such as child care and housing, in which the recipient and the provider can agree to what is essentially a kickback, legal or otherwise.

Voter resistance to refundable vouchers would, nevertheless, probably be substantial. In an innovative response, John Hood of the Reason Public Policy Institute has proposed that recipients "have the option of depositing any part of the [medical] voucher not spent on medical insurance or care not only into medical savings accounts but also in educational savings accounts, from which they could make withdrawals for their or their children's education, or individual development accounts, from which they could make withdrawals for housing, transportation, or other approved expenditures to help get themselves off public assistance."[49] The idea is particularly apt for medical vouchers, since they would be so large and the possible price reductions through competition so great. But this concept of modified refundability could be applied to other areas as well, such as food stamps.

One other possibility is the kind of bundled voucher recommended by Robert Lerman and C. Eugene Steuerle in this volume. They propose grouping together voucher amounts for several services to offer families "structured choice." Using this approach, "recipients can use a voucher in choosing from an expanded, though still limited, set of goods and services. . . . A broad form of structured choice would involve a voucher that could pay for a wide variety of goods and services, such as food, housing, education, child care, moving allowances for new jobs, and transportation. A narrow form might include only a couple of services, such as child care and transportation." Bundled vouchers offer recipients a wider range of choices, by deciding how much to spend on each service, while still targeting the financial assistance to certain goods and services.

Some may argue that it is not necessary to make vouchers formally refundable, because parents who really want to can work around the system. This makes them criminals, however, under highly questionable circumstances. (We recognize that providing refundable vouchers, or cash for that matter, may give a windfall to those families that can obtain free or low-cost child care. But that is how the nonwelfare world works, and it might even help stabilize otherwise weak household arrangements.)

Conclusion

A chapter on parental choice should not be closed without recognizing that parental decisionmaking is not appropriate in all situations. Parents must have a sufficient personal interest in the quality of the care the child receives and must function at an adequate level to make informed and responsible choices. Thus vouchers may be inappropriate for (1) involuntary interventions or authoritative services, such as those for child abusers, and (2) incompetent or dysfunctional recipients. Certainly, cash payments would be.

But these are minor limitations. This chapter has traced the apparently smooth implementation of child-care voucher systems in all states. Although there are real gaps in child-care services, especially for infants and toddlers, vouchers seem to provide a means to reflect the needs and preferences of the great majority of children—without central or government planning.

Why was the implementation of state voucher systems so easy? And why do vouchers seem to enjoy much broader support than, say, school vouchers? The main answer seems to be the size and diversity of the preexisting child-care market—with many providers wanting to participate compared to a small number of nonprofit agencies that already had grants and contracts. Many of these prospective providers were religious or sectarian and, without vouchers, would not have been able to serve publicly subsidized children. At the same time, the same concerns did not exist about the separation of church and state (for unclear reasons, since many child-care providers have a distinctly religious tone) or about undermining the public system (because there is none). Nor were there strong vested interests (in the form of a large unionized work force) to protect the status quo.

Moreover, there was wide recognition of the heterogeneity of parental tastes and needs. Many parents, for example, had a keen interest in informal care, especially for infants. Many wanted a system that kept the care within the family. Only vouchers and cash could respond to this desire for diverse and informal care. It also helped that the states realized that a voucher system could be less costly, because more parents would choose family day care and unlicensed care, and would be easier to administer, since parents are making the basic decisions.

The major disadvantage of voucher systems, of course, is the obverse of the last point. Vouchers make it more difficult to push children into regulated, center-based care, even though some experts believe that it is better for children. Some think that this is the crux of the issue. They say that parental choice should be constrained because the purpose of policy should be to improve the "quality" of child care.

We think this underestimates the centrality of parental responsibility for their children's well-being and raises the major question about vouchers: Can parents be trusted to make the right child-care choices for their children—especially if they are made moderately cost conscious through co-payments, refundable vouchers, or cash payments?

As we have seen, the evidence, although limited, suggests that parents can be trusted, that they make good choices for their children—often better than the government can. Other observers, however, review the same evidence and conclude that children need more "quality" in their child care and believe that, with enough money, the government can deliver that quality.

That raises an even larger issue: Given the ambiguous impact of expensive "quality" child-care programs on child development, how much money should be spent on them versus other programs for disadvantaged children? That is not a question that is often heard in the child-care debate, but it should be decisive.

Notes

1. In June and July of 1998, using contact information provided by the Department of Health and Human Services Child Care Bureau, we conducted telephone interviews with state Child Care and Development Fund administrators in the fifty states, the District of Columbia, and Puerto Rico. Administrators were asked to give program details about the method of distribution (cash in advance, reimbursement, electronic benefit transfer), eligible recipients (some states distinguished between Temporary Aid to Needy Families [TANF] and non-TANF families in providing cash subsidies), and type of care for which cash would be issued (some states provided cash for all types of care, some only for informal providers, and some only for emergency care). Administrators were further asked to discuss perceived successes, failures, or complications.

2. Children's Defense Fund, *Federal and State Government: Partners in Child Care* (Washington, D.C., October 24, 1997).

3. *Child Care and Development Block Grant Act of 1990*, H. Rept. 5835, 101 Cong. 2 sess. (Government Printing Office, October 26, 1990), sec. 658E(c)(2)(A)(i)(I) & (II).

4. Department of Health and Human Services, Office of Inspector General, *States' Child Care Certificate Systems: An Early Assessment of Vulnerabilities and Barriers* (February 1998), p. 3. Emphasis added.

5. June 30, 1999, telephone interview by Nazanin Samari with Kristine Iverson, legislative director for Senator Orrin Hatch.

6. In its January 1995 report on state child-care subsidy payment approaches, the Children's Defense Fund reported that twenty-two states "made direct payments to parents receiving general child care assistance in at least some situations." See Children's Defense Fund, *Pre-Welfare Reform State Child Care Policies: Original Data* (Washington, D.C., March 1999), p. 3. Our telephone survey of state child-care administrators indicates, however, that many states reevaluated and modified their child-care subsidy programs after the creation of the 1996 Child Care and Development Fund. Our survey indicates that at least sixteen states and Puerto Rico have continued to make direct payments to parents: Alabama, Alaska, Colorado, Connecticut, Hawaii, Idaho, Indiana, Kansas, Minnesota, Missouri, New Mexico, New York, North Carolina, Pennsylvania, Puerto Rico, Utah, and Wisconsin.

7. Researchers Thomas Kaplan and Ingrid Rothe of the Institute for Research on Poverty report that "some serious early problems with long delays in referrals and payments in Milwaukee appear to have been largely resolved after the state provided extra funds to the county to hire more administrative staff." Thomas Kaplan and Ingrid Rothe, "New Hope and W-2: Common Challenges, Different Responses," *Focus*, vol. 20, no. 2 (Spring 1999), p. 47. However, as recently as October 11, 1999, the *Washington Post* reported that the District of

Columbia government was having difficulty reimbursing day-care providers for vouchers given to foster parents and that "many day-care providers no longer accept D.C. payment vouchers." Sari Horowitz and Peter Slevin, "Foster Parents Protest Lag in D.C. Day-Care Payments," *Washington Post,* October 11, 1999, p.1, col. 1–2, at p. A18, col. 4.

8. See, for example, Helen Blank, director, Child Care Division, Children's Defense Fund, testimony before the House Committee on Ways and Means Subcommittee on Human Resources, 106 Cong. 1 sess. (Government Printing Office, March 16, 1999); Christine Ross and Stuart Kerachsky, "Strategies for Program Integration," in Douglas J. Besharov, ed., *Enhancing Early Childhood Programs: Burdens and Opportunities* (Washington, D.C.: Child Welfare League of America and AEI Press, 1996).

9. HHS, *States' Child Care Certificate Systems,* p. 7.

10. June 22, 1998, telephone interview by Nazanin Samari with David McCarley, director, Child-Care Subsidy Program, Alabama Department of Human Resources, Welfare Reform Division; Peter Palermino, program manager, Connecticut Department of Social Services, Division of Child Care; Connie Shorr, acting program administrator, Arizona Department of Economic Security, Child Care Administration; Jerry Allen, state child care coordinator, Nevada Department of Human Resources, Welfare Division.

11. Preschoolers are children age zero to five. Average cost includes paid arrangements only; average cost for family day care includes both licensed and unlicensed homes. Lynne M. Casper, *What Does It Cost to Mind Our Preschoolers?* (Bureau of the Census, 1995), table 2.

12. HHS, *States' Child Care Certificate Systems,* p. 8.

13. National Child Care Information Center, *Child Care and Development Block Grant: Report of State Plans* (Department of Health and Human Services, March 1998), p. 50.

14. June 22, 1998, telephone interview by Nazanin Samari with McCarley, Palermino, Shorr, and Allen.

15. Ross and Kerachsky, "Strategies for Program Integration," p. 56.

16. Susan Rose-Ackerman, *Unintended Consequences: Regulating the Quality of Subsidized Day Care* (Yale University Institution for Social and Policy Studies, 1983), p. 9.

17. August 2, 1999, correspondence to Nazanin Samari from Giovanna Stark, president, Government Action and Communication.

18. Possibly conflicting data come from what parents tell the Census Bureau about how much they pay for care. According to the census, the percentage of monthly income spent on child care for families with employed mothers who pay for care increased from 6.3 percent in 1986 to 7.3 percent in 1993. In addition, the weekly cost of care increased from $58 in 1986 to $70 in 1993. Census Bureau, *Who's Minding the Kids? Child Care Arrangements: Fall 1991,* Current Population

Report P70-36 (1991), table C2. However, there is no way of knowing if this reflects an increase in the price of care, an increase in the number of children families have in care, or an increase in the number of hours the children were in care.

19. Council of Economic Advisers, *The Economics of Child Care* (December 1997), pp. 12–13.

20. David Osborne and Ted Gaebler, *Reinventing Government: How the Entrepreneurial Spirit is Transforming the Public Sector* (Reading, Mass: Addison-Wesley, 1992), p. 181.

21. Even if government initially picked allowable providers, it could drop them based on the actual selections of clients: A rule could be established that a minimum number of clients must select that particular service provider over a designated period of time; otherwise the provider would be automatically dropped from the list.

22. January 26, 1999, telephone interview by Nazanin Samari with Kimberley Hubbard, executive director, Day Care Advocates of Milwaukee.

23. Ellen Kisker, Sandra L. Hofferth, Deborah A. Phillips, and Elizabeth Farquhar, *A Profile of Child Care Settings: Early Education and Care in 1990*, vol. 1 (Princeton, N.J.: Mathematica Policy Research, 1991), p. 7.

24. (1) A saturation work requirement that created a large market for child care, (2) tiered child-care vouchers that encouraged the entry of informal providers in the market, and (3) a co-payment scheme that made parents price-sensitive shoppers and that gave providers an incentive to compete for clients.

25. HHS, *States' Child Care Certificate Systems*, p. ii.

26. Lynne M. Casper, *Who's Minding Our Preschoolers?*, Current Population Report P70-62 (Census Bureau, November 1997), table 6.

27. Ellen Kisker and Rebecca Maynard, "Quality, Cost, and Parental Choice of Child Care," in David Blau, ed., *The Economics of Child Care* (New York: Russell Sage Foundation, 1991), p. 130.

28. Ellen Kisker, Rebecca Maynard, Anne Gordon, and Margaret Strain, *The Child Care Challenge: What Parents Need and What Is Available in Three Metropolitan Areas, Executive Summary* (Princeton, N.J.: Mathematica Policy Research, 1989), p. 17.

29. Sandra L. Hofferth, April Brayfield, Sharon Deich, and Pamela Holcomb, *National Child Care Survey, 1990* (Urban Institute, 1991), pp. 231–34.

30. David M. Blau and Naci H. Mocan, "The Supply of Quality in Child Care Centers," Working Paper 7225 (Cambridge, Mass.: National Bureau of Economic Research, April 1999), p. 21, n. 19.

31. See, for example, K. Alison Clarke-Stewart, "Predicting Child Development from Child Care Forms and Features: The Chicago Study," in Deborah A. Phillips, ed., *Quality in Child Care: What Does the Research Tell Us?* (Washington, D.C.: National Association for the Education of Young Children, 1987) (no correlation for staff-to-child ratios or staff training in child development; small but statistically significant correlation between group size and some measures of cog-

nitive development); Carollee Howes, "Quality Indicators in Infant and Toddler Child Care: The Los Angeles Study," in Phillips, ed., *Quality in Child Care: What Does the Research Tell Us?* (small correlation between staff-to-child ratios, low teacher turnover, staff training in child development, and some measures of social development; no correlation for others); T. M. Field, "Preschool Play: Effects of Teacher/Child Ratios and Organization of Classroom Space," *Child Study Journal*, vol. 10 (1980) (no correlation between staff-to-child ratios and social development); Hillel Goelman and Alan Pence, "Effects of Child Care, Family, and Individual Characteristics on Children's Language Development: The Victoria Day Care Research Project," in Phillips, ed., *Quality in Child Care: What Does the Research Tell Us?* (no statistical significance for centers for staff training in child development, a small but statistically significant correlation in family day-care homes); Susan Kontos and Richard Fiene, "Child Care Quality, Compliance with Regulations, and Children's Development: The Pennsylvania Study," in Phillips, ed., *Quality in Child Care: What Does the Research Tell Us?* (no correlation between staff turnover, staff-to-child ratios, group size, or teacher training and child development); Deborah A. Phillips, Sandra Scarr, and Kathleen McCartney, "Dimensions and Effects of Child Care Quality: The Bermuda Study," in Phillips, ed., *Quality in Child Care: What Does the Research Tell Us?* (no correlation between staff training in child development and children's cognitive development; small correlation between staff-to-child ratios and children's cognitive development); J. Travers and B. D. Goodson, *Research Results of the National Day Care Study* (Cambridge, Mass.: Abt Associates, 1980) (no correlation for staff-to-child ratios and teacher education, small but statistically significant correlation for group size and specialized training in child development).

32. Ron Haskins, "Reform of Federal Child Care Programs," December 1996, p. 10 (paper presented at Day Care and Early Childhood Programs under Welfare Reform conference at the American Enterprise Institute, Washington, D.C., March 24–25, 1997).

33. K. E. Bolger and Sandra Scarr, "Not So Far from Home: How Family Characteristics Predict Child Care Quality," *Early Development and Parenting*, vol. 4, no. 3 (1995); Haskins, "Reform of Federal Child Care Programs"; C. Howes and M. Olenick, "Family and Child Care Influences on Toddler's Compliance," *Child Development*, vol. 57, no. 1 (February 1986); Sandra Scarr, "Child Care Research, Social Values, and Public Policy," paper presented at the state meeting of the American Academy of Arts and Sciences, Cambridge, Mass., April 10, 1996.

34. Ellen Kisker and Rebecca Maynard, "Quality, Cost, and Parental Choice of Child Care," p. 129.

35. Sandra Scarr, "Child Care Research, Social Values, and Public Policy."

36. For example, the Urban Institute's National Child Care Survey 1990, based on a nationally representative sample of families with children under age thirteen, found that the hourly fee for regulated family day care was $1.64 an

hour, compared to $1.48 an hour for nonregulated family day care. Barbara Willer and others, *The Demand and Supply of Child Care in 1990* (Washington, D.C.: National Association for the Education of Young Children, 1991), p. 30.

37. William T. Gormley Jr., "Regulating Mister Rogers' Neighborhood: The Dilemmas of Day Care Regulation," *Brookings Review* (Fall 1990), p. 25.

38. Ibid., p. 24.

39. William T. Gormley, *Everybody's Children: Child Care as a Public Problem* (Brookings, 1995), p. 103–104.

40. 22 June, 1998, telephone interview by Nazanin Samari with David McCarley, director, Child-Care Subsidy Program, Alabama Department of Human Resources, Welfare Reform Division; and Nancy Dierker, Division of Child Care, Colorado Department of Human Services.

41. June 22, 1998, telephone interview by Nazanin Samari with Cathie Pappas, block grant administrator for child care, Utah.

42. Department of Health and Human Services, Administration for Children and Families, *Child Care and Development Fund, Final Rule* (July 24, 1998).

43. June 22, 1998, telephone interview by Nazanin Samari with McCarley, Palermino, Shorr, and Allen.

44. See, for example, Robert A. Robinson, General Accounting Office, "Food Assistance: Reducing Food Stamp Overpayments and Trafficking," testimony before the House Subcommittee on Department Operations, Nutrition, and Foreign Agriculture Committee on Agriculture, 105 Cong., 1 sess., (Government Printing Office, October 30, 1997), p. 3; Theodore Macaluso, *The Extent of Trafficking in the Food Stamp Program* (Department of Agriculture, August 1995).

45. "Helping Families Work—Alternatives to the Child Care Disregard," *Working for Change* (San Francisco: The Child Care Law Center, August 1994), pp. 3–5.

46. Department of Health and Human Services, Administration for Children and Families, Office of Family Assistance, Division of Performance Measurement, *Characteristics and Financial Circumstances of AFDC Recipients: Fiscal Year 1995* (1995), table 39.

47. September 15, 1998, telephone interview by Nazanin Samari with Darryl W. Kehrer, Department of Veterans Affairs. For more information, see generally Michael J. Bennett, *When Dreams Came True: The GI Bill and the Making of Modern America* (Brassey's, 1996). To receive the voucher, eligible service members and veterans must choose an institution and certify their enrollment. Students can receive their benefits either by a check that is issued to them directly or by the request that the benefit be deposited directly into their checking or savings account. (Department of Veterans Affairs home page, http://www.va.gov/benefits/Education/benefits.htm [September 9, 1998].)

48. John C. Weicher, "The Voucher/Production Debate," in Denise DiPasquale and Langley C. Keyes, eds., *Building Foundations: Housing and Federal Policy* (University of Pennsylvania Press, 1990), p. 266; April 14, 1998, written commu-

nication to Nazanin Samari from John Weicher: "Actual program outcomes show that about 24% of voucher recipients rent units for less than 95% of the Fair Market Rent [FMR]. 19% rent units for 95% to 100% of the FMR. The others pay more than the FMR, paying the difference out of their own pocket. That's another distinctive feature of the voucher: They can do that."

49. John Hood, *Solving the Medicaid Puzzle: Strategies for State Entitlement Reform* (Los Angeles: Reason Public Policy Institute, October 1997), p. 29.

BURT S. BARNOW

8 Vouchers for Federal Targeted Training Programs

R ECENT LEGISLATION authorizing new training programs makes an assessment of the use of vouchers for
government-sponsored targeted training programs timely. The Workforce
Investment Act, passed in 1998, requires that voucherlike instruments be
used for a new training program aimed at the nation's disadvantaged, and
voucher legislation also was recently enacted for vocational rehabilitation,
the major training program for people with disabilities. This chapter discusses training and why government is involved, presents arguments for
and against the use of vouchers for targeted training programs, and summarizes the current U.S. employment and training system. It also reviews
how well vouchers and voucherlike programs have performed and assesses
the voucher provisions in recently enacted legislation.

The term "occupational training" is used in this chapter to cover course
work, either full- or part-time, that is directly related to the preparation for
paid employment or for additional preparation for a career requiring other
than a baccalaureate or advanced degree.[1] This definition excludes such
employment and training activities as basic skills training, labor exchange
services, and public service employment.

The focus of the chapter is on *targeted* training programs, where the targeting is based on economic circumstances (such as income or welfare sta-

tus), demographic characteristics (such as being a Native American or an older worker), or the conditions surrounding unemployment (individuals with disabilities or dislocated workers). The intent here is to limit the scope of the chapter by not considering programs for the general population, such as vocational education.

The reasons government gets involved in training are similar to those applied to education. First, people who need training may not be able to afford it, so that appropriate training programs for them are not available. Second, training is considered a "merit good," which society might wish to make widely available without charge. Third, the government wishes to make training available to individuals with certain characteristics as a matter of equity, either to compensate them for individual losses or to enable them to compete better in the labor market. Fourth, workers might underinvest in training from a social perspective because of imperfect information or because of a divergence between private and social returns.

If the government is to be involved, it can play a number of roles. At one extreme the government can provide the training directly. Two good examples are the training of pilots and other specialists in the military and the provision of primary and secondary public education. With direct provision, the government is usually involved in all aspects of the training— recruiting, eligibility determination, selection (if there is excess demand), assessment, assignment to a specific training program, provision of training, and placement at completion. The front-end activities—recruiting, eligibility determination, selection, and assessment—can be undertaken by the responsible government program itself, delegated to a lower level of government, or contracted out.

Vouchers, in a training program context, may be used for any or all of these activities. Under an extreme version, once an individual is admitted to the program, he or she will receive one or more voucher certificates that can be used toward assessment (mandatory or optional), training, and placement. Vouchers could be restricted in a number of ways:

—To vendors that meet certain criteria in terms of quality of training (for example, curriculum used or placement rates)

—To particular occupations (for example, occupations with strong current or projected demand or with high wages)

—To occupations for which the participant has shown appropriate aptitude and interest through the assessment

—In how much tuition they cover.

Vouchers are not feasible for some types of training, such as that provided directly by the government or an employer. For direct provision, however, efficiency can be encouraged through the use of competition or performance incentive systems.[2]

The success of a training program with vouchers may depend critically on the nature of the vouchers as well as on the extent to which the program hands out voucher certificates to eligible persons, provides participants with information on the job market and on the effectiveness of potential vendors, and assesses and counsels participants. When examining the success of training programs with vouchers and voucherlike designs, it is important to look at the services that go along with the voucher. Providing information and guidance may be particularly important for some of the more disadvantaged populations served by some programs.

Rationale for Vouchers

Economists tend to favor vouchers over directed training because they maximize consumer choice. If consumers can select the training program they value most, it will generally maximize consumer utility and social welfare. Another potential advantage of vouchers is that they simplify the training process. Instead of a government agency trying to determine the most appropriate training program for a participant and arranging for the training, in the extreme case all the agency need do is provide the participant with a voucher and perhaps a list of acceptable training programs. Vouchers may also improve the performance of training organizations. By forcing training organizations to compete for participants, inefficient providers should be driven from the market, resulting in survival of the fittest.

Vouchers fit well with the movement to "reinvent" government. Three of the principles stressed by David Osborne and Ted Gaebler in their book on reinventing government are "empowering rather than serving," "injecting competition into service delivery," and "meeting the needs of the customer, not of the bureaucracy."[3] Osborne and Gaebler argue that governments should give decisionmaking power back to the citizens: "What Americans *do* hunger for is more control over matters that directly affect their lives: public safety, their children's schools, the developers who want to change their neighborhood."[4] Osborne and Gaebler stress the importance of customer choice and specifically call for vouchers in training programs: "The single best way to make public service providers respond to the needs of their customers is to put resources in the customers' hands and let them choose. All the listening techniques listed above are important, but if the customers do not have a choice of providers—schools, training programs, motor vehicle offices—they remain dependent on the goodwill of the provider."[5]

The Employment and Training Administration (ETA), which is responsible for the Job Training Partnership Act (JTPA), the largest targeted training program, has included customer choice as one of its values since 1993: "In short, we believe the people we serve are customers who must be pleased, not clients who need to be processed." In addition, ETA has established personal responsibility as a value: "We believe that ETA customers and employees possess both the right and the responsibility to make decisions about their work lives."[6]

Arguments against Vouchers

It is no accident that vouchers have rarely been used for targeted training programs. For almost every argument for vouchers, there is an argument to the contrary. First, the basic claim that increasing choice always increases utility can be challenged. If choice is such a good option, why not give people cash and let them decide if they want training or would rather spend the money on food, shelter, or something else?[7] (See the chapter by Robert Lerman and C. Eugene Steuerle in this volume.) Opponents of vouchers also point out that participants might not make the "right" choice of a training program from a social perspective for several reasons. First, although the taxpayers' goal is for the participant to maximize earnings gains, the participant may select a training program that provides more consumption value or an occupation that provides more consumption and less income than is socially desired.

Another potential problem with consumer choice is the lack of information available to those who would use vouchers. This information failure falls into three categories:

—information about occupations in demand and wages that are paid

—information about how successful various vendors are in placing their participants

—information about their own capabilities as applied to various occupations and training programs.

The first two information failures can be dealt with by providing information to the participants, but the third requires an assessment of aptitudes and interests as well as guidance to the participants.

Federally Sponsored Targeted Employment and Training Programs

Although a large number of targeted training programs are currently supported by the U.S. government, some disagreement arises regarding how many federally sponsored training programs exist.[8] The General Accounting Office (GAO) recently counted 163 employment and training programs, but the GAO definition of a "program" is very loose.[9] That definition includes demonstrations with a limited life span (such as the Job Training for the Homeless Demonstration) and funding streams used to reward good performance (in JTPA). Burt Barnow and Laudan Aron identified fourteen major training programs, but several of those programs are more geared to employment (for example, the Senior Community Service Employment Program), and others no longer exist (Aid to Families with Dependent Children, or AFDC, and the Work Incentive program).[10] Since the Barnow and Aron paper was written, the JTPA Title II-A program has been split, and a separate youth program established under Title II-C; a new dislocated worker program has been added for workers who lose their job because of the North American Free Trade Agreement (NAFTA); and the AFDC training programs have been largely devolved to the states with much more emphasis on employment than on training ("work first") under the Personal Responsibility and Work Opportunity Reconciliation Act of 1996.

This chapter focuses on JTPA Title II-A and Title III, the Trade Adjustment Assistance (TAA) program, and vocational rehabilitation. These programs are highly targeted, research is available on how effective vouchers might be for these programs, and legislation has been recently enacted that requires the use of vouchers.

Title II-A of the Job Training Partnership Act

Operated through a partnership of federal, state, and local government with the private sector, the program is funded by the federal government, with funds distributed by formula to over six hundred state and local units of government, called service delivery areas (SDAs). Amendments passed in 1992 established separate year-round programs for disadvantaged youths under Title II-C, operated under the same basic structure as the adult programs.

Each SDA must form a private industry council (PIC), comprising representatives of the private sector and other governmental and nonprofit organizations. PICs may choose to run the program or to serve more as a

---

Box 8-1. *Timeline for Federal Employment and Training Programs*

1962	Manpower Development and Training Act (MDTA) passed
1973	Comprehensive Employment and Training Act (CETA) passed
1982	Job Training Partnership Act (JTPA) passed to replace CETA
1983	JTPA programs authorized in Titles II, III, and IV implemented
1988	Economic Dislocation and Worker Adjustment Assistance Act passed, substantially modified Title III under JTPA
1992	JTPA amended substantially
1998	Workforce Investment Act passed to replace JTPA
1999–2000	WIA programs phased in

---

board of directors, providing guidance to the program. Private sector members of the PIC must constitute a majority of the membership.

MAJOR ACTIVITIES UNDER TITLE II-A. Participants engage in a number of activities, including

—Vocational training through programs that teach occupational skills in a classroom setting. Vendors are usually selected competitively by the SDAs and include community colleges, community-based organizations (CBOs), and proprietary schools. SDAs can offer training through special classes established for JTPA, or they can send participants to courses already offered by vendors.

Box 8-2. *Major Job Training Partnership Act Programs*

Title II-A	Training services for economically disadvantaged adults
Title II-B	Summer youth employment and training program
Title II-C	Training services for economically disadvanaged youth
Title III	Employment and training services for dislocated workers
Title IV-A	Employment and training programs for Native Americans and migrant and seasonal farmworkers
Title IV-B	Job Corps
Title IV-C	Veterans' employment and training programs

Each of the JTPA programs has specific eligibility requirements, although an individual may qualify for more than one program.

—Basic skills and remedial education through programs that provide participants with classroom instruction in reading, arithmetic, and other academic skills. The programs are often intended to lead to a GED or high school diploma.

—On-the-job training (OJT) through programs that encourage placing participants with individual employers. The employer typically receives a payment of 50 percent of wages paid to the participant for up to six months of employment to cover the cost of formal and informal training.

—Work experience through programs that place participants with government or nonprofit agencies and organizations. Work experience participants are generally paid the minimum wage. The intent of the program is for participants to gain work experience that will help them qualify for unsubsidized jobs.

—Job search assistance to help participants improve their job search methods and skills.

The original statute limited the amount of work experience that could be provided, and the 1992 amendments to the act placed significant limitations on the provision of OJT and stand-alone job search assistance.

EFFECT OF THE WORKFORCE INVESTMENT ACT. With enactment of the Workforce Investment Act (WIA), state and local areas may begin phasing in WIA requirements immediately, but full compliance is not required until July 2000. The Workforce Investment Act retains many of the features of the act it replaces, but there are some important changes relevant to training.[11] Local programs must

—Establish a one-stop delivery system that puts together WIA activities with related programs, including adult education and literacy activities, the employment service, vocational rehabilitation programs, welfare to work programs, postsecondary vocational education, trade adjustment assistance programs, veterans' employment and training programs, and HUD and community services block grant employment and training programs.[12]

—Provide core services, and make them available to the entire labor force, to include eligibility determination; outreach, intake, and orientation to the one-stop delivery system; initial assessment of skill levels, aptitudes, abilities, and supportive service needs; job search, placement, and career counseling services; labor market information; information on the availability of supportive services; and follow-up services for at least twelve months.

—Provide intensive services, which include comprehensive and specialized assessments, development of an individual employment plan, group counseling, individual counseling and career planning, case management for participants interested in training services, learning skills, interviewing skills, and training on professional conduct. The intensive services are to be targeted to recipients of core services who are unemployed or employed but assessed as needing intensive services.

—Provide training services, including occupational classroom training, adult education and literacy, and on-the-job training. Training is to be provided to individuals who receive intensive services but who are not able to obtain or retain employment, who are assessed as likely to benefit from training, and who cannot meet their training needs through other grant assistance, such as Pell grants.

—Establish individual training accounts (ITAs), which enable the training participant to select a provider and program among eligible candidates. Depending on the regulations issued by the Department of Labor, the new program could operate like a pure voucher system or like the individual referral system currently used by many local JTPA programs.[13] (This requirement is of greatest interest here because it will require local programs to use vouchers or voucherlike instruments for the first time.)

In addition, states must establish a performance-based certification system for determining which training programs are permitted to receive funding for training adults and dislocated workers. Performance criteria for providers include the following data on WIA participants served by the provider: completion rates, employment at termination rates, and employment retention six months after employment commences. States and local boards may add additional criteria for providers.

Programs for Dislocated Workers

There is one broad-based employment and training program for dislocated workers (Title III of JTPA) and several programs for dislocated workers who meet special eligibility requirements, including the Trade Adjustment Assistance program (the largest of the programs with special eligibility requirements).

TITLE III OF THE JOB TRAINING PARTNERSHIP ACT. The employment and training program with the broadest coverage for dislocated workers is Title III of JTPA, which was amended by the Economic Dislocation and Worker Adjustment Assistance Act. To be eligible for Title III, a dislocated worker must

—Have been terminated or laid off or have received notice of termination or layoff and be ineligible for or have exhausted unemployment insurance

—Have been terminated as a result of a plant closing

—Be a long-term unemployed worker with limited opportunities for reemployment in the same occupation or

—Be a self-employed individual (including a farmer or a rancher) who is unemployed because of general economic conditions or natural disaster. Under some circumstances, states may authorize services for displaced homemakers.

The governor of each state is required to establish a dislocated worker unit that has responsibility for administering the Title III program for the state, including responsibility for operating a rapid response unit for coordinating responses to major layoffs and plant closings. States must designate substate areas for service delivery under Title III but are not required to use the same substate areas used for Title II.

Title III programs provide several types of activities and services to eligible participants:

—Readjustment services may be services that do not involve vocational training, for example, front-end activities such as outreach and intake, early readjustment assistance, counseling, testing, orientation, assessment, determination of occupational skills, and provision of world-of-work and occupational information. Basic readjustment services also include services that generally would be provided after training, if training is needed. These activities include job placement assistance, labor market information, job clubs, job search, job development, and relocation assistance. Supportive services such as child care and commuting assistance are also considered basic readjustment services.

—Retraining services include occupational skill training, on-the-job training, out-of-area job search, relocation, basic and remedial education, literacy and English training, and entrepreneurial training. The only activity specifically prohibited is public service employment. Retraining services may be provided by certifying eligible individuals and providing them with vouchers.

—Needs-related payments can be made to individuals who fail to qualify or who have exhausted unemployment insurance so that they may enroll in occupational or educational training. The law places restrictions on when such individuals must enroll in training to qualify for such payments. These payments must not exceed the higher of the applicable level of unemployment insurance payments or of the poverty level.

TRADE ADJUSTMENT ASSISTANCE. The Trade Adjustment Assistance (TAA) program was established in 1962 to provide financial assistance and training to workers who lose their jobs as a result of imports.[14] The program provides cash assistance through trade readjustment allowances (TRAs), and workers are permitted to identify and select their own training program. The program has been amended significantly several times.[15] The qualifying criteria were liberalized in 1974. In 1981 TRA benefits were reduced to be equal to the worker's unemployment insurance benefits, and workers could only collect TRAs after they had exhausted their unemployment insurance. Training was made an entitlement and a requirement for workers under this program beginning in 1988. Although dislocated workers covered by TAA must have their training approved by the employment service, workers may choose their own training, and the employment service generally concurs with the workers' plans.

VOCATIONAL REHABILITATION. The vocational rehabilitation program, authorized under Title I of the Rehabilitation Act of 1973, provides grants to states for comprehensive vocational rehabilitation programs that meet the "needs of individuals with handicaps so that such individuals may prepare for and engage in gainful employment to the extent of their capabilities." Disabled individuals must satisfy a number of requirements to be eligible to participate in the program. Participants must have a physical or mental disability that can be medically described, have a substantial handicap to employment, and be capable of achieving employability (that is, they have rehabilitation potential).

All vocational rehabilitation activities are conducted at the state level, but they are reviewed and monitored by the Rehabilitation Services Administration of the U.S. Department of Education. Currently, there are over eighty agencies administering vocational rehabilitation in the fifty states, the District of Columbia, the territories, and other government units.[16] About half the states have two agencies, one for those who are blind and one for people with other disabilities. In the remaining states, a single agency is responsible for all vocational rehabilitation services.

Individuals receiving Social Security Disability Insurance (SSDI) or Supplemental Security Income (SSI) and who are considered good candidates for rehabilitation by social security officials are referred to the state rehabilitation agencies. The state agencies are reimbursed for the costs of their rehabilitation if a referred SSDI beneficiary or SSI recipient is continuously employed in substantial gainful activity (defined as earning at least $500 a month) for nine consecutive months. Beginning in 1996, SSI recipients and SSDI beneficiaries who were referred to state agencies but who were not served by the agencies may be served by alternate providers, who are reimbursed for the cost of services on the same basis as state agencies.

Approximately one million individuals are served by state vocational rehabilitation agencies annually, and approximately 200,000 are "successfully rehabilitated."[17] The program is supposed to focus on individuals with severe disabilities, and 65 percent of the individuals accepted are classified as severely disabled, compared to 35 percent of those not accepted. The most common disabling conditions among those accepted are mental and emotional (43 percent) and orthopedic (24 percent).[18]

Effectiveness of Vouchers in Training Programs

This section summarizes the evidence of the effectiveness of vouchers for training programs for economically disadvantaged and dislocated workers. Although Congress has authorized a voucher program for the vocational rehabilitation program, there is little evidence that vouchers for these workers are effective and that they are a better alternative than other service delivery mechanisms. (The term voucher is used loosely here to include examples where participants are primarily responsible for selecting their training program.)

Economically Disadvantaged

Only one experimental effort has been identified that rigorously examined the effectiveness of vouchers for disadvantaged populations—an experiment that was conducted in conjunction with the Seattle-Denver Income Maintenance Experiments. Some researchers have also drawn inferences from the Pell grant program, which essentially is a voucher program. But evaluations of Pell grants are generally more concerned with the impact on access and the effect of the extra education on earnings than they are with the effectiveness of the voucher delivery mechanism.

EVIDENCE FROM THE SEATTLE-DENVER VOUCHER EXPERIMENT. The Counseling and Education Subsidy Program (CESP) was implemented along with the Seattle-Denver Income Maintenance Experiments (often referred to as SIME/DIME).[19] The Seattle-Denver program was the largest and last of a series of experiments conducted in the 1960s and 1970s to learn about the feasibility and behavioral implications of a "negative income tax" program, where members of the treatment group were provided a guaranteed income, and any income earned by the participants was taxed at a specified rate. SIME/DIME was carried out between 1970 and 1978 in selected sections of the two cities. To be eligible, a person had to meet the following requirements:

—Income below $9,000 (in then-current dollars) for a family of four (adjusted for other family sizes)

—Family structure restricted to married couples and single parents with minor dependent children

—Head of family to be black or white in Seattle (black, white, or Chicano in Denver) and between the ages of eighteen and fifty-eight, capable of employment, and not in military service.[20]

For the counseling and education subsidy component of the experiment, treatment and control group members were randomly assigned to one of three counseling and training options: counseling only; counseling plus a 50 percent subsidy for the cost of any education or training in which the person enrolled; or counseling plus a full subsidy for the cost of any education or training in which the person enrolled.[21]

Participants were enrolled in the experiment for up to six years. Education was interpreted very broadly so that most occupational training and general education courses were approved. Most of the training was occupational classroom training, and the community college was the most common provider. Participation in subsidized training was moderate. For the group with a 100 percent subsidy, about 36 percent of the married men and women participated, and 47 percent of the single female heads of household took some education or training. Participation rates were lower for those granted a 50 percent subsidy—21 percent for the married men and women, and 35 percent for the single female heads.

The hypothesis underlying the CESP was that the subsidies for training would lead to increased participation in education and training programs, which would, in turn, increase earnings. The first part of the hypothesis was confirmed, with participants in the 100 percent subsidy group taking approximately one year of additional training compared to those with no subsidy. The surprising result was that in virtually all the analyses undertaken, the training led to either no change in subsequent earnings or an actual reduction in earnings, although the negative impacts often were not statistically significant. Katherine Dickinson and Richard West conclude,

Up to this point we have found that, as expected, the SIME/DIME counseling and training programs increased the amount of job counseling and the amount of additional schooling received. However, we have determined they also, quite unexpectedly, reduced the earnings of those eligible to participate, with the exception of the counseling-only program for single women. Further, we have found that these negative impacts are widespread and that the programs, on the whole, were not beneficial even for select subgroups of the population (again, with the exception of counseling only for single women). Since these results are based on a comparison of randomly assigned experiments and controls and thus are not a result of the self-selection and noncomparability problems that plague most other evaluations of employment and training programs, considerable reliance can be placed on these basic findings.[22]

Dickinson and West undertook a number of analyses to determine if their findings resulted from some type of statistical problem or nonrandom selection. In the end, they concluded that the problem was in the treatment itself: "The SIME/DIME programs were designed to maximize freedom of choice for participants. They offered nondirective counseling and a wide range of educational opportunities. Evaluation indicates that such programs in general are inappropriate for low-income individuals, causing at least some of them to form unrealistic expectations about their labor market prospects and to pursue overly ambitious goals."[23]

OTHER EVIDENCE. There is not a great deal of additional evidence on the use of vouchers for the economically disadvantaged. Some observers, such as Anthony Carnevale and Louis Jacobson, point to Pell grants, also known as Basic Educational Opportunity Grants (BEOGs), as effective voucher programs for individuals with low incomes, but care must be taken in interpreting the data.[24] Pell grants provide financial aid in the form of grants to low-income students for postsecondary education or training below the baccalaureate level. The size of the grant depends on the income and assets of the student and his or her family, whether the student attends full time or part time, and the tuition charged by the school. The size of the grant also depends on the amount appropriated. For the 1997–98 school year, the maximum grant was $2,700.

Carnevale and Jacobson claim in the title of their paper that the Pell grant program is "the voucher that works." What they mean by the program working is never explicitly stated in the paper, but it is clear that they do not mean to compare Pell grants to a JTPA-type program, where the activity assignment is the responsibility of a government agency. Instead, their statement that Pell grants "work" is based on evidence that these grants encourage postsecondary education and that postsecondary education, at community colleges as well as at four-year colleges, increases earnings.[25] Carnevale and Jacobson do not advocate a pure voucher system, where potential students are simply provided with voucher certificates good at the school of their choice. Instead, they call for individual assessments to determine student capabilities and interests combined with counseling to help students interpret the data on themselves and the training institutions open to them.[26] Thus, although Carnevale and Jacobson approve of the choice offered by vouchers, they stress the importance of trying to ensure that potential enrollees make their choices wisely.

Dislocated Workers

There is more evidence available on the effectiveness of vouchers for dislocated workers in such programs as the Trade Adjustment Assistance program, a voucher experiment called the Career Management Account (CMA) that the U.S. Department of Labor tested at thirteen sites, and several local programs that used vouchers or voucherlike instruments.

TRADE ADJUSTMENT ASSISTANCE. Mathematica Policy Research (MPR) completed an impact evaluation of TAA training in 1992. The evaluation included four groups of TAA recipients: participants who began receiving TRA benefits before the 1988 changes, participants who received TAA training before the 1988 changes, participants who began receiving TRA payments after the 1988 changes, and participants who enrolled in TAA training after the 1988 changes. The original design called for fifteen states to be included in the study, but six states refused to participate and only one was replaced, yielding a final sample of ten states. For comparison groups, the MPR researchers selected samples of unemployment insurance (UI) recipients matched to the TAA samples on several criteria. The UI samples were drawn from the same states and roughly the same time periods as the TAA and TRA samples and from manufacturing because the TAA population is drawn largely from manufacturing (85 percent in the TAA sample selected). Finally, because workers had to exhaust their UI payments to collect TRA, the analysis was restricted to UI exhaustees. The final analysis sample included 4,776 individuals, of whom 1,174 were UI exhaustees and the remainder were TRA recipients and TAA trainees. Data were gathered primarily through telephone interviews and covered approximately four years of experience.

The MPR study found that a substantial minority of TAA participants received training—37 percent in the pre-1988 sample (when training was neither an entitlement nor a requirement) and 47 percent in the post-1988 period.[27] About 70 percent of the TAA trainees completed their training, with a slightly higher proportion of the pre-1988 group (72 percent) completing training than in the post-1988 group (67 percent). As in most studies of dislocated workers, the MPR study found that participants in TAA generally suffered substantial reductions in wage rates and earnings following their job loss.

The MPR researchers used ordinary least squares regression analysis of the TAA samples and the UI exhaustee comparison group to estimate the effect of TAA training on the employment and earnings of participants. The researchers found that when differences in characteristics between trainees and others are controlled for, "our findings imply that, if training has a substantial positive effect on employment or earnings among all trainees, it is realized not earlier than three years after the initial UI claim."[28] In other words, the TAA program had no effect on earnings during the first three postprogram years. The study also found that individuals who received training had slightly lower wage rates than those who did not take training, but the differences were generally not statistically significant.

Although the TAA evaluation is another example of a voucherlike program that failed to produce significant positive effects on the employment and earnings of trainees, the evidence here must be interpreted with caution for several reasons.[29] First, the evaluation used a nonexperimental design, and the design may not have adequately controlled for differences between the treatment and control groups.[30] Second, the evaluation may not have followed up with the participants long enough to measure any gains. Finally, the failure of the program to produce significant effects may not have resulted from the voucher aspect of the program but from other features of the intervention. For example, in the post-1988 period, training was a requirement, so the results may not apply to a nonmandatory program. In addition, several other evaluations of training programs for dislocated workers failed to find significant positive effects.[31]

Career Management Account demonstration. This demonstration project was sponsored by the U.S. Department of Labor to learn about the feasibility, effectiveness, and cost-benefit attributes of vouchers for dislocated workers relative to the traditional approach used in Title III of JTPA. The Career Management Account (CMA) demonstration was conducted at thirteen competitively selected sites from 1995 through 1997. The sites differed significantly in the treatments offered, the activities and services covered by the vouchers, and in other services and activities offered to participants. Assessing the CMA is difficult because the evaluation mostly compares CMA results to regular Title III results at the thirteen sites.[32] Preliminary results from the evaluation indicated that participants in the CMA group had an 85 percent positive termination rate, which was 6 percent more than other Title III participants, and that thirteen weeks after termination, wages for CMA participants grew by 5 percent, which was 3 percent more than for other Title III participants. Surveys and focus groups also provided some positive evidence for the CMA approach. Staff members reported satisfaction with the approach and believed that the outcomes were better. CMA participants indicated slightly higher satisfaction than participants in the regular Title III program, but satisfaction levels were high (in excess of 85 percent) in both programs.

In addition to the lack of an experimental design (except at one site), the design of the demonstration makes it difficult to determine how useful the vouchers were in leading to the higher positive termination and wage growth rates for the CMA group. The biggest problem is that CMA programs spent significantly more per participant than regular Title III programs do. Part of the increased costs were one-time startup costs, but the evaluators were not able to determine how much more would have been spent on an ongoing basis. Although expenditures per participant were higher for the CMA participants, the amount spent on training was 13 percent less. Thus the mix of services varied between CMA and traditional Title III programs.

Overall, the findings from the CMA are too mixed to provide policy recommendations, but one would be hard pressed to recommend instituting vouchers for Title III based on the CMA results. There were small positive outcome differences in favor of the CMA participants, but the cost differentials were potentially large, and the lack of a strong evaluation design leaves open the question of how much any differences are explained by the treatment rather than by selection.

OTHER FINDINGS. Several local voucher-type programs for dislocated workers have also been evaluated. Robert Bednarzik and Louis Jacobson provide evidence on a voucher program funded by Allegheny County, Pennsylvania.[33] This program was open to virtually all dislocated workers in the county (which covers most of the Pittsburgh metropolitan area).

Notable features of the program included a requirement that participants be counseled before using their vouchers and that the vouchers be valid only at the Community College of Allegheny County. The training received through the voucher program was estimated to increase earnings by about 6.3 percent, but the estimate is based on a comparison with non-participants rather than with participants in an alternative program, and the evaluation uses nonexperimental methods. So it is possible that the estimates are biased.

Jacob Benus and colleagues are evaluating New Jersey's Workforce Development Partnership Program (WDPP), which includes a voucher component called individual training grants (ITGs).[34] Their interim evaluation indicates that individuals receiving these grants initially earn less than they would have earned without the training, but that after eighteen months, the ITG participants earn more. Benus and others note that they used nonexperimental techniques to draw their inferences and that long-term data are needed to determine if the benefits of the program outweigh the costs. They believe,however, that the voucher approach is promising. As in the case of Allegheny County, the New Jersey ITG program requires substantial counseling before participants are permitted to use their vouchers.

Conclusions and Applications to New and Proposed Legislation

This is an especially opportune time to review what we know about vouchers for targeted training programs. As this chapter was being prepared, legislation was enacted to replace the Job Training Partnership Act, and legislation is expected to amend the vocational rehabilitation program to include provisions for vouchers. The conclusions presented in this section are based on the theory and empirical research on vouchers for targeted training programs and can be applied to the recent legislation.

Vouchers in the Workforce Investment Act of 1998

It is too early to tell whether the voucher provisions of the Workforce Investment Act will enhance or hinder the effectiveness of the nation's targeted training programs. Until the program is fully implemented in July 2000, one can only speculate on the effects of provisions based on statutory language. The WIA classifies initial assessment of skill levels, aptitudes, and supportive service needs; labor market information; career counseling; and information about service providers' placement rates as "core services" that must be provided to participants. Conversely, the WIA states in Section 134 that "Training services provided under this paragraph shall be provided in a manner that maximizes consumer choice in the selection of an eligible provider of such services." But how will dilemmas where a participant wishes to enroll in a program in which he or she is unlikely to succeed be resolved?

Although we will not know for certain until regulations are issued, Department of Labor officials have indicated that the regulations are likely to permit "individual referrals" to meet the individual training account requirements of the WIA. This approach includes the consumer choice of vouchers, but participants are restricted to vendors with good performance and reasonable cost records, and they may only enroll in programs where the occupations are in demand and where they have the aptitude and skills required. In a recent study of the use of vouchers for JTPA training, John Trutko and Burt Barnow found over a dozen examples of individual referrals and only one example of a voucher program with pure consumer choice.[35] Thus, it is likely that the Workforce Investment Act will strike a good balance between the advantages of vouchers and the threats to their effectiveness.

Vouchers in Vocational Rehabilitation

In recent years a number of policy analysts have called for reform of the nation's vocational rehabilitation program to provide more choice for disabled individuals who would like to receive vocational training. Monroe Berkowitz described a "ticket to independence" program based on the premise that the current system works very poorly in getting people off the rolls who receive Social Security Disability Insurance or Supplemental Security Income.[36] Berkowitz estimates that only about one-half of one percent of the caseload is rehabilitated each year. Under Berkowitz's proposal, eligible individuals would be provided with a voucher, or "ticket," that they could use with a provider of their choice. Providers would be paid out of savings to the disability trust funds as the participants worked. Because the return to work rate now is extremely low, ticket proponents argue that the program could only result in savings to the taxpayer and more gainful employment for the disabled.

Many of the features of Berkowitz's proposal are retained in the Ticket to Work and Work Incentives Improvement Act of 1999, which was signed into law on December 17, 1999. Under the legislation, the Social Security Administration (SSA) will issue vouchers, or "tickets," to new beneficiaries at the time of award and to current beneficiaries following a disability review.[37] Providers would have a choice of reimbursement schemes. They can choose to receive a percentage of the average SSDI or SSI benefit for up to five years so long as the individual remains off the rolls for that period. Alternatively, providers can elect to receive some payments after achieving specified milestones, but subsequent payments would be reduced. Thus the legislation combines a voucher approach with a modified pay for performance component, although the pay for performance component is not as strong as in the original ticket proposal.

In a study conducted for the Department of Labor last year, individuals interviewed raised several objections to the original ticket proposal:[38]

—*Lack of clarity in the ticket proposal.* The legislation that has been proposed is short on details in a number of very critical areas and appears to leave much for the Social Security commissioner to determine by regulation. For example, the commissioner would (at a later date) prescribe when the tickets would expire, the duration for which the tickets may be assigned to an enrolled provider, as well as the allowable renewal periods, if any, of the tickets or assignments. The commissioner would also prescribe the total amount of the payment that will be made to the enrolled provider holding the ticket of a beneficiary who returns to work and the time(s) at which such payments shall be made.

—*No effect on incentives for disabled beneficiaries.* While the ticket approach could substantially encourage vocational rehabilitation providers to move SSDI and SSI beneficiaries into work, the initiative would not change the basic incentives to work for beneficiaries. Fear of loss of cash benefits and, particularly, loss of health benefits (that is, Medicare for SSDI beneficiaries and Medicaid for SSI beneficiaries) because of work are primary factors for unwillingness of beneficiaries to work. Critics of the ticket approach argue that the real barrier to employment is loss of benefits. For example, changing provisions with regard to guaranteeing continued health insurance would have a much more substantial impact on willingness to return to work for disabled individuals.

—*Difficulties faced by disabled individuals choosing providers.* Under a voucher system such as the ticket approach, a critical element would be to ensure that each disabled individual made an informed decision about the provider with which he or she would enroll. The legislation is unclear about how this would be achieved, and for some disabled individuals—especially those with mental disabilities—it will be difficult to develop a methodology that will ensure informed consent.

—*Predatory practices by providers.* Faced with strong financial incentives to place individuals into jobs, providers may place reimbursement considerations ahead of providing services that are most appropriate for the disabled individual. For example, in the interest of getting individuals into jobs quickly, training and other vocational rehabilitative services that may be of the greatest benefit over the long term for the individual might be given a back seat.

—*Potential for "buying the base" under a ticket approach.* In this scenario, payments under the ticket approach would be made for individuals who would have terminated SSDI/SSI anyway (that is, without the initiative).

—*Potential for "induced filers."* With strong financial incentives, vocational rehabilitation providers may induce individuals to file for SSDI and SSI benefits who might not have filed otherwise so that they can subsequently get these same beneficiaries into jobs and collect payments.

—*Same service providers used.* State vocational rehabilitation agencies already contract with many of the same providers to serve SSDI and SSI beneficiaries. Given the fact that many of the same service providers will be involved, the ticket approach is unlikely to have a major effect on availability of vocational rehabilitation services or return to work.

—*No effect on timing of services.* One of the problems of the existing system is that disabled individuals are referred for rehabilitative services either too early or too late. For example, SSDI and SSI beneficiaries are typically referred for services after they have been engaged in a nine-month to two-year effort to convince the SSA that they are disabled and cannot work. The ticket approach will not do much to change the timing with regard to referral for services.

For the most part, these criticisms focus on features other than the use of vouchers. As Jane Ross noted in her testimony before Congress, vouchers alone do not deal with problems such as providing clear work incentives and intervening as soon as possible.[39] In her CBO cost estimate, Kathy Ruffing summarizes the effects of S. 331 as "small early costs, giving way to small savings after 2003."[40]

On balance, a voucher program might help with the low return to work rate for SSDI and SSI. The programs currently have such little success that the use of vouchers can only lead to an improvement in the proportion of beneficiaries who return to work.

Conclusions about Vouchers for Targeted Training Programs

Interestingly, vouchers have not generated as much spirited debate for targeted training programs as they have for education. As noted earlier, the picture is mixed, with arguments for and against.

LIMITING USE. Although there are good arguments in favor of vouchers as a delivery mechanism for targeted training programs, there are also good reasons why some authority for determining or limiting the type of training and vendor should be vested in the government.

The theoretical case for vouchers rests on the arguments that vouchers maximize choice, thereby increasing utility to consumers, and that they promote efficiency by making vendors compete with each other. Conversely, for publicly funded programs, interdependent utility functions could result in vouchers leading to less social welfare than programs where assignments are made by the government or its agent. In addition, consumers will act to maximize their private gains, which may not be the same as social gains. Finally, participants in training programs may lack appropriate information about their own skills and aptitudes as well as the characteristics of training vendors. Providing information about placement rates of vendors will help eliminate the latter problem, but it will not deal with the former. Thus, economic theory provides no strong a priori reason to prefer vouchers with pure choice to a program—voucher or otherwise—that involves negotiated decisionmaking between the program and the participant. (See the chapter by Robert Lerman and C. Eugene Steuerle in this volume.) At a minimum, the evidence suggests that vouchers be restricted to training for which the participants show aptitude and background. This is the approach followed by JTPA programs using the "individual referral" approach, and it is unlikely to be permitted under WIA.

EMPIRICAL EVIDENCE MIXED. Previous studies provide only negative evidence on the effectiveness of past voucher programs for the economically disadvantaged and quite mixed evidence on the effects for dislocated workers—perhaps reflecting program design, the value of subsidized training per se, or the use of the voucher as a delivery mechanism.

Unfortunately, none of the empirical evidence on vouchers for targeted training programs is as strong as one might like. Evidence from the SIME/DIME voucher experiments for the economically disadvantaged is more than twenty years old, but it remains the best evidence currently available for this target group. Pell grants provide an example of a pure targeted voucher program, but there are no studies available to compare them with a nonvoucher alternative.

The programs for dislocated workers provide mixed evidence on the utility of vouchers, and none of the evaluations has as strong a design as is desirable. The major evaluation of the TAA program showed it to have little impact on the earnings of participants. The negative findings might stem from a weak evaluation design or from the ineffectiveness of training for this group rather than from any characteristics of vouchers. Preliminary findings from the recent Career Management Accounts demonstration indicate possible small, positive effects on employment and earnings, but the demonstrations spent significantly more per participant than the regular training program to which they were compared, and the CMA participants actually received less vocational training than did those in traditional programs. The mixed findings for dislocated worker training programs might reflect problems with the underlying training intervention itself rather than with the use of vouchers. Evaluations of a state (New Jersey) and local (Allegheny County, Pennsylvania) program indicated some potential evidence of gains from the voucher programs, but both programs involved counseling and restricted lists of vendors.

VALUE OF ASSESSMENT AND COUNSELING. A targeted training program should include assessment and counseling to determine what training is appropriate for the participants and screening of vendors for quality of training and appropriate placement rates. All of the voucher programs (as well as other programs) that have positive effects include assessment, counseling, and screening of vendors. The 1992 JTPA amendments required local service delivery areas to provide in-depth assessment for Title II-A participants, and most of the SDAs interviewed in the assessment of the amendments stated that although the increased assessment added to the cost and time required to serve participants, the benefits exceeded the costs.[41] Programs using individual referrals under JTPA have found that participants are generally satisfied with the choices they receive, and the programs believe that the outcomes are as effective as with traditional referral mechanisms.

For targeted training programs, vouchers can be useful, but they can also be deleterious. The evidence indicates that vouchers alone are insufficient to guarantee that training programs are effective. Research by the General Accounting Office indicates that Pell grants and guaranteed student loans are being used by students to train for occupations with at least twice as many aspiring entrants as there are job openings.[42] Conversely, training programs that do not take the preferences of participants into account are almost certainly doomed if people are enrolled in occupational programs regardless of their interests. For targeted training programs to work well, participant preferences must be taken into account. At the same time, a well-run training program can offer participants the assessment and guidance they are likely to require to ensure that they can benefit from the training.

In the case of the Workforce Investment Act, the ability to use individual referrals to meet the individual training account requirements is likely to include the best features of vouchers and to avoid the problems that have surfaced in past evaluations. Thus the new program appears to strike a good balance between permitting participants to have choice and restricting their choice set to programs that are likely to benefit them. In the case of vocational rehabilitation, the vouchers may not solve all the problems in the system. But given the poor performance of the current approach, vouchers probably only can benefit the eligible population.

Notes

1. This definition is based loosely on the definitions of vocational education from several editions of the *Digest of Education*.

2. For a discussion of alternative approaches to encouraging efficiency for government-provided services, see William Niskanen, *Bureaucracy and Representative Government* (Chicago: Aldine Publishing Company, 1971). For an assessment of the performance management system in place for government training programs, see Burt S. Barnow, "Exploring the Relationship between Performance Management and Program Impact: A Case Study of the Job Training Partnership Act," *Journal of Policy Analysis and Management* (Winter 2000).

3. See chapters 2, 3, and 6 in David Osborne and Ted Gaebler, *Reinventing Government: How the Entrepreneurial Spirit Is Transforming the Public Sector* (Reading, Mass.: Addison-Wesley, 1992).

4. Ibid., p. 74.

5. Ibid., p. 180.

6. See ETA's mission statement and values on their Internet home page (http://www.doleta.gov [June 24, 1999]).

7. Irwin Garfinkel shows that if we have interdependent utility functions, where the taxpayers' utility depends on the consumption of particular goods by (rather than the income or utility of) the beneficiaries, in-kind redistribution may well be more efficient than cash assistance. Thus programs such as food stamps, public housing, and training can be justified on these grounds. It is a logical exten-

sion of Garfinkel's work to place restrictions on the type of training participants obtain with government funding. See Irwin Garfinkel, "Is In-kind Redistribution Efficient?" *Quarterly Journal of Economics*, vol. 87 (May 1993).

8. I exclude programs that are untargeted, such as vocational education, and programs that do not provide or emphasize training, such as the employment service, which primarily provides labor exchange services, and the Senior Community Service Employment Program, also known as the Older Workers Program, because it primarily provides employment opportunities.

9. General Accounting Office, *Multiple Employment Training Programs: Information Crosswalk on 163 Employment Training Programs*, report HEHS-95-85FS (February 1995).

10. See Burt S. Barnow and Laudan Y. Aron, Commission on Workforce Quality and Labor Market Efficiency, *Investing in People: A Strategy to Address America's Workforce Crisis* (Department of Labor, 1989). The programs identified by Barnow and Aron are Job Training Partnership Act Title II-A training for the economically disadvantaged, the JTPA Title II-B Summer Youth Program, the JTPA Title III program for dislocated workers, the JTPA Native American Program, the JTPA Migrant and Seasonal Farmworker Program, the Job Corps, Veterans' Employment and Training, vocational education (which is mostly state funded), the Senior Community Service Employment Program, vocational rehabilitation, Trade Adjustment Assistance, the Refugee Resettlement Program, the Food Stamp Employment and Training Program, and training for recipients of Aid to Families with Dependent Children under the WIN program and related programs.

11. This description is based on Steve Savner, "Training Issues under the Workforce Investment Act of 1998" (Washington, D.C.: Center for Law and Social Policy, 1998), draft.

12. Optional one-stop partners include training programs authorized under Temporary Assistance for Needy Families (TANF), food stamp employment and training programs, and community service programs.

13. The individual referral programs used by many local JTPA programs permit a participant to select the service provider and program of his or her choice, provided that the participant has the appropriate education and aptitude as determined during assessment, that the service provider has an adequate record of job placement (overall and for the program being considered) defined by placement rate and wage at placement, that the occupation selected is considered in high demand, and that the costs for the program be in the range considered reasonable by the local program. See John W. Trutko and Burt S. Barnow, *Experiences with Training Vouchers under the Job Training Partnership Act and Implications for Individual Training Accounts under the Workforce Investment Act* (Department of Labor, 1999). ITAs are not required under certain circumstances: for on-the-job and customized training and when the local board determines that there are too

few providers available in the area or that there is a local program of demonstrated effectiveness serving a population with multiple barriers to employment.

14. Workers who lose their jobs as a direct result of NAFTA are served under the NAFTA Transitional Assistance program, which provides the same cash and training benefits as the TAA program.

15. See Walter Corson and others, *International Trade and Worker Dislocation: Evaluation of the Trade Adjustment Assistance Program* (Princeton, N.J.: Mathematica Policy Research, April 1993).

16. See Department of Education, Rehabilitation Services Administration, *Annual Report to the President and to the Congress: Fiscal Year 1992 on Federal Activities Related to the Rehabilitation Act of 1973, as Amended* (1992), and General Accounting Office, *Vocational Rehabilitation: Evidence for Federal Program's Effectiveness*, GAO/PEMD-93-19 (August 1993).

17. Closures from the active caseload are classified as rehabilitated if they satisfy all the following conditions: (1) have been declared eligible for services, (2) have received appropriate diagnostic and related services, (3) have had a program for vocational rehabilitation services formulated, (4) have completed the program, (5) have been provided counseling, and (6) have been determined to be suitably employed for a minimum of sixty days.

18. Figures in this paragraph are for individuals accepted into the program in 1988 (General Accounting Office, 1993). Data on cases rehabilitated in 1991 (Department of Education, 1992) provide similar but not identical findings.

19. Some of the material presented in this and the following section was originally presented in Burt S. Barnow and Christopher T. King, "The Baby and the Bath Water: Lessons for the Next Employment and Training Program," in Garth Mangum and Stephen Mangum, eds., *Of Heart and Mind: Social Essays in Honor of Sar Levitan* (Kalamazoo, Mich.: Upjohn Institute for Employment Research, 1996).

20. Gary Christopherson, "Locating, Enrolling, and Maintaining the Sample," in SRI International, *Final Report of the Seattle-Denver Income Maintenance Experiment, Vol.1: Design and Results* (Menlo Park, Calif.: SRI International, 1983).

21. Information on the counseling and education subsidy programs is from Katherine P. Dickinson and Richard W. West, "Impacts of Counseling and Education Subsidy Programs," in SRI International, *Final Report of the Seattle-Denver Income Maintenance Experiment, Vol.1*.

22. Ibid., p. 233.

23. Ibid., p. 253.

24. Unpublished manuscript by Anthony P. Carnevale and Louis S. Jacobson, "The Voucher That Works: The Role of Pell Grants in the Welfare, Employment Policy, and Training System," 1997.

25. See Thomas J. Kane and Cecilia Rouse, "Labor Market Returns to Two- and Four-Year Colleges: Is a Credit a Credit and Do Degrees Matter?" Working Paper 311 (Industrial Relations Section, Princeton University, 1993).

26. Regarding counseling, Carnevale and Jacobson state in "The Voucher That Works": "Counseling adds value to information; it provides an intermediary service to collect and interpret information on alternative learning and employment choices and on likely outcomes. Clients, especially disadvantaged clients with family responsibilities and multiple needs, require advice in making informed choices and customizing educational and career programs to their circumstances."

27. Although training was generally required in the post-1988 period, participants could obtain waivers if appropriate training was not available.

28. Corson and others, *International Trade and Worker Dislocation*, p. 155.

29. Office of the Chief Economist, U.S. Department of Labor, *What's Working (and What's Not)* (January 1995), p. 55.

30. Nonexperimental designs do not make use of random assignment to generate a control group with similar characteristics. In such designs the treatment and comparison groups may not be adequately matched, and there is a risk that any effects detected are an artifact of the design rather than of the treatment itself.

31. Department of Labor, *What's Working*, p. 55.

32. Information about the CMA evaluation presented here is based on material presented by Public Policy Associates at an April 23, 1998, briefing at the Employment and Training Administration.

33. Unpublished manuscript by Robert W. Bednarzik and Louis Jacobson, "Labor Training Policy in an Increasingly Competitive World but Shrinking Federal Budgets," 1996.

34. Jacob M. Benus, Jane Kulik, Neelima Grover, Steven S. Marcus, and Michelle Ciurea, *Third Annual Assessment Report of the Workforce Development Partnership Program* (Bethesda, Md.: Abt Associates, 1996).

35. John W. Trutko and Burt S. Barnow, *Experiences with Training Vouchers under the Job Training Partnership Act and Implications for Individual Training Accounts under the Workforce Investment Act* (Department of Labor, 1999).

36. Monroe Berkowitz, "Improving the Return to Work of Social Security Disability Beneficiaries," in Jerry L. Mashaw, Virginia Reno, Richard V. Burkhauser, and Monroe Berkowitz, eds., *Disability, Work, and Cash Benefits* (Kalamazoo, Mich.: Upjohn Institute for Employment Research, 1996).

37. This summary is based on Kathy Ruffing, "Congressional Budget Office Cost Estimate of S. 331 Work Incentives Improvement Act of 1999," prepared March 19, 1999 (http://www.cbo.gov [June 15, 1999]).

38. See Burt S. Barnow and John Trutko, "Inventory of Employment Rehabilitation Programs and Approaches for the Severely Disabled," final report submitted to the Office of the Assistant Secretary for Policy, Department of Labor (Urban Institute, 1997).

39. Jane L. Ross, *Social Security Disability: Improving Return-to-Work Outcomes Important, but Trade-Offs and Challenges Exist*, GAO/T-HEHS-97-186 (General Accounting Office, July 23, 1997).

40. Kathy Ruffing, "Congressional Budget Office Cost Estimate."

41. See John W. Trutko and Burt S. Barnow, *Implementation of the 1992 Job Training Partnership Act (JTPA) Amendments* (Department of Labor, 1997).

42. See General Accounting Office, Millions Spent to Train Students for Oversupplied Occupations, GAO/HEHS-97-104 (June 1997).

ISABEL V. SAWHILL
SHANNON L. SMITH

9

Vouchers for Elementary and Secondary Education

PUBLIC CONCERN about the condition of the schools is high and support for public education is waning. A large proportion of the public is now in favor of school vouchers. Minority parents are especially concerned about the public schools, with a majority (68 percent) now in favor of more school choice.[1] These sentiments have helped fuel a major debate about the benefits of choice as well as a number of ongoing experiments with school vouchers.

This chapter examines the issue of using vouchers to pay for elementary and secondary education in the United States. It begins with a review of the history of school choice in the United States and the arguments commonly made both for and against vouchers in that context. Some of the major choice proposals that have been advanced recently at the federal, state, and local levels are described, emphasizing that vouchers can take many forms. The devil is, as always, in the details—a point that both sides in the debate seem to have forgotten in their haste to either endorse or condemn the

The authors would like to thank Jane Hannaway, Jens Ludwig, Richard Murnane, Paul Peterson, Diane Ravitch, Bella Rosenberg, John Witte, and the editors of this volume for very helpful comments without in any way associating any of them with our conclusions.

251

basic idea of choice as a tool for improving children's education. By focusing on some of these details, we hope to show that vouchers are a flexible tool that can be adapted to achieve a variety of political or substantive purposes. The chapter also examines the kinds of choice plans that have actually been adopted (not simply proposed) and how they have worked in practice. In particular, the evidence on whether school choice improves the academic performance of children is reviewed.

Stated briefly, the chapter concludes the following:

First, contrary to much of the rhetoric about them, vouchers do not abandon the education of children to the market. Public funds are used to finance them, and wherever public monies are involved, some accountability for the use of these funds will always be required. The ability of vouchers to achieve various public purposes depends on the details of the program—for example, who is eligible, the level and variation of the subsidy, how schools are held accountable for performance, and what kind of information parents are provided.

Second, most voucher programs to date have been targeted on low-income families. These families have expressed great satisfaction with their new schools. The evidence on whether their children are performing better in these new schools than comparable students in the public schools is somewhat mixed, but the results to date are modestly encouraging.

Third, the fear that vouchers will resegregate schools along racial or economic lines is not unfounded, but the standard for comparison needs to be the high degree of segregation that already exists, not the nonexistent ideal. It is possible to design a voucher program that would provide much greater equalization of spending per student than the current system of school finance.

Fourth, vouchers may siphon students and resources away from existing public schools, creating short-term adjustment costs for these schools, but over the longer term they are likely to produce the kind of wake-up call to the public schools that their advocates have emphasized. Experiments with vouchers have thus far been too small to shed any direct light on this issue, but other research suggests that, on balance, more competition is likely to produce positive effects.

Fifth, vouchers are no panacea for what ails public education. Any notion that full-scale adoption of school choice is either feasible or desirable is misplaced. Just as higher education in the United States has become a mixed public-private system, so, too, is it likely that elementary and secondary education will evolve in the same direction. However, for the foreseeable future most students will continue to be educated in the public schools, making it imperative that these schools be improved and that the debate about vouchers not be allowed to block the needed public school reforms.

The History of the Debate about School Choice

Proponents of school choice can point to a long history of intellectual support for the idea that parents should be able to choose the schools their children attend. From the beginning, Americans were intent on maximizing individual freedom and limiting the power of the state. John Stuart Mill, the English philosopher, understood that a democracy required an educated citizenry, but also one that was not subjected to a state-controlled curriculum. In the end, he said, the state "might leave to parents to obtain the education where and how they pleased, and content itself with helping to pay the school fees."[2] Thomas Paine, among others, agreed. But no consensus among the founders existed on this issue.

The Constitution remained silent on the issue of how education was to be organized in the United States, implicitly leaving such decisions to the states. What evolved, of course, were schools that were not just publicly financed but also publicly run. The dominant public philosophy in the United States has seen public schools as places that would bring together children from diverse backgrounds, teach democratic values, provide opportunities for upward mobility, and help newcomers assimilate to the American way of life.[3] This vision of the public school as an incubator of democratic values and practices remains strong to this day.[4]

It was not until the 1950s, when the economist Milton Friedman first published an essay on school vouchers, that the idea of choice gained intellectual heft. Choice proponents such as Friedman do not dispute the idea that education is a public good that society should pay for, but, like Mill, they question why that good should be publicly produced. As Friedman noted,

> Governments could require a minimum level of education which they could finance by giving parents vouchers redeemable for a specified maximum sum per child per year if spent on "approved" educational services. Parents would then be free to spend this sum and any additional sum on purchasing educational services from an "approved" institution of their own choice. The educational services could be rendered by private enterprises operated for profit, or by

non-profit institutions of various kinds. The role of government would be limited to assuring that schools met certain minimum standards such as the inclusion of a minimum content in their programs, much as it now inspects restaurants to assure that they maintain minimum sanitary standards.[5]

In a free and competitive education market, according to this argument, schools that produce a desirable product will thrive, while those that produce a less than desirable product will drop out of the market, allowing more adaptable, innovative, and cost-efficient schools to take their places. Not only will schools be forced to improve, but also families will be able to choose from a variety of programs that may be more suited to their child's interests or learning style than the "one-size-fits-all" public schools. As in markets for most other commodities, parents will hold teachers and administrators directly accountable by their freedom to choose alternative providers. Advocates of choice contrast this with the current system in which schools operate as a public monopoly. And, as with any monopoly, there is the risk that too little will be produced, prices will be inflated, and the industry itself (teachers, administrators, and government bureaucrats) will benefit at the expense of parents and students. Public monopolies are, of course, subject to public regulation, which is supposed to prevent such abuses while permitting certain efficiencies associated with larger-scale operation. But in practice the regulators are often captured by those they are supposed to oversee. School boards, for example, may pay too much attention to teachers unions and not enough to the welfare of children.

Initially, these market-based arguments were anathema to those on the political left, but in the late 1960s some progressives decided that vouchers could be turned to more liberal purposes. Under contract to the U.S. Office of Economic Opportunity (OEO), Christopher Jencks and his colleagues at the Harvard Graduate School of Education designed a voucher proposal that involved providing more generous vouchers to parents with lower incomes, prohibiting parents from supplementing this amount, and requiring schools both to accept students on a random basis and to maintain racial and socioeconomic balance.

Despite its promotion and funding by the OEO, only one school district in the country—Alum Rock, California—was willing to test the Jencks idea. And by the time it was implemented, various local constituencies had insisted on a variety of limitations, such as job protection for teachers and no participation by private schools. When federal funding ceased in 1976, the district discontinued the program. Not surprisingly given the limitations under which it had to operate, an evaluation of the experiment by the RAND Corporation found that it had produced mediocre results at best.[6]

After the disappointing results in Alum Rock, interest in school choice waned. It was not until Ronald Reagan became president in 1981 that vouchers resurfaced on the policy agenda. The choice concept was consistent with Reagan's free market ideas, but choice legislation failed to win congressional approval three times during his tenure.[7]

In 1990 the idea of school choice got a new boost from the publication of John Chubb and Terry Moe's *Politics, Markets, and America's Schools*. While Friedman had emphasized the economic arguments for using markets to deliver educational services, Chubb and Moe focused more on the political environment affecting the current system. They argued that the central problem is the subordination of the schools to democratic political authority, which, in turn, has spawned a bureaucracy whose interests are not the same as those of parents and students. To break the hold of the bureaucracy, Chubb and Moe advocated a universal choice program that would include all existing schools.[8]

By the early 1990s voucher advocates had discovered a new ally in the battle for school choice: inner-city minorities frustrated by unsuccessful attempts to reform the public schools. What is particularly interesting about this alliance is an earlier history in which public school choice plans were adopted in most southern states (and private school choice in four of them) as a way around the U.S. Supreme Court's *Brown* v. *Board of Education* decision of 1954, which required an end to segregated schools. These laws were struck down by the federal courts on the grounds that they hindered desegregation. Later, when de jure segregation was followed by de facto segregation in most large cities in the country, school choice took another twist: the creation of magnet schools that became vehicles for stemming white flight and encouraging voluntary integration through parental choice within the public school system. As this history suggests, choice can be a vehicle for maintaining a racially segregated school system or a vehicle for encouraging integration, depending on the form it takes. Many present-day opponents of choice, however, fear that it will produce greater segregation unless special steps are taken to maintain racial balance, while proponents note the high degree of segregation that already exists since school assignment is so closely tied to residential location.

In fact, most parents already have at least some limited choice of schools, because they are able to choose where they live. It is mainly the poor, and especially the minority poor, whose children are locked into low-performing neighborhood schools. They can afford neither to move nor to send their children to private schools and may face discrimination in the housing market as well. By proposing to target vouchers on this group of low-income parents in the 1990s, advocates have begun to appeal to a broader constituency that believes a chance to send your child to a decent school is every American's birthright. In response to the argument that choice will merely lift a few motivated and talented students out of failing schools and leave the others behind, advocates decry the alternative of doing nothing. They prefer an immediate solution for a small population to a long and very uncertain process of reforming the public schools that, if it happens at all, will not affect the students trapped in the existing system today. For those concerned about existing fiscal inequities, vouchers could even become a vehicle for equalizing spending per child in a country where educational investments have traditionally depended heavily on the wealth of one's neighbors.

Although support for education vouchers has been growing, opponents continue to make a number of strong arguments against them.[9] First, they believe that vouchers will cause the most able students and the most motivated parents to leave the system, weakening the public schools and resegregating schools along economic or racial lines. Second, they note that parents, especially the most disadvantaged, lack the information and the ability to make wise choices and are likely to be overly influenced by such factors as the convenience of a school, frivolous or pedagogically questionable course offerings, and the degree to which the school is supportive of their own religion or ideology. Third, they question whether the supply of schools (either their quality or quantity) will respond to the new demand in the way that proponents expect. Fourth, they believe that the neighborhood school in which everyone participates and everyone has a stake is itself a public good in a democracy.[10] And finally, they note that choice is hardly a panacea for the very serious problems that currently afflict the schools and argue that a preoccupation with market solutions will divert resources and political energy from fixing the existing public schools.

As John Witte noted, "Decentralization and choice are not panaceas for solving the complex and very serious problems that affect overall achievement and inequity of achievement in the most problematic public school districts. To trumpet these policies as the road to salvation . . . could seriously damage the viability of both concepts."[11] A common theme of all these arguments against choice is the possibility that choice in practice will be quite different from choice in theory. As the Alum Rock episode illustrates, however, it is often the politics surrounding school choice that inhibit its being given a true test in practice.

Recent Choice Proposals

Proposals to provide parents a choice of schools have proliferated over the past decade. Although our focus is on those that offer parents funds to send their children to any school, public or private, it should be noted that choice can also exist within the public sector. Public school choice was first introduced in Minnesota in 1988[12] and is now available in fifteen states as well as in some individual districts (for example, Cambridge, Massachusetts).[13] Magnet schools and charter schools have further extended parental choice. Magnet schools exist in most large cities, are usually organized around an educational theme (for example, science or the arts), and receive extra resources that enable them to attract a diverse student body from a wide area. Charter schools are public schools that have been approved by, and are accountable to, state education authorities but that are not required to comply with most of the rules that govern regular public schools. By the fall of 1998, thirty-four states and the District of Columbia permitted the establishment of charter schools, approximately eleven hundred schools were operating, and two hundred and fifty thousand students were attending.[14] These experiments with choice within the public sector can shed further light on how choice works in practice but must be considered a more limited or constrained version of the voucher idea in its purest form.[15] Although magnet and charter schools do provide parents with additional options, they do so more by expanding the supply of publicly controlled schools than by directly empowering parents with the funds that would allow them to purchase education from a still wider array of existing providers.

Federal Proposals

Most federal proposals for school choice have sought to allocate funds to local choice efforts and demonstration projects. Although proposals during the Reagan and Bush administrations usually did not reach the floor of Congress, support for choice bills has been steadily growing throughout the 1990s.[16]

In 1996 presidential candidate Bob Dole strongly endorsed school choice during his campaign and proposed a joint state-federal initiative of private school vouchers for low- and middle-income students. The program allocated $3 billion a year for demonstration projects in eighteen states that were willing to match the federal scholarship.[17] In response to public support for the Dole plan, President Clinton advocated public school choice as a compromise to his constituency of parents, especially minority and urban parents, desiring school choice and to teachers unions, which staunchly oppose the rerouting of public money to private schools.[18]

In 1998 Congress passed, and the president vetoed, the "A+ Accounts" Bill, sponsored by Senator Paul Coverdell (R-Ga.), which would have allowed families with annual incomes below $95,000 to establish tax-free savings accounts of up to $2,000 per child to cover primary and secondary educational expenses.[19]

Another choice proposal, this one targeted on the District of Columbia, was also passed in 1998 and vetoed by the president. The District of Columbia Student Opportunity Scholarship would have allowed low-income public school students in Washington to attend any accredited school (public, private, independent, or parochial) in the District of Columbia or specified areas in nearby Virginia and Maryland. The vouchers would have covered the cost of tuition, fees, and transportation to school, not exceeding $3,200 in 1998, and students were to be permitted to supplement the voucher to attend more expensive schools. A *Washington Post* poll taken during the week before Clinton vetoed the bill found that 56 percent of all District residents and 67 percent of the parents of public school children favored federally funded vouchers for the District of Columbia.[20]

State Proposals

In 1992 Colorado introduced a constitutional amendment to provide private school choice to all students. This universal program, which did not pass, would have granted vouchers to students for any educational option, including home schooling. Since the proposal set the voucher amount as a percentage of district per pupil spending, large variations in vouchers would have existed between districts.[21]

In 1993 California voters overwhelmingly defeated Proposition 174, another universal tuition voucher proposal. Unlike the proposed Colorado voucher, this voucher plan would have covered a percentage of state and district per pupil spending, and it therefore would have been more similar for all students. The initiative would have permitted parents to supplement the voucher, however, and many critics feared the inequalities they believed would result.[22] Politically, it received weak support from business leaders and Republicans while being strongly opposed by the much better-organized teachers union.[23]

Arizona has devised still another variant on a choice program that doesn't involve vouchers at all. The state passed a law in early 1997 to grant income tax credits of up to $500 to those who donate money to nonprofit choice scholarship programs. Although some critics have called it a "back-door voucher scheme," it does not directly reimburse parents who send their children to private schools.[24]

Finally, families in Minnesota have been able to deduct education costs such as private school tuition, transportation, and extracurricular expenses from their taxable income since 1983, and as of June 1997, those with annual incomes below $33,500 may obtain a credit against state income taxes for certain school expenses (excluding private school tuition) up to $1,000 per child or $2,000 per family each year.[25]

Local Proposals

The federal and state initiatives are only the tip of a rapidly growing iceberg. It is at the local level that choice plans have proliferated most rapidly.[26] The best-known school choice plan in the nation began in Milwaukee, Wisconsin, in 1990. Targeted on public school students whose annual family incomes are less than 175 percent of the poverty line, the state-funded program granted $4,700 to each student in the 1997–98 school term to pay for tuition at private, nonsectarian schools. Students are selected randomly from eligible applicants to oversubscribed schools. Until 1998 only 1.5 percent of the total Milwaukee public school population could participate.[27] Although the state legislature voted to expand the program to religious schools and to fifteen thousand students (15 percent of district enrollment) in 1995, a contentious court battle questioned the constitutionality of the program and delayed its implementation until the fall of 1998.

Another notable choice program was established in Cleveland, Ohio, in 1996. It provides a sliding scale of scholarships of up to $2,500 each for students to attend either religious or secular private schools.[28] The scholarship, funded by the State of Ohio, can be used to cover up to 90 percent of tuition at a private school, with parents providing the difference.[29]

The first program in the wave of recent voucher experiments to be implemented with local public funds was unanimously approved by the Southeast Delco School Board of Delaware County, Pennsylvania, in

March 1998. The vouchers of $500 for grades 1–8 and $1,000 for grades 9–12 will reimburse parents who already send or wish to send their children to private schools.[30]

Private Proposals

Many private philanthropic organizations have initiated scholarship programs in cities around the country, including Indianapolis, Milwaukee, Albany, New York City, and Washington, D.C. The details of these programs are described in appendix 9B and in table 9-1, the latter of which has been adapted from Paul Peterson's excellent summary in *Learning from School Choice*. Virtually all of the current choice plans are targeted on lower-income families, permit attendance at religious schools, provide relatively low subsidies, and cover only a small fraction of all public school students in the cities where they are located.

Assessing the Debate: The Devil Is in the Details

Much of the political debate about school choice occurs in a vacuum in which exactly what is meant by school choice is never clearly defined. The common assumption is that education will be publicly financed, with the funds flowing directly to parents who would then be free to use them at the school of their choice.[31]

Left undefined by most contemporary discussions of vouchers, however, are a whole host of questions about which families will be eligible to participate, which schools can qualify for the vouchers, how students will be admitted to schools, what level of public subsidy will be provided, how that subsidy will vary (if at all) by location or need of the student, and what kind of information will be made available to parents. Yet it is impossible to assess a school choice plan without knowing the answers to these and related questions. Some of the key issues that must be resolved in designing a school choice plan are described below.

Student Eligibility

Two major variants of a choice plan have been widely discussed: a universal program and one targeted toward low-income families. A universal choice plan, such as that proposed by Friedman, would provide subsidies to all parents of school-age children, including those who are currently enrolled in private schools, and would thus extend subsidies to the 11 percent of all children whose education is now privately financed. Alternatively, eligibility for a voucher could be made conditional on income. Because most middle-class and affluent parents can afford to either pay for private school or move to a neighborhood with public schools more to their liking, and because inner-city schools are believed to be particularly deficient, a number of proposals and ongoing demonstrations have, as we have seen, focused on lower-income families. There is likely to be continuing debate, however, about whether to provide subsidies to all parents or to target subsidies on lower-income families only. Some current proposals would subsidize education through the tax system and would be regressive in their effect, since only families with sufficient incomes to owe taxes would benefit.[32]

Some geographic targeting would also be possible. A subsidy that favored big-city schools, or jurisdictions with low tax bases, over others might become a central element in a new urban agenda. This would give middle-class families with school-age children a reason to remain in the city and help to curb the abandonment of cities by everyone who is not rich, poor, or old.

Whatever the basis for targeting any new voucher plan, one reason that such targeting may be desirable is that, without it, private school capacity is unlikely to expand to meet the new demand—at least in the short run.

School Eligibility

Many fear that vouchers would encourage the establishment of schools that foster a particular religious or ideological agenda or that offer undemanding curricula or other activities that may appeal to parents and students but are clearly not in the public interest. It's inconceivable, however, that a voucher plan would operate without some government oversight. As Paul Peterson puts it, "No reasonable person can believe the American public would routinely turn over school dollars to extremist groups any more than it will allow airlines to fly unregulated or meat to be marketed without inspection."[33] However, some privately funded voucher plans do not regulate providers. In San Antonio, for example, five new private schools have opened in response to a scholarship plan. One of these schools, Sword of the Lord, is a ramshackle building with no telephone listing and a sign reading "Property of Jesus Christ" on the door.[34]

Table 9-1. *Characteristics of Big-City School Choice Programs for Low-Income Families*

City	Sponsor	Religious schools included	Grades	First school year	Initial enrollment	Enrollment 1996–97	Number of schools 1996–97	Maximum payment 1997–98[a] (dollars)	Selection method
Milwaukee	State of Wisconsin	No	Pre-K–12	1990–91	341	1,606	20	4,700	Lottery
Indianapolis	ECCT[b]	Yes	1–8	1991–92	746	1,014	70	800	First come
Milwaukee	PAVE[c]	Yes	K–12	1992–93	2,089	4,465	97	1,000 (e) 1,500 (h)	First come
San Antonio	CEO[d]	Yes	1–8	1992–93	930	995	49	One-half tuition	First come
Cleveland	State of Ohio	Yes	K–3	1996–97	1,996	1,996	55	2,500	Lottery
New York City	SCSF[e]	Yes	1–5	1997–98	1,200	1,200[f]	250	1,400	Lottery
Washington, D.C.	WSF[g]	Yes	K–12	1998–99	1,600	...	n.a.	1,700	Lottery
Dayton	PACE[h]	Yes	K–12	1998–99	650	...	n.a.	1,200	Lottery
San Antonio	CEO/Horizon[i]	Yes	K–12	1998–99	Over 1,000	...	n.a.	3,600 (e) 4,000 (h)	Unlimited

Sources: Adapted from Paul E. Peterson, "School Choice: A Report Card," in Paul E. Peterson and Bryan C. Hassel, eds., *Learning from School Choice* (Brookings, 1998), p. 14; Paul E. Peterson, "Top Ten Questions Asked about School Choice," *Brookings Papers on Education Policy, 1999.*

n.a. Not available.

a. (e) denotes elementary school, (h) high school.
b. Educational Choice Charitable Trust.
c. Partners Advancing Values in Education.
d. Children's Educational Opportunity.
e. School Choice Scholarships Foundation.
f. 1997–98 enrollment.
g. Washington Scholarship Fund.
h. Parents Advancing Choice in Education.
i. Children's Educational Opportunity/Horizon.

Nearly 80 percent of all private schools in the United States are church affiliated.[35] This raises concerns about whether educational vouchers would conflict with the First Amendment's separation of church and state provisions. If the courts should decide that religious schools cannot qualify for public subsidies, then the eligible pool of existing, nonsectarian private schools would be extremely small. If, conversely, religious schools are eligible, parents would have a much broader range of choices. Advocates of choice argue that because subsidies go directly to parents rather than to schools, church-state separation should not be an issue. They also point to the GI Bill, which allows veterans to use vouchers to attend any type of university, to child care subsidies that can be used for church-based programs, or to the new charitable choice provision in the 1996 welfare bill that permits religiously affiliated organizations to provide services to welfare recipients. But many state constitutions contain stricter separation of church and state clauses than the U.S. Constitution does. Thus court challenges have bedeviled attempts to establish choice plans in Milwaukee, Cleveland, and other areas and may not be fully resolved any time soon. (See the chapters by Michael McConnell and by Elliot Mincberg and Judith Schaeffer for summaries of legal issues.)

Another issue is what kind of standards schools must meet to qualify for vouchers and how this will be monitored. Experience with the Pell grants program has shown that private, for-profit operators running vocational programs can be quite unscrupulous about taking money from unsuspecting clients who get little of value in return.[36] Recent scandals in the home health care field tell a similar story. Thus the need for some kind of standards or monitoring of performance would seem to be essential. This could take the form of detailed regulation of inputs, but this might only succeed in duplicating the worst features of the current system. A second possibility would be to combine a much less prescriptive regulatory regime with some monitoring of outcomes achieved, a process that is now being used with the many charter schools springing up around the country. Finally, one could rely on private accreditation by respected professional groups, combined with some parental monitoring, a system that seems to work reasonably well for current private schools and institutions of higher education. But as long as there are substantial public monies involved, there will be concerns about accountability and a fear that parents may not exercise sufficient vigilance, especially if their own funds are not at risk. A set of nationally accepted content and performance standards could, of course, go a long way toward resolving this dilemma. Such standards would permit schools to be freed

from regulatory burdens as long as their students were performing satisfac-
torily or making progress toward achieving the standards.

Admissions

A major concern of choice opponents is their fear that schools will become
much more segregated by class, race, or ability. This can occur for two reasons. First, because more advantaged parents are the most likely to take
advantage of a choice plan and apply for a voucher (selective application
rates). And second, because if schools are allowed to choose students, they
will select the most able (selective acceptance rates). Either alone could
produce more sorting of students; both together almost certainly will. The
available evidence suggests that both phenomena are important.[37] A number of studies have shown that, given a choice, well-educated, affluent parents are more likely to move their children to better schools, while less-
advantaged parents are more likely to value the convenience of a
neighborhood school. And although schools may attempt to diversify their
student bodies somewhat, given an oversupply of applications they are
almost sure to choose the best students whether defined by academic ability, lack of handicapping conditions, leadership potential, or some other set
of criteria.

The effect of such resorting on academic performance is not clear, a
priori. The children who move to a new school are usually presumed to
benefit from the experience, while those who are left behind are presumed
to lose out as their more able or motivated classmates move on. However,
these so-called peer effects—that is, the tendency of individual academic
performance to vary with the composition of the group—are still being
debated in the literature.[38] Whatever its ultimate effects on school achievement, such segregation may be inconsistent with democratic ideals that
place a high premium on the kind of class and race-based integration that
allegedly occurs in the best public schools. We say "allegedly" because the
reality is that residential segregation now forces a large number of children
to attend schools in which there is little mixing of this sort.[39]

But assuming for the moment that greater segregation by income, race,
or ability would likely occur, it is possible to design a choice plan that min-
imizes its extent. First of all, parents can be required to make an explicit
choice of schools through a formal enrollment process in which their
choices are carefully delineated and explained and in which attendance at
a neighborhood school is simply one option. This would help to counter
the tendency of poorly educated or motivated parents to leave their chil-

dren in existing schools. Second, participating schools might be required to take all or a portion of their students based on a lottery or to use an admissions process that, at a minimum, preserved some kind of racial balance. In New York City, for example, magnet high schools are allowed to select some of their students but must take others on an assigned basis. Minnesota's open enrollment policy allows students to attend any public school in the state, provided that their transfer does not upset the racial balance of the school they are leaving or moving into. Similarly, Cambridge's program requires each school to be racially balanced.

This issue of admissions standards is obviously critical. A system that was so regimented that it attempted to closely control the selection process (by, for example, imposing a lottery system on participating schools) could have a chilling effect on the number of existing or new schools willing to participate in a choice plan. But in the absence of any rules or constraints, the worst fears of the opponents of choice could well materialize.

Subsidy Level

Average per pupil spending for public elementary and secondary education in 1993–94 was $6,492. Average private school tuition was $3,116 in the same academic year.[40] The variation of expenditures within each category is wide. Per pupil spending in public schools ranged from lows of $3,439 in Utah and $3,660 in Mississippi to highs of $9,677 in New Jersey and $9,175 in New York. Catholic school tuition during that year was only $2,178, while tuition at non-Catholic religious schools was $2,915 and at nonsectarian private schools was $6,631.[41] Private school tuition is kept low by competition from a zero-priced alternative in the public sector and by the willingness of many religious groups, most notably the Catholic Church, to subsidize education. The result is that most choice plans have been able to offer relatively low subsidy amounts that are well below public school levels but that still cover most or all of the cost of the typical private school. The marginal cost of enticing new school entrants may well be considerably higher than current tuition averages suggest, but is still not likely to be above current per pupil costs for public education.

The biggest issue in designing a choice plan is not so much the level of the subsidy as how that level should vary by location or student characteristics. A national or statewide choice plan that was linked to average per pupil spending in the public schools as a whole but that did not take into account the enormous variation in spending per pupil across districts and states would immediately create large numbers of potential winners and losers and likely would be politically dead on arrival. But a system that was linked to current district disparities would recreate all of the inequities that plague the current system of school finance in the United States, would be open to court challenge, and would encourage new private schools to locate in districts that already spend a lot per pupil. One way out of this dilemma would be to set a uniform subsidy rate (adjusted for geographic differences in educational costs) but at a level that was below spending in even the poorest public school districts. However, this might discourage new schools from forming and would likely require supplementation by parents (and create greater selection effects of the kind discussed in the last section). A possible compromise would be to set the subsidy level in such a way that it helped to equalize spending across districts but did not go all the way toward setting a uniform level within each state (or nationally, if federal funds were involved).[42] Such a compromise could lead to interesting new political coalitions in which liberals who have long espoused more equal spending on education made common cause with those conservatives who advocate choice.

An equally difficult issue is whether the subsidy level should vary with student characteristics. Just as Title I education funds are intended to compensate poorer school districts with educationally disadvantaged students, vouchers could be designed to provide more of a subsidy to these same students. Disabled students or those for whom English is a second language could be similarly helped. This would make such students more attractive to whatever school they attended and would offset some of the inevitable sorting effects described earlier. However, it would also greatly complicate the administration of the subsidies, and some inequities would undoubtedly remain.

Another question is whether subsidies should vary with student performance. Too often in discussions of education the role of student effort is forgotten. Yet students are not empty vessels into which more education can be poured; they must be involved in the process. The recent ending of social promotion in Chicago, for example, appears to have boosted test scores there. This suggests that some consideration might be given to basing voucher amounts on student academic gains as measured by an objective test during the preceding school year.

Finally, one could vary subsidy levels to achieve still other goals, such as improving urban education. Large concentrations of poor and minority children in urban areas have put an extreme burden on schools in such areas and contributed to the out-migration of white middle-class families. One way to slow this downward spiral would be to offer higher subsidies to families living in urban areas, although this clearly would be resisted by other jurisdictions.

Information and Counseling

A common criticism of vouchers is that they require parents to be informed consumers of education, even though most parents don't have the time, the ability, or the information that would enable them to make good assessments of their alternatives. The problem is likely to be most severe for parents with the least education. Thus information about choice schools will become increasingly important if vouchers become more widely available.

Currently, information exchange between schools and parents is sparse. A recent study found that few parents believe their child's school does "very well" at communicating with them about anything except their child's academic progress.[43] This will likely change in a free choice world, when all schools will have to market themselves to potential buyers and to maintain enrollment through better communication with parents.[44] For some schools, the temptation to present misleading or exaggerated information will be strong.

Because good information is important to making a voucher program work, and because schools themselves may not provide unbiased or comparable data on their programs, public information and counseling is likely to be needed. From the beginning, scholars such as Chubb and Moe have argued that centralized information is essential in any large voucher program.[45] Even with such information available, there is no guarantee that most parents will use it to guide their choices.

Finally, even with free government information, it will be difficult to accurately compare diverse schools without a common measure of student success. Most parents will have a difficult time comparing school A, a back-to-basics program that assigns nightly homework and bases grades on weekly tests, to school B, a progressive school that encourages new forms of learning and evaluates students on a broader set of criteria. Any parent quickly understands, however, that if school B's students experience more rapid gains on a national (or state) reading assessment, it probably has a better program than school A. A system of national or state-based standards backed up by good assessments would make such comparisons possible. Standards and assessments would also make detailed monitoring or regulation of individual schools less necessary while preserving accountability for the expenditure of public funds.

Transportation

Public schools, unlike private schools, spend a significant amount of money for transportation. In 1994–95 the average yearly cost of transporting a student to and from school was $417, and 58 percent of all public school students relied on such subsidized transportation to get to school.[46] The transportation issue has not gained much attention yet, as most voucher experiments are operating in large cities that have good public transportation systems. A study of the Cleveland voucher program, however, found that the most frequently cited reason that students declined to participate after being awarded a scholarship was lack of transportation.[47] If voucher programs expand to cover larger geographic areas, it may become a major issue, and lack of transportation funding could diminish the potential of vouchers to provide more opportunities for disadvantaged children to attend better schools.

Two Choice Plans

Using the program elements previously described as building blocks, an almost infinite number of choice plans can be designed. In table 9-2 just two such plans are illustrated. Plan X, described in column one of the table, is a more conservative plan that is low cost, emphasizes individual (student and parent) responsibility, and calls for minimal government regulation. Plan Y, described in column two, is a more liberal plan that is higher cost and that emphasizes compensatory funding of education for the disadvantaged, education standards, public accountability, strict separation of church and state, and the achievement of racial balance. Clearly, any number of variations on these two plans exists. The point is that they bear about as much resemblance to each other as either one does to the existing public school system.

The Evidence on Effectiveness

After all is said and done, the allure of choice plans is their promise to improve educational performance, especially among the most disadvantaged. Whether vouchers can do this or not remains controversial. And as the last section has emphasized, their effect may very much depend on the particular version of choice that is designed and implemented.

Table 9-2. *The Devil Is in the Details: Potential Design Elements in Two School Choice Plans*

Factor	Plan X	Plan Y
Student eligibility	Universal	Means tested
Average subsidy level	Low (some fraction of per pupil spending in public schools)	High (current per pupil spending)
Variation in subsidy level		
By school district	Linked to current per pupil spending in district	Linked to per pupil spending in state or nation
With student need	No variation	Varies with family income or educational need
With student performance	Extra subsidy tied to achievement gains/ no social promotion	No variation
With urban location	No variation	Extra subsidies for children in urban areas
School eligibility		
Religious included?	Yes	No
Accreditation process/regulatory framework	Less prescriptive, similar to independent schools	More prescriptive, similar to current charter schools
Accountability for results	No standards, let market determine outcomes	Standards, with loss of accreditation if fail to improve or achieve
Admissions	Students selected by schools from applicant pool (subject to current civil rights laws)	Students admitted by lottery from applicant pool
Counseling/ information	Parents inform themselves, no special effort to provide	Parents provided with information on how schools rank against national or state standards, individual counseling also available
Transportation	Not subsidized	Subsidized

There are three bodies of evidence with which to evaluate the potential of choice to improve performance. The first is studies that have compared the effectiveness of public and private schools. The second is evaluations of actual choice plans. And the third is studies that have looked at the effects of competition on public school performance.

The Effectiveness of Public versus Private Schools

Interest in school choice has been fueled by a perception that private schools educate children more effectively and at lower cost than their public counterparts do, so it is worth looking at the dimensions of the private school sector in the United States and the extent to which it is or is not outperforming the public schools.

About one-quarter of all elementary and secondary schools in the United States are private, but because they tend to be small, they enroll only 11 percent of all students. Most (79 percent) are religiously affiliated, and one-third of all private schools are sponsored by the Catholic Church. Although many of these schools serve poor, minority families in the inner city, private schools have student bodies that are, on average, more affluent and have fewer minorities than those in public schools.[48] Private schools are extremely heterogeneous, including the elite boarding schools in New England that have long been training grounds for Ivy League colleges, schools serving the handicapped or children with behavior problems, parochial schools located in urban neighborhoods, schools with experimental or progressive educational philosophies, and a rapidly growing number of Christian evangelical schools. Tuition can vary greatly as well, from $1,628 for Catholic elementary schools to $9,525 for nonsectarian secondary schools. As noted earlier, the average tuition for a private school was $3,116 in 1993–94. This contrasts with an average cost of $6,492 for public schools in the same year. The higher cost of the public schools is somewhat exaggerated by this comparison, because most private schools are elementary schools, which are cheaper to operate than secondary schools, and because public schools must pay for special and vocational education as well as comply with various rules from which private schools are exempt. (See table 9-3 for further comparisons of the two sectors.)

The question of whether private or public schools provide the better education has long been debated and has been addressed by numerous studies with no consistent results. Simple comparisons of public and private school students generally find that the latter outperform the former, but this may be because private schools are selective institutions.

One particularly influential study of high schools, conducted by Coleman and others in 1982, found that students in private schools had higher aspirations and higher levels of achievement than those in public schools, even after adjusting for differences in family background. The difference in average achievement was about one grade level. The authors of the study attribute the stronger performance of private schools to the fact that they are more likely to be academically demanding (for example, in having better attendance, more homework, and more rigorous courses) and to provide more orderly and disciplined environments. They note that where these conditions are present in public schools, those schools perform equally well, and that the differences among schools are much larger than any public-private differences.

Another conclusion from the Coleman study is that the availability of private schools has neither increased nor decreased racial segregation. On the one hand, the public sector has a higher proportion of minorities than the private sector. On the other hand, *individual* private schools typically have student bodies that are more integrated, both economically and racially, than the public sector.[49] Similarly, Jay Greene found both more classroom integration and greater racial tolerance in private schools, using data from a longitudinal study of students who were high school seniors in 1992.[50] However, the higher degree of integration found within the private school sector is probably related to the relatively small number of minorities enrolled in these schools. Any attempt to open private schools more broadly might be met with stronger resistance to integration on the part of white parents and to a higher degree of racial segregation than now exists.

Critics of the Coleman study have noted that it may not have controlled adequately for the tendency of more able, or more motivated, students to attend private schools. Numerous subsequent attempts to correct this flaw (using instrumental variables and value-added models) have produced inconsistent results and have not resolved the issue to anyone's satisfaction. As one recent study that has reviewed this literature concludes, "consistent estimates cannot be produced using the available data at this time."[51] Given the enormous heterogeneity that exists *within* each sector, overall comparisons may not even be particularly meaningful. A more interesting question is what happens when children from a particular school district are given a wider choice of schools to attend. To answer this question, we turn now to recent experiments with school choice that have been designed to answer this question.

Evidence from Existing Experiments

Ongoing experiments with school choice are producing two kinds of data relevant to assessing its effects. Data on parental satisfaction suggest that low-income families are extremely pleased with their new private schools. Data on whether children are actually achieving more in these schools are mixed.

Table 9-3. *Public versus Private Schools, 1993–94*

Characteristic	Public schools	Private schools			
		All private	Catholic	Other religious	Nonsectarian
Number of schools	80,740	26,093	8,351	12,180	5,563
Percent of all schools	75.6	24.4	7.8	11.4	5.2
Percent of all private schools	...	...	32.0	46.7	21.3
Enrollment	41,621,660	4,970,548	2,516,028	1,686,069	768,451
Percent of all enrollment	89.3	10.7	5.4	3.6	1.7
Percent of all private school enrollment	...	...	50.6	33.9	15.5
Average spending or tuition (dollars)[a]	6,492[b]	3,116	2,178	2,915	6,631
Elementary[a]	n.a.	2,138	1,628	2,606	4,693
Secondary[a]	n.a.	4,578	3,643	5,261	9,525
Average teacher salary (dollars)					
Bachelor's degree, no experience	21,923	16,239	16,603	15,232	18,054
Top of salary schedule	40,517	27,274	28,719	24,247	31,594
Base salary[c]	34,149	21,897	21,603	19,970	25,442
Percent of teachers with master's degree	42.0	29.8	29.7	25.8	36.4
Student-teacher ratio	17.3	15.0	19.0	14.0	9.8
Teacher experience (percent)					
Less than 3 years	9.6	20.2	17.4	23.9	19.7
More than 20 years	29.5	12.8	16.6	9.3	11.5

Percent of schools offering					
Programs for the handicapped	89.2	24.8	25.7	16.4	24.0[d]
Gifted programs	70.7	24.9	28.2	22.8	15.0
Vocational programs	12.4	3.6	1.3	4.1	5.9
Remedial reading	80.9	52.8	70.9	42.7	47.7
Remedial math	60.9	40.4	54.0	31.7	39.1
English as second language	42.7	11.3	12.4	9.5	13.7
Average graduation rate	93.0	98.0	99.0	98.0	96.0
Average college application rate	57.0	88.0	91.0	82.0	84.0

Sources: Sharon A. Bobbitt, Stephen P. Broughman, and Kerry J. Gruber, *Schools and Staffing in the United States: Selected Data for Public and Private Schools, 1993–94* (National Center for Education Statistics, Department of Education, 1995); and for spending and tuition data, Department of Education, *Digest of Education Statistics, 1997*, pp. 72, 172.

n.a. Not available.

a. Private school tuition listed is the average paid by students for attendance and does not necessarily equal total spending on behalf of each student. Therefore public school spending and private school tuition as reported here may not be comparable figures for the cost of educating a student.

b. Total expenditure per pupil in the public schools, equal to day-to-day operating costs of schools plus expenditures for construction, equipment, debt financing, and non-prekindergarten through grade 12 programs, such as adult education. Current expenditures, which reflect only the day-to-day operating costs of schools, were $5,767 per pupil in 1993–94.

c. Base salary does not include supplementary salaries, which some schools offer teachers during the summer; it represents ten months only.

d. Excludes special education private schools, all of which include programs for the handicapped.

PARENTAL SATISFACTION. Voucher programs are typically oversubscribed, suggesting considerable dissatisfaction with the available public schools and a strong latent demand for more parental choice.[52] Not only are the programs oversubscribed, but four different studies have found that parents are typically much more satisfied with the private schools participating in these plans than they are with the existing public schools. They are pleased with what their children are learning, with school discipline, and with opportunities for parental involvement.[53] Perhaps because of their enthusiasm, parents are also less likely to transfer their children to another school, with the result that mobility rates are lower than in the public schools.[54]

TEST SCORES. The longest running experiment, and thus the one for which the most data exists, is the publicly funded school choice program in Milwaukee. Three different studies of the available data from this experiment have come to three different conclusions. One study, by Paul Peterson and his colleagues, found that by the third and fourth year of the program, choice students had made sizeable gains relative to their public school counterparts in both reading and math.[55] Another study, by John Witte and colleagues, found no differences between the two groups.[56] And a third study, by Cecilia Rouse, found gains in math but not in reading.[57] There are several reasons for these differences, including how each research team selected its control or comparison group and how they chose to adjust for any remaining differences between students who took advantage of the voucher and those who remained in the Milwaukee public schools. After carefully reviewing these three studies, we conclude that each has advantages and disadvantages, and that it is simply not possible at the current time to render a clear verdict on the outcome of the experiment. (For additional details, see appendix table 9A-1.) A similar debate seems to be under way about the effectiveness of vouchers in Cleveland. Early evaluations by Peterson's team found gains in math and reading scores for the scholarship students, but a study by Indiana University researchers shows no academic improvement resulting from the program.[58] Once again, controversies exist about the quality of the available test data and the appropriate statistical techniques to use in analyzing them.

What should be concluded from this debate? Much depends, in our view, on whether educational gaps between disadvantaged and other children have been perceived to have normally grown or diminished over time. We think the evidence suggests the former—that children from poor families fall further and further behind with additional years of schooling.[59] If this is the case, then the results from Milwaukee, and also from Cleveland, are modestly encouraging, because they suggest some attenuation of this pattern among children attending private schools.[60] This interpretation is consistent with the findings of Coleman and others that Catholic high schools have had some success in narrowing achievement gaps by race and income. At the same time, the fact that the results from existing experiments are quite sensitive to various analytic and data choices suggests that they are not terribly robust and that the test score effects of offering a choice of schools to students are probably not very large, especially in comparison to differences in the effectiveness of existing schools within each sector. In fact, in a comparison of three different types of public schools in Milwaukee (regular, magnet, and enriched), Cecilia Rouse finds that the enriched schools—which have supplemental funding and smaller class sizes than the regular public schools—outperform choice schools in reading and are equivalent in math.[61]

Additional data from these and other experiments with vouchers should become available over the next few years, making somewhat firmer conclusions possible about the potential of vouchers to improve academic performance. Particularly notable in this context is a new experiment with vouchers in New York City, where 1,200 students accepted scholarships in the fall of 1997 to attend private schools. Because the sponsors of this program are committed to learning more about its effectiveness, it has been designed to produce clearer answers on the possible academic benefits of choice.

The Effects of Competition on Public School Performance

One of the putative benefits of choice is its effects on existing public schools. Indeed, if choice were widely available, one might expect to see many of the differences between public and private schools disappear as competition forced each sector to adopt the best practices of the other.[62] Thus far, however, choice experiments have been far too small to provide any direct evidence on this issue.[63]

Less direct evidence comes from studies that have examined how public schools respond when they face greater competition from either other public schools or existing private schools. To study this issue, Caroline Hoxby used the fact that parents have a greater choice of schools in metropolitan areas with many independent school districts (for example, Boston and Albany) than they do in areas with few or only one (for example, Miami and Albuquerque). She found that in cities where there is more choice among public schools (1) reading and math scores are higher, (2) per pupil costs are lower, (3) segregation by race, income, and ethnicity is unaffected,

(4) parents are more involved in the schools, and (5) the curriculum is more challenging and the environment more disciplined.[64] These effects are strongest in areas where schools face strong financial incentives to improve their performance because they rely heavily on property taxes (which are sensitive to housing values and thus to parental choice of district).

Competition with existing public schools can come not only from other public schools but also from private schools. Hoxby made use of the fact that the proportion of children enrolled in private schools is much larger in some areas (for example, over 25 percent in Philadelphia, St. Louis, and New Orleans) than in others (for example, less than 6 percent in Pine Bluff, Arkansas, or Pueblo, Colorado) to examine the effects of competition from this sector on the performance of the public schools. She found that competition from private schools also enhances achievement, educational attainment, and subsequent wages among public school students. And again, it does not appear to affect the degree of sorting or segregation by race, ethnicity, income, or ability.[65]

Several other studies appear to be consistent both with Hoxby's findings and with theoretical predictions from a choice model.[66] However, none of this research provides a very satisfactory test of the long-run effects of competition on public school performance, given its strong assumptions and the lack of an actual experiment with which to assess the theory.

Finally, it is worth distinguishing between effects on performance and effects on school productivity (performance per dollar spent). Theory suggests that competition should increase productivity, and Hoxby's results suggest it does. However, what matters most to public officials is performance per dollar of *public* funding, and there are four reasons why this narrower definition of productivity might decrease under a choice plan. First, public dollars might substitute for what parents are now spending out of their own pockets for private school tuition and fees. Second, religious or philanthropic contributions to private schools might decline in the face of more public support for vouchers. Third, private schools might increase their tuition in response to greater demand. And finally, the budgets of public schools that lose students might not decline in tandem with their enrollments, if political pressures shield them from fiscal competition or if they lose the economies of scale they currently enjoy. Offsetting these potential effects are two factors that work in the opposite direction. First, private schools cost less than public schools (mainly because they have less administrative overhead and pay lower salaries) and appear to be more efficient. Second, greater competition should force such economies in the public sector as well.

Broader Implications for the Use of Vouchers to Achieve Public Purposes

The experience with school choice suggests a number of lessons that may inform the broader debate about whether vouchers are a good way of achieving public purposes:

—First and foremost, the devil is in the details. Vouchers can be designed to accomplish almost any purpose. The debate about them has too often pitted those who believe in the efficacy of markets against those who believe in a stronger government role. But precisely because they are publicly financed, vouchers will always come with public strings attached. The question is how well the strings are designed to accomplish various purposes. The two voucher plans described earlier in this chapter illustrate the range of possibilities.

—Vouchers work best when consumers are adequately informed about their choices and receive some feedback on how their children are doing. Education vouchers without some means of holding schools accountable for results and making information about those results available to parents could lead to inappropriate use of public funds. Not every consumer needs to be attentive to such information. A small number is sufficient to make the system work. But without such information, vouchers could lead to very disappointing results.

—Provider groups (for example, teachers unions) are likely to oppose vouchers because they may produce competition that erodes job security or the wage premium associated with working in a protected market. This political opposition may lead to program rules that are suboptimal and undermine the effectiveness of the program. (Alum Rock is a case in point, as is Milwaukee to a lesser extent.)

—Where there is an existing private market for a good (for example, private schools), publicly provided vouchers may replace private expenditures (fiscal substitution) and increase government costs in the process. Offsetting this are possible savings of public funds if the private sector provides the same product at lower cost. The net effect is not clear at the present time, and it is likely to depend on the design of the voucher (for example, whether it is targeted just on low-income parents).

—Supply may not respond to the increased demand induced by vouchers, especially in the short run. Over the longer term, new institutions are likely to enter the market. There is little evidence to date on this question from experiments with school vouchers, because these experiments have been too small to have much effect on the number of private schools or their enrollments.

—Vouchers permit a greater diversity of suppliers of education. Whether this is a plus or a minus depends on whether it is believed that education should be a standardized product (an experience that all children share in common) or that it should be tailored to the specific needs and preferences of different groups. The public appears to hold ambivalent, if not inconsistent, views on this issue, and there is probably a middle ground between rampant multiculturalism on the one hand and a regimented curriculum on the other.

—Targeting vouchers on low-income groups has several advantages, including reducing the likelihood of fiscal substitution, limiting short-run pressures on supply, and improving opportunity by giving disadvantaged groups access to higher-quality services than they could otherwise afford. Offsetting this is the fact that this group may lack the information and ability to take advantage of such opportunities and that, in the absence of more sophisticated and powerful consumers, the market may not produce a very good product. In addition, another income-tested program might further reduce incentives to work or to marry.[67]

—Evidence from existing experiments with vouchers suggests that low-income parents are eager participants in voucher programs and have exercised this option enthusiastically. Whether the education their children receive is of higher quality as a result remains somewhat unclear, but the results to date are modestly encouraging. Rigorous evaluations of such experiments help to substitute facts for rhetoric in the debate about market-based solutions to social problems.

—Because both buyers and sellers in private markets can select one another, vouchers may lead to a *greater* segmenting of recipients by race, ethnicity, income, or ability. There is some evidence that school choice will produce this result, and it remains a serious concern. But the standard for comparison needs to be the high degree of segregation that already exists within the existing public school system, not some nonexistent ideal.

—When consumers are given a choice, they express greater satisfaction with the product chosen and become more involved in its use. There is quite clear evidence of this from several school choice experiments.

—Public institutions may improve under the spur of competition from the private sector. At the same time, they may lose some of their best customers. Applied to vouchers, the concern has been that they would drain away good students and involved parents from the public schools, thereby reducing the ability of those schools to educate the students that remain. Our reading of the evidence is that the positive effect of competition dominates the negative effect of a depleted public sector.

—Vouchers may be a good vehicle for restructuring the financing of a public good. Currently, education is funded by a mix of federal, state, and local funds, with the result that spending per child varies enormously from district to district. Greater federal or state involvement in the funding of vouchers could even out some of these disparities, replace categorical programs at the federal level, and still compensate schools for the extra burdens involved in educating some groups of children.

—In many areas, including education, vouchers are likely to operate side by side with continuing public provision of a good or service. Proposals to completely replace public provision with vouchers are often unrealistic, suggesting the need to think in terms of the costs and benefits of a mixed system.

Table 9A-1. *Milwaukee and Cleveland Effectiveness Assessment Summaries*

Study	Choice experiment	Experimental sample	Control group
Witte[a]	Milwaukee Parental Choice Program, 1991–95	Choice students	Random sample of MPS students
Greene, Peterson, and Du[b]	Milwaukee Parental Choice Program, 1991–95	Choice students	Nonselected choice applicants who remained in MPS
Rouse[c]	Milwaukee Parental Choice Program, 1991–95	Choice students	(1) Random sample of MPS students; (2) nonselected choice applicants who remained in MPS
Greene, Howell, and Peterson[d]	Cleveland Scholarship Program, 1996–97	Choice students enrolled in the two new schools established for the program	Each student's own test score at the beginning of the school year
Indiana University[e]	Cleveland Scholarship Program, 1996–97	Third grade choice students	Cleveland public school students

a. John F. Witte, Troy D. Sterr, and Christopher A. Thorn, *Fifty Year Report, Milwaukee Parental Choice Program* (University of Wisconsin, 1995).

b. Jay P. Greene, Paul E. Peterson, and Jiangtao Du, "School Choice in Milwaukee: A Randomized Experiment," in Peterson and Hassel, eds., *Learning from School Choice.*

c. Cecilia Elena Rouse, "Private School Vouchers and Student Achievement: An Evaluation of the Milwaukee Parental Choice Program," *Quarterly Journal of Economics*, vol. 133, no. 2 (May 1998).

d. Jay P. Greene, William G. Howell, and Paul E. Peterson, "Lessons from the Cleveland Scholarship Program," in Peterson and Hassel, eds., *Learning from School Choice.*

e. Kim K. Metcalf and others, "A Comparative Evaluation of the Cleveland Scholarship and Tutoring Grant Program" (Indiana University School of Education, March 16, 1998).

Method of controlling for background and ability	Findings	Issues
Statistical controls, including prior test score	No significant difference in math or reading between choice and MPS students	Statistical controls may not fully adjust for unobserved differences between two groups
Reliance on experimental data (with controls for fact that lottery was school specific)	Scores 3–5 and 5–12 percentage points higher in reading and math, respectively, in years 3 and 4	Small sample (40 by year 4) and possible nonrandom attrition from both experimental and control group (about half of rejects left the MPS; no test data available)
Individual fixed effects model comparing students to own projected scores over time if they had remained in public schools	Scores 1.5–2 percentage points higher in math, no difference in reading scores	Two groups of students assumed to have same test scores trajectories (no catch up or falling behind for disadvantaged in absence of program)
Method unclear; apparently based on individual gains (fall to fall) compared to Milwaukee low-income scholarship applicants and to typical inner-city students	Increase of 5 and 15 percentile points in reading and math, respectively; 5 percentile point decrease in language	Very preliminary findings based on limited data
Statistical controls, including prior test scores	No significant difference between choice and public school students in five subject area tests, accounting for background characteristics	Very preliminary findings based on limited data

Appendix 9B
Examples of Privately Funded Voucher Programs

The Educational Choice Charitable Trust, established by Indianapolis businessman J. Patrick Rooney in 1991 to provide half-tuition scholarships of up to $800 to low-income families, was the first such program. In 1996 over a thousand students attended seventy different private schools (including religious schools) thanks to the program.[68]

Several San Antonio business leaders, inspired by Rooney, developed the Children's Educational Opportunity Foundation of San Antonio (CEO San Antonio), a voucher program similar to the one in Indianapolis, in 1992. Two years later they expanded the organization (renamed CEO America) to provide information, support services, and financial assistance to existing voucher programs and to groups that want to start programs nationwide.[69] Recently, the group established CEO Horizon, a project that provides vouchers of up to $4,000 a year for ten years to every student who applies in San Antonio's largely poor and Hispanic Edgewood school district.[70] It also sponsors thirty voucher experiments, most of which began independently, including the well-known Parents Advancing Values in Education (PAVE) program in Milwaukee (the privately funded counterpart to the publicly funded program described above) and the Giffen Elementary School program in Albany, New York. Most CEO America-sponsored programs offer only partial scholarships, but they reached over 10,000 students in 1996–97.[71]

In 1996 philanthropists in New York City established the School Choice Scholarships Foundation to provide low-income students in kindergarten through grade four with half-tuition scholarships of up to $1,400. This experiment, designed to facilitate evaluation, selects students randomly from the eligible pool and maintains a control group so that achievement changes can be scientifically studied.[72]

The Thomas B. Fordham Foundation initiated a voucher program in Dayton, Ohio, beginning in the fall of 1998. The vouchers cover two-thirds of private school tuition for up to 650 children.[73] Another new program, the Washington Scholarship Fund, was established by philanthropists Ted Forstmann and John Walton in late 1997 and provides $1,700 scholarships to low-income students in Washington, D.C.[74]

Notes

1. Lowell C. Rose, Alec M. Gallup, and Stanley M. Elam, *The 30th Annual Phi Delta Kappan/Gallup Poll of the Public's Attitudes toward the Public Schools* (September 1998) (http://www.pdkintl.org/kappan/kp9809-a.htm [January, 29, 1999]).

2. John Stuart Mill, *On Liberty* (The Macmillan Company, 1986), originally published in 1859. This section of the chapter owes much to two excellent historical essays, one by Paul E. Peterson, "The New Politics of Choice," in Diane Ravitch and Maris A. Vinovskis, eds., *Learning from the Past: What History Teaches Us about School Reform* (Johns Hopkins University Press, 1995) and the other by John R. Henig, *Rethinking School Choice: Limits of the Market Metaphor* (Princeton University Press, 1994).

3. This philosophy was most strongly articulated by Horace Mann and John Dewey in the nineteenth century. However, as Paul Peterson notes in his review of the historical tension between libertarian ideals and the Hegelian arguments espoused by Dewey, the Supreme Court has tended to uphold the rights of parents against those of the state. The Court has struck down laws compelling children to attend only public schools, to salute the flag, or to comply with compulsory school laws when (as in the case of the Amish) this conflicts with their religious beliefs. Peterson, "The New Politics of Choice," p. 223.

4. See, for example, Henig, *Rethinking School Choice;* and Amy Gutmann, *Democratic Education* (Princeton University Press, 1994).

5. Milton Friedman, "The Role of Government in Education," in Robert A. Solo, ed., *Economics and the Public Interest* (Rutgers University Press, 1955), p. 127.

6. F. J. Capell and L. Doscher, *A Study of Alternatives in American Education: Vol. VI, Student Outcomes at Alum Rock 1974–1976* (Santa Monica, Calif.: RAND, 1981). The study of student outcomes in the Alum Rock district found "no appreciable differences" in reading achievement between students in regular and choice schools at the end of the three-year program.

7. Henig, *Rethinking School Choice*, pp. 71–72.

8. John E. Chubb and Terry M. Moe, *Politics, Markets, and America's Schools* (Brookings, 1990), pp. 219–25. Each school district would organize a central office to provide parental information and administer the vouchers. All students in the same state would receive the same voucher amount, and the voucher would be financed through a progressive state tax system in which richer districts would pay more than poorer districts. Individual parents would not be allowed to supplement the state voucher, but if a community decided collectively that it wanted to increase the amount, it could levy a local tax for that purpose. Schools would be allowed to admit students as they choose, subject only to antidiscrimination laws.

9. Support for allowing students to choose a private school at public expense has grown from 24 percent to 44 percent between 1993 and 1998. Rose, Gallup, and Elam, *30th Annual Phi Delta Kappan/Gallup Poll.*

10. The local school is the centerpiece of many communities, especially in rural and inner-city neighborhoods. In inner cities that have lost most services and industries, local schools are one of the few remaining "symbols of local order." A school choice program that would allow students to leave the neighborhood to attend school may decrease the importance of the community school and further alienate the residents of the neighborhood. Alan Ehrenhalt, "The Radical Idea of Neighborhood Schools," *Governing*, vol. 9, no 5 (February 1996).

11. William H. Clune and John F. Witte, *Choice and Control in American Education*, vol. 1 (Philadelphia: Falmer, 1990), p. 43.

12. Mike Malone, Joe Nathan, and Darryl Sedio, *Facts, Figures, and Faces: A Look at Minnesota's School Choice Programs* (St. Paul, Minn.: Humphrey Institute of Public Affairs, University of Minnesota, 1993), p. 4.

13. Nina H. Shokraii and Sarah E. Youssef, *School Choice Programs: What's Happening in the States* (Washington, D.C.: Heritage Foundation) (http://www. heritage.org/heritage/schools/[June 29, 1998]).

14. Personal communication with the Center for Education Reform, Washington, D.C., March 1999.

15. For further analysis of the differences between vouchers and charter schools, see Bryan C. Hassel, "Charter Schools: Politics and Practice in Four States," in Paul E. Peterson and Bryan C. Hassel, eds., *Learning from School Choice* (Brookings, 1998), pp. 249–71. As he notes, private schools, unlike charters, can set their own admission standards, can charge tuition, are less accountable to public authorities, and may be affiliated with religious institutions. However, as we emphasized in the section entitled "Recent Choice Proposals" in this chapter, these two types of choice can easily merge, depending on the particular design of a voucher program.

16. During his presidency, Bush endorsed three proposals: the Excellence in Education Act, which allotted $230 million to fund choice scholarships and experiments, in 1989; America 2000, a virtually identical program, in 1991; and the GI Bill for Children, a $500 million program of $1,000 scholarships for middle- and low-income students to attend the public, private, or religious school of their choice, in 1992. George Bush, "Remarks from the Presidency: 7 June 1990, 18 April 1991, 22 May 1991, 7 June 1991" (www.csdl.tamu.edu [February 3, 1998]).

17. Peter Passell, "An Economics Lesson: The Candidates' Plans for Education," *New York Times*, November 3, 1996, p. 4A. Though Dole said the program was for low- and middle-income students, his proposal did not require that states use an income measure in determining scholarship recipients. The proposal provided $500 to elementary students and $750 to high school students to pay for tuition at any private school.

18. Paul E. Peterson, "School Choice: A Report Card," in Peterson and Hassel, *Learning from School Choice*, p. 8.

19. Lizette Alvarez, "House and Senate Negotiators Agree on Education Tax Credits," *New York Times*, June 11, 1998, p. 24; Paul Coverdell, "Coverdell 'A+

Accounts': the Facts on Education Savings Accounts" (www.senate.gov/~coverdell/aplus/ [June 29, 1998]).

20. "District of Columbia Student Opportunity Scholarship Act of 1997," from S. 1502, 105 Cong. 1 sess., passed November 9, 1997. This proposal expanded upon the earlier, unsuccessful House amendment 891 (to H.R. 2546, appropriations bill for D.C. government) proposed by Gunderson on November 2, 1995, to offer scholarships to poor residents of the District of Columbia for private schools. See also Sari Horwitz, "Poll Finds Backing for D.C. School Vouchers," *Washington Post*, May 23, 1998, p. F1.

21. 1992 Colorado State Legislature, "Vouchers for Education," Amendment 7—Constitutional Amendment Initiated by Petition. The amendment included no provision for information or transportation and no variation in subsidy level attached to student need.

22. Michael A. Shires, Cathy S. Krop, C. Peter Rydell, and Stephen J. Carroll, *The Effects of the California Voucher Initiative on Public Expenditures for Education* (Santa Monica, Calif.: RAND, 1994), pp. 2–3; Peter Robinson, *School Days: An Essay on the Hoover Institution Conference "Choice and Vouchers—the Future of American Education?"* (Hoover Institution on War, Revolution, and Peace, Stanford University, 1993), pp. 10–11. The voucher would equal approximately $2,600 per student, religious and single-sex schools were acceptable under the law, and the legislation restricted the ability of the state legislature to regulate private schools after passage of the initiative.

23. Myron Lieberman, "The School Choice Fiasco," *The Public Interest*, vol. 114 (Winter 1994), p. 29. Lieberman quotes the explanation of the California Teachers Union of why the union fought against allowing the choice proposal to even go on the ballot: "There are some proposals that are so evil that they should never even be presented to the voters. We do not believe, for example, that we should hold an election on 'empowering' the Ku Klux Klan. And we would not think it's 'undemocratic' to oppose voting on legalizing child prostitution. Destroying public education, in our view, belongs in the same category."

24. Parents may not use the tax credit if their contribution is for "the direct benefit of their children." Lynn Schnaiberg, "Arizona Law Grants Tax Credit for Tuition-Aid Donations," *Education Week*, April 16, 1997 (http://www.edweek.org/ew/1997/29credit.h16 [June 30, 1999]).

25. "Minnesota Education Credit," *Laws of Minnesota: 1997 First Special Session*, chap. 4, art. 13, sec. 3 (290:0674), p. 3381.

26. Some of these local plans, such as the ones in Milwaukee and in Cleveland, were authorized by the state legislature and in this sense could be called state sponsored, although locally implemented.

27. Paul E. Peterson, "Top Ten Questions Asked about School Choice," *Brookings Papers on Education Policy, 1999*, pp. 14–15.

28. Students with family annual incomes of less than 200 percent of the poverty line receive $2,500 each and those with incomes greater than 200 percent

of the poverty line receive $1,875 each. Although any students in grades K–4 may apply for one of the 2,000 available scholarships, preferences are given to students with family annual incomes below the poverty line and students currently attending public schools.

29. Jay P. Greene, William G. Howell, and Paul E. Peterson, "Lessons from the Cleveland Scholarship Program," in Peterson and Hassel, *Learning from School Choice*, pp. 357–92.

30. Jeff Archer, "Pennsylvania District Gives Go-Ahead to Local Voucher Plan," *Education Week*, vol. 17, no. 29 (April 1, 1998), p. 3; William C. Smith, "Southeast Delco School District Sued over Tuition Voucher Plan," *The Legal Intelligencer*, April 22, 1998, p. 6.

31. As originally proposed by Milton Friedman, every parent would receive a voucher equal in value to the current cost of educating a child in the public schools (or a little less, since the vouchers would have to cover those currently attending private schools as well). Parents would then use the vouchers to enroll their children in any school—public or private—in any district, city, or state that was willing to accept their child. Milton Friedman and Rose Friedman, *Free to Choose: A Personal Statement* (Harcourt Brace, Friedman, and Friedman, 1980), pp. 160–61.

32. See Coverdell, "A+ Accounts." The Treasury estimates that 70 percent of the savings would go to those in the top income quintile and the Joint Committee on Taxation asserted that half the savings would go to families whose children attend private school anyway. "Wrong Way on Education," *Washington Post*, March 17, 1998, p. A20.

33. Peterson, "School Choice," p. 24.

34. June Kronholz, "Class Action: A Poor School District in Texas Is Learning to Cope in a Test Tube—Edgewood, on the Rebound, Becomes a Focal Point of Debate on Vouchers—Angst over 700 Defections," *Wall Street Journal*, September 11, 1998, p. A1.

35. Sharon A. Bobbitt, Stephen P. Broughman, and Kerry J. Gruber, *Schools and Staffing in the United States: Selected Data for Public and Private Schools, 1993–94* (National Center for Education Statistics, Department of Education, 1995).

36. General Accounting Office, *Higher Education: Ensuring Quality Education from Proprietary Institutions* (1996); General Accounting Office, *Proprietary Schools: Millions Spent to Train Students for Oversupplied Occupations* (1997).

37. For example, a survey of children in grades 3 through 12 in 1993 found that 20 percent were attending schools chosen by their parents (11 percent were in public schools; 9 percent in private schools) and that these parents were disproportionately well educated and affluent. However, somewhat surprisingly, black parents and those living in urban areas were more likely to choose their child's school than whites or those in nonurban areas. National Center for Education Statistics, *Use of School Choice*, Education Policy Issues: Statistical Perspectives (Department of

Education, 1995). Maureen Allenberg Petronio's 1996 study of the Cambridge, Massachusetts, controlled choice program found that minority and low-income parents were more likely to select neighborhood schools than were nonminority or more affluent parents. Maureen Allenberg Petronio, "The Choices Parents Make," *Educational Leadership*, vol. 54, no. 2 (October 1996), p. 33. David Armor and Brett Peiser's 1998 study of interdistrict choice in Massachusetts found that choice families were more likely to be white and had higher socioeconomic status and higher achieving children than nonchoice families. David L. Armor and Brett M. Peiser, "Interdistrict Choice in Massachusetts," in Peterson and Hassel, *Learning from School Choice*. For a more theoretical exploration of these issues, see Dennis Epple and Richard E. Romano, "Competition between Private and Public Schools, Vouchers, and Peer-Group Effects," *American Economic Review*, vol. 88 (March 1998), pp. 33–62. Using a simulation model, they found some support for the argument that students will sort themselves by income and ability, and in a sequel to their published article, they found that conditioning the subsidy on student income or ability is not sufficient to eliminate such cream skimming.

38. For further discussion, see Peterson, "School Choice," pp. 26–28. He pointed out that critics of choice plans worry that more privileged families will leave the public schools, that children learn from their peers, and that inner-city schools contain many middle-class students who have a positive influence on their less-advantaged peers and then goes on to argue that none of these assumptions is well supported by the data from existing experiments involving low-income children. Also see Christopher Jencks and Susan Mayer, "The Social Consequences of Growing Up in a Poor Neighborhood," in Laurence E. Lynn and Michael G. H. McGeary, eds., *Inner-City Poverty in the United States* (Washington, D.C.: National Academy Press, 1990), pp. 111–86.

39. In 1993 the minority proportion in central-city public schools was over 80 percent in Boston, Chicago, Dallas, Detroit, Houston, Los Angeles, New York, and Washington, D.C. Peterson, "School Choice," p. 13. More recent data published by Gary Orfield and the National School Boards Association show that racial segregation has not declined and may be getting worse in the 1990s. A total of 60 percent of all minority students in public schools attend a predominantly minority school. National Center for Education Statistics, *Profile of Children in U.S. School Districts*, statistical analysis report (Department of Education, 1996). Segregation is worst in Northeastern cities, where 50 percent of black students and 50 percent of Hispanic students attend schools that are over 90 percent minority. Peter Schmidt, "Desegregation Study Spurs Debate over Equity Remedies," *Education Week*, January, 12, 1994, p. 5.

40. Department of Education, *Digest of Education Statistics, 1997* (1997). The public school figure is from table 169, p. 172, in current expenditures. The private school figure is from table 61, p. 72. The private school figure is the most recent available. Public school current expenditure per pupil in 1996–97 was $6,564 in 1997 dollars.

41. Ibid., table 168, p. 171. All figures in 1993–94 dollars. Also see table 3. Note that tuition may not cover the full costs of educating children in private schools.

42. It should be noted that two-thirds of the variance in spending across school districts results from the variance across rather than within states. Some of this variance—but only a small amount—is related to differences in the cost of living in different areas. See William N. Evans, Sheila E. Murray, and Robert M. Schwab, "Schoolhouses, Courthouses, and Statehouses after *Serrano*," *Journal of Policy Analysis and Management*, vol. 16 (1997), pp. 10–31.

43. Nancy Vaden-Kiernan and Kathryn Chandler, *Parents' Reports of School Practices to Involve Families*, Statistics in Brief Series (National Center for Education Statistics, Department of Education, 1996), p. 3. Items surveyed included "helped parents understand what children at their child's age are like," "provided information about why their child was placed in particular groups or classes," "helped them help their child learn at home," "provided information about how to help with homework," and "provided information about community services."

44. Ibid. Private schools already engage in these sorts of activities. Private school parents are more likely than public school parents to report that their children's schools do a good job of keeping parents informed of school affairs.

45. Chubb and Moe, *Politics, Markets, and America's Schools*, p. 221.

46. Department of Education, *Digest of Education Statistics, 1997*, table 51, p. 64.

47. Greene and Peterson, *Learning from School Choice*, p. 369. This was the most important reason among families that were aware they had been awarded a scholarship.

48. Only 4 percent of private school students receive free or reduced-price lunches, while 29 percent of public school students do. In addition, 46 percent of private schools enroll fewer than 5 percent minority students. Peter W. Cookson Jr., "New Kid on the Block: A Closer Look at America's Private Schools," *Brookings Review*, vol. 15, no. 1 (Winter 1997), p. 23.

49. James S. Coleman, Thomas Hoffer, and Sally Kilgore, *High School Achievement: Public, Catholic, and Private Schools Compared* (Basic Books, 1982), pp. 182–83.

50. Jay P. Greene, "Civic Values in Public and Private Schools," in Peterson and Hassel, *Learning from School Choice*, pp. 83–106.

51. Jens Ludwig, *Educational Achievement in Public, Private, and Catholic Schools: New Evidence on What We Know (and Don't Know)* (Georgetown University Press, 1996), p. 26. Ludwig, in a summer of 1998 personal communication, has also noted that whatever the evidence on existing public-private school differences, it does not tell us anything about the quality of new entrants into the private market.

52. In New York City, for example, there were over 20,000 applicants for 1,300 slots in the program that began in 1997 despite the fact that the scholarships

were only $1,400, less than tuition at most parochial schools. Peterson, "School Choice," p. 15.

53. Ibid., pp. 17–18.

54. Ibid., pp. 19–20.

55. Jay P. Greene, Paul E. Peterson, and Jiangtao Du, "School Choice in Milwaukee: A Randomized Experiment," in Peterson and Hassel, *Learning from School Choice*, pp. 335–56; Jay P. Greene, Paul E. Peterson, and Jiangtao Du, *The Effectiveness of School Choice in Milwaukee: A Secondary Analysis of Data from the Program's Evaluation* (Harvard, 1996).

56. Witte published findings every year for the first five years of the Milwaukee experiment, each in December, beginning in 1991. John F. Witte, *Achievement Effects of the Milwaukee Voucher Program* (University of Wisconsin, 1997).

57. Cecilia Elena Rouse, "Private School Vouchers and Student Achievement: An Evaluation of the Milwaukee Parental Choice Program," *Quarterly Journal of Economics*, vol. 133, no. 2 (May 1998); Cecilia Elena Rouse, "Schools and Student Achievement: More Evidence from the Milwaukee Parental Choice Program," *Economic Policy Review*, vol. 4, no. 1 (March 1998), pp. 61–78.

58. Greene, Howell, and Peterson, "Lessons from the Cleveland Scholarship Program"; Kim K. Metcalf, William J. Boone, Frances K. Stage, Todd L. Chilton, Patty Muller, and Polly Tait, *A Comparative Evaluation of the Cleveland Scholarship and Tutoring Grant Program* (Indiana University School of Education, March 16, 1998).

59. For some suggestive evidence on this point, see Peterson, "School Choice," p. 12.

60. It should also be emphasized that the Milwaukee experiment may not have been a fair test of a voucher plan, since only a small proportion of all public school students were permitted to participate, religious schools were (until recently) excluded, half the students in participating private schools had to be nonchoice students, families could not supplement the scholarship of $4,700, and many parents who might have applied for the publicly funded voucher took advantage of a parallel voucher program (PAVE) that was privately funded.

61. Rouse, "Schools and Student Achievement."

62. Note that this expectation assumes parents have sufficient information about the effectiveness of different schools and that financing arrangements provide the right fiscal incentives for schools to improve.

63. One choice plan that has had some effect on at least one public school is philanthropist Virginia Gilder's offer of a scholarship to all of the students attending a poorly performing elementary school in Albany, New York. An even more extensive test has recently begun in the Edgewood district in San Antonio, where all children were offered a voucher in the fall of 1998 to attend the school of their choice.

64. Caroline Minter Hoxby, "Analyzing School Choice Reforms That Use America's Traditional Forms of Parental Choice," in Peterson and Hassel, *Learning from School Choice*, pp. 133–56; Caroline Minter Hoxby, *Do Private Schools Provide Competition for Public Schools?* (Cambridge, Mass.: National Bureau of Economic Research, December 1994); Caroline Minter Hoxby, *Does Competition among Public Schools Benefit Students and Taxpayers?* (Cambridge, Mass: National Bureau of Economic Research, December 1994).

65. Hoxby, *Does Competition among Public Schools Benefit Students and Taxpayers?* Although Hoxby uses a number of ingenious methods to control for factors that may simultaneously affect the quality of public schools and the amount of competition from either the public or private sector, we cannot be certain that she has resolved all of the problems. Her methodology involves using topographical features as an instrument for predicting the number of school districts in a metropolitan area and the historic proportion of the population that is Catholic to predict private school enrollments. For further comments on this approach and its pitfalls, see Thomas J. Kane, "Comments on Chapters Five and Six," in Helen F. Ladd, ed., *Holding Schools Accountable* (Brookings, 1996), pp. 209–17.

66. See, for example, Armor and Peiser, "Interdistrict Choice in Massachusetts"; Richard Arum, "Do Private Schools Force Public Schools to Compete?" *American Sociological Review,* vol. 61 (February 1996), pp. 29–46; Blair R. Zanzig, "Measuring the Impact of Competition in Local Government Education Markets on the Cognitive Achievement of Students," *Economics of Education Review,* vol. 16, no. 4 (1997), pp. 431–41; and Department of Education, *Study of Public School Choice in Minnesota* (1996).

67. C. Eugene Steuerle, Edward M. Gramlich, Hugh Heclo, and Demetra Smith Nightingale, *The Government We Deserve: Responsive Democracy and Changing Expectations* (Urban Institute, 1998).

68. Mark Walsh, "Indianapolis Study Documents Benefits of Vouchers," *Education Week,* March 20, 1996, p. 3.

69. Dorman E. Cordell, *Private Vouchers for Educational Choice,* Brief no. 265 (Dallas, Tex.: National Center for Policy Analysis and CEO America, April 29, 1998).

70. Carol Marie Cropper, "Texas Business Foundation to Pay for School Vouchers," *New York Times,* April 23, 1998, p. A14; and Fritz Steiger, "School Choice for an Entire District: $50 Million Horizon Project a Model for the Nation," (Dallas, Tex.: CEO America, April 22, 1998) (www.ceoamerica.org/horizon-news.html [June 17, 1998]).

71. "Voucher Programs Sponsored by CEO America" (www.ceoamerica.org/programs.html [August 3, 1998]).

72. Paul E. Peterson, David Myers, and William Howell, "Research Design and Initial Findings from an Evaluation of the New York School Choice

Scholarships Program," paper prepared for presentation before the Association of Public Policy and Management, Washington, D.C., November 1997.

73. "Putting Private Effort to the Test," *Columbus Dispatch*, June 4, 1998, p. 10A.

74. "Private School Scholarship Fund Gets $6 Million," *Washington Post*, October 14, 1997, p. B3.

JOHN H. BISHOP

10 | *Privatizing Education: Lessons from Canada, Europe, and Asia*

L EGISLATIVE PROPOSALS for vouchers and tax credits for attending private schools are now a regular part of political debate. Public support for voucher funding of private schools is growing. A 1998 poll showed that 44 percent of the public favored "allowing students and parents to choose a private school to attend at public expense," up from 24 percent in 1993. A tax credit has even more support. The poll reflected that 73 percent favored tax credits "that would allow parents who send their children to private or church related schools to recover part of the tuition paid."[1] This is a policy idea whose time may soon come.

Advocates of voucher funding of private schools argue that there are five mechanisms by which voucher funding of private schools will improve student achievement.

The research reported in this chapter was supported by the Center for Advanced Human Resource Studies and the Consortium for Policy Research in Education (funded by the Office of Educational Research and Improvement, U.S. Department of Education). The findings and opinions expressed in this report do not reflect the position or policies of the Office of Educational Research and Improvement or the U.S. Department of Education.

—*Competition for students.* Voucher funding forces schools to become more responsive to parents' wishes. Since parents' preferences are diverse, schools will become more diverse. Voucher advocates claim that parents will tend to select schools with more qualified teachers and higher graduation standards and that this will result in improved academic achievement.[2]

—*Innovation and diversity.* Voucher funding allows teachers and principals who are dissatisfied with the way existing schools operate to create a school reflecting their unique vision. Schools will no longer have to be all things to all people. They can seek out their own niche. Schools could specify up front what the school will provide and what is expected of students and parents and allow those who like the school's approach to choose it.

—*Competition for teachers and a more flexible employment relationship.* Advocates argue that the competitive market for students created by vouchers will force schools to compete more actively in the teacher labor market. Teachers unions will be weakened and the authority of principals will be strengthened. Talented teachers will be better rewarded (thereby being induced to remain in the profession) and incompetent teachers will be forced to seek employment elsewhere.

—*Avoiding the dead hand of public bureaucracy.* Vouchers will increase the size of the private school sector. John Chubb and Terry Moe argue that privately run schools will always be more effective than public schools because they are not subject to the bureaucratic controls and tight regulation that public schools are subject to.[3]

—*Bringing religion back into the schools.* Advocates argue that faith-based institutions are better at teaching values and good behavior than are secular institutions. This is an important function of schools, and success in such teaching values as honesty, hard work, and dependability is an important function of schools that carries over into the academic realm.

Opponents have responses to all of these arguments.

—*Competition for students.* Parents, they argue, are poorly informed about the academic quality of schools, so most will select schools on nonacademic criteria—for example, religion, school disciplinary environment, sports programs—not academic criteria. Parents may be happier with their child's school, but the public goal of higher academic achievement will not be served.[4]

—*Innovation and diversity.* Innovation and diversity can be obtained by public school choice—magnet schools and charter schools—and by contracting with private secular organizations such as the Edison project to manage public schools. Many nations offer different kinds of public schools and allow parents to choose their child's school but do not include private schools in the publicly funded choice regime.

—*A backdoor way of weakening tenure.* Opponents are aghast at the prospect of weakened tenure protection and will fight to retain such protections at voucher-funded schools. Countries that fund schools through voucherlike systems often negotiate pay, tenure protections, and conditions of work at the national level and sometimes leave headmasters with little discretionary power over their teachers. Opponents also argue that teachers are not receiving rents. If tenure is taken away, schools will be forced to pay more and costs will go up.

—*Voucher funding is a Trojan horse that risks destroying private schools.* Opponents point out that publicly funded organizations will have to be regulated to avoid fraud and ensure that higher-order values (such as curriculum, racial integration, nondiscrimination) are served. These regulations will grow over time and may weaken the effectiveness of private schools.

—*Religion back in the schools.* Opponents argue that publicly subsidized denominational schools are often not successful in instilling moral values. Quebec has had such a system for over a century, yet "church attendance among Catholics stands at 15 percent, the lowest rate in North America," and "53 percent of births in the province occur out of wedlock."[5] Religious schools, they argue, also sometimes teach intolerance and pseudoscience such as creationism.

Opponents also argue that a growing private school sector would weaken local voter support of publicly funded schools, causing them to be underfunded. To avoid this, per pupil funding levels of the two types of school would have to be formally tied together. Many nations that fund private schools equate per pupil public funding in the two sectors. American proposals for tax credits and vouchers typically do not tie per pupil grants for attending private schools to per pupil spending in the public schools. In a voucher system, parents dissatisfied with a school would simply "exit" rather than "voice" their concern by running for PTA president or school board. Another fear is that the best students would use choice to avoid having to share classrooms with lower-achieving students and those from low-income backgrounds.

The counterargument of proponents is that without subsidies, the private sector has already captured 11 percent of the market and tracking already allows the smartest high school students to spend little time with low-achieving students. The deleterious effects of the flight to private

Table 10-1. *Types of Public and Nonpublic Schools*

	Government funded (≥90%) and closely regulated	Independent: tuition dependent, limited public funding and regulation
Managed by secular organizations	Secular public schools run by locally elected or appointed boards and regulated by ministries of education	Nondenominational private schools
Owned and managed by religious organizations	For example, state-funded schools run by religious organizations in Belgium, Ireland, France, Israel, and the Netherlands; schools run by elected school board of religious organizations in Canada	Catholic schools, yeshivas, and Christian academies in the United States

schools on voter support for public schools may already be a reality. Tying the fortunes of the two sectors together and facilitating the expansion of the private school sector might generate a stronger pro-education coalition and help both types of schools improve.

Both sides of the debate have plausible a priori arguments for their positions. The issues of fact and causality that are debated by the two camps can be settled scientifically only by empirical evidence. It is time to take a careful look at how such systems work in practice, not just in theory. Isabel Sawhill and Shannon Smith's contribution to this book reviews American experience with voucher schemes. This chapter looks at Canadian, European, and Asian experience with voucher funding of K–12 education. Two kinds of questions are addressed: Do countries with large private school sectors have higher levels of average achievement? Do privately run schools outperform public schools? Private schools come in hundreds of different forms, and voucher schemes come in hundreds of different flavors. Different schemes will have very different effects and very different costs. Sawhill and Smith argue that vouchers "are a flexible tool that can be bent to a variety of political or substantive purposes."[6] Consequently, it is important to know which types of nonpublic schools are most effective and how context influences the effectiveness of different types of nonpublic schools. As outlined in table 10-1, the empirical analysis will distinguish three "nonpublic" types of school: independent tuition charging nondenominational private

Table 10-2. *Enrollment Share of Independent Private Schools,*
Selected Countries, 1990[a]

Percent

	OECD			IAEP		
Country	Primary school (1)	Lower secondary school (2)	Academic secondary school (3)	Religious independent (4)	Independent secular (5)	Religious state funded (6)
Australia	24.9	...	31.5	...	...	...
Austria	3.9	6.5	11.0	...	...	...
Belgium	56.0	...	65.0	...	...	...
Canada	3.6	6.7	4.8	5.0	3.3	19.6
China	...	...	...	0.0	0.8	0.0
Cyprus	2.5	10.0	...	...	...	...
Denmark	9.7	17.6	8.6	...	...	...
England	12.0	9.8	10.1	0.0	9.6	9.6
Finland	0.9	3.0	5.8	...	...	...
France	14.8	21.0	21.8	0.9	0.0	12.7
Germany	1.8	7.5	12.0	...	...	...
Greece	6.6	3.7	4.1	...	...	...
Hong Kong	93.6	91.7	91.7	...	...	...
Hungary	...	...	...	0.0	0.0	0.0
Iceland	1.8	1.8	1.8	...	...	...
Ireland	1.6	...	0.0	0.0	0.9	65.7
Israel	...	...	...	0.0	1.0	20.0
Italy	7.5	4.6	15.3	3.2	0.0	0.0
Japan	0.7	3.5	29.5	...	...	...
Korea	1.2	36.1	52.6	0.9	24.5	5.5
Netherlands	68.8	79.9	72.3	...	...	...

(continued)

schools, independent tuition charging denominational schools, and publicly funded and regulated schools that are run by religious organizations.

Table 10-2 presents data from the Organization for Economic Cooperation and Development (OECD) and from the International Assessment of Educational Progress (IAEP) on the size and character of the private school sector in thirty-five countries. A number of European governments pay for private or religious schooling on much the same terms as they pay for school-

Table 10-2. *Enrollment Share of Independent Private Schools,
Selected Countries, 1990 (Continued)*
Percent

Country	OECD			IAEP		
	Primary school (1)	Lower secondary school (2)	Academic secondary school (3)	Religious independent (4)	Independent secular (5)	Religious state funded (6)
New Zealand	2.5	4.4	5.5	. . .	. . .	. . .
Norway	1.1	1.2	11.1	. . .	. . .	. . .
Philippines	4.9	55.0	55.0	. . .	. . .	. . .
Portugal	6.5	9.7	5.6	7.5	2.2	0.0
Russia	0	0	0	. . .	. . .	. . .
Scotland	. . .	. . .	. . .	0.0	2.8	0.0
Singapore	28.8	28.8	. . .	. . .	. . .	. . .
Slovenia	0	0	0	0.0	0.0	0.0
Spain	34.5	35.1	28.7	30.2	2.6	0.0
Sweden	0.9	0.8	3.0	. . .	. . .	. . .
Switzerland	2.4	5.0	11.7	0.0	0.0	0.0
Taiwan	. . .	. . .	. . .	0.9	0.0	0.0
Thailand	9.0	12.0	7.0	. . .	. . .	. . .
United States	12.0	9.8	9.9	12.0	1.9	0.0

Sources: For most countries, data for columns 1, 2, and 3 are from OECD, *Education in OECD Countries—1988–90* (Paris, 1993), tables 2.2, 2.3, 2.4; data for Cyprus, Hong Kong, Iceland, Korea, the Philippines, Russia, Singapore, Slovenia, and Thailand are from an education encyclopedia. Columns 4, 5, and 6 are author's calculations from the IAEP data set.

a. Columns 1, 2, and 3 show the private school share of enrollment at each level. Columns 4, 5, and 6 show the proportion of the schools in the IAEP data set that are independent sectarian, nonsectarian independent, and state-funded denominationally controlled schools. OECD considers the Canadian and Irish schools in this final category as public but the corresponding French schools as private. In many nations—for example, Austria, England, and Ireland—state-run schools require that students take a religion course.

ing provided by state schools. This has resulted in private schools becoming very important in some countries. In 1990, for example, 69 percent of Dutch primary school students, 56 percent of Belgian primary school students, 35 percent of Spanish primary school students, and 15 percent of French primary school students attended schools run by church organizations. More than a quarter of the secondary schools in Japan and Korea are private, and some 90 percent of the schools in Hong Kong are private.

Choice and Privatization: Belgium, Britain, Canada, France, Ireland, and the Netherlands

Private schools differ across national boundaries at least as much as public schools differ. They differ because they have evolved in unique historical, cultural, and institutional environments. Their character is influenced by the number and size of religious communities, anticlerical political movements, the existence of curriculum-based external exit exams, the traditions and qualifications of the teaching profession, the regulatory and funding environment, and traditions regarding retention in grade and choice of public school.

Competition among Schools

Belgian, British, Canadian, Dutch, and French schools face a competitive environment that is more like the one faced by American colleges and universities than the one faced by American primary and secondary schools.

MIXED CHOICE AND CATCHMENT. In France and Britain, each public school has its own geographically defined attendance area (catchment area), but funding is on a per student basis, and students from outside the catchment area are admitted if space is available. Since marginal costs of instruction are lower than the per student payment, schools experiencing an increase in applications have an incentive to expand up to the maximum their physical plant can accommodate. Students living in the school's catchment area or with siblings at the school have priority when queues develop. Where students from outside the catchment area are admitted, students are typically selected primarily on a first-come, first-served basis. Schools retain some discretion, however, so stronger students and well-behaved students are more likely to be accepted. Schools also have the authority to expel misbehaving students, in effect forcing them to find another school to attend.

Historically, most Canadian provinces have funded schools partly from local property taxes and partly from provincial grants.[7] Negotiations over teacher salaries have often, however, been handled at the provincial level. During the past decade, many provinces have taken over the property tax and assumed complete responsibility for funding K–12 schooling. As a result, school funding in most of Canada will soon be based purely on enrollment—linearly in some provinces and for some expenditure categories and in discrete jumps in other provinces and for other expenditure categories. Generally, students may attend public school outside their catchment area if space is available and parents assume transportation costs.

Canada also has a very interesting alternative to public subsidy of quasi-independent denominational schools. Four provinces—Alberta, Newfoundland, Ontario, and Saskatchawan—have a Catholic school system (Newfoundland has a Protestant system as well) that is overseen by school boards elected by members of the religious faith. Before provincial assumption of K–12 funding responsibility, these schools were supported by provincial grants and property taxes paid by people who registered as Catholics and whose children were therefore eligible to attend those schools. The schools run by these religious school boards compete for students with schools run by secular school boards and educate over 15 percent of all students.

In Ireland, parents may choose between two publicly funded systems of education: secular schools run by local authorities and parochial schools run by church organizations. Parochial schools (almost always Catholic) are twice as numerous as secular schools. Local archbishops (there are forty in Ireland) appoint the board of governors for the schools in their diocese. These schools are owned by the church, but government closely regulates them and pays almost all current expenses. While parents are allowed to send their children to schools outside their own parish, it is unusual for them to do so. If queues develop, church members can be given preference, but student behavior and achievement are not supposed to be admission criteria. If a school wants to expel a student for bad behavior, it must first find him a space at another school. National labor contracts specify teacher wages and working conditions. When complaints arise about the competence of a particular teacher, principals have no formal role in evaluating the teacher's performance. The matter is turned over to inspectors employed by the Ministry of Education. These inspectors are spread so thinly, individual schools are seldom visited more than once every few years.

PURE VOUCHER SYSTEMS. The constitutions of Belgium and the Netherlands guarantee that any group or individual is free to establish a school. Governments provide equal per pupil payments to all schools that teach the national curriculum, hire qualified teachers, and are above some minimum level of enrollment.[8] Most Belgians are baptized Catholics, and schools run by various Catholic organizations educate roughly half of the nation's students. The Catholic schools are generally thought to have higher standards and tend to serve children from more advantaged backgrounds. An additional source of educational diversity is separate school

systems maintained by each of Belgium's three language communities—
Flemish, French, and German. Parents may send their child to any school
they want. Where queues develop, students are supposed to be accepted by
lottery, but family pull and the student's record apparently often influence
who is admitted. Primary schools and academic secondary schools are
comprehensive.[9]

The Dutch population is pretty evenly divided between the Catholic
Church and the Dutch Reform Church. Three parallel systems of
education—a locally administered public system, a Catholic system, and
a Protestant system—have evolved. Primary education is comprehensive. Secondary education is differentiated. There are three types of general secondary school and a system of lower vocational schools that prepare students for occupationally specific exams as well as general
education exams. The curriculum of the first year of secondary school is
supposed to be the same in all schools so students can transfer between
schools at its conclusion. In succeeding years, however, curricula and
rigor diverge. Rigor and workload are greatest at the six-year gymnasi-
ums that qualify students to enter research universities. The somewhat
less demanding five-year secondary schools qualify students for nonuni-
versity tertiary programs in applied professions. The still less demanding
four-year secondary schools prepare students for white-collar employment or entry into upper secondary applied professional programs.
Which and how many foreign languages are studied also differs across
school types. The vocational schools devote considerable time to occupationally specific curricula, so less time is available for academic
courses. Advice to parents about which type of school is appropriate for
their child is based on the pupil's record in primary school. Parents,
however, have the right to select the type of school and which school
their child will enter. If, however, the student fails two or more courses
in any year of secondary school, the student must either repeat the grade
or transfer to an easier school.

Essential to a competitive environment, of course, is the right of a family to send its child to the school of his or her choice if the child qualifies
academically. Barriers to attending a school other than the closest one are
low in Belgium and the Netherlands, because schools are small and consequently more numerous, population densities are high, public transportation is generally available, opportunities to participate in sports and music
are often organized by the community not the school, and centralized
funding of schools means that spending per pupil varies little and money
follows the student.

Since the most prestigious schools are often selective in their admissions decisions in Belgium and the Netherlands, enrollment in the best secondary schools is affected by a student's achievement in primary schools, not solely by a parent's ability to buy a house in a community with an excellent high school as is the case in the United States. The same comment applies to a lesser degree to Britain, France, and many Canadian provinces. This means that parents who want their child to attend and graduate from the best secondary schools must make sure their child studies hard in primary school.

Interaction among School Choice, Private Schools, and External Examination Systems

At the end of secondary school, students in most European and Asian countries take national or provincial external exit examinations that are curriculum based and that assess how well they learned what was taught. Student performance on these examinations influences university attendance and job opportunities.

Nine-tenths of English youths now take the General Certificate of Secondary Education (GCSE) exam at age sixteen, and an increasing number take "A levels" two years later. Scotland also has a system of external examinations. For the United Kingdom as a whole, in 1991, 23 percent of all nineteen year olds passed at least one A level (or the Scottish equivalent).[10] Performance on GCSE and A level examinations and the equivalent Scottish exams determines whether the student can attend university and which university and program he or she is admitted to. Grades on the GCSE and A level exams are included on resumes and requested on job applications, so employment opportunities depend on school results as well.[11] Completing an A level qualification lowers unemployment rates for those between twenty-five and thirty-four from 16.9 to 6.9 percent, and graduating from university lowers it further to 4.3 percent.

Ireland's examination system is similar to the British system. When some political leaders proposed replacing external exams with a system of teacher assessment, the Association of Secondary Teachers of Ireland opposed the change, arguing, as follows, that it would damage the pastoral role of teachers and produce grade inflation:

Major strengths of the Irish educational system have been:
  1. The pastoral contribution of teachers in relation to their pupils,
  2. the perception of the teacher by the pupil as an advocate in terms of nationally certified examinations rather than as a judge.

The introduction of school-based assessment by the pupil's own teacher for certification purposes would undermine those two roles, to the detriment of all concerned. . . .

The role of the teacher as judge rather than advocate may lead to legal accountability in terms of marks awarded for certification purposes. This would automatically result in a distancing between the teacher, the pupil and the parent. It also opens the door to possible distortion of the results in response to either parental pressure or to pressure emanating from competition among local schools for pupils.[12]

In France, 71 percent of the eighteen-year-old group took a *Baccalaureat* (Bac) exam in 1992, and 51 percent of the age group passed a Bac exam. A total of 38 percent of the Baccalaureats awarded were in vocational lines of study.[13] This is a major accomplishment, for Bac exams are set to a very high standard.[14] The job market prizes young people who have passed the Bac. There are alternative lower-level examined qualifications for employment such as the *Brevet d'Enseignment Professionnel* (BEP) and the *Certificat d'Aptitude Professionelle* (CAP), but the Baccalaureat confers greater access to preferred jobs. In 1987 unemployment rates for fifteen to twenty-four year olds were 37 percent for those without any diploma, 18 percent for those with a Bac, and 10 percent for university graduates.

The Dutch Ministry of Education also sets examinations for each type of school that influence access to tertiary education and job opportunities.[15] In both France and the Netherlands, questions and answers are published in national newspapers and are available on video text. The published exams signal the standards that students and teachers must aim for.

Six of Canada's provinces—Alberta, British Columbia, Manitoba, New Brunswick, Newfoundland, and Quebec—now have diploma exams in mathematics and language arts and, in some cases, other subjects. These exams are typically taken at the end of twelfth grade and account for between 30 and 50 percent of the grade in the course.[16]

In this regard, Belgium is an exception. It has no externally set exit examinations. The teachers at each school write their own examinations. Obtaining the Certificate of Higher Secondary Education is all that is needed to enter university in almost any field. As in France, however, university failure rates are very high, particularly in the more popular, better-paid lines of study. Consequently, students who want to complete a university education must develop a solid foundation in secondary school.

Where there are diploma examinations, newspapers publish the numbers passing or getting high grades. Administrators seeking to strengthen their school's reputation are thus induced to give teaching effectiveness (as assessed by the external exam) first priority. British schools also publish annual reports that are sent to parents of current and prospective students.

In 1984, two years after choice became operational in Scotland, 9 percent of pupils entering secondary school nationally (11 to 14 percent in urban areas) attended a school outside their catchment area.[17] Scottish parents who made this choice appeared to be behaving rationally, for they tended to choose schools that were more effective than the school in their own catchment area. An analysis of school choice in the Fife Education Authority found that the schools chosen by those leaving their catchment area had better examination results at age sixteen than would have been predicted given the pupil's initial test scores and social background characteristics and the average socioeconomic status of pupils at the school.[18] Consequently, the free choice of schools that prevails in these nations and most Canadian provinces generates a competitive pressure on schools to excel that does not have any counterpart in the United States outside of the cities with magnet school systems.

What Happens When a Student Cannot or Does Not Keep Up?

In Belgium, France, and the Netherlands, pupils who fail more than one of their required secondary school courses are generally required to *redoubler*. The American translation of redoubler is "to be held back," or "to repeat the grade." In France, decisions about redoublement (repeating a grade) are made by the *Conseil de Class*, made up of the teachers for that class. The teachers' "basic motivation is to help the child himself, to ensure that the pupil is sufficiently well prepared so that he may fully benefit from work at a more demanding level."[19] To them, redoublement is a form of mastery learning, a way of allowing some students extra time to achieve very demanding learning goals.

By British, Canadian, and American standards, redoublement rates are very high in Belgium, France, and the Netherlands.[20] In 1990 Dutch redoublement rates were 7.5 percent each year in academic lower secondary schools, 5.1 percent each year in the vocational lower secondary schools, and 13.3 percent each year in academic upper secondary schools.[21] French rates of redoublement ranged from 6.8 and 11.0 percent each year during the four years of general lower secondary education, ranged from

12.1 to 18.4 percent each year in the three-year academic upper secondary schools, and averaged 8.4 percent each year in the first two years of vocational upper secondary schools.[22] As a result, in 1994, 34 percent of French, 32 percent of Belgian, 46 percent of Dutch, and 26 percent of Spanish nineteen year olds attended secondary school full time compared to only 16 percent of British and of Canadian and 7 percent of American nineteen year olds.[23]

For Belgian, Dutch, and French teenagers, the threat of having to redouble is a strong incentive to study. When I asked how the students who must redouble feel about it, I was told that they feel "dishonored." Since redoublement is a public event, parents also feel stigmatized, so they have an incentive to see that their child studies hard.[24]

In the Netherlands, students who are having difficulty keeping up with the demanding pace of the more rigorous five- and six-year secondary schools often have a choice: either repeat the year or transfer to a less-demanding type of school. At the gymnasium I visited in the Netherlands, one-third of the entering class transfers to a less-demanding secondary school before the beginning of the third year. Parents who want their child to enter a gymnasium are generally accommodated even when primary school teachers advise against it. The child's performance in school determines whether the parents' aspirations are realized or whether a transfer to a less-demanding school is necessary.

Forced transfers do not foreclose university attendance. With good grades at the end of the five-year secondary school program, the student can transfer to a gymnasium, complete the final two years, and then enter a research university. In addition, numerous vocationally oriented higher education options are open to graduates of the less-rigorous secondary schools, and transfers to university are feasible with good grades. These alternative routes to university are open; they just take longer.

While other routes to university are possible, pupils who choose the fast track in seventh grade, a gymnasium or a top lycee in France or Belgium, do not want to be forced "to get off the train." Students in these countries are formed into classes that take most subjects together and often remain essentially intact for two or more years. This class is their peer group, the group with whom they spend most of their time. When I asked a Dutch student who, despite long hours of study, had been required to repeat a grade why she had studied so hard, she responded, "I wanted to stay with my class!" Students do not want to have to repeat the grade, because it threatens to sever the friendships they have made in the class. Apparently, trying to keep up academically (that is, accepting the academic goals of the school) is viewed positively by peers because it is an expression of commitment to the group. Those who refuse to study are apparently seen as rejecting the group. In these three countries, peer pressure seems to encourage lagging students to study, not discourage them as in the United States.[25]

The variation just described in the governance and funding of nonpublic schools and in the context in which nonpublic schools operate provides a setting in which to look for answers to many of the questions that have been raised in the U.S. debate over voucher funding of private and denominational schools. I begin, in the next section, by assessing the impact of the size of the private sector on the overall effectiveness of national educational systems. The rest of the chapter is devoted to three issues: how independent private schools differ from public schools, how denominational schools differ from secular schools, and how curriculum-based examination systems affect these differences. The analysis focuses on student achievement, family background, school resources, and teacher quality.

The Effect of Private Schools on the Effectiveness of All Schools

Advocates of voucher funding of schools frequently argue that providing subsidies to private schools will make them more effective competitors of public schools and that the strengthened competition will force public schools to become better. Thus a large private school sector is predicted to raise average achievement levels of all students. This prediction is tested below.

Two data sets are employed: Data on seventh and eighth graders in the thirty-nine-nation 1994–95 Third International Math and Science Study (TIMSS) and data from the twenty-five-nation 1990–91 IEA study of reading literacy of ninth graders.[26] Twenty national school systems were classified as having a curriculum-based external examination (CBEEE) system for both subjects in all parts of the country.[27] Curriculum-based external examination systems are externally set medium- or high-stakes exams keyed to the content of the core curriculum of the nation's secondary schools that are taken by almost all students. The private market share variable was defined as the average of primary school and lower secondary school shares in the first two columns of table 10-2.[28]

Does Private School Share Have a Linear Effect on
Average Achievement Levels?

The mean eighth grade science and mathematics test scores were regressed
on the enrollment share of private schools in compulsory education, the
log of the average ratio of the nation's per capita gross domestic product
from 1987 to 1991 to the U.S. per capita GDP, a dummy for East Asian
nations, and a dummy for a CBEEE in the subject. The results presented
in table 10-3 indicate that countries with large numbers of private schools
do not score higher on the TIMSS science or mathematics tests. Test scores
are significantly higher in more developed nations, East Asian nations, and
in nations with a CBEEE in the subject.

The analysis of achievement at a particular grade level may be biased,
however, by differing policies regarding grade retention, age of school
entry, and which grade was chosen for assessment. Private sectors, for
example, might be associated with high rates of grade retention. Therefore,
a preferable dependent variable is a measure of student achievement at
some fixed age. The second row of each panel presents estimated models
predicting the median test score for each nation's thirteen year olds.[29]
Switching to the age-constant achievement leaves the estimated impact of
the private school share of enrollment on science and mathematics achievement essentially unchanged.

The bottom panel of table 10-3 presents an identical analysis of IEA
reading achievement data. To avoid the problems of differing school entry
ages and grade retention policies, the age-standardized reading scores have
been used in the analysis.[30] The IEA study defined and measured three different types of reading literacy—narrative, expository, and document—
and an average of the three scores is the dependent variable. The specification is the same as that used to study science and math achievement. Here
the exam variable is an average of the math and science dummy variables
used in the analysis of TIMSS data. The results are similar as well. Diploma
exams and per capita GDP have significant positive effects on reading
achievement. Countries with larger private school enrollment shares have,
other factors being equal, significantly lower reading achievement.

Is the Relationship between Private School Share and
Average Achievement Levels Nonlinear?

The discussion of the pros and cons of voucher funding of schools at the
beginning of the chapter suggested that a small unsubsidized and unregu-

lated private sector may have negative effects on the quality of public schools, but that tying the per pupil funding levels and regulatory environment of the two sectors together might improve quality in both sectors. This suggests that the relationship between private sector share and average achievement levels may be negative over some range close to zero and then become positive above some threshold.

This can be tested either by adding a (private school share − 0.12)^2 term to the model or by allowing the slope of the relationship between private sector share and achievement to shift at some arbitrary kink point (that is, including a spline). The size of the U.S. private school sector, 12 percent of students in all school sectors, was selected as the kink point for the spline. This is above the median of the variable and slightly below the mean, which is 0.159. Both of these models are presented in table 10-3. The results are very similar across the three outcome variables. The square term is consistently positive and the linear term consistently negative. The linear term is statistically significant in the reading equation. This suggests that in the neighborhood of the current U.S. private school share, increases in that share will lower achievement. The minimum achievement level is reached at a private share of 0.48 for science, 0.44 for reading, and 0.295 for mathematics.

The spline model has substantially higher adjusted R^2, suggesting that it fits the data better than the square term model does. Two separate slopes are estimated; one for the region below 0.12, the current U.S. private school enrollment share, and one for the range from 0.12 to 1.0. (Figure 10-1 graphs the spline results.) The coefficients on the lower range are all significantly negative. They imply that countries that lack any private schools tend to have a more than one grade-level equivalent achievement advantage over the United States when other things—GDP, Asia, and exam systems—are held constant. The upper region coefficient from the mathematics regression is statistically significant and positive. This may be interpreted as suggesting that a shift to vouchers that substantially increased the proportion of students in private schools would improve math achievement but leave reading and science achievement unaffected. Doubling the private sector share to 0.24 would increase predicted math achievement by roughly one-third of a grade-level equivalent.

There are three possible reasons for this nonlinear relationship—one causal, the other two noncausal. The causal explanation proposes that a growing private school sector weakens support for public schools, causing them to be underfunded. This can be avoided by tying the fortunes of the two sectors together, by requiring students in both sectors to take the same

Table 10-3. *Effect of Size of Private School Sector on Science, Mathematics, and Reading Achievement*[a]

	Private share	Private share less than 0.12	Private share greater than 0.12	Square of (private share-12)	Diploma exam	Per capita GDP 1987–91	East Asia	Adjusted R^2 and RMSE[b]
TIMSS Science, 1994[c]								
8th grade mean	-19.7 (0.74)	...	...	...	41.6*** (3.13)	30.0*** (2.97)	15.1 (0.86)	0.286 36.3
Median, 13 year olds	-21.6 (0.79)	...	...	...	33.2** (2.44)	39.3*** (3.65)	23.1 (1.28)	0.306 37.1
Median, 13 year olds	-72.0 (1.20)	...	...	99.4 (0.94)	30.76** (2.21)	38.5*** (3.57)	24.1 (1.33)	0.303 37.2
Median, 13 year olds	... ...	-270* (1.83)	19.4 (0.54)	...	30.2** (2.26)	41.7*** (3.95)	31.0* (1.71)	0.343 36.1
TIMSS Mathematics, 1994[c]								
8th grade mean	7.8 (0.28)	...	...	...	37.9** (2.50)	39.1*** (3.51)	56.2*** (3.04)	0.383 38.5
Median, 13 year olds	17.7 (0.65)	...	...	...	27.0* (1.85)	46.9*** (4.37)	62.4*** (3.38)	0.451 37.1
Median, 13 year olds	-37.8 (0.62)	... (1.02)	... (1.44)	107.9 (4.29)	23.3 (3.56)	46.0*** 37.0	63.5***	0.451
Median, 13 year olds	... ...	-283* (1.95)	66.3* (1.90)	...	22.1 (1.56)	59.7*** (4.82)	71.9*** (4.09)	0.501 35.3

IEA Reading, 1990[d]

Average, age adjusted	−25.0* (1.79)	...	...	...	25.1*** (3.28)	27.2*** (3.97)	−13.1 (1.17)	0.655 15.8
Average, age adjusted	−68.3** (2.11)	...	...	80.7 (1.48)	21.5** (2.75)	25.5*** (3.77)	−13.0 (1.20)	0.674 15.3
Average, age adjusted	...	−207** (2.63)	−0.8 (0.05)	...	20.7*** (2.87)	28.3*** (4.51)	−6.1 (0.58)	0.713 14.4

Source: Author's calculations.

* Significant at the 10 percent level (two tail test); ** at the 5 percent level (two tail test); *** at the 1 percent level (two tail test). *t* values are in parentheses.

a. Grade-level equivalents are approximately 26 for science and 24 for math and reading.

b. RMSE = root mean-squared error.

c. The TIMSS analysis is based on thirty-nine nations.

d. The IEA reading data analysis is based on twenty-five nations.

Figure 10.1 *Relationship between Size of Private School Sector and
Test Scores in Lower Secondary School*

Test score[a]

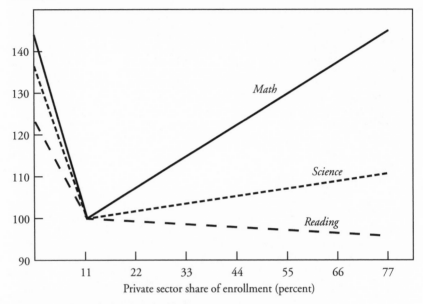

Source: Author's calculations as described in text.
a. Grade level equivalent = 24.

courses and the same exams, and by tying the subsidy of private school
students to the subsidy of public school students. This is what Belgium,
Hong Kong, and the Netherlands have done, and it has resulted in very
large private sectors. The second explanation is a misspecification problem
as a result of the absence of controls for public school choice. Public
school choice may be a more powerful way of generating accountability
and competitive pressure than public subsidies of private schools. Its omis-
sion from the regression may bias other coefficients. The final possible
explanation proposes that unsubsidized private sectors (such as the one
that has captured 12 percent of the market in the United States) spring up
when public schools do a poor job. If public schools are of uniformly high
quality, private schools have no market niche to fill. If the nation chooses
to fund private schools on the same footing as public schools, they end up
with over half of the market and their pressure forces the public schools to
become better.

How Do Independent Private Schools and Faith-Based Schools Differ from Secular Public Schools?

The differences between various types of nonpublic schools and traditional secular public schools are assessed in two international data sets on mathematics and science achievement of thirteen year olds in 1991. The first data set consists of 1,740 secondary schools from sixteen of the countries that participated in the International Assessment of Educational Progress (IAEP).[31] The second data set consists of 1,355 high schools from the nine Canadian provinces that participated in the IAEP.

Our objective is to assess the value added of different types of nonpublic schools, so the estimated models control for the finances and educational orientation of the parents of a school's students. The family status controls were the geometric mean of the number of books in the students' homes, the average number of siblings, and the proportion of students whose home language was different from the school's language of instruction. The models predicting mathematics achievement also controlled for the proportion of students who had a calculator at home and the proportion who had access to a computer for school work. Other control variables were the log of the number of students per grade, dummy variables for the nation, whether the school includes primary grades, and whether the school covers all grades—kindergarten through twelfth grade—in one building. The Canadian analysis has no controls for province but does control for French-speaking school systems and for provinces with diploma exams.

Student Achievement Differences in the Absence of Diploma Exams

The first group of hypotheses relates to student discipline, absenteeism, and achievement in nations that do not have a curriculum-based external exit exam system. In their influential 1990 book, John Chubb and Terry Moe argued that bureaucracy and democratic government inevitably result in public schools being less effective than independent schools that must compete for students and that are, thus, required to survive a market test. Independent private schools that charge tuition will not survive if they cannot convince many parents they are significantly better than public schools. This implies the following hypothesis:

Hypothesis one. Value added is greater at independent private schools. Holding student background constant, student achievement is higher and discipline and attendance is better.

Others have argued that faith-based institutions are inherently more effective at educating the young than are secular institutions. This implies a prediction:

Hypothesis two. Value added is greater at schools run by religious organizations than at schools run by secular organizations. Holding student background constant, student achievement is higher and discipline and attendance is better.

Those who oppose vouchers for denominational schools argue, to the contrary, that religious organizations will place lower priority on academics. They predict:

Hypothesis three. Private schools run by nonsectarian organizations will have higher student achievement than independent schools run by religious organizations when social background is held constant.

Hypothesis four. Publicly subsidized schools run by religious organizations will be less effective at teaching mathematics and science than secular public schools will be.

Results of testing these hypotheses are presented in table 10-4. The odd-numbered rows present the sixteen-nation analysis. The even-numbered rows present the Canadian results. Means and standard deviations of the dependent variables are presented in the first and second columns of the table. Column three presents an estimate of the effect of attending a school run by elected religious school boards rather than secular school boards in Ontario and Saskatchawan, two of the Canadian provinces that lack diploma exams. Column six presents an estimate of the effect of attending publicly subsidized denominational schools in nations or provinces that have a system of curriculum-based exit examinations (Alberta and Newfoundland, in the case of Canada). The schools run by elected religious school boards in Canada appear to have better discipline but significantly lower math and science achievement. For Canada, this is true in both the provinces with diploma exams and the provinces without such exams. In the sixteen-nation study, government-subsidized schools run by religious organizations are only found in nations with curriculum-based exit exams. In these nations, the subsidized religious schools are no more successful in achieving low absenteeism or in avoiding discipline problems, but they do have a statistically significant advantage in teaching math and science.

Thus we have contradictory findings in the two data sets. Hypothesis two is supported and hypothesis four is rejected in the sixteen-nation study. The Canadian data produce the opposite result. The explanation may be the unique character of the elected religious school boards in Canada. They clearly lack the independence and market sensitivity that plays such a central role in Chubb and Moe's theory of why private schools should outperform public schools. They were also not as well funded as the secular public schools in 1991. The independence and market sensitivity of the publicly subsidized, religiously controlled schools in the sixteen-nation study can also be questioned, but at least governing boards were not selected in local elections as they were in Canada.[32]

Columns four and five of table 10-4 provide evidence on hypothesis one—the effect of attending independent private schools in nations that lack curriculum-based exit exams. As expected, discipline and absenteeism problems are fewer at independent private schools. But attending such schools—ones that meet all of the Chubb-Moe tests—does not improve mathematics achievement and improves science achievement only in Canada and only when secular (not religious) private schools are attended.

Are secular independent private schools doing a better job of teaching academics than denominational schools as hypothesized in hypothesis three? This issue can be addressed by comparing column four to column five and column seven to column eight. There is no support for this hypothesis. None of the coefficient contrasts are statistically significant, and our estimates suggest that religious schools just as frequently surpass nondenominational schools as the reverse is true.

Student Achievement Differences in the Presence of Diploma Exams

The second group of hypotheses relates to the impact of curriculum-based external exit examinations on the relative effectiveness of private and public schools when all students must take curriculum-based external exams at the end of high school. I predicted in a 1996 study that

> If American parents and students were allowed to choose their high school, however, the Gresham's law of course selection [easy courses displace rigorous courses because rigor is not well signaled to colleges] might become a Gresham's law of school selection. . . . In order for school choice to generate an environment that induces schools to focus on upgrading instruction and improving learning, (1) the skills and competencies of individual graduates must be assessed relative to an external standard that is comparable across schools and (2) individual rewards—e.g., access to preferred university programs and better jobs—must be attached to these results. Only then are students and parents encouraged to select schools on the basis of their expected value added, rather than on the basis of

Table 10-4. *Private-Public Differences in Achievement, by Presence of Curriculum-Based External Exit Exam*

| Achievement variable | Data set[a] | Mean | Standard deviation | No exam system | | | Diploma exam system | | | | Adjusted R² |
				Religious school board	Independent religious	Independent secular	Religious school board	Independent religious	Independent secular	Exam* independent	
Math (percent correct)[b]	16 IAEP	0.514	0.176	···	−0.007	−0.044	0.033*	0.050**	0.064***	**	0.552
	Canada	0.473	0.125	−0.070***	0.042	−0.019	−0.037***	0.138***	0.077***	***	0.354
Science (percent correct)	16 IAEP	0.561	0.114	···	−0.009	−0.007	0.022*	0.025	0.031**	n.s.	0.427
	Canada	0.543	0.105	−0.044***	0.013	0.053*	−0.037***	−0.035	0.005	*	0.350
Discipline problems[c]	16 IAEP	0.98	0.74	···	−0.38***	−0.41	−0.104	−0.30**	−0.10	n.s.	0.097
	Canada	0.75	0.69	−0.25***	−0.46**	−0.33	0.00	−0.26*	−0.13*	n.s.	0.082
Absenteeism problems[c]	16 IAEP	0.77	0.75	···	−0.38***	0.02	−0.03	−0.42***	−0.163	n.s.	0.178
	Canada	0.80	0.71	−0.076	−0.40*	−0.33	0.092	−0.38***	−0.31***	n.s.	0.131

Source: Author's calculations based on 1991 IAEP data.

n.s. Not significant.

* Significant at the 10 percent level (two tail test); ** at the 5 percent level (two tail test); *** at the 1 percent level (two tail test).

a. Results for "16 IAEP" are based on analysis of data on 1,659 to 1,741 schools in China, England, France, Hungary, Ireland, Israel, Italy, Korea, Portugal, Scotland, Slovenia, Soviet Union, Switzerland, Spain, Taiwan, and the United States. This sample includes 106 schools run by religious school boards, 74 independent schools controlled by religious denominations, and 48 nonsectarian private schools. Results for "Canada" report analysis of data from 1,355 Canadian schools. Control variables not shown include logarithm of the average number of books in the home, mean number of siblings, proportion of the school's students whose home language was different from the language of instruction, logarithm of the number of students per grade in the school, and dummies for country, schools with primary grades, and schools that include K through eleventh grade in one building. The Canadian analysis does not control for province but does control for French-speaking school systems and provinces with diploma exams.

b. The models predicting math test scores have two additional controls for family background: share of students with access to a calculator at home and share of students with access to a computer.

c. Principal's report.

reputations that teachers are unable to change by doing a better job of teaching.[33]

This perspective predicts that the effectiveness of private schools should depend on whether all students are required to take curriculum-based external exit examinations at some time during secondary school. Therefore:

Hypothesis five. Being more sensitive to market pressures, independent private schools will respond more radically to an exam system than public schools will—that is, there will be a positive interaction between curriculum-based exams and independent private schools. The student achievement advantage that private schools have over public schools will be greater in nations or provinces with curriculum-based exit exams.

The statistical significance of the test of hypothesis five is given in the ninth column of table 10-4. For mathematics, hypothesis five is strongly supported in both data sets. Private school students learn more mathematics than public school students do but only when they face diploma examinations toward the end of secondary school. For science, however, there is no positive interaction between diploma exams and the effectiveness of independent private schools. In fact, science achievement of secular public school students in Canada responds more positively to diploma exams than does the achievement of private school students.

Background and Educational Orientation of Parents

The third set of hypotheses relates to the socioeconomic status and educational orientation of the families that choose to send their children to non-public schools:

Hypothesis six. The students at tuition-charging independent private schools come from socially advantaged families. There is no prediction regarding whether zero-tuition denominational schools serve a more or less socially advantaged clientele than secular public schools do.

Hypothesis seven. The parents of students at independent private schools spend more time talking with their children about school, and students perceive their parents as more interested in their doing well in school. Students at such schools will watch less television. No prediction is made regarding how zero-tuition denominational schools differ from secular private schools.

The geometric mean number of books in the home averaged across all students in the school is the best indicator of socioeconomic background and educational orientation of the parents of a school's students available in the IAEP data. Hypothesis six was tested by predicting this variable as a function of a series of dummies for the nation, the school's size and grade structure, and indicators for school governance. Results are presented in table 10-5. As expected, independent private schools serve a significantly more advantaged clientele than public schools in both Canada and the other sixteen nations do. The books in the home advantage of private schools is larger in nations that lack curriculum-based external examination systems (Portugal, Spain, and the United States).

Student reports that their parents want them to do well in mathematics are another indicator of parental interest in education. Here again the students at independent private schools have a significant advantage even when controls are introduced for books in the home, siblings, and the proportion of students whose home language is different from the school's language of instruction.

Television watching is a powerful negative predictor of student achievement. The relationship between school governance and television watching [while controlling for family background] is given in the fifth and sixth rows of table 10-5. Students at independent private schools watch significantly less television. The differential appears to be quite large in nations or provinces that do not have diploma exams. Given the strong taste for education among students attending private schools, the absence of a mathematics achievement advantage in their favor in nations or provinces without diploma exams is all the more noteworthy.

The table also reveals that students at Canadian schools run by elected religious school boards come from less-advantaged backgrounds and watch more television than do the students at secular public schools. This may be one of the reasons students at these schools performed so poorly in mathematics and science.

School Resources and Priorities

The fourth set of hypotheses relates to indicators of school quality: class size, teacher qualifications, administrative priorities, and academic press:

Hypothesis eight. Independent private schools have larger class sizes. Their limited access to public subsidy means they face financial pressures that force them to accept large class size.

Hypothesis nine. Independent private schools have a less-experienced teaching staff. This occurs because turnover is higher, because such schools often pay lower wages and are less encumbered by tenure.

Hypothesis ten. Independent private schools will have more qualified teachers and better facilities and will allocate more time to the teaching of mathematics and science than secular public schools. This will be particularly true in nations or provinces with diploma exams.

Hypothesis eleven. Religiously controlled schools will have less-qualified science and math teachers, poorer-quality science laboratories, and less school time devoted to teaching science and mathematics. This will be particularly true in nations or provinces without diploma examinations.

Hypothesis twelve. Teachers at independent private schools and publicly subsidized denominational schools assign more homework than teachers in secular public schools do.

The results of testing these hypotheses are presented in tables 10-6 and 10-7.

CLASS SIZE. As predicted in hypothesis eight, independent private schools have significantly larger class sizes than public schools do. This differential exists for both nonsectarian and religious schools. In Canada, the class size disadvantage of private schools is greater in provinces that have diploma exams. The schools run by elected religious school boards also have larger class sizes than secular public schools do.

INEXPERIENCED TEACHERS. As predicted in hypothesis nine, private schools are also generally more likely to employ teachers with under three years of teaching experience. The exceptions to this statement are the schools located in Canadian provinces with diploma exams. In these provinces, there are no differences between private and public schools in the proportion of inexperienced teachers.

SCIENCE LABORATORIES. As predicted by hypothesis ten, independent private schools in Canadian provinces with diploma exams tend to have better science laboratories than public schools in those provinces. In provinces without diploma exams, however, science labs are of considerably lower quality and are no better than the labs at public schools. Consistent with hypothesis eleven, a similar pattern prevails for schools run by religious school boards. In provinces without diploma exams, religious school boards invest significantly less in their science labs than public schools do. In diploma exam provinces, by contrast, religious school board schools invest significantly more in science labs and end up having better labs than do the public schools in the province.

Table 10-5. *Private-Public Differences in Student Background, by Presence of Curriculum-Based External Exit Exam*

Student background variable	Data set[a]	Mean	Standard deviation	No exam system			Diploma exam system				Adjusted R²
				Religious school board	Independent religious	Independent secular	Religious school board	Independent religious	Independent secular	Exam* independent	
Logarithm books in the home	16 IAEP	2.0	0.51	. . .	0.42***	0.58***	0.27***	0.056**	0.18**	**	0.560
	Canada	2.02	0.40	−0.007	0.22**	0.28***	−0.15***	0.29***	0.36***	n.s.	0.337
Parents want me to do well in math	16 IAEP	3.32	0.31	. . .	0.04	0.06	0.087**	0.106*	0.154***	n.s.	0.287
	Canada	2.53	0.22	0.15***	0.06	0.17**	0.035	0.04	0.17*	n.s.	0.106
TV hours per week[b]	16 IAEP	10.8	4.3	. . .	−1.4***	−1.9*	−0.45	−0.4	−0.4	*	0.709
	Canada	14.7	2.9	0.26	−2.8***	−2.1**	1.46***	−1.9***	−1.26***	n.s.	0.292

Source: Author's calculations based on 1991 IAEP data.

n.s. Not significant.

* Significant at the 10 percent level (two tail test); ** at the 5 percent level (two tail test); *** at the 1 percent level (two tail test).

a. For details, see table 10-4, note a.

b. School average.

Table 10-6. *Private-Public Differences in Teacher Quality, by Presence of Curriculum-Based External Exit Exam*

Teacher quality variable	Data set[a]	Mean	Standard deviation	No exam system			Diploma exam system				Adjusted R^2
				Religious school board	Independent religious	Independent secular	Religious school board	Independent religious	Independent secular	Exam* independent	
Class size	16 IAEP	28.7	12.3	⋯	8.3***	4.8	0.6	8.4***	6.7***	n.s.	0.637
	Canada	24.8	6.2	3.0***	1.0	4.7***	3.1***	3.0***	6.7***	*	0.369
Proportion of new teachers	16 IAEP	0.13	0.12	⋯	0.085**	0.055	0.032***	-0.003	0.103***	n.s.	0.187
	Canada	0.16	0.15	0.04**	0.12***	0.10*	-0.02	-0.02	-0.04	**	0.083
Specialist 8th grade math teacher	16 IAEP	0.77	0.42	⋯	0.102*	-0.019	0.066	0.141**	0.237***	n.s.	0.414
	Canada	0.45	0.50	-0.21***	-0.13	-0.19	-0.18***	0.17**	0.11**	**	0.282
Specialist 8th grade science teacher	16 IAEP	0.75	0.43	⋯	-0.01	0.036	0.112**	0.057	0.221***	n.s.	0.402
	Canada	0.46	0.50	-0.15***	-0.03	-0.03	-0.05	0.01	0.01	n.s.	0.279
Math teacher majored in math in college	16 IAEP	0.66	0.40	⋯	0.25***	0.33**	-0.04	0.09	-0.09	n.s.	0.560
	Canada	0.66	0.39	-0.22***	-0.10	-0.16	0.00	0.01	0.07	n.s.	0.136
Science teacher majored in science in college	16 IAEP	0.65	0.40	⋯	0.20***	0.13	-0.06	0.18**	-0.11	n.s.	0.709
	Canada	0.69	0.38	-.27***	0.11	0.21*	0.05	-.06	0.04	n.s.	0.210
Quality of science labs	16 IAEP	2.23	1.00	⋯	0.113	0.371	0.38***	0.217	0.114	n.s.	0.271
	Canada	1.95	0.95	-.30***	-.21	-.02	0.15	0.25***	0.44***	*	0.281

Source: Author's calculations based on 1991 IAEP data.

n.s. Not significant.

* Significant at the 10 percent level (two tail test); ** at the 5 percent level (two tail test); *** at the 1 percent level (two tail test).

a. For details, see table 10-4, note a.

Table 10-7. *Private-Public Differences in Instruction and Homework Time, by Presence of Curriculum-Based External Exit Exam*

Teacher pedagogy variable	Data set[a]	Mean	Standard deviation	No exam system			Diploma exam system				Adjusted R²
				Religious school board	Independent religious	Independent secular	Religious school board	Independent religious	Independent secular	Exam* independent	
Scheduled math class hours per week	16 IAEP	3.66	0.82	...	-0.01	-0.00	-0.02	-0.13	-0.17	n.s.	0.403
	Canada	3.98	0.89	-0.57***	-0.26	-0.47	0.85***	0.14	-0.07	n.s.	0.194
Scheduled science class hours per week	16 IAEP	3.53	1.66	...	0.21	0.27	-0.12	0.02	0.24	n.s.	0.545
	Canada	2.92	0.82	-0.70***	0.05	-0.46*	0.06	-0.04	-0.55	n.s.	0.159
Total homework hours per week	16 IAEP	7.27	2.66	...	2.02***	1.11	-0.65***	2.02*	1.10***	n.s.	0.187
	Canada	4.41	1.62	1.06***	2.16***	2.93***	.22	1.60***	2.37***	n.s.	0.171

Source: Author's calculations based on 1991 IAEP data.

n.s. Not significant.

* Significant at the 10 percent level (two tail test); ** at the 5 percent level (two tail test); *** at the 1 percent level (two tail test).

a. For details, see table 10-4, note a.

In the sixteen-nation study, the publicly subsidized religious schools located in nations with diploma exams also had significantly better science labs than the secular public schools in these nations did. Private schools also had better science labs than secular public schools did, but the differential was not statistically significant.

OUT-OF-FIELD TEACHING BY EIGHTH GRADE SCIENCE AND MATH TEACHERS. Principals of IAEP schools were asked whether eighth grade math and science teachers specialize in teaching their subject and whether they majored in the subject in their university studies. These questions provide us with four indicators of out-of-field teaching.

In Canadian provinces that lack diploma exams, schools run by religious school boards are significantly less likely than secular public schools to hire math and science teachers who majored in the subject and who specialize in teaching it. For example, the proportion of math and science teachers who majored in their subject in university is more than a third smaller at these schools than at secular public schools in the province. In diploma exam provinces, however, these schools make very different hiring decisions. Switching to a province with a diploma exam more than doubles the proportion of math and science teachers at religious school board schools who have majored in the subject they teach. Once again the Canadian religious school board schools are behaving as predicted by hypothesis eleven. But within the independent school sector, there is no tendency for the schools run by religious organizations to give less emphasis to hiring qualified math and science teachers. Furthermore, in the sixteen-nation data set, hypothesis eleven is clearly rejected. The only significant difference between publicly subsidized schools run by government and those run by religious organizations is a clearer focus on science teaching on the part of the schools run by religious organizations. Publicly subsidized religious schools are significantly more likely to have science teachers specialize in teaching science and are no different from secular public schools with respect to the other three indicators of out-of-field teaching.

Despite the constrained finances of private schools, out-of–field teaching appears to be less prevalent in most private schools than in secular public schools in the sixteen-nation data set. Eight of sixteen tests of hypothesis ten rejected the null hypothesis of no difference. In Canada, however, the tendency of private schools to hire more qualified teachers was much weaker. Statistically significant differences in favor of private schools were found in only three of the sixteen comparisons.

HOURS OF MATHEMATICS AND SCIENCE INSTRUCTION. Regressions predicting hours of math and science instruction per week are reported in the first four rows of table 10-7. Once again, the Canadian religious school board schools behave as hypothesis eleven predicts. In provinces without diploma exams, they schedule nearly 20 percent less time for teaching math and science than secular public schools do. When there is a diploma exam, they schedule more instruction time for these subjects than secular public schools do. But here again there is no tendency for private schools controlled by religious organizations to schedule less time for math and science teaching than private nondenominational schools do, and the publicly funded but religious organization-controlled schools in the sixteen-nation study do not allocate class time differently from state-run schools.

HOURS OF HOMEWORK. As predicted by hypothesis twelve, students at independent private schools do a lot more homework than students in secular public schools do. Canadian students in conventional public schools average about four hours of homework per week, while private school students average about six hours per week. In the sixteen-nation study, students in secular public schools average about seven hours of homework a week, while students in private nondenominational schools average eight hours and students in private schools run by religious organizations do nine hours of homework a week. The heavy homework assignments may be one reason why private school students watch television substantially less than public school students do.

Summary and Discussion

At the beginning of the chapter, I expressed the hope that lessons could be drawn from an examination of other countries' educational systems. Before I attempt to meet this obligation, however, the reader needs to be cautioned about the weaknesses of the evidence I have been able to gather. The IAEP data contain information on 3,201 middle schools, of which 190 are classified as independent and 395 are classified as denominationally controlled but integral parts of state-funded school systems. Nonpublic schools are extremely diverse. Environmental factors such as diploma exam systems and government regulations are likely to influence the effectiveness of nonpublic schools. This makes the small sample size troublesome. An additional problem comes from our inability to employ a value-added specification in the IAEP data. No claim is made that the controls for family background and tastes that were included in the models solved (as opposed to just reduced) the selection bias problem. Clearly, an analysis needs to be conducted of other large micro data sets such as TIMSS, SIMSS (Second International Math and Science Study), the IEA reading study, and country-specific data sets.

The analysis of the country mean achievement-level data from TIMSS and the IEA reading study also has its limitations. Sample size is smaller than one would like. With samples this small, results may be sensitive to specification and to which countries are included in the regression [the regression samples include every country for which I was able to obtain data on both private school share and student achievement]. The issue being addressed is a system level one, so the unit of analysis is necessarily education systems. This means that data points must generally be nations. Where K–12 education is run by local government (for example, Germany, Australia, Canada, and the United States), comparisons across provinces, states, and metropolitan areas are also useful.[34] This implies that the number of observations is inevitably going to be small. The issues at stake are of enormous importance and policy relevance, so every possible source of variation in private school regime needs to be studied. I hope this chapter will stimulate others to find and analyze other data sets.

Tentative Lessons

The caveats of the previous section imply that the "lessons" described below are tentative in nature.

CURRICULUM-BASED EXTERNAL EXIT (DIPLOMA) EXAM SYSTEMS. The use of diploma exams raises achievement in both public and private schools.[35]

PARENTAL CHOICE, COMPETITION, AND SIZE OF PRIVATE SECTOR ARE NOT THE SAME. Parental choice and competition (between schools for students or between students for admission to schools) depend more on the rules governing admission to public schools and whether parents can select the public school their child attends than on the size of the private sector. A total of 65 percent of Irish schools are run by the Catholic Church, a private organization, but parents influence which of these school their child attends only by moving to a different community. In Finland, the private sector is tiny, but choice within the public sector is complete. Where queues develop, Finnish secondary schools admit students partially on the basis of performance in primary school. If competition between schools is the goal, empowering parents to send their children to community colleges, charter schools, and public schools in other school districts, with public funds following the student through vouchers or other mechanisms, is likely to be more effective than providing vouchers for attending private schools.

EFFECTS OF SIZE OF PRIVATE SECTOR ON AVERAGE ACHIEVEMENT LEVELS. There is no *linear* relationship between the size of the private school sector and national average levels of student achievement in mathematics, science, and reading. There may, however, be a *nonlinear* relationship. Nations with a small private school sector, such as the United States, have significantly lower average levels of achievement than nations with no schools run by nongovernmental organizations. Once the private sector's share of enrollment exceeds 12 percent, a larger private sector is associated with greater achievement in mathematics but no change in science and reading achievement. One possible explanation of this result is that private schools siphon off the elite and the result is a loss of political support for public education. An alternative interpretation argues that causation runs in the opposite direction. If unsubsidized private schools are able to get a non-zero market share only where public schools are failing, the same result would be produced.

INDEPENDENT PRIVATE SCHOOLS. Tuition-charging independent private schools (on the right-hand side of table 10-1) account for 26 percent of American schools and 12 percent of K–12 enrollment. Private schools receiving only minimal public subsidy exist in other countries as well, but they typically account for a smaller share of enrollment than they do in the United States. How do these independent private schools compare to the secular public schools of their nation? There are a number of findings that appear to apply to both denominational and private nondenominational schools and to both Canada and the other sixteen industrialized nations participating in the IAEP:

—Parents of independent private school students have more books in their home.

—Principals of independent private school report fewer problems with absenteeism and discipline.

—Teachers of independent private school students assign more homework, and, perhaps as a result, students watch less television.

—Private schools have larger class sizes.

—Private schools employ less-experienced teachers (particularly as reflected in the sixteen-nation study).

—Private schools are more likely to employ math and science teachers who majored in the subject in college and to assign them to teach only that subject.

However, for the most important outcome indicator, student achievement, private school students do not consistently outperform secular public school students when research controls for family background are included. For science achievement there is no pattern. Of eight coefficients, two are significantly positive. Nondenominational schools in Canadian provinces without diploma exams have significantly higher science achievement than their public counterparts do. In the sixteen-nation study, nondenominational schools in nations with diploma exams also have significantly higher science achievement.

For mathematics, by contrast, there is a clear pattern. In nations and provinces that require students to take curriculum-based external exit examinations, mathematics achievement of private school students exceeds that of public school students by a large margin—more than one grade-level equivalent—controlling for family background. When there is no diploma exam system, math achievement of private school students is no different from the math achievement of public school students. In Canada, there is also a tendency for some of the input indicators to be high in diploma exam provinces and low in provinces without diploma exams: quality of science labs, share of teachers with more than three years of experience, share of math teachers specializing in teaching math. This suggests that private schools may be more sensitive to the incentive effects of diploma exams than public schools and are therefore more likely to stimulate high achievement when there are external exams parents can use to judge the quality and value added of schools.

PUBLICLY FUNDED DENOMINATIONAL SCHOOLS. Publicly funded and regulated schools run by religious organizations (the lower left hand box of table 10-1) are common in Canada and Europe. Schools of this type do not currently exist in the United States, but many of the voucher schemes being considered by state legislatures would change that reality. How do publicly funded denominational schools differ from secular public schools? There were 276 such schools in the Canadian data and 106 in the sixteen-nation study, a sample size sufficient to give us confidence about the reliability of our findings.

Since the vast majority of American states do not have statewide curriculum-based diploma examination systems, the first place to look for lessons are the two Canadian provinces—Ontario and Saskatchawan—that, like the United States, lack diploma exam systems but also have a system of tax-funded denominational schools run by elected religious school boards. Should American states or cities try to replicate this unique institutional arrangement? The answer is an unambiguous *no!*

The thirteen year olds attending these schools are about one grade-level equivalent behind their counterparts at secular public schools. This math and science achievement gap has developed despite parental attitudes that are more favorable to learning math and science. Holding books in the home, siblings, and home language constant, parents of the students in these schools are more likely to talk to their children about math class, more likely to insist their child do well in math, and more likely to be interested in science than the parents of secular public school students. Their students are more likely to have computers and calculators and more likely to say math and science are useful in everyday life and necessary to get a job.[36] Why, then, do these schools do such a poor job of teaching math and science? Apparently it is because they allocate less time to teaching math and science, hire less-qualified teachers, use nonspecialists to teach the subjects, and have poorer science labs.

When they are located in provinces with diploma exam systems, schools run by religious school boards do much better. Their propensity to hire qualified teachers increases significantly and science labs improve. Exam systems also appear to induce these schools to increase classroom instruction hours by one-third in math and by one-fifth in science. Total hours in the school year do not rise, so the increase in time devoted to math and science comes at the expense of something else. Schools run by religious organization school boards also appear to employ more experienced teachers and to give them more preparation time when they are located in provinces with exam systems. Public schools do not. Finally, math and science achievement of thirteen year olds attending schools controlled by religious organization school boards is about one grade-level equivalent higher when the province has diploma exams. However, diploma exams also improve achievement in secular public schools. The gap between the two types of schools closes somewhat, but it remains large and significant.

Why did the publicly funded denominational schools in Canada perform so poorly? The poor performance probably derives from the unique Canadian governance structure—school boards elected by members of a religious community. Chubb and Moe would not expect these schools to perform well. These schools lack the independence of democratic oversight and government regulation that Chubb and Moe believe are the key to effectiveness. Empirical support for this view comes from the fact that in the sixteen-nation study, students attending publicly funded church-administered schools in Ireland, England, and France have higher math and science achievement than comparable students at secular public schools. The governing boards of these schools are appointed, not elected. It is important to remember, however, that the countries with publicly funded church-administered schools in the sixteen-nation study all have diploma exam systems. Only a couple of American states have such systems, so it is doubtful that the findings regarding the effectiveness of European schools controlled by religious organizations apply to most U.S. states.

One cannot generalize findings from nations with diploma exams to nations without such exams, because the relative effectiveness of private schools depends on whether the schools are preparing students for a common set of curriculum-based external exit exams. Analyses of the TIMSS, IEA, and IAEP data have found that CBEEEs raise achievement levels. Private schools are particularly responsive to the incentive effects of exit exams. They outperform secular public schools only in jurisdictions with CBEEE systems. In nations and provinces without diploma exams, students at independent private schools did not have higher math and science achievement than students in secular public schools. This suggests that if tax credits and vouchers are to be offered for private school attendance (or publicly funded charter schools are to be established), subsidized schools should be required to participate in statewide assessment systems and require their students to take curriculum-based diploma exams.

PROMOTING ACADEMIC ACHIEVEMENT: ALTERNATIVES TO VOUCHERS. There are many different ways of building high-performance school systems. The ability of parents and students to choose among public schools funded through voucherlike mechanisms and the independence and authority of the headmasters of these schools may be more important than who owns the school. How schools respond when students fall behind is another critical feature of educational systems. If students are to try hard in middle school, there must be some immediate stakes attached to their effort. Getting into a good college is an effective incentive for only a small minority. The threat of having to attend summer school or repeat a grade may be an effective incentive for these early teens.

Appendix 10A
IAEP Data and Model Specification

The sixteen nations and one region study used in the cross-national analysis included China, England, France, Hungary, Ireland, Israel, Korea, the Emilia Romagna region of northern Italy, Portugal, Scotland, Slovenia, the Soviet Union, Spain, Switzerland, Taiwan, and the United States. First schools, and then students within the schools, were sampled. Sampling frames generally excluded separate schools for special education students and often excluded very small schools as well. Israel assessed only its schools that were taught in Hebrew. The Soviet Union assessed Russian-language schools in fourteen of the nation's fifteen republics. Switzerland assessed fifteen of twenty-six cantons. A school's likelihood of selection was roughly in proportion to its estimated number of thirteen year olds. School nonresponse rates tended to be very low. They were zero in Hungary, Slovenia, Korea, and Taiwan and 3 percent in Israel and the Soviet Union. The countries and region with high school nonresponse rates were Switzerland (17 percent), Italy's Emilia Romagna region (18 percent), Scotland (19 percent), the United Stages (21 percent), and England (48 percent). When sampled schools declined to participate, an alternate was selected from the same stratum.[37]

When the Educational Testing Service canvassed countries about participating in the 1991 International Assessment of Educational Progress (IAEP), Canada decided to collect sufficient data to allow valid comparisons among provinces and between the Anglophone and Francophone school systems of the five provinces with dual systems. The Yukon, the Northwest Territories, and Prince Edward Island did not participate. Stratified random samples of 105 to 128 secondary schools were selected from the French-speaking school systems of Ontario and Quebec and from the English-speaking school systems of Alberta, British Columbia, Manitoba, Saskatchewan, Ontario, Quebec, New Brunswick, Nova Scotia, and Newfoundland.[38] A school's likelihood of selection was roughly in proportion to its estimated number of thirteen year olds. All French-speaking schools in New Brunswick, Saskatchewan, and Manitoba were invited to participate. About 20 percent of the schools were controlled by religious organizations, and 2 percent were nondenominational.

Random samples of thirty to thirty-four thirteen year olds were selected from each school. Half were assigned to the mathematics assessment and half were assigned to the science assessment. The end result was data on about forty thousand Canadian thirteen year olds at 1,338 different schools.

Students also completed a brief questionnaire that asked about books in the home, number of siblings, language usually spoken at home, hours watching television, hours doing homework, pleasure reading, watching science programs on television, home availability of mathematics and science resources, attitudes towards math and science, and teaching methods used by teachers. The principals of participating schools also completed questionnaires describing school policies, school resources, and the qualifications of eighth grade mathematics and science teachers.

The student questionnaires provided data on the behavior and attitudes of students and parents and the instructional strategies of teachers. School means on each variable were calculated for the schools with at least nine students in the school sample, and these were the dependent variables analyzed.

Models were estimated predicting student background and attitudes, student achievement, teacher behavior, teacher quality, and school resource allocation variables. In the sixteen-nation study, the predictive model included five dummy variables for type of governance, a series of dummies for each nation, logarithm of the number of students per grade in the school, a dummy for schools with primary grades, a dummy for schools that include kindergarten through eleventh grade in one building, and three variables measuring the socioeconomic status of the children in the school. The three socioeconomic status and parental attitude variables were the log of the mean number of books in the home, the mean number of siblings, and the proportion of the school's students whose home language was different from the language in which the school gave instruction. The governance dummies were as follows: independent nonsectarian school, independent denominational school, independent nonsectarian schools in nations with a CBEEE system, independent denominational schools in a nation with a CBEEE, and denominationally controlled schools that are an integral part of a national school system that has a CBEEE. In every case secular public schools were the excluded category.

The analysis of Canadian data used an almost identical specification. The differences were the absence of dummy variables for nation, the addition of a dummy variable for French-speaking school systems, the addition of a dummy variable distinguishing provinces with CBEEEs in 1990–91, and a different set of governance dummy variables. There were three types of "nonpublic" schools: schools run by school boards elected by people of a particular faith (generally Catholic), a dummy for independent schools controlled by religious organizations, and a dummy for independent nonsectarian schools. The final two variables in the model were interaction variables: a dummy for independent private (both sectarian and nonsectarian) schools in diploma exam provinces and a dummy for schools run by religious organization school boards in a diploma exam province. Here again secular public schools are the excluded category.

At the time the data used in this study were collected, 1990–91, Alberta, British Columbia, Newfoundland, Quebec, and Francophone New Brunswick had curriculum-based provincial examinations in English, French, mathematics, biology, chemistry, and physics. Alberta's examination system was reestablished in 1984, so it was seven years old when the IAEP data was collected.[39] The other provinces had no curriculum-based provincial examinations in 1990–91. Ontario eliminated them in 1967, Manitoba in 1970, and Nova Scotia in 1972. Nova Scotia substituted multiple-choice norm-referenced achievement tests in reading, language usage, proofreading, mathematics, science, and social studies that do not influence student grades. Anglophone New Brunswick had provincial exams in language arts and mathematics, but exam grades were not reported on transcripts or counted in final course grades. They had little credibility and some students failed to expend much effort on them. In Ontario, some local school districts have district-level exams for core subjects, but most do not. In any case, one would not expect local district subject exams to have as powerful incentive effects as provincial or national exams.

Notes

1. Lowell C. Rose and Alec M. Gallup, and Stanley M. Elam, "The 30th Annual Phi Delta Kappa/Gallup Poll of the Public's Attitudes toward the Public Schools," *Phi Delta Kappan*, vol. 80, no. 1 (September 1998), pp. 41–58.

2. Rendigs Fels, "Making U.S. Schools Competitive," in William Becker and William Baumol, eds., *Assessing Educational Practice: The Contribution of Economics* (Cambridge, Mass: MIT Press, 1996), pp. 41–73.

3. John E. Chubb and Terry M. Moe, *Politics, Markets, and America's Schools* (Brookings, 1990).

4. The 1996 Phi Delta Kappa/Gallup poll found, for example, that by a 2-1 margin (60 percent to 28 percent), respondents said that, "if forced to choose, they would prefer their sons or daughters to make C grades and be active in extracurricular activities rather than make A grades and not be active." Lowell Rose, Alec Gallup, and Stanley Elam, "The 29th Annual Phi Delta Kappa/Gallup Poll of the Public's Attitudes toward the Public Schools," *Phi Delta Kappan* (September 1997), pp. 41–56.

5. Steven Pearlstein, "Quebec Schools May Exorcise Religion," *Washington Post*, May 10, 1999, p. A15.

6. See the chapter by Sawhill and Shannon in this volume.

7. In 1980 localities provided 28.5 percent of school funds in Canada compared to 43 percent in the United States. The average within-province coefficient of variation was 0.09 for Canada and 0.17 for the United States. Judith McDonald, "The Canadian Educational System," in Richard Aronson and Robert Thornton, eds., *The Economic Consequences of American Education* (New York: JAI Press, 1994).

8. Ministry of Education and Science, *The Dutch Education System*, Docinform no. 332E (Votermeer, Netherlands, 1988), p. 4.

9. Information about admission practices came from interviews with Belgian academics. Other information came from Ministerie van de Vlaamse Gemeenschap, *Education in Belgium: The Diverging Paths, Review of National Policies of Education* (Brussels, 1991), pp. 1–463; and Ministerie Van de Vlaamse Gemeenschap, *Educational Developments in Belgium, 1992–94: The Flemish Community* (Brussels: Centrum voor Informatie en Documentatie, 1994), pp. 1–42.

10. Government Statistical Service, *Education Statistics for the United Kingdom: 1992* (London: Her Majesty's Statistical Office, 1993), p. 8.

11. D. Raffe, "School Attainment and the Labor Market," in D. Raffe, ed., *Fourteen to Eighteen: The Changing Pattern of Schooling in Scotland* (Aberdeen University Press, 1984), pp. 174–93.

12. Association of Secondary Teachers of Ireland, Information sheet opposing changes in the Irish examination system (1990), p. 1.

13. Ministere de l'Education Nationale et de la Culture, *Reperes and References Statistiques sur les enseignmements et la formation* (Paris, 1992).

14. Bac exams in mathematics, history/geography, and French are set and marked by twenty-three regional academies. School-based assessments are used for other subjects. George Madeus and Thomas Kelleghan, "Student Examination Systems in the European Community: Lessons for the United States," report to the Office of Technology Assessment (June 1991), p. 17.

15. The Ministry of Education sets an exam that has both multiple-choice and essay components. The multiple-choice component represents half the written paper and is graded centrally. The essay component is marked by the student's own teacher and a teacher from another school, employing rubrics supplied by the Ministry of Education. Oral components are administered by the student's teacher.

16. Kathleen D. White, *Educational Testing: The Canadian Experience with Standards, Examinations and Assessments*, GAO/PEMD-93-11 (General Accounting Office, April 1993), pp. 1–74.

17. M. Adler and G. M. Raab, "Exit Choice and Loyalty: The Impact of Parental Choice on Admissions to Secondary Schools in Edinburgh and Dundee," *Journal of Educational Policy*, vol. 3 (Winter 1988), pp. 155–79.

18. Analysis of data on out-of-catchment school selections for the Fife Local Education Authority found that the Type B school effect estimates (measures of how well each school does compared to others serving pupils of similar ability and

social background) are significantly and substantially higher at the schools selected by parents choosing to leave their catchment area. Douglas J. Willms and Frank Echols, "Alert and Inert Clients: The Scottish Experience of Parental Choice of Schools," *Economics of Education Review*, vol. 11, no. 4 (October 1993), pp. 339–50. My summary sentence sounds different from Willms and Echols's summary of their own results because they unaccountably base their conclusions on estimates of school effects from models that did not control for the pupil's ability when entering secondary school that they acknowledge are biased. Luckily, they also present results based on correctly specified models with controls for initial ability in table 3 of their article.

19. H. D. Lewis, *The French Education System* (St. Martins Press, 1985), p. 3.

20. According to Lorrie Shepard and Mary Lee Smith ("Introduction and Overview," in Lorrie Shepard and Mary Lee Smith, eds., *Flunking Grades: Research and Policies on Retention* [Falmer Press, 1989], pp. 16–33), some state systems of education in the United States report retaining between 5 and 10 percent of their students each year. These reports are not, however, consistent with household survey data from the Census Bureau. For example, in October 1991, 33.7 percent of sixteen year olds were either enrolled below grade eleven or not enrolled. This is only slightly above the 27.8 percent of eleven year olds five years earlier who were below their modal grade, implying that about 8 percent of those at the modal grade at age eleven in 1986 were retained during the next five years. Retention rates are higher in elementary school. Five years earlier, in 1981, 10.6 percent of six year olds were in grades below first grade, so it appears that 19 percent of the pupils were retained during the first five years of primary school (Current Population Survey, *School Enrollment*, Series P-20, various issues).

21. Central Bureau Voor De Statistiek, *Educational Statistics for the Netherlands* (1993), pp. 19, 20, 29.

22. Ministere de l'Education Nationale et de la Culture, *Reperes and References Statistiques sur les enseignmements et la formation*, pp. 77, 93, 99. Redoublement is not something inflicted only on children from lower-class backgrounds. Often high aspirations can be achieved only by redoublement. The two Dutch professors with grown children with whom I have discussed this matter both had a child who was required to redoubler. In France, selective upper secondary schools serving upper-middle-class communities have grade-repeating rates that are nearly as high as schools serving lower-income communities. For example, Lycee Charlemagne, an upper secondary school serving one of the richest neighborhoods in Paris, asked 14 percent of its entering class to repeat the year in 1992.

23. Organization for Economic Cooperation and Development, *Education at a Glance* (Paris, 1996), table P3.3.

24. High goals—that is, high minimum achievement levels necessary for promotion—appear to simultaneously raise both age-standardized performance and retention rates. In the United States, student background and learning and teaching effectiveness vary a great deal across jurisdictions, and this will produce a

negative correlation between retention rates and age-standardized achievement within the United States. I am not aware of any empirical studies of the relationship between standards, achievement, and retention that take account of the simultaneous character of the system. For a formal analysis of this issue, see Suk Kang "A Formal Model of School Reward Systems," in John Bishop, ed., *Incentives, Learning and Employability* (Columbus, Ohio: National Center for Research in Vocational Education, 1985); and Robert Costrell, "A Simple Model of Educational Standards," *American Economic Review*, vol. 84, no. 4 (September 1994), pp. 956–71.

25. The argument against retention is that it lowers the learning goals being set for the retained student in subsequent years. Within-school cross-section studies suggest that subsequent learning is reduced by retention. Holmes, "Grade Level Retention Effects," pp. 16–33; and Arthur J. Reynolds, "Grade Retention and School Adjustment: An Exploratory Analysis," *Educational Evaluation and Policy Analysis*, vol. 14, no. 2 (Summer 1992), pp. 101–21. These studies, however, do not address the effects of ending social promotion on the students who study harder because of the threat of retention and who get extra instruction during the summer and the effect of higher standards in the next grade because students are better prepared. Failing a few courses does not sever peer relationships in U.S. high schools in the way it does in France, Belgium, and the Netherlands, so ending social promotion might have smaller incentive effects in the United States than it appears to have had in Europe. Requiring failing students to attend summer school would create strong incentives for students to study during the regular school year. Making graduation from primary to middle school and from middle to high school contingent on effort and achievement would have a similar effect.

26. Comparative education studies, government documents, and education encyclopedias were reviewed and education ministry officials, embassy personnel, and Cornell graduate students from the country were interviewed to determine which of the TIMSS nations have curriculum-based externally set exit examinations in secondary school and the importance and character of private schools.

27. Austria, Bulgaria, Columbia, the Czech Republic, Denmark, England, Finland, Hong Kong, Hungary, Ireland, Israel, Italy, Japan, Korea, Lithuania, the Netherlands, New Zealand, Russia, Scotland, Singapore, the Slovak Republic, Slovenia, and Thailand in both mathematics and science. Three countries—France, Iceland, and Romania—had CBEEEs in mathematics but not in science. Five countries—Australia, Canada, Germany, Switzerland, and the United States—had CBEEEs in some provinces and states but not in others. Norway has regular exit examinations in mathematics but examines science only every few years. Latvia had an external examination system until very recently, so it was given a 0.5 on the CBEEE variable. The countries classified as not having a CBEEE in either subject were Belgium (both Flemish- and French-speaking systems), Cyprus, Greece, the Philippines, Portugal, Spain, and Sweden. Following Madeus

and Kellaghan, "Student Examination Systems in the European Community," the university entrance examinations in Greece, Portugal, Spain, and Cyprus and the ACT and SAT in the United States were not considered CBEEEs. University entrance exams should have much smaller incentive effects, because students headed into work do not take them and teachers can avoid responsibility for their students' exam results by arguing that not everyone is college material or that examiners have set an unreasonably high standard to limit enrollment in higher education. John H. Bishop, "Do Curriculum-based External Exit Exam Systems Enhance Student Achievement?" Consortium for Policy Research on Education Research Report RR40 (Philadelphia: University of Pennsylvania, 1998), appendix A, pp. 1–32, provides a bibliography of the documents and individuals consulted when making these classifications. The TIMSS report's information about examination systems does not distinguish between university admissions exams and curriculum-based exit exams, so its classifications are not useful for this exercise.

28. OECD data on Israel was not available, so IAEP data on the share of middle schools run by publicly funded religious schools or by independent secular organizations was used instead. This made Israel's private share 21 percent. The publicly funded schools run by the Irish Catholic Church were classified as private for purposes of this analysis, so Ireland's private share was 67 percent. Substituting OECD's numbers for the 67 percent figure does not significantly change the empirical results.

29. Table 1.5 of Albert Beaton et al., *Mathematics [Science] Achievement in the Middle School Years: IEA's Third International Mathematics and Science Study* (Boston, Mass.: CSTEEP, Boston College, 1996). For countries not included in this table, the thirteen-year-old median was estimated by age adjusting the seventh and eighth grade means. The Philippines, for example, had a math score mean of 399 in eighth grade and a mean of 386 in seventh grade. The mean age of eighth graders was 14 and the mean age of seventh graders was 12.9. The math score for 13.5 year olds was estimated by interpolation between seventh and eighth grade means. Math13.5 = 386 + (399 − 386)*[(13.5 − 12.9)/(14 − 12.9)].

30. Appendix E of Warwick Elley, *How in the World do Students Read?* (The Hague: International Association for the Evaluation of Educational Achievement, 1992).

31. Data from Brazil, Jordan, and Mozambique were not used because of the low levels of industrialization there. Canada participated as nine different provinces, five of which were stratified into separate English-speaking and French-speaking school systems. The Canadian data are analyzed separately.

32. Catholic parish schools in Ireland accounted for 71 of the 106 publicly subsidized religiously controlled schools in the sixteen-nation study. If only Irish data had been used, the coefficient on subsidized religious schools would be 0.025 for math and 0.03 for science, little changed from the result obtained in the full sixteen-nation sample.

33. John Bishop, "Incentives to Study and the Organization of Secondary Instruction," in William Becher and William Baumol, eds., *Assessing Educational Practice: The Contribution of Economics* (MIT Press, 1996), p. 122.

34. Caroline Hoxby, "The Effects of School Choice on Curriculum and Atmosphere," in Susan Mayer and Paul Peterson (Brookings, 1999), pp. 281–316; and Caroline Hoxby, "Does Competition among Public Schools Benefit Students and Taxpayers?" Working Paper 4979 (Cambridge, Mass.: National Bureau of Economic Research, 1997).

35. This conclusion also rests on comparisons of New York with other states in the United States, comparisons of Canadian provinces with and without diploma exams, and cross-national analysis of IAEP data on geography, math, and science. John Bishop, Joan Moriarty, and Ferran Mane, "Diplomas for Learning, not Seat Time: The Effects of New York State's Regents Examinations," *Economics of Education Review* (forthcoming); John Bishop, "The Impact of Curriculum-Based External Examinations on School Priorities and Student Learning," *International Journal of Educational Research*, vol. 23, no. 8 (1995).

36. See table 1 of John Bishop, "Nerd Harassment, Incentives, School Priorities and Learning," in Susan Mayer and Paul Peterson, eds., *Earning and Learning* (Brookings, 1999), p 258.

37. International Assessment of Educational Progress, *IAEP Technical Report*, vol. 1 (Princeton, N.J.: Educational Testing Service, 1992).

38. Ibid. In Canada, the highest school refusal rates were for the English-speaking school systems in Quebec (15 percent), the English-speaking school systems in Saskatchewan (12 percent), and the French-speaking school systems in New Brunswick (12 percent). In the rest of the provinces, refusal rates were below 7 percent, and in many provinces all invited schools participated.

39. Three of the provinces that lacked CBEEEs in 1991 have now reintroduced them (GAO 1993). Manitoba introduced its twelfth grade examination in the winter of 1991, about the time the IAEP exam was being administered to eighth graders in the province. The new examination system was announced in June 1990, only seven months earlier. This system rotated the subject assessed on a five- or six-year cycle. Starting in 1996, Manitoba has assessed math and language arts every year and requires that the exams count for 30 percent of the student's final grade. Starting in 1995, Anglophone New Brunswick has required that exam results account for 30 percent of course grades. Exam results are also now included on the transcript and school-level results are published in newspapers.

ARTHUR M. HAUPTMAN

11 | Vouchers and American Higher Education

FOR MORE than half a century, American higher education has had a broad experience with federal programs that can be defined as vouchers. This chapter examines four principal federal vouchers in higher education—educational benefits under the G.I. Bill, federally sponsored student loans, Pell grants, and two tuition tax credits enacted in 1997, Helping Outstanding Pupils Educationally (HOPE) Scholarship and Lifetime Learning. Each of these four federal programs may be considered a voucher in that the aid may only be used for tuition and other expenses related to college attendance (although some students do use these benefits to pay for living expenses), benefits are portable to a broad range of institutions, and the amount of benefit is largely determined through a statutory formula in which institutions have little or no discretion in determining the amount students receive.[1]

Vouchers in Higher Education

Of all the domestic policy functions in the United States, higher education has among the longest and perhaps the most extensive experience with using vouchers as a means of financing. The American experience with

336

vouchers for higher education stretches back more than fifty years to 1944, when the G.I. Bill was first enacted. The following half-century has seen a progression of voucher efforts, including the extension of G.I. education benefits, the creation of the Guaranteed Student Loan program in 1965, and the Basic Grants program (now Pell grants) in 1972. Most recently, in 1997 the federal government enacted two tuition tax credits that represent the newest federal effort to use vouchers as a vehicle for government assistance for college students.

G.I. Bill benefits were first created to help returning World War II veterans pay for the costs of readjustment for housing, health, and education, including the federal payment of college tuition and related expenses. Subsequent versions were made available to the veterans of the Korean and Vietnam Wars. Although variations have occurred in the benefits provided and the rules of eligibility under the different iterations of the G.I. Bill, all versions have been federal entitlements based on service in the military. No need calculation is used to determine eligibility. The initial G.I. Bill legislation provided the full amount of tuition plus a stipend for living expenses. Subsequent versions of the G.I. Bill provided recipients with a set amount of monthly benefits typically matching the veteran's months of service.

Federal student loans were first established in the National Defense Education Act of 1958, but they did not exist as vouchers until 1965, when the Guaranteed Student Loan program was enacted to provide privately financed loans with a government guarantee against default.[2] The federally guaranteed loan programs operate as an entitlement in that all eligible students may borrow and banks and other loan holders are entitled to receive federal payments for interest subsidies and federal reinsurance for defaulted loans. Since 1993 some federal student loans have been made directly by institutions, using federal capital. These direct loans also are a federal entitlement (although there are no explicit payments to lenders because the loans are financed with federal capital). Two types of subsidies exist in both the guaranteed and direct student loan programs: the federal assumption of interest while the borrower remains in school for students deemed to be financially needy and an interest rate for all student borrowers below what the market would otherwise charge.

Pell grants, initially called basic grants, emerged out of legislation enacted in 1972 after a hot debate about the federal role in higher education. The issue was whether to provide students with vouchers or whether federal aid should continue to be provided principally to institutions and then distributed to students. Although both types of aid were included in the 1972 legislation and continue to exist, the voucher approach in the form of Pell grants has been the clear winner over time in terms of funding. Thus, for most recipients, costs of attendance play no role in the Pell award calculation. Although the program is not a federal entitlement, it has been treated in the appropriations process as if it were one.[3]

Tuition tax credits were established in 1997 in response to political pressures to make college more affordable for the middle class. President Clinton made tuition tax credits a centerpiece of his reelection campaign in 1996 and central to his 1997 balanced budget negotiations with the Republicans, who favored a more general tax cut. In addition to the two tuition tax credits, the 1997 legislation included a number of provisions designed to encourage parents to save more money for their children's college education as well as a partial reinstatement of deduction for interest on student loans. The two tuition credits focus on different groups of students. The HOPE Scholarship tax credit will benefit students enrolled at least half-time in the first two years of higher education. The other new credit for Lifetime Learning is intended more specifically for older students taking at least one course at the undergraduate or graduate level.

Differences among the Programs

In many ways, these four higher education vouchers are distinctly different. The GI Bill provides nonrepayable grants based on service in the military with no determination of financial need. Pell grants also require no repayment but are targeted toward students from lower-income families; the bulk of benefits go to students with annual family incomes that are less than $30,000. Federal student loans require repayment and are available to students from a much broader range of family incomes because eligibility for interest subsidies varies with a student's costs of attendance. The new tuition tax credits are the only higher education vouchers that are not a spending program; they operate through the federal tax code instead. The tax credits are designed to primarily benefit students with annual family incomes of between $30,000 and $80,000.

Common Goals and Principles

Although these four voucher efforts clearly are very different in their nature and their target populations, the legislation that created each of them also reveals the following important common goals and principles:

—The principal goal of each of the higher education voucher programs was to increase the college participation rates of groups of students targeted for assistance. In each program, improving the quality of education or the academic performance and degree completion of beneficiaries has been a distinctly secondary consideration.

—Federal aid dollars should not encourage institutions to increase their tuition and other charges. The framers of each of the higher education voucher programs expressed concern that the creation of the benefit not lead to higher tuition and other college charges. In some cases, steps were taken in the legislation to minimize the potential effect on tuition, while in other instances this goal of tuition restraint has not been accompanied by specific provisions.

—Steps should be taken to prevent the creation of low-quality institutions established mainly to capture federal aid. The issue of fraud and abuse has played a significant role in the debates over each of the higher education voucher programs. Student loan defaults have been the most prominent concern, but other quality concerns exist as well. A related concern is that existing institutions not relax their academic standards to keep students enrolled and thereby increase the federal funds they might receive.

—Students who receive federal student aid should be prepared to succeed at the postsecondary level. This principle may seem obvious, but under the so-called ability-to-benefit provisions enacted in 1976, students who are not high school graduates and who have not received a high school equivalency degree nonetheless are eligible to receive a wide range of federal benefits. Through these provisions, the growing numbers of college students who require remediation in basic skills are eligible for all forms of federal aid. These provisions have been a source of concern, however, because the tests used to determine whether a student could benefit were administered for many years by the schools with an obvious self-interest in seeing a high pass rate. More recent efforts require an independently administered test, but the standards of passage on the tests are still low enough to raise concerns about these provisions.

Why Have Vouchers Been Much More Acceptable in Higher Education than K–12 Education?

While vouchers have become a critical component in the financing of higher education in this country, they continue to pay a very small share of the bill in K–12 education. The following aspects of higher education may help to explain why it consistently has been a more receptive environment for vouchers than K–12 education:

—There is a highly competitive market for higher education services composed of diverse providers. In K–12 education, public schools are totally dependent on taxpayer support, and most students are restricted to local school providers. By contrast, higher education in this country is characterized by highly mobile students choosing from a natural market of more than thirty-five hundred widely diverse institutions that draw on a broad-ranging set of public and private resources. The concept of vouchers seems to fit far better into a market environment than a public monopoly.

—The principle of charging fees for service is well established in higher education. Because fees are regularly charged in higher education, it is easier to use a voucher to pay for them. In contrast, no fee structure exists for most K–12 education. In addition, the fees in higher education cover only a portion of the costs per student, and that makes vouchers more budgetarily feasible. If tuition and fees paid the total bill in higher education, the government funding necessary to provide vouchers covering full costs would be prohibitive.

—The notion of using vouchers to enhance access to a diverse set of public and private institutions has been politically and legally acceptable in higher education. Although most private colleges in this country initially had some religious affiliation and many still do, debates over the need to separate church and state have been far more muted regarding higher education vouchers than the very contentious debates over vouchers in K–12 education. Public subsidies in higher education have a different legal status than those provided in K–12 education. Given the long history and political strength of private colleges in this country, it also is difficult to imagine the adoption of any of the higher education vouchers if students attending private colleges and universities had not been eligible.

Perhaps because of these differences in the structures of K–12 education and higher education, the debates over vouchers have been remarkably different in their tone and content. These differences can perhaps best be seen by the relative emphasis placed on the goals of access, choice, and quality. Debates over the creation of the various higher education voucher programs have centered on the goals of providing greater access and, initially, choice of institutions. But the goal of providing more choice has faded in the past two decades in part because the student loan programs have been effective in allowing students to enroll in a broad range of institutions. As a result, access has become the primary focus of debates over higher education vouchers. The possibility of using vouchers to improve the quality of higher education institutions or students, however, has been conspicuously absent from the federal debates regarding higher education.

The emphasis on increasing access and, to a lesser extent, choice in higher education debates is in sharp contrast to the debates over creating vouchers in K–12 education, where the goal of providing greater choice of schools has been a predominant theme. This emphasis on choice in K–12 education relates directly to the issue of improving quality. Giving parents more choice in the schools their children attend and the competition that choice will engender are viewed as primary means for improving the quality of public schools and the academic performance of students. By contrast, providing basic access to K–12 education is less important because compulsory education assures everyone of some form of public education.

Assessing the Impact of Vouchers

The common goals and principles for the various higher education vouchers listed in the preceding section serve as benchmarks for measuring the effectiveness of these voucher programs as well as evaluating the impact of other forms of government support for higher education. To what extent has the introduction of various vouchers led to increased participation rates among eligible groups of students? Has the availability of the voucher had an effect on what institutions charge for tuition and other fees? Did the voucher lead to changes in the quality of education provided or in the academic performance of students? In short, vouchers and other public policies in higher education can be evaluated on the basis of their effect on enrollments, prices, and quality of institutions and students who attend them.

—*Enrollments.* Since improving access is the primary policy objective of all federal higher education vouchers, measuring their effect on enrollments is obviously critical. At least two measures of enrollment should be considered in this context. One is the effect on the overall level of enrollments at different types of institutions. The other is whether the composition of the student body changed during the period of review and the extent to which this change was attributable to some feature of the voucher.

Assessments of the impact of public policies on the levels of enrollments and the characteristics of students also should recognize both the supply and demand aspects of the equation. Most assessments of public policies in higher education, however, have been designed to measure the willingness and ability of students to enroll. Often lost in this focus on demand responsiveness is whether the number of seats provided by institutions has grown to absorb any increase in demand at different types of institutions.

—*Quality of institutions and students.* As in the case of enrollments, the question of whether federal vouchers and other public policies have affected the quality of higher education also should be divided into two parts. One issue of quality relates to whether vouchers have affected the quality of the institutions and the education and training they provide. Of greatest concern is the potential for inferior institutions to spring up primarily to take advantage of the availability of federal aid. A related concern is whether existing institutions debase their programs or courses to cater to more students who are eligible for the federal aid.

The other quality issue in postsecondary education involves the academic preparedness and performance of students rather than the quality of the education and training provided. Again, higher education's view of quality seems in contrast to K–12 school vouchers, where improving the academic performance of students is one of the primary goals of the effort. Students need only show "satisfactory academic progress" to maintain their eligibility for federal student aid, an ambiguous standard that is difficult to enforce. Quality also relates in part to the principle that students who receive federal aid should be capable of doing college-level work, whether in academic or more vocationally oriented programs. This principle has eroded over time as ability-to-benefit provisions have allowed students who were not high school graduates or were without a high school equivalency to qualify for federal aid.

—*Tuition and other charges.* As previously noted, in the debates leading to each of the federal vouchers, concerns were expressed that the availability of the voucher should not contribute to the growth of tuition and other charges. Despite this intent, some evidence suggests that the funds provided through vouchers have led to higher prices, particularly in the case of federal student loans. As with enrollments and quality, it is important to assess the possible impact that vouchers might have on prices for the different sectors of postsecondary education. Certain types of institutions may well have been more likely than others to raise their prices in reaction to the greater availability of federal aid for their students.

—*Interrelatedness of enrollment, quality, and price effects.* Enrollments, quality, and price obviously are related and cannot be viewed in isolation from one another. Assessments of the impact of vouchers therefore must consider the interaction of these variables. For example, efforts to open up higher education to traditionally underserved groups of students are likely to have an impact on quality in terms of the education provided and the average performance and proficiency of the students who go to college. While the federal goals in higher education have been tilted much more strongly in the direction of access than quality, trade-offs between quality and access form a more critical set of decision points for college and university officials. Similarly, institutional officials are intensely aware of the impact tuition may have on both enrollments and quality.

Difficulties in Measuring the Impact of Vouchers

Assessing the extent to which the various voucher programs have affected enrollments, prices, and quality measures would be greatly facilitated if we could compare the experience of students who received vouchers to a similar group of students who had not. In higher education, however, this kind of scientific inquiry is not feasible for the following reasons:

—Perhaps most important, each higher education voucher is a federal entitlement (or nearly so in the case of Pell grants). This means that the benefits are available uniformly and universally to eligible students. The only feasible comparison, therefore, is between groups of students who are eligible by dint of their service or financial need and those who are not. In short, there is no appropriate control group likely to yield viable statistical results.

—Although the effects of public policies may be as much or more on the supply side as the demand by the recipients of aid, most of the econometric work in higher education has focused on the demand side. For example, the impact of tuition increases is assessed principally on the basis of price elasticity of students' willingness to pay, with increases in price correlated with modest declines in college participation rates. Similarly, the student aid programs typically are evaluated on the basis of whether targeted groups of students increased their participation rates. Supply considerations, especially at public institutions, which may have played a more critical role in determining whether many of these students were able to meet their aspirations, have not been studied nearly as intensively. A number of studies also have been conducted on the effects of nonprice variables, such as the socioeconomic status of students and the availability of information on higher education participation rates.[4]

—There is little econometric analysis of the effects of any of the higher education voucher programs on variables other than enrollment, such as whether the availability of aid has affected the tuitions that colleges charge or the quality of the programs they provide. The evidence that does exist typically is in the form of simple correlations and anecdotes. Any effort to measure the impact of vouchers on the academic performance of students will be complicated by the fact that college officials traditionally have resisted the notion of assessing the added value of the education they provide. As a result, very little information exists, for example, on whether what students learn while they are enrolled in college is affected by what kinds of aid they received.

Relatively little analysis has been devoted to which programs in higher education have been most cost effective. The analyses of various federal and state student aid programs have paid very little attention to the potential effects of alternative policies, to what would have happened if the same funding had been devoted instead to the additional direct support of institutions or other ways of providing student financial aid. For example, despite the intensity of the debate when Pell grants were enacted in 1972 over the best way to provide aid, the relative cost effectiveness of vouchers compared with providing the aid indirectly through institutions has not been thoroughly investigated.

Little attention has been paid to how institutions alter their own aid policies in reaction to federal and state student aid policies. Most private institutions became more aggressive in using their tuition and aid policies as an enrollment management tool beginning in the 1980s. Many public institutions have followed suit in the 1990s, although not nearly to the same degree as their private counterparts. The issue is how institutions factor the availability of federal and state student aid as well as private sources of aid into the calculation of how much aid they provide to students from their own resources. There is reason to believe that many institutions may be awarding this aid in ways that blunt the effectiveness of government and private aid. But the extent of this displacement effect is just beginning to be more fully explored in the research literature.[5]

Speculating on the Effects of Vouchers in Higher Education

In the absence of systematic empirical analysis of the effects of higher education vouchers, other procedures must be employed to estimate their impact. The approach taken here is to examine trends in enrollments, quality, and price that have occurred while different vouchers have been in effect and then analyze whether the vouchers may have affected these trends. To aid in this process of inference, this chapter examines the following three categories of possible explanations: the program design of the voucher, the program coverage of the voucher, and changes in the condition of the higher education "industry" while the vouchers were in effect.

—*Program design.* A key factor in determining the impact of vouchers and other public policies is the program's structure. For example, certain design features could either stimulate higher tuitions or moderate their growth. Similarly, the voucher program could reward completion of a degree or do nothing on this front, emphasizing only college entrance. Some aid programs focus funds on students who demonstrate high academic performance or other merit factors, but most make no distinction among students on the basis of quality and merit considerations.

—*Program coverage.* Another obvious consideration in trying to determine the impact of vouchers is their size. Program coverage can be measured in one of two ways: first, by the proportion of students who receive a certain type of voucher; and second, by the proportion of the total bill paid for by the voucher. The higher the share of students who receive a voucher or the greater share of costs covered by a voucher, the more impact the voucher is likely to have on enrollments, price, and quality.

—*Industry structure.* The impact of vouchers or other public policies is also a function of the capacity of the enterprise while the policies are in effect. If, for example, competition among institutions for students is keen at the time that a voucher goes into effect, the voucher is likely to have less impact on tuitions than if it is enacted when there are more qualified applicants than available seats. Similarly, a widely available voucher is more likely to lead institutions to increase their capacity in a sellers' market than a buyers' market.

Industry conditions will, of course, change over time because of underlying economic and demographic factors with or without vouchers being in effect. Vouchers must be judged in the context of when they are enacted and, while they are in effect, on whether they may have had an impact on the structure of the industry. Thus, if the design of the voucher or the extent of its coverage contributed to pricing decisions among certain segments of the industry, that would represent an effect on the industry structure. Even though the industry structure probably would have changed without any voucher being enacted, this does not diminish the fact that the voucher may have affected the speed and the size of these changes.

The Experience with the Various Higher Education Vouchers

In this section the framework of program design, program coverage, and the condition of the industry is used to examine the possible impact of the three existing voucher programs. The same framework is also used to speculate on the future impact of the new tuition tax credits on enrollments, prices, and quality in higher education.

The G.I. Bill

The G.I. Bill, through the opportunities it provided to veterans in housing, education, and other services, is widely regarded as one of the most successful domestic policies in this country's history. In higher education, it allowed millions of veterans from three wars to further their education. The G.I. Bill also helped change the face of American higher education, as its education provisions, along with the decision of the states to greatly expand public higher education, are the two public policies most responsible for transforming America's colleges and universities from elite institutions to ones that provided opportunities for a much broader population. This expansion seems to have occurred without many of the negative consequences normally associated with programs of this magnitude. For example, there was no widespread run-up in tuition, nor was there a proliferation of low-quality institutions created to capture some of the billions of federal dollars being poured into higher education.[6]

What factors account for this apparent success of the G.I. Bill? Let's begin with how the program was designed. Each version of the legislation has been based on service in the military, with no assessment of financial need of the veterans. Under each G.I. Bill, veterans applied to colleges and were admitted through the normal processes. The Veterans Administration was responsible for determining eligibility and for mailing checks to the institutions and the veterans but otherwise did not exert much control over the process. Benefits typically were provided for as many months as the veteran served in the military.

The initial G.I. Bill legislation paid tuition, fees, books, and supplies, up to $500 a year (which was the amount that Harvard, the highest-priced institution at the time, charged). Single veterans in addition received a $50 monthly living allowance, while married veterans received $75 a month. There is evidence that this initial structure may have contributed to a run-up of tuitions at many institutions following World War II, especially those in the public sector. One particularly troublesome trend was that in some states veterans were automatically treated as nonresidents so that out-of-state tuition could be charged.

As a result of concerns about these increases in tuition, subsequent versions of the G.I. Bill paid veterans a fixed amount each month regardless of which institution they attended. Under this revised structure, when veterans enrolled in an institution that charged less than their G.I. Bill benefit, they could pocket the difference to pay for more of their living expenses. This change in program design seemed to have the desired effect; over time, an increasing proportion of veterans enrolled in lower-priced public institutions. Some have argued that this change in the G.I. Bill program led to the shift toward greater enrollments in the public sector. But it is more likely that this switch simply reflected the general trend in which the growth of enrollments in this country was financed primarily by the creation and expansion of public institutions so that they accounted for a larger share of overall higher education enrollments.[7]

A recounting of the G.I. Bill program suggests that the program structure had several advantages. It built on the large reservoir of public sentiment to help veterans who had served their country in wartime, thus avoiding the political class warfare that has surrounded many other domestic programs. The G.I. Bill's service-based structure also is much easier to administer than programs that require a needs test to determine eligibility. All that was required in the case of the G.I. Bill was for the government to know that the individuals had served in the military, how long they had served, and that they were attending an institution that qualified. This ease of administration should not be underestimated as a factor in the perceived success of the program.

When the G.I. Bill was created, a great deal of concern arose that it would lead to fly-by-night operations created to get rich quick off federal taxpayers and unsuspecting veterans. Although some of this did occur, it was not nearly as extensive as feared, and there was no proliferation of profit-making schools. It is not entirely clear in retrospect what the legislation or the Veterans Administration did to prevent program abuse that subsequent voucher efforts were unable to do. Schools had to be accredited, and the Veterans Administration apparently had some additional requirements, but the kinds of additional safeguards that now are required to ensure integrity in the student aid programs were not in place then.

Another concern when the initial G.I. Bill was enacted was that the increased presence of veterans on campus would cheapen the college degree. James B. Conant, president of Harvard University at the time, thought that the G.I. Bill would result in "the least capable among the war generation . . . flooding the facilities for advanced education." Robert Hutchins, the president of the University of Chicago, called the program "unworkable" and worried that colleges would admit veterans to capture federal dollars.[8] These concerns turned out to be largely unfounded. Most of the veterans were older and highly motivated by their war experience and intent on improving their lot through the educational opportunities provided to them.

Predictions of how many veterans would use the G.I. Bill also turned out to be low, as few people at the time thought that it would be as extensively used as it turned out to be. Initial estimates of participants were in the hundreds of thousands, but more than two million World War II veterans used the education benefits following the war, and total enrollment in higher education increased from 1.7 million in 1945 to nearly 2.5 million in 1950. Virtually all of that enrollment growth consisted of males, and almost all of those males were veterans. At the peak of G.I. Bill usage in 1947, more than 1.1 million veterans were enrolled, which represented half of total higher education enrollments and more than two-thirds of male college students in that year.[9]

Subsequent versions of the G.I. Bill also helped large numbers of veterans, although not as many or as high a proportion of enrollments as the initial version of the legislation. Higher education enrollments increased by more than a million students (an increase of roughly 50 percent) in the four years following the end of the Korean War in 1953. Males accounted for about one-half of the enrollment growth during that time, and veterans appear to have accounted for perhaps one-half of those enrollments. These figures suggest that the G.I. Bill had relatively little impact on enrollments in the 1950s, since female enrollments grew at roughly the same rate as male enrollments. The number of Vietnam-era veterans who enrolled in college was smaller still, constituting less than one-tenth of all higher education enrollments in the late 1960s and the 1970s.

There is some question about how many veterans would have enrolled in college in the absence of the G.I. Bill. One study indicated that one-fifth of enrolled World War II veterans would not have attended college without the G.I. Bill.[10] Other observers would peg the number of veterans who would have been unable to go to college without the G.I. Bill at a much higher level.

Regardless of the program's net effect on enrollments, its history suggests that whatever impact it had on enrollment levels and the quality of American higher education was a function of the condition of institutions when the benefits were made available. During World War II, many colleges and universities were transformed into facilities for the war effort. When the war ended, most higher education institutions, like many other organizations that were part of the national reconversion effort, were anxious to rebuild themselves through the participation of veterans. Despite the reservations of Presidents Conant, Hutchins, and others, most institutions (including Harvard and the University of Chicago) went to great lengths to accommodate the returning veterans, including establishing special offices to ease the transition from soldiers to students. Housing was another critical function provided by the institutions, often in very creative ways. The willingness if not eagerness of many institutions to provide a wide range of support services played a critical role in enabling World War II veterans to make this transition successfully.

A case also can be made that subsequent versions of the G.I. Bill were less successful because the commitment to provide housing and other support services was not as strong as it had been immediately after World War II. The kind of national mobilization that was evident in the years immediately following the end of World War II was not in evidence in society or in higher education following either the Korean War or the Vietnam War. Particularly in the case of the Vietnam War, neither the federal government nor the institutions made available the kinds of support services that were provided to World War II veterans. And this absence of commitment to services may be critical in explaining why Vietnam-era veterans did not fare nearly as well in advancement through higher education as their counterparts from earlier conflicts.

Federal Student Loans

Student loans have become an increasingly prominent form of financing higher education in this country over the past two decades. In 1975 borrowing in the federal student loan programs paid for less than 10 percent of the total costs of attendance that students faced. By 1995 federal student loans had grown to fund more than one-third of total costs of attendance. More than $30 billion in loan volume in the late 1990s is annually made available through the various federal student loan programs. This growth in reliance on loans occurred during the same time that tuition and other charges grew at twice the rate of inflation.[11]

Considerable disagreement occurs over the extent to which these two trends of increased borrowing and higher tuitions are related in a causal way. Many in the higher education establishment argue that student loans have not had a major impact on tuition setting at most colleges and universities. They contend that the growth in tuitions has had more to do with the escalating costs that colleges face for salaries and other compensation, utilities, periodicals, and the many other goods and services that colleges and universities must purchase.

The National Commission on the Cost in Higher Education, which was appointed by Congress in 1997 to investigate the growth in college costs, adopted the position that the cost factors discussed above have been the principal driver of tuition increases. The commission in its final report also emphasized that since tuitions in higher education nearly always are set below the cost per student as the result of public and private subsidies, higher education cannot be analyzed like most other industries in which price exceeds the cost of producing the good or providing the service.[12] By taking this cost-based view, the commission in effect rejected the argument that revenue levels largely determine costs per student, an argument that was dubbed by the late Howard Bowen as the revenue theory of higher education—colleges and universities raise all the revenues they can and spend all the revenues they have.

Whether recent rapid tuition growth is more cost driven or revenue induced is critical to the question of what role student loans may have played in the escalation of tuitions and other charges during the past two decades. If the higher education pricing structure is mostly cost driven, then the availability of loans is relatively unimportant in explaining the growth of tuitions. If, however, tuition pricing is driven more strongly by the availability of revenues, then the increase in borrowing over the past two decades is much more than a coincidence with higher tuitions.

In a paper I coauthored with Cathy Krop that was prepared for the National Commission, we argued the latter position: that growing reliance on loans had been a significant factor in the growth of tuitions.[13] We said that it was hard to imagine tuitions could have grown at twice the rate of inflation and roughly 50 percent faster than real family incomes over the past two decades without substantial increases in borrowing. We asked, if loans had not been available, could most colleges and universities have raised their prices so much faster than inflation without significant consumer resistance and enrollment erosion?

Our paper further argued that changes in program design may help to explain the connection between college tuitions and the availability of student loans. In the initial legislation, students qualified for interest subsidies in the federal student loan programs on the basis of their income falling below a certain specified level. In 1978 this income limit was removed as part of federal legislation to expand the student aid programs in lieu of adopting tuition tax credits. In 1981, in response to mushrooming loan volume, the law was altered again to limit which students could receive the federal interest subsidies. But the 1981 change, rather than reintroducing a straight income cap, limited interest subsidies on the basis of the need of the student. Need was defined as the costs of attendance minus other aid plus what families could contribute to education.

As a result, costs of attendance have become a factor in determining eligibility for student loan interest subsidies. Under this rule, every time tuition and other allowable charges increase, the family income that qualifies students for interest subsidies similarly increases. With this linkage between costs of attendance and loan eligibility, annual and cumulative dollar limits on how much students may borrow became the primary protection against a direct connection between loans and tuitions. But each time that loan limits increase, the potential connection between loan policies and tuition setting is strengthened.

There is also the related question of whether the growing reliance on student loans over time has had an impact on enrollment levels. On the surface, the answer would seem to be no. Enrollments overall in colleges and universities have grown relatively modestly over the period that federal student loan volume has exploded, suggesting little connection between the growing availability of loans and the overall levels of enrollment in higher education. But given the increase in tuitions and the decline in the size of the traditional college age group throughout the 1980s and into the 1990s, it would be reasonable to surmise that enrollments would have dropped in the absence of greater loan availability. Under this construction, the growing availability of loans allowed institutions to maintain or even increase slightly their enrollments in the face of higher prices and a demographic decline in the size of the traditional college age group of those between eighteen and twenty-four.

This seems especially true for many private colleges and universities, as the growing availability of federal student loans seems to have allowed many private institutions to maintain their enrollments in the face of higher prices. For example, between 1950 and 1975, private higher education enrollments as a proportion of total enrollments fell from one-half to less than one-quarter, principally the result of the public sector absorbing the bulk of the baby boomers. Since the mid-1970s, the private sector enrollment share stabilized between 20 and 25 percent, corresponding to the time when loans became the predominant form of financing. It is hard to believe these trends are simply a coincidence.

In short, during a time when private institutions were aggressively pursuing a high-tuition, high-aid strategy of rapidly increasing their tuitions while providing a higher proportion of their students with aid discounts, it is almost inconceivable that they could have maintained their market share of enrollments in the absence of growing loan availability for their students and their parents. Put even more strongly, the ready and growing availability of loans was a crucial component in the calculus that led most private colleges and universities to pursue a more aggressive pricing and discounting policy throughout most of the 1980s and the first half of the 1990s.

In the 1990s students at public institutions have borrowed more often, so that borrowing rates are now nearly equal among public and private college students. In each sector more than half of all students enrolled at least half time now borrow. Public college students have been particularly frequent borrowers in the unsubsidized loan program that was established in 1992 and now accounts for one-third of all federal student loans. These loans allow borrowing under federal auspices by students who failed to qualify for interest subsidies on the basis of their financial need.

Proprietary schools are the other sector of postsecondary education, and they clearly have benefited from the ready and growing availability of federal student loans. There is considerable evidence that a number of these schools have based their pricing policies on the availability of federal aid, particularly loans.[14] It also is fair to assume that enrollments at proprietary schools would be sharply reduced if loans were not available. In the alternative, their tuitions and fees would have to be sharply reduced to maintain enrollment levels.

There also is little question that federal student loans have been a source of considerable fraud and abuse through the creation of institutions providing education and training of marginal quality. Many (although not all) of these marginal institutions are proprietary schools, which are a major (although far from only) source of defaults in the student loan programs. Default rates at proprietary schools are typically several times higher than the rates of borrowers at nonprofit institutions. This higher default rate is partly a function of the fact that the students who enroll in proprietary schools come disproportionately from low-income families and circumstances. But it also is true that many proprietary schools have been aggressive in exploiting student aid policies, including encouraging a high proportion of their students to borrow. Recent declines in student loan default rates are mostly a function of trimming many marginal schools from federal aid eligibility as well as a booming economy that boosts all borrowers' ability to repay their loans.

Pell Grants

Pell grants are the principal federal program designed to increase access to higher education. Therefore, one way to assess Pell grants is to examine whether participation rates for students from low-income families have increased since the program was established as basic grants in 1972. In this regard, the proportion of high school graduates from low-income families enrolling in college more than doubled from 20 percent in 1973 to 45 percent in 1993. During the same time, however, the gap in college participation rates between poor and rich students remained about the same— students from low-income families remain roughly half as likely to go to college as students from high-income families.[15]

Some look at the persistent gap in college participation rates and argue that Pell grants have failed in their basic mission of expanding educational opportunities for traditionally disadvantaged groups of students. More optimistic observers suggest that doubling the rate of college participation for students from low-income families is a substantial achievement and that the gap between rich and poor students would have grown far more in the absence of the Pell grant program. Those with this view focus on the fact that the maximum Pell grant award has not kept pace with the increase in college costs and suggest that had the Pell grant program been more adequately funded, the gap in college participation rates would have been reduced.[16]

Advocates of both of these views may overstate their case. It is true that the Pell grant maximum award did not keep pace with the increase in college costs until 1996. The maximum award declined from a peak of 80 percent in 1979 to less than 40 percent in 1996 as a share of average costs of attendance at public four-year institutions. For private four-year institutions, it declined from 40 percent of the costs of attendance in 1979 to less than 20 percent in 1996.[17] From 1996 to 1999 it was increased by more than $700 over three years (an increase of roughly 25 percent in real terms). Even after these increases, the maximum award as a percentage of the cost of attendance is below the peak of the late 1970s.

Much of the decline in the purchasing power of the Pell grant maximum award, however, is a function of the fact that college tuitions and other costs of attendance have been increasing at twice the rate of inflation. Also often lost in the discussion about the purchasing power of Pell grants is the fact that appropriations for the program have increased in constant dollars over time. The decline in the maximum award while appropriations have grown in real terms is mostly the result of expansions in program eligibility designed to bolster its political support. With expanded eligibility, the real dollar increases in funding have been devoted to helping more students rather than increasing the maximum award for the most disadvantaged students. Although this may make for good politics, it may not be good policy.

The lack of more progress on improving college participation rates may also be a function of unrealistically high expectations being placed on the

Pell grant program. The fact that the maximum grant has declined in real terms and not kept up with college costs means that for the students who receive Pell grants, the program is increasingly unable to deliver sufficient resources to overcome the financial barriers that disadvantaged students face in thinking about college as an option.

Perhaps more important, as the preceding analysis of the G.I. Bill indicated, the availability of adequate support services is a critical element if vouchers are to succeed in changing the behavior of targeted groups of students. In the case of a program like Pell grants, which is specifically intended to help students who previously did not aspire to college, adequately funded and well-designed support services are even more critical to ensure that students are prepared to do college-level work and complete their degree.

The federal government funds a series of support services through the TRIO programs of Upward Bound, Talent Search, Educational Opportunity Centers, and Special Services, programs that predate the Pell grants.[18] But while Pell grants over the past quarter-century have grown to be a cornerstone of the federal role in higher education, with appropriations now exceeding $7 billion, funding for the TRIO programs has grown far more slowly, with annual funding in the late 1990s of roughly $500 million. And although the TRIO programs have generally received good marks for their effectiveness, they remain largely demonstration efforts, reaching only 10 percent or less of the eligible population. Thus, the growth in Pell grants over time has not been accompanied by a similar increase in funding or coverage of the support services that are critical for ensuring that Pell grant recipients are prepared to do college level work when they first enroll. Lack of adequate support services also means that disadvantaged students will not have the help they need along the way to improve their chances of graduating.

Pell grants seem to have contributed less significantly to the college tuition spiral of the past two decades than student loans. Pell grants provide far less coverage and have not played nearly as major a role in the college financing equation as loans. Pell grants have never financed more than 10 percent of the total costs of attendance, in contrast to federal student loans that now meet more than one-third of total costs of attendance. This is particularly true for private institutions, where the run-up in tuitions has been most pronounced. Unlike loans, Pell grants are not a significant source of revenue for most private institutions, and a small proportion of their students are Pell grant recipients because their higher prices net of aid historically have served as a barrier to many economically disadvantaged students. With this lack of coverage, it is hard to believe that Pell grants have had much of a role in the tuition-setting decisions of private college officials.[19]

There is ample reason to believe that Pell grants, like student loans, have been a factor in the pricing decisions of many proprietary schools that rely on federal student aid as a primary revenue source. The available evidence suggests that many of these schools use the Pell grant maximum award and federal loan limits to determine how much to charge their students.

Program design is another reason that Pell grants may have had less influence on tuition-setting decisions than student loans. For most students, the Pell grant now is calculated as the maximum award minus the family's contribution; costs of attendance play no role in the calculation. Under this formula, institutions thus have no incentive to raise tuition, since charges will have no effect on how much Pell grant a student receives. This is in sharp contrast to student loans, where increases in tuition and other charges can translate into more eligibility for interest subsidies.

The initial Pell grants legislation contained a provision that limited a student's award to 50 percent of costs of attendance. This provision, which was subsequently increased to 60 percent of costs, was inserted into the initial legislation to prevent students at low-cost institutions from receiving their total costs of attendance through the Pell grant program. It also was designed to minimize the incentives for officials at these low-cost institutions to raise tuition to capture more federal aid. Although some institutions did start charging tuition to capture more Pell grant aid—for example, the decision to impose tuition at the City University of New York in the mid-1970s—there is no evidence of widespread use of this practice, in part because only schools with no or very low levels of tuition and fees would reap any increase in Pell grant revenues. The cost limitation language was dropped in 1992, and a standard amount was provided for expense other than tuition and fees. Under this arrangement, virtually no student's award is affected by the tuition and fees charged by the institution he or she attends.[20]

In terms of possible effects on quality, many of the same concerns in the student loan program apply to Pell grants as well. For example, at many proprietary schools Pell grants are a primary source of revenue, and these schools probably could not survive if Pell grants did not exist. Although there are no defaults in the Pell grant program since recipients have no obligation to repay the federal aid they receive, the available statistics indicate that Pell grants share the problem with student loans that many recipients do not complete their educational program and receive a degree.

Although Pell grants have escaped the high level of scrutiny paid to federal student loans because there is no record of failure manifested in the form of defaults, the problems of noncompletion are probably just as pronounced for Pell grant recipients as for borrowers.

Tuition Tax Credits

The same construct of program design, program coverage, and industry structure that allows for an assessment of existing vouchers also can be used to speculate on the possible effects of the new tuition tax credits by identifying who is likely to benefit and the effect of the credits on enrollments, prices, and quality. Students from families with incomes of between $30,000 and $80,000 will be the primary beneficiaries of the new tax credits because both of the credits begin phasing out at $80,000 of family income, and students from families with incomes above $100,000 will be ineligible. The decision to limit the income of families who qualify for the tax credit was in response to concerns about the lack of progressivity in the distribution of benefits under the initial legislative proposals. Similar income caps were not put in place for the other tax provisions in the 1997 legislation designed to encourage families to save more for college, however, meaning that these savings provisions will be more regressively distributed than the two new credits.[21]

Students from low-income families will not benefit much from the new tax credits. Neither credit is refundable, so that low-income families whose tax liability is less than the credit for which they are eligible will not pocket the difference. Also, since grant assistance will be subtracted from tuition expenses in determining eligibility for the credits, students from low-income families eligible for grants will find their tax credits reduced as a result.

To the extent that middle-income students will be the primary beneficiaries of the new tuition tax credits, it seems unlikely that the credits will have a significant effect on college enrollments. College participation rates of middle-income students are at an all-time high—more than three-quarters of middle-income students attend some form of postsecondary education and training—and the funds received from the credits do not seem significant enough to raise these rates of college attendance substantially. Low-income students are the ones whose behavior would most likely be affected by the credits, but they typically will not be eligible for the reasons described above.

The one group whose college-going behavior may be significantly affected by the new tax credits are people in the work force who go back to college for a course or two for career advancement or personal fulfillment. For these individuals, the Lifetime Learning credit may well be sufficiently attractive and tailored to their needs to affect their enrollment decisions. These are also the individuals who currently do not qualify for most of the federal student aid programs because they do not enroll on a half-time or more basis. Thus, the Lifetime Learning credit may represent a significant improvement in the financing calculus of many older students.

A prominent criticism directed at the tuition tax credits during the debate leading up to their passage was that they would result in higher tuitions as institutions sought to capture federal tax benefits. The chief sponsors of the legislation addressed these concerns by revising the legislation so that neither of the new credits reimburses students and their families for tuition expenses on a dollar-for-dollar basis. The HOPE Scholarship credit covers only 50 percent of tuition above the first $1,000, up to a maximum of $1,500 credit a year. The Lifetime Learning credit covers only 50 percent of the first $2,000 in tuition. These provisions were put in place to limit the potential effect of the credits on institutional pricing decisions as well as minimize the federal budget cost. Although the new tax credits still provide some incentive for institutions to raise their prices— especially low-priced community colleges that can increase the eligibility of their students for the tax credits by increasing their fees to qualify for the maximum credit—the credits generally should have less impact on tuitions than federal student loans have had.

The potential impact of the new tax credits on tuitions also should be limited by their coverage. The Department of Education estimates that as many as fourteen million individuals will receive one of the credits when the provisions are fully implemented in 2002. Since this fourteen million figure is the same as current fall enrollments in higher education, the coverage of the new credits could be construed as 100 percent. But the total number of individuals taking at least one course some time during the year in some form of postsecondary education and training is roughly twenty million, meaning that two-thirds of eligible students could receive a tax credit, still a very high number. Of greater relevance, however, is the fact that the $10 billion in aggregate tax benefits when the credits are fully implemented would represent less than 10 percent of the total bill for tuition and related costs of attendance that these students face, thus sharply reducing the potential impact of the credits on pricing decisions. In addition, the fact that the credits will be received after the students finish the course work and pay taxes should reduce the potential impact of the credits on tuition-setting practices.

Most of the quality-related issues involved in establishing tuition tax credits are similar to those voiced about the other vouchers. Although little was said during the tax credit debates about preventing get-rich-quick operations from benefiting from the availability of new federal dollars, this certainly should be a concern. The one additional quality issue in the case of the tax credits involves the government determining whether students and their families actually paid the tuition they claim for purposes of receiving the credit. To prevent abuse on this front, the legislation imposes a series of reporting requirements on both families and institutions that the higher education associations opposed as being too onerous.

It is possible, of course, that in the future we may realize that the tax credits had far more effect than presently is anticipated. But at this point, it seems more likely that the tax credits will represent a modest bonus for most of the students and their families who receive them, with very little impact on their decisions of whether or where to enroll in college. The one exception may be older students, who may find their opportunities to enroll on a part-time basis greatly broadened. Although this assessment of the future effect of the tax credits may seem modest and benign, it can be hoped that a $10 billion annual federal investment would help far more in addressing very legitimate concerns about higher education access, affordability, and quality.

Lessons Learned from the Higher Education Voucher Experience

This review of the experience with federal vouchers in higher education suggests a mixed record of success. In some cases, vouchers appear to have had a substantial effect on students' decisions to enroll as well as on institutional decisionmaking. In other cases large investments of federal funds have had only modest effect. But in the case of each of the three traditional vouchers, it appears that program design, program coverage, and condition of the industry have mattered.

—The perceived success of the initial G.I. Bill after World War II was a function of an effective program design, the fact that at its peak usage the G.I. Bill was aiding one-half of all students and that the federal government and student-hungry institutions provided the necessary housing and support services to help veterans make the transition. The subsequent versions of the G.I. Bill were less successful in part because the program coverage was not nearly as great and institutions were not nearly as accommodating of veterans as students.

—Federal student loans by virtue of their growth during the past two decades have played a key role in allowing private institutions to stabilize their enrollment share, while their tuitions have been increasing at twice the rate of inflation over the past two decades. Loans may also have been an important factor in fueling this tuition growth, as they now represent one-third of the total costs of attendance that students face. Program design may also have contributed to the connection between loans and tuition growth, because under program rules in effect since 1981, tuition increases translate into larger program eligibility. This program design feature accounts for why students with family incomes in excess of $100,000 are eligible for valuable interest subsidies only if they attend high-priced institutions.

—Pell grants seem to have had less impact on both enrollments and tuitions than student loans, in part because Pell grants play a much smaller role in the financing of higher education than loans and benefit fewer students. This lower degree of program coverage, combined with the fact that costs of attendance play virtually no role in the calculation of the Pell grant award, lead to the conclusion that Pell grants have had little influence on tuition growth.

—Both Pell grants and federal student loans have played a key role in the growth of proprietary schools. The proprietary sector would probably be a shadow of what it now is if these two voucher programs did not exist or if they were not as available to proprietary school students as they have been. The size and growth of the proprietary sector have coincided with concerns about quality control in the student aid programs, most specifically the growth in student loan defaults as proprietary school borrowers default at several times the rate of borrowers at nonprofit institutions. But concerns about quality issues in the Pell grant and federal student loan programs are not limited to the proprietary sector. Another quality concern is that degree completion rates have declined and the time taken to earn a degree throughout higher education has increased. Both Pell grants and federal student loans, by emphasizing access over quality concerns, have most likely contributed to these trends.

Rules of the Road

Although there is relatively little systematic econometric evidence, this chapter suggests that a number of lessons can be learned from analyzing the

half-century of experience with vouchers in higher education in this country. These lessons can serve as "rules of the road" for assessing and improving the effectiveness of vouchers in higher education as well as other
domestic policy functions. They can best be summarized as the answer to
the following two questions:

First, what are the strengths and weaknesses of vouchers compared with
other public policies for financing higher education, namely, direct support
of institutions and institution-based student aid? Second, based on the
experience in higher education, under what conditions are vouchers most
effective?

Although vouchers have been prominent in the financing of American
higher education, they remain only one of several mechanisms that have
been used to finance colleges and universities and to help students and
their parents pay for college. The following discussion considers the effectiveness of vouchers relative to two other ways in which governments regularly reduce the price that students pay for higher education: direct support of institutions and institution-based student aid.

—*Direct support of institutions.* Despite the substantial investment the
federal government has made in vouchers of various forms, direct support
of institutions by the states remains the principal form of taxpayer support
of higher education in this country. In the late 1990s state governments
collectively spent roughly $50 billion annually in support of their public
institutions, compared with the roughly $15 billion in annual federal
expenditures for student aid.[22] Even if the $10 billion in annual tax expen-
ditures estimated to result when the tuition tax credits are fully implemented are added, the annual state investment in higher education will still
be twice as large as that of the federal government.[23] These state appropriations allow public institutions to charge tuitions and fees that are a fraction of what it costs to educate students in that sector. Even with rapid
increases in public sector tuitions through much of the 1990s, they still
average less than one-third of education-related expenditures per student in
the public sector.

—*Institution-based student aid.* The 1972 debate that led to the creation
of the Pell grant program was over whether to continue providing student
aid in the traditional manner of making allocations to institutions that, in
turn, would provide aid to students using federal guidelines or to shift to a
voucher approach similar to the G.I. Bill and the Guaranteed Student Loan
program. The 1972 legislation authorized both types of student aid approaches, but over time the funding and dependence on Pell grants has

grown, while funding of the campus-based student aid programs has increased far more slowly, barely keeping up with inflation.

The analysis in this chapter suggests that there are some situations in which the direct support of institutions or institution-based student aid may be more effective than vouchers.

—Vouchers may not work as well as direct support of institutions if adequate seats are not available to accommodate the voucher recipients. The experience in higher education over the past half-century suggests that if the policy goal is to ensure that sufficient seats are provided for all qualified students, the more appropriate public policy may be to provide direct support to public institutions than to provide vouchers. In the case of the G.I. Bill following World War II, the adequate supply of seats meant that vouchers were the appropriate policy response. But two decades later, when the states were faced with the prospect of accommodating the first wave of baby boomers, there were not enough seats to accommodate the exploding demand for higher education. In this instance, the states were probably right to create additional seats through the direct support of existing public institutions and the creation of new ones. This policy for expansion also allowed states to have greater control over the quality of the education being provided than if they had gone the voucher route.

—Vouchers tend to entail more administrative costs and structure on the part of governments than many other public policies. It is far easier for states to distribute funds directly to dozens of institutions to support their operations than to operate a voucher program that may require dealing with thousands or millions of students and their families. The same logic suggests that the federal campus-based student aid programs are easier to administer than vouchers—the government distributes funds to institutions on the basis of some formula, and the institutions distribute the funds to students on the basis of government guidelines. In effect, the institutions are picking up much of the administrative responsibility that would fall to government offices under a voucher approach. As a result, the number of government employees needed to administer an institution-based student aid program typically will be far smaller than a voucher program. This suggests that institution-based student aid may be more appropriate when the governmental unit is small relative to the size of the higher education institutions or when political and financial considerations severely limit the size of government.

Conversely, the tendency of these other public policies to reinforce the status quo is perhaps the strongest argument for the voucher approach.

Without the degree of competition and market forces that vouchers tend to introduce, colleges and universities may settle into patterns that best meet the needs of their administrators and faculty. By giving students more buying power, the experience in higher education has been that vouchers tend to serve the needs of students better than these other public policies.

The long experience with vouchers in higher education confirms that they create more marketlike incentives than other public policies designed to reduce the net price of the good or service being provided. Policies that distribute funds to institutions, whether for direct support of operations or for campus-based student aid, fail to create these kinds of competitive market pressures that spur greater efforts by institutions to attract students and to provide a quality education. State funding of public institutions typically is incremental, often reinforcing existing inequities in the distribution of funds. Institutions with the most resources continue to receive the bulk of state funding, and institutional officials have little incentive to achieve productivity gains since they are funded on the basis of their costs per student. Similarly, institution-based student aid programs provide little or no market-based incentives because allocations are based on the students who already are in attendance.

The first section of this chapter discussed some of the reasons that vouchers may have been more acceptable in higher education than in K–12 education, where the issue of vouchers is far more contentious. These differences between higher education and K–12 education also help to define the conditions under which vouchers tend to be more effective than other public policies.

—Vouchers are likely to work better when a market already exists for the designated good or service. The concept of vouchers seems generally incompatible with a nonmarket situation. Helping voucher recipients pay all or a portion of the cost entailed in participating seems to work best when a market already exists with a defined set of prices. The fact that higher education is a natural market with more than 3,500 diverse institutions competing for students has been an important consideration in the policy decision to use vouchers so extensively.

—Vouchers are a more feasible option when the prices in the existing market are set below the cost of providing the good or service. While vouchers seem to work better when a market exists, they are more affordable from a budgetary perspective when a portion of the cost of providing the service is borne by someone else. In higher education, the other groups bearing some of the costs are the state governments in the case of public institutions and the institutions themselves in the private sector by virtue of their endowments defraying a portion of the cost per student.

Beyond these differences between higher and K–12 education, the experience with vouchers in higher education also provides important insights into the conditions for success of vouchers.

—Vouchers work best when program design provides incentives consistent with policy goals and social norms. In higher education, the experience with vouchers indicates that incentives for students and institutions make a difference, both in a positive way as well as in negative, unintended consequences. Vouchers that reward institutions and students for enrolling but provide little or no incentive for graduation are likely to increase participation rates but lower graduation rates. The fact that no voucher in higher education uses graduation as a criterion for aiding students and their families also helps explain the decline in college completion rates. Similarly, if the voucher takes into account a student's costs of attendance in determining eligibility, as in the case of student loan interest subsidies, it is more likely to contribute to higher tuitions than in a program like Pell grants, where there is virtually no difference in award size based on cost differentials.

—Vouchers that benefit a high percentage of students or pay a high proportion of the bill are more likely to have an impact on both student and institutional behavior than programs with lesser coverage. The initial G.I. Bill following the end of World War II had a big impact on higher education in large part because at its peak it provided aid to half of all students enrolled. It was therefore large enough not only to motivate millions of veterans to further their education but also to motivate institutions to provide the necessary housing and support services to enable veterans to succeed in college. Student loans also have become big enough to make a difference, although one of the impacts may have been to enable institutions to raise their tuitions and other charges more rapidly than otherwise would have been the case. By contrast, the Pell grant program has never achieved a sufficiently large maximum award or targeted enough on low-income students to narrow the gap in participation between rich and poor.

—The condition of the industry is an important factor in determining the effectiveness of a voucher. Introducing a voucher program in a sellers' market, as was true when Pell grants were established, will have a much different result than in a time that many institutions are anxious to fill their seats, as was the case with the initial G.I. Bill. Institutions did not welcome Vietnam-era veterans with their arms as open, in part because many of them in the 1970s had many more applicants than slots to fill. Similarly, federal student loan volume exploded at the same time that private colleges were preparing to move to a high-tuition, high-aid strategy as a means for catching up from the 1970s when their tuition increases had lagged behind inflation.

—Vouchers are more effective if they affect the supply of seats as well as the demand side. If additional seats are not available in the long run, the introduction of vouchers will lead to shifts in who goes to college or how much they pay rather than increase overall participation rates. The experience with federal student loans also demonstrates that vouchers can influence the future structure of the industry, as loans have allowed private colleges to stabilize their market share. The argument that federal student loans have contributed to rapid tuition increases over the past two decades builds on the theory that providing a voucher when most seats are already filled is more likely to lead to a rapid buildup in prices. The experience with the various versions of the G.I. Bill reinforces this notion that changes in the industry structure are an important component in determining effectiveness of vouchers. Similarly, the inability of the Pell grant program to narrow the gap in college participation rates is attributable in part to restrictions on the number of seats at many institutions. In short, if supply is not altered, increasing the college participation of disadvantaged students requires reducing the participation of other groups of students.

—Vouchers tend to work better when they are combined with an aggressive effort to provide support services. It has become increasingly apparent in recent years that financial aid by itself is not enough to increase the college participation and degree completion of disadvantaged groups of students. If voucher recipients are not prepared to do college-level work, then no amount of financial aid is going to help them complete their educational program successfully. That is not to say that support services can supplant vouchers as a means for helping targeted groups of students improve their participation rates. Both are necessary components for success—the vouchers are needed to help students pay for their educational expenses, and the support services are critical to ensure adequate and improved academic performance.

This last condition for the success of vouchers in higher education is perhaps the most important. The experience over the past half-century reinforces the notion that vouchers by themselves are not the answer. They must be combined with adequate support services and information to maximize the power of the consumer in using vouchers. Successful voucher programs are ones that combine good program design and adequate coverage with sufficient services to make for a well-informed and prepared consumer. This is the essential lesson we have learned from a half-century of experience with vouchers in higher education.

Notes

1. Other, smaller federal student aid programs are not vouchers in that either they are not portable across institutions or the institutions have considerable discretion in determining how much aid a student will receive.

2. The Guaranteed Student Loan program was in sharp contrast to the National Defense Student Loan (NDSL) program enacted in 1958 and now called Perkins loans, which is federally financed, discretionary, and administered by the institutions as a nonvoucher program.

3. Pell grants are a quasi-entitlement in that the maximum award typically falls far short of the amount set in the law as the authorized maximum.

4. The results of a number of these studies are summarized in a recent report. See Karen Akerhielm and others, *Factors Related to College Enrollment*, final report prepared under contract for the U.S. Department of Education (Princeton, N.J.: Mathtech, 1998).

5. Sarah Turner explores this issue with specific regard to Pell grants in an unpublished paper, "Does Federal Aid Affect College Costs? Evidence from the Pell Program" (University of Virginia, 1998), and Jon Oberg provides a broader survey of the literature on this issue in "Testing Federal Student Aid Fungibility in Two Competing Versions of Federalism," *Journal of Federalism*, vol. 27 (Winter 1997), pp. 115–34.

6. Much of the information on the G.I. Bill in this paper comes from a special issue of *Education Record* that was entitled *The GI Bill's Lasting Legacy*. Of particular assistance was Keith Olson, "The Astonishing Story: Veterans Make Good on the Nation's Promise," *Education Record*, vol. 75, no. 4 (Fall 1994), pp.16–26.

7. These trends in tuition and G.I. Bill utilization are discussed in detail in Chester E. Finn Jr., *Scholars, Dollars, and Bureaucrats* (Brookings, 1978), pp. 62–64.

8. As quoted in Olson, "The Astonishing Story," p. 22.

9. Keith Olson, *The G.I. Bill, the Veterans, and the Colleges* (University Press of Kentucky, 1974), p. 44.

10. The study was conducted by Norman Frederickson and William Schrader, which examined the college performance of 10,000 veterans and non-veterans, as reported in Olson, *The G.I. Bill*.

11. These figures regarding whether student aid has had an impact on tuition trends are discussed at greater length in Arthur Hauptman and Cathy Krop, *Federal Student Aid and Tuition Growth: Examining the Relationship* (New York: Council for Aid to Education, 1998).

12. The National Commission on the Cost of Higher Education, *Straight Talk about College Costs and Prices* (Phoenix, Ariz.: Oryx Press, 1998).

13. An earlier version of Hauptman and Krop, *Federal Student Aid and the Growth in College Costs and Tuitions*, was published in National Commission on the Cost of Higher Education, *Straight Talk*, pp. 70–83.

14. The best example occurred when loan limits were reduced in the 1980s for supplemental loans, which proprietary school students participated in disproportionately. When these loan limits were reduced, a number of proprietary schools lowered their tuitions.

15. Department of Commerce, Bureau of the Census, *Current Population Surveys*, October files.

16. Data limitations may also be disguising the real impact of Pell grants. Episodic information suggests that the number of students from low-income families attending community colleges has increased substantially over the past several decades. But the Census Bureau, through its Current Population Report surveys, more than a decade ago stopped collecting data on the participation rates of students from different income groups by the type of institution attended. This prevents us from measuring the most likely impact of expansion in the Pell grant program over time—the increased ability of students from low-income families to attend postsecondary education in the form of community colleges.

17. College Board, *Trends in Student Aid: 1998* (New York: 1998). These percentages should not be confused with the figures on the percentage of total costs of attendance covered by Pell grants, which is calculated by dividing the appropriations for Pell grants by an estimate of the aggregate costs of attendance for all students for tuition, fees, room and board, and other expenses.

18. These programs were called the TRIO programs because initially there were three of them.

19. It was interesting that Princeton University, in a fifteen-page document that it sent alumni and others to explain its 1998 decision to revise its financial aid policies, never mentions the words Pell grants and hardly refers to federal aid at all. See Princeton Office of the President, "New Princeton Financial Aid Policies to Increase Affordability for Lower and Middle Income Students," February 1998.

20. A small proportion of part-time students have their awards reduced as a result of low costs because the standard living costs, which are now tied to the maximum award, are prorated, thereby subjecting them to a limitation that the Pell grant award cannot exceed the need of the student.

21. The income distribution of student aid benefits and tax credits and a series of policy issues are discussed in more detail in Arthur Hauptman and Lois Rice, *Coordinating Financial Aid with Tuition Tax Benefits*, policy brief (Brookings, December 1997).

22. Spending for student aid includes annual appropriations for Pell grants and campus-based student aid programs and the present value of federal interest subsidies, default-related payments, and other administrative costs associated with

the federal student loan programs. This figure is substantially different from the total amount of aid made available under federal auspices, which is now nearly $50 billion annually. The principal difference is that the aid figure includes the volume of loans guaranteed or financed by the federal government rather than the federal expenditures associated with these loans.

23. Data on federal student aid from College Board, *Trends in Student Aid* (New York, 1998). These calculations do not include federal funding of campus-based research that traditionally has exceeded what the federal government currently spends on student aid.

MICHAEL W. McCONNELL

12 | *Legal and Constitutional Issues of Vouchers*

A DISCUSSION ON the law and policy of vouchers could not be more timely. In the summer of 1998 the Wisconsin Supreme Court upheld the nation's most visible voucher experiment against claims that it violates both the state and federal constitutions.[1] Opponents of the program asked the U.S. Supreme Court to review that decision, claiming that it is inconsistent with the Court's precedents interpreting the Establishment Clause of the First Amendment. The Supreme Court rejected the petition, thus allowing the program to be implemented. But the underlying constitutional issue has not been definitively resolved. As a result of the Supreme Court's action, legislatures may feel more confident that they can experiment with educational choice. But constitutional uncertainty remains, with the near certainty that opponents of educational choice will file costly and debilitating lawsuits in an effort to discourage further reform. It is time to recognize just how weak the federal constitutional argument against educational vouchers is.

The Milwaukee program allows up to 15,000 poverty-stricken students in the public school system to attend accredited nonpublic schools of their choice. The state pays the per pupil cost of the nonpublic school, up to the per pupil amount of state aid. This is approximately $3,650. Payment is in the form of a check payable to the parent or guardian, which is sent to the nonpublic school, where the parent or guardian restrictively endorses the check for the use of the school. Schools must be fully accredited and must comply with all applicable health and safety laws as well as nondiscrimination laws. Although the program originally was limited to "nonsectarian" schools, in 1995 the legislature eliminated that limitation, thus significantly expanding the number of schools that could be chosen by participating students. The schools may use the funds so received, just like tuition, for any of the lawful expenses of the school, whether secular or religious. The only restriction imposed on the nonpublic schools with students in the program is a prohibition on requiring voucher recipients to participate in any "religious activity" over the family's objection.[2] These are the basic contours of the program.

At first blush, it may seem surprising that there is any doubt about the constitutionality of such a program. Vouchers are used, without serious legal controversy, at the preschool level and the college level, at religious as well as public and other secular schools. All across America students use federal grants and guaranteed student loans to attend Notre Dame, Brigham Young, and Texas Christian, just as they do to attend Harvard, Michigan, and Antioch. An estimated 40 percent of the kindergarten and preschool placements are under religious auspices; poor children attending these programs are eligible for government assistance under federal and state child care programs. Religiously affiliated organizations receive government grants to provide an extraordinary array of social services, ranging from foreign disaster relief to Head Start to substance abuse rehabilitation. Churches and other religious organizations receive substantial indirect subsidies in the form of tax exemptions and tax deductible contributions. None of this arouses much debate. Out of all the many contexts in which religiously affiliated groups participate, on equal terms, in publicly supported educational, health, and social welfare functions, only aid to church-related primary and secondary education seems to raise eyebrows.

Nonetheless, the questions exist. For almost a decade, starting in 1971, the Supreme Court held unconstitutional most, though not all, programs in which public money was used to support education in religious schools. The Court held that under most circumstances aid to religiously affiliated schools violates the Establishment Clause of the First Amendment, which forbids the government from passing laws "respecting an establishment of religion." In an attempt to clarify what this enigmatic phrase may mean, the Court used a three-part test, called the "*Lemon* test," after the case in which it was first announced: "First, the statute must have a secular legislative purpose; second, its principal or primary effect must be one that neither advances nor inhibits religion; finally, the statute must not foster an excessive entanglement with religion."[3] The Court consistently held that aid to nonpublic education has a secular purpose. But with exceptions to be discussed below, the Court generally held that aid to the educational function of a religious school has the effect of advancing religion, since religious instruction is part of the mission of the school. In cases where the state tried to ensure that the aid would not be used for religious purposes, the Court generally concluded that those enforcement efforts constituted "excessive entanglement," so the program was unconstitutional either way.

For example, in *Lemon* v. *Kurtzman* itself, the state sought to pay a portion of the salaries of teachers of secular subjects in religiously affiliated schools and required recipient teachers to agree not to allow any religious content to affect their teaching. The Court struck this down. In order for the aid program to be constitutional, the state had to be "certain" that subsidized teachers did not engage in religious instruction. This, needless to say, is difficult. But even if it were theoretically possible, enforcement of this condition would require extensive monitoring and censorship of the teachers' classroom performance—a form of "entanglement" that would be unconstitutional in itself. This brace of doctrines—the "certainty" standard for effects and the "entanglement" doctrine—was so potent that it resulted in a finding of unconstitutionality in every case in which it was applied honestly.

In recent years, the Court seems to have lost faith in the *Lemon* test. It has decided Establishment Clause cases without mentioning the three-part test, and five justices have called for reconsideration of some or all of its parts.[4] More fundamentally, the Court seems to be moving toward a quite different standard, based on neutrality toward religion. As Chief Justice William Rehnquist expressed the principle in *Zobrest* v. *Catalina Foothills School District*, "government programs that neutrally provide benefits to a broad class of citizens defined without reference to religion are not readily subject to an Establishment Clause challenge just because sectarian institutions may also receive an attenuated financial benefit."[5] Under a neutrality test, educational vouchers would almost certainly be constitutional, since they are distributed on the basis of neutral, secular criteria without regard to the religious or nonreligious character of recipients or of the institutions they choose for their children's education.

But *Lemon* has not been formally overruled.[6] Four justices oppose the shift to a neutrality standard at least as a general principle.[7] One justice—Justice Sandra Day O'Connor—refuses to be pinned down.[8] Thus no one can be certain what the outcome would be if the Court heard a case about educational vouchers in the near future. But for reasons I will explain shortly, it is likely that the Court would uphold a program similar to the Wisconsin Parental Choice Program.

That would not, however, resolve all legal questions about vouchers. There will remain at least three other legal issues to be resolved: the extension of the principle to noneducational contexts, state constitutional obstacles to educational choice, and applicability of the "state action" doctrine and its statutory analogs. I will turn to those questions, briefly, after discussing the first and most pressing question: whether state subsidies for education at a religious school chosen by individual students and their families violate the Establishment Clause.

School Aid and the Establishment Clause

The First Amendment to the U.S. Constitution forbids any law "respecting an establishment of religion, or prohibiting the free exercise thereof." Let us consider what that might mean. First, in light of the historical connections between established churches and compelled tax support, we might suppose that the amendment prevents the government from compelling financial support for churches or other institutions—including religious schools—that engage in religious teaching or ministry. Thus, in the first school aid case, *Everson* v. *Board of Education*, the Court explained: "No tax in any amount, large or small, can be levied to support any religious activities or institutions, whatever they may be called, or whatever form they may adopt to teach or practice religion."[9] This has been called the "no-aid" view.

Second, the amendment might be interpreted to require neutrality with respect to religion—to prevent the government from giving or denying benefits because of the recipient's religious character. As Justice Harry Blackmun wrote for the Court in *Roemer* v. *Board of Public Works*, "Neutrality is what is required. The State must confine itself to secular objectives, and neither advance nor impede religious activity."[10] Under this interpretation, which can be called the "neutrality" view, the government may subsidize the activities of religious organizations but only when funds are allocated for secular purposes, on the basis of secular criteria, to recipients without regard to their religious or nonreligious character.

A third possibility, called the "accommodation" interpretation, holds that the government may, and sometimes must, make special accommodations or exemptions where government practices would otherwise interfere with the exercise of religion. The key limitation is that the accommodations must lift a government-imposed burden on religious exercise, not create rewards or incentives for religious practice. This interpretation, while important for some public purposes, has not been relevant to the debate over funding of religious schools, and I will therefore not discuss it further.

The fundamental clash in the school aid cases has been between the insistence that taxpayers must not be compelled to support religious education and the notion that religious institutions must be treated neutrally. Obviously, these two principles cannot coexist. If aid must be denied to an otherwise eligible school because it teaches religion, that is not neutral treatment.

For the past fifty years the Supreme Court has attempted to find a principled middle-ground position, allowing some forms of aid to church-related schools while disallowing others. The reason for this attempt, I suspect, is that justices of the Supreme Court were persuaded of the soundness of the "no-aid" view as an abstract proposition, but in practice that interpretation turns out to be discriminatory, unfair, and unthinkable. If the no-aid position were applied unflinchingly, the government would be prevented from providing police and fire protection to churches and religious schools; churches would be barred from using the roads or the mails; and subsidies in the form of tax deductible contributions to churches would be forbidden. Indeed, given the pervasive character of public services, an unflinching application of the no-aid view would make the continued existence of religious institutions, hence of the exercise of religion, impossible. Advocates of the no-aid view realized from the start that *some* forms of aid to churches must be permitted. And thus began a long series of logic-chopping cases that sought to distinguish among different forms of aid, often on the basis of distinctions that only a medieval scholastic or a lawyer billing by the hour can appreciate.

Indeed, in the first school aid case, in 1947, the Court began the process of line drawing. At issue was a program in which parents of schoolchildren were reimbursed for the cost of public transportation of their children to and from school—whether they went to public or private (meaning Catholic) school. Weighty considerations of equity supported the program. The purpose of the program—to promote safety by enabling schoolchildren to ride a bus to school—applied to all the children. To hold that the Constitution requires the government to exclude religious school pupils from this program would have seemed rankly discriminatory. It would have been equivalent to imposing a penalty on those who choose to attend religious schools. Thus, the Court reasoned, "in protecting the citizens of [the state] against state-established churches, [we must] be sure that we do not inadvertently prohibit [the state] from extending its general State law benefits to all its citizens without regard to their religious belief."[11]

The difficulty lay in explaining why this form of aid was permissible, while still keeping the door closed to most aid to religious schools. If the state could subsidize one input to religious education—transportation— on the ground that it was extended to all school children on an equal basis, what principled objection could be made if the state subsidized other educational costs, provided it did so for all children on a neutral basis? There were four grounds on which this program differed from the classic form of established religion, the public subvention of churches. First, the economic beneficiary of the transportation subsidy was the child or the family—not the religious school. Second, the subsidy went to an entirely secular service, namely, public bus fares. Third, the money was paid to the family and not to the school. And fourth, the subsidy had a secular purpose (safety) and was allocated on the basis of objective criteria unrelated to religion.

Partly on the basis of these characteristics of the *Everson* program, the Court experimented with four approaches to line drawing between permissible and impermissible forms of aid. Three of them proved untenable. The remaining approach leads directly and inexorably toward the "neutrality" interpretation of the Establishment Clause. The debate over the Wisconsin educational choice plan is really a debate over whether the Court will recognize where its logic has led.

The first approach to line drawing was the "child benefit theory." The idea was to distinguish between forms of aid that benefit the child (or his family) and those that benefit the religious school. The *Everson* bus subsidy seemed a clear example of the former. The religious schools involved in the case had not previously provided transportation to their students. Thus, when the state began to reimburse parents for the cost of bus rides, this did not relieve the schools of any burden. The beneficiaries were the children, who got a safer, faster ride to school, or their parents, who were relieved of the cost of providing transportation.

This theory had a certain logic. If the purpose of the Establishment Clause is to protect taxpayers from being compelled to support religious teaching, the *Everson* bus rides were correctly upheld. Nothing protects taxpayers from being compelled to help families provide safe transportation to their children. If extended, the theory could be applied to any portion of the cost of education that had previously been paid by the parents— textbooks, locker fees, supplies, and so forth. Moreover, the theory could be extended to educational costs that previously were borne by parents of private school students but not by parents of public school students. Surely *Everson* would not have been differently decided if the program had been passed in two steps: the first year paying for transportation for public school students and the second year paying for transportation for all students. The distinction is based on historical happenstance—which costs were borne by parents at the time the program was enacted—rather than on economic realities.

The problem with the theory is that the distinction has no economic substance. The allocation of costs between parent and the school is purely arbitrary. Who is to say that transportation is not part of the basic educational package that should be paid by the school? Who is to say that parents should not pay for individual components of the education their children receive—such as elective classes? If the principle is that the state can pay for elements of the private school education that are paid by the parent, there is nothing to prevent schools and parents from shifting costs from the former to the latter. And it really does not matter which party— parent or school—is the direct beneficiary of the assistance. The two will share the benefit, according to their relative elasticities of demand and supply, without regard to the form that the assistance takes.

As applied to educational vouchers, the "child benefit" theory is ultimately indeterminate. The voucher reimburses the family for the cost of tuition, and the family thus appears to receive the benefit. But when its customers gain buying power, the school is able to extract some portion of the benefit. It is widely recognized that Pell grants and other forms of assistance to college students enable colleges to raise tuition. Indeed, the courts recognize aid to college students as a form of aid to the institution.[12] I would therefore not expect the Supreme Court to rest its decision regarding educational vouchers on this theory. In subsidizing the activity of nonpublic education, the government would be providing a benefit to *both* the child and the school, and the two benefits are inseparable. The underlying theory distinguishing between these benefits is incoherent, and has largely, and correctly, been abandoned by the Court.

The Court's second attempt to devise a principled middle ground was based on the idea that the government may subsidize secular components of nonpublic education, even though taxpayers must be spared any compulsion to pay for religious components. This is an alternative explanation for the result in *Everson.* The state could pay for transportation because bus rides are purely secular. It could not pay for chapels, hymnbooks, or instruction in religious subjects. On this logic, in later cases the Court allowed states to provide secular textbooks, school lunches, and public health services. However, the Court forbade subsidizing teachers' salaries, even in secular subjects, since there was no way to be sure that religious school teachers would not allow religious teaching to seep into their conduct even of secular courses.

Again, the problem with this distinction is that it lacked economic substance. Aid to any aspect of the religious school's operations necessarily was aid to the entire institution, since the budgets were united and the aid was fungible. If the government paid for public health services, the school had that much more money to use on religious education.

Even within the premises of the theory, moreover, the Court could never arrive at a consistent understanding of what aid to a secular component means. Specifically, was the issue whether the component itself was religious in nature, or was the issue whether the component contributed to religious instruction? Take the example of transportation, which was approved in *Everson*. The bus ride itself is secular, but the effect of the bus ride is to get the child to school, where religious instruction takes place. Transportation is an input into religious as well as secular aspects of religious school education. Implicitly, in upholding the program, the Court must have concluded that it is the character of the input being subsidized by the state that matters and not whether the input contributes to religious education. A few years later, however, the Court held unconstitutional a program that defrayed the cost of maintenance and repair of school buildings. To be sure, bricks and mortar are secular, just as bus rides are secular. But now the Court looked at the use of the input. It concluded that since religious instruction takes place in the places repaired and maintained with government assistance, this aid was unconstitutional. These results cannot be squared. Depending on which approach is taken, most forms of aid can be characterized as secular or as contributing to religious instruction. Thus the theory could be used to justify almost anything or almost nothing.

The results, predictably, were utterly arbitrary. The government could pay for buses to the religious school but not buses from the religious school to a secular site for a field trip. The government could pay for lunches but not water, for diagnosis of speech impairments but not for therapists, for remedial math and English teachers in portable classrooms parked outside the school but not for the same service inside the building, for textbooks but not science kits or maps, for state-mandated tests but not if they were composed by teachers at the school. There was neither rhyme nor reason to the pattern of results.

It would be more sensible to focus on outputs: are the schools that receive government money (directly or indirectly) producing students with a competence in reading, writing, mathematics, and other subjects that are the purpose of education? If the schools are producing the desired educational outputs, the government should be indifferent to whether, in addition, they are inculcating religion.

A third approach to line drawing was based on the nature of the recipient institution. The Court reasoned that in some religiously affiliated institutions, such as universities, the religious component of the activity was sufficiently minor, and sufficiently separate from the secular, that money given for secular purposes would have a predominantly secular effect. The only limitation on government funding of such institutions was that they must be forbidden to use the funds for "specifically religious" activities. In other institutions, which the Court dubs "pervasively sectarian," the religious component of their activities is so predominant and so intertwined with the secular that it is impossible to aid the latter without having the effect of aiding the former. The effect is to allow almost unlimited subsidies to some religiously affiliated institutions and to forbid almost all subsidies to others.

Under this approach, the outcome depends almost entirely on the characterization of the institution as "pervasively sectarian" or "nonpervasively sectarian." Surprisingly, however, the Supreme Court has never provided an authoritative definition of this term. Justice Blackmun has called it "a vaguely defined term of art."[13] Instead, the Court has looked to a number of characteristics: formal autonomy from control by a church, required participation in religious exercises, lack of academic freedom, acceptance of normal academic or professional standards, and religious criteria for admission or hiring. In practice, the courts have treated all religious primary and secondary schools as "pervasively sectarian" and all other religiously affiliated educational, health, and social service organizations as nonpervasively sectarian—despite powerful evidence that many inner-city Catholic schools are less religious in character than many publicly funded social service organizations.

Like the Court's other attempts at line drawing, the results of this one appear arbitrary and absurd. There is no apparent reason, for example, why education before the first grade and education after the twelfth grade is in one constitutional category, while the grades in between are in another. In a pair of cases decided two years apart, the Court held that it is unconstitutional for public school specialists to provide remedial English and math to educationally and economically disadvantaged children on the premises of religious high schools but constitutional to give money to religious groups to sponsor programs to encourage teenagers to practice sexual self-discipline.[14]

By any realistic measurement, the likelihood that remedial English and math instruction by public employees might have the effect of imparting religious doctrine is surely far less than that from counseling by religious employees regarding sexual morality. Indeed, while I can imagine arguments that both programs should be struck down, that both programs should be upheld, and that remedial English and math should be upheld while sexual morality counseling should be struck down, I simply cannot fathom an argument to justify the Court's pair of decisions.

But there *is* a pattern. Mainstream Protestant denominations commonly operate universities, kindergartens, hospitals, and other social service agencies, but they do not traditionally operate elementary or high schools. The tradition of funding religious educational and social service organizations other than schools dates to a time when anti-Catholic prejudice played a major role. By the time funding cases reached the courts, after World War II, there was a long-established tradition of funding religious hospitals, universities, and the like, and of not funding religious primary and secondary schools. For all its invocation of constitutional principle, the Court simply ratified the status quo, apparently unaware that in so doing it was perpetuating discrimination against a religious minority.

The final approach to line drawing turns out to be much more robust and sensible. Perhaps the result in *Everson* was attributable to the fact that the ultimate distribution of the aid was not determined by the government but by the free and independent decisions of private individuals. The government extended aid to all schoolchildren on a neutral basis; how the benefit of that aid was distributed between religious and secular schools depended on what schools the recipients selected. This approach, like the others, had a persuasive logic in the underlying purposes of the Establishment Clause. The Establishment Clause is designed to ensure that government does not use its authority to favor one religion over another, or religion over nonreligion, or to create incentives or inducements to participate in religion. By extending the same transportation subsidy to all schoolchildren in the district, the state achieved the necessary neutrality. This principle clearly supports the constitutionality of educational vouchers.

The most pertinent precedent is *Witters* v. *Department of Services for the Blind*, a unanimous decision holding that public funds could be used to pay the tuition of a student at a Bible college for training for the ministry, pursuant to a program of vocational assistance for the blind.[15] Justice

Thurgood Marshall's opinion for the Court identified several aspects of the program as "central to our inquiry."[16] First, he noted that funding goes to the recipient institution only through the choice of the individual student. "Any aid provided under Washington's program that ultimately flows to religious institutions does so only as a result of the genuinely independent and private choices of aid recipients."[17] The same is true of the Wisconsin educational choice program. Parents will receive grants that enable their children to obtain the education of their own choice. Any aid that flows to religious schools does so only as the result of the genuinely independent and private choices of the parents.

Second, Justice Marshall noted that "Washington's program is 'made available generally without regard to the sectarian-nonsectarian, or public-nonpublic nature of the institution benefitted,' and is in no way skewed toward religion."[18] Again, the same is true of the Wisconsin program. Whether parents choose public schools, private nonreligious schools, or private religious schools, the school of their choice will receive the student's per pupil share of state educational funds. If there is any "skew" to the proposal, it is in favor of public schools, which are eligible for the local as well as the state component of educational funding and thus receive a much higher per pupil sum.

Third, Justice Marshall stressed that the Washington program "creates no financial incentive for students to undertake sectarian education." Their benefits are neither "greater nor broader" if they "apply their aid to religious education" than if they apply it to secular programs. "The fact that aid goes to individuals means that the decision to support religious education is made by the individual, not by the State."[19] This is the crux of the matter. The principal purpose of the religion clauses is to ensure that decisions about religious practice, including education, are reserved to the private realm of individual conscience. The decision to choose religious or secular education should be made by the individual, not by the state. The government has no legitimate interest in discouraging free religious choices any more than in promoting them. In this respect, too, the Wisconsin educational choice program closely resembles the Washington program upheld in *Witters*. The benefits are neither broader nor greater for parents who choose religious education than for those who choose secular education. The proposal creates no incentive to undertake religious education; on the contrary, it is the usual system that creates a significant incentive to forego religious education.

Finally, Justice Marshall noted that "nothing in the record indicates that . . . any significant portion of the aid expended under the Washington program as a whole will end up flowing to religious education."[20] This is a somewhat more difficult point. The proportion of the aid that "ends up flowing to religious education" depends, in part, on what we use as the denominator. If we focus narrowly on the voucher program itself, disregarding the broader context of educational programs of which it is a part, a "significant portion" is likely to go to religious schools. If we look, more realistically, at the state's contributions to elementary and secondary education, then there is no reason to expect that any more than a modest proportion of the education budget will flow to religious schools in Wisconsin. The state pays about $3,650 per pupil. For those students who attend public schools, that sum is paid to the public school district; for those who choose to attend nonpublic schools, the sum is paid to the school of their choice. The vast majority of this money therefore will "flow to" public schools.

Indeed, under certain assumptions, which appear to be reasonable, the effect of a voucher program would be to increase the resources available to children in *public* schools. If the voucher is less than the marginal cost of public education, each child who previously attended a public school and now uses a voucher to attend private school will leave resources behind, for the use of the other public school children.[21] Indeed, one of the reasons states were so willing to experiment with school aid programs in the early 1970s was that, because of overcrowding, the marginal cost of serving additional children was very high, and it was cheaper to offer modest subsidies to keep private schooling attractive than to absorb the cost of additional schoolchildren.

There is no neutral or objective basis for determining what denominator to use, and the results will therefore hinge on the judge's characterization. That makes inconsistent results probable. It is therefore fortunate that the Court in more recent decisions has abandoned this part of the *Witters* analysis. In a 1997 decision, the Court stated that it was unwilling "to conclude that the constitutionality of an aid program depends on the number of sectarian school students who happen to receive the otherwise neutral aid."[22] That modification is sensible. Not only is the "significant portion" analysis dependent on the choice of a denominator, but it is inconsistent with the underlying theory under which the neutrality of a program matters. The theory is that when the government acts neutrally toward religion, any religious consequences are attributable to the choices of private individuals and not to the state. If that is true, it cannot matter whether those choices are numerous or few.

Even before *Witters*, in *Walz* v. *Tax Commission*, a 1970 case, the Court held, with only one dissent, that state property tax exemptions for religious organizations are permissible, even when the property is used "solely for religious worship."[23] Emphasizing the constitutional principle of "neutrality," the Court noted that the tax benefit was provided to churches "within a broad class of property owned by nonprofit, quasi-public corporations which include hospitals, libraries, playgrounds, scientific, professional, historical, and patriotic groups."[24] Unless there is a constitutionally significant distinction between tax exemptions and appropriations, *Walz* strongly supports the constitutionality of educational vouchers.[25] If the government may extend subsidies even to churches themselves, when done on a genuinely neutral basis, then surely it may extend subsidies to schools that serve the vital function of providing education to our children.

To be sure, some language in *Walz* suggested that the result turned on the distinction between a decision not to tax and a "direct money subsidy." But such a distinction would elevate form over substance. In a more recent decision, *Texas Monthly* v. *Bullock*, the Court treated a tax exemption as constitutionally indistinguishable from a "subsidy."[26] In a plurality opinion written by the late Justice William J. Brennan, who represented the wing of the Court most vigilant against Establishment Clause violations, the Court stated the operative principle. When a "subsidy is conferred upon a wide array of nonsectarian groups as well as religious organizations in pursuit of some legitimate secular end," Justice Brennan explained, "the fact that religious groups benefit incidentally does not deprive the subsidy of the secular purpose and primary effect mandated by the Establishment Clause."[27]

Widmar v. *Vincent* was another important precursor to *Witters*.[28] In *Widmar*, the Court held that it would not violate the Establishment Clause for a state university to make its facilities available, without payment, to a religious group on the same basis as other university student groups. Free facilities are, of course, a valuable benefit, and the group intended to use this benefit for specifically religious activities, including religious teaching, worship, and prayer. The Court reasoned, however, that when benefits of this sort are open to all on an evenhanded basis, there is no effect of "advanc[ing] religion." "The provision of benefits to so broad a spectrum of groups is an important index of secular effect."[29]

After *Witters*, the Court repeatedly embraced the neutrality principle. In each of these cases, as in *Witters* and *Widmar*, the Court reversed appellate decisions holding the programs unconstitutional under the three-part *Lemon* test. This is interesting, because it is a sign that the Court's jurisprudence was undergoing a significant change. In *Zobrest* v. *Catalina Foothills School District*, the Supreme Court upheld the provision of sign-language interpreters to deaf children attending religious schools.[30] The Court stated the operative principle as follows: "We have consistently held that government programs that neutrally provide benefits to a broad class of citizens defined without reference to religion are not readily subject to an Establishment Clause challenge just because sectarian institutions may also receive an attenuated financial benefit."[31] Significantly, the two justices who dissented on the merits (Justices Blackmun and David Souter) maintained that "the payment of cash," as in *Witters*, is a *less problematic* form of assistance than the sign language interpreter at issue in *Zobrest*. "When government dispenses public funds to individuals who employ them to finance private choices," Justice Blackmun wrote, "it is difficult to argue that government is actually endorsing religion."[32]

In *Rosenberger* v. *Rector and Visitors of the University of Virginia*, the Court held that a public university that subsidizes student publications need not, indeed *may not*, withhold funds from an otherwise eligible publication merely because it espouses a religious point of view.[33] The overriding principle, again, was neutrality. Indeed, *Rosenberger* suggests that it might be unconstitutional for a state to *exclude* religious schools from an otherwise neutral program open to private secular schools. Thus, in extending the Milwaukee program to religious schools in 1995, the Wisconsin legislature may have removed a constitutional problem, rather than created one.[34]

In the most recent in this line of cases, *Agostini* v. *Felton*,[35] the Court overruled several of its prior decisions restricting the ability of the government to provide certain forms of assistance to students attending religious schools, noting that the earlier decisions had been "eroded" by *Witters* and *Zobrest*. In so doing, the Court articulated "three primary criteria we currently use to evaluate whether government aid has the effect of advancing religion":

— It does not result in governmental indoctrination
— It does not define its recipients by reference to religion
— It does not create an excessive entanglement.[36]

Under these criteria, any well-constructed educational voucher program should easily be upheld. Since no government employees are involved in instruction, there is no danger of "governmental indoctrination." Since the program is open to all students on the basis of objective economic criteria, and since they are free to select from among a wide array of secular and religious nonpublic schools, in addition to their right to attend a public school, it is evident that the program "does not define its recipients by reference to religion." Finally, since the program imposes no additional regulatory burdens on the participating schools (with one exception discussed below), beyond the accreditation standards and nondiscrimination laws they are already required to meet, there is no reason to think that the program increases the level of "entanglement." Under current precedents, therefore, it is highly likely that the Wisconsin program will be upheld.

It is true that for almost a decade, beginning with *Lemon* v. *Kurtzman*, the neutrality principle seemed to have little weight in the Court's decisions. Before 1971 and after 1979, with the exception of two 1985 cases later overruled, the Court upheld every program of neutral aid to education. Between 1971 and 1979, the Court pursued the various line-drawing strategies already described and frequently reached results inconsistent with the principle of neutrality. Some of these decisions have been formally overruled; others are inconsistent with later decisions.[37] Until those inconsistent decisions are overruled or effectively distinguished, lower court litigation over educational choice programs will remain unsettled.

Committee for Public Education and Religious Liberty v. *Nyquist* is the case most often cited by opponents of educational choice.[38] In *Nyquist*, the Court struck down a New York statute that provided tuition reimbursements in the form of cash or equivalent tax credits to low-income families whose children attended accredited nonpublic schools. The Court began with the premise that if grants were given directly to the schools, "there can be no question" that they would violate the Establishment Clause, since there is no effective means of ensuring that the state aid would be "used exclusively for secular, neutral, and nonideological purposes."[39] The Court interpreted earlier decisions—the transportation and textbook cases—as resting on the secular nature of the aid rather than on the neutrality of the program. In *Nyquist*, by contrast, the tuition grants were "subject to no such restrictions. There has been no endeavor 'to guarantee the separation between secular and religious educational functions and to ensure the State financial aid supports only the former.'"[40] The Court then rejected the argument that "the fact that the grants are delivered to parents rather than schools is of such significance as to compel a contrary result."[41] Treating this as "only one among many factors to be considered," the Court held that "the effect of the aid is unmistakably to provide desired financial support for nonpublic, sectarian institutions."[42]

This reasoning is obviously at odds with later decisions.[43] In *Witters* there was no attempt to ensure that the state aid was used only for secular aspects of the recipient's education. Nor was there any such attempt in *Walz, Widmar, Zobrest,* or *Rosenberger*. The principle established in those cases is that there is no need to restrict the use of public aid when benefits are extended, for secular purposes, to a class of beneficiaries defined without reference to religion. When fire trucks pull up to fight a conflagration at a local church, they are not limited to saving parts of the building with secular uses.

Indeed, *Nyquist* itself suggests that the requirement of limiting aid to secular uses does not apply to neutral aid programs. In an important footnote, the Court differentiated between programs in which aid flows to "*all* schoolchildren" and those in which aid is restricted to those who choose to attend private schools, which are overwhelmingly sectarian. The Court suggested, in dictum, that it would approve of a genuinely neutral aid program like the "G.I. Bill," even though government funds in such a program would go to religious institutions and would presumably support sectarian teaching.[44] As discussed below, the distinction between the program struck down in *Nyquist* and the G.I. Bill program approved in the footnote is meaningless. But even taking it seriously, the Wisconsin program is more like the G.I. Bill than like the program struck down. The state of Wisconsin provides $3,650 per pupil for the benefit of every schoolchild in the state. For those who choose public schools, this sum is paid to the public school; for those who choose a nonpublic school, it is paid to the nonpublic school. Thus the state education subsidy is *not* limited to those who attend nonpublic schools. The Wisconsin program should therefore be upheld even under the logic of *Nyquist*.

In any event, the distinction drawn between the G.I. Bill program and the *Nyquist* program is without substance. Consider this hypothetical situation. State A has two separate programs, enacted in separate statutes. One program gives the parents of every public school student in the state a certificate for $5,000, which they must use to reimburse the local school district for the costs of education. The other program gives the parents of every nonpublic school student in the state a similar certificate for the same amount, to reimburse their school for the costs of education. State B has only one program. Under it, the parents of every schoolchild in the state are given a certificate for $5,000, which they must use to reimburse any accredited school, public or private, for the costs of education. If the *Nyquist* distinction were applied, the program in state A would be unconstitutional, since there exists a separate program that benefits only those who attend nonpublic schools, and the program in state B would be constitutional, since "the program," like the G.I. Bill, benefits "all schoolchildren." Yet the systems in the two states are in every substantial sense identical. The constitutionality of a program cannot hinge on whether the benefits provided to nonpublic schoolchildren are part of the same "program" as those provided to public schoolchildren. The question must be whether the benefits, taken as a whole, are "greater and broader" for those making religious choices or—the same point put differently—create an "incentive" to choose religious over secular education. The *Nyquist* program did not do that and should have been upheld.[45]

It follows from this analysis that it was not necessary for the Wisconsin legislature to protect voucher recipients from compulsory participation in religious activities. Indeed, this provision, while probably innocuous in practice, sets a bad precedent and may well be unconstitutional. Voucher recipients are free to choose the accredited school to attend, but they should not be free to force the school to change its policies, especially when those policies relate to its religious character.

I have not, thus far, paid much attention to the voucher form. Public aid to education can take many forms: tax benefits, in-kind contributions of materials or services, grants to the institution, or grants to the individual. In my opinion, the precise form of the aid should not be dispositive. I believe the Wisconsin Supreme Court correctly stated the legal principle: "State educational assistance programs do not have the primary effect of advancing religion if those programs provide public aid to both sectarian and non-sectarian institutions (1) on the basis of neutral, secular criteria that neither favor nor disfavor religion; and (2) only as a result of numerous private choices of the individual parents of school-age children."[46] There are, however, suggestions in some Supreme Court opinions that it may matter whether payments are made directly to the religious institution. For example, in *Rosenberger* v. *Rector and Visitors of the University of Virginia*, the Court referred several times to the fact that payments were made by the public university to "a third-party contractor" for printing services, rather than to the student group that published the religious magazine.[47] Apparently, "direct" aid is more suspect than "indirect"—even when the "indirection" is purely formal, as in *Rosenberger*. That is presumably why the Wisconsin legislature amended the program to make checks payable to parents, then restrictively endorsed over to the school, when it extended the program to religious schools.

In my opinion, it should not matter whether the check is made out to the parent or to the school. What matters is whether the allocation of funds results from the free and independent choice of private persons. If so, and if the government has been wholly neutral as to religion, the benefit is the product of private choice rather than government compulsion. Nonetheless, until that principle is formally adopted by the courts, legislatures can minimize litigation by casting educational assistance in the most "indirect" forms possible. Tax exemptions or deductions are probably the least vulnerable to challenge; vouchers paid to the ultimate beneficiary are next; and per capita payments to the institution for serving beneficiaries are the most likely to cause problems in court. Under current precedent, it still appears to be unconstitutional for the government to give direct grants (even on a per capita basis) to "pervasively sectarian" institutions, even though it could accomplish precisely the same objective in the form of vouchers.[48] Because that result makes so little economic or legal sense, I predict it will not last long; but in the meantime, legislatures should pay attention. Discretionary grants, where government officials determine the amount of the grants and the identity of the institutional recipients, will continue to present constitutional problems even if the neutrality principle is embraced and should be avoided wherever possible.

The issue of form might, moreover, have ramifications for the degree of regulation that would follow from the subsidy. Traditionally, the government has attached numerous conditions to direct grants, fewer conditions to indirect aid, and fewer still to beneficiaries of tax exemption. That may be a pragmatic reason to avoid the direct grant mechanism (assuming, as I do, that government regulation, on balance, would tend to make private education worse). But there is nothing inevitable about these differences. The Supreme Court has upheld regulation of beneficiaries of tax exemptions and indirect aid against constitutional challenge, implying that the forms of aid are constitutionally irrelevant to Congress's power to impose conditions.[49]

Ideally, the voucher concept should be viewed as a matter of substance and not of form. The key feature is that individuals have the ability to choose the service provider from an array of institutions. If so, and if the program is not skewed toward religion, the Establishment Clause is satisfied. Those criteria are not merely technical. They are rooted in the great American traditions of religious pluralism and individual conscience. The First Amendment exists to guarantee religious freedom to all. An important part of religious freedom is the freedom of the parents to direct and control the education of a child in accordance with their own faith and conscience—be that secular or religious. This is a freedom exercised by the wealthy, who can afford private schooling. It should be a freedom, no less, for parents of moderate or lower incomes.

Within these constitutional limits, there is a wide range of options that states may wish to consider. It is not obvious that educational choice should take the form of giving every child the same sum. There are good arguments for varying the amount of the voucher according to the educational needs of the child, thus creating an incentive for the private sector to develop effective ways of meeting these children's needs. (The problem would be that setting these voucher differentials would be an intensely political process, and there is no guarantee that the results would track any rational estimation of comparative need.) There might also be arguments for varying the amounts of the voucher to reward educational success and penalize poor performance. As long as the government is not discriminating on the basis of religion or other ideological factors, it has wide latitude to use the financing mechanism as a means for improving the quality of education.

Discrimination against religion, or religious institutions, was never a purpose of the religion clauses of the First Amendment. The framers of our Bill of Rights wanted to prohibit the practice of compelled contributions to churches. In Virginia, James Madison and Thomas Jefferson led the fight against a proposal sponsored by Patrick Henry (called "A Bill Establishing a Provision for Teachers of the Christian Religion") that would have required all citizens of the state to contribute to the church of their choice, or in the alternative, to the state educational fund. This was rejected on the ground that contributions to churches should be voluntary. But neither in Virginia nor elsewhere did anyone believe that the state should withhold support from schools or other institutions providing public services on the ground that they were religious in character. Until well into the nineteenth century, there were no public schools, and local governments contributed substantial sums to schools run by religious groups to provide schooling for the poor. This pluralistic practice was ended not because of constitutional principle but because of anti-Catholic prejudice.

The great principle of the religion clauses of the First Amendment is one of pluralism and religious choice. Allowing families to make the decision about the religious or secular content of their own children is entirely within that tradition.

Even under a comprehensive system of educational choice, many families (probably a large majority) will choose secular education. That is their right, and it would be unconstitutional to attempt to channel their children to religious schools. But some will choose religious education, if the option is available to them. That, too, should be their right. The government has no legitimate interest in directing this choice, one way or the other.[50] The Supreme Court has repeatedly upheld programs of financial assistance in which the aid flows to a wide spectrum of private organizations, including religious entities, through the independent choices of private individuals. There is no constitutional warrant for excluding religious schools from state education funding or for requiring them to stifle religious expression or observance. On the contrary, to open up state-funded education to a diverse set of providers, with different approaches to education (both religious and secular), will expand, rather than constrict, parental choice, in keeping with the spirit of the First Amendment.

Extension to Noneducational Contexts

The neutrality principle just discussed is not unique to the field of education. If it is valid here, it is equally valid for other forms of government-assisted health and social service programs. Indeed, historically religious organizations have participated in government-funded social welfare programs even when those programs give discretion to government officials regarding the allocation of funds. The Court has held that the funds may not go to a "pervasively sectarian" organization and may not be used for "specifically religious" activities.[51] No religiously affiliated social welfare agency has ever been found to be "pervasively sectarian," so the operative restriction is that funds may not be used for specifically religious activities.

Even that restriction is now being reconsidered by many figures in the social welfare community. Many social welfare programs, such as drug rehabilitation, job training, or delinquency prevention, have as their objective assisting individuals to gain control over their lives. They are directed at issues of personal character and not just at providing money to needy people. And it turns out that many people respond more readily and effectively when such programs are grounded in religious appeal.

Accordingly, one of the most interesting developments in the welfare reform legislation enacted in 1996 was its Charitable Choice provision. Under this provision, states are authorized to provide certain services through contracts with charitable, religious, or private organizations and to provide beneficiaries with vouchers that are redeemable at these organizations. Indeed, states are forbidden to discriminate against religious organizations as service providers, and participating organizations are given the right to practice and express their religious beliefs, display religious symbols, retain control over their internal governance structure, and retain control over hiring—including the imposition of religious restrictions on employees—all without restriction based on their status as service providers. Service providers are forbidden to discriminate against beneficiaries on the basis of religion, and any beneficiary who objects to the religious character of a service provider is entitled to an alternative placement.[52]

MICHAEL W. MCCONNELL

If the analysis above is correct, the Charitable Choice Act is clearly constitutional in its voucher form and somewhat more problematic as applied to state contracts. There are two differences. First, under current law, the contract portion of the program must be limited to "nonpervasively sectarian" organizations. This requires state administrators to undertake the highly subjective—and potentially discriminatory—assessment of the religiosity of otherwise eligible groups. Second, in the contract portion of the program, the service organizations must be able to show that they have not used government-derived funds for "specifically religious" activities. In the voucher portion of the program, it is necessary only to show that the funded activities are contributing to the purposes of the program. That is a more sensible focus. The government should be concerned about whether the programs accomplish their purposes—not whether, as a product of the choices of program beneficiaries, those purposes are achieved in ways that involve religion. Thus the voucher form of the Charitable Choice Act is preferable to the contract form.

State Constitutional Barriers

In light of the purposes of the Establishment Clause and recent decisions by the Supreme Court, it is likely that any federal constitutional obstacle to educational choice will soon be removed, if not in the Wisconsin case then in one of the other cases now under way in Ohio, Vermont, Maine, or Arizona. Attention will then shift primarily to state constitutional law. Roughly half of the state constitutions have specific prohibitions regarding the public funding of religious organizations or religious schools. Here are a few examples:

—*Colorado (Art. IX, §7)*. "Neither the general assembly, nor any county, city, town, township, school district or other public corporation, shall ever make any appropriation, or pay from any public fund or moneys whatever, anything in aid of any church of sectarian society, or for any sectarian purpose or to help support or sustain any school, academy, seminary, college, university, or other literary or scientific institution, controlled by any church or sectarian denomination whatsoever; nor shall any grant or donation of land, money or other personal property, ever be made by the state, or any such public corporation to any church, or for any sectarian purpose."

—*Florida (Art. I, §3)*. "There shall be no law respecting the establishment of religion or prohibiting or penalizing the free exercise thereof.

Religious freedom shall not justify practices inconsistent with public morals, peace or safety. No revenue of the state or any political subdivision or agency thereof shall ever be taken from the public treasury directly or indirectly in aid of any church, sect, or religious denomination or in aid of any sectarian institution."

—*Michigan (Art. VIII, §2).* "No public monies or property shall be appropriated or paid or any public credit utilized, by the legislature or any other political subdivision or agency of the state directly or indirectly to aid or maintain any private, denominational or other nonpublic, preelementary, elementary, or secondary school. No payment, credit, tax benefit, exemption or deductions, tuition voucher, subsidy, grant or loan of public monies or property shall be provided, directly or indirectly, to support the attendance of any student or the employment of any person at any such nonpublic school or at any location or institution where instruction is offered in whole or in part to such nonpublic school students. The legislature may provide for the transportation of students to and from any school."

—*New York (Art. 11, §3).* "Neither the state nor any subdivision thereof shall use its property or credit or any public money, or authorize or permit either to be used, directly or indirectly, in aid or maintenance, other than for examination or inspection, of any school or institution of learning wholly or in part under the direction of any religious denomination, or in which any denominational tenet or doctrine is taught, but the legislature may provide for the transportation of children to and from any school or institution of learning."

It is not possible to canvass the history and precedents of each of these provisions in this paper. Some states follow the interpretations of the Supreme Court in interpreting parallel provisions of their state constitutions; some do not. The language of some of the provisions is more ambiguous than that of others. And if the truth be told, some state supreme courts seem to decide state constitutional cases in accordance with policy preferences more than text, history, or precedent. This makes predictions very difficult.

But it should be noted that there is a federal constitutional argument that provisions of this sort are unconstitutional. Not only do many of these provisions discriminate against schools that teach a religious message, but also the history of these provisions is closely tied to anti-Catholic bigotry. This combination of textually demonstrable discrimination on the basis of religious viewpoint and a suspect history of animus against a religious minority makes these provisions vulnerable to challenge under the Free

Speech, Free Exercise, Equal Protection, and possibly even Establishment clauses of the federal constitution.

"State Action" Doctrine and Related Statutory Issues

Another set of legal issues revolves around the "state action" doctrine. There are a number of constitutional principles that apply only to the government and that are inapplicable and often inappropriate in the context of private groups or individuals. Under current doctrine, it is fairly clear that the receipt of governmental financial assistance does not convert a private organization into a state actor. In *Blum* v. *Yaretsky*, for example, the Court held that a private nursing home that derived 90 percent of its revenues from Medicaid payments was not a "state actor" for purposes of compliance with the Due Process Clause.[53] Similarly, in *Rendell-Baker* v. *Kohn*,[54] the Court held that a private school whose operating budget was underwritten by public sources by over 90 percent could exercise the usual authority of private employers to discharge their employees, without restriction under the Due Process Clause.

Conversely, some constitutional principles, as well as other statutory requirements, are imposed by statute on recipients of federal financial assistance. There is no doubt that direct grantees are covered by these statutes. But what is the status of organizations whose students, patients, or clients receive federal assistance in the form of vouchers? The Court grappled with this question in *Grove City College* v. *Bell*, a case involving a private religious college, some of whose students received federal educational grants or loans.[55] The Court came to the odd conclusion that the students' receipt of grants or loans constituted federal financial assistance only to the college's financial aid office. Subsequently, Congress passed a statute reversing this result with respect to four civil rights statutes, making those statutes applicable to the institutions in their entirety. This suggests that voucher programs will not subject recipient institutions to federal laws directed at recipients of federal financial assistance other than the four civil rights laws.

Conclusion

The Supreme Court's decisions pertaining to educational choice over the past fifty years have been riddled with inconsistencies, empty formalisms, and injustice. Much of this result is attributable to the Court's attempt to impose a "no aid" interpretation on the First Amendment's Establishment Clause. The effect of this interpretation, when rigorously applied, is to discriminate against religious institutions and even to deprive them of necessary public services otherwise available to all. When applied less rigorously, the effect was a jumble of illogical distinctions and arbitrary decisions.

Since the early 1980s the Court has taken a different path. Increasingly, the Court has abandoned its old "no aid" separationism and embraced neutrality as the dominant principle under the Establishment Clause. Under this principle, the government may extend benefits to religious as well as secular individuals or institutions on the basis of neutral criteria without violating the First Amendment.

Educational choice provides the major test of this principle. As applied to elementary and secondary schools, the principle of neutrality conflicts with the economic interests of powerful organizations, disturbs many who are satisfied with the educational status quo for their children, and revives long-standing fears about "sectarian" and "divisive" influences on the young. For many years, the idea of educational choice was on the fringes of public policy debates. It was a hard struggle for advocates of educational choice to win enactment of experimental programs in a few states and a hard struggle to surmount legal obstacles. Now, thanks to the Supreme Court's denial of certiorari, we can see what the effects will be in Wisconsin and presumably in other states.

Notes

1. *Jackson* v. *Benson*, 218 Wis. 2d 835, 578 N.W. 2d 602 (1998), petition for cert. filed September 1, 1998.

2. The law is set forth in Wis. Stat. § 119.23.

3. *Lemon* v. *Kurtzman*, 403 U.S. 602, 612–13 (1971).

4. See *Board of Education of Kiryas Joel* v. *Grumet*, 512 U.S. 687, 717–22 (1994) (O'Connor concurring); ibid. at 750–51 (Scalia, joined by Rehnquist and Thomas, dissenting); *Allegheny County* v. *ACLU*, 492 U.S. 573, 655–57 (1989) (Kennedy, dissenting in part).

5. 509 U.S. 1, 8 (1993).

6. See *Lamb's Chapel* v. *Center Moriches Union Free School District*, 508 U.S. 384 (1993).

7. See Rosenberger, 515 U.S. 819, 878–79 (1995) (Souter, joined by Stevens, Ginsburg, and Breyer, dissenting).

8. See ibid. at 846–52 (O'Connor, concurring).

9. *Everson* v. *Board of Education of Ewing Twp.*, 330 U.S. 1 (1947) at 16.

10. 426 U.S. 736, 747 (1976).

11. *Everson* v. *Board of Education of Ewing Twp.* at 16.

12. *Grove City College* v. *Bell,* 465 U.S. 555 (1984).

13. *Bowen* v. *Kendrick,* 487 U.S. 589, 631 (1988) (dissenting opinion).

14. *Aguilar* v. *Felton,* 473 U.S. 402 (1985); and *Bowen* v. *Kendrick,* 487 U.S. 589 (1988).

15. 474 U.S. 481 (1986).

16. Ibid. at 487.

17. Ibid.

18. Ibid. at 487–88 (quoting *Committee for Public Education and Religious Liberty* v. *Nyquist,* 413 U.S. 756, 782-83 n. 38 [1973]).

19. Ibid. at 488.

20. Ibid.

21. If for some reason only the lower marginal cost schoolchildren departed from the public schools, the effect could be negative. This would be less likely if special needs children, who are entitled to additional (and costly) educational services in public school, are permitted to receive those same services in private school. See *Peter* v. *Wedl,* 155 F.3d 992 (8th Cir. 1998).

22. *Agostini* v. *Felton,* 117 S. Ct. 1997, 2013 (1997).

23. 397 U.S. 664 (1970).

24. Ibid. at 673.

25. Whether tax benefits should be viewed as equivalent to cash subsidies and, indeed, whether various forms of tax benefit should be viewed the same way are complicated issues both as an economic matter and as they relate to institutional autonomy. Those questions are beyond the scope of this chapter. In its most recent decisions, the Supreme Court has treated tax exemption as equivalent to subsidy. See *Texas Monthly, Inc.* v. *Bullock,* 489 U.S. 1 (1989).

26. 489 U.S. 1 (1989).

27. Ibid. at 14–15.

28. 454 U.S. 263, 270–75 (1981).

29. Ibid. at 273–74.

30. 509 U.S. 1 (1993).

31. Ibid. at 8.

32. Ibid. at 22–23 (dissenting opinion).

33. 515 U.S. 819 (1995).

34. Before 1994 the Wisconsin program applied only to nonsectarian schools. Parents of otherwise eligible children who attended sectarian schools filed a constitutional challenge, based on the plausible theory that it is unconstitutional to discriminate against institutions on the basis of their religious viewpoint. *Miller* v. *Benson,* 878 F. Supp. 1209 (E.D. Wis. 1995). The case became moot when the legislature expanded the program to include all accredited schools.

35. 117 S. Ct. 1997 (1997).

36. Ibid. at 2016.

37. See *Agostini* v. *Felton*, 117 S. Ct. 1997 (1997), overruling *Aguilar* v. *Felton*, 473 U.S. 402 (1985), and part of *School District of Grand Rapids* v. *Ball*, 473 U.S. 373 (1985).

38. 413 U.S. 756 (1973).

39. Ibid. at 780.

40. Ibid. at 783, quoting *Lemon*, 403 U.S. at 613.

41. Ibid. at 781.

42. Ibid. at 783.

43. It was also inconsistent with the earlier decision in *Walz*. The *Nyquist* Court distinguished *Walz* on the ground that *Walz* involved a tax exemption rather than a direct subsidy. As noted, this distinction was abandoned in *Texas Monthly*.

44. Ibid. at 782 n. 38 (emphasis in original). This was followed by two summary affirmances of such programs. *Americans United for Separation of Church and State* v. *Blanton*, 433 F. Supp. 97 (M.D. Tenn.), affirmed, 434 U.S. 803 (1977); *Smith* v. *Board of Governors*, 429 F. Supp. 871 (W.D. N.C.), affirmed, 434 U.S. 803 (1977).

45. To be sure, the *Nyquist* program changed the incentives relative to the status quo ante; it became more desirable to use nonpublic schools. But that is only because the status quo ante skewed the incentives *against* nonpublic education.

46. *Jackson* v. *Benson*, supra at 617.

47. 515 U.S. at 843.

48. *Columbia Union College* v. *Clarke*, 159 F.3d 151 (4th Cir. 1998).

49. *Grove City College* v. *Bell*, 465 U.S. 555 (1984) (indirect aid); *Bob Jones University* v. *United States*, 461 U.S. 574 (1983).

50. There may be legitimate interests in encouraging public education over private education, but not secular over religious.

51. *Bowen* v. *Kendrick*, 487 U.S. 589 (1988).

52. 42 U.S.C. § 604a (Supp. II 1996).

53. 457 U.S. 991 (1982).

54. 457 U.S. 830 (1982).

55. 465 U.S. 555 (1984).

ELLIOT M. MINCBERG
JUDITH E. SCHAEFFER

13

Grades K–12: The Legal Problems with Public Funding of Religious Schools

IN THE aftermath of the Supreme Court's 1998 failure to review the decision upholding the Milwaukee school voucher program, the debate over the constitutionality of school vouchers will no doubt continue.[1] Even voucher advocates concede that the Court's denial of *certiorari* in the Milwaukee case has no legal effect, but nevertheless maintain that recent Court decisions should be read to support vouchers, despite the Court's 1973 decision striking down a New York voucher program.[2] In fact, given the nature of K–12 education in America, serious constitutional and other legal and policy defects are inherent in current K–12 school voucher proposals, particularly those involving religious schools.[3]

The Federal Constitutional Problems with K–12 Vouchers

Universal public education is a hallmark of our society. Across this country, a system of public schools ensures that all children have access to a primary and secondary education, no matter their race, gender, disability, intelligence, family income, social status, religion, or other personal characteristic.

And because they are free to all, in the sense that they do not impose out-of-pocket costs on students and families, public schools are unlike many other institutions. Higher education, health care, housing—all of these cost money. In the absence of vouchers, the baseline is free public education. For this reason, providing vouchers to educate students in grades K–12 is unlike providing vouchers for access to any other institution in our society and raises unique public policy and legal concerns.

Those concerns are compounded by the fact that the vast majority of this country's private schools—the schools where vouchers for grades K–12 would be used—are pervasively sectarian, which means that the religious mission of such schools permeates the entire education program. Indeed, the primary function of such schools is not the secular education of students, but education in accordance with the tenets of a particular religion.[4] Putting aside whether voucher programs are wise as a matter of public policy, there are strong arguments that the use of taxpayer monies to fund sectarian schools and subsidize religious education violates the fundamental principles of religious liberty and the separation of church and state that are the cornerstone of our Constitution.

Proponents of vouchers attempt to short-circuit the constitutional problem by claiming that vouchers are "neutral," that giving parents a government check to be used at the school of their choice is a purely neutral act, and that any "choice" to use the money at a religious school is made by the parents, not the state. As a constitutional argument, there are serious problems with this contention.

Because public schools are free, no government voucher or other financial subsidy is needed for a child to attend one. Providing a voucher is therefore not "neutral" at all but is, as the Supreme Court has already recognized, something "*in addition* to the right that [parents] have to send their children to public schools 'totally at state expense' [emphasis added]."[5]

In *Committee for Public Education and Religious Liberty* v. *Nyquist*, 413 U.S. 756 (1973), the seminal school voucher case, the Court struck down a New York state law that provided tuition reimbursement grants to parents who sent their children to private schools, the great majority of which (in New York as elsewhere) were sectarian. In so doing, the Court rejected the argument, still made by voucher proponents today, that government reimbursement (or vouchers) for private school tuition merely provides "comparable benefits to all parents of schoolchildren whether enrolled in public or nonpublic schools."[6] The Court recognized that because children already have the right to a free public education, government subsidization of private education through vouchers creates an "incentive" to send children to private schools.[7] Because public schools are free, vouchers immediately skew the "choice" toward private schools.

Although voucher proponents claim that public schools should be considered within the universe of "choices" that a parent with a voucher could make, this argument not only stands our education system on its head, it is also precisely what the Court rejected in *Nyquist*, where public schools in New York also were part of the universe of "choices" available to parents. Reimbursing private school tuition, said the Court, gives parents an "encouragement and reward" for sending their children to private schools.[8] The same is true of vouchers: they "encourage and reward" parents who send their children to private schools, since those sending their children to public schools do not need vouchers, because public schools are free.

Moreover, while voucher proponents are fond of claiming that a voucher program is just like the G.I. Bill, the analogy simply does not work: higher education is *not* free. Parents of children in primary or secondary school and parents of students attending college are not faced with equivalent "choices." The former have an option or "choice" that is entirely free; the latter do not. This point was illustrated in Justice Thurgood Marshall's opinion for the Court in *Witters* v. *Washington Department of Services for the Blind*, 474 U.S. 481 (1986), in which the Court upheld a state program providing postsecondary school vocational rehabilitation assistance that was used by one student to attend a religious school. As Justice Marshall explained, the program "creates no financial incentive for students to undertake sectarian education. . . . It does not tend to provide greater or broader benefits for recipients who apply their aid to religious education, *nor are the full benefits of the program limited, in large part or in whole, to students at sectarian institutions.* . . . Aid recipients' choices are made among a huge variety of possible careers, of which only a small handful are sectarian [emphasis added]."[9] In sharp contrast, given the nature of our primary and secondary education system, the benefits of a K–12 voucher program *are* "limited in large part" to students at sectarian schools.[10]

Even assuming, for the sake of argument, that a voucher program could be viewed as "neutral," it has never been the case that "neutrality" alone is the single touchstone for determining compliance with the Establishment Clause. As Justice Sandra Day O'Connor has put it, "Neutrality, in both form and effect, is *one* hallmark of the Establishment Clause [emphasis added]."[11] However, again in the words of Justice O'Connor, "[T]here exists another axiom in the history and precedent of the Establishment Clause. 'Public funds may not be used to endorse the religious message'.... Our cases ... provide no precedent for the use of public funds to finance religious activities."[12]

Compelled financial support of religion was a fundamental concern of the founders, and its prohibition lies at the heart of the Establishment Clause. Indeed, Madison's "Memorial and Remonstrance against Religious Assessments" was written in opposition to what may well have been the nation's first school voucher bill—the 1784 Virginia Bill of Assessments ("A Bill Establishing a Provision for Teachers of the Christian Religion").[13] At a time when public education as we know it did not exist and most schools were affiliated with religious establishments, this legislation would have levied a tax on Virginia property for the benefit of "teachers of the Christian religion." Each taxpayer would have had the right to decide "to what society of Christians" the money would be paid or could have declined to appropriate his taxes to any religious society, in which case his tax dollars would have been used "for the encouragement of seminaries of learning" in the counties of the property taxed—choices not unlike the "parental choice" argument being advanced by voucher proponents today. Madison's objections to the compelled support of religion were uncompromising:

> The Religion then of every man must be left to the conviction and conscience of every man. . . . Who does not see that the same authority which can establish Christianity, in exclusion of all other Religions, may establish with the same ease any particular sect of Christians, in exclusion of all other Sects? *That the same authority which can force a citizen to contribute three pence only of his property for the support of any one establishment, may force him to conform to any other establishment in all cases whatsoever* [emphasis added]?[14]

In *Nyquist*, the Court applied these fundamental precepts of religious liberty in striking down New York's private school tuition reimbursement statute. In so doing, the Court expressly noted that "'sponsorship, financial support, and active involvement of the sovereign in religious activity'" are "[p]rimary among those evils" against which the Establishment Clause protects.[15] The Court held that there is no constitutional difference between direct state aid to private schools, most of which are sectarian, and a program in which the aid is given to parents as reimbursement for private (and hence mainly religious) school tuition; in either case, "the effect of the aid is unmistakably to provide desired financial support for nonpublic, sectarian institutions."[16]

In his opinion for the Court in *Bowen* v. *Kendrick*, 487 U.S. 589 (1988), Chief Justice William Rehnquist reconfirmed these Establishment Clause principles, explaining that "*even when [a] challenged statute appears to be neutral on its face*, we have always been careful to ensure that direct government aid to religiously affiliated institutions does not have the primary effect of advancing religion. One way in which direct government aid might have that effect is if the aid flows to institutions that are 'pervasively sectarian' [emphasis added]."[17] In *Bowen*, the Court rejected a *facial* challenge to a federal program authorizing grants to public and private nonprofit agencies, including organizations with ties to religious denominations, for services in the area of adolescent sexual relations and pregnancy. The Court's ruling turned on the fact that "nothing on the face of [the statute] indicates that a significant proportion of the federal funds will be disbursed to 'pervasively sectarian' institutions" and expressly distinguished *Nyquist* as a case in which "'all or practically all' of the schools entitled to receive grants were religiously affiliated."[18] The Court remanded the case to the lower courts to determine whether the program was unconstitutional as applied, stating that it would be "open to appellees on remand to show that [statutory] aid is flowing to grantees that can be considered 'pervasively sectarian' religious institutions, such as we have held parochial schools to be."[19]

The Court's most recent decision involving religious schools and government assistance reinforces the constitutional ban on government funding of such schools. In *Agostini* v. *Felton*, 521 U.S. 203 (1997), the Court overruled its decision in *Aguilar* v. *Felton*, 473 U.S. 402 (1985), which prohibited public school teachers from entering the premises of religious schools, at public expense and under public supervision, for the purpose of providing secular, remedial services to disadvantaged children under the federal Title I program, as well as part of its decision in *School District of City of Grand Rapids* v. *Ball*, 473 U.S. 373 (1985), striking down a similar local program. The Court's ruling in *Agostini* was based on careful scrutiny of the remedial assistance program at issue and a conclusion that the assistance would not impermissibly advance religion because of the specific safeguards in place: the services were secular, they were provided solely by public employees acting under public supervision, no public funds were transferred to the "coffers of religious schools," and the assistance was purely supplemental and did not relieve the religious schools of expenses they would otherwise have had to bear. None of these safeguards is present in a voucher program.

Most important, the Court in *Agostini* let stand that part of *Grand Rapids* striking down a school district's "Community Education Program." Under that program, classes for nonpublic school students were paid for by the public school system and taught by teachers hired by the public school system in classrooms in the nonpublic schools; most of the nonpublic schools involved in the program were religious schools.[20] Justice O'Connor's opinion concurring in the judgment holding the Community Education Program to be unconstitutional is instructive:

> The record indicates that Community Education courses in the parochial schools are overwhelmingly taught by instructors who are current full-time employees of the parochial school. The teachers offer secular subjects to the same parochial school students who attend their regular parochial school classes. In addition, the supervisors of the Community Education program in the parochial schools are by and large the principals of the very schools where the classes are offered. *When full-time parochial school teachers receive public funds to teach secular courses to their parochial school students under parochial school supervision, I agree that the program has the perceived and actual effect of advancing the religious aims of the church-related schools. This is particularly the case where, as here, religion pervades the curriculum and the teachers are accustomed to bring religion to play in everything they teach* [emphasis added].[21]

The same can be said of the pervasively sectarian schools that would be the primary beneficiaries of a K–12 voucher program. In fact, such programs are, as a constitutional matter, even more problematic than the funding for "secular" classes struck down in *Grand Rapids*, because voucher funds for K–12 education are typically unrestricted and can therefore be used by religious schools to support any part of their religious mission, including religion classes and religious activities.

It is for all these reasons that many believe that *Jackson* v. *Benson*, 578 N.W.2d 602 (Wis. 1998), *cert. denied*, 119 S. Ct. 466 (1998), was wrongly decided by the Wisconsin Supreme Court. Indeed, the court's tortured effort to distinguish *Nyquist* reveals the fundamental flaw in its analysis. According to the court:

> In *Nyquist*, each of the facets of the challenged program directed aid exclusively to private schools and their students. The [Milwaukee

voucher program], by contrast, provides a neutral benefit to qualifying parents of school-age children in Milwaukee Public Schools. . . .
The amended [Milwaukee voucher program], viewed in its surrounding context, merely adds religious schools to a range of preexisting educational choices available to MPS children.[22]

But this was equally true in *Nyquist*, where the "surrounding context"
included a system of free public education available to all K–12 students in
New York; thus the tuition reimbursement program, like the Milwaukee
voucher program, provided a benefit "in addition to" the right to attend a
public school without cost.[23] It is difficult to discern any distinction of
constitutional significance between the Milwaukee voucher program and
the program struck down in *Nyquist*.[24]

Other Legal Problems with K–12 Voucher Programs

The Establishment Clause is not the only hurdle that K–12 education
voucher programs must overcome. Even if the U.S. Supreme Court ultimately overrules *Nyquist* or otherwise holds that the First Amendment does
not prohibit voucher programs that include religious schools, other legal
issues will remain. Most important, religious school voucher programs at
the state or local level will still have to pass muster under state constitutions, many of which have provisions explicitly prohibiting the compelled
support of religion or the use of public funds for the support of religious
schools.

The Vermont Constitution, for example, provides that "no person
ought to, or of right can be compelled to . . . support any place of worship"
(chapter 1, article 3). The Vermont Supreme Court has held that this provision prohibits the use of public funds for the payment of tuition at religious schools.[25] The court held that in pervasively sectarian schools there is
"no way to separate religious instruction from religious worship" and "no
line between these concepts." Other state constitutions have similar
"Compelled Support" clauses (see, for example, Pennsylvania Constitution,
article 1, section 3) as well as more express provisions prohibiting the public funding of religious schools.

The Pennsylvania Constitution, for example, expressly states that "No
money raised for the support of the public schools of the Commonwealth
shall be appropriated to or used for the support of any sectarian school."[26]
This provision is reinforced by article 3, section 29, which provides, "No

appropriation shall be made for . . . educational . . . purposes to any person or community nor to any denomination and sectarian institution." Similarly, the Florida Constitution provides that "No revenue of the state or any political subdivision or agency thereof shall ever be taken from the public treasury directly or indirectly in aid of any church, sect, or religious denomination or in aid of any sectarian institution."[27]

There is clear precedent for a government benefits program to be invalidated as a result of such state constitutional provisions even though it has been upheld under the Establishment Clause. In *Witters* v. *Washington Department of Services for the Blind*, 474 U.S. 481 (1986), the U.S. Supreme Court held that the Establishment Clause did not prohibit the state of Washington from extending vocational rehabilitation services, under a program providing special education assistance to the visually impaired, to a student who chose to attend a private religious college. However, in the same case on remand to the state supreme court, that court held that provision of such assistance to the student *would* violate article 1, section 11, of the Washington Constitution, which states that "[n]o public money . . . shall be appropriated for or applied to any religious . . . instruction."[28]

Voucher proponents, confronted with state court rulings or state programs excluding religious schools from voucher programs, would no doubt seek to challenge such exclusion as an alleged violation of the federal constitutional right to the free exercise of religion. Indeed, voucher proponents have filed lawsuits in Maine raising just such claims. To date, the courts have rejected them.[29] It has long been recognized that the government's failure or refusal to subsidize a right is not an infringement of that right.[30] Indeed, were the law otherwise, the government would be required, for example, to fund abortions for poor women, a subsidy program to which many voucher proponents would no doubt object.

In addition to state constitutional problems concerning public funding of religious schools, other state constitutional barriers could impede K–12 voucher proposals. For example, the Ohio Court of Appeals has held that enactment of a voucher program applicable only to students in the city of Cleveland violated the state constitution's "Uniformity Clause," which provides that "all laws, of a general nature, shall have a uniform operation throughout the State."[31]

A final legal problem that would survive even if the Supreme Court upholds religious school vouchers and that, in any event, exists now as to current school voucher programs, is the special privilege that private schools enjoy: the privilege of not being regulated by the state, or accountable to the public, with respect to most aspects of the operation and conduct of such schools. While this may be acceptable when such schools are truly private, the situation is vastly different when public monies are used to support them.

In contrast to the less regulated private schools, *public* schools are held accountable to the public in each state through a host of statutes and regulations that govern all facets of school operation, fiscal responsibility, and substantive performance. This is accomplished through such measures as the required certification of teachers, specified academic and graduation standards, student assessment tests, public reporting of test scores, and the like. By and large, private schools are not bound by such statutes or regulations, nor do they want to be.

Indeed, religious schools in Wisconsin taking public voucher monies have virtually rebelled against efforts by the state Department of Public Instruction (DPI) to have them confirm that they will abide by the same state and federal antidiscrimination laws and constitutional provisions that protect students educated in public schools. During the early years of the Milwaukee voucher program, before the inclusion of religious schools, DPI required private schools accepting voucher monies to sign a "Student Rights" form confirming that they would abide by such laws.[32] In the summer of 1998, however, when religious schools were first permitted to participate in the voucher program after the state supreme court upheld the inclusion of such schools in the program (see discussion of *Jackson* v. *Benson*, above), voucher proponents successfully applied political pressure through the legislature to get DPI to rescind this requirement.[33]

Clearly, religious schools in Milwaukee have sought special rights to which they have no legitimate claim: the right to take public education dollars, on the one hand, but the privilege, on the other hand, to be exempt from the rules that govern all other schools educating students with public funds. There is a strong argument that when taxpayer dollars are used to subsidize a school, all students should be able to attend it, and all students should retain the same legal rights and protections they would have if they were attending a public school. Public accountability should require no less. For similar reasons, increased financial and educational accountability requirements that apply to public schools have also been proposed for private voucher schools in Milwaukee.

Of course, the increased regulation of private and religious schools needed to ensure such accountability could well result in an undesirable and constitutionally problematic entanglement between government and religion. Without such increased regulation, the public cannot be certain of the quality or nature of the education that it is subsidizing. But increased regulation of religious schools could cause constitutional problems. Even putting the constitutional issues aside, most private schools will not welcome additional government controls. The alternative, however, is to provide public funding to private and religious schools without public accountability. Such is the inherent dilemma posed by K–12 school tuition vouchers.[34]

In conclusion, K–12 school tuition vouchers present significant constitutional and other legal and public policy problems. No matter what the courts hold as to the constitutionality of school tuition vouchers, the remaining problems will continue to raise legal and policy questions for K–12 voucher proposals.

Notes

1. *Jackson* v. *Benson*, 578 N.W.2d 602 (Wis.), *cert. denied,* 119 S. Ct. 466 (1998).

2. *Committee for Public Education and Religious Liberty* v. *Nyquist*, 413 U.S. 756 (1973).

3. This article was written in June 1999 and does not reflect legal developments since then. In particular, it does not reflect rulings in the federal court challenge to the 1999 Cleveland voucher program, *Simmons-Harris* v. *Zelman*, No. 1:99 CV 1740 (N.D. Ohio). And it does not reflect the United States Supreme Court's denial of *certiorari* in *Strout* v. *Commissioner, Maine Department of Education* and *Bagley* v. *Maine Department of Education*, 68 U.S.L.W. 3250 and 68 U.S.L.W. 3251 (Oct. 12, 1999).

4. Consider, for example, the mission statement of one of the religious schools currently participating in the Milwaukee voucher program: "At Holy Redeemer Christian Academy we believe that God has uniquely created each of his children and endowed them with gifts to be used to bring Him honor and glory. We consider it our responsibility to unfold this uniqueness and these gifts in each child and to motivate each child to do his utmost to achieve and exemplify excellence in every aspect of his life. *Thus, all learning will be rooted in the understanding of faith in God and power of His word* [emphasis added]." Mission Statement, Holy Redeemer Christian Academy, Milwaukee, Wisconsin.

5. *Committee for Public Education and Religious Liberty* v. *Nyquist*, 413 U.S. 756, 782 n. 38 (1973).

6. Ibid. at 782 n. 38.

7. Ibid. at 786.

8. Ibid. at 791.

9. *Witters* v. *Washington Department of Services for the Blind*, 474 U.S. at 488 (citations omitted).

10. As is clear from Justice Marshall's opinion, a pertinent fact for purposes of the Establishment Clause is the universe of choices actually available under a government assistance program, not the selections ultimately made by beneficiaries from among those choices. See also *Mueller* v. *Allen*, 463 U.S. 388, 401 (1983) ("We would be loath to adopt a rule grounding the constitutionality of a facially neutral law on annual reports reciting the extent to which various classes of private citizens claimed benefits under the law"). Voucher proponents, however, mistakenly focus *not* on the choice of schools available under a K–12 voucher program—thus ignoring the fact that most are sectarian—but on the theoretical ability of parents to make selections of nonreligious private schools from among those limited choices.

11. *Rosenberger* v. *Rector and Visitors of the University of Virginia*, 515 U.S. 819, 846 (1995) (Justice O'Connor concurring).

12. Ibid. at 846-47 (citations omitted).

13. The bill is reprinted in *Everson* v. *Board of Education of Ewing Twp.*, 330 U.S. 1, 72-74 (1947) (supplemental appendix to dissent of Justice Rutledge).

14. James Madison, "Memorial and Remonstrance against Religious Assessments," reprinted in *Everson* v. *Board of Education of Ewing Twp.*, 330 U.S. 1, 63-72 (1947) (appendix to dissent of Justice Rutledge).

15. *Committee for Public Education and Religious Liberty* v. *Nyquist* at 772 (citations omitted).

16. Ibid. at 783. The Court's later decisions in *Zobrest* v. *Catalina Foothills School District*, 509 U.S. 1 (1993); *Witters* v. *Washington Department of Services for the Blind*, 474 U.S. 481 (1986); and *Mueller* v. *Allen*, 463 U.S. 388 (1983) are not to the contrary. Although these cases are often relied on by voucher proponents, the situations they addressed involved education-related benefits or tax deductions available regardless of the type of school attended. As the Court said in *Mueller*, upholding a Minnesota tax deduction, the state program "permits *all* parents—whether their children attend public school or private—to deduct their children's education expenses." *Mueller* v. *Allen* at 398. Voucher programs are completely different: the financial benefit is available only to parents who send their children to private schools.

17. *Bowen* v. *Kendrick*, 487 U.S. at 609–10 (1988). Some voucher proponents claim that vouchers are constitutional because the asserted purpose of vouchers (improving education) is a secular one. This argument ignores the fact that a government program that has the primary *effect* of advancing religion—regardless of its intent—is unconstitutional, as the Court stated in *Bowen*.

18. *Bowen* v. *Kendrick* at 610, 611.

19. Ibid. at 621.

20. *School District of City of Grand Rapids* v. *Ball*, 473 U.S. at 375.

21. Ibid. at 399–400 (Justice O'Connor concurring in part and dissenting in part).

22. *Jackson* v. *Benson* at 614 n. 9.

23. *Committee for Public Education and Religious Liberty* v. *Nyquist* at 782 n. 38.

24. Although some voucher proponents have claimed that the Supreme Court's failure to grant *certiorari* in the Milwaukee case indicates the Court's approval of vouchers, most observers recognize that this is untrue and that nothing of substance may be gleaned from the denial of *certiorari*. Not only has the Court significantly reduced the number of cases it has heard in recent years, but it has also repeatedly stated that a "denial of *certiorari* imparts no implication or inference concerning the Court's view of the merits." *Hathorn* v. *Lovorn*, 457 U.S. 255, 262 n. 11 (1982). See also *Maryland* v. *Baltimore Radio Show*, 338 U.S. 912, 919 (1950) ("The Court has said this again and again; again and again the admonition has to be repeated").

25. *Chittenden Town School District* v. *Vermont Department of Education*, 1999 WL 378244 (Vt., June 11, 1999).

26. Pennsylvania Constitution, art. 3, sec. 15.

27. Florida Constitution, art. 1, sec. 3.

28. *Witters* v. *State Commission for the Blind*, 771 P.2d 1119 (1989). In *Jackson* v. *Benson*, 578 N.W.2d at 620-23, the Wisconsin Supreme Court effectively gutted a similar provision in its own state constitution, holding that the expansion of the Milwaukee voucher program to religious schools did not violate art. 1, sec. 18, of the Wisconsin Constitution, which states that "The right of every person to worship Almighty God according to the dictates of conscience shall never be infringed; nor shall any person be compelled to . . . support any place of worship . . . without consent; . . . nor shall any money be drawn from the treasury for the benefit of religious societies, or religious or theological seminaries." The state court ruled that this Wisconsin provision should effectively be interpreted in the same manner as the federal Establishment Clause. This decision, of course, is not binding in any other state and is contrary to the approach taken in state cases such as *Witters*.

29. See *Strout* v. *Commissioner, Maine Department of Education*, 13 F. Supp. 2d 112 (D. Me. 1998), *affirmed,* 1999 U.S. App. LEXIS 10932 (1st Cir., May 27, 1999); *Bagley* v. *Maine Department of Education*, No. CV-97-484 (Cumberland Cty. Super. Ct., Apr. 20, 1998), *affirmed,* 728 A. 2d 127 (Me. 1999).

30. See, for example, *Maher* v. *Roe*, 432 U.S. 464 (1977); *Brusca* v. *Missouri*, 332 F. Supp. 275, 277 (E.D. Mo. 1971) ("a parent's right to choose a religious private school for his children may not be equated with a right to insist that the state is compelled to finance his child's non-public school education in whole or in part in order that he may obtain a religious education"), *affirmed,* 405 U.S. 1050 (1972). As the district court said in *Strout,* "The plaintiffs certainly are free to send their children to a sectarian school. That is a right protected by the Constitution. . . . The law is clear, however, that they do not have the right to require taxpayers to subsidize that choice." 13 F. Supp. 2d at 114 (citation omitted).

31. *Simmons-Harris* v. *Goff,* 1997 Ohio App. LEXIS 1766, *34-*39 (1997), *affirmed,* 1999 WL 349689 (Ohio, May 27, 1999).

32. One such law is the Wisconsin Pupil Nondiscrimination Act, Wis. Stat. §118.13, which prohibits public schools from denying admission to or discriminating against any student in any program or activity based on the student's "sex, race, religion, national origin, ancestry, creed, pregnancy, marital or parental status, sexual orientation or physical, mental, emotional or learning disability."

33. See, for example, "Single-Sex Schools OK in Choice Plan, DPI Now Says," Milwaukee *Journal Sentinel*, July 31, 1998, p. 1.

34. The Wisconsin voucher law provides a good example of the regulation and accountability problem. In an effort to prevent private and religious schools participating in the Milwaukee voucher program from picking and choosing among voucher students based on religion or other factors, the law requires that voucher schools admit voucher students randomly. Wis. Stat. §119.23(3)(a). Nonetheless, according to a complaint filed with the Wisconsin Department of Public Instruction by People For the American Way Foundation and the NAACP-Milwaukee Branch, more than a third of the voucher schools have random selection plans that either violate this clear requirement or that are too vague for the department (which is charged with enforcing the random selection requirement) to be able to tell what selection process is used. See Letter of Complaint to Wisconsin Superintendent of Public Instruction John T. Benson (February 2, 1999); "Some Choice Schools Broke Rules, Foes Say," Milwaukee *Journal Sentinel*, February 3, 1999, p. 1.

ROBERT D. REISCHAUER

14 | *Medicare Vouchers*

THE MEDICARE program was enacted in 1965 to provide the elderly (people age sixty-five and older) with basic health insurance. In 1973 it was expanded to cover the disabled who received Social Security disability benefits and those suffering from end-stage renal disease. Before Medicare, only about half of the elderly had health insurance. Even among this fortunate half, the protection was limited because in many circumstances the insurance carrier could refuse to renew a policy or could raise the premium to an unaffordable level if the health of the covered individual deteriorated. Many of those who lacked coverage could not afford to buy insurance because their incomes were low and coverage was expensive, while others had chronic conditions that rendered them uninsurable in the private marketplace. No regulations at that time guaranteed the issuing of insurance or mandated even partial community rating of premiums so that those in poorer health did not pay a much higher individual premium than others in the community for individual policies. Medicare represented the federal government's response to these social problems and the failure of the market to deal with them.

Traditional Medicare was designed to provide the elderly and disabled with health insurance that was comparable in structure and scope to that received by the working population and its dependents through employer-sponsored plans. Like the prevalent employer-sponsored plan of the mid-1960s, Medicare consists of a hospital insurance (Blue Cross type) plan and a medical services (Blue Shield type) plan. The hospital insurance component (HI, or Part A) covers inpatient hospital services, posthospital care in skilled nursing facilities (SNF), some home health services, and hospice care.[1] It is financed largely by a payroll tax. The revenues from this tax are dedicated to a trust fund (the HI Trust Fund) from which HI benefits must be paid. The Supplementary Medical Insurance (SMI, or Part B) program covers physicians services, outpatient hospital services, laboratory and diagnostic services, durable medical equipment, and some home health services (after 1997). Notably absent from the Medicare benefit package are coverage of outpatient pharmaceuticals and long-term care for those with chronic conditions.[2]

Part A coverage is an entitlement available to all elderly and disabled workers who have paid HI payroll taxes for at least forty quarters, as well as to their spouses. Participation in Part B, however, is "voluntary." Those who choose to enroll in Part B—about 96 percent of the eligible population, because the program is heavily subsidized—must pay a monthly premium that currently covers about one-quarter of this component's costs. The balance comes from general revenues.

Like employer-sponsored insurance of the 1960s, Medicare is structured to provide indemnity coverage for unmanaged fee-for-service care. Participants are free to obtain their health care services from virtually any licensed provider. The type and amount of treatment is left up to decisions made by participants and providers, as long as they fall within broad standards of accepted medical practice. Traditional Medicare pays providers for services rendered according to set payment schedules and reimbursement rules.

Participants are responsible for certain deductibles, co-payments, and coinsurance that vary according to the type of service.[3] Medicare has no "stop loss" protection, which limits participants' out-of-pocket expenditures to some maximum amount. The vast majority of participants, therefore, obtain supplementary insurance that limits their financial exposure and pays for some of the services, such as outpatient pharmaceuticals, that Medicare does not cover.

While traditional Medicare might, under the broadest of definitions, be regarded as a type of voucher, for the purposes of this paper, it is taken to be a government-provided service—that is, government-provided health insurance.[4] Starting in the mid 1980s, however, Medicare began to offer participants a classic voucher option. Legislation enacted in 1997 expanded this alternative significantly. A number of policy experts have concluded that a complete shift to some type of voucher system represents the most promising approach to providing the elderly and disabled adequate health insurance that is affordable to society over the long run.[5]

This chapter reviews Medicare's decade-and-a-half experience with vouchers, examines the problems that policymakers have confronted in their effort to provide health insurance through the voucher mechanism, analyzes the changes that the Balanced Budget Act of 1997 (BBA97) made in Medicare's voucherized component, and discusses whether vouchers offer a realistic way to deal with the long-run problems that face the Medicare program.

The 1985–98 Experience

Section 1876 of the Tax Equity and Fiscal Responsibility Act of 1982 (TEFRA) provided Medicare participants with a new way to obtain health insurance. Rather than receiving services through traditional fee-for-service Medicare, they could choose to enroll in and receive their care through an approved private or nonprofit health maintenance organization (HMO). Under this option, the Health Care Financing Administration (HCFA) paid HMOs a fixed monthly amount (a capitated payment) for each Medicare participant they enrolled.[6] In return, the HMOs were required to provide these enrollees a benefit package that, at a minimum, covered all of the services provided by traditional Medicare. Thus starting in 1985, Medicare participants were offered the option of receiving indemnity health insurance administered by the government or accepting a voucher that could be used to obtain similar services from any Medicare-approved HMO that served Medicare participants residing in their local area.

Whereas vouchers are often seen as a mechanism for introducing greater consumer choice, spurring efficiency, or reducing costs for a government service, these objectives were not the primary forces motivating the TEFRA initiative. Consumer choice was not an issue. Traditional Medicare already was at the limit on this dimension because participants could obtain services from virtually any licensed provider. Nor was traditional Medicare regarded as particularly inefficient. It operated with far higher payout rates—payments for benefits as a percentage of total expenditures—than private insurance carriers because of its economies of scale in administration; its ability to operate without reserves, profits, or marketing expenses;

and its practice of hiring private-sector companies to act as payment inter-mediaries. Finally, because Medicare's provider reimbursements were set at the customary levels that providers received from other payers, it could not be argued that the government program was paying more than the private sector for services.

Instead, the primary motivation behind the TEFRA innovations was the conviction, shared by a small group of influential analysts and policy-makers, that the coordinated care HMOs promised to provide represented a higher quality of care than that provided by fee-for-service medicine, where a lack of systematic management of care often undermined effec-tiveness. These analysts and policymakers wanted the elderly to have an opportunity to access this emerging—and in their view, superior—form of delivering health care services. As advocates of HMOs, they also wanted to do all they could to help the nascent HMO industry expand. Access to Medicare, which accounted for 29 percent of the insurance market at that time, could provide a big boost for HMOs. Supporters of the TEFRA changes also were convinced that HMOs had the potential to develop into a more efficient delivery system. If so, this policy change eventually could save Medicare modest amounts of money. But this conviction was a sec-ondary consideration.

During the 1980s, the HMO voucher option created by TEFRA had little impact on the Medicare program or the HMO industry. Fewer than 5 percent of the program's participants chose to join HMOs. This was not surprising considering that over half of the recipients lived in areas in which no plan was offered. The situation began to change in the early 1990s. Medicare HMO enrollment grew by over 20 percent a year between 1990 and 1998. By mid-1999 over 16 percent of Medicare participants were availing themselves of the voucher option, and projections suggest this fraction will grow to 31 percent by 2009.[7]

Several factors help to explain the growing popularity of the voucher option during the 1990s. First, employer-sponsored plans increasingly turned to managed-care organizations to provide services for their workers, making this form of care both more familiar to younger Medicare benefi-ciaries and available in more local markets. The number of plans offering services to Medicare participants increased from 96 in 1990 to 346 in 1998, and the fraction of participants living in areas in which a Medicare HMO offered services increased to 72 percent by 1998.[8] Second, many HMOs began aggressive marketing campaigns to attract Medicare partici-pants. They were spurred on both because Wall Street favored the stocks of companies with rapid enrollee growth and because the level of Medicare's capitated payments in many geographic areas made this business very profitable. Third, soaring premiums for individual supplemental policies (Medigap insurance) made the low-cost sharing and additional benefits offered by most Medicare HMOs at no additional premium increasingly attractive to many participants. Finally, some firms shifted the supplemental policies that covered their retired workers, as well as the policies they offered active workers, to HMOs. Their former employees then had to select the voucher option if they wanted continued employer-financed supplemental coverage.[9]

Medicare's experience over the 1985–98 period illustrates the problems and complexities inherent in using the voucher mechanism to provide health insurance. These include the difficulties encountered in setting an appropriate unit value for the voucher, the inequities that vouchers can create if the government's objective is to provide a uniform level of service to individuals living in different geographic areas, the challenge in ensuring that the voucher empowers consumers to make better choices, and the consequences when vouchers bring new political forces into play. Medicare's inability to deal adequately with these issues under the TEFRA structure was one of the reasons Congress radically restructured Medicare's voucher component in the Balanced Budget Act of 1997.

Unit Value of the Voucher

It is far more difficult to set the appropriate unit value of a voucher for health insurance than it is to establish the correct unit value of a voucher for food, housing, education, or other services. Problems arise because the cost of providing health services to different individuals varies much more than the cost of providing individuals with an adequate diet, a two-bedroom apartment, or even a year of fourth grade education. Some of the variation, which is not unique to health vouchers, relates to geography. Input prices, medical practice patterns, and access to providers differ greatly across the country. These differences can be seen in the variation that exists across counties in the expenditures of traditional Medicare. After adjusting for differences in the demographic composition of each area's enrollees, average per-participant spending levels differ by more than three to one across the nation's counties.[10]

This geographic variation means that the unit value of a health voucher must differ by geographic location if the voucher is to provide participants with the purchasing power needed to obtain roughly the same level of health insurance services across the country. While this problem is present to some degree with all voucher and many nonvoucher programs, for some, such as food stamps, the geographic variation is not large in many programs. For others, like housing vouchers, which must reflect the wide differences in rents that exist across the nation's many separate housing markets, the challenge related to geography is as great as it is for health insurance.

The cost of providing health insurance, however, has another source of variation, one embodied in the individual. It derives from the tremendous differences that exist in individual health needs and the different proclivities people have to use health services when faced with a health problem. The magnitude of this variation is illustrated by the concentration of health spending among the few who have serious medical problems. In 1996 only 3 percent of Medicare's costs for the elderly were incurred by the 52 percent of participants with the lowest expenditures, while 45 percent of the program's costs were accounted for by the 5 percent of participants with the highest expenditures.[11] This variation creates the need to individualize—that is, risk adjust—the unit value of the voucher to reflect each participant's health status. Clearly, a voucher meant to cover the likely costs of a healthy sixty six year old would not be sufficient to cover the costs of serving an eighty-year-old diabetic who also suffers from arthritis. Furthermore, plans would have to be regulated to ensure that they did not discriminate against those whose vouchers were unlikely to cover the costs of their health care.

Problems related to the individual variation in service needs arise in other voucher applications. For example, it is inherently more expensive to educate a child with learning disabilities or one with behavioral problems than an average child. Similarly, a family of six will need a larger housing voucher than a family of two to rent an adequate unit in the same housing market. Presented with such variation, vouchers are usually adjusted, using objective measures, to reflect relative need and service delivery costs. For example, family size can be used as an objective measure of how large a housing unit a family needs. Readily accessible objective measures that can be used to adjust the unit value of a health insurance voucher are just beginning to be developed.

The adjusted average per capita cost (AAPCC) methodology established by TEFRA to set Medicare's voucher amounts attempted to address the need for both geographic and individual cost variation. Using this methodology, the base voucher amount paid to an HMO for an average enrollee is adjusted to reflect local conditions by relating it to the average per-participant expenditure on traditional Medicare in the enrollee's county of residence, excluding the effects of differences in the demographic characteristics of the county's Medicare population.[12] Specifically, the unit value of the base voucher is set at 95 percent of the adjusted per-participant fee-for-service spending in the county. This amount is then individualized, that is, adjusted for certain risk factors that reflect the likely health needs of the enrollee. These factors include the participant's age, gender, eligibility for Medicaid, and institutional status. As a result of these factors, the unit value of the Medicare voucher an HMO received in 1998 for serving an eighty-five-year-old, noninstitutionalized male who was also eligible for Medicaid was 3.63 times the amount it received for serving a sixty-five-year-old woman who was neither institutionalized nor a Medicaid enrollee.[13]

While large, the adjustments made for geographic and individual cost differences have proved to be neither accurate nor adequate. In fact, the demographic factors used in the AAPCC methodology explain only about 1 percent of the variation in health care costs across individuals.[14] As a result, this methodology creates incentives on both the demand and supply sides that affect participation. On the demand side, individuals who have chronic conditions or who expect to be heavy users of health services are often reluctant to leave traditional Medicare with its open-ended subsidy for all the care they and their providers deem desirable. They know that the voucher that an HMO would receive when they enrolled may not be sufficient to cover the costs of their health care needs. Understandably, they fear that the HMO may stint on care or limit their access to specialists. Furthermore, being heavy users of services, many put a premium on developing close relationships with particular doctors, which may be more difficult in a managed-care setting.

On the supply side, HMOs are not anxious to sign up those who are likely to have above-average needs for services, because the voucher payments they will receive from HCFA probably will not cover the costs of the care they will have to provide. Even though HMOs are required by law to accept any Medicare participant who wishes to enroll, plans can try to skew the composition of their enrollees toward those whose vouchers are most likely to exceed the costs of the care they require. One way HMOs can maximize the gap between the Medicare voucher amount they receive and the likely costs of providing services to the average enrollee is by limiting the geographic area in which they offer services. Under TEFRA, HMOs can define their service areas to include any county or zip code area within a county. By and large, they have chosen to offer services in areas where the voucher amounts are relatively high. In 1998 the monthly voucher amount available in counties where no Medicare HMO plan was available averaged less than $400, while the average Medicare HMO enrollee lived in a county in which the voucher was worth $518.

Because the unit value of the voucher is tied to traditional Medicare per-participant spending in each county area, significant differences in capitated payments can occur even within rather limited geographic areas. For example, in the Washington, D.C., metropolitan area in 1997, HMOs received $7,036 for serving the average participant in Prince Georges County, Maryland, but only $4,718 for enrolling residents of neighboring Fairfax County, Virginia. Within the five boroughs (counties) of New York City, annual voucher payments differed by as much as $1,280. Clearly, such variations are not related to differences in input prices or regional practice patterns.

Plans can also attempt to influence the composition of their enrollees by concentrating their marketing on participants who are most likely to be profitable. They can advertise in magazines that are read by active seniors or mail brochures only to those living in zip codes with many single family houses, where Medicare enrollees are most likely to be healthy because they are living independently.[15] Their marketing materials can be designed to appeal to healthy individuals by using illustrations that show active seniors playing tennis and golf. Plans can also structure their supplementary benefits to attract healthy participants by emphasizing preventive care, exercise classes, and nutrition counseling. Or plans might highlight their generous provisions for obtaining out-of-area care, assuming that the elderly who travel a lot or who are snow birds wintering in the South are likely to be quite healthy.

Services can also be skewed in ways to maximize the satisfaction of relatively healthy individuals and discourage participation of those with chronic or costly conditions. The number of specialists who treat expensive conditions—oncologists and cardiologists—can be limited. If HMOs control home health visits more tightly than is the case in fee-for-service Medicare, then those needing such services who are in poor health would be more likely to cancel enrollment and return to the fee-for-service delivery systems.

As long as the unit value of the vouchers paid to HMOs is less than perfectly reflective of the likely health costs of the individual Medicare enrollee, plans will have an incentive to seek healthier than average enrollees. They will engage in activities to attract such participants as long as the payoff from doing so exceeds the costs.[16] To expect otherwise, or to think that plans should advertise their excellent cancer center or superior record with organ transplants, would be naive. Adverse selection would quickly drive such an HMO out of business, because the HMO would soon attract disproportionate numbers of participants whose costs of care far exceeded their Medicare vouchers.

Because of the incentives on both the supply and demand sides, Medicare's voucher option has attracted participants who, on average, are less costly to serve than those who have remained in the fee-for-service component. In the six months before joining an HMO, the average managed-care enrollee cost Medicare roughly 35 percent less than the average participant who does not choose the voucher option. Those canceling enrollment in HMOs to return to traditional Medicare cost the program about 60 percent more than the average fee-for-service participant in the six months following enrollment cancellation.[17] The cost to the government from favorable selection into HMOs exceeds its gain from the 5 percent reduction from average fee-for-service spending made using the AAPCC voucher payment methodology. Thus one study estimated that the average voucher exceeds by about 6 percent the amount the average Medicare HMO enrollee would cost if he or she was covered by traditional Medicare.[18] This means that the voucher option, as it has functioned over the 1985–98 period, has cost, rather than saved, Medicare money.

Equity

Failure to set voucher payments at appropriate levels relative to the cost of providing services to those enrolling in Medicare HMOs has not only cost the government money, but it has also created inequities. Medicare was intended to provide uniform services to all of the elderly and disabled, no matter where in the nation they lived.[19] However, there are wide differences in the services available to Medicare participants across geographic areas under the voucher option, thus belying this objective. Some variation of this sort is unavoidable under any voucher scheme. For example, it would be technically infeasible to adjust food stamp allotments to account for the different purchasing power that $100 in food stamps has across the regions of the country, let alone across the neighborhood grocery stores of a single city. Furthermore, some voucher programs make no pretense that they are providing a uniform level of service everywhere. For example, while the maximum Pell grant may be sufficient to cover tuition and fees for a student at a state college in California, it covers only about half of such costs for a student attending a four-year college in Vermont.

The discrepancies that have emerged under Medicare's voucher option, however, are more extreme because in some areas the option is simply not available. In 1998 no Medicare HMOs offered services to Medicare participants in five states; the voucher option was available statewide in only six states. In that year, 28 percent of Medicare participants lived in counties where no Medicare HMO offered services. Of those who lived in areas where Medicare HMOs were available, 14 percent had only a choice between traditional Medicare and one HMO, while 54 percent had a choice among five or more managed-care plans.

The inequity inherent in the nonuniform availability of the voucher option is compounded by differences in the generosity of the benefits that HMOs offer from market area to market area. These differences arise from the interaction of TEFRA regulations and the poor correlation between the unit value of the Medicare vouchers and the costs of providing services to HMO enrollees in an area. Under TEFRA regulations, HMOs are not permitted to profit unduly from their Medicare business. Plans are required to estimate their cost of providing services to Medicare enrollees, and if the voucher payments they expect to receive from HCFA exceed this estimate—known as the adjusted community rate (ACR)—they are required to return the excess to HCFA, deposit it in a benefits stabilization fund for later use, or use it to provide additional benefits and reduced cost sharing.[20] Not surprisingly, all plans choose the third of these alternatives, which makes them more attractive to Medicare participants. Along with lower cost sharing, the most common additional benefits provided in 1998 were coverage for routine physical, vision, and hearing exams and immunizations. About 68 percent of Medicare HMO participants were also provided with some outpatient drugs coverage as an extra benefit.

But the types and value of the supplemental benefits provided to HMO enrollees vary tremendously from area to area. HMOs operating in markets with high voucher levels tend to offer more generous benefits than those operating in markets with lower AAPCC payment levels. For example, the typical plan operating in the Miami area provided all of the services mentioned above plus additional benefits without charging a premium. At the other extreme, the typical plan offered to Medicare participants in the Minneapolis-St. Paul market provided only reduced cost sharing, and some plans even had to charge additional premiums for this basic coverage.

Market Information

Vouchers empower individuals by allowing them to choose their service provider. Voucher recipients are assumed to be both adequately informed and able decisionmakers who can make choices that meet their needs better than would a "one size fits all" government program. There is no question that in the case of frequently purchased goods and services whose quality is easy to evaluate, like food, consumers tend to be well informed about their alternatives and capable of making decisions that maximize their satisfaction. Food stamp recipients know the relative strengths and weaknesses of the grocery stores in their neighborhood and the attributes of the foods they purchase. They are certainly better off with a voucher than they would be with direct commodity distribution. Even if a food stamp recipient makes a mistake by shopping at a store with high prices or poor quality, the consequences of the bad decision are small, involving only food for a few days. This is not necessarily the case with more complex services, such as education and medical care, where consumers make less frequent decisions and are often uninformed or ill informed about the quality of the services they purchase.

Despite the clear need for assistance, the government shied away from providing Medicare voucher recipients with information that might help them make more informed decisions as consumers. Through 1998, sixty five year olds signing up for Medicare were given literature that contained a general description of the voucher option.[21] HCFA, however, did not routinely inform enrollees about the various HMOs they were eligible to join. If asked, HCFA would provide a list of plans offering services to Medicare participants in the participant's local area, but the individual was required to contact each plan to obtain information about particular benefits, the composition of provider panels, cost-sharing requirements, and premiums. It was, therefore, a significant undertaking for an individual to gather comparative information on available plans. In some market areas, organizations serving senior citizens collect and disseminate such information. Nevertheless, it is not an exaggeration to say that the vast majority of Medicare participants were woefully uninformed about their options.[22] Even those who had enrolled in an HMO had only a rudimentary understanding of the benefits to which they were entitled and almost no knowledge of what was offered by competing HMOs.[23]

Of course, workers with employer-sponsored plans also often are not well informed about their health insurance plan options. However, their situations are somewhat different in that in most cases a benefits specialist has preselected, from the many available plans in an area, one or a few plans to offer to the firm's employees. The employer usually provides comparative information that allows its workers to make informed decisions. With Medicare, participants are dependent largely on the marketing materials distributed by HMOs and word of mouth for their information.

Not only did the government do little to inform Medicare participants about the choices available to them, but it also did nothing substantial to evaluate the quality of the HMOs that Medicare participants could access through the voucher option. The government's reluctance to play a role in this area is not surprising. It is explained primarily by the difficulties inherent in measuring the quality and efficiency of health plans. HCFA has taken a similar stance with respect to fee-for-service Medicare, where provider opposition and methodological hurdles have precluded most efforts to measure the quality of individual service providers and disseminate such information to consumers.

In theory, state regulators and professional licensing ensure that certain minimal quality standards are maintained. The TEFRA requirement that commercial enrollees make up at least half of the covered lives of any HMO wishing to serve Medicare participants was intended to be a further check on quality. Presumably, any HMO that could attract significant private business would be good enough to serve Medicare participants. In addition, a growing number of regulations, some arising from the recommendations of the Presidential Advisory Commission on Consumer Protection and Quality in the Health Care Industry, have been adopted in an effort to improve the quality of care provided by Medicare HMOs.

Because participants may be relatively uninformed about the limitations imposed by managed-care organizations when they decide to leave fee-for-service Medicare and because they may be unaware of the alternatives offered by competing HMOs when they select a specific plan, Medicare's voucher option has had relatively lenient lock-in rules. Unlike employer-sponsored insurance, in which workers usually are permitted to switch plans only once a year during a designated open-enrollment period, Medicare HMO enrollees are free to rejoin traditional Medicare or switch to a different HMO after thirty days notice. The consequences of a bad decision are, therefore, limited.

Not insignificant numbers of first-time HMO enrollees take advantage of this safety valve; in 1996 some 15 percent of new enrollees left their plan within the first year.[24] Some plans of dubious quality and some that have used deceptive advertising to attract enrollees have experienced enrollment cancellation rates of over 50 percent.[25] Notwithstanding this flexibility, some participants find themselves effectively locked into the voucher option. This occurs because most HMO enrollees drop their Medigap insurance. They do this because their HMO, as part of its basic benefit package, provides the extra coverage they previously obtained through supplemental insurance. If they become dissatisfied with their HMO and decide to return to traditional

Medicare, those who have canceled their enrollment discover that they face much higher Medigap premiums than they had previously paid. This occurs because Medigap rules allow carriers to underwrite, or risk-base, premiums for policies issued to those who have not maintained continuous Medigap coverage since their period of initial eligibility.

The lenient lock-in provisions may have had several interesting consequences. First, they probably have made HMOs less willing to invest in gathering basic health information or provide preventive care to their new enrollees than would be the case if plans were assured they could amortize these up-front costs over at least a twelve-month period, which would be the case if new enrollees were locked in for a year. Second, the flexibility has probably pushed up costs and reduced the range of benefits available to participants. Costs are higher because participants can switch to the plan that provides the most generous benefits for whatever medical problem afflicts them at a particular time. For example, if an individual began to develop a hearing problem and his HMO did not offer hearing exams, he could switch to one that did. While this may be good from the participant's perspective, it increases costs. There are anecdotal reports that some participants switch HMOs when they hit the annual limit on their drug benefit.[26] To protect themselves from such behavior, all of the plans operating within a market area will tend to offer similar benefit packages, thereby reducing choice.

Constituencies and Political Interests

The Medicare voucher option created surprisingly few political waves during its first decade, even though providers could have viewed it as a threat to their authority and independence. Their relative indifference can be explained by the option's limited appeal among participants and to the explosive growth in traditional Medicare payments providers were enjoying. When Medicare HMO participation began to grow rapidly in the 1990s, providers had bigger things to worry about—the Clinton health reform initiative and the rapid shift of employer-sponsored plans into managed care. Because managed-care penetration in Medicare has lagged well behind that in the employer-sponsored sector and because Medicare accounts for only a small part of the business of most HMOs, the battles between providers and plans have generally been fought out with little reference to Medicare.[27]

The Medicare voucher option has, however, created a constituency—HMO enrollees—that could play an increasingly important role in determining the program's future. Members of this incipient interest group have come to think that they are entitled to the additional benefits most HMOs provide; many also believe they should not have to pay supplemental premiums for these extra benefits. These expectations are one further repercussion of setting the voucher payments at excessive levels. As the rate of growth of the Medicare voucher payment is reduced and plans are forced to cut back or charge more for the additional benefits, Congress has begun to hear complaints from HMO enrollees. Because of the high and growing costs of Medigap insurance, many participants will feel trapped in the voucher component and unhappy about the rising supplemental premiums that plans will be forced to charge. Furthermore, faced with changed market conditions, plans have pulled out of some areas, leaving participants with no choice but to return to traditional fee-for-service Medicare.[28]

Fungibility

Problems of fungibility, or substitution, face all voucher programs. Most often vouchers are provided to increase the recipient's consumption of a particular good or service, but vouchers can also free up, for spending on other items, personal resources that the recipient would have devoted to the subsidized good or service. In the case of Medicare vouchers, the voucher option was not motivated by a desire to increase the consumption of medical services by Medicare participants. Traditional Medicare already allowed participants to consume health care services with few constraints. Rather, it was hoped that the voucher option would lead to a more appropriate mix of services delivered in a more efficient manner.

Surveys reveal that Medicare HMO enrollees consume less of some services, such as inpatient hospital days and specialists visits, than they would if they remained in fee-for-service care. Conversely, they consume more preventive care, including routine physicals, mammograms, flu shots, colon cancer screening, immunizations, and health education.[29] These patterns reflect the management of care by HMOs and the broader array of services covered by HMOs. Overall, the voucher option has probably had little impact on the aggregate volume of medical services consumed by Medicare participants and has increased the government's expenditures on Medicare because the payments made to plans exceed the likely costs that HMO enrollees would incur in fee-for-service Medicare. Nevertheless, the voucher option has freed up personal resources of participants for other consumption. This has occurred because HMO enrollees generally have broader insurance protection through their HMOs than they would have enjoyed had they remained in traditional Medicare and bought a supplemental Medigap policy and have had to devote less of their own money to supplementary premiums and cost sharing. Almost 70 percent of HMOs charged no premium in 1998, and among those that did, few imposed charges anywhere near the roughly $1,500 cost of the average Medigap policy.[30] What this implies is that the Medicare voucher has allowed HMO enrollees to increase their consumption of other goods and services while using at least as many health services as they would have used had they had to rely on traditional Medicare because the voucher option was not available. One study estimated that out-of-pocket spending by HMO enrollees in 1997 was $679 less than that of participants in traditional fee-for-service Medicare.[31] This is not an insignificant amount, considering that the median income of those sixty-five and older was only about $10,000.

Changes under the Balanced Budget Act of 1997

The Balanced Budget Act of 1997 radically restructured Medicare's voucher option. Many of the changes were designed to address the problems that had emerged during the option's first decade and a half; others were primarily intended to help balance the budget by reducing the rate of growth of Medicare spending. Under BBA97, the choices available under Medicare vouchers have been expanded, the method of setting the voucher amounts has been reformed, and HCFA is playing a more active role in providing information to participants. As the old problems are addressed, however, new difficulties are likely to develop.

Expanded Choices and Equity

The vouchers permitted under TEFRA could be used only to obtain health care through an approved HMO.[32] Under the Medicare+Choice (M+C) option created by the BBA97, vouchers can be used to pay for care provided by a variety of plan types, including three forms of coordinated-care organizations—HMOs (with and without the point-of-service [POS] option), provider-sponsored organizations (PSOs), and preferred provider organizations (PPOs)—private fee-for-service (PFFS) plans, and plans that offer catastrophic insurance backstopped by a medical saving account (MSA). The move away from an exclusive focus on managed care suggests that the primary impetus behind the TEFRA reforms—to allow Medicare participants access to what some thought was a superior form of health care delivery—has been abandoned. Cost reduction now appears to be the primary force driving the voucher component of Medicare.

Medicare participants should welcome the expanded range of delivery options. Many have been reluctant to join HMOs because they offer limited choice of providers and restrict direct access to specialists. The more flexible approach taken by PPOs, PFFS, and HMO-POS plans could attract many who now receive care through traditional Medicare.

The range of options, however, could create new problems for the program. Concerns about equity could intensify. While the huge interarea disparities in fee-for-service Medicare expenditures per beneficiary suggest that there are inequities in the basic program, vouchers make these inequities more visible and explicit. If the full range of delivery options is available in some markets while in others only a few types of organizations offer services, and in still other markets nothing but traditional Medicare is available, beneficiaries in areas lacking options will feel shortchanged. Access could also become a problem in some areas, if significant numbers of providers practice exclusively with one or several of the Medicare+ Choice plans and, therefore, are no longer available to serve those in traditional Medicare.[33] The difficulties inherent in setting appropriate voucher amounts could be magnified if Medicare participants with different health risks are attracted to the different types of plans. For example, disproportionate numbers of seniors who travel a lot and are likely to have few health problems might prefer the PFFS option.

At least for the next few years, these concerns are not likely to be important because plans and insurance companies have shown little interest in offering Medicare participants the new delivery systems. As of September 1999, only one PSO plan and no PPO, PFFS, or catastrophic/MSA plan had been approved by HCFA to provide services. Over the longer run, however, it is probable that this situation will change and that the shape of the health plan industry will be profoundly affected by the expansion of Medicare's voucher option. The industry could also be reshaped by the elimination of the TEFRA requirement that capitated Medicare plans have at least half of their total enrollment in the commercial sector. Under the Medicare+Choice structure, organizations could emerge that serve only Medicare enrollees. Plans that specialize in geriatric care and have facilities designed to meet the particular needs of older patients could develop, leading to better care for the elderly. However, plans that are structured to exploit the peculiarities of the Medicare administrative system could arise, and such organizations could provide Medicare participants with less adequate care.

Value of the Voucher

The BBA97 scrapped the AAPCC methodology for setting the voucher amounts in favor of procedures that are intended to better align the value of the vouchers to the costs of providing care to covered individuals. The new procedures are also intended to reduce the inequities that have arisen from the uneven availability of voucher plans across market areas and the intermarket discrepancies in the generosity of supplemental benefits offered where M+C plans are available. The BBA97 established a minimum monthly voucher amount of $367 for 1998, which is increased each year by the projected annual growth of per-participant fee-for-service Medicare spending.[34] Roughly one-third of the nation's counties are affected by this floor, which boosted payment levels in the counties with the least-generous vouchers by over 50 percent. It is hoped that the higher payment levels will attract Medicare+Choice plans to these counties, many of which had no voucher option under the AAPCC system. To reduce the year-to-year variation in payment rates, which created uncertainty that discouraged plans from entering low-payment counties under the previous system, the BBA97 also established a 2 percent minimum annual increase in the value of each area's voucher amount.[35]

The BBA97 procedures will gradually reduce the impact that geographic differences in fee-for-service practice patterns have on the unit value of the voucher paid to plans. This will be accomplished by moving the voucher over several years from a payment based solely on per-participant expenditures in fee-for-service Medicare at the county level to a fifty-fifty blend of county-level and national-level per-participant expenditures.[36] When fully phased in, this blended payment rate will raise the capitated payment levels in low-expenditure areas. Plans operating in areas in which high expenditures are related to high service use may encounter difficulties. Unless the doctors who provide care for these plans begin to follow national rather than local practice patterns, the Medicare voucher may prove insufficient to cover plan costs. Such behavioral changes are unlikely, however, because medical professionals tend not to vary their practice pattern to reflect their patients' insurance coverage. The blending of local and national expenditures was to have taken place between 1998 and 2003. The impact of this reform was delayed through 2000 because the BBA97 imposed a budget neutrality constraint—that is, the blended national-local payment adjustments could not increase total Medicare payments.[37]

The BBA97 required that payments to capitated plans be risk adjusted starting in 2000. This represents an effort to better align the payment made to a plan for providing health care to an individual with the likely cost of that individual's care. HCFA was given flexibility to design an appropriate method for risk adjusting payments and to modify the mechanism it selects as new data become available and improved risk adjusters are developed. Of the various mechanisms currently available, HCFA chose to use the Principal Inpatient Diagnostic Cost Group (PIP-DCG) risk adjuster. This measure uses diagnostic information from past inpatient hospital visits to predict an enrollee's future health care costs. When data relating to outpatient care become available in 2003, HCFA plans to incorporate them into the risk-adjustment mechanism. Researchers have estimated that the PIP-DCG adjuster is capable of accounting for about one-quarter of the variation in individual health spending that is explainable, that is, is nonrandom.[38] While far from perfect, the PIP-DCG adjuster represents a major improvement over the AAPCC adjustment mechanism, whose crude demographic factors proved to be a deficient predictor of individual cost variation.

Together with the other changes, risk adjusting the voucher could lead to significant reductions in the amounts that some plans receive, particularly those in high AAPCC urban areas. These reductions could force affected plans to impose or raise premiums, reduce supplemental benefits, or drop out of certain markets. Affected enrollees, who have benefited from past overpayments, will object and complain to their congressmen and senators. In some areas, the voucher option may become unavailable.

Even before risk adjustment was introduced, the reduction in the growth of payments and other market forces caused some plans to scale back or terminate their participation in the M+C program. In 1999 forty-five plans terminated their Medicare contracts and fifty-four others reduced the geographic areas they served, affecting some 407,000 M+C enrollees.[39] In 2000 forty-one contractors withdrew from the M+C program and fifty-eight reduced their service areas, affecting 327,000 enrollees.[40] These effects have been partially offset by forty-two organizations that have either begun offering services for the first time or have expanded their service areas.

Informing Consumers

The BBA97 required that HCFA begin to play an active role in providing Medicare participants with information about their options. The month of November is designated as an "annual coordinated election period," during which Medicare participants can choose how they will receive their care in the following year. Several weeks before this open season, the secretary of the Department of Health and Human Services must send each participant and prospective participant materials describing the traditional Medicare, Medigap, Medicare Select, and Medicare+Choice options. This information will also explain the participant's rights, the enrollment procedures, and the risks inherent in the new system. The information on Medicare+ Choice plans will compare the plans available in the participant's market area. It will lay out each plan's additional benefits, beneficiary cost sharing, out-of-network limits, regulations regarding emergency care, out-of-pocket cost limits, and other dimensions that are important to consumers. During the open-enrollment period, HCFA is required to hold Medicare+Choice information fairs around the nation and "to conduct a nationally coordinated education and publicity campaign to inform Medicare+Choice eligible individuals about . . . plans and the election process."[41] These requirements represent a significant departure from past practice and will constitute a formidable challenge to HCFA. Other than the advertising done to attract recruits to the volunteer military, no federal agency has mounted such an ambitious campaign to inform citizens about a federal program.

In addition to the federal information effort, plans will still be able to market directly to Medicare participants. They will be required, however, to submit their marketing materials to HCFA so that the agency can ensure that the materials are both accurate and not misleading. There are, however, no prohibitions against materials that are designed to have special appeal to subgroups of the Medicare population that might be particularly profitable to serve.

Measuring Quality and Disseminating the Results

The BBA97 also required that HCFA play a more active role in measuring the quality of care provided by coordinated-care organizations (but not PFFS or catastrophic/MSA organizations) and in sharing this information with participants. The materials disseminated during the open-enrollment period will include, to the extent they are available, plan quality and performance indicators, enrollment cancellation rates, participant satisfaction measures, and health outcomes information. Plans will have to establish quality assurance programs, and HCFA is required to set minimum levels of performance that all plans will have to meet. In addition, each plan will identify and pursue certain performance improvement projects designed to strengthen clinical or nonclinical aspects of the plan.

Given the data requirements and the methodological difficulties inherent in measuring plan performance, these quality initiatives could take a number of years to implement even partially. Nevertheless, they could have a significant impact on the non-Medicare, as well as the Medicare, market. Employers and their employees will begin to demand similar information from plans. In addition, the quality-related requirements are likely to affect the structure of the industry by making it more difficult for PPOs and HMOs with loose POS options or very extensive provider networks to operate. Not only will these plans have more difficulty collecting the necessary data, but they also will have a harder time successfully completing their performance improvement projects and affecting the practice patterns of their providers so as to improve measured quality. As a result, the recent trend toward plans with more open networks may reverse in favor of plans with more limited panels of providers. This would narrow the provider choice offered to M+C enrollees within any plan. An enrollee wishing to access the services of a particular doctor or hospital may have to switch plans. Those who travel a lot or who live in the north but winter in the south may have no choice but to remain in fee-for-service Medicare.

Switching plans, however, will become more difficult starting in 2002. In that year, participants will be able to shift into or out of traditional Medicare or change their M+C plan only once during the first six months; after that window, they will be locked in to the plan they selected until the beginning of the next year.[42] In 2003 this grace period will extend only for the first three months of the year. The more stringent lock-in rules might lead to lower costs and increases in the diversity of the benefit packages that plans offer in each market area. They almost certainly will increase dissatisfaction among some participants.

Are Medicare Vouchers the Long-Run Answer?

The BBA97 not only greatly expanded the scope and, possibly, the size of Medicare's voucher component, but it also significantly reduced the projected growth of Medicare spending over the 1999–2002 period.[43] While the measures enacted to reduce spending will buy time, they will not solve the program's long-run imbalance between its income and expenditures. Current estimates suggest that costs, driven by the retirement of the baby boom generation and expensive new medical technologies, will rise faster than receipts, depleting the HI Trust Fund by 2025. In addition to fiscal problems, further fundamental changes will be required because Medicare will become increasingly inadequate. Its failure to cover outpatient drugs, limited coverage of long-term care, high cost-sharing requirements, and lack of stop loss protection will leave increasing numbers of participants exposed to substantial financial risk. Currently, employer-sponsored retiree policies and individually purchased Medigap policies limit most participants' exposure to these costs. Such dual insurance coverage, however, is complex and confusing to participants and providers and is administratively inefficient. In addition, the system of supplemental insurance is eroding. Employers are scaling back their retiree coverage: between 1994 and 1998, the fraction of firms offering retiree health coverage to former workers who are Medicare eligible fell by 25 percent.[44] Medigap policies are expensive, and most provide no coverage for outpatient prescription drugs, which have become an increasingly important component of modern health care. Medigap premiums have begun to rise rapidly, making such coverage unaffordable to growing numbers of the elderly.

Some analysts and policymakers have concluded that Medicare's long-run problems could best be addressed by gradually expanding the voucher component until it encompasses the entire program. Proponents of this approach argue that if Medicare were gradually transformed completely into a voucher program, it would restrain cost growth, strengthen the incentives for participants to choose cost-effective, high-quality plans, and encourage providers to deliver efficacious care with benefits that exceed costs. However, numerous technical, practical, and philosophical issues would have to be addressed before such a reform was practical. The following discussion reviews a number of these and identifies some of the questions that would have to be answered before a full voucher system could be implemented.

Benefit Package

Under a voucher structure, plans could be required to provide a standard package of benefits, as Medicare currently mandates, or they could be free to design different benefit packages as the Federal Employees Health Benefit Plan (FEHBP) allows.[45] While the latter would allow consumers to choose the benefit package that best fit their needs, resources, and taste for risk, it would make the task of risk adjusting the voucher more difficult. Healthier individuals and those who tend to believe that "watchful waiting" should be the first response to most of their maladies will be drawn to bare-bones plans, while the infirm and those who turn to medical professionals whenever they feel a bit under the weather will seek more extensive coverage. Available risk-adjustment mechanisms may not be capable of handling such segmentation. Moral hazard could also become a problem if those who gravitate to relatively Spartan plans do not have the personal resources necessary to pay for necessary care their plans do not cover. They could become a burden on Medicaid, increase the uncompensated care burden placed on providers, or become public health problems because they chose not to obtain needed care. Furthermore, if a wide variety of benefit packages is made available, consumers, most of whom have little ability to estimate health risks and limited knowledge of available medical technologies, will find it difficult to evaluate the merits of the options available to them.

If a minimum benefit package is required, the question becomes, "How generous should that package be?" If the required package is no broader than that of the current Medicare program, the overwhelming majority of participants will continue to demand a supplemental policy. If plans are permitted to integrate their basic and supplemental coverage into a single package, they will be able to use benefit design to attract participants who are the most profitable to cover—namely, the healthy. To avoid these problems, it would be wise to establish a standard benefit package that the vast majority of participants—say, 80 to 90 percent—would regard as adequate. Those who wanted to supplement this package could do so, but all plans would have to offer the standard package separately and would have to include in the premiums charged for the supplemental policies the added costs that the supplemental coverage imposed on the standard plan. These costs arise because supplemental insurance usually induces greater use of the benefits covered by the standard package.

Service Area

Medicare+Choice plans can offer services county by county unless a state requests that other market areas—metropolitan statistical areas, other groups of counties, or the entire state—be used. Few believe there is any logical reason to continue to use county areas as the geographic domain of Medicare's voucher component. If Medicare were to be gradually transformed into a voucher system, larger health market areas should be created. The boundaries of these areas may or may not follow county lines; they should reflect the catchment areas for hospitals and other facilities and encompass both the workplace and residential locations of the bulk of the population. New plans and small plans may have a harder time competing in larger geographic areas. This disadvantage could be mitigated if such plans were not required to provide accessible facilities throughout a market area.

Unit Value of the Voucher

The unit value of the voucher is currently based on the per-participant costs of traditional Medicare. Whether or not this practice makes any sense, this benchmark would no longer be available if traditional Medicare were phased out. The voucher could be set administratively or by using market forces. HCFA could negotiate with plans in each market area as employers now do and as the Office of Personnel Management does to set the rates for the local FEHBP plans. These negotiations would lead to a uniform acceptable premium for each area. Such a system could be complex and require a large staff of negotiators whose effectiveness might vary across markets. Alternatively, HCFA could require plans to submit a bid specifying the amount they would have to charge to provide the average Medicare participant with the required benefit package. The uniform acceptable premium would then be set according to some fixed rule, such as the median bid, the 30th percentile bid, or the lowest bid.[46] Plans bidding above the federal contribution could be excluded from the market, could be required to charge a supplemental premium equal to the difference between their bids and the federal payment, could be permitted to divide their excess bid between a supplemental premium and a lower federal contribution, or could be allowed to lower their bid without consequence. Plans bidding below the uniform acceptable premium could be required to provide extra benefits, could be allowed to provide premium rebates to their enrollees, or could be permitted to keep the difference as added profits.

The average amount paid to a plan under either the administrative or competitive system should be adjusted to reflect the health risk of each enrollee; it could also be modified to reflect other factors, such as measured plan quality. If available risk adjustment mechanisms proved inadequate, payments to plans could be based partially on capitation and partially on actual costs incurred for certain expensive procedures.

Participant Contributions

The uniform acceptable premium amount in each market area would have to be divided between a federal (Medicare) contribution and a participant premium. If the basic Medicare benefit package were enriched so that only a small fraction of participants felt the need for a supplemental policy, Medicare's costs would rise, unless participants were asked to pay more than the projected Part B premium, which was $45.50 a month in 1999. Because most participants or their former employers are paying added premiums for individual Medigap or retiree policies that provide the reduced cost-sharing and expanded benefits that would be part of the new basic Medicare benefit package, it would be equitable to increase Medicare's Part B premiums to incorporate the average amount paid for supplemental coverage. Those enrolled in a no-premium Medicare+Choice plan could face a significant increase in out-of-pocket costs from such a change. Mechanisms would have to be developed to protect those with modest incomes.[47]

Equity and Political Considerations

While the number of taxpayer dollars devoted to the average Medicare beneficiary's care varies widely across the nation today, these differences are largely invisible to participants. Even if this were not the case, it could be argued that the differences reflect the varying costs of buying a uniform indemnity health insurance product in different locations. If Medicare were transformed into a voucher program, however, the variation in the federal contribution would become more visible and more controversial. Because of market conditions, the full range of health organization types will not be available in all market areas. Those living in markets with relatively low federal voucher payment levels may feel that they have been treated unfairly relative to those living in markets with more generous vouchers and a full range of plan types. Similarly, in some areas, PPOs, PFFS plans, and other plans with greater choice of providers may be available for little or no additional costs, while in other markets such plans will have to impose hefty additional premiums. If areas with low or no supplementary premiums also enjoyed high federal payment levels, participants in the area with high supplemental premiums might feel unfairly treated.

Participants living in rural areas may, as they do now, have very limited choices. HCFA would have to ensure that Medicare beneficiaries living in such areas are not faced with the choice between a highly restrictive managed-care plan with no additional premium and a costly fee-for-service plan. For these areas, it might make sense to require that HCFA maintain traditional Medicare, with its more limited benefit package, as an option.

Reform Proposals in 1999

Two initiatives that would move Medicare in the direction of greater reliance on voucherlike mechanisms were proposed in 1999. Senator John Breaux (D-La.) and Representative William Thomas (R-Calif.), in their roles as chairmen of the Bipartisan Commission on the Future of Medicare, crafted a plan to restructure Medicare that, along with other changes, would pay M+C plans *and* fee-for-service Medicare with vouchers. Under their proposal, both M+C plans and fee-for-service Medicare would submit bids to the government that reflected their costs of providing health care to Medicare participants. The government's maximum contribution to the plans—the voucher—would be tied to the average bid submitted by all competing plans with adjustments for local differences in input prices. Participants who enrolled in an average-priced plan would be required to pay a premium that covered 12 percent of the plan's costs—about the fraction of total Medicare costs that Part B premium will cover in the future. Participants joining less-expensive plans would face lower premiums. No premium would be charged to those enrolling in plans charging 85 percent or less of the average. Those joining plans costing more than the average would pay all the additional costs.

All plans, including traditional fee-for-service Medicare, would be required to offer both a standard-option and a high-option benefit package. The standard option would cover Medicare's current mandated benefits, although plans could, with the approval of a newly established Medicare board, vary benefits and cost-sharing requirements within specified limits. The high option would include a prescription drug benefit as well as a cap on catastrophic out-of-pocket spending. Those with incomes over 135 percent of the poverty line would bear the full costs if they chose the richer benefit package. The federal government would, however, pay the high-option premium for those with incomes below this threshold if they chose the high-option benefit package offered by a low-cost plan.

After criticizing the Breaux-Thomas proposal, in part because it could lead to higher costs for those relying on fee-for-service Medicare, President Clinton developed a major initiative to strengthen and reform Medicare. Under the president's "competitive defined benefit" approach, M+C plans would be paid according to their bids as long as their bid was 96 percent or less of the costs of fee-for-service Medicare. Participants choosing the traditional fee-for-service Medicare would continue to pay current-law

Part B premiums. Participants who joined M+C plans that charged below 96 percent of the cost of fee-for-service Medicare would pay reduced premiums; those joining plans that charged 80 percent or less of the fee-for-service costs would pay no Part B premium. Participants joining plans with costs over 96 percent of fee-for-service costs would pay the Part B premium plus all costs above that threshold.

Under the president's proposal, all plans would be required to submit bids based on their costs of providing the standard Medicare benefit package, although M+C plans could price into their bids reduced cost sharing. The standard Medicare benefit package would be modified to eliminate cost sharing on preventive services such as mammography screening, impose 20 percent coinsurance on clinical laboratory services, and increase the $100 Part B deductible annually with inflation. M+C plans would be able to offer additional benefits, but they would have to market and price these supplements separately. In addition, all plans would have to offer as a voluntary high option the standard Medicare package plus a prescription drug benefit. The government would pick up both the premium and coinsurance costs for drug coverage for those with incomes below 135 percent of the poverty line. Those with incomes above 135 percent of the poverty line would pay 50 percent coinsurance and a monthly premium that would be heavily subsidized for those with incomes between 135 percent and 150 percent of the poverty line and would cover only half the program costs for those with higher incomes.

Conclusion

Although it is probably more difficult to design and operate a voucher program for health care than a voucher program for any other government service, vouchers are coming to play a greater role in the Medicare program. In their first incarnation—the TEFRA system—they created a large number of problems. The BBA97 legislation addressed some of these problems, but it created new, equally vexing problems for the future. While restructuring Medicare into a full voucher program holds some promise for addressing the program's long-run problems, the complexity of this challenge should not be underestimated. In all likelihood, it would take at least a decade to implement a workable Medicare program that relied solely on vouchers. Even after that, problems needing the attention of policymakers would persist.

Notes

1. Hospice care was not part of the original' benefit package. It was first authorized in P.L. 97-248, the Tax Equity and Fiscal Responsibilities Act of 1982 (TEFRA).

2. Unlike most employer-sponsored plans, Medicare provides relatively generous home health and posthospital SNF coverage.

3. The participants' contributions are not systematic. For example, Part B services are subject to a $100 annual deductible, after which the participant must pay 20 percent of approved charges. However, laboratory and diagnostic services and home health care do not require any coinsurance, and coinsurance for outpatient hospital services, until recently, has been close to 50 percent of total charges. Legislation enacted in 1997 will reduce gradually that figure to 20 percent. Under Part A, participants in 1999 are required to pay an initial deductible for hospitalization of $768 and co-payments of $192 a day for days sixty-one through ninety of hospitalization. After twenty days in an SNF, participants are required to pay $96 a day. There are no deductibles or coinsurance for home health services.

4. In their chapter in this volume, David F. Bradford and Daniel N. Shaviro have chosen to treat traditional Medicare as very close to a voucher. If Medicare is viewed as health insurance, it is an example of a government-provided service that, because of certain market failures and the limited incomes of the elderly, was unavailable to many participants before the government stepped in. All participants receive the same basic insurance plan. Viewed from the individual participant's perspective, Medicare is an open-ended subsidy for the purchase of certain medical services. Following the definition of a voucher in Steuerle's chapter, moreover, traditional Medicare does not grant "limited" purchasing power because it is uncapped.

5. Henry J. Aaron and Robert D. Reischauer, "The Medicare Reform Debate: What Is the Next Step?" *Health Affairs*, vol. 14 (Winter 1995); Stuart M. Butler and Robert E. Moffit, "The FEHBP as a Model for a New Medicare Program," *Health Affairs*, vol. 14 (Winter 1995); David Kendall, *A New Deal for Medicare and Medicaid: Building a Buyer's Market for Health Care* (Washington, D.C.: Progressive Policy Institute, 1995).

6. Plans accepting capitated payments are known as risk contractors. Until 2000, plans could also participate as cost-based contractors, which HCFA would reimburse for the costs of providing services less the estimated value of participant cost sharing. Only a small fraction of enrollment is accounted for by cost-based plans.

7. Congressional Budget Office, *An Analysis of the President's Budgetary Proposals for Fiscal Year 2000* (Government Printing Office, April 1999), table 3-2.

8. Medicare Payment Advisory Commission, *Health Care Spending and the Medicare Program: A Data Book* (Washington, D.C., July 1998), charts 2–8 and 2–10.

9. In such cases, the employer-sponsored retiree policy usually provides the retiree with more benefits than the HMO offers to other Medicare participants. Between 1993 and 1997, the fraction of employers with retiree health plans that offered their former workers a Medicare HMO option rose from 7 to 39 percent. American Association of Health Plans, "Employer Use of the Medicare HMO Program," policy brief, May 1998.

10. In 1997 the average monthly Medicare voucher varied from $221 in Banner and Arthur counties in Nebraska to $767 in the borough (county) of Richmond (Staten Island) in New York.

11. Health Care Financing Administration, *A Profile of Medicare: Chart Book* (May 1998), figure 18.

12. This is a somewhat stylized description of the actual calculations, which are complex and involve estimated amounts. The 5 percent discount is designed to achieve cost saving, and the average expenditures are adjusted to reflect the program's demographic characteristics nationwide. Vouchers are calculated separately for Part A and Part B services. For a more complete description of the methodology, see Leslie M. Greenwald, Al Esposito, Melvin J. Ingber, and Jesse M. Levy, "Risk Adjustment for Medicare Program: Lessons Learned from Research and Demonstrations," *Inquiry*, vol. 35 (Summer 1998), pp. 193–209.

13. *1998 Green Book*, Committee Print, House Committee on Ways and Means, 105 Cong., 2 sess. (Government Printing Office, May 19, 1998), p. 187.

14. Medicare Payment Advisory Commission (MedPAC), *Report to the Congress: Medicare Payment Policy*, vol. 1 (Washington, D.C., March 1998), chap. 3.

15. Patricia Neuman, Ed Maibach, and others, "Marketing HMOs to Medicare Beneficiaries: Do Medicare HMOs Target Healthy Seniors?" *Health Affairs*, vol. 17 (July–August 1998); Kaiser Family Foundation, *Medicare HMOs Pitch Better Benefits and Lower Costs: But Ads Appear to Seek Healthier Seniors*, paper 1417 (Menlo Park, Calif., July 13, 1997).

16. Attempts to skew enrollment can be costly and, at some point, are not worth the effort. A good portion of an individual's health needs over a two- or three-year period are unpredictable, and it is not easy for plans to ascertain even the more predictable portion for prospective enrollees.

17. Physician Payment Review Commission, *1996 Annual Report to Congress* (1996), chap. 15.

18. Randall S. Brown, Jeanette W. Bergeron, Dolores G. Clement, and others, *The Medicare Risk Program for HMOs—Final Summary Report on the Findings from the Evaluation*, report to HCFA (Mathematica Policy Research, February 1993). In addition to favorable risk selection, the AAPCC payment levels are excessive in some areas because the traditional Medicare expenditures include the program payments to hospitals for graduate medical education (GME) and for the care for low-income uninsured populations (disproportionate share payments, or DSH).

19. This is not to suggest that the program promised a uniform quality or quantity of health care services but rather that it provides insurance covering the same services with the same cost-sharing requirements.

20. Plans calculate the ACR using the administrative cost rates and profit margins on their commercial business. Since these rates are based on the much lower capitated payments of the nonaged population, the gross margins on Medicare business are much larger than those on their commercial business. This gives plans considerable leeway to add even more benefits for competitive purposes and still earn healthy profits.

21. For a discussion of the lack of assistance provided Medicare participants and its consequences, see General Accounting Office, *HCFA Should Release Data to Aid Consumers, Prompt Better HMO Performance*, GAO/HEHS-97-23 (October 1996).

22. Consumers Union attempted to fill the void by evaluating the Medicare HMOs and Medigap policies available in the nation's major metropolitan areas. "Medicare: New Choices, New Worries," *Consumer Reports*, vol. 63 (September 1998), pp. 27–38.

23. Susan Kleinmann, "Inundated by Information: Consumer Information Provisions of the Balanced Budget Act of 1997," testimony before the Senate Special Committee on Aging, May 6, 1998.

24. Medicare Payment Advisory Commission, *Health Care Spending and the Medicare Program* (Washington, D.C., July 1998), chart 2-3.

25. General Accounting Office, *Medicare: Many HMOs Experience High Rates of Beneficiary Disenrollment*, GAO/HEHS-98-142 (April 1998).

26. In many market areas, over half of the individuals canceling enrollment in an HMO join another HMO rather than returning to traditional Medicare. See GAO, *Medicare: Many HMOs Experience High Rates of Beneficiary Disenrollment*.

27. Medicare enrollees constituted over 10 percent of the covered lives of only two of the eleven largest plans with national affiliation, which enroll 76 percent of all Medicare HMO participants. Medicare Payment Advisory Commission, *Health Care Spending and the Medicare Program*, chart 2-11. In most states and metropolitan areas, Medicare managed-care penetration is half or less than in the employer-sponsored market. Health Care Financing Administration, *A Profile of Medicare: Chart Book*, figure 49.

28. For an analysis of the reasons why plans have withdrawn from certain markets, see General Accounting Office, *Medicare Managed Care Plans: Many Factors Contribute to Recent Withdrawals; Plan Interest Continues*, GAO/HEHS-99-91 (April 1999).

29. Physicians Payment Review Commission, *Access to Care in Medicare Managed Care: Results from a 1996 Survey of Enrollees and Disenrollees*, Selected External Research Series 7 (Washington, D.C., November 1996).

30. About 5 percent of Medicare HMO enrollees have supplemental insurance coverage. Some have employer-sponsored policies that offer more generous

coverage than the HMO's standard benefit package, and others may keep their Medigap policy to ensure lower premiums if they choose to rejoin traditional Medicare. Physicians Payment Review Commission, *Access to Care in Medicare Managed Care*, pp. 131–33.

31. AARP Public Policy Institute and the Lewin Group, *Out-of-Pocket Health Spending by Medicare Beneficiaries Age 65 and Older: 1997*, AARP Policy Paper 9705 (Washington, D.C., December 1997).

32. Starting in 1995, the voucher could be used for HMOs with a point-of-service option (POS). Under the POS options, HMO members can seek out-of-network care but are responsible for higher co-payments for such care.

33. This might occur if providers received higher payments from PSO, PFFS, or other plans than they did from traditional Medicare and these plans provided them with a high volume of business.

34. The BBA97 reduced the growth factor applied to payments to all plans by 0.8 percentage points for 1998 and by 0.5 percentage points a year for each of the following four years.

35. Even though the AAPCC used a five-year average of each county's fee-for-service per-participant expenditures, there was a good deal of year-to-year variation in payment levels, especially for counties with small numbers of Medicare participants. This provision was also designed to protect high-payment counties, which, using the new methodology, could have experienced declines in their voucher amounts.

36. The national expenditure amount will be adjusted to reflect area-specific input price differences.

37. As a result, the minimum payment and annual 2 percent increase constraints will govern the payments.

38. About 20 percent of the variation in individual health expenditures is believed to be explainable. The PIP-DCG methodology is able to account for 5.5 percent of the total variation. Greenwald and others, "Risk Adjustment for Medicare Program: Lessons Learned from Research and Demonstrations," pp. 193–209.

39. GAO, *Medicare Managed Care Plans*.

40. Health Care Financing Administration, *Medicare+Choice: Changes for the Year 2000, an Analysis of the Medicare+Choice Program and How Beneficiaries Will Be Affected by Change* (September 1999).

41. P.L. 105-33, Section 1851 (e) 3 (C).

42. There are exceptions to this rule. For example, participants can choose another plan if they move to a different market area, if the plan fails to provide minimally acceptable care or promised benefits, or if the plan becomes insolvent. In addition, those first becoming eligible for Part A benefits who initially select a M+C plan can cancel enrollment and join traditional Medicare at any time during their first twelve months of participation. However, plans can expel partici-

pants who fail to pay any required supplemental premium in a timely fashion or who are disruptive.

43. The Congressional Budget Office estimated that, as a result of the BBA97, the average annual Medicare spending growth in this period will slow from 8.5 percent to 6 percent. Congressional Budget Office, *The Economic and Budget Outlook: An Update* (Government Printing Office, September 1997), p. 41.

44. National Economic Council, Domestic Policy Council, *Disturbing Truths and Dangerous Consequences: The Facts about Medicare Beneficiaries and Prescription Drug Coverage* (July 22, 1999).

45. This is a bit of an overstatement, because the FEHBP requires coverage of hospitalization, physician services, and other basic services as well as some particular preventive measures (breast cancer screening). It does allow plans a good deal of flexibility to offer other coverage beyond the core.

46. Many complex issues would have to be dealt with in designing any bidding rule. For example, the capacities of the bidders would have to be considered. If they were not, the plans with bids at or lower than the federal contribution might have the capacity to enroll only a small fraction of the area's participants. To reduce this possibility, bids could be weighted by enrollment.

47. Under current law, Medicaid pays the Part B premium and cost-sharing amounts for those with incomes under the poverty threshold (Qualified Medicare Beneficiaries, or QMBs), the Part B premiums for those with incomes between the poverty threshold and 120 percent of that level (Specified Low-income Medicare Beneficiaries, or SLMBs), and the increase in Part B premiums attributable to the BBA97 (Qualified Individuals, or QIs) for those with incomes above 120 percent of the poverty threshold up to a higher level. Dual eligibles—those with very low incomes who are eligible for Medicaid as well as Medicare—receive whatever additional services Medicaid provides in their state as well as QMB benefits.

LINDA T. BILHEIMER

15 Subsidizing Health Care for the under Sixty-Five Population

T HE FEDERAL AND state governments subsidize the purchase of health care for the under sixty-five population
through a variety of means. Public programs to provide health insurance
coverage include Medicaid, which provides coverage for certain poor and
near-poor population groups, the recently enacted State Children's Health
Insurance Program (S-CHIP), which provides coverage for uninsured low-
income children who are ineligible for Medicaid, and programs for other
low-income population groups that the states establish and fund themselves.[1] In addition to public programs that provide insurance coverage, the
federal and state governments also subsidize the purchase of private health
insurance through the tax system. Despite such an extensive system of subsidies, over 40 million people under age sixty-five remain uninsured, raising
questions about the efficiency and equity of existing health care subsidies.

Those subsidies generally lack what many economists would view as the
desirable features of vouchers. In principle, vouchers would provide beneficiaries with choices as well as incentives to seek lower-cost plans, attrib-

The views expressed here are those of the author and do not necessarily represent the views of the Congressional Budget Office.

438

utes that are thought to promote competition, enhance beneficiary satisfaction, and control government costs. Under a voucher system, anyone who met a standard set of eligibility criteria would be eligible to receive a defined contribution for health insurance coverage from the government. That contribution would vary according to people's income and possibly health status but not with the cost of the plan that they chose. Beneficiaries would have the freedom to select from a range of health plans and providers, bearing the responsibility for paying the additional costs of more expensive plans. Everyone would be able to purchase coverage in well-regulated markets.

In practice, however, establishing a system of health care subsidies based on vouchers would be difficult, could conflict with other public goals, and might not produce the intended outcomes. This chapter explores these issues from the perspective of the Medicaid and S-CHIP programs, recent proposals to expand coverage to certain targeted groups in the population, and proposals to change the tax treatment of health insurance.

Competition and Consumer Choice in Medicaid

The Medicaid program, which is jointly funded by the federal and state governments, provides a comprehensive package of health benefits to certain poor and near-poor population groups, primarily the elderly, the disabled, and single-parent families. Despite extensive federal requirements for the program, states retain considerable discretion in establishing income eligibility standards, covered benefits, and payment rates for providers.

In recent years, the program has extended coverage to many low-income children and pregnant women. About 37 million people under age sixty-five were enrolled in the program at some time during fiscal year 1997. More than half of them were nondisabled children. Disabled children and adults composed less than one-quarter of nonelderly Medicaid enrollees but accounted for more than 60 percent of the approximately $100 billion in benefit payments that the federal and state governments made on behalf of nonelderly enrollees.

For many Medicaid enrollees, the 1990s have seen the transformation of the program from a traditional open-ended fee-for-service model to a managed care system. The majority of nondisabled children and adults under age sixty-five are now enrolled in a managed care plan. But states have moved much less quickly to enroll disabled Medicaid beneficiaries in managed care, owing in part to concerns about the ability of managed care plans to care for patients with complex conditions and the incentives for plans to restrict services in the face of financial risks. Under fee for service, beneficiaries were nominally free to choose their providers. But exercising that right was often difficult because many providers would not accept Medicaid patients. In a managed care system, beneficiaries may have a choice of plans, primary care providers, or both.

Yet despite the transformation of the program and the shift of the state's role from payer to prudent purchaser, establishing a competitive model for Medicaid based on beneficiary choice is difficult and could prove costly for the state and federal governments. Several factors contribute to that difficulty. States have multiple, and sometimes conflicting, goals for the program; they want to ensure access to care, improve the quality of care, control costs, and protect "safety net" providers, those that have traditionally served the Medicaid and uninsured populations. Attracting commercial plans to participate in the program can be a problem. And some beneficiaries are unable or unwilling to choose a health plan when more than one choice is available to them. Partly because of those factors, managed care has evolved differently in Medicaid than in the private sector. That evolution highlights some of the complexities of developing a competitive model for the program.

Evolution of Medicaid Managed Care

The use of managed care in Medicaid lagged behind its adoption by the private sector. Although a few states had long-standing experience with managed care models, it was not until the late 1980s that many states began to consider shifting beneficiaries from traditional fee-for-service into managed care plans.[2] That slow development resulted in part from the difficulties of attracting commercial plans into a program with low payment rates, volatile enrollment, and beneficiaries who were not familiar with managed care and often lived in areas with few providers. Federal restrictions were another obstacle. To require beneficiaries to enroll in managed care plans, states had to obtain a waiver from federal Medicaid rules, which could be a time-consuming and cumbersome process; otherwise, enrollment had to be voluntary. Getting health plans to participate was difficult if states could not guarantee a minimum level of enrollment, as was the case under a system of voluntary enrollment.

MANAGED CARE MODELS IN MEDICAID. The managed care models that Medicaid uses differ somewhat from those in the private sector. They are of essentially three types:[3]

—Primary care case management (PCCM) programs under which enrollees sign up with a primary care physician who acts as their case manager and receives a small monthly fee per enrollee for acting as a gatekeeper. All reimbursement is on a fee-for-service basis, and providers bear no financial risk.

—Full risk capitation plans that receive a monthly capitation payment per enrollee and are at full financial risk for a comprehensive package of health benefits. Most of those types of plans are health maintenance organizations (HMOs), but Medicaid programs in a few states also use health insuring organizations (HIOs), which receive capitation payments from the state and then contract with other plans and providers to provide care.

—Prepaid health plans (PHPs) that contract with states to provide a limited range of services to an enrolled population, either on a capitation or a nonrisk basis. Such plans are usually sponsored by clinics or large group practices.

GROWTH OF PCCM. Among those models, PCCM is almost unique to Medicaid and formed the basis for much of the growth in Medicaid managed care in the early 1990s. For some states, the initial impetus for shifting to managed care was to improve access to care for Medicaid beneficiaries rather than to contain costs. Low Medicaid fees often made it difficult for beneficiaries to find providers who accepted Medicaid patients. Shifting to managed care meant that providers had a contractual obligation to serve their enrolled clients, and beneficiaries knew they had a place where they could receive care other than the hospital emergency room. PCCM provided states, especially those with limited experience with managed care, with a low-cost and low-risk way of establishing contractual obligations between physicians and Medicaid beneficiaries. It also served as a transition mechanism for beneficiaries from fee-for-service to more constrained forms of managed care such as HMOs.

Also contributing to the growth of PCCM programs were the federal waiver requirements. The waiver criteria incorporated some voucher principles by explicitly requiring that beneficiaries should have the right to choose either among plans or primary care providers when a traditional fee-for-service option was no longer available to them. Under the most common form of waiver that would allow mandatory enrollment in managed care (known as a "freedom-of-choice" waiver under section 1915[b] of the Social Security Act), states had to give beneficiaries at least one of two options: a choice of health plan from two or more plans; or a choice of primary care provider in a PCCM program. So a state could mandate enrollment in PCCM without offering any other plan choices, which some states regarded as the simpler of the two options.

SHIFT TO FULL-RISK PLANS. Growing numbers of states obtained waivers in the 1990s, and enrollment in managed care plans soared from less than 10 percent of total Medicaid enrollment in 1991 to more than 50 percent in 1998.[4] By mid-1998 every state except Alaska and Wyoming was using some form of Medicaid managed care.[5] PCCM, which accounted for only about 12 percent of managed care enrollment in 1991, grew to account for 31 percent in 1995 and then fell back to 22 percent in 1997. That decline reflects attempts by the states to shift more beneficiaries into full-risk capitation plans as controlling costs became an increasingly important goal.

The move to mandatory enrollment in full-risk plans meant that more states were obligated to provide their Medicaid beneficiaries with a choice of plans—a situation that, from the beneficiary's perspective, is similar to having a voucher. That federal requirement continues today, despite the provisions in the Balanced Budget Act of 1997 (BBA) that eliminated the waiver requirement for mandatory enrollment in managed care, making it much easier for states to expand their managed care initiatives. The BBA requires states to offer beneficiaries a choice of at least two plans, except in rural areas and in certain counties in California.

As states are eager to continue to shift beneficiaries into managed care, including now their disabled populations, this arguably would be an ideal time to convert the Medicaid program into a full voucher system. Under that approach, beneficiaries would receive a broad choice of health plans. The state and federal governments would make a fixed contribution to the premium, regardless of the plan chosen, and allow competition among private health plans to control costs. But there are several barriers to the development of a voucher system.

Barriers to Implementing a Voucher System in Medicaid

Developing a competitive market in Medicaid is a much more complex undertaking than the recent surge in managed care enrollment might suggest. The number of health plans from which Medicaid beneficiaries may choose varies widely both within and among states, depending on the willingness of commercial and noncommercial plans to participate. Key factors affecting participation are payment rates, the volatility of Medicaid enrollment, the experience of plans in serving low-income and disabled clients, and the willingness or ability of plans to provide services in traditionally underserved areas. Those factors have contributed to the growth of Medicaid-dominated plans that have few commercial clients. Effective development of a competitive model has also been hindered on the demand side, as many beneficiaries do not exercise their right to choose.

MEDICAID PAYMENT RATES. As with many types of voucher-like programs, establishing appropriate payment rates for Medicaid managed care plans is difficult. States want both to control Medicaid costs and to ensure that beneficiaries have access to appropriate care—goals that inherently conflict.

The rates that states pay managed care plans have generally been based on Medicaid fee-for-service payment rates, which are often low. Moreover, because states are seeking to generate savings from managed care, they typically negotiate rates or cap bids at a percentage of the average fee-for-service per capita amount. Currently, anticipated savings on the order of 5 to 10 percent of average fee-for-service costs are fairly typical, although some states have sought considerably higher savings.[6] Not only are payment rates low, but also any adjustments to reflect differences in the characteristics of enrolled populations are rudimentary, and few states have developed systems that adjust payments to plans to reflect the health status of their enrollees.[7]

In setting payment rates, states face a potential trade-off between price and choice. In a noncompetitive world, guaranteeing plans a minimum volume of patients enables states to pay relatively low rates. As more plans enter the marketplace, that guarantee no longer exists, making it difficult for states both to drive hard bargains and to keep multiple plans in the system. Illinois, for example, announced in August 1998 that it was raising payment rates for managed care plans to improve access to care for Medicaid beneficiaries. That action followed the withdrawal of four Chicago plans from the Medicaid program because of low payment rates.[8] Low patient volume was a particularly serious problem for those plans because Illinois did not require Medicaid beneficiaries to enroll in managed care plans.

States face a similar trade-off between price and quality of care. Health plans complain that they are being squeezed by low Medicaid payment rates and growing regulatory requirements that increase their costs.[9]

Consequently, some of them are dropping out of the program. Such complaints are likely to increase as the BBA established several new patient protection standards that plans will have to meet. Some experts believe that those provisions will trigger a further exodus from the Medicaid program if states do not raise their payments to cover the additional costs.

VOLATILITY OF ENROLLMENT. Volatility of enrollment is also a significant factor affecting the interest of plans in participating in Medicaid. Many low-income families rotate on and off Medicaid as their income fluctuates. But few states have taken advantage of the federal option to grant a minimum period of eligibility to children, regardless of changes in their family income—presumably because of the cost.

Enrollment volatility is a particular problem for plans serving Medicaid beneficiaries, because the program allows eligible people to sign up at any time during the year. Consequently, people tend to enroll when they are sick and need health services. If they drop out of the plan shortly thereafter, plans that are receiving capitation payments and are at financial risk may not be able to recoup their costs. From a quality of care perspective, moreover, plans have little incentive to provide preventive health services to beneficiaries who are likely to be enrolled for only short periods.

As a result of the BBA, however, more states may guarantee a minimum period of eligibility for Medicaid enrollees in managed care plans.[10] Before the act, states could guarantee up to six months of eligibility for children. They also had the option of guaranteeing six months of eligibility to Medicaid beneficiaries enrolled in federally qualified HMOs and certain other types of prepaid health plans. The BBA extended that option to cover all types of managed care, including PCCM, and also allowed states to raise the guaranteed eligibility period for children to twelve months.

CHARACTERISTICS OF MEDICAID BENEFICIARIES. The sociodemographic and health status characteristics of Medicaid beneficiaries pose major challenges for health plans. Poverty and fragmented lifestyles make it difficult for Medicaid beneficiaries to keep medical appointments, comply with treatment regimens, or fully understand the constraints that managed care imposes. Inappropriate use of emergency rooms tends to be high. In addition, states have now enrolled most of their nondisabled Medicaid populations in managed care, and some are now enrolling the disabled. Many commercial plans have little experience in serving disabled beneficiaries, who typically have complex and expensive health care needs.

SERVICE PROVISION IN MEDICALLY UNDERSERVED AREAS. Adding to the complications of serving Medicaid beneficiaries is the fact that many of them live in areas such as the inner city, which have few medical providers except for those that have traditionally served low-income neighborhoods, such as community-based health care organizations and large public hospitals. Commercial health plans, therefore, sometimes have few providers with whom to contract, other than traditional providers, who may have little experience in contracting with managed care plans or may have set up competing plans of their own.[11]

Some states require commercial plans, as a condition for Medicaid participation, to contract with traditional, or safety net, providers, which are heavily dependent on Medicaid revenues.[12] Such requirements reflect the concerns of states that those providers should not be squeezed out of the market when Medicaid contracts with commercial plans. But forcing plans to contract with safety net providers makes it more difficult for them to control their costs.

Other Medicaid beneficiaries live in rural areas where there are fewer potential enrollees among whom to spread risk, providers are sparse and often resistant to managed care, and the commercial managed care market is relatively undeveloped.[13] Consequently, managed care plans in rural areas are more likely to use a PCCM model than those in urban areas. Some states are using a variety of contracting strategies to encourage the development of risk-based Medicaid managed care plans in rural areas. Those strategies range from sharing financial risks with plans to requiring plans to serve rural Medicaid markets as a condition for participating in the Medicaid program. States are also loosening their access standards for managed care plans in rural areas and giving plans more flexibility to determine who may be considered a primary care provider. Whether such strategies will encourage more plans to move into rural areas is uncertain. It seems unlikely, however, that voucher models could function effectively in rural areas or that efforts to expand Medicaid managed care in those areas would result in lower costs.

COMMERCIAL VERSUS MEDICAID-DOMINATED PLANS. Despite the apparent disincentives for health plans to participate in Medicaid, the number of participating HMOs and HMO-like plans—those that are at financial risk for providing a comprehensive package of services—has grown rapidly, rising from 166 in 1993 to 355 in 1996, with enrollment growing from 8 percent of beneficiaries to 23 percent.[14] Recent indications suggest, however, that those plans did not always anticipate the difficulties they would experience. Some major commercial plans, citing low payment rates and other difficulties, are withdrawing from the Medicaid program or reducing their coverage in several states, including Arizona, California, Connecticut, Florida, Illinois, Massachusetts, Missouri, New York, North Carolina, Ohio, Oregon, Texas, and Utah.[15]

Most of the rapid growth of Medicaid enrollment in risk-based plans has occurred among plans in which the large majority of enrollees are Medicaid beneficiaries. Some of those plans are sponsored by community-based health organizations and public hospitals. Others are sponsored by private companies seeking to serve the Medicaid population. More than 60 percent of the risk-based plans entering the Medicaid market between 1993 and 1996 were new enterprises, and the large majority of those new plans were Medicaid-only plans, with more than 90 percent of their enrollees in Medicaid.[16]

The surge in plans that primarily serve the Medicaid market raises important policy questions for states about competition in the marketplace, the survival of safety net providers, and quality of care for Medicaid beneficiaries. In principle, the increase in the number of plans offers beneficiaries more choice. But Medicaid-only plans tend to be relatively small and, hence, vulnerable to swings in enrollment. With low payment rates, their financial viability is threatened if states cannot guarantee them some minimum level of enrollment, effectively limiting the number of plans with which the state may contract if it wants them to survive.

California, for example, has adopted a two-plan model for Medicaid managed care in twelve counties in the state. Under that model, the state selects a single commercial plan to operate in each county, and the county establishes a competing nonprofit health plan; Medicaid beneficiaries may choose from one of the two. But declining overall Medicaid enrollment in California is causing the state to consider dropping the two-plan model in some counties, because enrollment is falling to levels at which plan solvency is threatened.[17] Several California counties are now pushing to have the county-sponsored plan as the only choice for Medicaid beneficiaries. While that change would, in theory, eliminate beneficiary choice, it may make little practical difference, because in many counties the provider networks for the two plans are essentially the same.

Predicting the future course of Medicaid managed care markets is difficult because considerable churning seems to be occurring at present, with new plans entering the market and others leaving or consolidating. Researchers at the Urban Institute maintain that the use of commercial HMOs is becoming more common in the thirteen states that they are studying, but those plans may be more costly than Medicaid-only plans, reducing any potential savings from managed care.[18] Other industry experts believe that commercial plans are the most likely to withdraw from Medicaid markets if payment rates do not rise to cover the cost increases resulting from the new regulatory requirements in the BBA.[19] They anticipate that community-based plans, which are often run by traditional Medicaid providers, will stay in the market and get an enrollment boost if commercial plans drop out. In the future, therefore, some Medicaid markets will probably be served by plans with few or no commercial enrollees, and in some markets there may be little or no choice of plan.

Experts disagree on the impact of those outcomes on the quality of care for Medicaid beneficiaries. Medicaid-only plans that are sponsored by safety net providers are familiar with the needs of low-income patients and are more willing to serve disabled beneficiaries. But lack of choice raises the possibility of having a separate system of care for Medicaid beneficiaries, with no competitive incentives for plans to provide higher quality care. Moreover, plans with a low percentage of commercial enrollees have few alternative sources of revenue, making it difficult for them to maintain services if states freeze or cut Medicaid payment rates.[20]

BARRIERS ON THE DEMAND SIDE OF THE MARKET. Characteristics of the demand as well as the supply side of the Medicaid managed care market affect the feasibility of establishing a consumer-choice model. For such a model to function effectively, beneficiaries have to be able and willing to make informed choices about their health plans. But for various reasons, many Medicaid beneficiaries who are required to enroll in managed care plans do not exercise their right to choose, resulting in states assigning them to plans—a process known as "autoassignment." Because of definitional differences, comparing autoassignment rates among the states is difficult. Nonetheless, there appears to be considerable variation, with some states and areas reporting rates in the range of 40 to 50 percent.[21]

High rates of autoassignment may indicate that states have not provided beneficiaries with appropriate information and assistance, and some states are now using enrollment brokers to help address that problem. But failure to choose a plan may also reflect that, for some beneficiaries, choice of plan is not particularly meaningful, which would be understandable in areas in which plans are using essentially the same provider networks. Or choice of provider may be more important to Medicaid beneficiaries than choice of plan.[22]

Under ordinary circumstances, the failure of some beneficiaries to choose health plans would reduce competition. But some states are now using the autoassignment process to further their policy goals, as plans seem eager to enroll beneficiaries who do not voluntarily select a plan. Some states apparently believe that such beneficiaries have better health status than Medicaid enrollees overall, making them attractive to health plans. A recent study on autoassignment, however, argues that there is little evidence to support that claim. Rather, plans want to increase their covered lives, and that is why they are interested in enrolling autoassignees.[23] According to the Urban Institute researchers, states may establish autoassignment policies that reward higher quality plans, those that have lower premiums, or those that have higher enrollment rates before autoassignment.[24] Thus at least some states are attempting to inject competitive forces into a system in which individual choice may not be a particularly effective tool at present.

Those state policies may have to change in the future, however, as a result of the BBA, which grants states new flexibility to establish mandatory managed care programs. The default enrollment process for those programs must meet certain criteria. (Existing programs established under waivers would not be affected.) Autoassignment policies for new mandatory programs must "take into consideration" maintaining existing provider-beneficiary relationships or relationships with traditional Medicaid providers. If those providers are not available, states must distribute enrollees equitably among the available, qualified managed care organizations. States establishing new mandatory managed care programs under the BBA provisions will, therefore, have more difficulty in using default enrollment processes to generate competition among plans.[25]

Competition and Consumer Choice in S-CHIP

Since the demise of the president's health care reform initiative in 1994, both the president and Congress have moved away from comprehensive proposals to expand health coverage for the uninsured. Instead, they have pursued more incremental approaches that target particular subgroups of the population. Reflecting that philosophy, the Balanced Budget Act of 1997 provided about $40 billion over the 1998–2007 period to establish the State Children's Health Insurance Program (S-CHIP). Because the funds are capped, the program is an entitlement for states but not for individuals.

S-CHIP provides federal matching funds to states, with higher federal matching rates than in the Medicaid program, to expand health insurance coverage for uninsured low-income children who are ineligible for Medicaid. States may cover children with family income up to the greater of 200 percent of the poverty level or 50 percentage points above the state's income eligibility standard for Medicaid that was in effect before the BBA.

The program gives the states considerably more flexibility than they have in the Medicaid program. They may choose to cover uninsured children by expanding Medicaid, establishing a separate health insurance program for children, providing services directly through community-based organizations (although only a limited amount of S-CHIP funds may be used for that purpose), or using a combination of those approaches. States that adopt a Medicaid approach must follow all of Medicaid's rules and restrictions on covered benefits and cost sharing. But those adopting a separate model may use a less comprehensive benefit package (provided that covered benefits meet certain standards specified in the act). They may also impose premiums and cost-sharing requirements, within limits, for children in families with income above 150 percent of the poverty level.

Approaches Adopted by the States

As of February 1999, forty-eight states, the District of Columbia, Puerto Rico, and three of the territories had submitted S-CHIP plans to the Health Care Financing Administration (HCFA), of which fifty had been approved.[26] More than half of the plans proposed to expand Medicaid, while others proposed either to establish separate health plans for children or to use a combination approach. Several of the states that submitted Medicaid expansion proposals indicated that those expansions were just the first step of a two-stage process and that they might adopt private programs in the second phase. Some of them have subsequently submitted amendments to their original plans. Alabama, for example, the first state to have an S-CHIP plan approved by the HCFA, proposed initially to expand Medicaid coverage for all poor children up to age nineteen. In August 1998 Alabama became the first state to have the second phase of an S-CHIP plan approved. That state is now establishing a separate health insurance program for children between 100 percent and 200 percent of the poverty level.

The S-CHIP plans indicate that states are employing a wide variety of approaches for covering children. Benefit packages, premiums, and cost-sharing requirements, for example, differ among the states' programs. Some states are giving children no choice of plan, while others allow families to choose from several qualifying plans. And some states want to use their S-CHIP funds to subsidize employer-sponsored insurance.

ALLOWING CHOICE OF PLAN. Many states are building their S-CHIP programs around the same network of providers that Medicaid uses, even if they are establishing a separate children's health insurance program. In those states, choice of plan depends on the choices that Medicaid allows. Because of volatility of income and the requirement that children who are eligible for Medicaid should be enrolled in that program rather than S-CHIP, children are likely to bounce between Medicaid and S-CHIP. Using the same provider networks allows children to stay with the same plan when their eligibility status changes, which is a priority for some states.[27]

Other factors also affect states' decisions on whether to restrict or encourage plan choice. As in Medicaid, being able to guarantee volume gives states and localities considerable market power in negotiating with health plans or in soliciting competitive bids. It also keeps the administrative costs of plans low, because they incur minimal marketing costs. But guaranteeing volume means limiting choice.

The Florida S-CHIP program, for example, is an expansion of the state's existing Healthy Kids initiative. The program now accepts competitive bids from health plans to serve uninsured children ages five to eighteen who are ineligible for Medicaid and whose family income is less than 200 percent of the poverty level.[28] Plans bid on a county-by-county basis and, until recently, only one contract was awarded per county. In 1998, however, the directors of the program decided to allow a choice of health plans in areas or counties in which enrollment was likely to exceed ten thousand children. By the fall of 1999, three of Florida's largest counties were to have a choice of plans. Other, smaller, counties will continue to have a single plan.

Other states that are establishing separate children's health insurance programs are encouraging multiple plans to participate. In those states, allowing choice is a priority. Michigan, for example, plans to contract with any licensed HMO or PPO that is willing to sign a contract.[29] And California plans to establish a health insurance purchasing pool modeled after the California Public Employees Retirement System (CalPERS).[30]

SUBSIDIZING EMPLOYER-SPONSORED COVERAGE. A few states have expressed interest in using S-CHIP funds to subsidize employer-sponsored family coverage. The BBA allows states to use that approach if they can demonstrate that it is more cost effective than covering the children alone in a separate program. But that cost-effectiveness criterion is difficult to meet.[31] As of January 1999, the HCFA had approved plans from Massachusetts and Wisconsin to use S-CHIP funds to provide coverage for families but had not ruled on a request from Illinois, which enacted legislation to cover families in August 1998. The approval of the Wisconsin request came only after months of wrangling between the state and the HCFA, which initially rejected the Wisconsin proposal.

From the perspective of the states, subsidizing employer-sponsored coverage gives them the biggest "bang for the buck," because for the same expenditure of state dollars, they can provide coverage for uninsured adults as well as their children. Over time, however, program costs could rise significantly because of the potential for public subsidies to displace private premium payments.

Subsidizing employer-sponsored coverage also lacks most features of a voucher model. In particular:

—As many employers offer only one health plan, enrollees may have no choice of plan;

—The government's contribution varies for families at the same income level, as do the benefits that they receive and the cost-sharing that they incur; and

—If an employer's plan is self-insured, it is subject to much less state regulation than the other plans in which S-CHIP beneficiaries may enroll.

Oregon is offering low-income families an intriguing choice between employer-sponsored and other coverage, the results of which will be interesting to track. In the summer of 1998 the state initiated a state-funded program, independent of S-CHIP, to subsidize family coverage for uninsured families with income up to 170 percent of the poverty level.[32] To participate in the program, families must insure their children—that is, they may cover themselves only if they cover their children, but they may elect to cover their children and not themselves—and those with access to employer-sponsored coverage must enroll in their employer's plan. Premium subsidies are on a sliding scale.

The state has determined that many children who will be eligible for the state's S-CHIP program, which will essentially parallel the Medicaid program, will also be eligible for the family subsidy program. But unlike the family program, S-CHIP will charge no premiums and have no cost sharing. The state intends to allow families who qualify for both programs to choose between enrolling their children at no cost in S-CHIP; paying an income-related premium to enroll their children in a private plan; or paying a higher income-related premium to enroll the whole family in a private plan. In that way, the state is hoping to use subsidies to preserve rather than undermine employer-sponsored coverage in the state. But there is considerable uncertainty about the choices that low-income families will make and how those choices may change over time with swings in the economy.

Displacement of Private Coverage

The BBA required states to take measures to ensure that insurance programs established under S-CHIP do not displace private insurance. Nonetheless, some displacement is inevitable, which will raise the costs of the program.

To limit the substitution of public for private insurance, most states are requiring a minimum waiting period of several months without private coverage before a child may enroll in S-CHIP. But such policies do not really address the underlying ways in which displacement is likely to occur. In the short term, one would not expect low-income workers with family coverage, or their employers, to drop coverage of dependents as a result of S-CHIP. But the target population for the program is near-poor children (those with income between 100 percent and 200 percent of the poverty level), many of whom have private insurance coverage some of the time. If such children enroll in the program after their parents have lost access to employer-sponsored coverage, they may well stay enrolled in S-CHIP when their parents regain access to private coverage. One might argue that establishing stable coverage for children whose insurance status is inherently volatile is a positive outcome for the program, but it is an outcome that involves some displacement of private coverage.

Over the long term, labor markets will adapt to the presence of federal subsidies for health care. Newly established small firms will be less likely to offer dependent coverage if a subsidized program is available for children. And low-wage workers, knowing that they can get public coverage for their children, will seek out firms that offer higher cash wages in lieu of health insurance.

Evaluating the S-CHIP Program

The different strategies that states are adopting in S-CHIP provide health policy researchers with a rich social experiment to assess the effects of price and choice on the participation of low-income families in health insurance programs and on their satisfaction with those programs. But some states are going to be hard pressed to conduct extensive evaluations of their programs, and many policy questions will be answerable only through comparative studies conducted at the national level. One hopes, therefore, that the health policy research community will rise to the challenge of evaluating S-CHIP, focusing on important policy questions for improving the program in the future.

Tax Subsidies for Employer-Sponsored Coverage

In addition to direct outlays for Medicaid and S-CHIP, the federal government subsidizes health insurance coverage for the nonelderly population through the tax system. Employers' contributions for employee health insurance are exempt from both federal income and payroll taxes. The Joint Committee on Taxation estimates that those exemptions, which largely benefit people under age sixty-five, will reduce federal revenues by about $92 billion in fiscal year 2000.[33] That amount is about $20 billion more than the federal government will spend on Medicaid benefits for the nonelderly population in the same year.[34]

Current tax exemptions for health insurance generally have none of the attributes of vouchers because of the way in which they are structured and because of the contribution strategies of employers. The exemptions benefit workers whose employers contribute to their health care coverage. Workers whose employers do not contribute, people who purchase in the individual market, and the uninsured are ineligible, raising concerns about equity. Moreover, the value of the exemptions varies inversely with income. High-income workers typically gain more from the exemptions than low-income workers because they are in higher tax brackets, their employers are more likely to offer coverage, and that coverage typically has richer benefits and is more costly. In 1994 the Congressional Budget Office estimated that the federal income and the payroll tax exclusions for employer-sponsored insurance, in conjunction with the corresponding exemptions from state income taxes, could reduce the after-tax cost of health insurance by half for some taxpayers in the upper brackets.[35]

Effects of Firm Size on Choice

The amount of choice among plans and providers that workers have, as well as the likelihood that their employer offers coverage at all, varies significantly by firm size. In 1993 fewer than half of all establishments with fewer than 50 employees offered health insurance to their workers, compared with more than 90 percent of establishments with 50 or more employees.[36] (Note, however, that employees of firms that do not offer coverage are not necessarily uninsured. Many of them obtain coverage elsewhere, frequently through an employed spouse.)

Moreover, in 1996, 80 percent of firms with fewer than 200 employees that provided coverage offered only one plan.[37] Enrolling in that plan was the only way that employees could benefit from a tax subsidy if they did not have access to employer-sponsored coverage through a spouse. If, for example, they wanted indemnity coverage and their employer offered only an HMO, they could, in theory, purchase coverage in the individual market. But not only would the premium be considerably higher, they would also have to pay the full amount out of after tax-dollars.[38] Large firms, by contrast, are much more likely to offer their employees a choice of plans.

Although choice of plan is severely constrained in most small firms, the majority of workers who obtain coverage through small employers retain the right to choose their providers, albeit sometimes at considerable additional cost to themselves. In 1996 between 20 and 25 percent of firms with fewer than 200 employees that offered coverage to their workers offered only an HMO.[39] The remainder offered indemnity, PPO, or POS plans, all of which allow freedom of choice of provider. Being able to choose a provider presumably mitigates some of the dissatisfaction that employees express when they have no choice of plan.[40] But enrollees who seek care outside a PPO or POS plan's network may face significantly higher cost-sharing payments than if they stay in the network.

In several states, including Florida, Colorado, California, and North Carolina, small employers have been able to expand the plan choices available to their employees by joining consumer-choice health insurance purchasing groups. While most health insurance purchasing cooperatives offer choices to employers, the consumer-choice groups offer choices to individual employees. Typically, those groups establish a set of standardized benefits that health plans must offer plus reporting requirements and other criteria they must meet.[41] (Standardized benefits facilitate price and quality comparisons among health plans.) The purchasing group solicits bids from health plans, contracting with those that offer the best value, and provides employees with comparative price and performance information. Employees may select the plan of their choice, and the employer makes a single premium payment to the purchasing group.

Such purchasing groups provide workable models for expanding competition and choice in the small group market. How closely they approximate voucher systems depends on the contribution strategies of their member employers. Developing those strategies can be quite complicated, because the participating health plans are selling to individual employees, not employers. Consequently, they want to charge premiums that vary according to age and other factors, insofar as state rating laws allow such variation. Employers, however, want to be able to make a composite contribution for each of their employees. The simplest strategy of tying the employer's contribution to some reference plan offered through the cooperative may result in an approach that is close to a voucher model, although it is unclear how widely that strategy is used.

Selling directly to employees also raises the possibility that plans will experience adverse selection. For that reason, some insurers are unwilling to participate in purchasing cooperatives that offer consumer choice.[42] The purchasing group, however, provides a vehicle for making risk- adjustment payments to health plans that enroll higher percentages of costly patients. The consumer-choice purchasing cooperative in California is leading the way in attempting to develop such adjusters, although much more research is needed.[43]

Contribution Policies of Large Firms

Although large firms typically offer their employees more choice of health plans than do small firms, the contribution policies of most large employers do not foster price sensitivity among their employees when selecting plans. Consequently, federal tax subsidies are typically larger for employees who choose costlier plans. A recent study of employers' contribution practices in 1995, for example, found that most large employers who offered multiple plans made larger contributions for plans with higher premiums.[44] In that year only 7 percent of large firms offered multiple plans and made a level contribution to the premium, regardless of the plan chosen by the employee. A further 40 percent offered one plan only, and 53 percent offered multiple plans and made higher contributions for costlier plans.

Even the Federal Employees Health Benefits Plan (FEHBP), which offers employees a broad choice of health plans and is often viewed as a prototype of a competitive model for other groups in the population, is not a defined-contribution plan. Employees who choose more costly plans receive a larger subsidy than those who select plans with lower premiums, although the amount contributed by the federal government is capped.

Employers may be cautious about switching to a flat contribution policy because of the adverse selection among plans that may result in the absence of risk adjustment. Adverse selection can cause premiums for higher-cost plans to spiral, eventually forcing employers to drop them. That phenomenon has occurred in the FEHBP and also in the University of California's employee benefits program, which uses a flat contribution.[45]

Changes in Health Care Markets

Current tax exemptions for employer-sponsored health insurance encourage people to purchase insurance and also provide incentives for that coverage to be more comprehensive than otherwise.[46] Despite those incentives, however, health care markets saw a significant slowing of premium growth in recent years, following several years of double-digit rate increases. That reduction in premium growth resulted from employers shifting away from indemnity coverage to various forms of managed care plans, and from plans competing to maintain or expand their market shares.

Now a backlash against managed care plans is emerging from several quarters. Employees increasingly resent the constraints that strict managed care plans impose. Stockholders in managed care companies, by contrast, are concerned about the weak financial performance of plans, which have held their premiums down in an effort to gain market share. Premiums, therefore, began to rise more rapidly in 1998, and higher growth is predicted for 1999, as employers shift to less tightly managed options and plans raise premiums to bolster their profit margins.[47] If higher premium growth persists, policymakers may begin to focus their attention again on the incentives that current tax exemptions provide. Equity concerns are also coming to the fore as growing numbers of Americans lack insurance coverage and receive no subsidy, and those numbers will increase if premiums rise significantly.

New Strategies and Policy Options

Concerns about the growing numbers of people who are uninsured and the inequities of existing tax subsidies have prompted a range of proposals to expand health insurance coverage. Some of these proposals target specific subgroups of the insured population, while others focus on changing tax incentives.

Targeting Specific Population Groups

Some policymakers view S-CHIP as the first step in an incremental approach to expanding health insurance coverage to the entire population and have proposed a variety of initiatives targeting other groups in the population. In 1998 the Clinton administration proposed new health insurance subsidies for two groups that lack access to employer-sponsored insurance: displaced workers fifty-five to sixty-one years old, who have exhausted their benefits under COBRA (the Consolidated Budget Reconciliation Act of 1985, which required employers offering group health plans to allow workers leaving their jobs to continue coverage under the employers' plans); and people sixty-two to sixty-four years old who lack coverage from other sources. The president included similar proposals in his proposed budget for 2000.

BUYING INTO MEDICARE. The administration proposed that people in both of those groups be allowed to buy into Medicare. Displaced workers would be implicitly subsidized by Medicare because the premiums they would be required to pay would not cover the costs of their care. People aged sixty-two to sixty-four who chose to purchase Medicare coverage would receive an explicit up-front subsidy, which they would pay back gradually after reaching age sixty-five.[48]

As the Medicare+Choice program develops, opening up Medicare to other population groups would be a way to offer people receiving subsidies a choice of health plans, although in some parts of the country those options might be limited. But enrollees would be constrained to Medicare's limited benefit package and would have to pay for supplements unless they could enroll in a managed care plan that offered additional benefits.

ALTERNATIVE APPROACHES. Instead of opening up Medicare, the federal government could give people vouchers for the subsidy amount and let them choose from all the insurance options available in the individual market. But Medicare provides what the individual market does not, a mechanism for pooling risks. Left to fend for themselves in the individual market, people would face a wide range of premiums as well as exclusions for preexisting conditions, reflecting their individual health risks. Some people might not be able to purchase coverage at all.

Some states now impose limits on premium variation in the individual market, have guaranteed-issue requirements, or prohibit preexisting condition exclusions. But those states are the minority. In addition, the Health

Insurance Portability and Accountability Act of 1996 (HIPAA) guarantees that people losing group coverage will have access to coverage in the individual market, but it does nothing to protect people seeking coverage from high premiums. Not only is coverage likely to be costly in the individual market (because those who seek coverage there tend to be sicker than average), but high administrative costs result in only about 60 percent of a premium dollar being spent on benefits.

A subsidy program based on a fixed voucher amount would probably be politically untenable if people faced different premiums for the same coverage. To address that problem, the federal government could adjust the voucher amounts to reflect the relative health status and expected health care costs of individual enrollees. But given the current limitations of risk adjustment techniques, that approach seems unlikely to overcome insurers' resistance to covering potentially high-cost people—at least in the near term.[49] Moreover, even with improved methods of risk adjustment, premiums for comprehensive coverage are likely to be high in the individual market, making this form of subsidy model a costly option.

Modifying the Tax System

Because of concerns about efficiency and equity, health policy analysts frequently propose modifying the tax treatment of employer-sponsored health insurance.[50] Some proposals would essentially establish a voucher system for the purchase of health insurance with low-income individuals and families receiving the largest subsidies.

In the early 1990s, for example, Mark Pauly and colleagues suggested restructuring the tax treatment of health insurance by establishing a system of refundable, fixed-dollar tax credits.[51] People could use those credits to buy health insurance through their employers or through any other purchasing mechanism, but any payments for health insurance made by employers would be subject to income and payroll taxes. The amount of the credit would vary only by income, not by the cost of the health plan chosen, with credits phasing out as income rose. The proposal would require everyone to purchase insurance, with the minimum amount of coverage required also being inversely related to income. (The authors argued that lower-income people should be required to have more comprehensive coverage because they are less able to pay out of pocket for health care.)

C. Eugene Steuerle and Gordon Mermin have suggested using a flat tax credit for the purchase of health insurance, which would be less complex to administer and would also avoid the potentially high marginal tax rates that an income-related credit would impose.[52] Their approach would limit the existing tax exclusion for employer-sponsored coverage and substitute a uniform credit for everyone. People who did not purchase insurance would be liable for income-related penalties, and employers would be required to offer coverage for which the credit could be used.

If everyone was eligible for the same credit, however, the credit amount would have to be quite low. Otherwise the subsidies would be extremely costly. Consequently, such a credit might not purchase much coverage for low-income families who could not afford to supplement it. The same issue would arise if the tax credits were purely redistributional and only reallocated the existing tax exemptions. Recognizing that problem, the authors suggest that a compromise proposal might focus on covering children only.[53]

A major concern with any proposal that would provide subsidies for people to buy health insurance is whether efficient markets would exist in which they could purchase coverage. Today, the only alternative available to most people who do not have access to employer-sponsored insurance is to purchase coverage in the individual market. Premiums in that market are high because of adverse selection and high administrative costs, and individuals purchasing coverage are usually subject to medical underwriting. Some policy analysts who advocate shifting to a system of individual tax credits envision that many workers would still obtain coverage through their employers under the new system, as the workplace provides an effective means of pooling risks and reducing the administrative costs of insurance. Other means of pooling risks might also develop, through churches, trades associations, and schools, for example. But without government intervention, some people would probably have access to limited high-cost options only.

In a recent paper, Lynn Etheridge and Stanley Jones attempted to address that problem in a proposal to subsidize health insurance for full-time workers whose employers do not offer coverage.[54] Under their approach, the federal government would establish a fairly lean benefits package, modeled on current Medicare benefits, and invite insurers and health plans to offer that coverage through an administrative mechanism similar to that used by the FEHBP. Participants could deduct all of their premium payments from their federal taxable income, and those with no tax liability could claim a 15 percent refundable tax credit. Administrative costs would be considerably lower than in the individual market, as employers could withhold premium payments, even if they did not offer coverage. The government would also provide start-up subsidies to counteract the effects of initial adverse selection, which the authors project would decline over time.

Although such a model does not meet all of the criteria for a voucher plan—subsidies would rise with income and also with plan premiums—it could be modified to base subsidies on the premium of some average or low-cost plan. A more serious concern would be the response of employers who currently provide coverage. Erosion of employer contributions would be likely, increasing the potential costs of the subsidy program.

LEGISLATIVE PROPOSALS. As the number of people lacking insurance coverage has grown, policymakers have become increasingly interested in restructuring tax subsidies to lower the cost of insurance to uninsured people who cannot afford coverage. The 105th Congress enacted legislation to accelerate the phase in of full deductibility of premiums for the self-employed and considered proposals to allow people who purchase coverage in the individual market to deduct their premiums. Similar proposals are likely to be introduced in the 106th Congress.

Some members of Congress are considering a more radical shift in policy, comparable to the proposals to provide tax credits to individuals described above. They advocate replacing the current tax exemption for employer-paid premiums with a system of refundable tax credits for the purchase of health insurance.[55] People would have the choice of obtaining coverage through an employer (if that option was available), the individual market, or other organizations. Such a proposal would create a need for greater regulation of the individual market to limit the amount of medical underwriting and to reduce the incentives of insurers to avoid bad risks. A similar tax credit proposal has been endorsed by the American Medical Association, which envisages the establishment of alternative insurance markets in which individuals and small employers could form pools to purchase insurance.[56]

EXPERIENCE WITH THE HITC. Tax credits for the purchase of health insurance are not, in fact, new. Experience with the short-lived health insurance tax credit (HITC) established by the Omnibus Budget Reconciliation Act of 1990 provides valuable insights into the complexities of designing and implementing such programs.[57] The HITC, which existed between 1991 and 1993, allowed taxpayers who qualified for the earned income tax credit (EITC) to claim an additional tax credit if they purchased health insurance coverage for their children. The credit was 6 percent for earned income up to $7,125. Taxpayers with earned income between $7,125 and $11,275 could claim the maximum credit of $428, and the credit phased down to zero at an earned income of $21,250.

The HITC was much closer to a voucher than other existing subsidies, with beneficiaries having, in theory, an open choice of plans. But for several reasons it failed to have much impact on health insurance coverage.

—The credit was small, even for extremely low-income families. On average, it paid for less than one-quarter of the taxpayer's share of a family health insurance premium. Hence, it provided little incentive for uninsured families to purchase coverage.

—Information about the program was limited and sometimes misleading, and many people did not know that they were eligible.

—Some beneficiaries sought coverage in the individual market, and abuses by unscrupulous insurers were widespread.[58]

—The income of taxpayers who claimed the credit was 30 percent higher, on average, than that of other EITC recipients. Thus, claimants were primarily in the phaseout range of the credit, and their credit amounts were sufficiently small that they probably would have purchased coverage anyway.

The HITC program demonstrated that tax credits would have to be quite generous to encourage uninsured people to purchase coverage. That finding is consistent with other research on the impact of health insurance subsidies. (A study by researchers at RAND, for example, found that subsidies of as much as 60 percent of the premium would cause only one-quarter of uninsured working families to buy insurance.)[59] But generous subsidies give rise to a difficult policy dilemma as they increase the likelihood of imposing high marginal tax rates on some families, unless the subsidy phases out over a broad income range or is not phased out at all (as with the Steuerle and Mermin proposal). A broad phaseout range, however, increases the probability of subsidizing people who would have purchased coverage anyway.

In addition, a subsidy program based on tax credits would have to address the cash-flow problem that tax credits raise for low-income families. Otherwise tax credits would not be available until after a family had incurred a year's health insurance costs. Outreach to low-income families to explain the tax credit option and close monitoring of insurers' practices would also be essential.

What Have We Learned about Health Care Subsidies?

Over the past decade the federal and state governments have undertaken many initiatives to expand health insurance coverage for low-income uninsured people and debated multiple other initiative proposals. The HITC experiment in the early 1990s and broad expansions of Medicaid for children and pregnant women preceded the Clinton administration's failed attempt at comprehensive health care reform in 1994. Following that watershed in public policy, federal and state governments returned to more incremental approaches—further Medicaid expansions, new state programs for the uninsured, subsidies targeted at particular population groups, greater portability of health insurance, purchasing options for small employers, and changes to the current system of tax subsidies for private health insurance. Experience from the initiatives that have been enacted, as well as the debates over other options, highlight many of the complications of establishing subsidy systems for health care.

The Clinton administration's 1994 proposal was essentially a voucher system. It would have allowed everyone to have a choice of health plan, provided subsidies for low-income families, and required people who selected costlier plans to pay higher premiums. The designers discovered, however, that developing a program of universal health coverage based on choice required a fundamental restructuring of the entire health care system, which many people found to be too complex and politically untenable—hence the return to incremental approaches.

An abiding lesson from that experience is that the proposal was complicated because the existing system of health care financing is complicated. It has become even more so since 1994, with the wave of new federal and state subsidy programs as well as the dramatic changes that have occurred in private health care markets as both employers and public programs have shifted to managed care. Incremental proposals to expand health insurance coverage or to redesign existing subsidies now have to build on an extraordinarily complex financing infrastructure, and it is difficult for policymakers to foresee all of the potential responses and unintended consequences. Nonetheless, certain principles have emerged from the ongoing debate over options.

—With the rapid development of medical technologies, the potential demand for health care services is almost limitless. The growing demand for costly treatments pushes up the price of health insurance, making coverage increasingly inaccessible to low-income families.

—Subsidies or tax credits for health insurance have to be generous to encourage low-income families to purchase coverage. Because many near-poor families (those with income between 100 percent and 200 percent of the poverty level) have coverage already, at least some of the time, subsidy programs may be extremely costly as subsidies extend up the income scale, if eligibility qualifications are based solely on income. But that problem is inherent in the existing tax structure, which is both inefficient and inequitable, as well as costly. The people who benefit the most from current tax exclusions are higher-income workers, most of whom would be likely to continue to purchase coverage without a subsidy.

—In developing initiatives to subsidize health insurance, policymakers face a difficult trade-off between imposing high marginal tax rates on low-income families and incurring high subsidy costs. To reduce marginal tax rates, subsidies could be phased out over a broad income range. But the broader the range, the greater the probability of subsidizing those who would otherwise be covered.

—Building subsidy programs around employer-sponsored coverage, for those who have access to such coverage, is potentially a way to reduce public costs. But such an approach is likely to displace some existing employer contributions, causing subsidy costs to rise over time. In addition, covered benefits, premiums, and subsidy amounts will vary from individual to individual; some people receiving subsidies may have no choice of plan; and those with choices may have little incentive to be sensitive to price because of their employer's contribution policy.

—Giving low-income, uninsured people purchasing power in the market does not necessarily promote competition, lower subsidy costs, or enhance beneficiary satisfaction. People have to be able and willing to make choices. Experience in Medicaid suggests this frequently is not the case. In addition, exercising choice may be difficult if the price people face is a function of their health status, as often occurs in the individual insurance market. Government regulation can reduce price variation in the individual market but may also drive plans out of that market. Adjusting subsidy amounts for the health risks of individuals is a process that is still in its infancy.

—More generally, the market for individual insurance does not provide low-cost options for people who lack access to employer-sponsored coverage and are ineligible for public programs. Administrative costs tend to be high for insurance that is marketed to individuals, and the cost of covered benefits is high because of adverse selection in the individual market. Partly for that reason, some states have developed alternative options for uninsured people to obtain coverage, and the administration has proposed offering Medicare as an option for early retirees who lack access to employer-sponsored coverage.

—Allowing beneficiaries to have a broad choice of plans in Medicaid may require states to pay considerably more per enrollee than under a restricted managed care model. Many commercial HMOs are unwilling to serve the Medicaid population because of low payment rates, the complex social and medical needs of Medicaid beneficiaries, and the volatility of their enrollment. States cannot guarantee a minimum level of enrollment for a plan, which may help to offset the effects of low payment rates if multiple plans are participating and beneficiaries may enroll in the plan of their choice.

—The existing system of subsidies serves multiple functions, and economic efficiency may not be the highest priority for policymakers, especially those at the state level. States use the Medicaid program, for example, to subsidize providers who serve other uninsured people. Maintaining those subsidies may be an important priority as long as significant numbers of people remain uninsured.

Notes

1. Certain disabled people under age sixty-five, and most people with chronic kidney disease, are eligible for Medicare. That program is not the focus of this chapter.

2. Robert E. Hurley and Susan Wallin, "Adopting and Adapting Managed Care for Medicaid Beneficiaries: An Imperfect Translation, Assessing the New Federalism," Occasional Paper 7 (Urban Institute, June 1998).

3. Diane Rowland and Kristina Hanson, "Medicaid: Moving to Managed Care," *Health Affairs*, vol. 15 (Fall 1996), pp. 150–52.

4. Health Care Financing Administration, "Medicaid Managed Care Plan Type and National Enrollment—June 30, 1998" (http://www.hcfa.gov/medicaid/trends98.htm [June 28, 1999]).

5. Health Care Financing Administration, "Medicaid Managed Care Plan Type and Enrollment by State—June 30, 1998" (http://www.hcfa.gov/medicaid/plantyp8.htm [June 28, 1999]).

6. John Holahan and others, "Medicaid Managed Care in Thirteen States," *Health Affairs*, vol. 17 (May–June 1998), pp. 43–63.

7. In 1998 Colorado became one of the first states to implement a diagnosis-based risk-adjustment system for Medicaid managed care. See Marilyn Moon and

others, "Health Policy for Low-Income People in Colorado," Assessing the New Federalism: State Reports (Urban Institute, July 1998).

8. Bruce Japsen, "Medicaid HMO Pay Rate Raised," *Chicago Tribune*, August 27, 1998 (http://chicagotribune.com/business).

9. Geri Aston, "Widespread HMO Defections Starting to Hit Medicaid, Too," *American Medical News*, December 14, 1998, pp. 5–6; Robert Cunningham, "For Better or Worse, Medicaid Shakeout Foreshadows Aspects of M+C Exodus," *Medicine and Health, Perspectives*, November 16, 1998.

10. Sally K. Richardson, letter to state Medicaid directors on guaranteed eligibility, March 23, 1998 (www.hcfa.gov/medicaid/bbagelig.htm [June 28, 1999]).

11. Cara Lesser, Kathryn Duke, and Harold Luft, *Care for the Uninsured and Underserved in the Age of Managed Care*, report prepared for the Commonwealth Fund (New York: Commonwealth Fund, March 1997).

12. Sara Rosenbaum and others, *Negotiating the New Health System: A Nationwide Study of Medicaid Managed Care Contracts*, vol. 2, pt. 2 (George Washington University, Center for Health Policy Research, February 1997).

13. Rebecca T. Slifkin and others, "Medicaid Managed Care Programs in Rural Areas: A Fifty-State Overview," *Health Affairs*, vol. 17 (November–December 1998), pp. 217–27.

14. Suzanne Felt-Lisk and Sara Yang, "Changes in Health Plans Serving Medicaid, 1993–1996," *Health Affairs*, vol. 16 (September–October 1997), pp. 125–33.

15. Peter T. Kilborn, "Largest HMO's Cutting the Poor and the Elderly: A Managed Care Retreat," *New York Times*, July 6, 1998, p. 1; Bruce Japsen, "U. of C. Pulls Out of Medicaid Business," *Chicago Tribune*, August 18, 1998 (http://chicagotribune.com); Charles Ornstein, "Texas Blues Will Not Join Medicaid HMO in Dallas Area," *Dallas Morning News*, February 3, 1999 (www.dallasnews.com/business-nf/biz45.htm).

16. Felt-Lisk and Yang, "Changes in Health Plans Serving Medicaid, 1993–1996."

17. Leigh Page, "Medicaid Managed Care, California Style: Innovative or Ill-Conceived," *American Medical News*, vol. 42 (January 1998), p. 1.

18. Holahan and others, "Medicaid Managed Care in Thirteen States."

19. Aston, "Widespread HMO Defections."

20. Kilborn, "Largest HMO's Cutting the Poor and the Elderly."

21. General Accounting Office, *Medicaid: State Efforts to Educate and Enroll Beneficiaries in Managed Care*, GAO/HEHS-96-184 (September 1996); Len Nichols and others, "Health Policy for Low-Income People in Washington," Assessing the New Federalism: State Reports (Urban Institute, November 1997); Joshua M. Wiener and others, "Health Policy for Low-Income People in Texas," Assessing the New Federalism: State Reports (Urban Institute, November 1997).

22. Page, "Medicaid Managed Care: California Style."

23. Center for Health Care Strategies, *Auto-Enrollment into Health Plans: An Analysis of Select Provisions in Medicaid Managed Care Contracts* (http://www.chcs.org/srexec.htm [June 28, 1999]).

24. Holahan and others, "Medicaid Managed Care in Thirteen States."

25. Sally K. Richardson, letter to state Medicaid directors on enrollment, termination, and default assignment, January 21, 1998 (www.hcfa.gov/medicaid/bbadisn.htm [June 28, 1999]).

26. Health Care Financing Administration, "Child Health Insurance Program State Plans" (http://www.hcfa.gov/init/chipBmap.htm [June 28, 1999]).

27. See, for example, State of New York, *State Child Health Plan under Title XXI of the Social Security Act: State Children's Health Insurance Program* (http://www.health.state.ny.us/nysdoh/child/childhe2.pdf [June 28, 1999]).

28. *Healthy Kids Annual Report* (Tallahassee, Fla.: Florida Health Kids Corporation, 1999).

29. Denise Holmes, "Structuring Service Delivery Systems with the Capacity to Serve Children," presentation at *CHIP: Implementing Effective Programs and Understanding Their Impacts*, meeting sponsored by the Agency for Health Care Policy and Research, 1998.

30. National Conference of State Legislatures, Forum for State Health Policy Leadership, "Delivery Systems under Approved Title XXI Plans," June 8, 1998 (http://www.stateserv.hpts.org [June 28, 1999]).

31. Bureau of National Affairs, "HCFA Official Acknowledges Difficulty in Meeting CHIP Rule for Family Coverage," *BNA Health Care Daily Report*, August 31, 1998.

32. *Oregon Title XXI State Plan-Part I*, February 28, 1998.

33. Unpublished data from the Joint Committee on Taxation, January 1999. The expected revenue loss would be higher if the Department of the Treasury's estimation methods were used.

34. Congressional Budget Office, "Medicaid and State Children's Health Insurance Program, March 1999 baseline."

35. Congressional Budget Office, *The Tax Treatment of Employment-Based Health Insurance* (March 1994).

36. Centers for Disease Control and Prevention, *Employer-Sponsored Health Insurance: State and National Estimates* (Hyattsville, Md.: National Center for Health Statistics, 1997). These rates, which are based on a random sample of employers nationwide, are considerably lower than those reported by KPMG Peat Marwick in its annual surveys of employers.

37. Jon R. Gabel, Paul B. Ginsburg, and Kelly A. Hunt, "Small Employers and Their Health Benefits, 1988–1996: An Awkward Adolescence," *Health Affairs*, vol. 16 (September–October 1997), pp. 103–10.

38. Self-employed taxpayers may, however, deduct part of the cost of their health insurance premiums when determining their adjusted gross income. As a result of the Omnibus Consolidated and Emergency Appropriations Act for fiscal

1999, those taxpayers may deduct 45 percent of the amount they paid for health insurance in 1998. That percentage rises to 60 percent for the period 1999–2001, 70 percent for 2002, and 100 percent for 2003 and thereafter.

39. Thomas Rice and others, *Trends in Job-Based Health Insurance Coverage*, report for the Henry J. Kaiser Family Foundation (Los Angeles: UCLA Center for Health Policy Research, June 1998).

40. Karen Davis and Cathy Schoen, *Managed Care, Choice, and Patient Satisfaction*, report for the Commonwealth Fund (New York, August 1997); Karen Davis and Cathy Schoen, "Assuring Quality, Information, and Choice in Managed Care," *Inquiry*, vol. 35 (Summer 1998), pp. 104–14.

41. Institute for Health Policy Solutions, "Consumer-Choice Health Purchasing Groups (CHPGs)" (http://www.ihps.org/CHPGs.html [June 28, 1999]).

42. "Reforms Don't Protect Group Purchasing Schemes from Marketplace Vicissitudes," *Medicine and Health Perspectives* (May 17, 1999).

43. John Bertko and Sandra Hunt, "Case Study: The Health Insurance Plan of California," *Inquiry*, vol. 35 (Summer 1998), pp. 148–53.

44. Kelly A. Hunt and others, "Paying More Twice: When Employers Subsidize Higher-Cost Plans," *Health Affairs*, vol. 16 (November–December 1997), pp. 150–56.

45. Walton Francis, "Federal Employees' Health Benefits Program: Promises and Pitfalls," presentation at the American Enterprise Institute conference "Medicare Reform—What Can the Private Sector Teach Us?", 1995; Thomas C. Buchmueller, "Does a Fixed Dollar Premium Contribute to Lower Spending?" *Health Affairs*, vol. 17 (November–December 1998), pp. 228–35.

46. Congressional Budget Office, *The Tax Treatment of Employment-Based Health Insurance*.

47. Ron Winslow, "Measurement of HMO Membership Falls for First Time," *Wall Street Journal*, January 26, 1999, p. B7; Andrea Gerlin, "Health Costs Soar for Area Employers," *Philadelphia Inquirer*, January 26, 1999 (www.phillynew.../inquirer/99/Jan/26/city/HMO26.htm).

48. Congressional Budget Office, "The Administration's Medicare Buy-in Proposals," *An Analysis of the President's Budgetary Proposals for Fiscal Year 1999* (March 1998), app. B.

49. The experience of the Medicare program demonstrates the difficulties of developing adequate mechanisms for risk adjustment. Medicare adjusts payments to managed-care plans to reflect demographic and other characteristics of their enrollees. Those adjustments, however, account for just 1 percent of the variation in health care costs among beneficiaries. The BBA required the HCFA to implement an expanded risk adjustment system in 2000. The first phase of that system, however, will be based on inpatient hospital use only because data for other sites of service are not yet available. Such an adjustment could introduce perverse incentives for inpatient treatment.

50. Congressional Budget Office, *The Tax Treatment of Employment-Based Health Insurance*.

51. Mark V. Pauly and others, *Responsible National Health Insurance* (Washington, D.C.: AEI Press, 1992).

52. C. Eugene Steuerle and Gordon B. T. Mermin, "A Better Subsidy for Health Insurance," in Grace-Marie Arnett, ed., *Empowering Health Care Consumers through Tax Reform* (Alexandria, Va.: Galen Institute, forthcoming).

53. A similar proposal to subsidize children's coverage through tax credits was the subject of an earlier article by Steuerle. That article also discusses former president Bush's tax credit proposal. See C. Eugene Steuerle, "Beyond Paralysis in Health Policy: A Proposal to Focus on Children," *National Tax Journal*, vol. 14 (September 1992), pp. 357–68.

54. Lynn Etheridge and Stanley B. Jones, "Affordable Health Benefits for Workers without Employer Coverage," *Research Agenda Brief*, Health Insurance Reform Project (George Washington University, February 1998).

55. Marilyn Werber Serafini, "An Overture, Again, on Health Reform," *National Journal*, December 12, 1998, pp. 29–33.

56. Geri Aston, "AMA Access Plan Stresses Individual Choice," *American Medical News*, January 4, 1999, pp. 5–6.

57. General Accounting Office, *Health Insurance Tax Credit Participation Rate Was Low*, GAO/GGD-94-99 (May 1994); General Accounting Office, *Administrative Aspects of the Health Insurance Tax Credit*, GAO/GGD-91-110FS (September 1991).

58. House Committee on Ways and Means, Subcommittee on Oversight, *Report on Marketing Abuse and Administrative Problems Involving the Health Insurance Component of the Earned Income Tax Credit*, WMCP: 103-14 (Government Printing Office, 1993).

59. M. Susan Marquis and Stephen H. Long, "Worker Demand for Health Insurance in the Non-Group Market," *Journal of Health Economics*, vol. 14 (May 1995), pp. 47–63.

PART THREE

Design

ROBERT LERMAN
C. EUGENE STEUERLE

16

Structured Choice versus Fragmented Choice: Bundling of Vouchers

Vouchers to help low-income families purchase necessities or merit goods have attractive properties. They provide increased purchasing power and a choice of providers for a particular service or good.[1] When structured appropriately, vouchers can meet high standards of horizontal and vertical equity so long as they offer equal benefits to families in the same circumstances and the voucher benefits (less taxes paid) decline gradually with increased income. Using vouchers, the government can openly choose how best to reconcile conflicting goals of concentrating benefits on those with greater needs and providing reasonable financial incentives to work.

Although a single voucher may have these and other advantages, the issue becomes more complicated when the government creates multiple income-related vouchers and other subsidies. Each additional program—whether in education, child care, or any other service—magnifies coordination problems with respect to the amount of choice offered, restrictions on what is still proscribed, level of income support, effective tax rates on additional income, administrative duplication, and transaction costs. In this chapter, we examine one way out of the dilemma: pulling together two or more programs into a "bundled voucher." As one of us has argued, *structured choice* is a suitable label for a bundled or combined voucher,

471

because it allows more choice than a set of individual vouchers yet still requires more structure than cash assistance.[2]

Structured Choice and the Negative Income Tax Paradigm

In the 1960s proposals for a negative income tax began to gain momentum. The arguments that were used were the following:

—More choice: recipients could better determine how to spend their money, thus creating an efficiency gain for society

—Less bureaucracy: less interference and involvement in the lives of the poor, thus creating cost efficiency in programs

—A more rational tax structure: all the implicit taxes and explicit taxes faced by recipients would be combined together

—Universality: greater equity across households with equal incomes would result from a single program that had no queues to limit the number of eligible recipients receiving benefits

The negative income tax (NIT) movement reached its heyday when President Nixon proposed his family assistance plan, although cousins to the NIT were proposed by presidential candidates George McGovern in 1972 and Walter Mondale in 1984 as a flat credit for each person, later labeled a "demogrant." The NIT never achieved success, in no small part because some taxpayers feared that recipients might spend money on items other than basic necessities, while others thought that benefits ought to be linked to work. A good indication of the nation's preferences is the shift in spending from cash assistance toward in-kind benefits for necessities. Cash assistance under Aid to Families with Dependent Children (AFDC) and its replacement, Temporary Assistance to Needy Families (TANF), has declined as a percentage of national income since about the mid-1970s. Conversely, vouchers for food and housing have increased significantly in real terms, and Medicaid has grown continually in both its voucher (capitated) and nonvoucher forms.[3]

The NIT left its mark through the adoption and expansion of two cash programs. Supplemental Security Income (SSI)—essentially a federal NIT for the aged, blind, and disabled—became a reality in 1974 and provided benefits of $28.4 billion in fiscal year 1996.[4] Meanwhile, the Earned Income Tax Credit (EITC), another cousin to the NIT, was adopted in 1975 and expanded three times (1986, 1990, and 1993). EITC provides cash payments of about $27 billion, mostly to families with children, but establishes the equivalent of a "work" test by phasing out benefits as earnings increase across a modest range.[5] Thus in recent decades income assistance has expanded along three lines: toward the provision of particular services and goods for nonworking welfare recipients, toward vouchers for many of those services and goods, and toward cash for those working and for those elderly, blind, and disabled not expected to work.

Vouchers for individual goods and services usually are designed to provide more choice than direct government provision. However, bundling vouchers over a range of goods and services widens the scope for choice and offers the possibility of meeting many goals espoused for vouchers and even for the NIT. Yet the structured choice approach does so without abandoning the main reasons for rejection of the NIT: subsidized goods and services still can be forced to meet some "merit" or "necessity" test, and distinctions can be made between those who work and those who do not work.

Under a structured choice approach, recipients can use a voucher in choosing from an expanded, though still limited, set of goods and services. Consider, for example, two programs provided to families with no other income or resources: one that provides a $2,000 voucher for service A and a second that provides a $3,000 voucher for service B. This family would be unable to spend on anything other than A or B, and the family could not spend more than $2,000 on A or $3,000 on B. Now, suppose instead the family receives a bundled voucher allowing up to $5,000 to be spent on any combination of A and B. In this case, the family gains the freedom to choose not only among providers of A or providers of B, but also how much to spend between A and B.

A broad form of structured choice would involve a voucher that could pay for a wide variety of goods and services, such as food, housing, education, child care, moving allowances for new jobs, and transportation. A narrow form might include only a couple of services, such as child care and transportation. At a minimum, the narrow form seems most appropriate when separate subsidies have roughly the same purpose. For example, states trying to help low-income parents find and keep jobs could combine subsidies for transportation and child care into one voucher and allow recipients to choose how much to allocate to each service.

Certainly, some people favor a pure cash system, while others advocate using the in-kind approach to constrain all the choices of the poor or to attract political support from suppliers of specific goods or services. From this perspective, the bundled voucher represents a political compromise that is suboptimal from each end of the social policy spectrum. In contrast, we see the bundled voucher as superior for policy reasons to either the pure cash or pure in-kind strategy.

In the next sections, we consider the rationale for structured choice in the context of U.S. income-support programs. We discuss problems of the existing model of "fragmented choice" within in-kind programs to help low-income families. We then turn to examine the conditions under which the modified paradigm of a more broadly structured choice might better meet the needs of both beneficiaries and taxpayers. In our final section, we elaborate on alternative types of bundled vouchers, as well as on how they might be combined with other options to increase choice or minimize anti-work and antimarriage effects of the system as a whole.

Issues Raised by the Structured Choice Model

Many of the issues surrounding the structured choice approach arise in considering a single voucher. For those who believe low-income people are able to set their own spending priorities more sensibly than the government can, there is no reason why government programs should dictate the precise nature of the consumption or who produces it. For those who favor a model where taxpayers have good cause to limit the types of services that they finance for others, government proscriptions remain important. With structured choice, the government would still limit the subsidies, usually to the same set of prescribed goods and services, but would offer recipients much greater flexibility in choosing within the prescribed set.

EFFECT ON CHOICE AND SUBSTITUTABILITY. Perhaps the major advantage of bundling services into a single package is greater choice and flexibility for recipients. By itself, this implies efficiency gains that increase the value of a given voucher or allow a program to provide equal levels of benefits at lower costs. Since beneficiaries vary in their ability to obtain certain necessities, such as inexpensive housing or child care, restrictions that prevent substitution across categories can add to economic hardship, especially at low incomes. Such limitations also prevent beneficiaries from reallocating their spending over time in response to changes in prices or other market conditions that affect the relative value of the goods or services that government already subsidizes.

While more choice generally means less proscription, a bundled voucher is likely to free up options that were never meant to be proscribed. If the public is indifferent between how much low-income families spend on food versus housing or how much on different types of work expenses, then widening the choices of recipients does not conflict with following the preferences of donors (taxpayers). The structured choice approach still limits the subsidy to necessities or merit goods.[6] Of course, the more specific donor preferences are, the greater likelihood there will be of a trade-off between consumer and donor preferences.

Bundled vouchers present interesting possibilities for reallocating the increased flexibility not simply to the beneficiaries but also to caseworkers attempting to reach mutually agreeable compacts with recipients. For instance, suppose that job-guidance and job-search requirements for low-income families represent a sound investment of scarce dollars.[7] In Wisconsin's new welfare program, Wisconsin Works, or "W-2," for example, intensive planning with recipients is one of the mechanisms used to encourage job participation.[8] In such a program, structured choice could be designed so that the selection of services and goods within the bundled set must be agreed to by those directly advising and guiding recipients. Thus social workers might be empowered to agree on a plan with the recipient in which voucher dollars for one item could substitute for other voucher dollars if both parties thought that such a transfer would improve the probability of maintaining a job.

CONSUMER KNOWLEDGE, QUALITY, AND ADMINISTRATION. Since structured choice generally means more choice or more options,[9] it requires recipients not only to choose among suppliers or items within a given category but also to decide among categories. In this sense, recipients must have a greater understanding of the match between their consumption decisions and their welfare than they would under a single voucher system. In programs with intense involvement with recipients, the mechanisms may already be in place to meet this additional requirement. But more monitoring and advising—one consequence of recent welfare reform efforts—could mean higher administrative costs.

In one way, structured choice might lessen the demands on participants to become knowledgeable about suppliers. In a program world with separate vouchers for good A and for good B, participants must learn a good deal about suppliers of both goods. Under a combined voucher, participants who chose to focus their spending only on good A may have less need or concern with gathering information about suppliers of good B.

Sometimes quality standards are enforced independently from a voucher program, as in the case of safe food, health, and educational standards. Quality standards might be easier to enforce if structured choice could generate administrative savings from coordinating the income verification process and work requirements. However, administrative costs could rise, because obtaining receipts to verify expenditures on a variety of approved items could be cumbersome.

CASH ASSISTANCE VERSUS BUNDLED VOUCHERS. Bundled vouchers can be stacked up against one of the alternatives—cash assistance. As we noted, the EITC indirectly adds a work requirement in exchange for fewer restrictions on what can be bought with assistance. A bundled voucher (or sets of bundled vouchers) covering a broad enough range of basic necessities could be used to reduce further the role of cash assistance under programs like the Temporary Assistance to Needy Families. Such a substitution is interesting because it would involve increased choice through the bundled voucher as a partial offset to the reduced level of choice because of the cutback in cash. It would help increase the incentive to work as long as individuals wanted to buy items not considered necessities and not covered by the voucher but otherwise purchasable with cash assistance. Already, some members of Congress and state legislators have proposed to provide vouchers for basic necessities to families dropped from cash assistance because of the time limits on TANF. Compared to separate vouchers, a bundled voucher could provide a better mix of prescription and proscription for long-term recipients for whom cash is not going to be provided or is provided only in limited amounts.

DONOR PREFERENCES. The shift toward broader choice among merit goods might or might not weaken donor support for transfer programs. So long as the primary concern of donors is on the proscription side—that recipients spend the transfers on a set of goods and services the donors consider appropriate and worthwhile—the change from individual programs to a structured choice model should not reduce the appeal of in-kind support for low-income families. We suspect that most voters would not object to offering low-income families the opportunities to make some choices, such as sacrificing housing quality to spend more on education. However, since programs dealing with specific needs—such as reducing hunger, homelessness, and ill health—generate an emotional appeal, a structured choice model might elicit less-passionate public support.

In economic theory, some goods are labeled as merit goods, defined as goods or services that have a meritorious purpose from the standpoint of donors. Treating the structure of U.S. benefit programs as a set of revealed preferences, the presumption might be that donors define food, housing, child care, and medical care spending as meritorious in comparison to spending on other goods and services, such as entertainment. The idea that raising the poor's consumption of essentials also makes donors feel better is sometimes called an "external benefit." What is unclear is whether the external benefit experienced by donors from the knowledge that recipients are spending on essentials depends on a highly specific allocation (as with today's programs) or whether external benefit would not change if recipients were allowed to allocate their spending among agreed upon merit goods. Donors, for instance, might consider health care a merit good worthy of separate treatment but be indifferent between transportation and child care as mechanisms for providing work support. Also, donors might be more concerned about minimum levels of purchase than with setting precise amounts. To the extent recipients would buy at least the minimum levels appropriate for their families, donors may well be indifferent about further allocations across essentials.

A more direct form of externality relates to the experiences of donors rather than to their views on how the poor should spend money. A good example is slum housing that might be an eyesore and thus might lower a donor's welfare even if the individual cares nothing about the poor. Alternatively, the presence of dilapidated housing might lower the land values of other homes in the area. In either case, the externality relating to a particular good or service strengthens the rationale for restricting the program to specific goods. The problem is that such externalities apply to almost all subsidized and even some unsubsidized areas. High-quality child care may produce external benefits (lower social costs because of reduced crime and reduced spending on schooling) as great as improved housing. The extent to which one good or service produces more externalities may well vary by geographic area or by family. Moreover, one form of externality gain might increase if the family is able to spend the available assistance more efficiently. This would be the case if the donors derived positive utility from the well-being of recipients and the well-being of recipients rose with greater choice.

INCENTIVES AND CUMULATIVE TAX RATE. A combined voucher would integrate the combined tax rates that result from the phaseout of uncoordinated programs. Policymakers and recipients would then be better able to determine the combined structure directly, rather than accidentally. We will return to this issue below.

MORAL HAZARD AND ADVERSE SELECTION. Structured choice may prove difficult to implement where either moral hazard or adverse selection is present. It would be inappropriate, for instance, to allow Medicaid beneficiaries to shift resources away from even a low-cost health insurance plan if they were expecting to substitute access to free care supported by other tax dollars. Similarly, healthy Medicaid recipients should not be allowed to spend the difference between the "average" cost of Medicaid and the cost of a health care plan that somehow includes only healthier, less costly individuals. Less severe but similar problems could arise in other programs, such as the school lunch program. Recipients might divert resources from the school lunch program to housing in the expectation that the school will not permit their child to be without food during the school day. Because regulations usually limit the amount of selection that can take place, such regulations would have to apply in a cross-program way under a structured voucher. While it is difficult to comment generally on the feasibility of such efforts without looking at specific program design, in general restrictions on flexibility are more likely where adverse selection and moral hazard are consequences to be avoided.

REORIENTING POLICY TOWARD IMPORTANT DESIGN ISSUES. Consolidating multiple vouchers is likely to permit policymakers to focus on design issues often submerged in a multiprogram world. Currently, each of several programs must develop its own work requirements, asset tests, accounting period, and treatment of income. Today, any gain from developing improved policies for a single program can be offset unintentionally by interactions with other programs. Under a structured choice approach, policymakers would know that investing their time and attention to improving program design will have broad consequences for the primary benefit to low-income families. As an example, instead of having separate evaluations of a food stamp employment and training program, a housing employment program, and a TANF employment program, the government could sponsor one or two high-quality research projects on the structured choice employment and training program.

OTHER ISSUES THAT DO NOT GO AWAY. Many of the issues in a world of multiple vouchers and programs remain in the case of structured choice. Asset tests will lower the incentive to save. The quantity or quality of goods supplied by the market may be unsatisfactory. Families may choose unwisely, increasing their chances of eviction or hunger. Given all the issues that must be confronted under a structured choice model, is a shift away from our multiple program world worthwhile? To examine this question, it is worth examining some of the problems of the current system of "fragmented choice" in a bit more depth.

Receipt of Multiple Benefits

While the number of welfare recipients has declined substantially in recent years, many former recipients continue to receive government support in the form of one or another in-kind program and the EITC. As of 1995, over 70 million Americans lived in households in which someone received an income-tested cash or noncash benefit (not including the Earned Income Tax Credit).[10] By income-tested benefits we mean public benefits that are limited to those with low income and that decline with increased income. Nearly all recipients of the former Aid to Families with Dependent Children program participated in Medicaid, 82 percent reported receiving food stamps, 54 percent reported receiving school lunch benefits, and nearly 30 percent reported receiving housing subsidies of one form or another. In addition, most recipients have access to subsidized child care, child support collection services, employment and training services, or other social services. Under recent welfare reform, with its emphasis on jobs and time-limited welfare, the availability of child care, training, and transportation is often directly or indirectly under the discretion of case-workers. Despite government spending on selected programs for low-income children of $8,600 per poor child in the median state in 1995, about 20 percent of the nation's children were counted as poor.[11]

Limited Flexibility to Tailor Benefits to Family Needs

Within the current system, limitations on recipient choices are prevalent within categories, especially in housing and medical care, but even more so between categories. Although policymakers and the public certainly favor linking benefits to necessities, some efforts to restrict benefits to specific purposes weaken the ability of families to achieve an adequate living standard. They also restrict recipients from making the types of sacrifices that are required of most families not only to advance in society but also to understand how to advance—for example, spending less on food or housing in order to provide an even better education for one's children. Since the other chapters in this book take up questions of flexibility within benefit categories, we focus here on flexibility among categories.

In assessing the practical impact of constrained choice across categories, the political question of whether a less restrictive set of choices would generate the same government outlays cannot be ignored. From the standpoint of taxpayers in general, the constant outlay assumption makes sense, because taxpayers may well approve of methods that can improve family functioning at no added costs. From the standpoint of lobbies for farmers, doctors, child-care providers, and real estate and construction companies, however, taking away a program specifically targeted on the goods and services they provide could cause political support to erode. Despite this political reality, our discussion begins with the constant cost assumption, and we will not address political feasibility issues further here.

The primary in-kind benefits available to low-income families are food stamps, other nutrition programs, medical care, housing subsidies, education and training benefits, and child-care subsidies. How might the inability to spend across categories inappropriately restrict the choices of low-income recipients?

At least for those with modest amounts of earnings, food stamps probably restrict choices only moderately. In the late 1970s, the law eliminated a requirement that recipients purchase the gross amount allotted per family of any given size. Before then, a family of four that qualified for, say, $300 a month in food stamps and had an income of $500 a month would have to pay about $140 to buy the full $300 in stamps. Since 1977, low-income recipients have received only the net allotment—$160 in food stamps in the example—and pay nothing to the government. Current rules are thus much less likely to restrict the actual choices made by food stamp recipients. Evidence from experiments with cashing out food stamps suggest that the food stamp program induces modest, not large, shifts in expenditure patterns.[12] Still, the restrictions are real in some cases, especially at very low income levels. Otherwise, we would not observe cases of illegal trading in food stamps.[13] Finally, the whole notion of providing choice is related to opportunity. Even if only a small portion of food stamp recipients found a better use for their funds in any one year—for example, better education or living in a better environment or better coverage of work-related expenses—that shift may be more than sufficient to justify a change.

Housing programs may or may not constrain the choices of recipients. Until recently, most housing benefit programs (public housing and the former rental certificate program) operated with what is the equivalent of the food stamp purchase requirement. A recipient obtained an amount that had to be devoted to housing (either in the form of a public housing unit or voucher) and then paid 25 percent to 30 percent of his or her income in return. The gross subsidy, not the net subsidy, had to be allocated toward housing. If we simply wanted to expand choices toward purchasing anything, the voucher could instead operate like food stamps. Families would receive as their housing-conditioned benefit an amount equal to the difference between the maximum allotment and the family's contribution. Thus if fair market rent in an area were equal to $600 per month and the family's income were $700 per month, the housing-conditioned benefit would be $600 less 30 percent of $700, or $390. This result could not be achieved with public housing since the units are indivisible. Note that a structured choice approach could be designed either way; that is, it could include some minimum amounts that had to be spent on some items like health care or housing.

Today's rental voucher program already allows some substitution of the subsidy for purposes other than housing. Families with vouchers can keep the difference between fair market rent and the actual rent paid to the landlord. However, their choices of units are limited by Department of Housing and Urban Development (HUD) provisions requiring that the subsidized dwelling be of a certain size and physical standard. Such restrictive aspects of housing assistance may be reasonable for the "average" family, but no family is precisely average, and the restriction may have a worst effect on families seeking to advance themselves. For example, recipients may not be able to combine with other families in a unit or even make the trade-off of more children per bedroom in exchange for living in a better neighborhood. Such moves would violate HUD's standards for the "quality" of housing recipients should have.

One of the most problematic aspects of housing assistance has been the restriction of large and important housing subsidies to specific geographic areas, at least in practice if not in law. As of 1997, of the 5.8 million households receiving some form of housing assistance, 1.7 million lived in public housing and 1.4 million received restricted Section 8 rental subsidies tied to a specific housing unit. Unfortunately, these recipients cannot take their subsidies with them if they find another job or cheaper housing in another jurisdiction. Only those with less-restrictive Section 8 tenant vouchers can do so. Federal rules allow tenant vouchers to be used anywhere in the nation, but there is a limited supply of suitable low-cost housing. As noted by George Peterson in this volume, a substantial but diminishing proportion of jurisdictions had residency preferences for accessing low-cost housing built with public support and for awarding Section 8 vouchers. Nonetheless, even a jurisdiction without residency preferences will hardly move to the top of their queue someone who already has adequate subsidized housing in one jurisdiction and decides to move to another region or state.

Usage of vouchers outside the issuing authority's boundaries is increasing because of court decisions and the encouragement of some local housing authorities, but most local administrators or state officials do not do much to try to assist those who live elsewhere, nor, in the presence of queues, would they support a system if most of their vouchers ended up going to people who lived out of their state or jurisdiction. For all these reasons, in practice most housing assistance still is not portable, nor is it likely ever to be adequately portable for most people as long as the system as a whole operates with queues, especially with local or regional, rather than state or national, administration.

A related problem is the inability of some beneficiary families to use their vouchers because they cannot find a rental unit where they want to live that is affordable (even with the voucher) and that still meets HUD standards. Some families turn in their housing voucher for this reason, thereby losing a substantial supplement to their real income as a result of program restrictions.

A bundled voucher does not get around all geographical and programmatic limitations. For example, even if families allocated more funds to housing, well-off communities may still try to keep out low-income housing simply through zoning or other rules. Still, because a bundled voucher would less likely be granted through a queue, it would do less to impede mobility. Queues typically discourage movement, because leaving an area shifts the recipient back to the bottom of a queue. There is a strong case for making both individual and structured vouchers transportable over boundaries. Among other reasons, this would give recipients the ability to spend more efficiently in lower-cost areas.[14]

A range of other programs in the nutrition field limit the recipient's ability to determine spending priorities. These often overlooked programs provide a substantial amount of in-kind support. Outlays in the school lunch; school breakfast; and Women, Infants, and Children (WIC) programs reached over $10 billion in 1996. The WIC program served an average of 7.2 million persons, about 1.7 million families, at a cost of over $2,200 per family. Whether families would be able to reallocate their spending toward more valued necessities under a bundled voucher is unclear, but the sums involved clearly represent a significant proportion of family income.

There is no simple way to determine the proportion of families that might find themselves better off with a less restricted set of food and housing subsidies. Existing studies have found mixed results on the extent to which families reallocate their food spending and other spending when allowed to do so.[15]

The case of child care and Headstart is complicated in two ways. First, no single approach determines gross benefits, net benefits, and implied restricted amounts. Second, some of the outlays are intended as investments in the education of children and not simply to offset work expenses so that low-income parents can make ends meet. Still, in many cases the agency pays the full fees of the child-care center, possibly in return for some contribution by the parent. The result is similar to the purchase requirement model, because it is often the gross subsidy, not the net subsidy, that must go toward the designated purpose. Some child-care programs, however, do permit the parent to keep the difference between the gross subsidy and the net costs of child care.

Overall, the amounts strictly allocated to child care can be a substantial share of the incomes of recipients. For cases in which the state pays to send children to institutional care or in which the federal government provides Headstart funding, the outlays often reach over $400 a month per child and can easily represent one-third of the family's gross income. State officials estimate a statewide average of $4,800 per child in Wisconsin, but over $7,000 in Milwaukee.[16] Many of these families might choose a less expensive form of child care if they could spend the remaining portion of the subsidy.

The education and child-care issue is especially complicated by the ambiguity over goals. If the purpose is educational, for instance, the goal of structured choice would not be more ability to withdraw resources *from* Headstart, say, any more than from primary education. Conversely, the goal might be to allow recipients to reallocate resources *toward* other education or child-care programs to enhance the quality obtained. Still another complication is that in some cases payments to grandparents are substitutable for payments to other child-care providers, which in many families converts the in-kind benefit into a cash supplement. All this may argue more extensively for a particular type of structured choice model where decisions can be made in one way—that is, to allow shifts toward education (for example, only from "lower" to "higher" levels of services) but not away from the amount of education that would otherwise be included in a separate voucher or grant program.

One of the largest allocations is for Medicaid. In 1995 over 17 million children and over 7 million parents of dependent children obtained Medicaid benefits, and that number may expand under new entitlements for children. The outlays on behalf of eligible families are clearly restricted to reimbursements for care. As of 1995, average Medicaid payments on behalf of children and an adult in a family amounted to about $3,800 a year. However, the amounts varied widely across states—for example, $5,800 in Maryland and $2,700 in California. For individuals over age sixty-five, the national average outlay per person was $8,900 a year, partly reflecting nursing home expenses.[17]

How might families effectively substitute Medicaid payments on their behalf for other basic needs? Clearly, there are substantial limits. The government might permit families to choose among competing health plans that provided a similar degree of health coverage, but perhaps with differing deductibles and co-payments. The existing range of variation across states suggests there may be considerable scope for shifting between health care and other needs. If Maryland's low-income families could attain the same health coverage at about the same costs as are now paid in California and keep a significant portion of the difference between what is spent on their behalf and the amounts spent in California, they would certainly do so. Similar differences sometimes apply within state borders also.

Of course, if all that is provided is that recipients can pocket some saving by choosing lower-cost plans, then that can be achieved with a simple, not bundled, voucher. The main additional feature of a bundled voucher in this case is to restrict the goods and services that can be purchased with those savings.

The ability to shift from medical care dollars toward other goods or services could actually improve the health of low-income people. For example, if recipients used some of their savings to move from dangerous neighborhoods, they might well end up healthier as well as enjoying a higher standard of living. As a bottom line, however, it appears that medical care would be one of those items for which some minimum quality of insurance would probably be required, thus restricting how far a move could be taken toward including this particular service in a structured choice option.

Administrative and Transaction Costs of Separate Programs

The administrative costs of government income support programs are high, though not necessarily excessive relative to the tasks program staff must perform. Unfortunately, too often policymakers see administrative costs as overhead unlinked to the program's broader purposes. Ideally, we should value administrative costs in relation to the effectiveness of implementation of the program.

Administrative demands vary widely across programs. Some deal mainly with determining eligibility, calculating benefits, and delivering the benefits, while others involve counseling, enforcement of work requirements, and regulating the quality of suppliers. Administrative outlays can be a high percentage of program costs. WIC administrative expenses amount to about 25 percent of costs, but this figure includes provision for nutrition assessment and nutrition education. Even a program like food stamps, the primary responsibility of which is the determination of benefits, spends significant sums on administration. In 1996 the administrative costs of the food stamp program were nearly $4 billion, or 14 percent of total costs.

A key question is whether operating separate programs instead of consolidating programs in part or in whole wastes administrative expenses. The answer is not unambiguous, although the odds of waste may increase the more programs are multiplied, and especially if they are directed at similar ends. Nonetheless, although the country could avoid duplication in many tasks—such as eligibility determination, payment calculations, and work requirements—other administrative functions will still have to continue and possibly will have to expand. If the program requires landlords to provide housing that meets an adequate standard in order to receive public funds, then officials will have to spend administrative time auditing landlords. As long as the voucher mechanism is used, whether bundled or not, it will still be necessary to limit what can be purchased through administrative mechanisms such as the printing of script or determining which providers can accept vouchers for reimbursement.

Often ignored in discussions of program implementation are the transaction costs of recipients. When recipients have to interact with a number of programs and deal separately with multiple sets of requirements, the costs can be substantial. With increasing shares of welfare, food stamp, and housing recipients working outside the home, high transaction costs in terms of time can be even more onerous. The wide variation in take-up rates on some programs is itself an indicator that recipients have trouble negotiating existing labyrinths. As a first approximation, costs borne by recipients add nothing to the program's effectiveness. If they are intended to raise the cost of not working relative to working, or simply to control costs, they are not a very efficient way to go about achieving those objectives. Consolidating existing programs into one or more systems of structured choice almost certainly would reduce the transaction costs.

Horizontal Inequities in the Distribution of Benefits

The world of multiple programs leads to many inequities among low-income families. Some differences in benefits among families with the same incomes may be justifiable as adjustments for family size or special circumstance, as for families with infants (through the WIC program) or for those living in a high-cost area of the country. However, programs that depend on queues miserably fail the test of equal justice or horizontal equity.

Queuing is almost inevitable in a multiprogram world, where there are strong political incentives to appear to tackle a problem or to announce the enactment of new programs but not to pay the full freight of achieving the purpose. If outlays were consolidated into fewer programs with structured choice of in-kind benefits, it would be more difficult to exclude families systematically without a broad justification.

The use of queues in income assistance programs, whether using vouchers or not, is pervasive. It arises in housing assistance, child care, job training, Headstart, social services, and presumably under the new TANF program. Not surprisingly, the impact of current exclusions on low-income families varies across programs. The case of housing is clearest. As of 1996, fewer than 30 percent of poor families with children received a housing benefit that averaged over $400 a month. Waiting lists for support for child care are also said to be common in large states, despite the availability of federal funds from several sources and even though tax credit and deduction aspects of tax-related federal child-care funding are open-ended and thus cover almost all middle-income taxpayers. Overall, Sharon Long and Sandra Clark, in their recent study of the new child care block grant, estimate that even under the expanded programs for child care, fewer than half of the low-income children in paid child care will obtain any subsidy at all. Moreover, the child-care or Headstart subsidy amounts vary widely across families.[18]

The new TANF program provides the flexibility to remove some benefit disparities across families. As noted above, the law allows states to shift up to 30 percent of TANF dollars to child care, thereby allowing most states to offer subsidies to all eligibles.[19] New Mexico recently passed a law under which TANF recipients not receiving any housing subsidy will receive an additional $100. Thus there are at least some efforts by states to use social welfare dollars in a way that offsets the inequities that arise in the distribution of other benefits. But few states have begun to use their authority in a significant way to offset differentials in the receipt of benefits.

Take-up Rates in a Multiprogram Context

Even welfare programs funded to cover all eligibles are typically unable to reach many eligible families because people lack knowledge, face high transaction costs, or are unwilling to bear the stigma of accepting public charity.

For example, only about 74 percent of those persons eligible actually participated.[20] The multiprogram world adds to the problem of low take-up rates because of the high ratio of transaction costs to benefits. For any one program, the transaction costs may be high relative to the benefits. In a structured choice model offering a combined benefit, the combined benefits to families would become more visible and would probably rise relative to the transaction costs of participation. This could help increase efficiency, as well as remove some of the horizontal inequities arising from different take-up rates. By the same token, it could expand overall take-up rates and increase costs or lower average benefits under a fixed overall budget.

Escalating Tax Rates and Vertical Equity

One of the critical problems of the multiprogram world of vouchers and other income assistance programs is the complexity of the financial incentives embedded in the combination of programs. Today, benefit reduction rates often escalate in unintended and unknown ways because of many disparate and uncoordinated programs. A consolidated program likely would increase the transparency of the system and lead to a more rationalized structure. However, consolidating benefits per se would not be sufficient to prevent sharp financial penalties on work and marriage over significant ranges of income.

In a comprehensive analysis of all programs available to welfare recipients, C. Eugene Steuerle and Linda Giannarelli, in a paper from the proceedings of the 1995 National Tax Association annual conference, demonstrated that effective tax rates—direct tax rates plus benefit reduction rates—often approached 100 percent when taking into account EITC, food stamps, income taxes, Social Security, housing, Medicaid, and what was then AFDC.[21] From earnings of about one-fourth of minimum wage to two and a half times minimum wage, the combined marginal tax rate for all welfare recipients was close to 70 cents for each dollar earned. What has stretched these high tax rates so far into the middle class is that long after leaving traditional welfare (then AFDC, now TANF), there remains the phaseout of food stamps, EITC, housing, and Medicaid, and the application of federal and state income taxes and Social Security taxes. What essentially used to be a high tax rate regime for lower-income welfare recipients has moved in recent times into the lower-middle class, with social consequences that are yet to be learned.

Changes in the income support system have improved work incentives for recipients moving from no work to full-time work at low wages ($6 an hour and below). However, cumulative benefit reductions remain high for many groups. A 1988 study by Robert Lerman, Gregory Acs, Keith Watson, and Norma Coe showed recipients who raise their wage from $5.15 an hour to $9 an hour will gain only about 15 to 40 percent of the rise in earnings, thus implying about a 60 to 85 percent marginal tax rate.[22] Financial incentives to work are substantially lower among recipients of public housing, and policymakers rarely consider how interactions among programs can affect these incentives.[23] Food stamps and housing benefits, together with payroll taxes,[24] lead to benefit reduction rates reaching over 70 percent.[25]

Other in-kind programs operate on a sliding scale or suddenly drop benefits as income rises above some threshold level. Medicaid, child care, WIC, and school lunch are among the programs in this category.[26] The Medicaid cutoff and its relationship to earnings is particularly complex.[27] School lunch benefits decline from free lunches to reduced-price lunches as the family's income moves above 130 percent of the poverty line and to no subsidy at all when family income reaches 185 percent of the poverty line. Attempts to employ a gradual phaseout of child-care benefits can easily lead to a significant rise in tax rates.

Since the 1986, 1990, and 1993 EITC expansions, EITC subsidy rates offset a significant portion of benefit reductions from other programs through about $9,000 in annual earnings. However, the EITC begins to phase out at incomes beyond $12,000, adding tax rates of 16 percent for one-child families and 21 percent for families with more than one child. These phaseout rates add to the high benefit reduction rates already facing those receiving food stamps and housing benefits.

Overall, the current system of transfers embodies only moderate work disincentives at earnings levels through $9,000. However, as earnings rise from $9,000 to $12,000 a year, the combined effect of higher taxes and benefit reductions from several programs is at least a 76 percent cumulative tax rate on earnings. Beyond $12,000 and until food stamps and housing benefits phase out completely, the added benefit reduction from EITC is 21 percent, and recipients face nearly a 100 percent cumulative rate on earnings. The rate is even higher if potential losses of Medicaid are added in.

In this context, adding new vouchers that phase out with income forces difficult choices. Consider an education voucher worth about $3,600 a year. Imposing even a small 10 percent co-payment with no initial income exclusion would require that benefits extend to families with incomes up to

$36,000 a year. A 15 percent rate and a $24,000 income limit are more plausible parameters from a narrow program cost standpoint. But families with two children in school might then be subject to a 30 percent education voucher rate. Even for families with incomes below $9,000 and receiving a 40 percent earnings subsidy through the EITC, the cumulative tax-benefit rate would reach 51 percent. Beyond $9,000, the cumulative rate would jump beyond 90 percent. Families with one education voucher would still face a 75 percent cumulative rate. The addition of transportation or child-care vouchers would generate similar problems of cascading tax rates.

To the extent that the complexity confuses recipients, the extreme financial penalties on added earnings may be thought by some not to induce large reductions in work effort. By the same token, confusion may induce even larger reductions. But ultimately, recipients almost surely come to understand how little their net income changes in response to significant increases in their work effort. Once that social understanding is reached, some recipients are likely to reduce their hours of work, accept an easier job at a lower wage, or not report added earnings to at least some of the programs.

The effect of significant tax rates may work their way through social effects on whole segments of the population. As an example from another context, it is possible that earnings tests and other signals in Social Security send strong messages that lead large segments of the population to retire at the same time as others in their age cohorts. A similar process may occur in welfare programs, especially where welfare recipients are congregated in close proximity. Work on the books and (as discussed below) marriage on the books, so to speak, become understood socially as unproductive and money-losing propositions. Work off the books and single-parent families become more the norm in those situations.

Offsets to Single Sanctions When Multiple Programs Operate

Administering welfare programs increasingly involves sanctioning recipients for noncompliance with program rules. In a multiprogram world, each benefit may be subject to sanctioning separately and for varying reasons. More important, benefits lost as a result of noncompliance in one program may be largely offset by benefit gains in other programs. Reductions in cash payments resulting from sanctions applied under the TANF program lower countable income and thus can raise benefits from other income-tested programs.

Marriage and Family Formation Incentives

Few analysts have systematically examined the impact of the nation's tax and transfer system on the financial gains or losses from marriage.[28] Nevertheless, the high benefit reduction rates apparent in the U.S. system of multiple income-tested programs inadvertently reduce or eliminate the financial gain from marriage as they reduce the gains from work. Marital disincentives arise in transfer programs via the highly progressive benefit schedules and the attempt to assess benefits, benefit reductions, and taxes on a household, rather than individual, basis.[29]

Consider a single mother with two children who is working full time at the minimum wage and receiving TANF, food stamps, Medicaid and the EITC. If she simply marries someone earning $8 an hour and does nothing else, their combined income falls by over $8,000, or more than 25 percent of their combined income if they remain unmarried. Essentially what happens is that the marriage wipes out all or almost all of the food stamps, Medicaid, and EITC benefits.

A recent paper by Stacey Dickert-Conlin and Scott Houser examined the impact of food stamps, SSI, the tax system (including EITC), AFDC, state income taxes, and payroll taxes on samples of American families by marital status.[30] They concluded that as of 1990 the nation's transfer system provided significant financial penalties for unmarried mothers who marry and financial gains for married couples who split up. The reductions in transfers here amounted to about 25 percent of incomes of poor families, which was only partly offset by about a 8 percent to 9 percent tax savings. These last figures actually understate the disincentives to marry for low- and middle-income families, because they leave out a number of transfer programs, the most important of which are housing assistance, Medicaid, and child-care benefits.

In a study on how tax and transfer programs create marriage penalties, Steuerle notes that the very highest marriage penalties for modest-wage single workers occur now in almost precisely the economic situation in which recent welfare reform aims to put actual or potential welfare recipients.[31] In other words, the work requirements in welfare reform may have reduced work disincentives, but they have added to marriage penalties for working recipients. An exception occurs for those recipients who work little or not at all even in the presence of potential or actual loss of TANF benefits; for this group, marriage may then be more financially attractive than under AFDC partly because there are fewer AFDC or TANF benefits over time. Also, EITC benefits might be brought into some households with the introduction of a working spouse, and those EITC benefits will offset some of the loss of foods stamps and other benefits from marriage. Conversely, if the welfare reforms stimulate single parents to work and earn moderate wages, then marriage introduces large penalties from the EITC, food stamps, housing, and Medicaid.

In sum, there are serious problems evident in the nation's fragmented transfer system. Overall spending is already high enough to reduce child poverty significantly—even in the absence of AFDC, which in recent years had already become a smaller and smaller share of total income-conditioned assistance. However, channeling funds in a more rational way, either by caseworkers or by recipients, has proved elusive. Choice remains unduly limited, work and family formation disincentives are extremely high over important ranges of income, inequities can be substantial, and the system's complexity makes it difficult to identify and solve these and other problems. Moreover, the high tax rates present in the existing mix of programs limits the scope for simply patching on additional vouchers (for example, a more universal health care voucher or an educational voucher) that would add further to combined tax rates and make them almost confiscatory.

Structured Choice within a System of Fragmented Choice

While most in-kind programs offer limited flexibility to recipients, two significant programs have given discretion to government—and perhaps indirectly to beneficiaries—in choosing how to spend across a variety of services. In some ways, they set a precedent for a structured voucher approach, albeit with discretion on the part of caseworkers as well. State and local governments allocate about $6 billion under the Social Services Block Grant to pay for a whole range of qualifying services so long as the expenditures help maintain self-support, reduce dependency, prevent neglect and abuse of children, and prevent excessive use of institutional care while still helping individuals obtain it where appropriate. These supported services are not supposed to substitute for normal government functions (services in the health and education normally provided by the state).

Under this grant program, states are given wide latitude. They have taken advantage of this flexibility to spend on everything from case management and counseling to day care and services to protect adults and children against abuse. While the power technically lies in the hands of government agencies, caseworkers likely allocate some resources in ways that reflect negotiations with recipients. Formalizing this arrangement into one involving structured choice might involve nothing more than empowering recipients to suggest alternatives that could not be dismissed by case managers without cause. In well-developed programs, this may involve little change in what is already happening implicitly, while in other programs the formal requirement to offer recipients such opportunities could significantly change program design.

Until 1996 the Emergency Assistance (EA) program also allowed state and local governments wide discretion to spend on a range of in-kind benefits and temporary cash support. Before the passage of the Personal Responsibility and Work Opportunity Reconciliation Act (PRWORA), which folded EA into the block grant to states for Temporary Assistance to Needy Families, agencies used EA funds to help families affected by evictions, homelessness, utility shutoffs, emergency medical needs, victim assistance, and natural disasters. Spending on these purposes was modest through the early 1990s. In 1991 EA outlays were $306 million. However, between 1991 and 1996, spending under EA surged tenfold, reaching $3.2 billion in 1996. The shift from EA to TANF generally will not alter the ability of state and local agencies to use federal and state resources in a flexible manner.

The overall shift from AFDC (and EA) to TANF widens the scope for state flexibility in the provision of necessities. States can use TANF dollars to develop a wide range of program options other than cash assistance so long as the funds are aimed at reducing dependency and illegitimacy, promote two-parent families, and aid needy families so that children can be cared for in their homes. For example, the legislation authorizes states to shift up to 30 percent of TANF funds to child care. Again, one might think that with a bit more empowerment of recipients, some of these "variable" funds could be built into a system of structured choice.

Plans such as Wisconsin Works arguably already provide a lot of discretion to both caseworker and recipient, even though the greater decisionmaking power is with the caseworker. At least during the 1997–98 phase of welfare reform, average total assistance per recipient was rising across the country even as caseloads were falling. Many supplements, such as child-care and transportation assistance, are available on a fairly discretionary basis. This planning flexibility, while somewhat informal and of uncertain duration, offers modest opportunity to move in the direction of structured choice.

The Structured Choice Model

Under a structured choice model, the government would provide a single voucher (or a reduced number of vouchers) that recipients could use for a range of goods and services considered necessities or worthwhile investments in human capital.

Alternative Approaches to Structured Choice

The structured choice model involves at least three sets of design issues. One is the range of programs whose benefits would be combined and among which choice would be expanded. The second is whether recipients exercise choice over the reallocation of benefits through negotiation with caseworkers or at their own discretion. The third set concerns whether to use existing benefit levels and eligibility rules and expand each person's choice to reallocate benefits already obtained or to pool the spending into a new, more coherent program. Maintaining existing benefit levels and eligibility rules would widen the scope for choice and is a more incremental approach to reform, but it does not tackle the inequities in benefits or the work and marriage penalties. In contrast, the broader reform would create winners and losers, making it more difficult politically to achieve.

Beginning with the first issue of what programs to combine, a first step toward a system of structured choice would be to combine benefits under work-enabling programs such as child-care, transportation, and training assistance, allowing recipients to change their allocation across spending categories but maintaining existing eligibility and benefit rules. Michigan's Tool Chest program is a limited example of structured choice in use that permits eligible individuals to choose from a range of services that would help them do better in the job market.[32] A variation of this plan that engages the second design issue would allow for reallocations across categories only with approval of case managers. Suppose, for example, that a working mother heading a family could avoid or reduce child-care costs by moving to a neighborhood near close relatives or nearer a subsidized local facility, but that this would raise transportation costs. The mother could propose to use some of the child-care savings to pay for the additional transportation costs. If the caseworker approved, the mother could reallocate the use of her subsidy. The success of this policy of encouraging interactions between caseworkers and recipients would depend partly on the ability of caseworkers to make sensible judgments about what is constructive for the family. In this respect, the policy operates along the lines of the "New Paternalism," espoused by Lawrence Mead and said to work well in Wisconsin.[33] Granting veto power to the caseworker offers protection against significant reductions in quality of child care or a reallocation that is clearly unhelpful.

Once an initial combined voucher proves effective, the next issue is whether to broaden the benefits programs embedded in the program. A broader based reform might add food stamps, housing, and school lunch to the training, transportation, and child-care benefits. Again, under the structured choice program, the recipient would be able to reallocate existing benefits, possibly with the approval of a caseworker. Legislatures would also need to allow authorization and allocation limits to be flexible. Otherwise, if spending switches from transportation to child care, total child care spending would exceed its initial authorized limit.

Medical benefits are a special case. The moral hazard argument is that some individuals would substitute away from spending on health insurance and take a chance that if they require medical assistance, local clinics and hospitals would still provide them care. Such a strategy could prove more costly from a purely medical standpoint if people rely less on primary and preventive care. The adverse selection argument is that, since those shifting away from Medicaid might be the healthiest within the group, providing the option to transfer an "average" amount of Medicaid expenditures to other purposes would increase average costs for the remaining participants. Still, within limits, some health insurance options might be included in a well-constructed system of structured choice. For example, the recipient might be permitted (by the caseworker or by regulation) to reallocate some of the savings made possible by his or her willingness to participate in selected qualified heath insurance policies. Another option might be to allow some reallocation by recipients willing to accept some level of co-payment.

Engaging the third design issue requires consideration of consolidating the outlays on a number of benefit programs into a voucher provided on a common basis to all eligible families. Consider a family consisting of a single mother and two children that is eligible for a voucher providing a maximum of $9,000 a year in purchasing power ($750 a month), subject to a benefit reduction rate of 75 percent. Assuming the current EITC remains the same, the voucher and combined benefit reduction rate, along with the Social Security tax, would equal 42 percent through $9,100 in earnings. Over the $9,100 to $12,000 range, the marginal tax rate would equal 82 percent, but it would fall back to 28 percent on earnings above $12,000 a year up to the income tax threshold of $19,683 a year, at which point an additional 15 percent federal income tax rate would apply.[34]

An indirect result of this structure is that as recipients increase their market work and earnings, the mix of benefits would gradually shift from the voucher (which limits spending to selected necessities) to unrestricted cash benefits. The idea of making benefits more restrictive for recipients least able to help themselves may underlie some congressional and legislative proposals to provide vouchers instead of cash to TANF recipients who have stayed on welfare beyond the five-year time limit.

This movement toward limitation on choice at lower earnings levels has a twofold rationale. First, since recipients would prefer cash, the shift at low or zero earnings levels from unrestricted grants to a restricted voucher could increase their incentive to work without depriving them of basic necessities. If cash is valued more highly, the effective tax rate on additional earnings is "effectively" lowered, or, said another way, the increased flexibility is like an additional return to work for the beneficiary. Second, considered as a unit, the households of adult recipients unable even to obtain a low-wage job for five full years might do better with a restricted set of benefits. These recipients often have social or familial problems that demand the close involvement or supervision of caseworkers, as well as greater insurance that the benefit flows through to children.[35]

Incorporating into the bundled vouchers such nonentitlement benefits as housing and child care would require a transition period. Otherwise, either expenditures would have to rise substantially (as coverage at existing benefit levels expanded) or benefits to existing families would have to decline sharply (as the government spreads a fixed amount of money across a substantially larger number of families). The transition could occur through a combination of attrition and some increase in outlays. As families exit from housing or child-care benefit programs, newly eligible families could be provided with a supplement to their bundled voucher.

Expanding Choices while Reducing Income Testing

Widening the scope of reforms that accompany a broad voucher could also involve strategies that reduce the system's reliance on income testing. Combining programs into fewer systems or even a single system offers simplicity, reduced transaction costs, administrative savings, flexibility in the purchase of necessities, and transparency with regard to incentives. However, a combined approach does not overcome the fundamental conflict between adequacy of benefits, work and family incentives, and program costs.

One way to reduce these conflicts is to tie programs not directly to income but rather to other indicators of deservingness. For example, the government might relate benefits to a good proxy for low economic status.[36] We should remember that the annual or monthly income measure used to determine benefits in most programs is itself an imperfect indicator of economic status. Other attributes—wealth, leisure, income variability, income averaged over a longer period than a month or a year, as well as access to relatives—clearly affect economic status but do not alter benefits in most programs. Thus there is justification for some benefit differentiation for families when they are comparable only in terms of monthly or annual income.

A good example of the use of proxies is the practice of providing higher returns under public retirement programs to those with low *prior* earnings. Suppose that the incomes of senior citizens were highly correlated with their preretirement earnings. Then, paying higher benefits (or a higher rate of return) to those with lower preretirement earnings can channel resources toward low-income elderly without imposing an income test that may discourage saving for retirement.[37] Another example is the potential interaction between large families and low incomes relative to needs. If the vast majority of larger families have lower incomes or simply lower ability to pay because of family size, then paying reasonable child allowances (or making child tax credits refundable) could be distributionally efficient without generating disincentives to work or marriage. Of course, if it is of sufficient size, the payment would increase the incentive to have larger families, but not necessarily more than under existing welfare laws and with fewer work and marriage disincentives.

One other type of reform needs to be considered because it fits in well with the theory behind structured choice, even as it moves beyond a voucher per se by enhancing cash assistance for those who work. The suggestion is a wage rate subsidy paid on the basis of individual earnings rates, not household income. The subsidy may or may not be confined to those workers who have dependent children. For example, the subsidy, which could be targeted to up to two adults in a family with children, could pay a fraction of the difference between $10 an hour and the worker's actual wage.[38] Canada is currently experimenting with a generous but temporary wage subsidy aimed at encouraging families to leave welfare.[39]

The presence of this subsidy would allow for a lower guarantee under a system of structured or fragmented choice using vouchers, and it could increase work incentives without harming low-income families. Although wage subsidies result in different payments to families with the same incomes and family size, such an approach can still be justified on a variety of equity grounds.[40] Wage rate subsidies essentially pay the highest benefits to those willing to work longest at low wages. Indeed, the ability of an adult earner to earn only low wage rates may be a better indicator of economic status than reported income.

One of the great advantages of individual wage rate subsidies is that we can avoid marriage penalties altogether, as suggested by C. Eugene Steuerle in a recent study.[41] Moreover, the wage subsidy embodies the principle that the more people work, the less restrictive is their government assistance. Implementing a wage rate subsidy in the context of a broad-based voucher might also allow some substitution for an EITC that currently provides subsidies on the basis of annual earnings regardless of wage rates and is the source of many marriage penalties itself. The subsidy could also be designed to keep benefit reduction rates moderate for those with low wages and low income.

Child support assurance (CSA) is another way to help mostly low- and lower-middle-income parents without an income test.[42] If the government were unable to collect child support from noncustodial parents—either because it cannot find the parent or because the parent has very little income—the custodial parent would be eligible for some minimum payment. Although the payment would be subject to the income tax and thus would lower the tax threshold, it would not have a phaseout range. All custodial parents cooperating with child support collection agencies would qualify. The philosophy underlying this program is that absent parents have an obligation to pay for child support, but the government also has a responsibility to enforce that obligation. When both fail, the custodial parent should not have to pay for the entire shortfall. The government's inability to collect, not poverty, would trigger benefits. Still, the vast bulk of the outlays under CSA would go to low-income families.[43]

Conclusions

The logical first step of considering vouchers as a means of income assistance leads to examining under what circumstances choices should be expanded or restricted. The case for subsidizing each particular necessity or merit good through a separate voucher is generally dependent on very selective circumstances. First, donor preferences must be quite strong for the precise amount of good purchased by recipients, perhaps because there are side effects or "externalities" that benefit the donor himself, or the donor's view of the marginal "merit" of the good declines rapidly when more or less of it is purchased. Second, sometimes there are considerable administrative difficulties, such as adverse selection and moral hazard, that cannot be avoided through other regulations or subsidies of risk pools. Absent either of these two conditions, structured choice or the bundling of vouchers offers a powerful way to operate within the voucher paradigm, because it directly expands opportunity within a set of goods and services that society has already decided to subsidize and prescribe.

Bundled vouchers expand choice outside the prescribed set only when the individual already has other resources that can be more easily shifted. However, when there are sufficient earnings and income, substitution is easier no matter how the vouchers are designed. In any case, almost any level of proscription, effective or not, entails some administrative costs and reductions in value for beneficiaries. Society seems to recognize these additional burdens and often tries to avoid them; thus it is more willing to provide cash directly through earned income tax credits or child credits for those who work and have sufficient earnings.

A variety of design options are available under structured choice: the number of goods and services covered, the involvement of caseworkers in choices made, and a more thorough integration of plans rather than a simple combining of choices under existing eligibility and benefit reduction rules. Small, incremental reform would involve combining vouchers aimed at some common goal, such as covering expenses related to work. A higher level of reform would involve more services and goods, at least in cases that expanded opportunity in the view of caseworkers, as well as recipients. In the ideal, a system of structured choice would be integrated with earned income tax credits or wage rate subsidies, child credits, and child assurance payments not only in a consistent fashion, but in a way that finally tackled the huge work and marriage disincentives under current law.

Notes

1. See other chapters in this book for a more thorough list of advantages and potential disadvantages of vouchers.

2. C. Eugene Steuerle, "Uses of the Negative Income Tax Framework," *Focus*, vol. 12, no. 3 (Spring 1990), pp. 30–32.

3. C. Eugene Steuerle and Gordon Mermin, "Devolution as Seen from the Budget," Series A, no. A-2 (Urban Institute, 1997).

4. *Green Book*, Committee Print, House Committee on Ways and Means, 105 Cong., 2 sess. (Government Printing Office, 1998).

5. Ibid.

6. We do not address the issue here of whether increased choice makes it easier for the recipient to displace spending he or she would have done anyway. Obviously, the more resources the recipient has on the side, the easier it is to substitute government spending for that spending.

7. Lawrence Mead, *The New Paternalism: Supervisory Approaches to Poverty* (Brookings, 1997).

8. For information on Wisconsin Works (W-2), see the web site at <http://www.dwd.state.wi.us/desw2/w2home.htm>.

9. One might argue that if greater discretion is also given to caseworkers, the recipient does not necessarily have greater individual choice. However, the number of feasible options on which they could agree still has increased.

10. *Green Book*, p. 410.

11. See Toby Douglas, Kimura Flores, and Deborah Ellwood, *The Children's Budget Report: A Detailed Analysis of Spending on Low-Income Children's Programs in 13 States* (Urban Institute, 1998).

12. See the discussion in chapter 4 of this book by Robert Moffitt.

13. Benjamin Weiser, "Food Stamp Fraud Cited in New York," *New York Times*, August 11, 1998, p. A1.

14. Rent subsidies depend on fair market rents (FMR), which vary widely across geographic areas. In many locations, fair market rents reach well beyond the family's entire income. For example, in the San Francisco metropolitan statistical area, the FMR for a two-bedroom unit is $987 a month. Admittedly, this level is far above average, but FMR values in other metropolitan areas are often high relative to the incomes of recipients. In Detroit, the FMR is $618 for a two-bedroom unit. For a recipient not working and receiving cash income only from the Temporary Assistance for Needy Families, this gross housing benefit would constitute nearly half the family's total income, including food stamps and the net value of housing subsidies. Those with a full-time minimum wage job in Michigan would have to allocate at least 36 percent of their gross income to housing.

15. See Robert Moffitt, chapter 4 of this volume.

16. John Weicher, "Child Care and Welfare Reform: The Wisconsin Experience," presented at the conference on "Day Care and Early Childhood Programs under Welfare Reform," American Enterprise Institute, Washington, D.C., March 24, 1997.

17. *Green Book*.

18. Sharon Long and Sandra Clark, *The New Child Care Block Grant: State Funding Choices and Their Implications* (Urban Institute, 1997).

19. With declines in overall welfare roles, increases in federal funding and state maintenance of effort requirements under TANF have also led to significant increases in child-care funding.

20. *Green Book.*

21. C. Eugene Steuerle and Linda Giannarelli, "The True Tax Rates Faced by Welfare Recipients," in National Tax Association, *Proceedings of the Eighty-Seventh Annual Conference, 1995* (1996), pp. 123–29.

22. Robert Lerman, Gregory Acs, Keith Watson, and Norma Coe, *Does Work Pay? An Analysis of the Work Incentives under TANF* (Urban Institute, 1998).

23. Benefit reduction rates cumulate fastest when each program ignores the benefits provided from the other program. For example, food stamp benefits generally do not decline with changes in housing benefits and housing programs do not count food stamps as income. As a result, the benefit reduction rates from the two programs alone are additive and add up to about 54 percent of added earnings.

24. To the extent that social security contributions count as part of earnings records, they bring at least a reasonable rate of return to low-wage workers. If workers were to recognize this reality, they may not view the Social Security tax as a reduced incentive to work. However, the cost of taxes paid by employers on behalf of low-wage workers may be borne by the workers themselves and thus reduce financial rewards for work. In addition, low-wage workers may bear the cost of other payroll taxes at a higher rate than others. Employers are subject to the tax only up to some specified, often relatively low, earnings amount per worker.

25. Food stamps and housing programs count welfare income, but income counted against the welfare grant generally does not include food stamps or housing benefits. In these cases, the combined benefit reductions equal the TANF reduction rate (say, 50 percent, as in California beyond a modest earnings disregard) plus the product of TANF rate and the food stamp reduction rate (0.5 × 0.24). Even with these two programs, additional complications arise as a result of the "excess shelter deduction" in food stamps. Added income lowers the extent to which a recipient is considered to have an excess housing burden, thereby lowering a deduction from income and reducing benefits. As a result, families subject to shelter burdens face a combined benefit reduction rate from these two programs of 63.5 percent.

26. The income cutoff often depends on the poverty line, implying that the earnings threshold at which benefits suddenly fall will vary across families.

27. States must cover pregnant women and children under age six so long as the family's income is no more than 133 percent of the poverty line (about $17,700 for a family of three in 1997). All children (up to age fifteen in September 1998) in families with incomes below 100 percent ($13,300 for a family of four) qualify for Medicaid. In these cases, the cutoff of Medicaid benefits would take place at wage levels as low as $6.65 an hour (which equals $13,300 at 2,000 hours of work annually) or at levels up to $8.84 an hour ($17,700 at 2,000 hours) or

higher if the individual works fewer than 2,000 hours annually. A few states, including Hawaii, Minnesota, Tennessee, and Washington, have used sliding scale fees that add a low (under 4 percent) benefit reduction rate over a range of earnings. Leighton Ku and Teresa Coughlin, *The Use of Sliding Scale Premiums in Subsidized Insurance Programs* (Urban Institute, 1997).

28. A notable exception is James Alm and Leslie Whittington, "Income Taxes and the Marriage Decision," *Applied Economics*, vol. 27, no. 1 (1995), pp. 25–31.

29. C. Eugene Steuerle, "The Effects of Tax and Welfare Policies on Family Formation," the Family Impact Seminar, "Strategies to Strengthen Marriage, What Do We Know? What Do We Need to Know?" Washington, D.C., 1997; C. Eugene Steuerle, *A Comprehensive Approach to Removing Marriage Penalties* (Washington, D.C.: The Communitarian Network, 1999).

30. See Stacy Dickert-Conlin and Scott Houser, "Taxes and Transfers: A New Look at the Marriage Penalty," Institute for Research on Poverty, Discussion Paper (1997), pp. 1146–97.

31. Steuerle, *Removing Marriage Penalties.*

32. The Internet site for Michigan's "Tool Chest" program is located at <http://www.thumbworks.org>.

33. See, for example, Lawrence M. Mead, "How Should Congress Respond? If Waivers Are Granted, Congress Must Monitor Results," *Public Welfare*, vol. 50 (Spring 1992), pp. 14–17.

34. The income tax threshold for 1998 was calculated by adding the standard deduction ($6,250), three exemptions worth $2,700 apiece, and two child credits valued at $5,333.

35. In truth, if we count the assistance of the caseworker to be of value for the longer term, then their total benefit package is worth more than the short-run consumption that it allows to be purchased.

36. Robert Lerman, "Separating Income Support from Income Supplementation," *Journal of the Institute for Socioeconomic Studies* (Autumn 1985), pp. 101–25, makes the argument for this approach and develops a mix of programs that builds on the concept. Also, see George Akerlof, "The Economics of 'Tagging' as Applied to the Optimal Income Tax, Welfare Programs, and Manpower Planning," in *An Economic Theorist's Book of Tales: Essays that Entertain the Consequences of New Assumptions in Economic Theory* (Cambridge University Press, 1984), pp. 45–68.

37. Jack Habib and Robert Lerman, "Options in Income Support for the Aged: A Critique of the Two-Tier Approach," *Journal of Public Economics*, vol. 11, no. 2 (April 1979), pp. 159–77.

38. Recently, Robert Lawrence and Robert Litan, in *Globalism: The Wrong Debate over Trade Policy*, Policy Brief 24 (Brookings, September 1997), have suggested a similar subsidy to those displaced by trade.

39. See Social Research and Demonstration Corporation (SRDC), *When Work Pays Better than Welfare* (Ottawa, Canada, 1996).

40. For example, we would want to take account of leisure as a part of a measure of ability or need. Also the "equitable" unit of taxation or benefit receipt is never precisely clear. If defined as the household rather than the individual, for instance, it almost inevitably leads to treating married couples differently than cohabitating couples or adults sharing living space even when their combined income is exactly the same.

41. Steuerle, *Removing Marriage Penalties*.

42. Irwin Garfinkel, Sara S. McLanahan, and Philip K. Robins, *Child Support Assurance: Design Issues, Expected Impacts, and Political Barriers as Seen from Wisconsin* (Urban Institute, 1992).

43. To offset some of the costs of CSA, the government could count CSA payments as income, thereby triggering benefit reductions in income-conditioned programs, including the broad-based voucher.

PAUL POSNER, ROBERT YETVIN,
MARK SCHNEIDERMAN,
CHRISTOPHER SPIRO,
ANDREA BARNETT

17 | *A Survey of Voucher Use: Variations and Common Elements*

A WIDE VARIETY of voucher programs are currently in use in the United States at the federal, state, and local levels. This chapter discusses the results of a survey on the use of vouchers across a wide range of programs. The various levels of government and private-sector entities covered in the survey permit identification of the rich variation in vouchers as they are used across major program areas. Appendix 17A at the end of the chapter reveals the cases identified in this survey, organized by program area. The survey also captures common features of the vouchers covered, which both help define the voucher tool and highlight its key design dimensions. Among other features, variations were identified in the range of choice provided to recipients, the methods of payment, and types of accountability and control mechanisms. Using these examples as a base, some common challenges faced by those charged with designing and managing vouchers can be drawn out.

The survey used a broad definition of vouchers. Any assistance that allows program participants to choose a service provider within a limited set of choices and within limited total costs is considered a voucher, even if no formal certificate is issued or no formal reference to "voucher" is used in the program.

We approached our work by identifying leading voucher examples from a variety of sources. To identify programs using vouchers at the federal

503

level, we spoke with federal officials in departmental planning and evaluation offices for the departments of Health and Human Services (HHS),
Housing and Urban Development, Education, and Defense. We also sent
out written questionnaires to major federal grant programs listed in the
Catalogue of Federal Domestic Assistance to ascertain whether vouchers were
part of federal, state, or local program delivery strategies. In addition, we
searched reports from the General Accounting Office and the Congressional Research Service on a variety of domestic programs for cases where
vouchers were used.

At the state and local level, we searched state and city web sites and newspaper articles for notable examples. We looked at case studies on income
support and social services conducted by the Urban Institute as part of its
Assessing the New Federalism project, which described major state employment and training, child care, child support, child welfare, emergency services, housing, and health programs. We spoke to representatives of associations of state and local officials, such as the Government Finance Officers
Association and the Council of State Governments, to obtain any studies and
examples those groups have identified. We also searched private foundation
sources for innovative voucher initiatives sponsored or recognized by those
organizations, and we reviewed books, articles, and case identifications on
vouchers in several program areas for additional background.

Once voucher cases were identified, we followed up by conducting a
telephone survey with staff members from many of the programs we chose
to include in our matrix. These conversations added depth to our work and
helped clarify many of the issues outlined in this chapter.

These various strategies enabled us first to build a long list of potential
cases and then to screen out those examples that failed (1) to meet our definitional criteria, (2) to offer any distinguishing features beyond those
already listed for a program area, or (3) to provide sufficient information
on program characteristics and activities. In deciding which cases to
include in the matrix at the end of this chapter, we gave special weight to
voucher programs that highlighted innovative approaches to voucher
design and implementation. The survey and resulting matrix of examples
is only intended to illustrate voucher use and suggest variations and is not
designed to be comprehensive or to portray the universe of vouchers used.

Major Program Areas that Use Vouchers

Our survey found that vouchers are used across a wide and diverse range of
program areas. These programs were catalogued into ten major areas: child

care, criminal justice, education, employment and training, environmental protection, general assistance, health care, housing, nutrition, and transportation. For many of these areas, such as child care or low-income housing, vouchers are intergovernmental initiatives, funded by federal and state governments and implemented by a diverse array of local governments and nonprofit and for-profit entities. In some areas, like criminal justice or environmental protection, vouchers are often grassroots innovations launched by local governments or nonprofits through a combination of public and private funds.

Vouchers, however implemented, have several rationales. We typically think of a voucher program as offering a coupon to an individual or family that enables them to choose providers to obtain a specific and limited good or service, such as food or child care. Indeed, the majority of voucher programs in our survey fell into this category. Many of these programs also targeted their benefits on lower-income people.

In addition to traditional voucher programs, we also identified vouchers whose primary goal was to provide incentives to change behavior of participants and to promote broader community goals. Vouchers are used to encourage compliance with air quality goals, to promote water conservation, to advance public health goals, and to promote public safety objectives such as rewarding the disposal of guns. Voucher programs are also used as a tool to facilitate compliance with new laws and regulations.

Programs differ in the scope of services and goods covered. Most traditional voucher programs target use to one category (for example, housing or food) but also offer several goods or services within this category (for example, vouchers for education may include a subsidy for books, fees, and tuition). Several programs, however, provide a more flexible range of goods and services to better meet the needs of recipients. State welfare reform initiatives have generated new case-managed voucher programs that offer a range of services from transportation to child care to education to allow the participant additional choices of services necessary to move from welfare to work.

Child Care

The 1996 federal welfare reform established a new consolidated federal child-care program. Parental choice is a key goal of this program, and states are required to give families the opportunity to obtain child care from a broad range of providers through a form of voucher the program calls "certificates." As with federal child-care assistance before the 1996 welfare reform program, states still provide care through contracts with specific service providers, but vouchers have become the primary vehicle for financing care in most states. Parents are given a choice of using their vouchers at state-licensed day care facilities or hiring informal care providers such as relatives, neighbors, or friends. Nationwide, over half of poor parents use these informal care arrangements. These providers are exempt from state licensure requirements, and most states have not chosen to actively monitor this sector, relying instead on self-certifications of compliance with health and safety standards. Although child-care assistance is no longer an entitlement for welfare recipients, most federal funds must be used for Temporary Assistance for Needy Families (TANF) recipients, public assistance families in work activities, or families at risk of becoming dependent on public assistance.

Our survey showed some variations in how states implemented voucher programs. South Carolina has transitioned to vouchers as a result of the federal program mandate but maintains a system where state-licensed day care facilities get contracts from the state for a specific number of children. As vouchers have enabled parents to use informal providers to meet their needs, the state-contracted facilities have had problems competing and some may be forced to consolidate or go out of business. Wisconsin, however, has relied on vouchers for many years for day care and has not experienced these transition problems.

Criminal Justice

Programs in criminal justice use vouchers as incentives to reward behavior that promotes community public safety goals. We found programs that encourage people to turn in illegal guns for vouchers to purchase groceries or other products. We also found a voucher program for persons who successfully maintain their probation status.

The Pittsburgh Goods for Guns program (similar programs were identified in Columbus, New Orleans, Santa Rosa, New York, and Philadelphia) provide an incentive to reduce the number of guns in the community. The program is privately supported and uses grocery and department store certificates as vouchers. Individuals are rewarded with $25 certificates for turning in an operating handgun and with $50 certificates for turning in a long gun. The programs collect an average of a thousand guns a year.

The Thrift Store Vouchers for Children's Hospital of Orange County, California, provide low-income probationers with vouchers to obtain items such as clothing, furniture, and appliances from ten thrift stores. Examples include clothes vouchers for teenagers who participate in long-term drug rehabilitation programs and "baby showers" for pregnant women.

Education

Vouchers for higher education and K–12 typically serve different purposes. In higher education, vouchers are used as a financial means to access education for millions of students, with voucher awards often based on both financial need and merit. Financial access is not an issue for K–12 education, since public school is available to everyone. So K–12 vouchers typically provide greater choice and improved opportunity. While largely limited to choice within public schools, including magnet and charter schools, several local and state voucher programs expand the student's choice to private and religious schools. Some of these programs have the dual goals of directly improving the education of participating students in the short run while fostering competition to indirectly improve the public education system for all students in the long run. Also, K–12 vouchers have been used to enable students who live in a district without a public school to attend private schools.

For example, the Cleveland Tutoring program, funded by the Ohio Department of Public Instruction, provides vouchers for up to $500 ($10 an hour) for before- and after-school tutoring for children in grades K–3, with eligibility based on a sliding income scale. The student may be tutored by any individual who has an Ohio teaching certificate and who is approved by the state. Each student's regular teacher evaluates the quality of the instruction and provides a report to both parents and instructor.

The Cleveland Scholarship program, also funded by the Ohio Department of Public Instruction, reimburses parents up to $2,500 for the tuition costs of K–3 students to attend the public or private school of their choice, provided that school meets certain criteria. Students from low-income families have priority, with awards made by lottery. The Cambridge, Massachusetts, Controlled Choice program also awards vouchers by lottery to promote choice among public schools, with the goal of promoting desegregation across the schools within the city.

Employment and Training

Traditional job training vouchers typically enable the participants to choose the type of training they receive from any number of vocational schools, colleges, or private firms. Several federal and local area programs use vouchers as part of their work force development strategy. In some cases, vouchers are provided for participants who are permitted to choose courses and providers on their own without the help of a counselor, while other programs provide for case managers to serve as career counselors and facilitators.[1] Vouchers are also used for employment retention by providing a package of goods and services to persons currently employed but at risk of losing their job.

Several voucher programs in our survey target dislocated workers. Funded by Title III of the Job Training Partnership Act (JTPA) program, San Bernardino County, California, provides up to $4,000 in training for each worker displaced by cutbacks in the aerospace and defense industries. The county auditor writes eligible individuals a check to be presented to qualified providers. This same federal program underwrites a program in Phoenix that awards up to $7,500 per person for education, training, and support services for occupations in high demand, coupled with an incentive payment of $500 should the individual remain employed for six months. Payments are made directly to vendors, who qualify based on approval by the local Chamber of Commerce or other local entities.

Vouchers have also been used for job retention. In the District IX Welfare to Work program in Montana, a job retention specialist approves a package of goods and services specially designed for the participant. This bundled voucher program offers goods and services that will support the client's employment or retention needs, including child care, clothing, gas for a car, or computer classes as support to the employee. (For a discussion of bundled vouchers, see the chapter by Robert Lerman and C. Eugene Steuerle in this volume.)

Environmental Protection

Environmental concerns have led to voucher programs that provide incentives for compliance with environmental laws and regulations. These programs address specific program goals, such as water conservation or clean air.

The Mow Down Pollution program in Tucson, Arizona, creates an incentive for persons to turn in their old gas-powered lawnmowers and replace them with electric-powered mowers. This program uses funds appropriated by the state legislature for new, EPA-approved electric lawnmowers, and area residents may purchase a new mower from any of twenty-four participating stores. The Tucson Electric and Power Company helps promote this program by advertising it on its monthly electric bills.

Last year the program collected 1,676 mowers, which will yield an estimated 439 tons in pollution reduction a year.

The Ultra-Low Flush Toilet Voucher program in San Diego is supported by the San Diego Water Authority and provides area residents with vouchers for new low-flush toilets or rebates if they turn in their old high-water-usage toilets. This program is designed to help residents comply with a California law that mandates 1.6 gallons-per-flush toilets. The program estimates that households will save around $48 per year on water and sewer bills and 11,000 gallons of water a year. Persons can purchase the new toilets from most wholesale and retail plumbing stores.

General Assistance

In the area of general assistance, many states have incorporated the use of vouchers into their programs in response to welfare reform. The 1996 welfare reform legislation ended the tradition of welfare cash entitlements, which has provided states the opportunity to employ other mechanisms, including vouchers, to target resources as they deem appropriate to meet the new program's goals. In most cases vouchers replace cash assistance and are provided for the "necessities of life," including shelter, utilities, food, and clothing. Vouchers are often used in situations where welfare recipients fail to meet certain conditions of assistance, including obtaining work within the time limit, not having additional children, and being convicted of drug offenses. Because the introduction of these vouchers into general assistance programs follows a tradition of cash assistance, vouchers are often viewed as limiting choice and involve oversight by caseworkers. Other programs, however, use vouchers as an add-on to traditional general assistance by providing supplemental assistance to welfare recipients on either a one-time or short-term basis.

Oklahoma's Vouchers for Infants and Toddlers program provides two $30 vouchers monthly to mothers who give birth to a child while receiving TANF. The program was a compromise between those seeking to protect the state's family cap policy and those fearful that the family cap policy of limiting benefits to families with additional children could result in abortion or child neglect. Recipients use the vouchers like cash at any store for food, clothing, and other articles of necessity for the child up to age three. The Family Independence Act of South Carolina provides assistance for TANF families that move to become more self-sufficient, for example, to an area with increased employment opportunities. Clients work closely with a caseworker, who approves each voucher use. Payment is made in a variety of ways, including reimbursement to the vendor, reimbursement directly to the client with proof of payment for the good or service, and even cash to the client in some cases.

A number of localities are using vouchers to provide assistance to panhandlers. To gain some control over what the recipients purchase, a Berkeley, California, program enables people to give vouchers instead of change to panhandlers. Vouchers can be redeemed for food, laundry, or bus passes, but not for alcohol or tobacco. National legislation has been proposed to extend these initiatives throughout the nation.

Health Care

Vouchers for health care are used to provide either medical services—prescription drugs or vaccinations for example—or incentives for employers or employees to purchase health insurance coverage. In both cases vouchers target low-to-middle-income persons who would otherwise have minimal access to health care. Vouchers are not as common for health care as in other areas, since public funding primarily involves direct payment of health care costs for Medicaid and Medicare rather than subsidizing consumer purchase of health insurance from a choice of health care plans. As the Medicaid and Medicare programs move toward providing their recipients a choice of health insurance coverage (that is, through health maintenance organizations or other managed-care arrangements), they move closer to becoming a voucher program.

One innovative private health voucher program targets prescription drugs for children whose parents do not qualify for government health care programs and who cannot afford to purchase prescription drug coverage. The Pasco Pediatric Foundation's Prescription Voucher Program was created when it became apparent that lower-income parents not eligible for Medicaid were not obtaining drugs prescribed by doctors for their children because they could not afford to do so and were ashamed to tell their doctors this. This program gives these parents a voucher to purchase prescription drugs from several pharmacies in the Pasco County area in Florida.

Some vouchers help provide a subsidy to purchase health insurance coverage for the uninsured. A proposed Massachusetts state program available under a Health Care Financing Administration waiver will provide a voucher payment that allows employers and employees to purchase health insurance coverage in the private market. An Oregon program subsidizes the purchase of either individual or employer-sponsored health insurance by lower-income families. Officials associated with both programs have expressed concerns that these vouchers might prompt employers to drop or reduce existing health coverage for participating workers.

Public health services are also provided through vouchers. In Los Angeles, vouchers are provided for pet owners to neuter their pets at veterinarian offices, funded by a $2 surcharge on dog licenses. Several cities are providing vouchers as incentives for former cocaine addicts to remain drug free.

Housing

Housing voucher programs offer recipients greater housing choice than traditional project-based public housing programs do. These programs seek to permit families to move from high poverty areas to middle-class neighborhoods. The largest of such programs is the federal Section 8 housing voucher program, which serves over 1.4 million households, with annual federal spending estimated at $16.7 billion. Vouchers coexist with other federal housing subsidy tools, including public housing, project-based assistance for construction of private low-income housing, and the low-income housing tax credit that subsidizes low-income housing developers through the tax code.

Other housing voucher programs initiated by states and localities, sometimes with federal support, tend to target specific groups, such as persons with AIDS, the homeless, or the mentally ill, in an effort to address either permanent or temporary housing needs. For instance, the state-funded Bridges program in Minnesota provides temporary housing vouchers for severely mentally ill persons who are awaiting Section 8 housing vouchers or certificates. Through this program, the recipient may choose any housing unit as long as the landlord accepts the vouchers. The program has been received very well by landlords, since both the housing agency and the mental health agency provide support if problem situations arise. In addition, the program will pay rent and utilities for up to ninety days if recipients are hospitalized because of their illnesses. This has proven to be very helpful during hospitalization, since the recipients are assured that their belongings will be safe and that they will have a place to return to after discharge.

Several cities have used federal Community Development Block Grant funds to implement a voucher tool lending program. Lower-income families in targeted neighborhoods receive vouchers for up to $500 in tool rentals to renovate their housing units.

Nutrition

Nutrition voucher programs provide essential food products to low-income families. Vouchers for food, rather than cash assistance, limit choice of foods to those that program designers believe will encourage healthy eating habits. The $27.6 billion federal Food Stamp Program and the $3.7 billion Women, Infants, and Children (WIC) program dominate food voucher programs.

The federal Food Stamp Program, administered at the state and local levels, provides food vouchers to low-income households—generally families with incomes below 130 percent of federal poverty guidelines. Electronic benefit transfer cards will soon replace coupon vouchers to reduce the potential for fraudulent trafficking, where food coupons are exchanged for cash. The program sanctions states if they have significant error rates in determining eligibility and benefit levels and financially rewards states that perform this task well.

The WIC program is administered by states, which provide vouchers for low-income pregnant and postpartum women and their children for the purchase of specified food items such as infant formula, cereals, and fruit. The WIC Farmer's Market Nutrition Program provides vouchers to eligible low-income recipients to purchase fresh fruit and vegetables at authorized farmer's markets. For both programs, vouchers are provided directly to participants, who exchange them for authorized food items at designated retail outlets or farm stands.

Transportation

Transportation voucher programs provide individuals or special groups with access to specific transportation services while also seeking to achieve corresponding goals such as environmental protection, traffic control, and public safety. Mass transit vouchers, which provide employers a tax incentive to offer vouchers to their employees, have the multiple goals of subsidizing the cost of employee travel to work as well as reducing automobile traffic problems and air pollution. Other programs target people who need transportation because of a disability. Transportation vouchers are also provided to welfare recipients as part of the general assistance package of services and vouchers to encourage work.

The Los Angeles Police Department sponsors a program that provides taxi rides to individuals who are intoxicated to prevent motor vehicle accidents. The program provides 50,000 taxicab vouchers for use with ten city cab companies during the holiday season for rides up to seven miles each within the Los Angeles city limits.

The Immediate Need program, also in Los Angeles, provides vouchers for low-income and homeless individuals for taxi rides to doctor's offices, food banks, battered women's shelters, and other important locations. Administered by social service agencies throughout Los Angeles county and supported by a one-half cent per gallon tax increase, this program has distributed 60,000 vouchers worth about seven dollars each. Similarly, the Massachusetts Medicaid program provides vouchers to eligible participants for transportation to doctors and other health service providers.

Voucher Program Implementation Observations

Our survey of vouchers across these ten areas also surfaced some common implementation issues. Our discussions with program administrators at federal, state, and local levels suggest that officials face a number of key decisions and trade-offs in administering voucher programs. The following discussion, drawn from the matrix of voucher examples included in this chapter, suggests that different approaches have been articulated to address these common challenges. It describes some of the important administrative issues but is by no means exhaustive.

Choice of Providers

Choice is one of the defining characteristics that distinguishes vouchers from other tools of government. Although limiting participants to particular goods or services, vouchers often give recipients an expanded choice among providers, particularly when compared to previous delivery approaches they replaced.

Our survey suggests, however, that voucher programs vary considerably in the range of choice available to recipients in the selection of providers. Several programs allow the individual to receive a good or service from nearly any provider. Certain general assistance programs in our survey, for instance, provide vouchers to welfare clients that can be used at any provider for specific goods. The federal child-care program enables parents to receive care from a wide range of informal providers who are exempt from state regulation, such as relatives, neighbors, and friends. As more parents choose these informal providers, the expanded choice in day care is forcing providers that formerly received exclusive state contracts to compete for clients and may prompt consolidation of centers as a result.

Most of the cases in our matrix limit choice to providers certified or licensed by either a government agency or private accrediting body, although in many cases the choices available were quite extensive. Food stamps, for instance, can only be used in USDA-approved stores, although the range of choice is quite extensive in urban areas. Other programs limit choice to a narrower group of providers. For example, the RESTART job training program in Palm Beach County, Florida, limits vouchers to thirty public and private providers that are approved by the county through a competitive process. The Prescription Voucher Program in Pasco County, Florida, limits choice to Kmart pharmacies only.

Various rationales have been offered for the selection of providers participating in voucher programs. In some cases officials have sought to control costs by selecting a limited number of providers through competitive bidding. For example, every two years Delaware's WIC program selects a limited number of vendors that bid the lowest prices and meet minimum qualification standards. In a recent study, most states reported limiting the number of vendors in the WIC program to constrain costs.[2]

Quality was also an important consideration in regulating the participation of providers. Section 8 housing voucher rules require that rental units meet HUD standards for health and safety. Health care vouchers to purchase insurance are generally limited to health care plans that meet certain benefit plan and fiscal standards. In Massachusetts, a proposed voucher for employer-sponsored health insurance would disqualify health insurance plans that failed to meet certain benefit levels and fiscal solvency standards.

Vouchers have raised some unique regulatory challenges for officials as a consequence of the expansion of the types of providers involved in public services. Although promoting greater choice for program participants, the subsidization of new types of providers has raised new questions about the quality of their programs and invited a debate over the extension of regulatory standards to their operations. In the day care program, for instance, vouchers have made public subsidies available for a range of informal providers—for example, neighbors, relatives, and friends—that have largely been exempt from state licensing and standards. States in our survey have chosen either not to regulate this sector or to apply certain minimal checks on informal providers, such as criminal background tests. Controversy continues as a federal HHS inspector general report has recommended state inspections and background checks of all informal providers by states.³ In the education area, vouchers raise sensitive issues about the regulation of religious schools that are participating in some voucher experiments. As with any subsidy, there is a risk that the subsidy itself may elicit the participation of opportunistic providers that lack sufficient commitment to quality or service goals of the program.⁴

Accountability and Controls

Vouchers raise the potential for fraud and abuse. For instance, vouchers such as food stamps or WIC can be misused when coupons are used to acquire nonauthorized goods from retailers, such as beer and wine.⁵ Vouchers can also be exchanged for cash through "trafficking," where the participant and the retailer collude in a process involving falsification of billing claims to government agencies. This problem has become particularly acute for food stamps, where one 1995 study estimated that $815 million, or 4 percent of all vouchers, were trafficked.⁶

A wide variety of administrative controls has been used to deter fiscal abuse and misuse of voucher funds by both providers and recipients. These concerns were addressed in our cases through payment mechanisms, oversight processes, transactional controls, and design constraints governing the range of goods and services offered.

We found several different payment approaches that were being used to provide vouchers for services. In some cases vouchers were provided directly to individual participants. Programs like food stamps and WIC and certain job training vouchers provide coupons or other types of authorization directly for the acquisition of a good or service. Many vouchers intended to serve as incentives for some kind of behavior change, such as for handgun turn-ins and pet neutering, are provided directly to consumers. Providers typically obtain reimbursement from state or local agencies.

In a number of other voucher-type programs, formal vouchers are not provided to individuals. Although individuals are free to choose among a range of providers, payment is made directly to the provider, typically on a reimbursement basis. Some officials believe that paying providers limits the potential for fraud and misuse. A Wisconsin child-care official, for instance, said that when vouchers were paid directly to parents, many providers never received sufficient payments, prompting the state to switch to direct provider payments.

Direct payments to providers or vendors cannot always eliminate fraud. The Section 8 housing program sometimes attracts participants and landlords who attempt to establish eligibility or increase benefits by falsifying information. State day care officials in our survey expressed concern that nonlicensed informal providers might bill for services for days children were not attending.

A range of approaches has been adopted to address these potential problems. State agencies conduct monitoring visits to half of the vendors for the WIC program each year, and they frequently sanction stores found to be overcharging the program for covered items. The food stamp program has long relied on U.S. Department of Agriculture inspections of retailers suspected of trafficking, based in part on profiles of store sales patterns. By 2002 states will be required to use electronic benefit transfers as the method of payment for food stamp vouchers, which will enable program overseers to better track retail store records to discover cases of fraud. This change in program design also serves to lessen the stigma for food stamp recipients, since they will no longer need to show a food stamp coupon at the grocery store.

State and local housing authorities have adopted several approaches to address fraud and abuse. Minnesota requires annual recertification of eligibility for its Rental Assistance for Family Stabilization Program, a temporary housing voucher for families transitioning to work. Some housing authorities have created fraud detection units to weed out such problems as unreported spouses or other adult wage earners in the household, unreported or underreported client income, and unreported side-payment agreements between tenants and landlords. Initial tips come from agency staff members who encounter inconsistent statements during interviews, from inspection findings, and from anonymous telephone calls. With online access to other state information, such as the Department of Motor Vehicles, the fraud unit can quickly investigate possibly fraudulent behavior by tenants or landlords.[7]

State day care officials in our survey review child attendance reports and social security numbers from all providers. Inspections are triggered when providers report suspect data, such as 100 percent attendance by all children. Milwaukee's education voucher experiment requires private schools to submit an independent financial audit each year.

Some voucher programs have controls over voucher payments to reduce potential for abuse. Some voucher programs, such as the Ultra Low-Flush Toilet Voucher program, provide payment on the voucher only when an original sales receipt is submitted. Most states pay day care providers only on a reimbursement basis once claims are submitted for actual expenses, contrary to the prospective payment that many providers receive in the private market.

Other programs review voucher-funded activities from a performance perspective on both a prospective and retrospective basis. Oklahoma's Flexible Funding general assistance program requires local caseworkers to authorize each use of vouchers by welfare clients for specific work transitional services. Staff members with the Texas Panhandle job training program provide assessment and counseling and must provide preapproval for all uses of vouchers. This program as well as other employment and training vouchers, such as the Michigan Tool Chest program, also measure the performance of vendors against such criteria as job placement and wages achieved by clients. Similarly, the Cleveland Tutoring Program provides for an evaluation of the quality of tutoring services acquired with the voucher, and these reports are submitted to both parents and providers.

Program design limiting the use of vouchers or of the providers participating can also be viewed as a way to control misuse. For instance, in the Goods for Guns program, vouchers are only available from specific stores for certain kinds of merchandise. Similarly, vouchers for cocaine abstinence can only be redeemed at specific stores for particular goods or services purchased by a clinical team. In some states, general assistance vouchers for welfare clients can only be used for child-related commodities such as food and clothing.

Resource Trade-offs

In most cases resources for voucher programs were limited, often necessitating difficult trade-offs. Officials in our cases developed various ways of rationing vouchers among eligible beneficiaries and constraining payment levels and costs. Some programs chose voucher payment levels to ensure that as many eligible people as possible would receive some level of goods or services. For example, the Senior Pharmacy Program in Massachusetts set the maximum annual voucher amount at $750 so that thousands of potentially eligible elders would receive at least some benefit from the program, even though the voucher amount would not, in most cases, cover a year's supply of drugs nor be related to actual expenses in a given year. The Rental Assistance for Family Stabilization program in Minnesota sets a fixed "shallow subsidy" voucher amount of $200 a month to supplement housing costs for family members who are in the process of finding stable jobs. This program has decided, however, to provide an additional $50 a month to families living in the more expensive Twin Cities area.

Officials also have chosen several ways to ration vouchers to eligible program participants when resources were scarce. For example, because the supply of Section 8 housing is limited and there are so many eligible house-holds, families must wait several years before receiving assistance. Housing authorities are finding innovative ways to manage waiting lists by estab-lishing reciprocal waiting list agreements with neighboring communities and using innovative voice response systems to inform participants of wait-ing list status.[8] The Cleveland Scholarship Program uses a lottery to deter-mine which children will participate in the voucher experiment. In the day care area, states limit eligibility to an income level below federal eligibility maximums and require higher parental co-payments. Wisconsin decided to target eligibility to serve all families at a lower level than the federal maxi-mum, thereby eliminating waiting lists for this limited group but at the same time constraining participation by families falling outside this group that are eligible in some other states.

Other programs have developed numerous cost containment strategies as a way to stretch available program dollars. In the WIC program, savings generated by rebates from suppliers, use of generic brands, and home deliv-ery or direct distribution systems enable participation levels to increase by holding down the average food cost per person. The WIC program's most successful strategy has been competitive rebate contracts between state agencies and infant formula companies. In fiscal year 1997, for example, the rebate savings were estimated to be about $1.3 billion.[9] The Prescrip-tion Voucher Program in Florida contains costs by requiring that partici-pants receive only generic drugs when they are available. States do market surveys in setting payment rates for day care, and the level of payment depends on the level of supply. Massachusetts, for instance, pays at 55 per-cent of the rates in each of six geographic areas, which is sufficient to induce continued participation in the program by providers.

Concerns have been raised that overly stringent participant co-payment requirements, shallow subsidies, and limits on provider reimbursements could prevent some needy or worthy individuals from participating in the program. While these limits may indeed have this effect, co-payments and provider cost controls can induce more efficiency in the system. Moreover, they also extend limited funding to more participants. Unless additional resources are forthcoming, officials face a trade-off between serving more people and providing larger and more sufficient subsidies to fewer people.

Complementary Strategies and Tools

Vouchers were accompanied by the use of other governmental strategies and tools to enhance their effectiveness as a governmental tool. These strategies could be viewed as initiatives designed to improve the market conditions—both the demand and supply sides—under which a voucher can operate.

On the demand side, we identified voucher programs that sought to help recipients improve their knowledge of the market and of their own needs. In the day care area, for instance, states frequently contract with resource and referral agencies at the local level that, among other tasks, develop guides for parents on choices of providers available in their local area.[10] In the employment and training area, programs often provide extensive career counseling and mentoring to voucher participants as well as information assessing the performance of providers in the area. Some studies suggest that "pure vouchers" may lead individuals to make inappropriate choices among careers and training providers.[11] Among our cases, the Michigan Tool Chest voucher program, which provides employment and training, has included an "Enhancement Network" to provide voucher recipients with career counseling, job banks, mentoring, and outreach to employers. The Cambridge, Massachusetts, Controlled Choice education voucher enables Family Liaisons to provide families with the information needed to make an informed choice on schooling options for their children.

As the foregoing suggests, voucher recipients often require auxiliary services to successfully benefit from the program. Some may need help with voucher choice, others with supportive services that enable them to take advantage of the voucher. In the Minnesota Bridges program, it was necessary for the mental health agency to provide intensive support to mentally ill persons receiving housing vouchers. More broadly, Peterson observes in this volume that housing authorities strengthen the market position of voucher holders by providing information about the market, enforcing quality standards on housing units, and serving as an ombudsman to hear consumer complaints.

Vouchers also depend on a viable market of suppliers to promote the goals of improving choice and efficiency in service delivery. Although the voucher can elicit greater competition as a result of the subsidy itself, sometimes public agencies work to encourage a market to emerge. For instance, although vouchers are available for child care to assist welfare recipients in making the transition to work, the supply of child care is often insufficient in many communities to meet the needs of parents with infants or those working jobs at night or on weekends. Accordingly, programs have sought to fill this niche by contracting with providers to enhance coverage or providing separate grants to augment the equipment of day care centers to meet the needs of infants. For instance, one of the local sites in Michigan's

Project Zero—an innovative program to place welfare recipients in work— has entered into contracts with the local Camp Fire Boys and Girls in Midland, Michigan, to provide child care to program participants at nights and on weekends.

Also on the supply side, public agencies have taken on the responsibility in some cases to articulate quality standards and enhancements for the market as well. Previously, we discussed some of these initiatives in the housing, health, and nutrition areas. In day care, some states, including Wisconsin and South Carolina, give incentives to providers to receive training and upgrade their licensure status by providing an enriched reimbursement rate.

Conclusion

The foregoing discussion suggests that vouchers are by no means a simple governmental tool to administer. Although perhaps less administratively burdensome than direct public provision of services, the effective implementation of vouchers nonetheless requires considerable skill and initiative.

In fact, when compared to contracting with providers, some administrators have suggested that vouchers are as complex and challenging in their own way and that they possibly involve higher transaction costs. Administrators have noted that instead of dealing with a limited number of contractors through negotiation and regulation, officials have had to articulate a process to deal directly with thousands of clients with differing needs and capacities. The process of ensuring that public funds are targeted to those most in need and are only used for their authorized purposes can also be a daunting one. These concerns play out against a backdrop of limited public resources, where accountability for public resources has become an increasingly important concern. When viewed against this backdrop, it is not surprising that vouchers are rarely implemented alone in their pure form, but rather call forth a rich variety of public institutions and processes to address multiple public goals.

Notes

1. Ann Lordeman, *Employment and Training: Using Vouchers to Provide Services* (Congressional Research Service, 1997), p. 6.

2. General Accounting Office, *Food Assistance: A Variety of Practices May Lower the Costs of WIC*, GAO/RCED-97-225 (September 1997).

3. Department of Health and Human Services, Office of Inspector General, *States' Child Care Certificate Systems: An Early Assessment of Vulnerabilities and Barriers*, OEI-05-000320 (February 1998).

4. See Arthur Hauptman's chapter in this volume.

5. Even when applied for authorized purposes, vouchers are economically fungible instruments and can have the effect of freeing up income for purchase of other goods and services not covered by the program.

6. General Accounting Office, *Food Stamp Program: Information on Trafficking Food Stamp Benefits*, GAO/RCED-98-77 (1998).

7. Department of Housing and Urban Development, Office of Policy Development and Research and Office of Public and Indian Housing, *Learning from Each Other: New Ideas for Managing the Section 8 Certificate and Voucher Programs* (September 1996), pp. 17, 22, 23.

8. Ibid., pp. 12–15.

9. Department of Agriculture budget justification documents for fiscal year 1999, pp. 27g–53.

10. A recent HHS Inspector General audit revealed that such efforts frequently fall short of providing sufficient information to parents. See Department of Health and Human Services, Office of Inspector General, *States' Child Care Certificate Systems*, pp. 11–14.

11. Ann Lordeman, *Employment and Training*.

Appendix 17A

Program location and description	*Eligibility*
Child Care	
Child Care and Development Fund Block Grant (national). Requires states to give families an option of either enrolling with eligible providers or receiving child care certificates.	Children under thirteen with family income below 85 percent of the state or tribal median income and whose parent(s) are transitioning to work or in need of protective services; 70 percent of funds must be targeted to families that are Temporary Assistance for Needy Families (TANF) recipients, transitioning to work, or at risk of public dependency; states may set sliding fee scales to determine parents' contributions, but all families above the federal poverty level must contribute; eliminates previous entitlement for welfare families; states can set more restrictive guidelines.
Wisconsin Child Care Program. Vouchers are the principal tool for delivering publicly assisted child care.	TANF families and non-TANF families with income below 165 percent of the federal poverty level; parental copayments based on a sliding scale.
Massachusetts Child Care. Vouchers for child care.	TANF families: vouchers cover the full amount at licensed and exempt providers and for posttransitional care for a year; non-TANF families with income between 50 and 70 percent of the median state income; parental copayments based on a sliding scale.
South Carolina Day Care. ABC child care system includes both vouchers and contracted slots.	All TANF families; low-income working families share costs based on a sliding scale.
Criminal Justice	
Goods for Guns (Pittsburgh). Similar programs in Columbus, Ohio; Florida; New Orleans; Santa Rosa, Calif.; New York City; and Philadelphia. People trade in their guns for vouchers to purchase food or retail merchandise.	People who turn in operating guns; $25 certificates for handguns, $50 certificates for long guns; no geographical restrictions.
CHOC Thrift Store Vouchers (Orange County, Calif.). Vouchers for probationers to purchase items at thrift stores, including clothing, furniture, appliances, and other items.	Indigent probationers.
Education	
Federal Pell Grants (national). Need-based grants to low- and moderate-income undergraduate students to improve access to postsecondary education.	Financial need determined by a standard formula based on students' and parents' income and assets, household size, and the number of family members attending postsecondary institutions.

Degree of provider choice	Method of payment	Comments
Any legally operating provider as defined by the state; about 50 percent of vouchers are used for informal providers (neighbors or relatives); some states may offer in-home care as an option on a restricted basis (since in-home care tends to be more expensive).	Child care providers are reimbursed by the administering state or local agency.	Result of the consolidation of funding for the three Title IV-A programs in the 1996 amendments. Informal providers are mostly license exempt, making safety and quality of care difficult to monitor; conflict exists between providing for all eligible families and ensuring an adequate subsidy level—access for low-income families is sometimes limited because of the low value of the vouchers; concern that the use of vouchers makes achieving other program goals (that is, parental education) more difficult; fiscal year 1998: $3.1 billion appropriation; fiscal years 1996–2002: $21 billion appropriation.
Licensed centers and exempt providers (that is, neighbors, relatives); state is attempting to expand the supply of evening and weekend care and of care for infants and special needs children.	Directly to providers with a maximum reimbursement of 75 percent of market prices; formerly, payments went to parents, but providers complained they were not being paid.	State accountability controls include reports on attendance, inspection of all providers (including exempt providers), and reporting of social security numbers.
Licensed and exempt providers.	Directly to providers through resource and referral agencies; licensed providers receive a higher reimbursement of 55 percent of the market rate	Federal consolidation in 1996 prompted the state to consolidate day care so that clients have expanded choice among voucher and contract slots; vouchers for TANF recipients: 14,922 licensed care slots, 5,447 exempt provider slots.
Licensed and regulated centers or exempt providers; lists of providers and other information are given to parents.	Directly to providers, with higher payments for state-regulated and accredited providers as an incentive to upgrade care.	Vouchers challenge day care centers, which formerly relied on contracts and now have to compete for clients; 22,000 children served (half TANF and half non-TANF).
Grocery store chain or department store chain.	Program purchases certificates from stores.	Guns collected the first two Saturdays in December; guns accepted with no questions asked; collected guns are usually melted down; approximately 1,000 guns collected each year.
Ten thrift stores.	Deputy probation officers purchase the items.	Examples of voucher use include clothes for teenagers who participate in a long-term residential drug rehabilitation program; baby showers for pregnant women; clothes for a probationer and her five children whose father is in prison.
Any of approximately 6,000 participating postsecondary institutions; student must first be accepted by the institution.		Fiscal year 1997: $7.6 billion for 3.9 million students, with an average grant of $1,882 and a range from $400 to $2,700.

Program location and description	*Eligibility*
Minnesota K–12 Education Credit and Education Subtraction. Tax deductions and credits for K–12 education expenses, including tutoring, enrichment programs, instructional materials, and computer hardware and software.	Families with income under $33,500 receive credit and deduction; families with income above $33,500 only qualify for the deduction.
Enrollment Options Program (Minnesota). Enables students to attend a school or program outside their district of residence.	K–12 students; resident district consent is required in the three districts with approved desegregation plans.
Postsecondary Enrollment Options (Minnesota). Allows high school juniors and seniors to take courses at a postsecondary institution for high school credit; includes aid for tuition, fees, required textbooks, and transportation for qualified families.	All high school juniors and seniors.
Vermont. Towns without public schools pay tuition for students to attend a public or approved private school.	Any student from the roughly 74 (of 246) towns without public schools.
Houston Tex. Allows elementary and secondary students to attend a school other than their neighborhood school.	Low-performing students (as measured by the TAAS test) in low-performing schools (as identified by the TEA); parents are informed of a child's eligibility and must submit an application.
Cleveland Scholarship Program. Up to $2,500 in tuition for elementary and secondary education.	Residents of Cleveland in grades K–3; scholarships are awarded by lottery, with amount depending on family income.
Cleveland Tutoring Program. Up to $500 in tuition for before and after school tutoring in reading, writing, math, science, and citizenship.	Residents of Cleveland in grades K–3; scholarships are awarded by lottery, with amount depending on family income.
Milwaukee Parental Choice Program. Allows K–12 students to attend the school of their choice.	Up to 15 percent of Milwaukee's students from families with income below 175 percent of the federal poverty level.

Degree of provider choice	Method of payment	Comments
Any qualified instructor (defined as having at least a baccalaureate degree), including at private schools.	Directly to provider by recipient, with reimbursement through a tax deduction or credit; dollar-for-dollar tax credit or reduction, with a maximum credit refund of $1,000 per child and $2,000 per family and a maximum tax deduction of $1,625 (K–6) or $2,500 (7–12).	Families are not required to itemize deductions but are encouraged to keep receipts.
Any Minnesota public school where space is available.	Directly to provider; state per-pupil funds follow the student, but district funds do not.	
Any nonsectarian post-secondary institution.	Directly to provider by either the state or the district, using state funds; vouchers for books; reimbursement of families for transportation costs.	High schools are required to provide information about the program; schools must accdept $136/credit, but some limit available classes if funds are insufficient
Any public or approved private school located either within or outside Vermont.	Directly to district or private school by district of residence; district of residence pays full tuition charged by public schools, but is only required to pay private schools the average tuition charged by the state's high school districts.	
Any public school or accredited private school.	Directly to vendor.	Program began in the 1998–99 school year.
All public schools surrounding Cleveland and nonpublic schools within Cleveland; all schools must meet certain eligibility criteria.	Reimbursement of parents or guardians.	
Any individual who holds an Ohio teaching certificate and is approved by the state.	Reimbursement of parents or guardians with receipt of payment signed by provider.	Each student's regular teacher evaluates the quality of tutoring services and reports to both parents and providers.
Approved private or religious schools; awards made by lottery.	Family receives vouchers in quarterly payments in the amount of the per-pupil equalized state aid to Milwaukee public schools ($4,500 in 1997–98).	Original requirement for the collection and evaluation of student performance data was eliminated; each year, private schools must submit an independent financial audit based on uniform accounting standards.

Program location and description	*Eligibility*
Controlled Choice (Cambridge, Mass.). Parental choice of Cambridge public schools.	All K–8 students.

A Better Choice (ABC) (Albany, N.Y.). Privately funded vouchers for private school education.	Anyone attending Giffen Memorial Elementary School in Albany, N.Y.

Employment and Training

Employment and Training for Dislocated Workers (Title III-A) (national). Local training and employment assistance for dislocated workers; includes basic readjustment services (that is, job counseling) and retraining services (that is, occupational skills training).	Dislocated workers who (1) have been terminated and are unlikely to return to their previous occupation, (2) have been terminated as the result of the closing of a facility, (3) are long-term unemployed, or (4) are self-employed and were displaced as a result of general economic conditions.
Title III Dislocated Workers Career Management Grants (national). Thirteen demonstration sites. Transitional employment training and other assistance for dislocated workers.	Dislocated workers.
Trade Adjustment Assistance (TAA) (national). Aid for education and training, and partial coverage of travel, lodging, and meal expenses for job interviews and relocation for workers whose employment is adversely affected by competition from foreign imports.	Individuals unemployed as a result of foreign competition.
Michigan Works! Tool Chest ("thumb" region of Michigan). Recipients receive a "tool chest" packet of blank vouchers to improve their employability in the labor market; services include postsecondary and vocational education, public health services, transportation services, supportive employment job coaching, behavioral health and counseling services, private placement services, family and child care services, job training-related activities, and financial counseling services.	Residents of the four-county "thumb" region who are low-income public assistance recipients, veterans, laid-off workers, displaced homemakers, over age fifty-five and unemployed, or handicapped; value range of $500 to $2,500, depending on the characteristics of the recipient.
Skills Plus program (Massachusetts). Aid for occupational, vocational, preemployment, workplace, and personal skills enhancement training.	Individuals receiving transitional Aid to Families with Dependent Children who have some recent work history and need training; twenty-eight-day limit.
Career Account Management Program (CAMP) (Phoenix). Educational, training, employment, and support services for occupations that are in demand.	Same as Title III; hard-to-serve individuals as identified by the state profile.
San Bernardino County (Calif.). Training for long-term dislocated workers from the aerospace and defense industries who experience difficulty reentering the labor market.	Mostly unemployed aerospace and defense professionals who have had a single employer for at least ten years; participants recruited, screened, and assessed.

Degree of provider choice	Method of payment	Comments
Assignments are for the most part based on lottery, but racial balance, sibling preference, and proximity to home are taken into account.		Purpose is to promote desegregation, providing equal opportunity to students of all racial and ethnic groups; registration centers and family liaisons provide information to enable families to make informed decisions.
Local private elementary schools.		100 students receive vouchers worth up to $2,000 a year.
Any approved Title III-A program.	Recipients receive certificates to be used within forty-five days of the date of application.	Fiscal year 1997: $1.03 billion appropriation.
Varies by program.	Varies by program.	Purpose is to demonstrate the feasibility of greater flexibility through the use of vouchers; $10 million appropriation.
Degree of provider choice: Varies among states.	Varies among states.	$80 million annual federal appropriation.
Any service provider; information is disseminated through established referral networks and assistance in making decisions is available.	Vouchers co-signed.	Authorized services are determined on a case-by-case basis in consultation with a case manager. Voucher system was established to (1) deal efficiently with multiple sources of funding and (2) remove the stigma attached to other funding mechanisms; benefits claimed for the program include cost savings, a simplified and user-friendly system of delivery, and greater flexibility in meeting clients' needs; 1997–98: adult follow-up employment rate of 73.6 percent.
More than one hundred approved vendors; vendors' program proposals are reviewed by committee.	Vouchers issued directly to individuals.	Augments the 1995 welfare reform in Massachusetts by providing job training; local coordinators counsel individuals, issue vouchers, and track progress; $2 million appropriation; 1996: 1,514 clients served, 1,366 voucher recipients, 720 clients found employment, average program stay of twenty-six days.
Over one hundred public and private providers approved by the local chamber of commerce; if available, free in-house services must be used.	Directly to vendor.	Supplements Job Training Partnership Act (JTPA); program is designed as a limited experiment using random assignment; $500 cash incentive for job retention; first thirty months: 200 clients served, 97 percent job placement rate.
More than forty-seven providers with a federal tax identification number.	County auditor writes checks for individuals to present for payment to training providers.	Limited demonstration program; response to changes in the labor market resulting from the heavy impact of base closings and aerospace layoffs.

Program location and description	*Eligibility*

RESTART (Palm Beach County, Fla.). Education and training for employment.

District IX Welfare to Work program (Gallatin and Park Counties, Mont.). Individualized job retention case management, skill training, and employer networking.

70 percent distributed to hard-to-employ individuals and 30 percent to long-term TANF recipients at increased risk of remaining in poverty, targeting teen parents.

Training Assistance (Texas Panhandle). Postsecondary training in occupations likely to provide good opportunities for employment, including aid for tuition, books, fees, supplies, child care, transportation, work clothing, and support services.

Mentally disabled residents of the county.

Vouchers for the mentally disabled (Lehigh Valley, Pa.). Aid for job training, transportation, counseling, recreation, life skills programs.

Residents of twenty-six panhandle counties that qualify for JTPA; two-year limit

Environmental Protection

Ultra Low-Flush Toilet Voucher program (San Diego). Vouchers to purchase approved low-flush toilets using 1.6 gallons per flush (gpf).

All residential, commercial, and industrial water consumers, except those who only pay for sewer service; purchase of toilets for new construction or renovation projects does not qualify.

Mow Down Pollution (Tucson). Similar programs in Sacramento and Phoenix. People trade in their gas-powered lawnmowers for vouchers to purchase EPA-approved new electric lawnmowers.

County residents who trade in their gas-powered lawnmowers; people who trade in commercial lawnmowers receive vouchers of higher value.

Vouchers for individuals who reduce household water consumption (Singapore). People who reduce their household water consumption receive certificates for the purchase of sports merchandise.

Anyone who reduces household water consumption; consumers must bring their Public Utility Board bills to any RSH outlet.

Food and Nutrition

Food Stamp Program (national). Food for home preparation and consumption, not including alcohol, tobacco, or hot foods intended for immediate consumption; seeds and plants for use in gardens to produce food for personal consumption; elderly and disabled individuals may purchase delivered meals or meals prepared and served in approved dining halls.

Individuals with family incomes below 130 percent of the federal poverty level; income criteria may be partially waived for elderly or disabled individuals.

Degree of provider choice	*Method of payment*	*Comments*
Thirty public and private providers approved by the board of commissioners following competitive RFQ.	Individual debit accounts.	Limited demonstration program; pilot for a self-directed, computer-based employment guidance system; participants must keep records of their activities.
Must be approved by job retention specialist.	Individual bills agency, or payment made directly to vendor.	Aid for any good or service that supports the client's employment and retainment needs, provided no other options exist.
Public institutions that develop an agreement with the PRPC.	Directly to vendor.	Staff provides assessment and counseling and must approve all requests; invoices are cross-checked with matching payment authorization forms in participants' files; vendors' performance as measured by placement and wages is reviewed annually; 1997–98: 600 participants, 70 percent job placement rate, jobs had an average wage of over $9 per hour, exceeding all federal and state performance standards.
Recipients can compare programs at "employment fairs"; portions of the voucher can be redeemed at different agencies.	Reimbursement.	One goal of using vouchers is to reduce the cost of providing the programs.
Most wholesale and retail plumbing stores.	Residents who replace their old toilets with low-flow toilets receive a rebate; application with original sales receipt must be submitted. In other programs, customers apply for vouchers before buying their new toilets and vouchers are redeemed at the time of purchase.	City will pick up the old toilet. 1992 National Energy Policy Act mandates that household toilets manufactured in the United States must be limited to 1.6 gpf. California state law mandates that 1.6 gpf toilets must be installed in all new construction; 225,000 units installed so far; households can save an estimated $48 and 11,000 gallons a year.
Twenty-four participating stores.	Directly to the vendor.	Seven-week collection period; Tucson Electric Power Company helps promote the program by advertising it on electric bills; 1998: 1,676 lawn-mowers collected; program estimated to reduce pollution by 439 tons each year.
RSH sports stores.	Certificates.	Water gauge publicly displays the amount of water saved as a result of the program.
Any of approximately 209,255 providers approved by the U.S. Department of Agriculture.	Food coupons; states are required to implement electronic benefit transfer systems, which allow individuals to access their food stamp allotments at the point of sale.	Errors in determining recipients' eligibility and benefit levels result in nearly $2 billion in overpayments each year. Many food stamps are sold or used for nonfood purchases (generally referred to as trafficking); fiscal year 1997: $27.62 billion appropriation.

Program location and description	*Eligibility*
Women, Infants, and Children Program (WIC) (national). Supplemental nutrition program for lower-income pregnant and postpartum women and infants and children to purchase nutritional food products such as milk, cheese, eggs, infant formula, cereals, and fruit.	Pregnant and postpartum women, their infants, and children up to age five with family income below 185 percent of the federal poverty level and who are judged to be nutritionally at risk.
WIC Farmer's Market Nutrition Program (national). WIC-eligible women and children submit vouchers for farm produce, such as fresh fruits and vegetables.	Same as WIC.

General Assistance

Vouchers for Infants and Toddlers (Oklahoma). Assistance for food, clothing, and other necessities for children born while their mother was enrolled in TANF.	Welfare recipient with a subsequent child up to age three.
Family Independence Act (South Carolina). Assistance for child-related commodities for children born while their mothers were enrolled in TANF.	Welfare recipient with a subsequent child.
Family Independence Act (South Carolina). Assistance for relocation expenses, child care, and first month's rent for families relocating to find employment.	TANF recipient.
Flexible Funding Source (Oklahoma). Temporary one-time aid for gaining or maintaining employment, including a wide range of goods and services, such as car repair.	TANF recipients.
Clothing vouchers (West Virginia). Vouchers of $100 for clothing or sewing materials for clothing; vouchers may not be used for hair accessories, jewelry, or school supplies.	Children from families with income below the federal poverty level enrolled in the state's public and private schools in grades K–12.
Project Zero (Michigan). Vouchers used as a major tool to transition welfare recipients to work in selected sites, with a goal of zero unemployment; includes vouchers for relocation, clothing, transportation, car purchase and repair, child care, training, and supportive services (that is, mentoring and counseling).	All TANF recipients at twelve selected sites.

Degree of provider choice	Method of payment	Comments
Any authorized retail food store.	Grocery store clerk writes dollar amount of purchase on the voucher, participant signs the voucher, and administering agency reimburses the store (the vast majority of agencies use checks that are reimbursed after deposit in the store's bank account); about one-fourth of all states do not require any documentation of income eligibility.	Cost containment initiatives include contracting with manufacturers to obtain rebates on WIC foods, placing greater limits on the choice of food items, restricting the number of vendors, and ensuring that prices are competitive. In fiscal year 1996: 7,187,800 participants, of which 1,618,000 were women, 1,827,300 were children, and 3,712,300 were infants; $3.7 billion appropriation; average food package valued at $31 a month, average administrative cost of $11 a month.
Any state-approved farmer's market.	Either coupons or checks— markets submit coupons to the state for reimbursement; checks are deposited in the markets' bank accounts and are reimbursed through the banking system.	Farmers occasionally express concern about slow reimbursements for coupon vouchers; when checks are used instead, farmers receive payments directly through the banking system, as with any other check
Any provider.	Store submits voucher coupons for reimbursement.	Represents a compromise to maintain the goals of a family cap while preventing harm to children.
Any provider.	Varies by county—either reimbursement of the provider or payment to the mother upon proof of payment for goods and services.	Represents a compromise to maintain the goals of a family cap while preventing harm to children; caseworker oversight.
Any provider.	Vouchers or cash.	Aim is to move the family toward self-sufficiency by improving its location; approval of caseworker.
Any provider.	State authorization presented by the client to the vendor, who is later reimbursed by the state.	Approval of caseworker.
	Reimbursement of provider.	Goal is to remove the stigma that children often face because of their financial circumstances; 30,000 children expected to apply at a cost of $2.5 to $3 million a year.
Any service provider; day care has been expanded in some sites through contracts with Camp Fire Boys and Girls to provide night and weekend care.	Primarily reimbursement of providers.	Vouchers are tailored to meet individual needs.

Program location and description	*Eligibility*
Berkeley Cares (California). Similar programs in New Haven, Conn.; New York City; Boston; Boulder, Colo.; San Diego; Seattle; Chicago; Houston; Portland, Ore.; San Francisco; and Santa Cruz; national legislation has been proposed. Vouchers for panhandlers to purchase food, laundry services, or bus passes; restrictions on alcohol and tobacco.	

Health Care

Migrant Health Program (national). Vouchers are used to procure direct health services (that is, dental or primary care) in organizations that do not provide direct care themselves; health centers that do provide direct clinical care often use vouchers when referring patients for specialty care.	Migrant and seasonal farmworkers.
Family Health Insurance Assistance Program (Oregon). Subsidy for low-income families to purchase individual or employer-sponsored private health insurance coverage.	Working individuals with income below 170 percent of the federal poverty level who are uninsured for six months and who do not qualify for Medicaid; sliding scale from 70 percent to 95 percent of cost, depending on family income.
Employer-sponsored family coverage (Massachusetts). Vouchers to subsidize the purchase of health insurance coverage for low-income employees.	Employees with income below 200 percent of the federal poverty level who do not qualify for Medicaid.
Senior Pharmacy Program (Massachusetts). Subsidy for seniors to purchase up to $750 in prescription drugs a year; certain drugs are restricted.	Elders sixty-five years and older who have been state residents for at least six months, are not enrolled in Medicaid, have an annual income below $12,084, and lack drug insurance.
Vouchers for medical services (St. Louis, Mo.). Subsidy to purchase needed medical services that city clinics and hospitals are unable to provide.	Underinsured individuals with medical conditions that city hospitals are unable to treat.

Degree of provider choice	Method of payment	Comments
Nine area homeless service providers, 200 organizations and businesses.	People buy vouchers for $0.25 and distribute them to panhandlers; cash from sale of vouchers distributed to nine area homeless service providers.	Purpose is to enable people to give vouchers instead of change, so that they can have some control over what recipients purchase. (In New Haven, where recipients were turning vouchers into cash, vouchers that are only redeemable in emergency shelters will replace the original multiuse vouchers.) 1993–94 Berekeley Cares: 111,000 vouchers sold with a redemption rate of 96 percent.
Any service provider who will accept vouchers.	Reimbursement at a reduced rate.	Vouchers enable organizations to serve isolated pockets of migrant and seasonal farmworkers for whom a full clinic program would not be feasible; they also give full service clinics the opportunity to refer patients for specialty care; each grantee has a primary care effectiveness review every three years.
Recipients required to choose workplace-based coverage if offered and subsidized by the employer; otherwise, the employee may seek individual insurance; limited to family health insurance, and children must be covered.	Directly to employee.	Program intended to fill the gap in health insurance coverage for the working poor; concern that employers might reduce their contribution to health insurance coverage; 10,000 to 20,000 recipients.
Qualified providers (including health maintenance organizations, preferred provider organizations, regular indemnity).	Vouchers for qualified employees are provided to the employer, who sends the vouchers along with a payment of at least 50 percent of the insurance premiums to carriers, who are then reimbursed by the state; tax credits for employers providing health insurance coverage are also provided.	Program intended to reduce the number of people who would drop out of private insurance, but there is concern that it covers low-income workers who might have been covered by private insurance anyway; carriers cannot cash in the vouchers until the employer pays its full share; approximately 190,000 to 200,000 individuals or 100,000 families covered at an annual cost of about $150 to $250 million.
Any pharmacy registered by the DMA (that is, almost all pharmacies in Massachusetts).		More than 24,000 have enrolled in two years.
	Directly to vendor.	Program replaced the city's safety net hospital that had been closed.

Program location and description	*Eligibility*
Prescription Voucher Program (Pasco County, Fla.). Vouchers to purchase prescription drugs, and in some cases medical supplies, for uninsured children.	Uninsured children whose families do not qualify for Medicaid; county pediatricians and physicians determine family need, based on the state criteria for income, and award grants ranging from $5 to $60; if families qualify for Medicaid, the foundation will initiate a Medicaid application; first-time applicants receive vouchers to ensure that children receive needed medications.
Vouchers for treatment of cocaine dependence (Baltimore; San Francisco; New Haven, Conn.; Burlington, Vt.). "Clean" patients receive vouchers to purchase "reinforcers" (any item that promotes healthy living or the formation of new habits, for example, membership at a health club, paintbrushes); items are approved by a clinical team.	Patients who accumulate points for negative test results.
Vouchers for pet neutering (Los Angeles). Low-cost spay and neuter surgeries.	City residents.
Hope for Kids (national). Launched in Harlem, N.Y. Vouchers for immunization; vouchers for food and toys are also distributed as an incentive for parents.	

Housing

Section 8 Housing vouchers and certificates (national). Rent for housing for very low-income families ("left over" money from vouchers may be used for any purpose).	Determined by housing authorities based on income and family size; families with income below 50 percent of the median area income, or families with income between 60 and 80 percent of the median area income who meet other, specialized requirements; preference given to families that are homeless, or living in substandard housing and paying more than 50 percent of their income in rent, or involuntarily displaced.
Rental Assistance for Family Stabilization (Minnesota). Temporary housing vouchers for families transitioning to work.	Families eligible for TANF that are in the process of finding full employment (for example, moving off welfare) and do not participate in any other housing programs; vouchers expire after thirty-six months; annual recertification.

Degree of provider choice	Method of payment	Comments
Several Kmart pharmacies in the county; initially only one pharmacy was eligible, but the foundation quickly realized that this made accessibility too difficult.	Pharmacies bill foundation for reimbursement of vouchers.	Program intended to meet the need of parents who admitted their children to hospital despite receiving prescriptions, because they could not afford to fill them; foundation has donated $12,000 over three years; between 200 and 300 families served each year; average voucher award of $20.
Participating stores.	Clinical team purchases items for patients.	Voucher-based therapy is the only proven method of reliably reducing cocaine use in controlled studies; however, vouchers and cash have been found to be equally effective in terms of the percentage of patients successfully completing a tuberculosis regimen.
	Veterinarians exchange vouchers for cash.	Vouchers are being scaled back with the addition of a new city sterilization clinic; 1996–97: 9,600 of 12,000 vouchers redeemed. Comments: In New Jersey: 11,200 vouchers distributed statewide by 7,000 volunteers
Various hospitals.		Program intended to enable families to move out of primarily low-income areas (16 percent of Section 8 families live in very poor areas, compared to 59 percent of public housing families); many housing authorities operate fraud detection units and use automated verification systems; some housing authorities arrange installment payment plans or find other sources of funds to help recipients with security deposits; over 1.5 million households served (400,000 with vouchers), 68 percent of which include children; fiscal year 1997: estimated $16.7 billion.
Any single-family homes, townhouses, apartments, or public housing units; rental units must meet minimum standards of health and safety as established by housing authorities. Vouchers: no limits on the amount of rent tenants may pay. Certificates: rent must not exceed a predetermined maximum.	Vouchers: housing authority share of rent calculated, and families make up the difference (fixed payments). Certificates: family share of rent calculated, and housing authorities make up the difference (floating payments). In both cases the rental subsidy is paid directly to the landlord.	Families sanctioned if they do not have a full employment plan; approximately 600 households served, with a program budget of $5.5 million each year.
Any rental housing unit within the third of counties with the highest market rents, as determined by the Department of Housing and Urban Development.	Directly to landlord by housing authorities (like Section 8); fixed subsidy of $250 a month in the Twin Cities area and $200 a month in Greater Minnesota.	Program may pay rent and utilities for up to ninety days if the recipient is hospitalized, to maintain the unit and ensure the safety of recipient's property; approximately 400 individuals served a year, with a biannual program budget of $3.2 million.

Program location and description	*Eligibility*
Bridges (Minnesota). Temporary housing vouchers for severely mentally ill individuals; most recipients also receive support services.	Severely mentally ill individuals awaiting permanent Section 8 housing; income criteria based on gross rather than net income (in contrast to Section 8); annual recertification.
Massachusetts Rental Voucher Program. Mobile vouchers (assigned to a tenant rather than to a location) and project-based vouchers (assigned to a particular rental unit, so that tenants lose the voucher if they move).	Families with income below 200 percent of the federal poverty level (in contrast to Section 8); recipients of mobile vouchers must find a suitable housing unit within 120 days or forfeit the voucher; replaced a program with more generous eligibility standards; annual recertification.
Alternative Housing Vouchers (Massachusetts). Mobile housing vouchers for young disabled individuals.	Anyone under sixty and disabled (usually, mentally disabled).
AIDS rental subsidy (Boston). Housing rent and support services for HIV-positive individuals, including financial assistance with rental start-up, moving expenses, legal assistance, frozen meals, furniture donations, individual and group support therapy, and a number of other HIV-related, volunteer-based programs	Based on public housing guidelines; clients are put on a waiting list at the BHA, and the AAC is contacted when certificates become available.
Voucher tool-lending program (Long Beach, Calif.). Similar programs in Anaheim and Santa Ana, Calif. Tool rentals of $500, restricted to tools that would be used to renovate exterior surfaces.	Residents of designated neighborhoods that need cleaning up; families with income less than $59,750; residents of properties in which units are at least 50 percent residential and rental.

Transportation

Los Angeles. Vouchers for taxi rides of up to seven miles for intoxicated individuals.	Anyone.
Commuter Check (Boston). Mass transit vouchers worth $60 a month.	Employers buy vouchers for employees.

Degree of provider choice	Method of payment	Comments
Any rental housing unit in forty-four of eighty-seven counties, as long as the landlord accepts the applicant.	Directly to landlord by housing authority.	Fixed voucher payments have failed to keep pace with rising rents; administrative fees per unit have been reduced, straining housing authorities' ability to process vouchers; inspections of both mobile units and project-based units have been discontinued; approximately 9,000 mobile vouchers and 9,000 project-based vouchers at a cost of $40 million a year; mobile vouchers have been "frozen" (anyone coming off the program cannot be replaced) and so have declined relative to project-based vouchers.
Mobile vouchers: any apartment, single-family home, or condominium certified by the Board of Health, but tenants may have to leave if the unit is sold. Project-based vouchers: limited to the unit designated by the voucher, which is guaranteed. Housing authorities may grant waivers allowing recipients to pay the difference between the voucher amount and the rent charged.	Directly to landlord by housing authority; recipients pay roughly 35 percent of their income and vouchers make up the difference; landlords are not guaranteed tenants' share of the rent.	Response to the perception that younger disabled individuals should not have to live in housing complexes designed primarily for the elderly; 800 vouchers statewide, on a pilot basis.
Any rental housing unit certified by the Board of Health.	Directly to landlord by housing authority; recipients pay between 26 and 30 percent of their income.	Average monthly subsidy of $405; $118,800 budgeted per year; program monitored by housing authorities, the Department of Housing, and the state auditor's office.
Any rental housing unit.	Certificates.	
Two rental companies.	Community Development Department reimburses stores.	Only available during the holiday season; 1996: 50,000 vouchers available.
Ten authorized city taxicab companies.	Taxicab companies pay for rides.	Many winners: cheaper transportation for the employee, tax benefits for the employer, less crowded roads, and cleaner air; Federal Clean Air Act of 1990 mandates that companies with more than 100 employees must reduce the number who drive to work alone.
Mass transit systems.	Federal law allows employers to give up to $65 a month in tax-free vouchers.	

Program location and description	*Eligibility*
Vouchers for disabled individuals (Palm Beach, Fla.). Night-time transportation; four one-way trips a month to scheduled destinations within a fifteen-mile radius of home.	People with disabilities.
Need Program (Los Angeles County). Taxi rides to doctors' offices, food banks, battered women's shelters, and other locations.	Needy county residents; each client receives four vouchers a month.

Miscellaneous

Specialized Telecommunications Devices Assistance Program (Texas). Vouchers for deaf, blind, hard of hearing, and speech-impaired Texans to purchase specialized telecommunications devices, such as telebraillers and voice carry-over telephones.

Vouchers for market shares to encourage privatization (Russia). Shares in specific companies and in mutual funds, through auctions.

Any Russian citizen, including children.

Degree of provider choice	Method of payment	Comments
		Requires social security number; 60,000 vouchers each worth $7 available.
Thirty vendors statewide.	Vouchers distributed by social service agencies.	1998: 1,400 vouchers redeemed in four months.
	Public Utility Commission reimburses vendors.	
		Vouchers worth 10,000 rubles each; 144 million of 147 million Russians received their vouchers; by the end of the program, 40 million people were shareholders. (Vouchers became so popular that the song "Wow Wow Voucher" reached number five on the hit list.)

Contributors

Andrea Barnett
Urban Institute

Burt S. Barnow
Institute for Policy Studies,
  Johns Hopkins University

Douglas J. Besharov
American Enterprise Institute

Linda T. Bilheimer
Congressional Budget Office

David F. Bradford
Woodrow Wilson School, Princeton
  University

Arthur M. Hauptman
Council for Aid to Education

Robert Lerman
Urban Institute

Burdett Loomis
University of Kansas

Michael W. McConnell
University of Utah
  College of Law

Elliot M. Mincberg
People For the American Way
  Foundation

Robert A. Moffitt
Johns Hopkins University

George E. Peterson
Urban Institute

Paul Posner
U.S. General Accounting Office

Hugo Priemus
Delft University of Technology

541

Robert D. Reischauer
Urban Institute

Nazanin Samari
American Enterprise Institute

Isabel V. Sawhill
Brookings Institution

Judith E. Schaeffer
*People For the American Way
    Foundation*

Mark Schneiderman
*Council of Chief State School
    Officers*

Daniel N. Shaviro
*New York University
    School of Law*

Shannon L. Smith
Cornell University

Christopher Spiro
Urban Institute

C. Eugene Steuerle
Urban Institute

Robert Yetvin
*U.S. General Accounting
    Office*

Index